WITHDRAWN

The Andros Papers

1674–1676

The New York Historical Manuscripts Series
Volumes XXIV–XXV

**Sir Edmund Andros (1637–1714), Seigneur of Sausmarez,
Governor of New York, 1674–1681**

Engraved prior to 1868 from a photograph of a portrait then in the possession
of Amias Charles Andros of London. One source attributes the engraving to
"Kilburn," perhaps George Goodwin Kilburne, 1839–1924.

The Andros Papers

1674–1676

*Files of the Provincial Secretary
of New York During the Administration
of Governor Sir Edmund Andros
1674–1680*

Edited by
PETER R. CHRISTOPH and FLORENCE A. CHRISTOPH

With translations from the Dutch by
CHARLES T. GEHRING

SYRACUSE UNIVERSITY PRESS

First Edition, 1989

99 98 97 96 95 94 93 92 91 90 89   6 5 4 3 2 1

The paper used in this publication meets the minimum requirements of American National Standard for Information Sciences—Permanence of Paper for Printed Library Materials, ANSI Z 39.48–1984. ∞™

Produced with the support of The Holland Society of New York and the New Netherland Project of the New York State Library

The preparation of this volume was made possible in part by a grant from the Division of Research Programs of the National Endowment for the Humanities, an independent federal agency.

Library of Congress Cataloging-in-Publication Data

The Andros papers.

(The New York historical manuscripts series ; v. 24)
Bibliography: p.
Includes index.
Contents: [1] 1674–1676.
1. New York (State)—History—Colonial period, ca. 1600–1775—Sources. 2. New York (State)—Archives.
3. Andros, Edmund, Sir, 1637–1714—Archives.
I. Christoph, Peter R. II. Christoph, Florence A.
III. Andros, Edmund, Sir, 1637–1714. IV. Series.
F122.A5   1989   974.7'02   89-4409
ISBN 0-8156-2457-3 (v. 1 : alk. paper)

MANUFACTURED IN THE UNITED STATES OF AMERICA

Peter R. Christoph is a graduate of Hartwick College and holds the degrees of master of arts and master of library science from the State University of New York at Albany. In 1988 after eighteen years as administrator of Manuscripts and Special Collections at the New York State Library he joined the library's New Netherland Project staff as editor of English documents. His eight previously published volumes include six in the New York Historical Manuscripts series. He has written some two dozen articles and gives frequent talks on colonial history. He was elected a fellow of the Holland Society of New York in 1979.

Florence A. Christoph is a graduate of Hartwick College. She is a historical editor employed by The Holland Society of New York for the New Netherland Project, and has coedited three of the New York Historical Manuscripts volumes. In addition, she has edited two books of local records from the Albany area. She is also a certified genealogist specializing in the colonial period of upstate New York, on which she researches, teaches and lectures. She has compiled a published genealogy of the Schuyler Family, 1650–1800; a volume of later generations is in progress.

Charles T. Gehring was born in Fort Plain, an old Erie Canal town in New York State's Mohawk Valley. After completing his undergraduate and graduate work at West Virginia University he continued with post graduate studies at Albert–Ludwigs–Universität in Freiburg, Germany. There he began his study of the Dutch language and first realized that his future research lay much closer to home. He eventually received a Ph.D. in Germanic Linguistics from Indiana University with a concentration in Netherlandic Studies. His dissertation (1973) was a linguistic investigation of the survival of the Dutch language in colonial New York. He is presently director of the New York State Library's New Netherland Project, which is responsible for translating the official records of the Dutch colony and promoting awareness of the Dutch role in American history. He has been a fellow of the Holland Society of New York since 1979.

Committee on Publication

Contents

Acknowledgments

There are a number of people and organizations to whom we are indebted, particularly to Charles T. Gehring, director of the New Netherland Project, for all the translations from the Dutch. Linda J. Pike has provided all French translations except for one by Kenneth Scott: we are grateful to them, and to Dederick Kramers whose transcriptions of the Dutch records facilitated translation. The staffs of the New York State Library's Manuscripts and Special Collections, and of the New York State Archives and Records Administration have been helpful both in permitting access to these and related records and in providing advice and counsel. Members of the New Netherland Project staff have been helpful in innumerable ways, the most apparent of which is the visible text: camera-ready copy was prepared by project staff using the publishing program *Ventura Publisher*.

We particularly want to express our debt to the man to whom this set is dedicated: Ralph L. DeGroff, Sr. The entire program of translating the early Dutch records and editing the early English records of New York over the past sixteen years would not have happened without his interest, support, and leadership. That the project continues after him is a tribute to his vision and planning. Still, he is missed: he was a friend. It is particularly appropriate that this particular publication be dedicated to him for he was most interested in Governor Andros, the original DeGroff having been among the colonists who arrived with Andros's party.

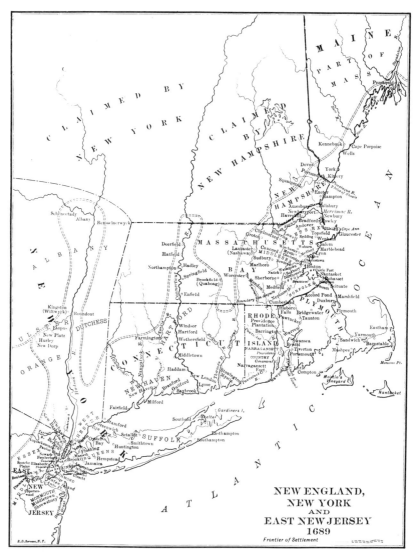

New England, New York, and East New Jersey, 1689

Map by R. D. Servoss from the American Nation: A History, by Charles McLean Andrews (New York and London: Harper and Brothers, 1904).

This pictures the colonial situation during the second Andros administration. The most notable change from 1676 is that Permaquid is shown here as part of Massachusetts, a change ordered by King James in 1686. The council protested, the Glorious Revolution intervened, and the issue was finally setled by King William in 1692 in favor of Massachusetts.

Introduction

We have impowered Our Trusty and Welbeloved Major Edmund Andros, and, in case of his death or other accident Anthony Brockhurst Gent. in Our name and for Our use to demand, and to take into either of their possession the place in the West Indies called by the Dutch New Netherlands, but by Our Subjects New York.

King Charles II to Heneage Lord Finch,
Keeper of the Great Seal, July 30, 1674*

Edmund Andros: Origins and Background

The Andros family on the Island of Guernsey had a long history of service to the English Crown. John Andros, great-great-grandfather of Edmund, was the first of the family on the island: born in Northamptonshire (where the rest of the family spelled the name as Andrews), he was sent to Guernsey as lieutenant governor. In 1543 he married Judith de Sausmarez, heiress of the seigneur of Sausmarez,‡ which title passed to John and Judith's son, John.

Thomas Andros, son of the younger John, was born in 1571, succeeded to his father's titles, and was appointed lieutenant governor. In 1606 he married Elizabeth, daughter of Amice de Carteret, former lieutenant governor and bailiff of Guernsey. Presumably Edmund Andros was related through this grandmother to the Carterets of the Island of Jersey, and thus to Gov. Philip Carteret of New Jersey.

Amice Andros (1610–1674) was the eldest son of Thomas. He married Elizabeth Stone whose brother Sir Robert Stone was cupbearer to Queen Elizabeth of Bohemia. The queen's brother, King Charles I of

---

* Pictured in "What is the Worth of a Unique Historic Rarity?" by Herman Herst, Jr., *Forbes* 139 (1987): 26; reprinted from *Stamps.* The original document is in the Forbes Magazine Galleries, New York.

‡ The title is somewhat less impressive when rendered into English: lord (of the manor, or fief) of Saltmarsh.

xiii

England, in 1632 named Amice his Marshall of Ceremonies. Thus began the Andros family's service to the Stuarts. Edmund Andros, eldest surviving child of Amice, was born December 6, 1637, in London, but was taken to Guernsey at the outbreak of the Civil War. Amice held Castle Cornet there for the monarchy as long as possible but in December 1651 took his family into exile in Holland (Edmund's mother had been captured by the enemy but escaped to Jersey in 1645 and went with Charles II to Holland in October 1651).

At the stadhouder's court in the Hague, Edmund became fluent in Dutch and perfected his French. He also became acquainted with three present and future kings of Great Britain: the royal refugees Charles II and James the duke of York and their nephew William III of Orange (son of the stadhouder, William II, prince of Orange, and Mary, sister of Charles and James).

At the age of 18, Edmund Andros joined a troop of horse under his uncle Sir Robert Stone, part of the Dutch army of Prince Henry of Nassau, and served in the First Northern War (1655–60) in Denmark against the Swedes. In 1660 Edmund became gentleman in ordinary to his uncle's patroness Queen Elizabeth of Bohemia.

After the Restoration in 1660, King Charles confirmed Amice Andros as bailiff of Guernsey, among other offices. In pardoning the people of Guernsey for having submitted to the Commonwealth government, the king pointedly named five loyal men who needed no pardon, including Amice Andros, his son Edmund, and Amice's brother Charles, a veteran of the Civil War who had later served in France in the duke of York's army.

In 1661 Edmund accompanied Elizabeth of Bohemia to London. Following her death in 1662, Andros received his first commission from the king, as ensign of Captain Sir John Talbot's company in the king's household troop, the First (the Grenadier) Guards. His battalion policed London during various crises, fought the Great Fire of London, escorted the king to the historic meeting of Parliament at Oxford, and helped to garrison Guernsey. In September 1665, the Isle of Wright suffered an uprising of republicans and Quakers and mutiny by the militia. Andros was dispatched with one hundred Guardsmen and put down the rebellions in quick order.

His military career advanced sharply when in 1667, during the Anglo-Dutch War, he was commissioned as a major and sent out with Col. Sir Tobias Bridge's regiment of foot to Barbados and the Leeward Islands. Over the next sixteen months the regiment fought the French, engaged in police work, negotiated a military treaty with the Carib Indians of St. Lucia and St. Vincent, and made a grand triumphal tour of the Lesser Antilles, returning to Barbados late in April 1668. Andros was then dispatched to London to seek supplies and clothing for the troops and to negotiate for back pay for his superiors and regiment, which occupied much of his time over the next three years. He was also commissioned by the king in August 1669 to supervise a diplomatically sensitive salvage operation in Ostend Harbor, the Netherlands, where a ship loaded with Cornish tin had sunk in August 1665. His success at this task earned him the royal thanks and a grant of £250.

By September 1671, two hundred men of the Barbados Regiment had returned home and were reorganized as four companies of foot under Andros. They served at first as the king's own but in November were incorporated into a regiment of dragoons led by Prince Rupert, the king's cousin and son of the late queen of Bohemia. The dragoons—mounted infantrymen used primarily as military police—were a new type of soldier, and Rupert's were the first English troops to be armed with a new form of weapon, the bayonet.

That autumn Andros was also given another diplomatic assignment. The widowered duke of York sent him in October and December to visit the eligible princess of Holstein, a close relative of the king of Sweden. Although the duke eventually decided to marry Mary of Modena, Andros was thereafter treated by the duke as one of his household.

Andros, in February 1672, married Marie Craven, a thirty-seven-year-old spinster and niece of William, earl of Craven, Edmund's military commander under Sir Robert Stone and the former chief advisor to the queen of Bohemia. After the wedding they lived at Lord Craven's house, and in 1672 Andros, through Craven's influence, became a landgrave of Carolina with baronies of forty-eight thousand total acres (a venture that, however, never came to anything).

On March 17, 1672, King Charles declared war on the Dutch again, and on March 30 the officers of the Barbados Regiment of Dragoons received their commissions. While Col. Prince Rupert and Lt. Col. Sir John Talbot attended to duties elsewhere, Major Andros led the regiment to Yarmouth and took command of the garrison. He fortified the town against possible Dutch assault and supervised the policing of both the town and a nearby army camp. Andros also had to react to rumors of Dutch invasion plans; he spent much of his time that year on coast-watching duty, turning up at various posts on the Channel as well as along the east coast facing Holland. A military association of future importance began at this time when Andros took on as one of his junior officers Anthony Brockholls, who had previously served in the duke of York's own troop of Horse Guards.

The Peace of Westminster, signed on February 9, 1674, returned the colony of New York, captured by the Dutch in 1673, to the English Crown. In that same month, Edmund Andros was commissioned major and captain of the Barbados Regiment serving in Ireland, but more offices were in store. After King Charles had regranted New York to his brother, he commissioned Edmund Andros as the duke's lieutenant and governor in New York and as captain of the company of foot that would accompany him. Andros, in addition to his salary as governor of New York and captain of the garrison at Fort James, would continue to receive his pay as major and captain of the Barbados Regiment.

Why had Andros been selected as governor? There are several possible reasons. Both Charles II and the duke of York favored military governors, and Andros had spent eighteen years in the army. He was loyal to the Stuarts and indebted to them for his several advancements. He spoke Dutch and French, important in New York with its mixed population and with New France as a neighbor. Undoubtedly in conversation he had expressed attitudes concerning administration and authority that met with the duke's approval. He was hard-nosed, did what he was told instead of what was popular, and could be expected to put the lid on the Dutch, the democrats, the Puritans, and the Indians.

During this period, Edmund's father died. Amice Andros had held the titles of seigneur, bailiff, master of the ceremonies to the king, hereditary cupbearer to the duke of Normandy (the king) in his island fief, and castellan of Jerbourg. The title of seigneur of Sausmarez passed to Edmund, but the local nobility wanted the office of bailiff to go to the governor of Guernsey. Support from Sir Heneage Finch, lord keeper (of the great seal), led to Andros's appointment by the king. The new bailiff quickly replaced local rule with royal prerogative. On departing he appointed his uncle Charles as his lieutenant.

He sailed for New York on his majesty's ship the *Diamond*. He was accompanied by his wife and their household staff, his officer corps, and the usual noncombatant gentlemen attached to a garrison including a commissary, a surgeon, and a chaplain. Noteworthy among the officers (besides Captain Andros) were lieutenants Christopher Billop and Deputy Governor Anthony Brockholls, and Ensign Caesar Knapton, Andros's brother-in-law.[*] Numbered among the other passengers were customs collector William Dyre, New Jersey Governor Philip Carteret, and the unfortunate former deputy governor of New York, Capt. John

---

[*] Several historians of colonial New York have called Knapton the nephew of Andros. However, Andros mentions no nephew by that name either in his will or in his genealogy submitted to the College of Arms, but he does name in both documents his brother-in-law Caesar Knapton, husband of Carterette Andros. Carterette was too young to have had a son in the army as early as 1674, in fact the genealogy says that her only child was a daughter.

Manning, who faced court-martial for having surrendered Fort James to the Dutch the year before. An important advisor on the military staff was Capt. Silvester Salisbury, a veteran of the two previous English administrations in New York. Accompanying the *Diamond* was the frigate *Castle*, which carried some of the one hundred enlisted men and several new settlers, including a number of English merchants and some French Protestant refugees.

The Situation at New York, 1674–1676

New York, which was originally part of the Dutch colony of New Netherland, had been taken by an English fleet in 1664 and retaken by a Dutch one in 1673. The Dutch residents had demonstrated during the battle for Manhattan where their loyalties lay after nine years of English rule: civilians swarmed to the fleet to supply military information, the New York City burgher guard joined the battle on the Dutch side, and the Dutch towns on Long Island threatened to sack neighboring English towns if they should send militia to join the battle on Manhattan. Threats against the Puritan towns were hardly necessary: they demonstrated no zeal to defend the royalist government. Fifteen months later the royalist government was back, and Andros was not arriving with the spirit of compromise that his English predecessors had demonstrated in their efforts to pacify the inhabitants.

Upon Andros's arrival at New York, the Dutch military governor Anthony Colve engaged him in lengthy discussions over the rights to be accorded the Dutch residents before agreeing to surrender the city and depart. Once Andros was in place, however, he quickly demonstrated that his interpretation of the terms of the agreement was to be considered definitive, and there would be no further discussion. He squelched protests from community leaders by economic intimidation: the protestors were treated as resident aliens without any of the property rights of English subjects. At the same time, he advanced and rewarded pliable residents, particularly among the principal merchants.

One of the first acts of Governor Andros upon arrival at New York was to swear in Matthias Nicolls as secretary of the province, mayor of the city, and member of the council. One of the most important figures in early New York government, Nicolls had originally arrived with the first English army of conquest in 1664 and had served in several major offices until the fall of New York to the Dutch in 1673. During the fifteen-month interregnum he had resided in Connecticut, probably supported in part by Governor Winthrop and his son Fitz-John (Nicolls's close personal friend, as was Silvester Salisbury), and kept up a correspondence with various persons as he looked after the duke's interests. A barrister by training and profession, Nicolls served in Andros's administration as judge, justice, and secretary (clerk) for virtually every type of court—the courts of sessions in the three ridings on Long Island, the mayor's court in New York, the general court of assizes, and special courts of admiralty. He was in addition captain of the Long Island volunteer troop of horse (also apparently a commissioned captain of regulars), and when he was not mayor of New York he served as alderman. For the researcher, his most important role was as provincial secretary: he decided what records were worth keeping, endorsed most of the documents himself, and is the author of nearly all the court and council minutes, administrative memoranda, and notes in the files from 1664 to 1680.

Much of the material in the documents of this time period is taken up with Andros's efforts at reestablishing the authority of the government—making contacts with neighboring colonies, trying to settle boundaries, squelching the Yankees on Long Island endeavoring to unite with Connecticut, and making treaties with the various Indian tribes within New York's sphere of influence. There were questions about confirming land titles issued during the Dutch interregnum and about New Yorkers' cargoes seized at Boston as the property of enemy Dutch and therefore as prizes of war.

Building on the colony's mercantile base, Andros embarked on a broad-scaled program to develop the commercial situation of the colony. He undertook several building projects to improve New York City and her harbor. He also increased government regulation of trade, favoring the principal centers to the disadvantage of the smaller communities and New Jersey.

During the Colve administration, the English towns of eastern Long Island eagerly accepted magistrates from Connecticut. Andros brought the towns quickly back into the New York fold. Martha's Vineyard and Nantucket had fallen under the authority of Massachusetts but were under Andros' control by April 1675, a change in law and government welcomed only by those settlers whose land titles derived from the duke of York's patent.

In May 1675, Andros rode down to Delaware to establish control there in the face of Maryland opposition. When John Fenwick set himself up as governor of West Jersey and voided land patents issued by Andros, he was summarily seized and taken to New York for trial. Problems with East New Jersey were still in the future: Philip Carteret administered the colony as a dependency of New York and was a member of Andros's council.

When Connecticut in 1675 pressed claims to territory east of the Hudson occupied by New Yorkers, Andros responded with a letter calling on Connecticut to surrender the disputed territories its colonists occupied west of the Connecticut River. Two months later, King Philip's War broke out in New England, and Andros led a military expedition to the Connecticut River to protect the settlers from the Indians. Given his recent claims to that territory, it is not surprising that when he arrived at Saybrook on July 8 he found the militia drawn up and ready to repel him. He retreated to Southold, Long Island, where he reviewed the militia, disarmed those Long Island Indian tribes with close ties to Philip, and sent munitions to the more receptive New Englanders: Major Winthrop at New London, Governor Coddington in Rhode Island, and the duke of York's subjects on Martha's Vineyard and Nantucket.

In August Andros went to Albany, met with the local court and then with leaders of at least some of the Five Nations, affirming to the sachems the treaties and policies of special relationship instituted by his predecessors, both Dutch and English. He apparently hoped to use the Iroquois to protect New York from the Puritans, the New England Indians, and the French and their Indian allies to the north, policies that the Iroquois found consistent with their own interests. When he returned to New York, he left behind a military detachment commanded by Ensign Caesar Knapton, and in October he sent reinforcements under the recently promoted Captain Brockholls.

In January 1675/6, Andros received word that Philip and several hundred of his fighting men were near Hoosick, only a few miles from Albany on the east side of the Hudson River. He ordered Brockholls to provide arms to the Mohawk, who with other Iroquois attacked Philip's encampment, sending the Abenakis fleeing to the north and Philip's own people toward the Connecticut River. As soon as the ice on the Hudson broke, Andros took as many troops as could be spared from the defense of Manhattan and sailed to Albany, arriving there the day after the triumphal return of the Mohawk. He sent Lt. Gerrit Teunisse of Albany to warn Philip not to come back and to promise to any peaceful Indians he might encounter a place of refuge. At the end of the month, Andros returned to New York but in May 1676 went to Schaghticoke in the Hoosick Valley to sign a treaty settling the refugees of the various Algonquian tribes there as wards of the Mohawk. Caught between simultaneous campaigns of the Connecticut militia and the Mohawk that summer, Indians by the hundreds fled New England for New York, many to accept the offer of peaceful settlement. Some of Philip's Wampanoag tried to escape back home to Mount Hope in Rhode Island and were killed, as was Philip himself on the twelfth of August.

At the same time but far to the south, the Susquehanna nation was being decimated as it fought two wars simultaneously against Maryland and the western Iroquois. The Mohawk, hoping through peaceful negotiations to snatch the spoils of victory away from the rest of the Five Nations and Maryland, made several offers to the Susquehanna to adopt them into their tribe. Governor Andros, equally desirous of control over the people and territory of the Susquehanna, sent Capt. John Collier to Delaware to negotiate with them. In the end, all of the Five Nations filled their depleted ranks of warriors through adoption and collectively increased the area of the confederacy's hegemony. Andros's program was successful to the extent that he prevented Maryland and Virginia from expanding into the Delaware region, and through Iroquois successes, he realized a strengthened position for New York in colonial-Indian trade.

Edmund Andros had arrived in New York at a time of great upheaval in colonial affairs. He was the right man for the job, not excited by difficult circumstances but able to examine them calmly to see what advantages might be wrested from each situation. He not only reacted to events but had vision: definite ideas on how to improve the territories under his authority; he was glad to accept the mercantile development and Indian relations established by earlier governments but intended to go farther and accomplish more, always to redound to the advantage of his patrons the king and duke. Those who criticize his administration of New York do so in terms of his suppression of democratic tendencies and his disinterest in playing to the crowd or accommodating the common man. None of this was what he was sent to do; judged according to his patrons' interests, he accomplished a great deal. The first two years were a difficult time to govern, but Edmund Andros governed certainly and with clear direction.

The Andros Papers

It should be noted what the papers are, and what they are not. Although they have long been popularly known as the Andros papers, they are to be understood as one of several series of records from his administration as governor of New York. They are the papers that the government received and the provincial secretary filed in the records office during the administration of Edmund Andros. In modern archival terms, these are papers of the executive department of the colonial government, not the personal papers of the governor himself. There is little in here of his handwriting, and almost nothing to indicate what he was thinking. Of the documents in the hand of an official of the provincial government, almost all are written by Matthias Nicolls, either on orders from the governor or in fulfillment of his administrative duties as provincial secretary, council secretary, and secretary of numerous courts.

Originally filed in bundles by subject, these records were reorganized in the nineteenth century in supposedly chronological order. They include minutes of council meetings with Long Island Indians and records of the New York mayor's court, the magistrates' court at Albany, the Long Island courts of sessions, and the court of assizes. There are petitions from private citizens for relief from various problems and for hearing cases on appeal. There are reports from persons commissioned to evaluate buildings, land, ships, cargoes, or other property that the government wished to improve, tax, or seize. There are notes intended to be rewritten in the copybooks—sometimes no fair copy was ever made, but when such exists we have noted any significant variations in text. There are copies of correspondence with governors and other officials of other colonies, both English and French. For the most part there are no general entries, council minutes, land patents, or land papers, which were kept in separate series. What appears here often does not provide a complete picture of events and should be taken together with records in other provincial series, with local records, with private papers, and with records of other colonies.

The amount of material that has survived from the Andros period is prodigious. This series for the six years that he was in the colony contains some 1,275 documents, as compared to 156 documents for the nine years of Governors Nicolls and Lovelace. The records in this book are from volumes 24 and 25 of the New York Colonial Manuscripts series in the New York State Archives; the only documents not included here are those previously published in our volume, *Records of the Court of Assizes for the Colony of New York, 1665–1682.* Two more books are planned for next year, which will contain the rest of the papers of the Andros administration in this series, volumes 26–29.

Most of this material has not previously been printed. The state historian published volume 24 in his annual report for 1897, lacking the numerous Dutch documents for which no translation was then available, and skipping over anything hard to read or incomplete. Errors of transcription and from misunderstanding are common in that edition. Similarly, those manuscripts included in the *Documentary History of the State of New York* and in the *Documents Relating to the Colonial History of the State of New York* often contain editorial suppositions in place of missing or indecipherable text. This of course reads nicely and avoids messy-looking blank areas; we have sacrificed elegance of that sort in the interest of accuracy.

We have made use of whatever versions of the materials we could find in print, particularly early transcriptions made before some of the damage occurred. However, we do suspect, and can occasionally demonstrate, that some of what is published is pure guesswork. We include such information in brackets, noting when it seems contrary to other information. The reader should of course always carefully evaluate all the bracketed material.

As might be expected, persons writing to the governor exhibit a variety of handwriting styles and spelling conventions. We have strived in every case to discover the exact word that the writer intended, and where the spelling is so far afield as to render the word incomprehensible, to suggest in a footnote what we think was the intended word.

It might be noted that the governor's handwriting was even worse than that of many of his humbler correspondents, especially when he scrawled with a red crayon or a blunt pencil: in the latter case one sometimes suspects him of using a piece of lead shot instead. Andros apparently had little formal education: he wrote in a semiliterate scrawl and showed little awareness of the spelling conventions of his day. One can find similar writers among the humbler artisans and farmers, but among the gentry only Sheriff Edmond Cantwell in Delaware is comparable.

Secretary Nicolls's draft copies of documents, often difficult enough to read because of insertions and deletions, are much more scrawled than similar documents of his from previous administrations. An ever-increasing work load is probably the chief cause, although in the past he had mentioned a session of some duration when pain in his arm prevented him from writing.

The editing rules followed in this volume are the same as for previous volumes in this series: abbreviations with the word's end letter have been expanded, and the letters used indifferently in the seventeenth century (as *i* for *j*) have been regularized. Minor mental lapses (writing the same word twice) have been corrected silently, but otherwise the original spelling and grammar have been preserved. Within the limits of our medium, our page layout suggests the appearance of the documents. Blank areas in brackets are of the approximate size of the lost material. We have avoided footnotes except when a particularly obscure term occurs. A glossary of recurring terms has been provided .

There is a fair amount of Dutch material, perhaps 10 percent of the whole. Much of it is tax valuations from western Long Island, business accounts of John Shakerly, and copies of Albany court records. There are also a few French documents from Michael Hainelle of Brooklyn and official correspondence with Quebec. All of this material is presented here in English translation, much of it for the first time.

In seeking to comprehend the gist of documents, two books on the general period have proved especially useful: John Romeyn Brodhead's *History of the State of New York,* and Robert C. Ritchie's *Duke's Province.* For writing this introduction, we have found them helpful and Stephen Saunders Webb's *1676: The End of American Independence.* All references cited are included in the bibliography.

Abbreviations, Terms, and Editorial Method

anker	Dutch measure: 10.128 gallons of wine; 9.812 gallons of brandy.
BGE	*Books of General Entries. See* Bibliography for full information.
burgher	(Dutch). Town resident with the rights and privileges of the community.
burn't wine	a literal translation of (Dutch) *brandewijn*, brandy.
C.	captain.
CA	*Records of the Court of Assizes. See* Bibliography for full information.
carsey	kersey: a coarse, ribbed woolen cloth.
CD	*Documents Relative to the Colonial History of the State of New York. See* Bibliography for full information.
cill	sill. Groundsill: "a timber serving as a foundation to carry a superstructure"—*Oxford English Dictionary.*
clipcunt	a type of shell; perhaps a term for the shells used in making seawant.
commissary	magistrate. A mistranslation from (Dutch) *commissaris.*
copia	(Latin) copy; *copia vera* (true copy).

DH	*Documentary History of the State of New York. See* Bibliography for full information.
deal boards	pinc planks.
domine	minister of the Dutch Reformed Church; by extention used also for Lutheran clergy.
duffel	blanket cloth, popular in the Indian trade. Duffel coats: coats of this material.
EAS	Edmund Andros, seigneur of Sausmarez. Used by the governor for initialling documents.
ERA	*Early Records of the City and County of Albany. See* Bibliography for full information.
ells	a cloth measure; 45 inches.
f	symbol for Dutch guilders (originally florins). In the seventeenth century 6 guilders were equal to an English pound sterling.
farm	a leasing of the office of excise farmer, with authority to license tapsters, brewers, and distillers, and to collect and retain excise taxes from them. The office was purchased annually at auction.
fathom	(of wampum): six feet of strung seawant.
G	English symbol for Dutch guilder. *See f.*
groundbrief	(Dutch) *grondbrief.* Land patent.
Hollants	(short for Hollants value). The price of goods according to the stable value of Dutch coin, rather than the inflationary seawant value. *See* seawant.
Hough, F. B., 1858	*Narrative of the Cases Which Led to Philip's Indian War. See* Bibliography for full information.
In presentia	(Latin). In the presence (of).

juffrou	(Dutch) lady. Conventional title of courtesy for a woman.
kan	plural, kanne(n). Also spelled *can*. Dutch liquid measure: 1.266 quarts.
£ s d	pounds, shillings, and pence.
lapp	(Dutch) *lap*; a fragment, usually of cloth. In the beaver trade a piece less than a full pelt.
MN	Matthias Nicolls.
major, mayor	two words spelled interchangeably by both Dutch and English (both pronounced the same in Dutch).
mole	(of the harbor). A pier or breakwater. The Great Dock on the East River in New York City.
morgen	Dutch land measure: 2.103 acres Rhineland measure; 2.069 Amsterdam measure.
Mr.	shipmaster, mister, and sometimes *meester*, for (Dutch) *heelmeester* (barber-surgeon).
mutsje	Dutch liquid measure: 2.15 oz.
NYSHAR	Annual Report of the New York State Historian. *See* Bibliography for full information.
Orania, New Orania	English spelling of (Dutch) *Nieu Oranje* (New Orange), the name given to the city of New York during the Dutch reoccupation, 1673–74.
packt	(Dutch) *pacht*; lease, especially the annual lease of the excise office. Great pacht: the liquor excise; and little pacht: beer excise.
paertie	Dutch liquid measure: two pints.
pintie	Dutch liquid measure: pint.
qt.	sometimes an abbreviation for quarter.

quod attestor	(Latin); bearing witness to that.
rate(s)	local tax(es).
sack	white wine from Spain or the Canary Islands.
sarge	serge cloth.
schepel	Dutch dry measure: 0.764 bushel wheat; 1.29 bushels salt.
schout	Dutch court officer with responsibilities for administration, law enforcement, criminal prosecution, and civil adjudication.
seawant	Known in New England as wampum; strings of beads made from clam shells by the Indians, used by the settlers as scrip in the absence of hard cash. It was usually worth less than the stated value, 16 guilders in seawant being equivalent to 5 guilders in coin.
s	symbol for (Dutch) *stuiver*, $1/20$ of a guilder, or (English) shilling, $1/20$ of a pound. A slash (/) is also used for the shilling.
ss	(Latin), *scilicet*, it is permitted to know: To wit, namely.
singell thicks	shingle thicks; thick here is probably derived from the verb (variant of thatch) meaning to cover.
staff	plural, staves. Emblems of office of constables.
stave	(of lead). An oblong mass of metal; an ingot or pig.
stuff coat	a coat of wool or worsted material.
teste	(Latin) witness. "Often used to indicate what immediately follows is named as authority for what precedes."—*Webster's Third New International Dictionary*.

vaatie   (Dutch) a barrel or keg (in a brewery); a tub (of butter).

Vlissinge   The Dutch village on Long Island, now called Flushing.

[   ]   Empty brackets indicate loss of text within a damaged document. When text appears within the brackets it has been supplied from another source, either a contemporary copy or an early transcript of the present document. In the latter case the reader should be wary: generally we cannot know whether earlier editors were working with the document prior to its being damaged, or simply guessing at missing words.

The Andros Papers

1674–1675

The New York Historical Manuscripts Series
Volume XXIV

[24:1b][*]

1674 July 1	Rates established By his Royal Highnes For the Custes at New York.

Forraigne goods Imported to New Yorke are to Pay as Follueth (vizt)

All Goods (Exept Such as are here particularly Rated) Shipt in England, or in any of the English Plantacions, when Imported to New Yorke are to pay two per Cent ad Valorem; Butt if it shall apeare, that any ship, come from, any other Cuntry to Ingland, with a Cargo of goods, and paying her Custums there proceed, thence for New Yorke with the said Cargo of goods then the Goods of such Cargo to pay ten per cent *ad valorem.*

All These goods going up Hudsons River to pay Thre per cent ad Valorem over and above the Two per Cent For Inportacions to New Yorke.

Wines from any Port to pay ten Shelings per Butt or Pipe.

Brandy or other Spirits to pay 15: shelins per Hoghead:

Rum to Pay Six Shelings per Hoghead

All these Liquors going up Hudsons River, to pay the Same Rates again at going up the River as they paid comming unto New Yorke

Goods of the Cuntry, coming into New Yorke are to pay as Folloueth (Vizt.)

Beaver per Merchandable Skin, to pay one Sheling thre Pence per Skin

All other Furs, Skins and Peltry to pay proporcionable to Beaver.

Tobacco, of the growth of the Place, if it goes for Ingland to pay two Shelings per Hoghead; Butt Tobacco of that Please, if it do not give Bound to come for England According to the Statute of 25 Regis Carol: Second:[‡] is to pay in Tobac: one penny per pound.
All goods both of the Cuntry and Forraigne goods, to be under the same

---

* This is the first document listed in E. B. O'Callaghan's Calendar of New York Historical Manuscripts. The present 24:1a may be found after 24:56.
‡ i.e., The twenty-fifth [year of the reign] of King Charles II.

Regulacion and Payments in Delaware River as in Hudsons river.

These Rates to hold good for Thre yeares to Commence from the Arival and Publicacion of them att New York.

Provided Neverthelesse, that all utensilles Such as Spaides, Axes, Plough Shares Shovels, and Such Like, as shall be Necessary and Enployed about The Improvement of Plantacions shall be exempt from the Paym. of Thre per Cent ad valorem; att theire going up the river.

[E Andros. S.]*

[ENDORSED:] A copie of the Rates payable at the Custom[es] house

[24:1c]

[COPY OF 24:1b]

[24:1d]

Councills Opinions concerning Colonell Nicholls Pattent and Indian Purchases‡

The Land Called N. York and other Parts in America now Called N. East Jersey was First Discovered by Sebastian Cobbitt a Subject of England in King Henery the 7ths time about 180 Years Since and afterwards Further by Sir Walter Raliegh in the Reign of Queen Eliz: and after him by Henery Hudson in the reign of King James and also by the Lord delaware and begun to be planted in the year 1614 by Dutch and English the Dutch Placed a Governour there but upon Complaint made by the King of England to the States of Holland the said States Disown'd the Bisness and Declard it was only a Private Undertaking of the West India Company of Amsterdam so the King of England Granted a Commission to Sir Edward Layden to Plant these parts calling them New Albion and the Dutch submited themselves to the English Government but in King Charels the 1st Reign the troubles in England breaking forth the English not minding to promote these New Plantations because of the troubles the Dutch Pretended to Establish a Government there again untill the year 1660 when afterwards it was Reduced under the English Govern-

* The signature appears in the copy 24:1c.
‡ This appears to be the king's council.

ment and included and Ratifyed in the peace made between England and Holland then it was Granted to the Duke of York 1664 who the same Year Granted it to the Lord Barckley and Sir George Cartrett betwixt the Dukes Grant to the Lord Barckly and Sir George Cartrett and Notice thereof in America severall Persons took Grants of Lands from Colonell Nicolls the Dukes Governor. Severall of the Planters have purchased of the Indians but Refuse to pay any acknowledgment to the Kings Grantees.

Q:1st. Wither the Grants made by Colonell Nicolls are good against the Assigns of the Lord Berckley and Sir George Cartrett.

Q:2d. Wither the Grant from the Indians be sufficient to any Planter without a Grant from the King or his Assignes.

Ans: 1st. To the first Question the Authority by which Colonell Nicholls Acted Determined by the Dukes Grant to the Lord Berckley and Sir George Cartrett and all Grants made by him afterwards (tho according to the Commission:) are void for the Delegated Power which Colonell Nicolls had of making Grants of the Land could Last no Longer then his Majesties Intrest who gave him that Power and the having or not having notice of the Dukes Grant to the Lord Berckly and Sir George Cartret makes no Difference in the Law but the want of Notice makes it Great Equity that the Present Propritor should Confirm such Grants to the people who will submit to the Condissions and payments of the Present Proprioters Quitt rents other wise they may Look upon them as Desseizors and treat them as such

Answ: To the 2d Question by the Law of Nations if any people make Discovery of any Contry of Barbarians the Prince of that people who makes the Discovery hath the Right of the Soyle and Government of that place and no people can plant there without the Consent of the Prince or of such Persons to whom his Right is Devoulved and Convayed the Practice of all Plantations has been according to this and no People has been suffered to take up Land but by the Consent and Lycence of the Governor or proprietors under the Princes title whose people made the first Discovery and upon their submition to the Laws of the Place and Contribution to the Publick Charges of the place and the payment of such Rent and other Value for the Soile as the Proprietors for the time being Require and tho it hath been and still is the usuall Practice of all Proprietors to give their Indians some Recompence for their Land and so seems to Purchase it of them yet that is not done for want of sufficient

title from the King or Prince who hath the right of Discovery but out of
Prudence and Christian Charity Least otherwise the Indians might have
destroyed the first planters (who are usually to few to Defend themselves) or Refuse all Commerce and Conversation with the planters and
thereby all hopes of Converting them to the Christian faith would be Lost
in this the Common Law of England and the Civill Law doth agree and
if any planter be Refractory and will Insist on his Indian Purchase and
not submit to this Law of Plantations the Proprietors who have the Title
Under the Prince may deny them the benefit of the Law and Prohibitt
Comerce with them as Opposers and Enemys to the Publick peace
Besides t'is Observable that no man Can goe from England to plant in
an English Plantation without Leave from the Government and therefore
in All Pattents and grants of Plantations from the King a Particular
Lycence to Carry Over Planters is incerted which Power in Prohibitting
is now in the Proprietors as the Kings Assigns and therefore tho some
planters have purchased from the Indians Yett having done soe without
the Consent of the Proprietors for the time being the title is good against
the Indians but not against the Proprietors without a Confirmation from
them upon the usuall terms of Other Plantations.

Wm.Leek	John Hoyle	Richd. Wallop
Wm.Williams	Jo: Holt	Hen: Pollexfen
Jo: Holles	Wm. Thomson	

A True Coppy

Gawin Lawrie Robt. West

[ENDORSED:]   Councills Opinion
                   Concerning Col. Nicolls
                   Patent and Indian Purchases.

[24:2]

[PETITION BY WALTER WEBLEY FOR LAND]

[ ] Right honnorable Edmond Androsse Esquire Seignieur
of [ ]ns Marez and Governor Generall under his Royall
highness; [ ]ames Duke of Yorke and Albany of all his
territories: In America

The humble Peticion of Walter Webley,
agent and Attorney to Collenell Lewis
Morris:

That your Peticioners Employer, hath for some yeares [   ]Consider-
ably in this Port from Barbadoes, and purchaced [   ]within this his R.
Hs Government for the setleing a Plantacion [   ] Harlam and hath had
very great Losses by the Duches taking Country [   ] and being speedely
designed hither in Order to bring his [   ]lly and Setle thereupon May it
please your honnor there is a Small [   ] of Land next adjoyning to his
bounds North East, or Northerly from [   ] which Neck was formerly
promised to him by Governor Lovelace, [   ]e another parcell of Land
Lyeing and adjoyning to his betweene [   ] Archer and Spyting Divell
River: both which (as your Petitioner is [   ]ormed) was never granted
Purchased, or settled by any man and should [   ]eighbours settle
therupon it might greatly dammage your peticioners [   ]oyer by the
sheltring servants and Slaves emproving opportunities [   ] to desert
his worke, and flye from him, as alsoe for that hee [   ] 14 hands
allready upon his Land, and more dayly expected with [   ]llonell
which induceth him to feare hee hath not Land enough [   ]eploy his
people haveing not one foote given him but what hee hath [   ]hased,

Which constreyneth him on behalfe of the said [   ] Morris to suplicate
your honnor favourably to grant him the [   ]eco[ ]d Neck, with the
other Land for the enlarging the said [   ]and preventing the inconveniences that may attend him [   ]ers settle upon the same, which
favour will greatly oblidge [   ]id Collonell Morris,

To pray for your honnors
Long life and Prosperity,

Walter Webley

[ENDORSED:]   G[ ]t [   ]
M. Nicolls Sec.
[   ] Satu[ ]day
1674
Mr. Webley

[24:3]

[LETTER OF JOHN SAFFIN, ENTERING A CAVEAT AGAINST
THE SALE OF A HOUSE]

New Yorke 2d November 1674.

Capt. Nicolls
Sir

Whereas Henry van de Water hath Seruptitiously Obtained A Mortgage
of old Sander Lenderson of Albany on the Stone house Scittuate in the
Smiths fly, which was long before made over to, and hath been in the
possession of Capt. Tho. Willett Deceased, and Now of Right pertaines
to his heires as shall in Due time be made Appeare: I Say the premisses
Considered my humble Request to you is, that you would be pleased to
Doe me the favor as to give Check to any farther proceedings of him the
said Henry: Either by his Attempting to Expose the said house to sale,
or otherwise to Deprive the said heires of their Just Right; untill they may
have Oppertunity to Defend their Interest. Sir if in anything I may bee
in A Capacity to Doe you any Real service Either att Boston or Elsewhere
bee pleased to Command him who Assuredly is

> Sir
> Your most humble Servant
> John Saffin

Sir
Be Pleased allso to put aside, or note that protest Capt. Willett made
against Quaker Smith Concerning a tract of land att Long Island Called
Neshequage that it may be Ready in time Convenient.

[ADDRESSED:]   Jno Saffin

To Capt: Matthias Nicolls
Secretary of State.

[ENDORSED:]   Memorandum Nov. 2. 1674
Mr. Saffin.

[24:4]

[PETITION OF MARGARET BAKER TO BE
RELEASED FROM DEBT]

Citty of   To the Worshipfull Court of Mayor and Aldermen etc.
New York

The humble Peticion of Margt. Baker

Sheweth

That your peticioners husband Jacob Baker about 8 years since Departed
from your Peticioner leaving your Peticioner with three small Children
in a very poor Condicion without making any provision for satisfying
his debts or for the maintainance of his family but now Mr. Gerritt Van
tright who is one of the Creditors hath sued your Peticioner for his debt
the which will undoubtedly provoke the rest of the Creditors to doe the
like whose Just demands the Estate is not able to satisfie. And whereas
your Peticioner doth very much despaire of her husband being in Life
shee haveing had in severall yeares noe Letters or Advice from him but
only by various Reports that he is deceased since his departure from
hollond to the East Indies the which not being Certainly Knowne no
Administracion can be taken out.

Therefore humbly prays your Worshipps (your Peticioner
making a full and true discovery of her husbands Estate to
your Worshipps or to such person as to that end you shall
appoint) shee may be wholly cleared and quitted from the
said Estate and no further Molested or Sued by the sayd Van
tright or any other and that the same may be decided
amongst the Creditors or otherwise Disposed of as to your
worshipps shall seeme most agreeable with Equity and
Justice etc.

And shee shall ever pray etc.

[ENDORSED:]   1674
Coppy of Margtt. Bakers
Peticion.

[24:5]

To the right Honorable and highly Esteemed Lord, the honorable Edmund Andros, Governor on behalf of his-Royal Highness the Lord Duke of York etc.

Right Honorable and Highly Esteemed Lord.

Jacob Mauritsz, skipper on the ship *de Beurs* van Amsterdam, most humbly shows how he sailed to this place from Amsterdam and arrived here during the Dutch administration, carrying diverse merchandise for the inhabitants here, and furthermore in order to collect some outstanding debts for his superiors and for himself; and whereas the administration of this province is to be relinquished to your honor, and various merchants desire to ship goods and other persons have themselves transported from here to Holland; therefore, the petitioner turns to your honor reverently requesting that your honor be pleased to allow and permit him to do the same, and to depart from here therewith directly for Holland without any hindrance or obstruction. Anticipating your honor's favorable recommendation hereon, I remain in the meantime

Your honor's humble servant

Jacob Mauritsz

[ENDORSED:]   Jacobus Mauritz
Petition
Novemb. 3d 1674

[NOTATION:]*   Dutch Skiper

[24:6a]

---

*   Both the notation and the endorsement are in English.
‡   This document is missing.

[24:6b]

[PETITION OF TRISTRAM COFFIN AND MATTHEW MAYHEW ABOUT
THEIR GRANT, AND RELATED DOCUMENT INQUIRING ABOUT A
MANOR COURT]

To the honourable Major Edmund Andros Govournor of his Royall
highness Territories in America:

May it please Your honour to understand that divers gentlemen having
heertofore obtained liberty from Mr. Thomas Mayhew and Thomas
Mayhew his sonne by vertue of a right they had of the Right honourable
William Earle of Sterlig: to plant settle and inhabit upon the Ile of
Nantuckett, they prosecuted the same to a good effect and made lawfull
purchase of the Indians then inhabiting there; under which constitution
they the said first purchasers continued and admitted of divers other
inhabitants, allotting them such lands, as their quallitie, and way of living
might require; to some more, to some less; with divers in injunctions as
to your honour shall appear: and have since obtained a Confirmation
thereof by charter, from Collonell Lovelace, late Govournour under his
Royall Highnes, the Duke of Yorke which said charter or pattent, being
composed in generall termes: the said first purchasers, and not without
cause, have feared a disturbance in their quiet and peaceable injoment
of their said interest: by those they had formerly admitted in among them:
the cause whereof ariseth from their misconceiving, (as the first purchasers humbly conceive) of the pattent, or charter: supposing the said
charter to intend to have proportioned each person there inhabiting, a
like and equall interest, with the first purchasers: the said purchasers
conceiving the intent thereof only to be the setling and confirming of
each person in that Right and interest he before had in his Just tenure and
occupation; of which your petitioners humbly intreat your honours
resolution; as likewise whither any person having land, there, may not
inhabit and be said so to doe, by his substitute: your honours Resolve
heerof shall be a guide to such as might endeavor, to abridge the first
purchasers of their interest, to inlarge their own: we shall not further
inlarge but in behaulf as well of the said first purchasers as others there
inhabiting, declare to your honour the perfect state therof and therefore
conclude subscribing our selves
Honoured Sir

Your honors humble servants

Tristram Coffyn
Matthew Mayhew

[. . .]hether* or [   ] such pur[   ] [ ]andes, be not in the .
[   ]per power, of the pur[ ]hasers; and such others, as they have
admitted, as their Associates:

whether the purchasers and Associates, have not, by vertue of their
pattent, liberty, and power, to erect a Court o[ ] meeting, as a Mannour
Court: that such other landes, conditionally, or otherwise graunted them
in a way of Associateship, be accordingly held, a[ ] injoyed.

whether a man, may not inhabit and be properly [ ] [ ]nd so to doe by
his Substitute.
[   ]674

Tristram Coffyn
Matthew Mayhew

[ENDORSED:]   Mr. Tristram Coffin
Mr. Mathew Mayhew
A Peticion to the Governor
from Nantucket.

Nov. 4th 1674

[24:7a]

[LETTER FROM GOVERNOR ANDROS TO GOVERNOR COLVE
RELATING TO THE SURRENDER]

I have received yours of the 13th new style by Capt. Carel Episteyn and
Lieut. Charles Quirinsen, together with the Orders for the respective
places of this Government to bee delivered to mee, pursuant to the
Articles of Peace: And now have onely to adde my acknowledgments
and thankes for your further kind Expressions to mee in your said letter:

As to your Postscript concerning pressing I doe hope my former Answer
will bee satsfactory for quieting the minds of the Inhabitants. But for
your owne further satistion I doe further assure you, that I shall [   ]er
impose, nor desire their bearing Armes against their Nation.

As to Mr. Wm Darvalls molesting in words a person posses't of a
Confiscated house, As soone as I heard it, I did check the said Darvall
for soe doeing, letting him know, that all were to have the free benefitt

---

* Brackets indicate an unknown quantity of text lost at the top of the page.

of the law and Articles of Peace, and did assure the other of Right and Justice pursuant thereunto, which in all Cases shall bee my endeavor, as it is my Orders:

This is By Capt. Matthias Nicolls who will tell you the same verbally: and by whom (having had many addresses) I have sent you such demands as have been given mee in writing for damages susteyned, from those under your Command, since the time limited for Peace in these parts; upon which I pray and will not doubt your effectuall Answer; If there bee any thing yet remaining wherein I may serve you before your voyage, I shall bee ready further [   ]stify how much I am

                    Sir

                                        Your most humble servant
                                        November 7th 1674.

[ENDORSED:]   Letter to Go:
                   No. 7–1674.

[24:7b]

                   Losses and Damages sustayned by divers persons as
                   Masters of Vessells etc. by their being taken by the
                   snow[*] and brought to this place.

An Account brought in by
Richard Patteschall Master of
Ketch   211:19:00

An Account from William
Lewis Master of [ ] Vessell—
Damages   71:17:00

An Account of Robt. Edmunds
Merchant in William Lewis his
Vessell   87:15:10

* Snow: a square-rigged ship.

An Account of Samuell Wood-
berry Master of a Vessell   107:07:11

An Account of the losse and
damage of Samuell Crosse—
wounded on board Samuell
Woodberry   75:02:06
                                                                  554: 2: 3

[ENDORSED:]   Losses sus[   ]
                 severall Mast[   ]
                 Vessells from [   ]
                 here, after the [ ]

[NOTE:]   Put in by Capt. Davenport and Mr. Patteshall to Go:
                 Andros, but the Dutch Go: Colve went away before
                 it came to his hands.

[24:8]

(Copia)   The First Proclamation Confirming Rights and Proper-
                 tyes.

                        By the Governour

Whereas it hath pleased his Majestie and his Royall Highnesse to send
mee with Authority to receive this place and Government from the Dutch
and to Continue in the Command thereof, under his Royall Highnesse,
who hath not onely taken care for our future Safety and Defence, but also
given mee his Commands for securing the Rights and Propertyes of the
Inhabitants, and that I should endeavor by all fitting meanes the good
and wellfare of this Province and Dependences, under his Government.
That I may not bee wanting in any thinge that may conduce thereunto,
and for the saving of Trouble and Charge of any coming hither, for the
Satisfying themselves in such doubts as might arise concerning there
Rights and Propertyes, upon this change of Government, and wholly to
settle the mindes of all in Generall, I have thought fit to Publish and
Declare, That all former Graunts Priviledges, or Concessions heretofore
granted, and all Estates Legally posses't by any under his Royall Highnesse, before the Late Dutch Government, As alsoe All Legall Judiciall
Proceedings during that Government to my arrivall in these parts, are
hereby confirmed, and the Possessors by vertue thereof, to remaine in
quiet Possession of their Rights; It is hereby further declared That the

knowne Booke of Lawes formerly Establisht and Confirmed by his Royall Highnesse, is now againe in force and Confirmed by his Royall Highnesse, the which are to bee Observed and practised together with the manner and time of holding Courts therein mencioned as heretofore, And all Magistrates and Civill officers Belonging there unto to bee chosen and Establish't Accordingly. Given under my hand in New Yorke, this 9th day of November in the 26th yeare of his Majesties Raigne, Annoque Domini 1674.

Edmund Andros.

A True Copy Examined by mee.
Matthias Nicolls Secre.

[ENDORSED:]*   Copie of the Governors proclamacion
                   about Rights and Propertyes.

[24:9]

[PETITION OF JAMES MATTHEWS TO BUILD A WOOD
HOUSE AND PRIVY]

To the Right H[   ]und Andros Esqr. Governor
Generall under his Ro[   ]gnesse, James Duke of
Yorke and Albany[   ] his Territoryes in America.
The hu[   ] Peticion of James Matthews.

Humbly sheweth.

That your Peticioner is (and a long [   ] been) an Inhabitant and a Victualler within this City, and ha[ ] not long since) been at great charge and expences, in rebuilding and fitting of his House, with such convenient and necessary reparations, as are suitable for the accommodacion of Strangers and others, who may and do resort thereunto; yet notwithstanding all good con[ ]rivance us'd, your Peticioner is extreamly straitned for want of a little [   ]nient place to secure Firewood in, and to build a P[r]ivy House on h[ ]ving no private place of Evacuacion or Easment, belonging to his said [ ]abi[ ]acion, to his great damage.

Your Peticioner humbly [   ] your Honor to consider his
great necessity in this partic[   ], and grant him Liberty for
the Building of a small House for the security of his Wood,

---

* The endorsement appears on a separate piece of paper.

and to make a privy on, upon some part of the wharfe fronting the Road, which properly appertaines to himselfe, with such Allowance of dimencion for the performance thereof, as your Honor shall adjudge mee[ ]. And your Peticioner doth promise and engage, that the said N[   ]ry building shall no wayes (or as little as possible may be) prejudice the prospect of the street, towards the Harbour.

And your Peticioner shall pray etc.

[24:10a]

[PETITION OF JACOB MAURITSZ FOR PERMISSION TO SAIL. TRANSLATION]

To the right Honorable, Valiant and highly Esteemed Lord, the honorable Edmund Andros Governor General of New York etc.

Right Honorable, Valiant and Highly Esteemed Lord.

Jacob Maurits, skipper of the flyboat *de Beurs van Amsterdam*, riding at anchor before this city, most humbly shows how he, the petitioner, about 12 days ago presented and submitted to your honor a petition which in substance contained a request for permission to unload and sell the rest of his goods here; to receive payment for them as well as other outstanding debts; and permission to take on his cargo here and depart therewith directly to Holland. Until now the petitioner has yet to receive a definitive reply. And whereas the petitioner is staying here with the ship under his command at great expense; therefore, the petitioner turns once more to your honor, humbly requesting a speedy and favorable response to his aforesaid petition by which he can regulate himself. However, if it is beyond hope to obtain such permission, the petitioner requests consent to take on some wood and pipe staves* here and [   ] his outstanding debts and effects and to depart therewith to the [   ] islands, and wherever it may please him [   ] thereafter.

Thus, doing, I shall remain
Your honor's humble servant,
Jacob Mauritsz

---

* These are staves for a barrel used in shipping wine. A pipe could contain anywhere from 62 to 126 gallons depending on the origin of the wine.

[ENDORSED:]   The Petition of Jacob
               Mauritsz Master of
               the Pinck.
               Nov. 9, 1674.*

[24:10b]

[PETITION OF LUTHERANS AT NEW YORK CONCERNING THE CALL
AND SALARY FOR A MINISTER. TRANSLATION]

To the Right Honorable and Highly Esteemed Lord
Edmund Andros, Governor General of New York etc.

Right Honorable and Highly Esteemed Lord.

The underwritten elders and promoters of the Augsburgh Confession
here show with proper reverence how they, the petitioners, find much to
their sorrow that some members of their church remain in arrears with
regard to their promises to contribute and donate that which they have
pledged, first for the summoning and bringing over of a minister; and
secondly for his annual salary. For these pledges they, the petitioners,
have been constrained to turn to your highly esteemed honor, humbly
requesting that your honor be pleased to issue such an order as his honor
may find appropriate. Thus doing we remain
                       Your honor's humble and
                       faithful servants,
                                      Davit Wessels
                                      Lourens Andresz
                 The Mark of M M Marten Meyer

                                      Casper Steinmets

[ENDORSED:]   [   ]
               the elders and promoters of the
               Augsburgh Confession
               The like Ord[   ]‡
               Deacons upon the [   ]
               A Request from the Lutherans
               to the Go: at his first Arrival in 1674

* The endorsement appears in English in the hand of Matthias Nicolls, the provincial
secretary.
‡ Beginning with this line the endorsement is written in English.

[24:11]

An abstract of a Letter from the Governor of Roade
Island and assembly to his R. Highnesse Governor,
dated the 11th of November 1674.

The first part is congratulatory, for the Governors safe arrivall, and
reducing of New Yorke, desiring a friendly Correspondence and Commerce betwixt the Colonys

The next relates the occasion and time of the first settlement of Roade
Island their Endeavors to gaine a Patent from King Charles the first,
which was obstructed by the breaking out of the civill warres in England,
and their obtaining a Charter from his present Majestie at his Res-
tauracion, wherein they were like to bee circumvented by Conecticutt
Agents, who thought to have swallowed up part of that Colony within
their bounds, their Patent having the first date, but upon Complaint was
arbitrated betweene the Agents of the two Colonyes, by the kings advice,
and the bounds betweene them stated, and by his Majesties Graunt
determined, That Pawcatuck alias Narrigansett should bee the bounds
betweene the two Colonyes.

And further declares the said bounds to bee allowed and approved by the
Kings Commissioners the land betweene which and what those of
Conecticutt would imagine to bee Narragansett River, they called the
Kings Province, and betrusted the Jurisdiction thereof to the Officers of
Roade Island Colony untill the Kings pleasure was further knowne,
whereupon they had possession of that Jurisdiction for ten yeares at least.

After which Conecticutt disturbed one of Roade Isl: Townes next them
and would force them to remove in the winter, but tooke their promise
to submitt in the spring and so gott them under them.

The last summer Conecticutt would have forced the Kings Province to
come under their Jurisdiction, but for that time were withstood by the
Governor of Roade Island and Councell in person.

It was lastly offered by Roade Island that if Conecticutt were not
satisfyed they would referre it to the Kings determinacion, that would
not bee accepted, but they would referre it to the United Colonyes, which
were as to themselves, It was also offered by Roade Isl. to bee referr'd
to his R. Hs Governor.

So with civill Expressions Concludes

signed William Coddington Go.

[24:12]

[ORDER TO THE SHERIFF OF NEW YORK TO SEIZE
ESTRAYED PROPERTY]

Whereas Informacion hath beene given that there are severall things
concealed in the hands of private persons of this City which did formerly
belong to the stores of the Garrison in the Fort, As fire armes crosse barre
shott,* pick axes, spades sh[ ]ells etc., which have beene convey'd away
and embezelled, since the arrivall of his His R. Hs Governor in these
parts, These are in his Majesties name to require you with one of the
Constables and what other Company as shall bee requisite, to bee ayding
and assisting to Captain William Blagge Mr.‡ Gunner of the Fort, in the
looking after and finding the said materialls or any others belonging to
the stores of the Fort, to which End to repaire to such places and houses
as you shall have notice of to bee suspected, there to make search for
them, or any of them, and the same to seize and secure, for his Royall
Highnesse use, of which you are to returne an account, And for the doeing
hereof this shall bee your warrant. Given under my hand in N.Y. this 11th
day of November 1674.

By Order of the Governor

Matthias Nicolls Mayor.

To Ens. Thomas Gibbs
sheriffe of th[   ] of N.Y.

[ENDORSED:]   An Order from me as Mayor to Mr. Tho:Gibbs,
sheriffe, to searchsome houses for Armes etc.No: 11
1674
No: 75

* A cross bar shot was a spherical shot that unfolded into a cross, each arm of which ended
in a quarter sphere.
‡ master

[24:13]

[RETURN OF THE SHERIFF TO THE PRECEDING ORDER]

These are to Certifie, that by vertue of a warrant from the worshipfull Capt. Matthias Nicholls Major of the Citty of New York itt was ordred the making search and inquiery after severall abilliments of warr which have binn Embezeld out of the foart. Vizt—fire armes, crossbarr shott, pick Axes, spades, shovells, etc. since the arrivall of the Honourable Governor Andros. In persuance of the said warrant we have acted and done what was ordred to any suspitious hoases and have founde as followeth.

In the hoase of Low the smith
  14 Pick Axes
   6 spades
   2 Carbines
   1 crosbarre shott
   1 holberts picke
In the house of Peeter Mead.
   2 Carbines
   1 Pick Axe
   2 Spades
In the house of John Speegellar.
   1 Carbine
   1 round shott

as witnes our handes
this 11th day of November 1674.

William Blagge   Thomas Gibbs

[ENDORSED:]   The returns of C. Blagge
                and the sheriffe—
                about their search
                with the Constable
                for things belonging
                to the stores.

[24:14]

[WARRANT TO ATTACH PROPERTY OF FORMER
GOVERNOR LOVELACE]

By vertue of an Order directed unto us from the Right Honorable the
Governor willing and requiring us to Issue forth an Attachment, upon
the Lands, Houses and Estate of Francis Lovelace Esqr., within this city
and precincts, for the reasons therein set forth upon account of debt due
to, and by order of his Royall Highnesse. These are in his Majesties Name
to require you to Attach the Lands, Houses and Estate, both reall and
personall, Posses't and belonging to the said Francis Lovelace, of which
you shall herewith receive the particulars, in Order to further
p[roce]edings according to Law. And for so doing this shall be your
Warrant. Dated at the Court House in New Yorke, this 13th day of
November, 1674.

To Mr. Thomas Gibbs, Sherriffe of the City of New Yorke, who is to
make return of this Warrant, to the next Court.

[ENDORSED:]   A warrant from
                     the Mayor and
                     Aldermen
                     to the Sheriffe,
                     about an Attachment upon
                     Coll. Lovelaces Estate.

[24:15]

[COPY OF 24:14]*

By order of the M[ayor] and Aldermen

                         John Sharpe
                         Clearke of the Court.

* This is a damaged copy with additional closing information.

[24:15 *verso*]

[THE SHERIFF'S RETURN ON THE PRECEDING DOCUMENT]

New Yorke Saturday the 14 of November 1674.

I attached the great house near the State hous[ ] that [   ]* lives
in and the garden house in the broad way that Governor Carteret Is which
Formarly belonged to Coll. Francis Lovelace in presence of Mr. Hum-
phery Davenporte and Henry Newton by mee

Thomas Gibbs Sheriff

Munday the 16 Nov. 1674

By vertue of an order, I have Attached two parcells of land for his Royall
Highnesse Use from Coll. Francis Lovelas which formarly belonged to
C[ ] Willet and the Domine which lay betwe[   ] Derrick Seckars and
Mr. Abram Tony thes being [   ] with mee Derrick Seckars

Thoms Gibb[ ]

[ENDORSED:]   The Order of Attachment of
                   Colonell Lovelaces Estate
                   Nov. 13. 1764.
                   And the Sheriffs
                   returne 14 &16 Nov.

[24:16]

[LETTER FROM MATTHEW MAYHEW AND THOMAS DAGGETT
CONCERNING AFFAIRS AT MARTHA'S VINEYARD]‡

To his honor Major Edmund Adros, Govournor of his Royall Highness
territories in America:

May it pleas Your Honour to understand: that Mr. Thomas Mayhew of
Marthas Vineyard, having received Commission from Collonell Fraunces Lovelace late Govournor under his Royall highness, of his Territories
in America; to Govourn and hould, the said Ile of Marthas Vineyard, for
his Royall Highness, accordingly Continued, in the quiet and peaceable

* The name is faint and unreadable. It appears to be "Mr. nan Crlyfe." It is not Herbert
Cruyff.
‡ Part of the following text comes from *NYSHAR* vol. 3.

manage[   ] until the unhappie time of the enemies possession of this Cittie: [t]he [N]ews [w]hereof no sooner arived there, but
sundrie the inhabitants affirming [t]hat Ile to [be] vertually taken and be
under the govourment of the duch disclaimed [th]e Govourme[nt t]here
Established under his Royall Highnes; the Govournour giving them [to
un]derstand his Resolution to hould and Defend the place untill it should
be forceably t[ ]en out of his handes; some more principall putting the
matter forward, about ho[ ] the people in a Mutinous manner rose, with
many contumelious words and threats against the s[aid Go]vournour,
daring him in the prosecution of his Royall Highness his govourment
and sometime after sent Messengers to Boston, to transfer the Govourment of the place thither; of which they likewise, giveing the Govournor
notice; he, informed the Govournour of B[   ]n, that he held the Iland
for his Highne[s t]he Duke of Yorke: which [prevent]ing their intention,
they proceded to Ere[ct a] Govourment in opposition [to his] Royall
Highness govourment affirming the [govour]nour [tha]t the longest
[sword] [   ] bear Rule; tearing of [w]arr[ants] abusing officers [dis-
taining] [. . . one line lost . . .] [m]uch as at any in[timation] [ ] Right
and title of [interest from] his Royall Highness [and have ever since
ma]nage[d the island] with s[uch a high h]and as to live according to
t[hei]r profession, by the [   ] fists
thretning the govournour, challenging the [for] [   ]f him I
and [other his] majesties good subjects [t]here, they have not Refr[ai]ned
al[l ri]otous practices, in so [much] that they have in[tr]eated and hardly
been disswaded by the Govournour, from using of the sword in their
defence; bu[t] now h[op]e by your honours care, they shall be releived;
for whose safe arivall they hav[e patien]tly weighted as time of great
drouth for the latter Raine; of which it pleased the Govournour to Order
my self, together with Mr. Thomas Dagget, who is one of his assistants:
to give your honour a more particular accompt; and shall not farther
trouble your honour, But entreating your honours favourable Construction, and pardon for the prolixitie of these unpolished lines, I Remaine,
and subscribe myselfe to be

Novemb. 14th: Your honours most humble
1674   willing and obedient Servants

                                    Matthew Mayhew
                                    Thomas Daggett

[ENDORSED:]   Ma[   ] Mahew
                   Mr. [ ]ho: Dogget
                   [ ]he Vinyard Nov. 4. 1674

[24:17–18]

[ ]e originall right of Nantucket was obtained by Thomas Mahew and Thomas [ ]ahew his son of James Forett agent to William Earle of Starling the thir[ ]eenth of october 1641 and granted by them to the ten first purchasers the 2.5:1659 And the right of the indian sachims the tenth day of may [ ]660 before which time the said Mahew could not obtaine any land of the sachims upon the said Iland

[ ]t a meeting of the owners and purchasers the first originall [ ]roprieters of Nantukett upon the said Iland of Nantukett the 8: of June 1674 first for as much as there appeared severall grounds of suspistion of an [ ]deavour by som lately admitted to the said Iland and severall that for [ ]erly had been admitted and stated there by the alsoe said propriators supplaint the said propriators of their rights both generall and particular both by the defective recording and uncertain keeping [ ]f the said records as also by a passing two severall sorts of laws one against the other and both over throwing and takeing away the former [ ]hat did proceed in before thay were called to give an accompt to Fort Loukas by what right we held the said Iland who upon his being fully satisfied about our said intrest as by a charter or pattent under his hand and seale doth appear wherein he hath given testimony [ ]f his understanding our Just right derived origenally from my lord [ ]tarling as also our Indian purchas of the said land then in our tennure and occupation as by the said wryting bearing date the 28 of June 1671 may appear by pretence of which or under coller of which authority the said opposition is acted and carried on and a new power pretended to undertake the desposall of our said Intrest and the acting of severall things prejuditiall to the same by means of which interruption we canot with peace and quiatnes amend the same and whereof [ ] applied ourselves to the generall court of the said Ilands at the [ ]eason thereof for thair assistance of us by their advice or otherwise if it should belong to thair cognisence in the stating of our said manner or intrest for the future who returned us answer t[ ] thay were not in the capasity of a Court to answer by reson that [ ]he majestrats of Nantukett were not there Namely Thomas Macy, Mr. Richard and John Gardiners with whome we had severall times [ ]ndeavors to understand thair reasons and in an amicable way to [ ]ompose the matter but all in vaine and whereas there have been severall [ ]ltnations of right from the tenn first purchasers unto others and [ ]lso som of the assotiats and partners of the said tenn purchasers [ ]ere not named in the first records at Salsbury weareby it may appear who are now owners of the said lands

the premises considered togather with severall other good causes we the afforesaid purchasers owners and Freeholders of the said Iland of Nantukett have mutually agreed [ ]oted and subscribed being all present on the said Iland that an accompt shall presently be taken and recorded of those that are now the present owners of the said land whether of the first ten purchasers or of their [ ]en associats and partners who are in record called the twenty purchasers and owners to whome the sale proper and equall right doe belong of the said Iland and appurteynances and of the manner and order of all transaction that have past for the conveyances of any of the said rights untill the time and also that the like orders shall be observed from time to time for the recording of all such alenations as shall be made for the futur that soe every mans right may be orderly known and distinguished for time to com by perpetuall sucsestion

Thomas Mayhew	Robert Pike	Tristram Coffyn senior	
the mark of Richard Swyan senior		Steeven Grienlese	
Steeven Hussey	James Coffin	Tristram Coffin junier	
Nathaniell Starbuk	John Swain	John Coffin	John Billop
Nathaniell Barnard			

Accordingly At the same meeting it did appear by the perusein[ ]
[   ]rds of salsbury of 1659 amd 1661 that these tenn
pers[ ] na[   ] Thomas Mayhew Tristram Coffin senior Mr. Christopher Hussey Richard Swayn Thomas Barnard Peeter Coffin Steven Greinle[   ] John Swayn Thomas Macy and William Pike were the first tenn to whome the said Iland and appurtaynances did belong solely

Secondly that at the said meeting in the same records doe appear that Robert Pike was owned by Christophar Hussey to be his partner

Robert Barnard to be Thomas Barnards partner

Edward Starbuk to be Thomas Macys partner

Tristam Coffin junior to be Steeven Greinleses partner
James Coffin to be Peeter Coffins partner

Att the same meeting on nantuckett 8:4:1674
Itt is farther declared and owned that these are also assotiats the rest of the ten purchasors namely that Thomas Colman was partner to John Swayn as by deed Nathaniell Starbuk was partner to Tristram Coffin Senior John Smith the other 20th part with Mr. Thomas Mayhew

Thomas Cook partner with Richard [ ]wayn as by deed: the right of
William Pike was sould unto [ ]chard Swayn as by deed: Richard Swayn
conveyed the one halfe thereof to nathaniell Coulter and the other halfe
to his son in law and daughters in law namely William Bunker mary
Bunker Ann and Martha Bunker as by deed 18:4:1667 Also Nathaniell
Coulter sold his said right to John Bishop senior as by deed Capt.
Christopher Hussey have sold his owne part unto his sons Steeven
Hussey and John Hussey as by deed John Smith deceased left his right
to his two sons John Smith and Samuell Smith by equall devision as by
will appear 14:feb 1670 Tristram Coffin senior have conveyed one halfe
of his owne proper right unto his son Steeven Coffin as by deed Thomas
barnard conveyed one halfe of his proper right to his son Nathaniell
Barnard as by deed. Thomas Colman conveyed one halfe of his right
purchast of John Swayn unto his son John Colman

It is to be taken notis that this list of the 20 first purchasers should have
been inserted before these Alinations made by Capt Hussey John Smith
Tristram Coffin Tho Barnard and Thomas Colman that being the most
proper place for it: Namely

Mr. Thomas Mayhew
Mr. Tristram Coffin Senior
Richard Swayn
Mr. Christophar Hussey
Thomas Barnard
Nathaniell Starbuk
John Bishop Senior
Peeter Coffin
Steeven Greinlese
Thomas Macy
John Smith

William Bunker and his
  sisters Mary Ann and
  Martha in the one halfe
  right of William Pike
Mr. Robart Pike
Robart Barnard
Mr. Edward Starbuk
Tristram Coffin Junior
James Coffin
Thomas Colman
Thomas Look

These are the twenty first purchasers who are called the first purchasers
and their assoctiats to whome the right was sold by Mr. Mayhew and
which also bought the Indian right and the alinations above said and all
other alinations whatsoever have ben derived from them when it is
general or one of them when it is perticular

At the same meeting Tristram Coffin Junior acknowledged the one halfe
of his right to be conveyed to his son Henory Coffin as by deed bearing
date May the :29: 1674:

It is also acknowleged at the said meeting that the neck called [   ]catuk upon Nantukett which was by Mr. Thomas Mahew reserved [   ] himselfe when he sold the pattent right of Nantukett to the twenty purchasers is no part of the sail but doe remain to him the said Mayhew according to the right that he obtained of the Indians there according as it doe appear in the deeds that we had of the said Mr. Mayhew bearing date 2: 5: 1659

It doe also appear by a wryting in the manner of a morgadge under the hand of Thomas Macy unto Tristram Coffin of that part or so much of it belonging to Thomas Macy being his twentieth part as will pay the said Tristram Coffin for such some as the said Coffin was to pay for the said Macy as by the said wryting may appear bearing date 27: 7: 1660 but noe farther proceeding did then appear about it

At the same meeting Nathaniell Starbuk was appoynted to keepe this book according to the order therein exprest with respect to recording all such alinations as shall be made for the future.

This to continue till farther order

This is a true Coppy by mee Nathaniel Starbuk
the 24: of the 4 mo: 1674

[ENDORSED:]   Entred in the Office of Records
                     in New Yorke the
                     [blank] day of [blank] 167[blank]

                     Martins Vineyard and Nantucket.
                     Entred.
                     Accounts hereupon from
                     severall persons. 1660.

[24:19]
[EXTRACTS FROM THE RECORDS OF NANTUCKET]

Whereas there was a Purchase made of the patten Right that the honoraball lord Starling [   ]d of or in the Ile of Nantucket By Mr. Tho Mayhew of Martas Vinyard: whoe sould his Intrest Thearof unto, Tristram Coffyn senior—Thomas Macye and Richard Swayn Thomas Barnard Peeter Coffyn Christopher Hussey Steeven Grenlef John Swayne and William Pike, the aforesaid Mr. Mayhew, Reserving unto himself a Twentyeth part of the pattins Right, As also Became a purchaser with those nine men before named: of all Indian Rights that have bin

purchased. So that the tenn bee, Mr. Thomas Mayhew Tristram Coffyn
Thomas Macy: Richard Swayn: Thomas Barnard Peeter Coffyn Chis-
topher Hussye Steeven Greenlef John Swayn and William Pike, had the
whole and sole Interest disposall power and priveledge of the id Iland
and appurtenances tharof, etc.

Att a meetinge of the said purchaseres or the major parte of them
appeared as aloued [   ] the Rest together with some others that weare
owned for associates as will heareafter [   ] was agreed and determined and appoy[ ]ted as followeth: viz that thes tenn owners will admit
[   ] tenn more partners: whoe shall have Eq[   ] proportions power and
Intrest with Themselves: and that Ether: of the purchasers afore mentioned shall have libertie to tacke a partner whoe hee pleas not beinge
Justlye Excepted against By the Rest, att the meetinge was owne partner
with Christophel Husye Robbert Lyck, Robert Barnard was owned a
partner with Tho Barnard Edward Starbucke was owned to be Thomas
Macyes partner: And Tristram Coffyn Junior partner with Steeven
Greenlef and James Coffyn Junior partner with Steeven Greenlef And
James Coffyn partner with Peeter Coffyn,

Att The same meetinge It was ordred and determined that theare shall be
tenn other Inhabitants admitted Into the Plantation Whoe shall have such
accomodations as the owneres or purchasers shall Judge meet as namlye
[ ]essesarye Trades men and sea men, Att a meetinge of the owners of
the Ile of Nantucket att Salsburie, may the ninth a Thousand Six hundred
Sixtye one It was ordred that all the lands: that Its fitt for Areable, Land:
Convenient for hous lotes shall bee forthwith messured that the qantetye
thareof may Bee knowne which beinge donn shall bee devided By Eqall
proportion, that is to say fower fivght[*] Partes to the Owners or purchaseres: And the other fivght Partes to the tenn other Inhabitantes:

Att a meetinge on Nantucket of the owners or purchasers Inhabitinge
weare Mr. Mayhew beinge Present: and Peeter Folger: It was agreed and
concluded that Each man of the owners or purchaseres shall have libertie
to chuse his hous lott on any place within our limetes: not formerlye taken
up: and that Each house lott shall Contayn Sixtye Rod sqare to a whole
accommodation or share or the vallew of It.

They wittnes that wee whose names ar under writen doe give and grant
unto William Worth sailer halfe a share of land and meadowes and

* fifth

marshes Wood and timber and all manner of priveledges and appurtenances Theareto [ ]longinge, upon the Iland of Nantucket Bouth hous lot and all other divitiones of land and meadowes wood and timber: and commoneges [ ]* say halfe as much as any on of the Twentye first purchasers have both in plantation and patten Right to him the said William Worth his heares and assignes forever, upon Condition that hee pay his proportion of all Charges of purchasinge the patten and Indian Right And also other nessearye Charges Concerninge the Einglish Rightes also to com and dwell on The Iland and to Imploye himselfe or Bee Imployed on the sea for him selfe or shuch person or persones as ar inhabtinge on the Iland or any of the purchasers att shuch sesones as ar convenient: and for shuch hiere as the shall agree upon which shall bee accordinge to Resons and not to leave the Iland for Three Yeares time After the date hearof:

John Bishop	John Swayn
John Holt	Tho Macy
Edward Starbuck	Robart Barnard
Richard Swayn	Tho Collman
Nath: Starbuck	Thomas Mayhew

Tristram Coffyn Senior
for myself and five more
Impowered Imprimes

Petter Coffyn Jon Grenlef

Tho Coffyn Junior, and for
Will Pike ten shares‡

[ ]omas Macy doth Ingage himselfe as on of the number of the Trades men [ ] namely to supplye the occasiones of the Iland in the trade of wevinge for [ ] benefit of the inhabitantes as well as of himselfe: and hath a trades mans [ ]lfe share of accommodations granted to him, in concidration Theareof: answerth William Worth and the Rest

Att a meetinge of the Inhabitants a grant was made to Joseph Colman of halfe a share of accomodation: out of the grant made to the sea men [ ] Trades men on Condition that hee shall attend the occations of the Iland whyle hee liveth on the Iland and If hee shall att any time Thinke meet

* indecipherable
‡ These are copies; they are not the original signatures.

to leave the Iland delever up all his accommodation to The Company [   ]te will pay him for It as much as a Stranger and If hee leave the Iland [   ]ell els wheare his grant Is forfit.

[   ]tinge of the Inhabitantes a grant was made to Richard Gardner [   ]dations, accordinge to The [   ]ts mad[ ] to sea men and Trades men [   ] condition that hee Exercise himself as a sea man and that he Com to Inhabite heare with his fammelye before the end of May: 68: and after that his Entrance [   ] not to depart the Iland in point of dwelinge for the space of Three yeares upon the fortiture of the grant aforsaid.

Att a meetinge of the Inhabitantes a grant was made to Joseph Gardner halfe a share of accommodations answerabell to the other Trades men on Condition that hee suplye the occasiones of the Iland in way of shoumacker: and lickwise that hee shall not leave the Iland in poynt of dwellinge for the space of fower yeares or it is to fall out that hee shall remove ofe from the Iland within the aforsaid terme that then hee shall leave the said accommodation to his brother Richard: unto [ ]e said Richard the Company doth grant the accomodations aforementioned [ ] the termes aforementioned that hee supplye the occasiones of the Iland in way [ ]f a shou macker.

[   ] was made Nathaniell Holland of a tradesmans accommodation upon condition [   ] hee imploies himselfe in the trad of a tayler and Bringe his fammelye to the Iland before next winter and that hee bild and settell amongst us as an Inhabitant.

Al Theese particulars are True Copies
Peter Foulger
Clarke

[ENDORSED:]   A Copie of ordres and grants of [. . .]

Entred in the Office of Records in New Yorke the [*blank*] day of [*blank*] 167[*blank*]

[   ] by Mr Coffin
Nov. 10. 1674
Entred.
1674.

At Salisbury February. 59.

Att a meeting of the sayd purcha[*]

A Copie of our Grants and
disposall of laws.

[24:20]

[POWER OF ATTORNEY FROM GOVERNOR COLVE TO NICOLAES
BAYARD. TRANSLATION]

Whereas upon delivery of the province of New Netherland unto the
hands of the lord governor general, Major Edmund Andros, on the 10th
of this present month, pursuant to the peace treaty concluded on the 19th
of September between his majesty of Great Britain on the one side and
their high mightinesses, the lords states general of the United Netherlands etc., on the other side, and also pursuant to orders from my lords
superiors, it is still necessary for me to leave behind in this country, many
effects and outstanding debts and therefore necessary that a capable
person be commissioned for the collection of debts and the administration of the effects, which, according to the account and inventory books,
are still outstanding here in this country; and to make everyone, who is
in any way so concerned, aware of all of these matters that I, the
undersigned, by virtue of the commission from my lords superiors, their
noble mightinesses, the commissioned lords of the council, on behalf of
the province of Zeeland and their noble mightinesses, the lords of the
admiralty at Amsterdam, have commissioned, authorized, and completely empowered the person of Nicolaes Bayard, former secretary and
receiver general of New Netherland, as he is hereby commissioned,
authorized, and empowered, after my departure, hereafter to demand,
receive and, for the good of my superiors, manage and administer the
estate, effects, and outstanding debts here in this country, according to
the instructions already received from me or hereafter still to be received
from my lords superiors, as the respective commissioners have already
been specified or are still to be specified by the constituent, by virtue of
this, to urge the settlement of the respective confiscated estates, to
promote their liquidation for account and balance, and to assess that
which shall be found due to my lords superiors from the confiscated
estates; at the same time to enter upon them together with the other
aforesaid effects of my lords superiors, and to manage and administer
them; and upon receipt of the same in the name and on behalf of my lords
superiors to confirm receipts and other documents of release for the

* Probably intended as an abbreviation for purchasers.

same, and to guard against any false claims; in case of refusal to constrain the unwilling parties or false claimants to pay according to law and the rigor of justice, in which cases the constituent shall have to address himself to the aforesaid lord Major Edmund Andros and request, in the name of those stated, the firm hand of justice, which his honor has promised to me, just as he has accepted to do with further power and authority by delegating under himself, by virtue of this, one or more persons of similar or more limited authority; and furthermore to do, carry out and execute everything which the aforesaid Nicolaes Bayard shall deem useful and most beneficial for the aforesaid, my lords superiors, promising for all time to approve, praise, and consider good and beneficial everything which shall be done and executed by the same representative, by virtue of this, without any contradiction, with the constituent liable to justify his management and receipts upon request.

Done aboard the country's warship *de Suriname* at anchor below the Sandy Point of the North River of New Netherland, the 18th of November 1674, was signed: A. Colve, and as witnesses on his part: Charles Quirinsin, J. Vandewater, and Egidius Luyck.

[ENDORSED:]   Power of attorney of the honorable
                lord Anthony Colve to Nicolaes Bayard,
                18 November 1674.

[24:21]

            [ANOTHER COPY OF 24:21, WITH VARIATIONS]*

[WITNESSES:]   Charles Quirynsen
                J. Vander Water
                Agidius Luyck

[ENDORSED:]   A copie of N[   ] Bayards Procura[   ]
                from Go. Colve. Jan. 22, 1674
                No: 18, 1674‡

---

* Both copies are damaged and incomplete. Together they provide the complete text for the translation in 24:20.

‡ The entire endorsement is in English.

[24:22]

[PETITION OF NICOLAES BAYARD CONCERNING THE ABOVE DEBTS]

To the Right Honnorable Mayor * Edmund Andros Governor Generall of all his Royall Highnesses, James Duke of
Yorke, Territori[ ] in America;

Right Honnorable Sir.

Sheweth with due Respect and subbmiss[ ] unto your Honnor Nicolaes
Bayard as atturnie of the heer Anthony Colve Late Governor of the New
Netherlands, that Your Honnors Petitioner by Speciall Instructions from
the said Heer Colve was Recommended [   ] Your honnors favorable
answer [   ] the following particulers;

Imprimis: Whereas the said heer Colve uppon his departure from hence,
was forced to Leave here in the Country for the accompt of his Supperiors
the States of Zeeland, and the Colledge of admirality at amsterdam
several[ ] debts (as by the bookes Remaining in my Custody, at Large
may appeare;) for the Receipt and paiment whereof, I am by him
impouwred) My humble Reque[ ] is therefore in the behalfe aforesaid,
that Your Honnor will bee pleazed, to graun[ ] Your Petitioner an order,
Signifying [ ] the Respective Courts within Your honnors Government,
that your Petitioner Impouwred for the Receiving and Paying of the said
debts; and withall (if desiered) to bee aiding and assisting unto Your
Petitioner therein;

Secondly: That an order may bee graunted by Your Honnor, whereby the
Petitioner may bee authorized to take Possession of the houses Lands
and other Effects wich according to an act of Confiscati[ ] and the
annexed Inventory, are Confiscat to the use of the Late Dutch Govern[
] with freedom to dispose thereof according to the Instructions of th[ ]
said heer Colve;

3dly. That Your Honnor [ ]ill [   ] favour to somme of
the [   ] of this place, to endeavor a Re[   ] of the vallue
of about £300: Sterl[ ] which in the Last warre was sent, [   ] from
Enghland to this place, but by Reason of its being taken, Landed at
Boston, and there seized on, by the Govern[   ] in whoes hands it still
Remaines; wich Releasement if itt may bee effected, Your Honnors

* major

Petitioner hath order Likewyse to Release severall Confiscated Effects here under arres[ ] of his Majesties of Great Brittain Subjects, amounting as per Inventory here annex to the vallue of above £[ ] Sterling;

4thly. That the petitioner with Your Honnors Leave may take some Course according to the Tennor of his order, that the debts of the west india Company here may be paid and satisfyed out of their Effects here; as it was agreed uppon in the Yeare 1664 uppon the Surrender of this place, but hetherto omitted;

5thly. Whereas the said heer Colve hath graunted to the late Burgemasters of this place, that the Remainder part of the Townes Debts made during the tyme of his Government should bee paid out of the produce of the C[ ]fisc[ ]ted house and Lot of ground [   ]g and being within this Citty, on the Broadway formerly belong[ ] unto governor Francis Lovelace, wich now of Late was in the possession of Capt. Epstein: wich house the said heer Colve hath orderred mee to make sale of to that purpose, wherefore this Petitioner humbly Craves Your honnors Consent soo to doo; and Your Petitioner shall as in duty bound pray for your honnors happynes etc. and Remaine

Right Honnorble Sir
Your Honnors most humble Servant

N. Bayard

[   ] Yorke this
[   ] november 1674.

[ENDORSED:]   Mr . Bayards
Petition and answer.

[24:23]

[PROCLAMATION THAT ALL TRANSACTIONS REMAIN VALID]

These are to Certifie all whom it may concern That whatsoever Bargaine and Sale,Contract or Agreement hath been made, by any person or Persons, or any thing [   ]d sold in Open Vendue, [   ]blick Sale. either before the Dutch came into these Parts, in July 1673 or during their Government here, the same is to bee and remaine of full force and Power, as at the time of the making thereof, Notwithstanding the late alteracion of government, according as is set forth in two Proclamacions, bearing date the 9th and 16th days of this present Moneth, and consonant to the Treaty and Articles of Peace. Dated at New Yorke, the 24th day of November, in the 36th yeare of his Majesties Reigne, Annoque Domini 1674.

By order of the Go:
M: N:

[   ]ake a certificate of Mr. Bayards demands from Go: Colve for Mr. Dervall.

[ENDORSED:]   Certificate to Capt. Jaques Cortelyou
                    about the Vendue.Nov. 25th 1674

[24:24]

[PETITION OF THE INHABITANTS OF HEMPSTEAD CONCERNING
SUPPORT OF THE GOSPEL]

Honowred Sir

Right Honorowed Govenour Generall Edmond Andros G[ ]vcnor of new york in his magisties teritoris under his Royall highnes Jeames duck of york, wee your humble petichonors in the behalfe of sume others doe humbly petition unto your Honour that your Honour would be pleased to be mindfull of your petitioners most humble request, which is that the honour of god might be promotid and that his saboths may be obsarved for the honour of god and the good of us and our posterrity and to that end your honour would be pleased to install such athority amongst us which may be a meanes under god for the upholding and maintaing of the minestry an[ ] worship of god amongst us, your h[ ]our being the father of h[ ] coman[ ] which th[ ] hope you [   ] be unmindfull of your petitioners bu[   ]ill be anin[   ]der god for the uphold[   ] maintaing of the gospell of the lord Jesus Christ, so hoping you will be pleased to draw a favorable constroction from this our petitione we shall not farther truble your honour at preasant but leave this our petetion to your honnours serious consederation, we rest and remain your very humble sarvants and petichonors to the best of our pouer and for your honour we shall ever pray: farwell

from Hemsted
November the 30th
anno. 1674

Thomas Champin ⌐ his mark

Richard Gildersleve

Simon Saring

Williem Jecocks

Jems pine 𝕁𝕡 his maark

Richard Gilderslave junior

Jeremiah Wood 𝒢 his mark

[ON BACK:]   3dele: left to furder
information att
next sessions.

[ENDORSED:]   A Petition from divers
of the inhabitants
of Hempsteed about
their Minister.
James Pine etc.
1674.

[24:25]

[PETITION OF THE INHABITANTS OF JAMAICA FOR REPRESENTATION
IN GOVERNMENT]

To the Honorable Edmud Andreus Esquire Governer of
New Yourke and all the rest of his Royall Highnesses
Teritoris In America.

The petition of the Inhabetants of Jamaica Humbly sheweth to your
honere That wheras you have sent unto our towne to Establish Constable
and overseers under his Majestes Authoryty for our present benifitt and
preservation of our peace for which we do acknowledge our selfes
greatly obleiged To your honer: and forasmuch as you have decleared
your willingness to be Informed what may be Nessesary as we conciev[
] for the good of our Towne as allsoe our Confidence that your honer will
Endevor what you Can for the good and benifitt of us whom you are now
brought In Savty to be Ruller and governor over whom we shall Redily
and Chierfully Recieve and Imbrace not only as our governer but In A
sence our Father: we therfore make bould to petition your honer: first
that In such Conveniant time as your honers Ocatians will permitt that

the Country may be Called togethere before your honer: that therby your petitioners with the Rest of our Neighbors within this goverment may genarally have A full and Right Understanding what his Majestis pleasure is concierning our future settlement.

2ly That the Country may therby have full opertunity to give your honer Information of what may be best for the Advancment of the publicke Interest In these parts.

And farther we beg: Your honers pardon to declear that when Collenall Richard Nicolls Cam first by his Majestes Comistion to Reduce these parts to his obedience we being then Redy and willing to the hazard of our livs to Assist him therin had this Incurage he did decleare and gave under his hand that we should Enjoy as great priveledges as any of his majesties subjicts In America did: we humbly Concive: that very few if any of his Majesties subjicts ar debared of the liberty to have there deputys which are represenatiffs of there townes to sitt In there High Courts at the least once A yeare with the governer and his councill and have there Votes in the makeing and Repealling such laws and Orders as they concieve may Conduce to the publicke good: which thing we humbly desier your honer will grant us:

And farther we thought good to decleare to your honer that whereas there hath been bleam layd upon us for not Endeovring to defent his Majesties Interest In Repearing to the defence of the fourt: we do heare: decleare to your honer that we ar greatly wronged therin and do Engage to maintaine Against any that shall Charge us before your honer that the Country Can never be justly blamed therin: we should be to prolix to Releat heare to your honer the transactions of that matter: we pray god there may never be the like acation but In Case the be we hop you will see that we your poor petitioners shall cherfully and Redily do what In us lys to the hazard of our lifs In the defense of his Majesties Intrest Against any foraigne Invation we leve the premises to your honers wise and serius Consideration most humbly desireing you will be pleased to make the favorablest Construcktion hearof thus hoping your honer will grant these our Resonable Requests wee Rest In all sumistion to yours To Command the Inhabitants of the Towne of Jamaica who for your honer

        shall ever pray

        Nathaniell Denton Clerke
        In the behalfe of the Towne

Received Dec. 1st. 1674.
After the settlement of
Constable and Overseers.

[ADDRESSED:]   To the honerable Edmud
Andrews Esquire Governer of
Newyorke and all the Rest
of his Royall Highness
Teritoris In America.

[NOTATION:]   1st December 1674
AlreadyAnswer'd
by Proclamation
9 November fol.

[ENDORSED:]   A Petition from
Jamaica, not much
unlike that of Newtowne
Dec. 1st. 1674.

[24:26]

[PETITION OF ROBERT RIDER TO BE PAID FOR HAVING
SURVEYED STATEN ISLAND]

To the Right honorable Edmund Andrews Esqr. Governor Generall of all
his Royall highnesses Territorys in America.

The humble petion off Robt. Ryder

humbly sheweth

Whereas your petitioner was imployed by Collonell Lovelace with
several others For the laying out of Staten Island and afterwards was
Further imployed by himselfe for the taking an accomp of all the meddow
grounds upon the said Island and to make draught of the same all which
your petitioner hath performed according unto the warrants unto him
directed For which service (not withstanding his great labor and charge
he hath receaved noe compensation

These are therefore humbly intreating your honor to consider your humble petitioner he being much debillitated in
the time of pubblicke Calamity being aloane with Fowre
small children to provide For beesides himselfe: and your

honors christian Charity shall ever oblidge your petitioner
to pray For your Honors prosperity and happinesse.

Ro: Ryder

[ENDORSED:]   Mr. Robert Riders
Peticion.
Dec. 9: 1674

[24:27]

[SECURITY BOND OF WILLIAM DARVALL]

Know all men by these presents, That I William Darvall, of the City of
New Yorke, having received the Boat and Appurtenances, which was in
controversy between mee and Peter Alricks, of New Castle in Delaware,
and lately had a verdict and Judgment in the Court of Mayor and
Aldermen, for her; From the which, hee the said Peter Alricks hath made
his Appeale to the Governor, who hath ordered it to be heard in Equity,
at the next Generall Court of Assizes, I do hereby oblige and binde my
selfe, my Heires, and Executors to bee answerable for the said Boat and
Appurtenances, at the said Court, and the same shall make good, unto
the said Peter Alricks or his Assignes, in the like or as good condicion,
as I have receiv'd her, if at the said Generall Court of Assizes, I shall bee
Cast in the Suite, and adjudged there unto; In witnesse whereof, I have
here unto set my hand and Seale, in New Yorke aforesaid, the 2d day of
December, 1674.

Signed and acknowledged   Wm Darvall
before mee.
Matthias Nicolls. Secr.

[ENDORSED:]   Mr. Wm. Darvalls bond of
security about the pleasure
boate, to answer for her,
at the Assizes.
Dec. 2. 1674.
At the Assizes. 1675.

[24:28]

[ROUGH DRAFT OF COUNCIL MINUTES]

December 4th 1674

At a meeting in the Fort

The matter under Consideracion was a Lett[   ] sent from the East End
of Long Island ref[   ] to submit to his Royall Highnesse Governmen[ ]

[   ] Mutually [   ] That a m[   ] forthwi[   ]
[   ]mand the thre[   ] of their
Ap[   ] before the Gov[   ] the terme of dayes; and
that the old Constables and Overs[   ] bee ordered at their perills to
reassume the [   ]

To write to John Archer about a Gun [ ] Coate and hatchet taken from an
Indy[   ] Tapan for cutting a Chestnutt tree.

[   ] Radney had his Commission of [   ]
this date.

[   ] Ashowokan Sachem of [   ] Indyans
with his brother and Clar the Indyan[   ]ych and two
more came to give a visitt [   ] the Governor and to offer friendship, the
which was promised to them likewise they living quietly and friendly as
good Neighbors ought to doe.

The Governor presented the Sachem [   ] one of h[   ] worth
[   ] wi[   ] Sachems [   ]me
Is C[   ] hee hath given him a duffells Coa[ ]nd Clar
another. His Indyan na[ ]e [ ] Nascowaneet.*

[24:29]

Beforenoone.   At a Court of Sessions held at Gravesend,
            beginning the 16th day of Dec. 1674

Wednesday.

---

* The endorsement and the marginal note have been lost.

The Justices called. all present.
the Constables called who appeared all, but a Contest about Staten Island.

Thomas Walton the old Constable not out of Office untill the Dutch came, though Richard Doddiman was chosen, who being removed and having sold his accomodacion the Towne proceeded to a new Election, [ ] chose Obadiah Holmes, which is returned.

The Court will consider of it.

The Causes call'd over.

The Jury sworne.

The Court dismist till afternoone.

The Staten Island buisnesse order'd first to bee heard in regard of the dista[ ].

Afternoone.

The Jury call'd over.

Staten Island buisnesse called upon, That of the Constable first.

Richard Doddyman confirmed and sworne so were the Constables of Flatbush and Flattlands, as also two Overseers of Flattbush of which Aukey Jans was one.

John Sharpe Pltf.
Nath: Brittaine Deft.

The plt. putts in a declaracion about a servant sold to the deft.

A testimony to prove it, by the deposicion of Herman Wessells.

John Kingdome offers to take his Oath that hee demanded money of Nath: Brittaine from Mr. Sharpe that is an Oxe or 2 Cowes.
An Arbitracion upon it by the Governors Order—referred to
Tho: D[ ]vall, Matth: Nicolls: Tho: Lo[ ]lace, and Richard Morris.

The Contract of the man to serve Mr. Sharpe. His pretence to deliver him at Staten Island to the Deft.

The deft. putts in an Answer by his Attorney Mr. John Teudor. Hee alleadges the servant was taken away by Monsr. Minville, and the Governors order about it, so the deft. cleared of him. Tho: Walton sworne saith Hee saw the young man at Staten Isl: when Mr. Sharpe brought him to N. Brittaines, and a Chest at the doore, but whose it was, hee could not tell.

The defts. Att. saith Mr. Sharpe brought the fellow there in his owne service, and had him with him [   ]fter horses etc.

Richard Doddeman sworne saith That hee saw Mr. Sharpe tender this servant to Nath: Brittaine upon Staten Island but it was 3, or 4 dayes after hee had beene there.

Obediah Holmes ⎱   sworne—declare the damage N.
John Kingdome ⎰   Brittaine
                         sustayned for want of the servant

Its referred to the Jury.

Tho: Walton by way of Complaint declares that Peter Bilieu after the dutch came in, hee being Schout tooke two Guns away from him.

Peter Biliou puts in answer, [   ] if hee had order to doe it from Mr. v: R[   ]

Two dutch papers to bee translate[   ] against tomorrow morning, when the [   ] will give their Judgement in it.

Tho: Walton makes returne of the Attachment of Go: Lovelaces Estate upon Staten Island, with the warrant whereby hee acted: ordered to bee recorded.

The Proclamacions 1st and 2d read about Rights and propertyes etc. of the 9th and 16th Nov. last.

The Court dismist till tomorrow morne by 8 a Clock.

Thursday. December 17th. 1674.
Before noone.

John Sharpe Pltf.
Nathaniel Brittaine Deft.

The Jury find for the Pltf. but withall find the Deft. hath received damage[
]hich they cannot adjudge of, but referre it to the bench.

The Complaint of Thomas Walton against Peter Bilieu: ordered to bee
sett downe in writing.

A petition from Jan Jansen Verrin abo[ ] his being troubled by Timotheus
Gabry.

Gabry had no notice, however upo[   ] propasall of Mr. Sharpe Att.
for the Pet[   ] the bench allowed the hearing all for[   ] Orders to
bee read, and by that to Judg[   ] farre they can recommend the Case
to the Governor, It having beene decided in o[   ] severall Courts,
under the Engl. Government.

The Arbitracion before the Engl. Goverment read.

The order of Governor Nicolls, to confirme the Award. Oct. [*blank*]
1664.

The proceedings of the Court of Sessions here June 1665 given for the
Pltf.

The Judgment of the Court of Assizes in September following— Confirming the Award still and proceedings at Sessions.

Another order and Judgment at the Court of Assizes in 1666 Re=inforc-
ing the former Nothing being performed by the Deft.
To recommend the whole case with the damage to the Governor, with all
former Proceedings.

Tho: Waltons complaint in writing about 2 Guns taken from him etc.
No proofe being made that hee had order to take them: The Court adjudge
him to returne the Guns or make satisfaction.

George Wood Pltf.
Josias Firman Deft.
Some objection made as if this Cause h[ ] beene formerly tryde here, but said to bee of another nature by the Pltfs. Attorneys Mr. Cooke and Mr. Teudor.

The Att. putts in a Declaracion. The difference about some meadow Gro[ ] and Accounts.

The Newtowne men in the Jury excepted against by the plt. and others put in.

Ralph Hunt
John Smith   sworne

Ralph Hunt saith Hee was one of the first layers out of the Meadow, and the stakes being gone or markes worne out, hee was desired to give his Judgment of the old bounds, which hee did to the best of his knowledge, but the pltf. and defts. bro: quarralled and fell together by the Eares.

Afterwards upon some Agreement they ditched in their proporcions.

John Smith sworne saith being employed 7 yeares agoe by Josias Firman to make a ditch betweene the land of plt. and deft. etc. hee did it and Geo: Wood being sent for they agreed about making the Ditch, hee farther sait[ ] hee made all the Ditchs for the persons [ ]cerned who were 7 and no differen[ ] appeared then.

C. Tho: Laurence sworne and saith [   ] 11 yeares [ ] C. [ ] Laur: sold the plt. the Meadow in question [ ] that hee knowes hee hath not the full proporcion hee enjoyed. The occasion as he supposes was a division made by thre Lotts who had Controversy, the other 4 agreeing as being separated from them. A Cod* of meadow that was in C. T: L: portion, is now in Josiahs Firmans, upon what account hee knowes not.

The Deft. puts in an Answer by the Dr. at the Fort, and denyes all.
John Firman his bro: speakes for him. The order of a former Court of Sessions read, whereon the Deft. was plt. and the now pltf. was cast.

Two orders of Towne Courts read.

---

* *Webster's Third New International Dictionary* (Merriam, 1964) has "now dial.: a bay-shaped area of water or land; esp. the inmost recess of a bay, marsh, or meadow."

Its all refer'd to the Jury.

A Complaint of Nath: Brittaine against Nathan Whitmore and Will: Brittaine, for pulling up of fence upon Staten Isl: to his damage. The fence to bee made good by the persons in fault, and the Complainant hath his Remedy at Law for the damage.

A peticion from the wid: of Adriaen Heggeman, to have Go: Lovelaces order renewed about Goods sold by his father at the vendue to bee distrayned for.

It is to bee recommended to the Governor for a Confirmacion etc.

Jan van Kirke by Mr. Sharpe his Att. confesses Judgment by a *nihil dicit*[*] etc. for the payment of 60 scheple of winter wheate to Asser Levy; the which is ordered to bee entred—with cost of Court.

Capt. Tho: Laurence Plt.
Cornelys Mattys Deft.

The Plt. puts in a declaracion by his Attorney Mr. Arth: Waters.

About a bargaine for land at Nutons point neare C. Laurences plantacion.

By consent suspended till next Court, neither party being ready.

The Court adjourned till afternoone.

Afternoone.

George Wood Plt.
Josias Firman Deft.

The Jury find for the pltf. with Costs etc. The fence standing, refer'd to the Court.

Gabriel Minviele Pltf.
Jan van Kirke Deft.

---

[*] A judgment rendered against a defendant charged with a refusal or neglect to plead or answer.

A declaracion put in by Mr. Sharpe [   ] 2. summes of money due by bills. the one [   ] 633 G. 15 st. sewants value, the oth[   ] 310 G by assignacion of Mary Teller.

He hath nothing to object but of one hundred Guilders paid in part of the last b[   ] to Nich: Bayard but shews no Receit. Its referr'd to a Jury who find for the Plt with Costs.

Asser Levy Plt.
Jan van Kirk deft.

The deft confesses Judgment for principall and Interest for payment in 2 mo.—It is 490 G. Principall.

In the Case of
John Sharpe plt.
Nath: Brittiane deft.

The Court agree with the verdict of the Jury, and give Judgment accordingly, but will endeavor what may bee to mitigate the losse of the deft about his servant.

George Wood Plt.
Josias Firman Deft.

In this Case The Court agree with the Verdict of the Jury and give Judgment accordingly.[*] But if the deft shall loose by this Judgment any part of the Meadow hee hath had in possession, whereon hee hath beene at charge in fencing It shall bee lawfull, for the said Deft. peaceably to take or remove his fence, if they cannot agree for the same otherwise.

A Complaint against Jaques Guyon brought in by severall of Staten Island upon pretence of damage done to him. The Court doth recommend the Examinacion of the matter to the Constable and Overseers of the place, and to endeavor a Regulacion the which if it shall not bee attended by the person complayned against, They are desired to present the Case to the Governor who wee doubt not will take effectuall Order therein.

The Court dissolved

---

* Matthias Nicolls added the last four words to the sentence and crossed out the following: "but will endeavor to procure some other satisfaction for the Deft., if it shall really appeare that hee comes short of his proporcion of Meadow, according to their first laying out."

Decr. 18—But upon other Consideracions thi[   ] met againe
being within the time lim[   ] by the law.

To recommend to the Governors Consideracion, some currant Coine.

The like to reduce all payment to a certaine value of money.

To have a fayre for Cattle, which will prevent many Inconveniences, and
long Attendance at killing time at the Ferry.

This from severall of the best Inhabitants of Gravesend, by some of them
intended to bee presented to the Governor at the Assizes

Before noone. Dec. 18, 1674

The Constable of Gravesend tax't for not giving his Attendance; To bee
considered of.

Albert Cornelissen Wantenaar Plt.
Andries Juriansen Deft.

Their was a pretended Agreement yesterday, but upon second thoughts
agr[   ] send for plt. and deft. and the 2 Justic[   ] home, to bee here
againe this mornin[ ]

Accordingly they appeared and by Co[   ] proceede to Tryall.

A Jury empanelled and sworne.

The Plt. putts in a declaracion by Mr. Sharpe, against the Deft., for
Defamacion.

Mr. Allard Anthony Att. also for the Plt.

The transaction at the Court of Schepens at Breucklyn, with the defts.
Accusacion read.

Severall testimonyes translated from Dutch into Engl., read in Court.

A difference about the day of the month, one saying it was on the 17th
day the other the 18th but agree in the day of the weeke.

Cornelys van Nes ⎫
George Heynelle ⎰   sworne
Egbert Stevens ⎭

The deft. excepts against Cornelis and Egbert as Cousen and servant of the plt. and against the other as under age (Mr. Heynells son) but not allowed of.

A deposicion of Tunis Dircks that hee was with Albert at worke the day the informacion saith the fact was done, and declares the matter to bee otherwise.

Andries Juriansen—the Deft, Answers by word of mouth, and Justifyes his Informacion, Relating a long story thereof.

Hee puts in two papers wherein some persons declare quite contrary to what is sworne to by the former.

Some others discourst of words betweene Egbert Stevens and them, as if hee were prest by Mr. Anthony and Mr. Haynelle to take his Oath for the plt, upon which hee endeavoured to bee excused by reason of his youth.

The matter of the Defamacion was referred to the Jury.

The Court adjourned till afternoone.

Afternoone.

The Jury desiring to speake with th[ ] before they bring in their Verdict, th[ ] came and asked some questions.
Upon their farther Consideracion, They [   ] bring in their verdict, and find for the Pl[ ] There being no legall Evidence to prove his Charge.
The deft. desires an Appeale from the verdict.
The Pltfs Attorney Mr. Sharpe crav[ ] Judgment which is graunted accord[ ] to the verd[   ]
The Deft. appeales from that likew[   ] which is allowed of according to the directions in the law.
Security is given by the Deft. for 100 [   ]

The Court dismist.

[ENDORSED:]   Gravesend Sessions
beg: Dec. 16. 1674.

[24:30]

[MINUTES OF A COURT OF SESSIONS AT JAMAICA]

Before noone.

At Court of Sessions held at Jamaica the 9th day of Dec.
1674

Present.

The Governor.
The Secr.
Mr. Robert Coe
Mr. Richard Cornell } of this Riding
abs=   Mr. John Pell
Capt. James Hubbard
Capt. Richd Betts
Capt Elbert Elberts } of the West
Capt. Jaques Cortelyau
ab   Mr. Jonas Wood   of the East.

The Constables of
Hempsteed
Westchester
ab.   Oysterbay
Huntington

The Justices called.
The Constables
A Jury empannelled and sworne.
The Causes call'd over.

The court dismist for an houre—

Afterwards.

James Gumfields Case.

To consider it.

The Ferry at Westchester.
price to bee regulated.

Sam: Andrews of Oysterbay about a piece of land.

To enquire of the constable.

Mrs. Halletts Peticion.

To send to the husband to appeare and know his Reasons why hee makes not good his Covenant, and to doe Justice therein.

By directive of the Governor.

Capt. Sill: Salisbury agreed upon by the governor and all present to bee High Sheriffe of Long Island and to have a Commission for it.

The Countrey Rate proposed and agreed to bee a penny in the pound as formerly.

Afternoone

Present.

The Governor
The Secr.
Mr. R. Coe
Mr. R. Cornell.
C. James Hubbard.
C. R. Betts.
C. Elb: Elberts
C. Jaq: Cortelyau

The Jury called.

Tho Lovelace Esquire Plt.
John Hawes Deft.

Mr. Cooke Att. for the Plt. putts in his Declaracion for 10£ and by bill.
The Deft. denyes the debt.
The plts. Attorney not having the bill, is adjudged by the Court to bee

nonsuited if the bill bee not sent before the Court shall bee dismist.

John Coomes Plt.
Henry Taylour as Adm. to Nich. Davis Deft.

The plt. putts in his declaracion by John Teudor.
The Deft. produces his power of Administratorship

The plt. endeavors to prove his debt by Nich: Davis and Mr. Pells notes
for 5£ 10s

Referrd to the Jury.

Jacob Abrahams Plt.
John Smith   deft.

Put off till tomorrow upon motion of Mr. Cooke for the absence of his
Att.

Mathew Beagle Plt.
William Thickston Deft.

Mr. Cooke appeares for the Plt.
pretends the want of C. Seamans a[ ] a witnesse to proceede.

Mr. Teudor putts in the Defts. answer to make the contract null.
Putt off till tomorrow.

A Complaint from Peter Smith and Wm. Foster against John Baily as a
Trustee of Dan: Lanes Estate.

Put off till tomorrow.

Before noone. Dec. 10th 1674.

John Coomes Plt.
Henry Taylor Deft.

The Jury find for the Plt. with Costs of suite.

To make an Order about it for the Trustee, to come to account.

Matthew Beagle Plt.
Wm Thickston Deft.
The Declaracion read.

not sworne—ab—	Capt. Seamans.	} witnesses sworne
[ ]hen appeard	Wm. Jeacocks.	
	John Tredwell.	
	Cor: Mott	
	Moses Emery.	

C. Seamans that the Deft. owned the bargaine and receit of the Cow, but being excepted against, hee offer'd another more sufficient, and that the other pay was ready. Wm. Jeacocks the same. There was a Contest about the cow.

Mr. Teudor put in the Defts. Answer. That the Cow was insufficient. The other pay not brought, and would disanull the bargaine.

Mr. Wood being in Court the Justice pleads the Defts. Incapacity.

sworne   John Ellison—witnesse for the deft. declares his knowledge about the deceit in paying the Cow, and the woman offred a pair of stockings release the bargaine.

sworne   Herman Floure—testifyes the insufficienty of the cow, the hoofes after and hipshed.[*]

Richd Gildersleeve being not well, his deposicion was admitted.

Its referred to the Jury.

---

[*] Perhaps "aft and hipshot" (?). Hipshot: having a dislocated hip.

Jeremiah Wood   Plt.
John Seamans
John Townesend } Defts.
John Hinchman

The Plt. putts in a declaracion by Mr. Waters: A very scandalous one.
The Jury not to intermedle.
The bench to consider of it.

Adjourned to the afternoone.

Afternoone.

Mathew Beagle Plt.
Wm Thickston Deft.

The Jury find for the deft. The court give Judgment accordingly.

Mr . Woodhull
Mr. Bayly   } upon a Complaint of Mr. P. Smith—about Mr. D. Lane

Mrs. Lane present.

The accounts to bee brought in, what hath beene charged, and they ld.*
out etc.

Capt Newtons complaint against John Scudamore.

Scudamore to pay what hee hath in his hands.

James Gumfield Case referr'd to the Const. and Overseers of the place,
to provide for his subsistance. His losse valued at about 10£.

The Ferry recommended to Justice Pell and Justice Cornell to pitch upon
a fitt person; of Consider Wood or John Marsh.

The Charge 4 s horse and man single, 2 s each other: single man 1 s two
1 s 6 d and so proporcionable.

A complaint of the Indyan C. Ramrock—

* loaned

Mr. Tho Hicks Interpreter. Its about a Hogge of his stolne; of which the feet being found by him, they were brought in to Court.

Cor. Mott charged with it, who telling a very lame story, was ordered to bee committd into the Const. hands.

Abigail Darnell about a divorce.
Recommended to the Governor as above the cognizance of this court.

Mrs. Hallet complaynes against her husband for not paying her according to Contract.

In the Case or Complaint brought into this Court by Mrs. William Hallet, for not performing a certaine Contract made betweene them for the payment of a summe of money yearely by the husband to the wife, occasioned by their mutuall disagreement of Living together: The which was recommended by the late Go: Coll: Lovelace to the Consideracion of the Court of Sessions to bee held for this Riding And the said court held in the Month of June 1669 finding all endeavors of Reconciliacion betweene the partyes to bee fruitlesse, The one and the other being totally averse from Cohabiting together, or performing Conjugall Rights the one to the other: The Court did not then see Cause to make voyd the Marriage Relacion betweene them not finding sufficient grounds for the same, but did referre them to the contract to bee kept betweene them for quietnesse and peace sake, This court having now heard the Allegacions on both parts, the woman demanding payment of the yearely summe agreed upon and the husband offering to Cohabit with her which she still refuseth as hee doth to make any such payment, alleadging the Contract to bee voyde and contrary to Law: Upon consideracion had hereunto that the Case seemes to differ from what it formerly was, and is a buisnesse of extraordinary Concernment, wherein the Court of Sessions have former-ly given their Judgment They doe not think fitt either to reinforce or dis[a]null that Judgment, as the Case now stands but referre the same to the Governor for his farther direction or determinacion therein.

Fryday Dec. 11th 1674.

The buisnesse of Ramrock the Indyan about some hoggs stealers.

Cor. Mott accused confest the same to Mr. Cornell and Mr. Hicks.

Thomas Daniel called, hee was sent for last night to Mad Nans neck.

Hee denyes the Fact, but Cor. Mott maintains it to his face.

Richd Comes sworne — declares severall Circumstances against them, but especially against Tho: Daniel.

Hee is ordered to bee committed, and to bee bound over to the Assizes if he find security.

Cor. Mott hath entred into a Recognizance of 20£ to appeare at the Assizes.

Tho: Daniel the like summe. Mr. Cornell and Mr. Hicks are security. Mr. Pruddens buisnesse, ordered for his Contract.

The Court hereupon dissolved.

[24:31]

[BILL OF THE TAVERN KEEPER AT JAMAICA FOR THE BOARD OF THE COURT OF SESSIONS]

Court
December   The Acompt for diate for thous that wear
1674   At the first table

The first day att diner			£	s	d
	thear was	31	01	11	00
	At Super	27	01	07	00
2d day	At diner	29	01	09	00
	At Super	24	01	04	00
3d day	At diner	36	01	16	00
	And for drinke drane*		07	07	00
for The same Company			07	04	02

Captain Salliesbury going
downe
        [   ] Paid
        for d[   ]r A[   ]
        hors[   ]   00 10 00

* Apparently a misspelling of "drawn."

five Constables for drinke and vittles	03	07	06
4 Jurymen for drinke and vittles	02	02	00
Mr. Platt of Huntington	00	06	06
	00	06	00
	06:	12:	00

the two serv that waited upon his honor 2 meals	01:06
Michall	03:04
5 meals	00:08
1 muchtz *	00:06
1 Can ber ‡	06:00

[ENDORSED:]   Jamaica Sessions
                Expences.
                Dec. 1674.

[24:32]

[VERDICTS RENDERED AT THE GRAVESEND SESSIONS]

At a Court.

Assur Levy Plt.
Jan Jansen Van Kirk Deft.

The Deft. by Mr. Sharpe his attorney confesses Judgment to the plt. by a *nihil dicit*[†] for the sum of four hundred and ninety Guilders principall. Whereupon the [   ]able Court orders that the Deft. should pay the plt. the said summ of 490 Guilders with the Interest there within two moneths with Costs of court.

---

* Perhaps intended for *mutsje*, a Dutch liquid measure equal to 215 ounces.
‡ Perhaps a misspelling of "beer."
† Latin for "he says nothing." A refusal or neglect by the defendant to plead or answer; a judgment rendered against a defendant charged with *nihil dicit* (*Webster's Third New International Dictionary*).

By order etc.

Peter Smith etc.

Entring the accion and summons	00:05:00
Filing the Declaracion	00:01:00
Copy	00:02:00
Sheriffes Fee	00:06:00
Cryer and Marshall	00:01:04
Entring Judgment	00:03:00
To the publick	00:15:00
Attor: Fees	00:10:00
Execucion	00:05:00

Execusion given out
12th Mar. 1674/5.

At a Court of sessions held at Gravesend by his Majesties Authority beginning on the 16 day of Decemb. in the 26th yeare of his Majesties Raigne Annoque Domini 1674.

Albert Cornelisen Wantanaer Plt.
Andries Juriansen Deft.

The accion of Defamacion wherein Albert Cornelis wantanaer was plt. and Andries Juriansen deft. being referr'd to a Jury and who haveing heard both partyes with the Evidence on both sides, went out to conferr about the matter but after some time sent to have liberty to speake with the worshipfull Court, and aske some questions which was allowed of who upon their farther consideracion They bring in their verdict for the plt. There being no legall Evidence to prove his charge The worshipful Court ordered that Judgment should be enter'd accordingly with costs of such.

The Deft. desired an appeale from the Verdict of the Jury, and Judgment of court which was allowed of by the worshipful Court according to the Direccions in the Law giveing in 100£ prosecuty to prosecute the plt. at the Next Court of Assizes.

By order etc.

Peter Smith Clarke etc.

Entring the accion and sum:	00.05.00
Filing the declar:	00.01.00
Copy	00.02.00
Sher. Fees	00.06.00
6 witnesses	00.06.00
Cryer and marshall	00:03.10
Entring Judgment	00:09.00
Jury	01.04.06
The publick	00:01.15
Attorneys Fees	00:00.10
	04.16.04

[24:33]

[PETITION OF JURIAEN THEUNISSZ, HARMAN VAN GANSEVOORT
AND GERRIT THEUNISSZ FOR PERMISSION TO PURCHASE A TRACT
OF LAND AT CATSKILL FROM THE INDIANS. TRANSLATION]

To the Right Honorable Lords Schout and
Magistrates of Albany, the Colony of
Rensselaerwyck etc.

Juriaen Theunisz, Herman van Gansevoort amd Gerrit Theunisz
reverently show how they, the petitioners, are very desirous to buy some
land in Katskil, for which they already have a promise from the Indians,
who are very much inclined and desirous thereto; and having noticed
that all trades are becoming slack they would settle themselves and more
families there in order to cultivate, till, and plant the aforesaid land.
Therefore, they, the petitioners, humbly request and petition for permission
to be allowed to purchase the aforesaid land for a promise of
residency according to such orders drawn up thereto. Whereupon they
rely, awaiting a favorable recommendation. In so doing etc.

Your honors devoted servants,

Jurrejan Teunisen

Harman Harmans Gansevort

The mark of ✶ Gerrit Theunisz
done with his own hand.

[MARGINAL NOTATION:]

The honorable magistrates refer the petitioners to the honorable lord governor general of New York. If his right honorable lord [   ] to grant it, the Court shall have nothing against it.

Done in Albany the 17th of December 1674
By order of the court,

Johannes Provoost, secretary.

[ENDORSED:]   Petition for
               Juriaen Theunisz
               Herman van Gansevort
               and Gerrit Theunisz

[RECOMMENDATION:]*

The Governor doth consent unto and allow of the within written purchase Provided the Purchasers doe forthwith settle it as they ought and not hinder others by having greater Quantityes then they can improve.

[24:34]

[PETITION OF NICOLAES BAYARD AS ATTORNEY FOR GOVERNOR
COLVE, COMPLAINING OF PARTIES WHO REFUSE
TO FULFILL THEIR OBLIGATIONS]

To the Right Honnorable Mayor Edm. Andros
Governor Generall of all his Royall
Highnesses Territories in America.

[   ] Humbly Sheweth Nicolaes Bayard Atturny [   ] Anthony Colve, that Mr. Isaacq [   ] at Kings Towne in the [   ] [   ] Colves Government hath sold [   ] Cambrits and Mr. George Hall [   ] and other goods for the account of the [   ] Colve, which payment they not only refuse to make, but they being the Magistrates there do forbid others soe to doe, and hae alsoo taken in arrest the Mounies Collected there for Excise in the time of the said Hr. Colves Government, And Your petitioner Complaynes further that he hath alsoo received advice from Albany, that from Mr. Marten Kregier formerly Collector there, is fetshed away the Bookes and accounts of the Excize in that place due to the said Hr. Colve; but by what

* The recommendation is written in English.

order Your petitioner Knowes not; By Which Meanes your honnors petitioner is Hindered to Satisfy here the Creditors of the said Hr. Colve; Wherefor your Honnors petitioner doth hereby make his addresse to Your honnor Requesting that Your honnor will be pleased to order the said Magistrat[   ] and Albany to take of the said arrest [   ] payment of the said Negros and [   ] in outcry from the said Hr. Colve [   ]oner shall ever pray etc. and remaine.

Honnorable Sir

> Your Honners Verry Humble Servant
>
> N: Bayard.

[ENDORSED:]   Mr. Nicholas [   ]
                   Petition
                   Jan: 19. 1674 An[   ]
                   The petition is
                   To have all legall [   ]
                   and dispatch in the respective [   ]
                   due regard to the [   ]
                   of peace
                   By order of the Gov[   ]
                   M. N.

[24:35]

[ORDER ON THE PRECEDING PETITION]

The Merrits of this Peticion being taken into consideracion, It is left by the Governor to legall Judiciall proceedings and decision by Law, with due Regard had to the Articles of Peace, And the same is recommended to the Magistrates in the severall Courts to bee expedited without delay accordingly.

The said Mr. Nicholas Bayard in the first place recording his Procuracion or letter of Attorney from Governor Colve, in the Secr. office as is usuall. And [   ]cuting his action or Claymes before the first [   ] next which will bee in the yeare of our [   ]

> By order of the Governor
> in Councell.

[   ] 1674

[24:36]

[ADDRESS BY CAPTAIN JOHN MANNING CONCERNING HIS
EXAMINATION BEFORE THE KING AND DUKE]*

To the Right Honorable
Major Edmund [Andrews]
Governor Generall of all his Royall
High[nesses Territoryes] in America

The Address of Capt. John [Manning]

In all humble manner Sheweth,

That your Honors Addresser Arrived at Portsmouth [in Old England]
the 5th day of January in the Yeare 1673 where Qua[rters] [*were
provided*] for your Honors Addresser and the 23 Soldiers By order of
[   ] The 8th day your Honors Addresser had
passage for [London] [*and*] arrived their the 10th And without Stop or
Stay y[our Honors addresser] applied himselfe unto the Right Honorable
Governor [Legg and] imediately his Honor took your Honors Addresser
and Cap[t. Dudley] to his Royall Highness who was gratiousy please[d
to tell your] Honors Addresser that a greate informacion was come in
[against] him and that your Honors Addresser should answer it before
[his] Betters The meane time that your Honors Addresser may repai[re
to] his Lodging but be ready to attend his R: H: his [further Commands,]
the morneing following at which time his R: H: was furth[er] pleased to
Comand your Honors Addresser to give his attenda[nce in] the Afternoone, being their your Honors Addresser was ad[mitted] into the Private
Closset of his R: H: who was gratiou[sly] [*pleased*] to peruse the paper
of the whole Proceedings a[nd in] [*perticular*] his Royall Highnesse was
pleased to blame your [Honors Addresser] for sending 3 persons aboard
the enemies Sh[ipps to] [*make terms*] your Honors Addresser in all
humble Manner replied un[to his R: H:] that it was in hopes to have Stopt
the said Shipps one [Tide] and in that time expected the Governor or
more assistance [within] the Fort: The morneing following his R: H: was
further g[ratiously] pleased to Command your Honors Addresser to
weight up[on Sir] John Worden with the said papers the next morneing
[your Honors] Addresser was Comanded to give his further attendan[ce

* This document comes partly from *DH* 3; documents 36–51 appear in this printed source.
Material in brackets is missing in the original, but was presumably still present when E. B.
O'Callaghan edited *DH* 3. However, material in italics was already missing in O'Callaghan's
time and should be considered an educated guess on his part as to what had been lost.

upon] his Royal Highness who was gratiously pleased [to] [*Comand*]
your Honors Addresser to attend at the hower of Six [o clock] at the Right
Honorable the Lord Arlingtons and about the [hower] of Seaven your
Honors Addresser was admitted into the [presence] of the Kings Majestie
his Royal Highness His gra[ce the Duke] of Ormond the Lord high
Treasurer of England Th[e Lord] Keeper the Lord Arlington and one
Peere more [of] his [Majesties] Cabinett Counsell; And upon the Examinacion of y[our Honors] Addresser the King was gratiously plea[s]ed
to Co[mand] [*to be read*] an Account how the Fort of York was Loste
Soone [after] the Clerke of that supreme Court after he had [rede the]
papers The King amongust other Questions [was most] [*Gratiously*]
pleased to Command an Account to be render'd how [many Bastions]
was belonging unto the said Fort your honors Addresser an[swered]
[*four*] and allso how many Gunns belonged to each Bastia[n, and] his
Royal Highness was gratiously pleased to ans[wer] in the Behalfe of your
Honors Addresser that their was te[*n to*] everry Bastian; Further the King
was gratiously [pleased] to Demand how long the Curtaines* were your
Honors Ad[dresser] Humbly Answered that to the Best of his memory
7[0 paces] or upward and allso how many men was in the Fort, [And
was] answered 70 or 80 Whereupon the King was furt[her gratiously]
pleased unto his Royall Highness (to say) Brother [the] Ground could
not be maintained with soe few Men; [And it] was further demanded of
your Honors Addresser concer[ning] his knowledge of the Enemies
Fleete and their Strength a[nd] [*what*] loss they had at Viall;‡ Which
accordingly your Honors [Addresser] humbly answered; And at the same
time your Honors [Addresser] humbly besought his Majestie that care
mought be ta[ken] of the said Souldiers which the King imediately gave
Order to [be] listed in the Severall Companies at Portsmouth i[mmediate-
ly] after your Honors Addresser prayed to the Secretary to acquaint him
[what] [*Order*] was made who replied that he was to h[ave your Honors]
Addressers name and where he lodged Whi[ch] [*he gave*] never
remooveing from thence dureing his abo[ad] his R: H: was further
gratiously pleased to Comman[d your Honors] Addresser to gi[ve] his
constant attendance, which he d[id often] times after, when sickness did
not prevent And allso at [the] latter end of the moneth of March following
his R: [H: as he] was gratiously pleased Signed a Warrant upon the
Tre[asurer] for the Summe of 56£ to pay for the passage of your Honors
A[ddresser] for his family and Soldiers from Viall to London your
H[onors] Addresser still attending his Royall Highness his furth[er]
Commands untill the Court remooved from Whitehal[l to] Winsor where

---

* Curtain: the portion of a palisade connecting two bastions.
‡ Faial in the Azores.

allso your Honors Addresser th[ei]r [had] [*attended*] had not providence
soe decreed it that being [*sufficient*] money was wanteing your Honors
Addresser further S[*aith*] that in the moneth of August Sir John Worden
well kne[w your] Honors Addresser being aboard the Dimond Friggate
[*when*] she was ready to depart being bound for thiese pa[rtes] which
your Honors Addresser Averrs for a truieth as he sh[all] answere before
the Great God your Honor and your Honors [Court] Witness my hand
this 21 of Jan: Annoque Domini 167[4]

Your Honors most obed[ient servant,]

Joh[n Manning]

[ENDORSED:]   Capt Manning
                     No. 1.

                     The Address.

[24:37][*]

> Persons summansed to Apeare before the
> Governor about the Axamination of Capt. Jno.
> Manning on Fryday the 29 of Jan: 1674.

Mr. Jno Sharpe X
Mr. Tho: Berryman X
Mr. Tho: Tailer X
Mr. Edward Ellitt X
and his man   } Volanteers
Mr. Jno Worsencraft X
Mr. Jno. Cooly
Mr. Herry Newton X

Mr. Jno Thomson   Then Sodgars[‡] but
Mr. Churcher   now out of   } dismis't
Mr. Jno Ray pipe maker   Servis

---

* See the first footnote in 24:36.
‡ soldiers

Baynes
Fitz Gerald } Serjeants before, being cal'd upon appeared
Dowdale

[ENDORSED:] The Persons Sumans
About Capt. Jno.
Maning

[24:38]

> Articles against Capt. John Manning Commander in cheife
> in James Fort in New Yorke and Government at the taking
> thereof by the Dutch in July 1673

1. First, that on or about the 28th day of July 1673 the said Capt. John Manning having notice of a fleete of Ennemyes ships coming into the bay, Hee did not endeavour as hee ought, nor put the Garrison in such a fitting posture of Defence as hee might and slighted such as proffer'd their service.

2. That on or about the 30th day of July the said fleete of ennemyes being under Staten Island at Anchor, Hee the said Capt. John Manning treacherously sent on board to treate with them, to the Encouragement of the said Ennemy, and discouragement of the Garrison,

[3.] That upon the same 30th day of July, hee suffered the said Ennemyes with their Fleet to come and moare their ships under the fort without firing at them, which hee forbid, upon paine of death:

4. That sometime after the ennemyes fleet being so moared, Hee suffered them to send their boates on shoare loaden with Men and to land them without opposicion.

5. That a while after having sent out several times to treat with the Ennemy, hee strooke his Majesties Flagge before the Ennemy (that had Landed) were in sight of the Fort, though the Fort were in a Condicon, and all the Garrison desirous to fight.

6. That hee treacherously caused the gate to bee open'd and cowardly and basely let in the Ennemy, and yielded them his Majesties Fort without Articles, unlesse to himself[e]

Feb. 2. 1674.

[ENDORSED:]   [ ]rticles and Examinacions
against Capt. John Manning.
Feb. 4 and 5. 1674

[24:39]

Examinations concerning the surrende[r] of New Yorke
Fort to the Dutch, in Ju[l]y 1673, taken February 4th 1674.

[1.] To the 1st. Mr. John Rider, to the whole.
Thos: Taylor to the first Part, but not of slighting those etc.
William Palmer to the 1st parte.
Mr. John Sharpe, to the first, sayes nothing to the last part.
Mr. Thomas Gibbs to the 1st part, but not to the last.
Henry Newton, to the first. John Cavalier, to the 1st.
Mr. Thomas Lovelace, to the 1st.
Mr. Gabr: Minviele ⎞
Mr. Walter Webley ⎠   To the whole

[2.] To the 2d., Mr. Rider
Thomas Taylor was twice with those sent
William Palmer, that some were twice sent.
Mr. Sharpe, That hee was commanded to put off his Buff [C]oate, and
go on Board with others, the 1st time, and afterward[s] by himselfe, for
to Treat and gaine time.
Mr. Gibbs, That he sent twice on Board.
Mr. Lovelace. that hee was Commanded on board with others to Treat
and gaine time,
Henry Newton, John Cavalier, That hee sent on Board.

[3.] To the 3d. Mr. Rider.
Tho: Taylor. except forbidding upon paine of death.
Willm Palmer, John Cavalier, to the whole.
Mr. Sharpe, to the 1st part.
Mr. Gibbs, To the 1st part.
Mr. Lovelace, To the 1st parte.
Henry Newton, To the 1st, And heard Willm Palmer, and
Charles Bollen, Gunners, say they were; And did pull their Haire for
Anger.

[4.] To the 4th
Thomas Taylor
William Palmer
Thomas Gibbs
Mr . Sharpe
Mr . Lovelace
Henry Newton

5. To the 5th Tho. Taylor, That the Flagg was str[uck] a Flagge of Truce
put up, and a Parly Beat.
William Palmer.
Mr. Sharpe, That the Flagg was struck.
Mr. Gibbs, John Cavalier.
Mr. Thomas Lovelace   That the Flagg was struck [and]
Henry Newton   Parly Beat

6. To the 6th. Thomas Taylor, that the Gates wer[e opened] and the
Enemy Let in.
Willm Palmer.
Mr. Sharpe, That the Gates were open'd [and him]selfe being then out,
sent to propose Artic[les to] March out as Souldiers with their Baggage,
w[ich were] not signed.
Mr. Gibbs, That the Gate was open'd and the [Enemy] Let in, hee being
detained at the head of [their party where he] being sent with Mr.
Lovelace and Capt Car[re to make] Articles, and found the Enemy at the
New [Burial] place, without the Towne.
Mr. Tho. Lovelace, That the Gate was open'd [etc. as] Mr. Gibbs, being
with him, at the head of the enemy det[ayned.]
Henry Newton, That the Enemy was Let in b[efore he] came off the
Flagge Mount, etc.
John Cavalier, That the Gates being open [and the] Enemy Marching,
hee went out before they cam[e in.]

[ENDORSED:]   Examinacions against [   ]pt.
                 John Manning.
                 Taken Feb. 4 and 5th
                 1674

[24:40]

[24:41]*

[PETITION OF JOHN MANNING CONCERNING THE ARTICLES
AGAINST HIM]

To the Honored Governor And Court [Assembled.]

Since Providence has soe Order'd it, That I am Charged with six Seveer
Articles In all submissio[n] I acknowledge my selfe blame worthy to all
(but Treachery maeking of Articles for myselfe onely and Cowerdise
which I humble conceace I am not Guilty of or which if the words of a
dyeing Man m[ay] be Credited I take the greate God to Witness I [am]
not directly or indirectly in any Measure gui[lty] Had I entertained but
such a thought death [had] beene to good for me much less to Imagin[e]
or dare to Act such a Villinous deepe dyed [   ] unpardinable Crime but
to exhonerate myselfe soe farr as I cann In all humble maner upon the
bended Knee of my harte I pray that the following reasons which w[as
according] too my unadvised Judgment Cheefely [Induced] me soe to
Act May be pondred [and taken] into your Honors Pious and Grave
Consi[deracion] Humbly craveing a perdon for Errors [that may] be
theirin which may be occasioned by m[y poor] broaken head and
disquieted Spiritt In h[opes] of some Mittigacion of my charge I f[urther]
pray that all persons may be heard to s[peake] that can say any thing to
my advantage I haveing noe Advocate to make intercession but my
inocency and doe wholy relye upon your Honors Clemency, and Bowells
of Compation and Mercy.

A your Honors Supplicant as in duty bound shall ever pray etc.

[ENDORSED:]   A petition to the Governor
to Accept my Answers.

Capt. Manning.

* See the first footnote in 24:36.

[24:42][*]

[RESPONSE OF JOHN MANNING TO THE ARTICLES]

[my A]nswere [to the Articles drawne] against [me, which I] doe in [all hum]ble and Submissive [Man]ner [ten]der unto your Honors serious Considera[cion] not to Justify my Selfe but to shew your Honor how farr I Indeavered for the preservacion of this place.

Inprimis, I Answer, That I did not know the Shipps to bee Enemies before the 29th of July at five a Clock in the Evening, but aboute five Moneths before heareing of an Enemys Fleete that was bound for Verginia, and from thence to this place; Governor Lovelace being then at Mr. Pells at Anhookes neck I imedately sent notice to him of the same who imediately came and seeing noe Enemy slited my care and said this is one of Manning's Larrums, which newes I thought would have Caused him forthwith to prepare the Fort, and procure such necessaryes as would have beene Convenient and were wanting to withstand an Enemy, He haveing received into his Custody the Contribucion money that was gathered for that Intent. Notwithstanding the said Newes the money soe received he did not make any preparacion in the Fort, onely sent for the Soldiers from Albany and other places, and upon the first of May mustered them and they did amount to neare 130 Listed men. And upon the 29th of May did mak another m[uster] and then with Volunt[eer]s and Souldiers we did amount to 330 After which said Muster the Governor dischargeing some and dismissing others sent back all that came from Albany with Capt. Salsbury and Just before the Enemeyes Comeing here takes his Jurney for Conetticott and leaves mee in the Fort without any order to repaire the same for to make defence against an Enemy; But I heareing Newes of the Shipps being upon the Coaste did send notice with all expedicion to the Governor at Connetticott and did to the Best of my Indeavor send out my Warrants for aide to come to the Fort and likewise caused the drumms to beate up for Vollunteers and of all those that before proffered their service but few came which was discouragement to the whole Garrison I likewise Caused a Smith forthwith to repaire 100 fyrelocks ready upon the works for such as Should come in; and Sent out the Commesary Mr. Barker to fetch all sorts of provisson which was in the Towne into the Fort for feare we should have occasion for it, Soe that haveing but eighteene howers time after I Knew them to be an Enemy before they attackt us and being dismay'd at soe [su]daine surprisall [we w]ere not Capable to make mo[re] [*defence*] then [*we did*] I alsoe sent Mr. [   ] [to] go to the

---

* See the first footnote in 24:36.

Luthern Domin[ie] [   ] then [
] it But Could not.

2ly. To the [Sec]ond Article I [Answere] that the said Gov[ernor being Absent and the] Fort being s[oe Uncap]able of defence [I di]d in hopes of the Governors Returne and the Countrys Co[mei]ng in For [my] Better Assistance send on Board the said Shipps Mr. Tho: Lovelace Mr. Sharpe and Mr. Carr to know upon what Account they came etc. Thincking thereby to Stopp them one tide at Straton Iseland till further defence could be made against them, which I did out of a reall thought to delay their Comeing and not out of Treacherry; And for my Innocency thereof I referr my selfe to their Sayings that were sent wheather they thought or knew I sent them upon any Treacherous designe or noe.

3ly. To the third Article I Answere that the said Lovelace Sharpe and Carr being a Board and not returned a Shoare before the said Shipps did com to an Anckor I did not fyre thincking it is Not usuall when Ambassadors were on Board soe to doe; But that I should Comand upon Paine of Death noe man to fyre that I cannot well remember.

4ly. To the forth Article I answere that after the said Embassadors were retur'd and Account was given why they came, In hop[es and with an] Intent to have the Advise of the Major and Aldermen I sent Mr. Sharpe a Board the second time to demand liberty till 10 a Clock the next day to give them an Answere thincking still to prolong the time in expectacion for the Governors and the Countryes comeing in for Assistance dureing which time of his being a Board they did land their men which was unknowne to me Soe that Sharpe being upon a second Embassage caussed me not to fyre expecting their Answere to be According to my demand.

5ly. To the fifth I answere that Understanding the Enemy had Landed near 800 Soldiers and Mr. Lovelace and Carr giveing such an Account that we were not able to withstand soe greate forse I did by the Instigacion of Capt. Carr Concent that the Flagg of truice should be putt upp but not the Kings Flagg to be pull'd downe But Mr. Carr without my order or Concent struck the Kings Flagg to putt out the Flagg of truice. And I hope that Your Honer and Councell will Consider in what Condicion the Fort was to withstand soe greate an Enemy Armed as they were with Hand Granadoes ready for a Storme their being but about 70 or 80 men in the Fort and but foure Ladles and [sp]ung[es t]o all the Gunns in the fort without any Platformes or a[ny other necessaryes fitt for defen]ce.

6ly. To the sixth Article I answere that I did Neaver make any Articles for my private Intrest neither did I directly or Indirectly hold any Correspondence with the Enemy either by private Messengers or Papers neither did I Treacherously cause the Gates to be opened without Articles sent to be signd bud did send Mr. Sharpe with Articles that we should March out with our Drums beateing Cullors flying Bagg and Baggadge etc. Who brought word to the best of my knowledge before the Gates were opened we should have them Graunted whereupon the Gates were opened but not otherwise but in Considerracion of the Articles being graunted and for want of men to keepe it Longer against soe greate an Enemy as they were; The truieth of all these my Answeres I referr my selfe to the papers formerly Given in to your Honor and Councell, hopein You will make a favorable Construction of what Errors I Comitted it being for want of discrecion to manage it better and not out of any Intention of Treachery to Defraud his Majestie his Royall Highness or any of their Subjects, of any of their Right or Intrest in the leaste Measure.

[ENDORSED:]   Capt. Mannings
               Answer to his Char[   ]
               2.

               My Ans[   ]

[24:43]*

    [CERTIFICATE OF SOLDIERS IN DEFENSE OF JOHN MANNING]

Wee whose names are under written [are re]ady to mak oath that when the dush [floe]t cam to New York we had in the Fort Jeams but four Spunges and Ramers [that of all the Guns in the Fort and we Could] not get but sixe to beare upon the [Ennemy when] they were fird for want of [platforms] all the men upon the [bastian] Could not Bring them to [beare A]gaine or else the Carridge [brook]e and thier was neither Bed not [Koyn] plank spad Hand spick or anny [mat]eriall to help to defend us And [Ca]ptain Carre never returnd to [tell] us we wer prisoners at Ware when [Car]re Lovlas and Mr. Gibs wer then [pris]ners under thier Standard [Whe]n three were sent to mak Articl[es for] us

Patrick Dowdall ⎰   Thomas Gwinne
[Jo]hn B Gerratt ⎱ Sargeants

_____

* See the first footnote in 24:36.

[B]en: Comly
[Thom]as Bassett   Corporalls   David Thomas [*blank*] his marke
[ ][ ] Cantuell
                                        Joseph Stanton ⨎ $ his marke
[   ] Copstaffe [   ] marke
                                        the marke of Andrew ⌡ Stocker
[Lewis] [   ] Collens [   ] marke
                                        the marke of William ─┼─ Hatter
Jn[ ][ ] Wattkens 𝓙𝓦 his marke
                                        the marke of John ⟋⟍ Tayler
[   ] Perry 𝓃𝓎 his marke

[ ]ert Brayday ⟨⟩ his marke

[SIGNED:]*   John Massingale
                  Peter Good
                  Edward Suter
                  Tho: Chesmans
                  Niclos Pamer
                  Roberrt a Gardner

[ENDORSED:]   The Souldyers Certificate
                  No. 3.

[24:44]

[ACCOUNT BY JOHN MANNING OF EVENTS LEADING TO THE
SURRENDER]

An Exact Account of all the Proceedings of the [Military]
Officers of Fort James from the 28th 29th and 30th of July,
1[673.]‡

Coronell Frances Lovelace Governor of New Yorke ha[veing] urgent
occasions to John Wintrupt Esqr. Governor of Cornec[ticut] and had not
beene absent but eight daies, But upon Mun[day] July the 28th at 5 a
Clock at night we received an Alaram that t[here was] a Fleet of ships
upon the Coasts under Saile Standing f[or new] York; Wee dispatcht an
Express with Letters to his Honor with [word] to press horses and to
make all expedicion night and da[y] [*till he*] came to him to acquaint him
with it.

---

* The signatures appear on the back of the document.
‡ The Dutch are using new-style dating, the English old-style dating.

A Warrant with a Letter was likewise sent to Lieut: Willit [*and Correnett Doughty*] to draw up their truipe to Utrecht and the Coaste to ma[k discovery] or give resistance as occasion should require and to sen[d down an] officer to the Ferry to attend further Orders.

Stoffolo[*] was alsoe sent out with a Boate to discover [their Cullors] and the number of their Fleet and he brought us nu[se of 2 ships] but could not discover their Cullors about 2 a Clock [the 29th of July.]

Alsoe their was Warrants and Letters to acquaint [them of the] Alaram and to send us in what force they could out of [their] companies to Strengthen the Garrison.

> To Capt. Coe of New towne
> To Capt Lawrence of Flushing
> To Capt Panton of Westchester
> To Capt Seamons of Hempstead
> To Capt Carpender of Jamaica

Noe force comeing from the said Captaines According to the [tenor] of the said Warrants and the Fleete of the Enemie apeard in the [Bay at] 3 a Clock in the Afternoone the 29th of July other Warrants was direc[ted] and sent by Mr. Wm. Osborne to the said Captains upon pa[i]ne of D[eath] to march in with their Cullors and Companies which they whol[ly] neglected and Slited And Imediately sent the Serjants [with] drums and beete up for Volenteires in New York but verr[y few] appeard and then spict up the Guns at the Stait [howse.]

A warrant to Mr. Backer to Seize on all Breade flo[ur and] all other provissions which was accordingly putt in Exec[ucion when the] Fleet was come under Staten Island and Ancored in sight o[f the Fort] I myselfe Orderd the Sheriffe to bring all the Ladors[‡] of [the town] into the Fort which he alsoe neglected and kept them for the Ene[mie.]

July 30th

In hopes of the Governors Returne and the Countryes C[omeing] and that they might have Stopt a Tide when th[ey were at] Anckor Capt. Carr Tho: Lovelace Esq. and Mr. John Sharp [went on board] to Demand why they came in such a hostile mann[er to disturb] his Majestyes Subjects

---

* Perhaps "Stoffel, " the Dutch nickname for Christoffel.
‡ Probably intended for "ladders."

in this place who in the [way met] a Boate that brought this Summons each Bo[ate notwithstanding] keepeing on their way the one to the Fleet the other to the [Fort.]

The Sumons sent us was as Followeth

[Sir]

The force of Warr now lying in your Sight are Sent out by the [High] and Mighty States and his Serene Highness and Prince [of] Orange for to destroy their Enemies: We have sent you [ther]efore this our Letter together with our Trumpeter to the end [that you u]pon sight hereof Doe Surrender unto us the Fort called [Jam]es promiseing good Quarter or by refusall wee shall be [oblig]ed imediately to proceed both by water and Land in such [man]er as we shall finde to be most advantageous for the [High a]nd Mighty States dated in the Ship Swanenburgh [Anckor]ed betwixt Staton and Long Ileand New York the 09th of August [1673]

Cornelious Everson   Jacob Banques.

[An]swere by the same Trumpeter.

[I have] received by your Trumpeter a Summons for Surrendor of this [his Majesti]es Garrison of Fort James, which are sent (as you alleage) from [the High] and mighty States Generall of the Unighted Provinces [and his] serene Highness the Prince of Orrange, But their [are s]ome Gentlemen with you from hence to know why such [a Fleet]e of Shipps should come here to disturb his Majesties [Subjec]ts in these his Royal Highnesses Territoryes I therfore [*give you th*]is Answer that upon returne of those Gentlemen who are [   ]ng with your Lordshipps I shall send you a possitive Answere [*either*] [o]f the Surrendring of this His Majesties Garrison or nott. [Given at] Fort James in New York this 30th of July 1673.

John Manning.

[Whereup]on they gave us halfe [an how]ers time after our Men were landed [for our] finall Answere.

[They b]eing Anckored under the Fort and the halfe howere Expired [I sen]t this second Answere

[For the] preservacion of the Burgers of this Citty whome we [havi]ng promised to protect we desire you to forbeare any [   ] Hostillity untill

tomorrow at 10 a Clock at which time [we sha]ll by the advice of the
Major and Aldermen send you [our Ar]ticles of Resolucion their upon
Dated at New York this [30th of] July 1673.

[Upon t]his Letter they returned Mr. Sharp with this Answere.

[That th]ey would give us halfe an howers time longer and [noe more]
an accordingly they turned up the Glass.*

The time being nere Expired before Mr. Sharpe retu[rned they] [*turned*]
10 gunns to the Leward and imediately began to make [the same] [*bear*]
upon the Fort and when they had fyred 2000 Greate Shott [*from out*] the
boutes upon us and Killed and Wounded us some men, they [then] landed
about 600 Men and upward which had Granadoes with all [materials]
ready for a Storme and then we finding their power to greate [for us] they
advanceing wee beete a Parly and putt out a Flagg of [truice] yett they
fyred many gunns Afterward notwithstande[ing we] sent out Capt. Carr
Tho. Lovelace Esqr. Mr. Gibbs to meet [them] to make the best Condicions they could for us who f[indeing] them all drawne up and theire
forlorne‡ Marching th[ey] tould them they were all prisnors at Warr and
that if they had anything to say they must speake it Quickly.

After some little Discourse Capt. John Carr of Dellaw[ayre went] away
to the Fort and the rest remaineing prisnors under the [Standard] to
acquaint the Garrison they were all prisnors at Warr [and] they should
returne an Answere within a Quarter of an ho[wer] which he promised
upon the word and Honor of a Gentleman and [gave] his Hand upon it
but he never came neare the Garrison [and] has not been seen since;

The quarter of an hower being Expired they send a [trumpeter to] Know
why Capt. Carr did not returne with our Answere, Cap[tain] Manning
and Capt. Lovelace replied that Capt. [Carr had not been] their and that
we had Gent. with them to mak[e Condicons] [*to this*] Answer when the
Trumpeter returned to th[em they] replied this is the third time they have
playe[d] the [fool with us] march on and give the English noe Quarter
this the Gen[tlemen] informed us that was then prisnors under the
Standard.

They advanceing nearer the Fort they espyed Mr. Sharpe [coming]

---

* Meaning an hourglass (or to be precise, a half-hourglass).
‡ Probably short for "forlorn hope," from Dutch *verloren hoop*, a band of volunteers
detached for perilous service such as scaling walls or attempting a breach. These men were
in fact marines, a new type of soldier that the English had not yet encountered.

towards them with a paper in his hand wherewith [*upon*] Halt he brought to them 2 Articles

1. That all the Officers and Souldiers in Fort James sh[ould march] out with our armes, Drumes Beateing, Cullers flying Bag[g and] Baggage without Hindrance or Molestacion.

2. That the Fort with the Millitary Armes and Amu[nicon] be delivered to the Dutch Generall or any other Offi[cer]

I John Sharp being sent out by our Deputy Go[vernor Capt.] John Manning the 30th of July about 7 a Clock in [the] [   ] with the above said Articles Read them in Dutch to Coll. [Calvert and the] other Commanders marching with him in the Broad[way] and towards the Fort where I found Mr. Lovelace a[nd Mr.] [*Gibbs*] in the head of the Redgements.

The said Coll. Calvert took the said Articles and after s[ome] Capulacions[*] he putt them in his pockett and ing[aged his] hand on his Brest that upon the word and Honor [of a Gentlemen] they should be puncktually performed but perfid[eously] breakeing his faith and his word.

[When we] had Marcht out of the Fort with Drums beeteing and [our A]rmes Grounded contrary to their faith and their Honor they [put] a Guard upon and made us prisnors in the Church and fell [plu]ndring of all the Bagg and Baggage and the next morneing [put] us on Board severall of their Shippes of Warr and soe [carri]ed us some to Newfoundland and the Portinguall Ilands[‡] [where t]hey Inhumanly left us and some to Cales[†] which we have [not] heard from as yett

[When] ther fleet was come within Sandioock several of the Dutch [we]nt on Board them from Utrecht and Flatbush upon Long [Ilan]d and Informed them of the absence of our Governor [and] weekness of our Garrison and the number of our men [and] ingaged that if they would

---

* Perhaps "caperlash," a North English dialect for abusive language (*Century Dictionary*).

‡ The Portuguese Azores, which the Dutch fleet reached on Nov. 4, according to Captain Evertse's journal (De *Zeeuwsche Expeditie naar de West onder Cornelis Evertsen de Jonge 1672–74*, ed. by C. De Waard; 's-Gravenhage: Nijhoff, 1928).

† Perhaps "Cadiz," which the Dutch sometimes called *Cales Males*. Evertse's journal recounts the fleet's adventures in the Bay of Cadiz throughout the winter. Certainly Cales could not have been Calais, an enemy port.

attack that they would [be ha]ngd up if they would not win the place.

[The] Dutch in the Towne being all Armed Incouragcd thcm [to a] Storme and while they stormed ingaged that we should [not] look over our Workes and they were about 400 Armed Men.

[The] Condicion of the Garrison their was but 4 Spunges Ramers [for] all the Gunns of the Fort the Platformes and Carriges was [alsoe] Badd either the Carriges Broake or they Could not bring them [to pass] againe their was neither Bedd Spade Hanspike [or other mater]iall to help to defend us

[*There was*] [4] Bastians 10 gunns upon every Bastion 4 Curtains [each Curta]ine neare 80 paces long and we had but betweene [70 a]nd 80 men to maintaine the whole Ground

Finis.

[ENDORSED:]   Capt. Mannings
                   Relacion of Proceedings

                   No. 4.The Procedings in
                   t[ ] Govt

                   A Coppie.

[24:45]

To the Right Honorable the Governor and Counc[ell]

A Narretive of Capt. John Manning

Sheweth unto your Honor that before the Enemies F[leete] [*came*] heare we had Intelligence by one who was a prisono[r] Capt. Dellincourt and one Mr. Hopkins gave informac[on that] their was a fleete of Shipps comeing from the [West] Indies intending to make Spoile at Verginia an[d] thence to New Yorke as they was certainely In[formed] abaoard the said Capts. Shipp at that Instant Co[ll.] Lovelace was at Mr. Pells to whome imediately an ex[press was] sent and his Honor returned the day following [*and*] [with all] expedicion sent a dispatch for Capt. Sallsbury and [ ] men from Albany alsoe Issued out a Warrant to [Capt.] Chambers of Sopus for 20 men who was Ord[ered to] return soone after their comeing and likew[ise 9 men] and a Corporall came from Dellaware which co[mpleted] 130 men of Officers and Soldiers in the [muster] [*roll*] (in the 1st of May 1673) and upon th[e 29th of] [*May*] with Vollunteers that came out of the [Country] promised to be ready upon all occass[ions] [*to*] the number of 300 or their aboutes. [Soone after the] Garrison soe decreased some being di[scharged] [*some*] dismist and in July Capt. Salsbury and [*his men*] by Order returned to Albany Then the [whole] [*number*] was reduced to 15 or 16 with a Sarjant to [every] [   ] and of that Number their was 12 effective So[uldiers] [*with*] the Governor and absent upon the approa[ch of the] Enemie (in soldiers (besides) Officers there exc[   ] not above 50 And not one halfe of them [*ever had*] their heads over the workes while we w[*ere there*] They still crying out wheres the Country [*people*] [What] shall we do for men and at the Losse of the [said Fort it] was soe plundred that if Mr. Munveale ha[d not] Suplyed him with Shirts he had none to his [back.] When his Wife heard we were to be carried [as] prisnors she preferred a Peticion to the A[dmirall] for some few necessaryes which was graun[ted] [*as by*] the said Peticon appeareth at which time [our] Creditors aplied themselves to the Admiralls [*stating that*] the said Capt. was Indebted to them whereupo[n he] Commanded an Inventory of what Estate he left and it amounted unto 15413 Gilders and the Debt[s to] not above 5000 Gill. or their aboutes besides 100[£] losst in the Fort; Besides the Totall Ruin of [the Reall] Fortune he left behinde and after 4 M[oneths] Imprisonment one board their Shipps of him[self and] family and souldiers he was put a Shore at [Vaill] [*] where necessity inforst him to sell the nece[ssaryes] he had to lay in wine for the Securyty of [   ] and in our way for England it pleased God [to take] away his Wife which was his onely Comfort in [*this world*] after my arrivall in England with all speed [I went] to his Royall Highness and calls God to Wit[ness] [*that*] it was his cleare Concience that Carried [him] before his Majestie and his Royall Highness [*for if*] he had either the thoughts of Unfait[hfullnesse] Treacherry or Cowerdise he neave[r durst have] presumed to have come in the presen[ce of] [*his Majestie*] or Royall Highness much less dare h[ave] [*ventured*] to have paid 30 or 40£ for his passages [he felt not] any guilt in the least upon him all [which he] [*wishes*] to make appear to your Honor and Counce[ll.]

[ENDORSED:]   Capt Mannings Narrative.
                No. 5.

---

* Faial in the Azores.

[24:46]

[WARRANTS TO ASSEMBLE TROOPS FROM JOHN MANNING TO
CAPTAIN CARPENTER AND WILLIAM OSBORN]

Capt. Carpenter

You are hereby required in his Majesties Name [immediately] upon
Sight hereof to draw up your Compa[ny of Fuzileers] together By beete
of Drumme, and all [such volunteers] as are willing to serve his Majestie
that you caus[e] forthwith to repair with their Armes to this Garr[ison]
where they shal be straightway Entertai[ned] and have due Satisfaccion
made them for t[heir] paines. And for soe doeing this shall be your
[Warrant.] Hereof you are not to faile at your Perill, and [as] you tender
the welfare of his Majesties Service Da[ted] at Fort James in New York
July the 29th [1673.]

To Capt John Carpenter at
Jamaica upon Long Island
or Samuel Riscoe his Ensigne.

A true Copy per Peter Smith

Whereas their was last night Warrants sen[t for] the respective Captains
and Officers of the Foote [Companyes] upon Long Island requireing
them for his Majesties Service to draw up their severall Companye[s] by
Beate of drum upon sight of the said W[arrants] the Cuntry being then
allarm'd of an Ene[my] at Sand=Hooke and Whereas the said
Com[panyes did] not yett come heather according as 'twas e[xpected]
and the Enemie lyeing now in sight of the [Fort,] These are to impower
and require that as y[ou] tender the Welfare of his Majesties Service and
the [safety] of his Subjects you forthwith upon receptio[n] hereof repaire
to the Townes of Jamaica and [Hempstead] and give Charge to the
Captains and officers of the Foot Co[mpanyes] their, to betake themselves in all [speede to this] Garrison with their Companyes, We[e] [*Expect*]
each houre to be attaqut by the Ene[my,] [*See*] that you send the like
Warneing [to the] Townes of Flushing and Newto[wne] [*for the*] doeing
hereof this shall be your W[arrant Dated] at New York this 29th day of
July [1673] at nine a Clock at night
To. Mr. Wm Osborne
These.

A True Copy per Peter Smith

[ENDORSED:]   Copies of Capt. Mannings
                   warrants.
                   No. 2
[24:47][*]

[ANSWER OF ENSIGN RUSCOE TO THE PRECEDING WARRANT]

Captt. Maning

Worshipfull Sir yours we Received by Mr. Osbur[n upon which] The
Towne ar much Amazed and Trubled Tha[t they] should be Totally
destitute of men: yet notwit[hstanding] officers have don ther utermost
In Obedien[ce to your] Comand They have Required all There soul-
dier[s] [*to be in readiness*] Expecting the Coming of the other townes
[according to] your worships [or]der but we make bould To Inform[e
you] The Towne is [alto]gether destitute of powder and s[hott] wher[eby
t]hay conceive Themselves very Uncapable [*to proceed*] without
E[mi]nent danger but we shall do our [*best*] in this de[str]acted Time so
far as [o]ur power and [*capability*] will Reach: We have sent Two
messengers on [purpose] To bring us farther Intelligence There are
Thretening [sp][*eeches*] newly proseeded from the Dutch Amoungst us
wherby w[e] Concieve ourselfes in great danger: When the Tow[ne is]
[*left exposed*] by the Absence of all The men We Rest you[r Worships]

                                        Servants

                                        Sam [Ruscoe]

                                        Joseph Thirs[ton]

Jamaica this 30th
July 1673.

[ADDRESSED:]   To the worshipfull
                   Captt John Manning
                   For[   ]mes
                   These.

[ENDORSED:]   The Jamaica
                   Letter

---

* See the first footnote in 24:36.

[24:48]

[ORDER TO THOMAS WILLET OR ELIAS DOUGHTY
TO ASSEMBLE TROOPS]

You are hereby required in his Majesties [name] imediately uppon receipt hereof for to draw your troope togeather and m[ ] towards Utrecht or Gravesend to obse[rve] the motion of the enemy and make [all the] discovery or resistance you canne, and send [an officer] downe hither to receive such orders [as] shall bee thought necessary, Hereof yo[ ] [must] not faile as you will aunswere the [contrary] att your Uttermost perrill: Given und[er] my hand this 28th Day of July: [1673] past 11 of the clock att night:

John M[anning.]

[ADDRESSED:]   To Lieutenant Tho Willett or to
                   Corrinett Doughty or to either of them:

[24:49][*]

[ORDER TO THOMAS WILLET TO SEND AN OFFICER]

New York this 28th of Ju[ly 1673 at] halfe an hower past
10 at n[ight]

Lieutenant Willett

In the absence of the [Governor] and Your Capt. haveinge recieved r[ecent] intelligence of 10 Saile of Shippes [arived] within Sandy=Hook, I have [thought proper] to accquaint that you fortw[ith bring] your troope together, and, that [to night you] faile not to sende downe an Off[icer] [*to the Ferry*] to receive farther orders, and [in the mean time] you will doe good Service, to God, [your King and] your countrey and

Your humble [Servant]

John [Manning.]

[ADDRESSED:]   To Liuetenant Tho Willett
                   delliver

_____
* See the first footnote in 24:36.

[24:50][*]

[LETTER FROM JOHN MANNING TO ELIAS DOUGHTY CONCERNING
THE EXPECTED INVASION]

New Yorke this: 29th of July 1673:

Cornett Doughty

Yours I have received [by Mr.] Whitehead and returne you thanks fo[r
your readi]nes in the execution of the Warrant [to you]

I could heartyly wish you doe not [spend] time too longe least the enemie
tak[e] [*advantage*] thereby, as for those persones that refus[e I wish] not
but you will make a severe return[e. I] [*wish*] that soe wee may know
our friendes from [our Enemies] For powder such as wee have you may
cou[nt on] as likewise Muskett bullettes to bee [runned into] bulettes as
to newes our boate is return[ed] with the discovery of :21: saile greate
and [small] their coulers apeared to bee blew and a whit[e]

Thus leavinge you to the protection o[   ] God I remaine as ever

Yours to serve you [   ]

John Man[ning.]

All Subordinate Men:

As for your Orders, you are to observe the Warr[ants.]

[ADDRESSED:]   To His Esteemed Friend
Cornett Elyas Doughty
at Flushing.

These present.

* See the first footnote in 24:36.

[24:51]*

[LETTER FROM ELIAS DOUGHTY TO JOHN MANNING REPORTING THE
MILITARY STATE OF PREPAREDNESS]

Captt. Maning.

Sir My humble sarvis pres[ented to] Your Worship in the liftena[ntes]
[*absence*] I reseved yourr warrant to ge[th the] troope togethar and to
March t[owards] Gravesand or Utrik the lif[tenante is] absent Nithar a
Martar‡ musk[itt] nere to asist Mee yet in obed[ience] to youar wharrant
I have sen[t] to all the troopars and the Su[rjant] uppone resayt and sight
here[of to] repire with theyr hors and arms [to] Jamaco uppon thayr perell
not to fail to be redy to etent thayr[at] Command I have sent bost a wh[ay
to] the Liftenant acording to you[ar] [*order*] I have sent one of ouar
troapars Daniell Whithed in obedianc to [your] Command to whait one
you for f[urther] ordar Sir I humble desiar y[our] worshep to send hus
poudar and [*shott*] for whee ar unprovided and [unable] to defend ouar
selves if whe [should] Meet With an Enemy Nothing [els] but My prayers
to the Lo[rd] to give you wisdom and va[liant][*arm*] to Maneg and defend
his M[ajesties] intrest and ouar oune Lives [from] the Enimy that Shall
apose [them.]

Jemaca this 29 of July 1673.

> ur moyst
> Humble Sar[vint to]
> Command to [death]
>
> Elias D[oughty.]

[24:52]

[PETITION OF JOHN MANNING TO THE GOVERNOR]

> To the Right Honorable Major Edmund Andrews Governor
> Generall of all his Royall Highnesses Territoryes in
> America.
>
> The humble Peticon of Capt. John Manning

---

*   See the first footnote in 24:36.
‡   mortar

Humbly Sheweth.

That your Honors Peticioner is the most deplorable of all Men if your Honor out of your aboundant goodnesse pleaseth not to take his Miserable State into your Honors Pious Consideracion hopeing and prayeing that all the paypers may have a favorable Construction which shewes in what Condicion the Fort was in the weakeness of our Strength what Enemy was in our Bowells the Potent Enemy without us your Honors Peticioner being wholy left without advice or Councell and haveing but eighteen howers before the Enemy came to attack us besides the greate discouragement and dismaying Capt. Carr gave to our Men when he came from aboard the Shipps he saying how greate their strength was and that we were not able to resist them and his neaver returneing when he went to make Condicions for us all which Sudaine surprisalls brought such straige amaizements and Confusion amongst the Men not being able to withstand the Storme was the cause of the Loss of the Garrison as your Honors Peticioner Humbly conceaveth.

> Therefore humbly prayeth that your Honor out of a deep sence of your distressed Peticioners Sufferance will be pleased to take the premises into your Honors grave Consideracion and that if through ill managements and diserecion or imprudent Acting that any parte of his duty was wanting he Humbly implores your Honors Cleamency and mercy which he wholy relyes upon

> And your Peticioner shall ever pray etc.

[ENDORSED:]   Jan. 29 1674
                No. 6.

[24:53]

[PETITION OF JOHN MANNING TO THE COURT-MARTIAL]*

> To the Right Honorable Edmund Andrewes Esquire Governor Generall Under his Royall Highness of all his Territoryes in America and the Rest of his Majesties officers now Assembled with him in a Court Marshall.

---

*   See the first footnote in 24:36 on p. 61.

The humble Peticion of John Maning

Sheweth in all humble Manner that your Peticioner is the most deplorable of all men if your Honors out of your abundant goodness pleaseth not to take his Misserabel State into your Pious Consideracion hopeing and prayeing that all the payper[s] may be veiwed and have a favorable Construction which shewes in what Condicion the Fort was in, the weekness of our Strength the aprehencon of Enemies in our Bowells the potent Enemy without u[s] your Honors Peticioner being wholy left without Advice or Councell and haveing but eighteen howers before the Enemy came to attack us [be]side the Greate Discouragement and dismaying Capt. Carr ga[ve] to our Men when he came from aboard the Shipps he saying how greate their Strength was and that we was not able to wit[hst]and them and his not Returneing when he went to make Condicion All which sudaine surprisall occasioned strainge amaisements disorders and Confusion Amongust the Men as to our insufficiency for defence in Serious Examinacion I highly blame myselfe for first my unadvisedness and indiscrecion in takeing the Charge of the Garrison at Governor Lovelace his goeing away and allso that I did not see the Articles Signed before the Surrender which I do to my greef Acknow-ledge through the Suddaine Hurry of State Your Honors Peticioner had not those Consideracions in [   ] minde as was meete for his owne Wellfare and the wellfare of his neighbours and friends

Therefore doeth humbly crave your Honors favorable op-pinion on this State [o]f his their being nothing intended of disloyalt[y] or unfaithfullness to his Majestie or his Royall Highnesses Intrest Nor detriment to the Inhabitants heare Soe leaveing my selfe to your Honors Mercy and Clemancy.

[ENDORSED:]   [   ] Manning
                   to the Governor and
                   Court Marshall,
                   at the time of
                   his Tryall.

                   No. 7.

[24:54]

[COMPLAINT OF EDMUND GIBBON AGAINST PETER DE LA NOY]*

> The Co[   ] Edmu[   ] Gibbon against
> Peter De la Noye, the True, Case is here
> Stated

That the said Gibbon Did at Boston Lade on Bord the Bark Rebecca and Did Condishon and agree with the Marchant and Master That they should Deliver the said Goods one Bord any Vesell at New York: Bound for Virginia that being the said Gibbons intended Voyage as said Marchant and Master Cann Testifie — coming to New York and Going to said Peter Delanoyes at the Custome house for a permit To Take said Goods out of the Barke and to Loade them on bord A sloope which was Redy to saile to Verginia wich said Gibbon humbly Conceves [   ] was not Obleiged to Doe. [ ]he said Peter DelaNoye ref[   ]ed To Deliver said Gibbon any permitt and alsoe Tould the Master [ ]f the Bark that the Goods [   ] Entrered a[   ] pay the Customes or Else [ ] the said Delanoye [   ] Cease Upon the vesell where upon the Ma[   ] put m[ ]ny Goods on Shoare upon the Brigg[ ] and so was put into the Cus[ ]me house Where one hogshead is yet remaineing Peter Delanoye Telling said Gibbons he would Keepe it for the Customes the said Gibbon humblie Conceveth he being a free borne Su[   ]ect to the King of England is noe Wayes Obleiged To pay any Customes or Trubit‡ for Coming Through the Sound and p[ ]ssing by the Citty of New York but may without pa[   ] any Customs proceed one his Voyage To Virgini[. . .]

[ENDORSED:]   [   ]und Gibbons
                     Complaint
                     against
                     Mr. Peter de la Noy

---

* This undated document may not belong in this volume, since it appears to relate to a suit won by Gibbon at the mayor's court on Nov. 12, 1680, confirmed at the assizes on an appeal, Oct. 5, 1681. The relevant minutes of the mayor's court are lacking, but see *Records of the Court of Assizes*, p. 279, where de la Noy as deputy collector (of customs) has seized Gibbon's cargo bound for Virginia.

‡ tribute

[24:55a (1a)]

[JUDGMENT AND COURT FEES IN RICHARD LOCKWOOD'S SUIT
AGAINST JOHN CAVALIER FOR PASSAGE MONEY]

Richard Lockwood Plt.   New York the
John Cavelier Deft.   19th Jan.1674/5.

The Plt. declared the deft. is indebted unto him for his wifes passage
from Virginia to Boston with her Childe forty shillings the[   ]e
give [   ] for the sa[   ] both par[ ]s being heard,
the Worshippfull Court Past Judgment that the Deft. pay the Plt. the said
forty shillings and Cost.

                                            By order of the Court

                                            John Sharpe
                                            Towne: Clearke.

Clearkes fees.

for a Summons.   £0.2.6
for 2 testimonys   £0.2.0
for Judgment   £0.3.0
for a Coppy   £0.1.0
                           £0.8.6

To the Marshall.   £00.01.04
To the Sheriff   £00.01.00
for the Judgment.   £00–10.10

[ENDORSED:]   Mr. Lockwoods
                   bill and order
                   about John Caveliers
                   wives passage.

                   Rich[ ] Lockwood Plt.
                   John Cavalier Deft.
                   At the Mayors Court
                   Jan. 1674/5.

[24:55a (1b)]

Capt. Lockwoods account Debtor to Antony Johnson

| For meat, drinke washing and Lodgeing | Gldrs | St. |
| Sixty nyne Guilders and ten styvers | 69 : | 10 |

[24:55a (2)]

For Eight dayes lodging and diate For James of West chester and his wiffe at 2g per day 32 gilders

January 15th 1674.

Anthony Johnson.

[24:55a (3)]

Capt Nicolls Mayor as Debtor by order of the Constable have Lodged and Diated one man and his wife from Westchester

24 mar.	8 daies at 1 guilder per day	ƒ32
	To the Post from Delleware bay	14
	To New Yorke	ƒ46

This 8th of Aprill 1675

Anthony Johnson

[24:55b]

[DEPOSITION OF JOHN PRICE IN THE ABOVE SUIT]

[ ] ye 18th   The Deposition of John Pri[ ] Aged about 24 years or
1674.   their abouts.

The Deponant doath testifie and say that about 21 months agone or their abouts, that I being then a seaman one Board the Keitch Johns Returne of Boston in new England Richard Lockwood Master and alsoe Declaires that the said Lockwood did Carry in the aforesaid Keitch the wife of John Caverleire and her Child from Virginia neare Boston: and the said

Caverleires wife did Engage to pay unto the above said Master the Just summ of forty shillings in moneys for her and her childs passedge, which was the sayd masters one proper debt for any thinge I know:

[24:56]

[ORDER FOR A CANVASS OF VACANT BUILDING LOTS]

At a Councell held in Fort James, the 22th day
of January 1674.

Upon a Proposall made concerning vacant Ground, in this City, fitt to build upon, It is Ordered that the Mayor and Aldermen bee desired to cause an account to bee taken, of all the vacant Places in this city, fitt for Building; and what shall bee found to belong to particular Persons, that notice be given to them, and the same Apprized, that if the Proprietors shall not forthwith build themselves there upon, that then any other who shall desire it, may have Leave so to do, Paying the value at which the said Land shall bee apprized: The Apprizers to bee appointed by the Mayor and Aldermen, who are also desired to take into consideracion, the Manner of Building most proper for the towne, and advantageous for the Publicke good thereof.

By Order of the Governor
in Councell.

Matthias Nicolls.
Secr.

[ENDORSED:]   Order of Councell
to view the
Waste Ground
about the City etc.

Jan. 22. 1674.

[24:1a]

[COUNCIL MINUTES ABOUT A VISIT BY TWO SACHEMS]*

Feb: 10. 1674.

[   ]his day [   ]stacann[   ] Sachem of [   ]
[   ] Amman[   ] Sachem of [   ]
[   ] to give[   ]
[   ]wo stri[   ]
[   ] about [   ]
piece:
[   ]our presen[   ] them wi[   ] two Coates [   ]
some pouder and lead and bre[ ]d and drinke [   ]ant
say they will come once a yeare to [   ]heir friendship.

[24:57]

[BILL FOR A SIGN. TRANSLATION]

Municipal Account

By order of his honor Captain Mattias Nicols, mayor: repaired
or mended the King's arms before the city hall   f80
For the frame put around it   15
                                   Guilders in sewant   95

New York   Jan Cavelier
January 30, 1674/5

[24:58]

[PETITION OF THE BROTHERS OF BALTHAZAR DE HAART AGAINST
THE TRUSTEES OF HIS ESTATE]

            To the Honorable Edmund An[   ]
            Maior Leiftennant and Gov[   ]
            Roy[   ] Heighnesses Territor[   ]

                        The Hu[   ] of Daniell

* The document is not mentioned in E. B. O'Callaghan's calendar of the documents. When
the records were rebound in 1911, this one was placed first, although chronologically it
belongs here.

                    Mathia[   ] Brothers
                    [   ]lhasar De H[   ]

Sheweth
That your [   ]s P[ ]titione[   ]
Balthasar, who is his l[   ]fe[   ]
arived here Jacobus, and Ma[   ] you[ ]ger Brothers,
who[   ] personall of the said Deceased, w[   ]pers writtings and
Bookes, se[   ] and Jewells, etc: possessed and mos[   ]
legally disposed of, by Jacob C[   ] and Jaques Cosseau, or
some them, without giving in Security [   ] appraisment made
according to Law, and the remainder part of the said [   ] to
their totall impoverishment they giving the Younger Brothers what
[   ] the heire appearent arived not here, untill the month of
June last pas[   ] all, yet such their Confidence to sett the said
heires att Defiance, not-wi[   ] and disposed of the said
Estate, as aforesaid, thereby enriching the [   ]
Petitioners, all which evill practices, being Contrary to Law an Equite,
[   ] our Honnors Petitioners Bill in Equite, for
discovery (as w[   ] or to prevent further em-
bezellments and that the D[   ] and
more lost for want of Speedy Securing, they be [   ]

                Therefor humbly prayes that [   ] petitioners
                Sufferings will bee pl[   ] Consideration, and that
                all f[   ] said Estate, may bee stayed
                [   ]ered your Petitioners Bill
                [   ] all papers, writtings
                [. . . *last line and signature lost* . . .]

[ENDORSED:]   Daniel Mattys [   ]
                   Jacobus D'Haarts
                   Peticion, against the Trus[   ]
                   of their brother Balth[   ]
                   D'Haarts Estate.
                   [   ] Febr. 15th.

[24:59]

To the Right Honnorable Major Edmond Andrew Governor Gennerall of all his Royall Highnes his Territories in America etc.

The Petitioners f[   ]ll the
Inhabitance of M[   ]eeto Cove
and Mettinicoke on Long Island.

In all humble manner
Sheweth

That your honnors petitioners with much difficulty and greatte Labour has reduced part of a Wildernes into C[ ]rne feildes besides the greatte expence and toyle the inhabitance of Muskeeto Cove hath benn at in makeinge up a Dame and building of a Saw Mill which exhausted the most of there substance = they beinge now in the Infancey of there improvements it n[ ] much exceeding six yeare si[ ] they attempted that designe — but soe it is May please your honnor that your petitioners are informed that some persons would reepe the benifite of theire honest industry by indeavoring to obtaine a grant to purchase of the Indians land adjeacent: soe may thereby not only Monopolize the tymber to the great hurt and detriment of the publique = but alsoe soe straiten = the rainge that of nesesity the whole Inhabitance must unevitably be ruined, for that Muskeeto Cove Much relyes upon getting of hay in the place amed Att = more then what they goe 20 milds for.

Therefore most humbly pray that your honnor out of a deep sence of your petitioners suffering and will be pleased to take the premisses into your honnors Grave consideracion = and hope upon good resons shewne that your petitioners may be prefferd to have Lycence to purchase before any other the meane tyme they besech that which may incurrage the two settlements and they there wifes and Children shall as in Duty bound

Ever pray for your honnor

[ENDORSED:]   27th decer. 74
                   no Permision for purchase

without notice first
given to the Petitioners.

Muskitoe Cove
Peticion about purchasing
land neare them.

Dec. 27. 1674.

None shall be graunte[ ]
till they have notice.

[24:60]

[LETTER FROM INHABITANTS OF BROOKLYN REQUESTING A PATENT. TRANSLATION]*

Sir.

According to the purchase that we made previously from former governor Lovelance of the lands and water meadows situated between Breuckel and the Wallebockt we would lay stress on security for us and before entering into possession of the said lands and water meadows to have a patent signed by the governor E. Andros. So we ask you to secure for us the said patent as soon as possible, we the undersigned, each for his own part to give you, as soon as we shall have said patent, the satisfaction that remains for you. We hope for this favor from your kindness and we shall be deservedly grateful for it.

We judge that Lambertt and Dierck Stoorm should not have any share in the said lands and water meadows, since they have previously refused to pay what you had ordered to the widow of Johanes Nefius. We shall do however, in that matter what you will judge advisable.

We are in a hurry for the said patent since it is now time to have it trenched or enclosed in order to avoid the loss that these lands cause all the livestock in the spring. Thus, we once more beg you to let us have this patent as soon as possible and this favor will be duly appreciated by

At the ferry on Long Island
February 22, 1674/5.

* Translated from the French by Kenneth Scott.

Your devoted servant Dierck Janssen

this is   the mark of
Raeffe   Warnaer
                  Jeronimus Rapa[lie]
                  Michel Hainelle

[ADDRESSED:]   Sir
                   Mister Matth: Nicols
                   At Nieu Yorck*

[ENDORSED:]   Mons: haynelle
                   Feb. 2[ ] 1674
                   Breucklyn

[24:61]

[PETITION OF DOMINE JOHANNES THEODORUS POLHEMUS FOR PAYMENT OF SALARY. TRANSLATION]

[   ], Esteemed, Wise [   ] very [   ] Lord, My Lord Governor [   ]

After respectful greetings and cordial [   ] wishes of all blessed [   ] in his administration, I hereby extend my humble services as predicant to [   ] and his churches in these lands lying under the crown of Great Britain, requesting and praying that the same may be favorably and [   ] accepted, pledging myself to all due obedience and loyalty according to my vocation, which [   ] in the villages of Midwout and Amersfort on Long Island [. . .3 lines missing. . .] in addition to concern for the congregation in Breuckelen, which was taken under my care by the blessing of God; therefore, I hope to be able to enjoy a good testimony therefrom.

And because I am still owed f150 from the year 1672, which was promised me, I hereby request, in order to [   ] such, that your honor be pleased to inform them by displaying this and to help me [   ], I commend your honor [   ] to God's holy grace [   ]

25 Febr.   Your honor's humble servant,
1674

                   Joh: Theodo[ ] Polhemus

* This line is in Dutch.

[24:62a]

[DECLARATION OF JOHN SHAKERLY AGAINST SAMUEL WINSLOW]

[   ]
Samuel Winsilow Deft.

The plt. declares that at his laste being at Boston hee was unjustly molested arrested and imprisoned by the Deft. for the Summe of 178£ Sterling, through which unjust Molestation the plt. was forced (being a Stranger there) to Reunloade the Vessell by him loaden — which not onely doth redound to the plts. great loss and damage but also breake his credit, by which hee as a young Merchant must live all which hee esteemes more then 500£ besides the damage Susteined by the Sale of his goods here, hee Staying soe long untill the place was overstored with all sorts of goods: as also the hire of the vessell the wages and victualls which likewise doth amount to One hundred pound Sterling: Wherefore the plt. craves Judgement against the Defendant for the paying the abovementioned Summes amounting together to 600£ sterling and to restore unto him an Obligation of 48£ which the Deft. unjustly constreined the plt. to give to him together with costs.

This is a true Coppie as Attests
Isa: Addington Cler.

[ENDORSED:]   Shakerlys complaint
              against Winslow

[24:62b]

[BOND OF JOHN SHAKERLY AND PIETER JACOBSZ MARIUS
TO SAMUEL WINSLOW]

Know all men by these presents that wee John Shakerley of New Orania late New yorke in America Merchant and Peter Jacobsen Marius of the same place Marriner doe stand firmely bound and obliged unto Samuel Winslow of Boston in New England Merchant in the full and whole Summe of Forty eight pounds three shillings and three pence Sterling, to bee well and truly paid unto the saide Samuel Winslow his heires or assignes, the one Moity thereof in good Merchantable bisket bread at Eleven Shillings and six Pence per hundred, the other moity in good Merchantable Flower in Caske at ten Shillings and six pence per hundred, both the bread and Flower to bee approved and liked off by two of the inhabitants of New Orania or yorke who have skill in such commodities being chosen buy the saide Winslow or his order, the saide bread and

Flower to bee paide and delivered to the saide Winslow his heires or
a-signes upon the Weigh house in New Orania or yorke aforesaide on or
before the Fourteenth day of August nexte being the date hereof, the said
Shakerly and Jacobson Marius or theire o[ ]der or some one of them
giving the saide Winslow or his assignes Notice twenty four houres
before the saide time to make provition for the recipt thereof: hee the
saide Winslow allowing them twelve pence for every barrell hee shall
receive his Flower: which payment is the full ballance of all Accounts
between the said Shakerly and Winslow: To the true paiment of which
saide Summe of Forty eight pounds three Shillings and three pence in
the saide Species for time place and condition as aforesaide Wee saide
John Shakerly and Peter Jacobson Marius doe binde ourselves our heires
Executors and administrators jointly and severally for the whole and in
the whole unto the saide Samuel Winslow his heires and assignes firmely
by these presents. In Witness whereof wee have hereunto Set our hands
this eight day of July Anno Domini One thousand six hundred Seventy
and four. 1674.

Signed and Delivered   John Shakerly
in the presence of us   Peter Jacobson Marius
Edward Dyer
Claes Bording
Isa. Addington.   Verte.

Edward Dyer deposed on his Oath that hee was present at the day of the
date of this bill and was a Witness to the sigening and delivery of the
same by the Subscribors there named.

19.8.74   Before Wm. Davis Comissioner

Isa. Addington made Oath in Court 27.8br. 1674 that hee set his hand as
a Witness to this Instrument and saw the Subscribors Signe and deliver
it as theire act and Deed on the day of the date thereof as Attests

Is. Addington Cler.

This is a true Coppie
of the Originall on file
as Attests
Isa. Addington Cler.

[ENDORSED:]   Shakerleys bill

[24:63]

[BOND OF JOHN SHAKERLY TO PIETER JACOBSZ MARIUS]

Boston

Know all men By these Presents that I John Shakely: of Newe Aroyna doe make over Unto Petter Japosson of the aformenshed Place for to Secger him of A oblidge. which hee Is Jontley bound with mee for the Summe of Forty Eight Pounds three Shilling and three Pence Paiveth Unto Samuell Winsloo of Boston: that is to say to bee Paid In Newe arayna, In Bred att Elleven Shillings, and Six Pence per Hundred and flower att tenn Shillings and six Pence per Hundred, and for his Segeretey Bee itt Knowne to all them that itt may Consarne that the Said Shakerly Doe make over one Negro Woman and one Scowe one Greet Boote and one open Boote: and the movers and unmoveable of the Said Shakerleys Astatte, and when Satafacshon Is made for the Princeseceserys aforsaid this Oblidgs. to bee Void and of Noe Afect.

Is Wittness   My Hand   John Shakerly
July the 8th 1674.
witnesse
Edward Dyers
Claes bordingh

[ENDORSED:]   John Shakerlys bill

[24:64]

[WRIT ISSUED AGAINST JOHN SHAKERLY AND PIETER
JACOBSZ MARIUS]

To the Marshall of the County of Suffolk or his Deputy

You are hereby required in his Majesties Name to Attach the goods and for want thereof the body of John Shackerly or Peter Jacobson Marius and take bond of them or either of them to the value of One hundred pounds in money with sufficient Surety or Sureties for either of theire apperance at the next County Court to bee held at Boston in the last tuesday in October next then and there to answer the complaint of Richard Middlecot or John Williams attournies to Samuel Winslow in an action of the case for witholding a debt of Forty eight pounds three Shillings and three pence Starling; which was to bee paide the one halfe in bread at Eleven Shillings and six pence per hundred and the other halfe in Flower at ten shillings sixpence per hundred, all which was to have been delivered the saide Winslow at the Weigh house in New Orania or yorke upon the fourteenth day of August last past as will appeare by a bill under theire hands, dated the eigth day of July 1674; wherein the said John Shackerly and Peter Jacobson Marius are bound jointly and severally for the payment of the abovesaid summes in the Species abovementioned to the saide Winslow, and due interest and all o[   ] due damages and soe make a true return hereof under your hand. Dated the 19th of August 1674.

By the Court Jonath. Negrus.

The Return of

I have attached the body of Peter Jacobson this 29th of August and have take bond of him to the value of One hundred pounds in mony.

per mee Rich: Wayte Marshall

Wee Peter Jacobson and Rober Orchard doe binde our selves heires and Executors unto Richard Wayte Marshall in the Summe of One hundred pounds upon condition the saide Peter Jacobson shall appeare at the next County Court to bee held at Boston on the last tuesday in October next then and there to answer Richard Middlecot or John Williams Attournies to Samuel Winslow according to the tenor of this Attachment and that hee shall abide the Order of the Court and not depart without Licence as Witness our hands this 29th of August 1674.

Peter Jacobson Marius

Robert Orchard.

This is a true Coppie of the Originall on file

As Attests
Isa. Addington cler.

[ENDORSED:]   Attachment

[24:65]

[BOND OF SAMUEL WINSLOW]

Copi[ ]

Know all men by these Presendts thatt I Samuell Winsslow of boston Marchardt doe acknowledge my Selfe to ouwe and stand Indebted Unto te Right Honorable anthony Colve Esquire Govern. of N: Orangien — Sume of Six hundred pounds Current Mony to be paid to the said Govern. or his sucsesse to the Which payment Well and truly to be Made I binde Me My heires Executor and administraeter firmly by these Presents Sealed with My seale Dated this first day of September 1674.

The Condition of this obligaetion is such that Whereas the above bounded Saemuell Winsslow was arrested in New Orangien at the suite of John Schakerly merckt butt Nott beingh prepared to answer the said suiete for Want of some papers Which the left in Baston Which the Court thought for to give him liberty to goe or send for It there foore the said Samuell Winsslouw Schall att the first Court, hold in New Orangien after his Next arrievall there, Maecke his appeareance to answer the said suite he maekingh Convenient haste to performe the saeme then this obligaetion to be Void otherwise to Remaine in force.

(Signed:)
Samuel Winslow
S L

Signed sealed Delivered
in Presence of us
Richard Cornwel
Thom: Hickes

[24:66 (1)]

[ORDER OF THE COURT AT NEW ORANGE (NEW YORK CITY) IN THE CASE OF JOHN SHAKERLY VS. SAMUEL WINSLOW]

At a meeting of the Bayle Freemen and Townesmen holden in the Townehouse of the City of Orange the 4th September anno 1674.

John Shackerly the arrester and plaintiffe
Against
Samuel Winsloo arrested and Defendant

The defendant answers by Writeing to the plaintife for his petition delivered in and beseecheth you to Weight soe long till hee can procure his Evidence from Boston. It is Ordered that each party give in bond according to the Judgment given and that the defendant shall forthwith send for his Evidence from Boston.

By the order of the court abovenamed

Ephraim Herman Secre.

This is a true Coppie of that on file as Attests.

Isa Addington Cler.

[ENDORSED:]   Shakerly against Winslow
                     and order for Winslow.

[24:66 (2)]

[ORDER FOR HOLDING COURTS OF SESSIONS IN THE NORTH
AND WEST RIDINGS]

                Edmund Andros Esquire Governor Generall:
Copie   under his Royall Highness James Duke of Yorke and
                Albany of all his Territorys in America.

Whereas [   ]th the advice of my councell [   ] Court of sessions to bee held in the severall Ridings upon Long Island as formerly hath been Practised, According to the directions in the Booke of Laws confirmed by his Royall Highness, and the usuall time of holding the said Courts mor[ ] Particulerly in the North and West Ridings Drawing nigh, that is to say in the Approaching Month of Decemb: these are to advertize and give notice to al Persons, concerned, whose duty it is to give their Attendances at the respective Courts, or who may have suitt or plaints to make, That on the second Wednesday of Decemb: next which will bee on the 9th day of the said month, the Court of Sessions for the North Riding to bee held att the Town of Jamaica shall beginne; and the Wednesday following the Court of Sessions for the West Riding to bee held att [ ] T[ ]w[ ]e of Gravesend, which will bee the [   ] the said Month; the said Courts to[   ] as formerly, and Clarkes of the said [   ] Courts of Sessions to bee held as aforesaid are hereby required forthwith after Receipt hereof to give notice to the severall Townes of each Jurisdiction, that they may Conforme themselves hereunto accordingly. Given under my hand att new Yorke this 27th day

of Novemb. in the twenty Sixt yeare of his Majestys Raigne Annoque
Domini 1674.

Signed

E. Andros:s

To Mr. Anthony Waters
Clarke of the Sessions for the
North Riding [ ] Yorke-
shire upon Long [   ]

[ENDORSED:]   An Order about the Sessions
to bee held in Dec. 1674.
to Mr. Anth: Waters.

Queens County*

[24:67a]

[JUDGMENT IN THE CASE OF SHAKERLY VS. WINSLOW]

At a County Court held at Boston October 27th 1674

Richard Middlecot or John Williams Attourneys to Samuel Winslow
plaintiffs against John Shakerly and Peter Jacobson Marius or either of
them Defendants in an action of the case for witholding a debt of forty
eight pounds three Shillings three pence Starling; which was to bee paide
the one halfe in bread at Eleven Shillings and six pence per hundred and
the other halfe in Flower at ten Shillings six pence per hundred; all which
was to have been delivered the saide Winslow at the Weigh house in New
Orania or yorke upon the fourteenth day of August last past as well
appeare by bill under theire hands dated the eigth day of July 1674
wherein the saide John Shakerly and Peter Jacobson Marius are bound
jointly and severally for the payment of the abovesaide Summes in the
species abovementioned to the saide Winslow and due interest and all
other due d[ ]mages according to Attachment Dated August 29th 1674:
the Attachmen[ ] and Eviden[ ]s in the case produced being read
committed to the Jury and remaine on file with the Records of this Court
the Jury brought in theire Verdict, they founde for the plaintiffe Viz: the
bill forty eight pounds three Shillings three pence and damage for
nonpayment at time and place twenty five pound one Shilling and costs

* Added after the counties were formed in 1683.

of Court, allowed by the Court Nineteen Shillings; Robert Orchard as surety for the Defendant appealed from this Judgment unto the next Court of Assistants and the said Robert Orchard as principall in Seventy four pounds and Arthur Mason and Tho: Bingley as Sureties in thirty Seven pounds apeice acknowledged themselves respectively bound to the Treasuror of the County of Suffolke and party concerned on condition that the said Defendant shall prosecute his appeale from the Judgement of this Court at the next court of Assistants to Effect.

This is a true Coppie of the County Courts Judgment and bond for appeale.

as Attests.
Isa Addington Cler.

[ENDORSED:]   County Court Judgement

[24:67b]

[PROSPECTUS FOR A JOINT STOCK COMPANY IN THE COD-FISHING INDUSTRY]

1675. Jan. 8[*]

The Governor desiring and resolving by all Fitting meanes in his Power, to Promote and Encourage Codfish Fishery in this Government, And finding Upon enquiry, and the best Informacions and Advice, that the Most probable menes to effect it, is by a Company and Joynt Stock, doth by the advice of his Councell, allow and Authorize the Sale, in the manner after Exprest, to witt.

That all Persons within the Government, that will Subscribe to it before, and be ready to pay what they Shall so Suscribe, eight dayes after the 9th of February next, shall bee admitted.

That Every fifteen Bevers, or the Vallue, be a Share and have a Vote in the said company.

That Upon the 9th of February, every member of the said Company, or his Sufficient Deputy, shall meet together at New Yorcke to consult, and by the Plurality of votes make all orders, Rules and officers and so from time to time, and take all Accounts for the mannageing, improving and

---

* Added in another hand.

ordering all things relating to the said Company, and Joynt Stock as above, for the said Fishery, and them appoint or give Direccions for another generall meeting or Mcctings as shall bee thought necessary.

That all who are willing to bee concerned may bring or send the Subscription to the Secretaryes office In Fort James at New Yorcke, where they Shall be received and Kept till the above 9th of February, and then delivered to Such as the Company Shall appoint.

That this Company bee not Understood any wayes to debarre or hinder any other Person or Persons, from Fishing by themselves or in Companys, as they shall like best.

By order of the Governor.
Matthias: Nicolls. Secr.

[ENDORSED:]   Subscriptions about
the Cod Fishery.
23.

[24:68a]

[RELEASE OF CLAIMS AGAINST PIETER JACOBSZ MARIUS AND JOHN
SHAKERLY BY RICHARD MIDDLECOTT]

Know all men by these presents that I Richard Midlecot as Attorney unto Mr. Samuell Winslow of boston mariner doe Aquit Release and fully Discharge Peter Jacobson Marius and Jno Shakerly boath of New Yorke marinors there and either of their heirs Executors and Administraters and their and Either of their security of and from any demands sute or Action debt or dues Judgment or Execution that shall or May hereafter Arise from An Action now pending between the said parteys at the next Court of Asistance in Boston Upon appeale and of and from any other matter and thing in any maner Relating there Unto any wise what soe Ever the said Winslow or his Attorney haveing Received full satisfaction for the same to Content for the said Winslows Use; in testimony whereof in behalfe of said Winslow and as Atorney aforesaid I have here Unto put my hand and seale this three and twenteth day of february one Thousand six hundred seventy and fower.

Signed sealed and delivered   Richard Middlecott [*seal*]
in presence of Us

Arthur Mason
Humph: Hodges
Richard Way

[24:68b]

[SETTLEMENT OF PAYMENTS DUE TO SAMUEL WINSLOW]

Where as there is A suet depending upon [   ]
Winslow and Peter Jacobson Marius and J[   ]
or one of them; the which Case is Determined [   ]
order and consent of the said partys Attorneys; the award bee[   ]
[   ] the said Peter Jacobson Marius or his Attorney shall pay
or Cause [   ] payd Unto the said Winslows Attorney; Mr. Richard
Middlecot the some of fifty six pounds twelve shillings in mony by the
25th of this instant February as finall Isue of the Case of matter: aforesaid
which said some of mony is paid Unto the said midlecot to his content;
and whereas it is posible the said debt or matter may bee payd or
Compounded, for at new yorke or Elsewhere Which is soe the said
Richard Midlecot doe ingage himselfe his heir Executor and administrators that the said Composision shall bee Voyd and what payment
that is made Into the said winslow Excepted; or to his Asignes; they
paying frayght thereof if transported and Charges of shiping and Landing
said goods: in witnes here of the said Richard Midlecot have put to his
hand this 24th of febuary 1674

Witnes   Richard Middlecott
Arthur Mason
Humph: Hodges
Richard Way

[24:69]

[RECEIPT OF ROBERT ORCHARD FOR MONEY
TO PAY TO SAMUEL WINSLOW]

I Robert orchard as Attorney to Peter Jacobson marius of new york have
Receved of Arthur Mason the some of fifty six pounds [   ] I say fifty
six pounds and Twelve shillings, in mony which said some is paid unto
Mr. Rich: Midlecot Attorney to Mr. Samuell Winslow for a debt or Action
depending at the Court of asistance next in boston betwene said Winslow
and said Jacobson and Jno: Shakerley but said debt is properly sayd

Shakerley: and said Jacobson but security for said Case or debt as witnes
my hand this 24th of febuary 1674.

Witness   Robert Orchard
Richard Middlecott
Humph: Hodges

[24:70]

[ACCOUNT OF ROBERT ORCHARD AS ATTORNEY TO
PIETER JACOBSZ MARIUS]

march 5th 74/5

An account of the Charges about John Shakerlys Caes as being inployd
By Peeter Jakobesan marys

For making the Bond of apeaell   00:01:00
for taking out the Caes   00:06:10
for Entrying the accion   00:10:00
Exspenc at arbitracion in mony   00:08:00
for the Resuns of apeaell)
and other wrightings   )   01:05:00
                                                      02:10:10

For preparing for the County Court and at the County Court
and preparing for the Court of Asistanc and at it which was
about a fortnits time and other exspences 5 pounds If Peeter
Jakobs be sekeured other wies what he pleases

[ENDORSED:]

Resived of Mr. Arther Mason   56 12
the Sume of 2 pounds 10 shillinges   2 10
one the Account of Peter Jacobes   59. 2
I say Resived this 7 day of March 1675/4   25. 6
                                                      54. 8

Robert Orchard.   56–12
                                                       2–10
                                                          2

[24:71]

[MINUTES OF A MEETING OF THE GOVERNOR WITH TACKPOUSHA
AND OTHER SACHEMS]

March 9th 1

[   ] came to the Fort [   ]
[   ]ong Island to give a visitt to [   ]
[   ]atha Sachem of Massapeag[   ]
[   ]ka Sachem of Sequata Ma[   ]
[   ] Sachem of Mencock of R[   ]
[   ]ll othe[   ]
[   ] saith [   ]
[   ]Ship s[   ]
[   ] has [   ]
[   ] former [   ]
[   ] Governor promises the continuance[   ]
[   ] and saith as long as they are quiet [ ]
[   ]otect them from their enemyes [   ]
[   ]asha presents the Governor [   ]
[   ] about 40 or 50 Guilders.

[   ] governor proposes a renewing [   ]
[   ] Lovelace about br[   ]
[   ] them by the [   ]
[   ] was proposed by Go: Love[   ]
[   ]overnor offerrs to give them some [   ]
[   ] space of one yeare [   ]
[   ]an doe, but in the meane[ ]me will [   ]
[   ]ll protection and desires of them no[   ]
[   ]y can well accomplish.

[   ]ld have them to sett some dayes ab[   ]
[   ] to ty[   ]
[   ] wher[   ]
[   ]red to [   ]
[   ] appointed to, vizt. [   ] rece[   ]
[   ]romise to goe out 6 dayes in the [   ]
[   ].

[   ] promises they shall bee [   ] all[ ]
[   ] they kill, and if the Cons[   ]
[   ]rates refuse or neglect to [   ]
[   ]de they shall have right[. . .]

[ENDORSED:]   [. . .] will inquire
                   [   ] and hearing

[24:72a]

[WARRANT FOR ATTACHMENT AND APPRAISAL OF FRANCIS
LOVELACE'S ESTATE, WITH THE AUDIT]

By the Governor.

Whereas upon an Action of Debt for the summe of seven thousand
pounds sterl., due from Colonell Francis Lovela[   ] unto his Royall
Highnesse, there issue[ ] f[   ]h an Attachment from the Court of [   ]
Mayor and Aldermen of this City, bear[   ] date the 13th day of November last, upon all the Estate of the said Colonell Lovelace within the
precincts of the said City; And none yet appearing on the said Col.
Lovelaces behalfe; These are therefore to authorize and require you on
his Royall Highnesse behalfe forthwith to prosecute the Attachment
aforesaid to Execucion, and that the said Estate bee legally apprized and
an Inventory of every particular and value therof returned to the Court,
there to bee recorded as so much in satisfaction upon Account: And for
soe doeing this shall bee your Warrant: Given under my hand in New
Yorke this 13th day of March, 1674.

                                                   E Andros. s.

[   ] Mr. Thomas Gibbs
[   ]eriffe of the City of
[   ]ew Yorke.

Wee whose names are he[   ] being appoynted by the
[   ] and Aldermen of this City to [   ] Surveigh and Appraise the hou[   ] and accommodation belonging
[   ] Francis Lovlace upon this Island [   ] discharge of that
trust [   ]ding [   ] best of our Knowledge or else find[   ] is a
fo[   ]

Imprimis. The house Garden with the accomodations ⎫
Lyeing in the Broad street at   ⎬   £175.00 [   ]
                                                   ⎭

The hous and accomodations nex[   ]
the Citty hall — Vallued at   [   ]

The Domines Land—at—   £1[   ]
The Land formerly Rutt Jac[   ]   [   ]800[ ]

Wittness our hands
In N. Yorke the 27o   Sam[   ]
March 1675.   Adolf [   ]
                             Allard [   ]

[24:72b]

The persons nominated and Appoynted to make an appraisment of
Colonell Lovlaces estate are, Mr. Samuell Edsall, Mr. Allard Antony, Mr.
Thomas Lewis and Mr. Adolph Peiterson, who have taken their Oathes
Accordingly, this 27o March 1675.

By order of the Mayors court

John Sharpe
Towne Clearke.

[ENDORSED:]   March. 13, 167[ ]
                   and Mar. 27. 167[ ]
                   Warrant of Apprizement

                   Warrant of Apraysment of Gouvernour
                   Lovelaces Estate to his Royall Highnesse

[24:73]

[PETITION OF EIGHT DUTCH RESIDENTS OF NEW YORK CONCERNING
THE OATH OF ALLEGIANCE. TRANSLATION]

To the honorable and highly esteemed Lords
Mayor and Aldermen of the City of New York:

We, the undersigned petitioners, make known with [   ] reverence how
we, petitioners, to our great sorrow and sadness, have been unwarren-
tedly mistrusted today by our most honorable and highly esteemed lord
governor, as if the petitioners were leaders in agitating and inciting the
community to disobey his order to take the prescribed oath of allegiance.

In order to remove such suspicion from us, his honor's servants, as much
as possible, we make so bold as to ask his honor's forgiveness for this
[   ] by this petition; and at the same time humbly request that his
highly esteemed honor continue our previous privileges of not being
pressed to arms, especially not against our own native land. Therefore it
is our humble request that your honors (who sufficiently know, without
a doubt, that some of us have comported ourselves here as loyal servants
of the lawful authorities of this province for twenty years, others for thirty
years), as superiors and protectors over us, your honors' petitioners,
intercede with the highly esteemed lord governor on our behalf so that
your honors' petitioners may be [discharged] of the aforesaid suspicion
by his honorable [   ] requested freedom [
] be permitted them. By so doing we remain

New York, the 16th   Your highly esteemed honors'
of March 1674/5   humble petitioners
                            and servants,

              N. Bayard   Corn. Steenwyck
              Johannes van Brugh   Agidius Luyk
              Johannes de Peyster   Wilh . Beeckman
                                     Anthony de Milt

                            Jacob Kip

[24:74]

[OBLIGATION OF SOPHIA VAN LODENSTEYN TO PAY DEBTS OF HER
SON JACOBUS DE BEAUVOIS. TRANSLATION]

Today, the twenty sixth of March in the year sixteen hundred and seventy
five, English style, appeared before me, Michil Hainelle, appointed clerk
of the five Dutch villages in the west riding of Yorkshire on Long Island
by the most honorable lord E. Andros esq., lord of Santmeres, governor
general under his royal highness, James, duke of York and Albany and
in all his territories in America, Soffia van Loodesteyn, widow of Carel
de Beauvois, resident of Breuckel in the west riding of Yorkshire on Long
Island, who has promised, as she hereby promises in the presence of the
undersigned witnesses, that if in the absence of her son Jacobus de
Beauvois who, with God's help, is of the intention to depart for Holland
with the ship *de Beurs*, whose skipper is Jacob Stenwyck, any debts in
this country are revealed or come to light after his departure, to assume
the same as her own debts and to pay them honorably; placing herself

hereby completely in his stead in order to settle any outstanding claims against him in this country and to give satisfaction to everyone in his stead as if he himself were present. In order to insure this is carried out I pledge [   ] goods, done in good faith without guile or deceit in the presence of the undersigned witnesses at Breuckel, day and date as above.

Witnesses: Sophia va[   ]
                                                  Lodensteyn

This is the mark   of
Johannes   Marcuse
made with his own hand.   Acknowledged by me

George Hainelle   Michil Hainelle, clerk.

[ENDORSED:]*   [   ]rtificate of wi[   ]
                  some of Breucklyn for
                  a young man; whereby
                  hee had the Go: perm[   ]
                  to goe in the Flye boate
                  March 26. 1671.

[24:75]

[UNSIGNED LETTER FROM INHABITANTS OF MARTHA'S VINEYARD
ABOUT THOMAS MAYHEW'S PATENT]

Worthy sir we Intreat you to Except and piruse our Rude and Uncomly Loins‡ yet trew: for our Oppertunity will not Admite of [   ] [ ]ew draught as our Intent was our desires is allso that you w[   ] be pleased to bestow a few loins upon us in way of Counsall and advise and if you disire it we will kieep your Advise a[   ] seacret; Sir if you see it your way to Answer our Request you may be plesed to direct your Letters with James Readfield now Resadent in New haven who we doubt not but will be [ ] Careful of them and faithfull to us in sendeng them.

[ADDRESSED:]   The[   ]
                  To the Worshipfull
                  Captain Mathias N[   ]
                  now Resadent in Strat[   ]rd
                  in N[ ]w Engla[   ]

* The endorsement is written in English.
‡ lines

[ENDORSED:]   A letter from so[ ]
                         Inhabitants of Mar[   ]
                         Vinyard about Mr. Mah[ ]
                         and his Patent.
                         May 5, 1674.

[24:76]

[ROUGH MINUTES OF THE MAYOR'S COURT, WRITTEN BY
MATTHIAS NICOLLS]*

To advise upon the buisnesse of the Prisoners in the Fort.

To recommend the boatemens Imprisonment.

To give our Judgment about the seamens [   ]‡

The warrant about Mr. Bayard and Mr. Luycks papers.
to appoint about it.

           The Court having taken into their serious Consideracions
           the Case of the Prisoners now in the Fort, recommended
           unto them by his honor the Governor

It is humbly presented as their opinion that the said Prisoners having all
subscribed to and owned the petitioners shall give in to the Secretarys
office security to the value of 200£ a piece to answer what shall be
alleadged against them, at the generall Court of Assizes, or at a speciall
Court of Assizes to bee held sooner (if the [ ]vernor shall see cause).

Fryday night or Even.   Quare whether of the good
Mar. 19th 1674.   behavior.

                              left to the Governor

[ENDORSED:]   At a Mayors Court.

---

* A list of the imprisoned petitioners was struck out. It reads: Mr. Cornelis Steenwick, Mr.
Johannes Va[ ] Brugh, Mr. Johannes d[ ] Peyster, Mr. Egidius Luyck, Mr. Nicholas Bayard,
Mr. Willi[ ] Beekman, Mr. Jacob Kip, Mr. Guyluyn Verplanke, Mr. Antonis De Mill, Mr.
Oloffe Stevens[ ].
‡ Perhaps "shares."

[24:77]

[BOND OF JOHANNES VAN BRUGH TO APPEAR AT
THE NEXT ASSIZES]

Know all men by These Presents that wee Johannes Van
Brough of this City Merchant, and Cornelis Van Borsum
doe Stand and are firmely bound unto our Soveraigne Lord
the King in the Summe of two hundred pound of Good and
Lawfull Money of England, to be paid Unto his Royall
Highnesse present Lieutentant Governour in these his Territoryes or his Successors, his or their order, or Assigns to
the which payment well and truely to bee made, Wee do
bind us and either of Us, Joyntly and Severally for and in
the whole our and Every, and either of our Heires, Executors
and Administrators and every of them firmly by these
Presents; Sealed with our Seals, Dated the 22th day of
March, in the 27th yeare of his Majesties Reigne, Annoq.
Dominy 1674.

The Condicion of this obligation is such that if the Above bounded
Johannes Van Brough shall well and truely make his personall appearance at the next Generall Court of Assizes to be held in this City,
then and there to make answer to what shall be alleadged against him,
as to the matter for the which he hath by the Governours speciall warrant
stood lately Committed, and doe abide the determinacion of That Court
therein, and in the meane Time to bee of the Good behaviour that then
this Present obligacion to be void and of noe Effect otherwise to remaine,
and be in full force Power, and Vertue.

Sealed and delivered in the
Presence of   Johannes van brug. [*seal*]
J. Van de Water   Cornelis van Borsum   [*seal*]
Dirck van der Clyff

[ENDORSED:]   Mr. Johannes van Brughs
                 bond of security, to appeare
                 at the Assizes.

                 200£

[24:78]

[A SIMILAR BOND FOR EGIDIUS LUYCK, MERCHANT, SIGNED BY
AEGIDIUS LUYCK AND BONDSMAN NICOLAES BAYARD]

[24:79]

[ANOTHER BOND FOR NICOLAES BAYARD, SIGNED BY NICOLAES
BAYARD AND GABRIEL MINVIELLE, MERCHANT]

[24:80]

[ANOTHER BOND FOR ANTHONY DE MILL BAKER, COSIGNED BY
JAN VIGNE, BREWER]

[24:81]

[A BOND FOR WILLIAM BEEKMAN, COSIGNED BY ISAAC VAN VLEEQ]

[24:82]

[A BOND FOR JACOB KIP, COSIGNED BY ABRAHAM JANSE]

[24:83]

[AN UNSIGNED COPY OF THE BOND FOR NICOLAES BAYARD, IN
MATTHIAS NICOLLS'S HANDWRITING]

[24:84]

[*Missing*]

[24:85]

[TWO DOCUMENTS IN A SUIT BROUGHT BY JOHN LAURENCE
AGAINST NICOLAES BAYARD]

[   ]as Beay[   ]
an Accion of Trovere and
Conversion.*

The Plt. declares [   ] of a Subject to the [   ]
[   ] Majestie, and a freeman of [   ] which
Capacity, may justly [   ] Protection to his person and
[   ] thereunto upon the 27th day [   ] Old
Style the Plts. house was [   ] and his shopp unlocked, and
div[   ] taken Plundered and Carryed away f[   ] By

---

* An action to recover the value of goods wrongfully converted by another to his own use.

what Power to the Plt. unkno[   ] Order, fo[   ]he Same
produced [   ] Assured it cannot bee by any Lawful[   ]
being directly contrary to the 6th Artic[   ] Peace, Concluded betweene
the Kings Mos[ ] Excellent Majestie and the estates Generall of the
United Netherlands, the perticulers [   ] the Goods are as followeth,
Vizt.

20 Els 1/4 Kersey at f14 per ell is	2[ ]
21 Ells blue [ ]e at ƒ6: is	[ ]
19 ell[ ] stuff at ƒ8: is	1[ ]
24 [ ]nlett at ƒ7 is	160[ ]
[ ] Kerzey at ƒ18 is	108[ ]
[ ]ge at ƒ9 is	29:00[ ]
[ ]es at ƒ4 is	45:6.[ ]
	1322.[ ]

[   ] the Defendant [   ] Considera[   ]
[   ] selfe or his order, at half [   ]duce
whereof was by his [   ] disposed off, and fraud away
[   ] to whom this plt. owed, [   ] Upon
which Injury and [   ] this his suite, and humbly
[   ] Judgement, that his goods may bee [   ]
the Value, with Costs of the [   ] hee shall Pray etc.

John Sharpe Towne Clearke.

A Mayors Cou[   ]
15 Aprill 1675.

Mr. John Lawrence Plt.
Mr. Nicol. Bayard Deft.

that the deft. had not [   ]
the worshippfull Court order [   ]
against the deft. according [   ]

By order of [   ]
John S[   ]
Town Clea[   ]

[24:86]

[JUDGMENT IN THE SUIT OF WALTER WEBLEY, TRUSTEE OF THE
ESTATE OF RICHARD MORRIS, AGAINST PIETER ALRICHS]

At a Mayors Court [   ]
Pr[   ] D[ ]e.
[   ] Dominy 1674.

[   ]ter Web[   ] T[ ]testator [   ]
Deceased, Plt.
Peter Aldrix Deft.

The Plt. declared that the Deft. detey[ ]d a [   ] Woman, which
[   ]as commonly called or kn[   ] Name of Bess [   ]d
produced an order under th[   ] hand that all good[ ] belonging
to the Orphane Childe [   ] delivered and returned to [   ]Trustees
of said Orphaine, a[   ] under Coll. Morris [   ] hand that
the said [   ] Controversye was absolutely allienated from his [
] given to the wife of C. Richard Mo[ ]ris withou[   ]Provizo
or Exception; [   ] W[   ] the said Negro was in
Verity tr[   ] Lewis Morris gave Capt. Richard
Mor[]is [   ] The Worshippfull Court having [   ]ard
the debates [   ] Parties and their Eviden[   ]hey g[ ]e the
charg[   ] the Jury of twelve men w[   ] bro[ ]ght in their Ver[   ] for
the Plaintiff with costs of [   ]

The Court ordered Judgment to be [   ]tred accordingly.

T[   ] Sherriff of New Yorke.

By order of the court.

John Shar[   ]
Towne Clea[   ]

[24:87]

[LIST OF AVAILABLE BUILDING SITES IN NEW YORK CITY]*

Mar. 25th 75.

Behind the Perle streete on the south side of the Fort it may be inclosed to Pearle street.

2 houses or 3 to the water side if enclosed at pearle street End and Mr. Delavalls yard, no way for them to pass to and fro.

A voyde piece of ground betweene Mr. Delavalls and Leyslers, fit to build upon

Shops or sheds for flesh and fish, at the Corner over against Stephanus van Cortlands.

The way from hence to the state house to bee levell'd, and paved next the wall.

The great ditch to bee ordered to bee cleansed, according to former orders.

Behind the halfe moone by the State house on the East side, a fitt place for a Common house of‡ office.

The halfe moone there wants repaire, by roling stones out of the water neare the foundacion.

The passage to bee closed or paved goeing to Mr. De Meyers, hee formerly promis't to pave it.

To fill up to the south wall by levelling the rubbish.

A place for a house next to C. Salisburyes.

The corner at Trintye Clocks belong[   ] to Mr. Paterson — voyde, fit to build.

* The document was written by Matthias Nicolls in ink over a penciled version. The reverse of the first page is numbered 3; there is no page 2 with the present record. There are two additional leaves, with entries in columns numbered 4, 5, 6.
‡ He probably intended to write "or."

A Very old house against it — ready to fall, fit to build: by Mr. Bayards Its Der: Smiths.

Tom Lewis brings the front of his house to Mr. V: Brughs.

Ground for 4 or 5 houses at Mrs. Goverts besides that building upon. The wall defective by Caarstens etc.

A space betweene Mr. Balthazer and mother Daniels and another on the other side at the Corner.

Besides theres Roome along mother Daniels Garden to the Eastward for 3 or 4 houses.

another next to it a voyde lott of Mr. Darvalls.

A house of Dirck Smiths like to fall, nobody lives in it.

the next hath no Chimney.

A voyde lott next of Christop. Amyes.

Another old house of Dirck Smiths next to that of Moosemans where hee dwells.

A parcell of rotten old houses next towards the fortification and a Garden fronting of Do. Drisius Here's much vacant ground.

The Gate here not thought convenient.

A Corner Lott on the Northwest side — a little house too farre in — Then very pitifull houses to the Governors stables.

a fitter place thought for the Port against the broade way.

A spare place next betweene the Luthers Church and the works.

A voyde place against the Luthers Church on t'other side.

Voyde ground there by C. Mannings.— for 4 or 5 in front.

If the place to bee left open to the litle halfe moone for a street Steph: V:

Cortlands offers to build towards the broade way and towards the halfe moone.

T'other side capable of the like.
Fitt for 2 or 3 houses on each side besides to the broade way.

Another Voyde place of about 60 feet betweene Mr. Rombouts and the Sheriffs.

The Church yard where Couvenhovens wid. is building I have forbad them to proceede.

Two voyde places against it small houses with Gardens behind.

Home — Dircks small house voyde places on both sides

backside of John the Coopers and another of Mr. Minviells by Antonie de Milles.

[ENDORSED:] An Account of the voyd places about
the Town viewed Mar. 25th 1675.

Present.
The Mayor
The Dep: Mayor
Mr. Fr: Philips
Mr. Ga. Minvielle   Aldermen
C. Salisbury and Severall others
Tho. Lewis etc.

[NOTE :]*

Mate
Deliver to Cornelius this barrer 100 bush. of salt
[   ]

---

* Written in another hand.

[NOTES:]*

Apr. 26. 1675

To appoint officers for 3 Companies — 3 times 6.

To view the [   ]‡

To rememb. Jacob Couwehovens widdo. for a house lot.

The officers of the Church for a Couple of Ladders etc.

[24:88]

[BILL OF CORNELIS COERSENS AGAINST THE GOVERNMENT.
TRANSLATION]

[. . . . . .about 29 lines missing . . . .]

8   [   ] 1674 in the [   ] men
           [   ] gone [   ] Jamicke,†
           with a pack of beavers for the lord governor.

15 —   [   ] verbal order from
           Capt. Nickels, pressed one horse for his
           servant Charleton [to go] to Vlissinge;+ gone 6 days.

5 —   [   ] de Coerst of Jamicke a horse;
           gone two days.

8   For Capt. Nickels son Willem. Mr. Coker @ 2 days.

1–2–6   24 Feb., according to the order of Capt. Nickels,
           pressed one horse for Mr. Clercq; gone 9 days.

---

* These notes have been canceled.
‡ It appears to be "watte Grue," but is probably intended for "water gate." Nicolls's notes
after 1673 are carelessly written and very difficult to interpret (not that his earlier notes to
himself are deciphered easily).
† Jamaica, Long Island
+ Flushing, Long Island

5   27 March, two horses pressed by order of the lord gover-
             nor for his servant when he went to the whale.

2–15– 6
2– 7– 6
£5– 3s–0d

8– 3   For Dierck Jansen Verman

2– 6   For Jan Aerse
5– 13– 9

7– 4   For Albert Cornelise
6– 1– 1

9– [ ]   Theunes Jansen
[   ]

This bill allowed this 29th day of March
1675.   2£–15s–6d

                              Silvr . Salisbury
                              High Sheriff

[ENDORSED:]*   [   ]
                   about pr[   ]

I have allowed Corn Coersens Accounts in Capt.
Salisburyes time for the yeares 1674 and 1675 part
one and part t'other.

Apr. 28. 1677.

The bills are herein [   ].

---

* Endorsed in English.

[24:89]

[PETITION OF NICOLAES BAYARD, APPEALING THE VERDICT
IN FAVOR OF JOHN LAURENCE]

Humbly Sheweth, that [   ] hath bene unjus[   ]
Molested by Mr. John Lawrence [   ]ed this Petit[   ] the
Worshipfull Mayors Court [   ] Citty New Yorke [   ]
Parcel of goods by this Petitioners Clarcq as Vendu Master in the time
of the late Dutch Government sold att a Publicq Vendu and outcry held
within this Citty, for the account of the Shreave or Sherif of that
Government unto whom and by whoes order this Petitioner before Your
honnors arrival here, alsoo had made the full payment of the produce of
the said goods; Neverthelesse the said Mr. Lawrence hath obtained a
Verdict of the Jury (some of them being no Merchants, and without doubt
alsoo ignorant what the office of a Vendu Master is) Whereby this
Petitioner should be lyable to returne the said goods to the said Mr.
Lawrence, or the vallue thereof, amounting according t[ ] Mr. Lawrence
V[ ]lluation to the summe of ƒ1322:15, But sold in outcry for ƒ728:1
for Wampum or £20:4:5 in Beavers; By which Verdict of the Jury this
Petitioner finds himselfe much wronged, the Petitioner haveing never
had any of the said goods in his Possession, but where only as aforesaid
by his Clarcq as Vendu Master sold for the account of the said fiscael, as
by the former English and Late Dutch Government, hath been Customary; Wherefore the plt. humbly Craves that Your honnor will be
pleased to graunt the Petitioner the favour of an appeale from the said
Verdict, to have a hearing in Equity before Your honnor and Court of
assizes.

And Your honnors Petitioner shall ever pray etc.

[   ] Yorke 30th of March
   1675.

N: Bayard

[ENDORSED:]   [   ]
                   Petition of Appeale
                   Mar. 30. 1675.
                   The Judgment of Court to bee first
                   given and then graunted.

[24:90]

[LETTER FROM LUDOVICUS COBES, SECRETARY OF THE COURT AT ALBANY, CONCERNING A MORTGAGE GIVEN TO JAN CLUTE BY SOME CATSKILL INDIANS. TRANSLATION]

Albany. 7 April 1675

My Lord and Friend Capt. Nicolls,

Lieutenant Clute has disbursed over several years a considerable quantity of merchandise amounting to eighty whole beavers and fifteen otters, and that to some Catskill Indians, because an Indian named Schermerhorn persuaded him that he had a special bond which was executed for the rightful half of his and the aforesaid participants' land for recovery of his arrears by failure to pay at the expiration of the term.

This serves then only to inform you of this and to have the inclosed mortgage registered by you so that hereafter no more ignorance can be claimed here and he, Clute, is not cheated out of his property rights; your honor shall be compensated well by Lt. Clute. In closing I commend your honor and his wife to the protection of God Almighty, and I am

Your honor's devoted servant,

Ludovicus Cobes

[ADDRESSED:] To the honorable Lord
Capt. Nicolls,
Major ofN. York
and Secretary
of Fort James.

[ENDORSED:] Lodovicus Cobes
Alb. Apr. 7, 1675.

[24:91]

[AFFIRMATION MADE IN COURT BY QUAKERS]

The Engagement subscribed to, by those called
Quakers at or neare Oysterbay.

Wee whose names are hereunder written, doe promise to bee true Subjects, and faithfull to this Government, under his Majestie and his

Royall Highness, as long as wee shall continue within this same: In testimony whereof wee have hereunto subscribed our Names: The 9th and 10th dayes of Apr. 1675.

John Weekes etc.

The voluntary Engagment and
subscription of Henry Townesend
senior.

I doe by these presents, subject to Charles the second, King of England etc., and to live quietly under his Government, without plotting or contriving anything against him: And if I breake this Engagement, to suffer as those that breake an Oath.

Oysterbay.   Apr. 10th 1675.

Henry Townsend.

The usuall Oath or Engagement of a
Jury, impos[ ]d by the Quakers at
Rhoade Island, for Life and death.

Wheareas you are nominated and chosen, to goe upon this Inquest of Tryall, betweene our Soveraigne Lord the King and the Prisoner at the Barre, you are to make a due return thereof, to the present court sitting according to Law and Evidence, and Light of your Conscience upon the penalty of Perjury.

To the like purpose a Jury in
Causes with the same penalty.

[ENDORSED:]   1675.

[24:92]

[Upon Martin's] Vynyard,
this 12th Aprill, 1675.

[Deservedly
honoured Sir:]

[I have] written to your Honor by Steven Hussy, the which I hope is come
to Hand synce, by Way of Boston, which I doubt not [were]‡ [carefully
sent, to both] which I humbly [desire]† your Honour, not [questioning]+
[in the least but th]at they shal be considered according to the Worth of
the [C]ontents: My earnest Desire now is, to crave patience to reade and
Weigh the ensueing lines in a speciall Manner whereby unto your honour
I shall be Much Obliged: In 1641, I had a graunt of Mr. James Forret[t,]
Agent to the Lord sterling for these Isles, and I forthwith indeav[our]ed
to obtaine the In[dian] Right of them; Mr. Richard [Vy]nes, [S]teward
Gen[erall] to Sir [F]erdynando [Gorges,] heareing of it, Enterrupted
showing me his [Master's] pa[tten]t and his power insomuch that I was
Convinced by him [and] [   ]** gorges, who was then governour
of the province of Maine th[   ] realy Sir Ferdynandoes right
And for a some of Money did obtaine from said Vynes a Graunt also: It
came soe to pass that Mr. Forrett went sudden[ly] for england before he
had shewed me his Masters pattent whome after[wards] I never saw:
some yeares after this Came over one Mr. Forrester furnish[ed with]
power who was here with me, and told me that he would Cleare upp all
things and that I should be one of his Counsel But he from [hence]‡‡
went to Long Iland and from thence to the dutch Where the govern[our
put] him in prison and sent him a prisoner into holland, as I heard and I
never saw him more; soe Wee Remained under gorge ha[d] [noe]††

* The document is badly damaged. Material in brackets is from a published transcript,
Franklin B. Hough: *Papers Relating to the Island of Nantucket* (Albany, 1865), 68–75.
Another transcript, prepared by George R. Howell in 1897, is bound with the manuscript.
The following footnotes indicate Howell's reading where it differs from Hough's and where
the original is now lost or unreadable.
‡ will be
† referre
+ presuming
** that
‡‡ here
†† haveing

Newes of either Lord proprietor till his Majesties Commissioners[*] came over and then Mr. Archdale sent me printed paper Whereby his Majestie had by his [   ] Counsell in the [   ] most strongly Confirmed Ferdynandi Georges Esquire to be the Lord of the provynce of Maine of which Nantuckett and this be a parte: withall he [wrote me] that generall Nycolls did clayme these Iles but at theire fir[st Meeting] that would be taken of etc: now after this generall [Nicholls wrote to] me that Mr. Archdale haveing gorges pattent for to p[resent an]d he not haveing the Lord Sterlings the Kings Comis[sioners] refered the Decision to his Majestie: whereof he had not any I[ntel]ligence but a litle before he went home for England: generall Nyc[olls] did acknowledge that the power of these Ilands was proper in the heires of sir fernando gorges: I have the testimony of the generall Court of boston for it: which Court sent to the gentlemen of the provyence of Maine Whose Answer was that it was in myselfe, etc: Now after all this Co[ ]es Collonell Lovelace he sends for me in a loveing [Manner,] to come to yorke to shew by What Tytle I held these Ilands whereuppon I ga[ve] him to understand as is above written; And at length went to him and shewed him my graunts which he approved of and the printed paper from his majestie, at w[hich he] stumbles Much: allso I shewed him what generall Nycolls [had] Written me of his not being Informed what his Majestie had donne thereat he stumbled Very Much likewise: then I asked him yf he had the Lord St[erl]ings p[att]ent by him he saied noe: I answered then I was at a losse I [went][‡] to Captaine Nycolls and acquainted him with our discourse and [   ] prayed him to search in matters of long Iland to see yf he could [not find] the date of Lord Sterlings pattent yf not I could doe nothing at yorke [which he did] finde and it was more antient then gorges: if not I had no[thing but about] Elizabeth Iles: I questioned allso in myselfe whether safe for to med[le, I say med]le touching any thing without a publique a Warrant to [declare][†] [Gorges] government as I had to obey it [   ][+] his majestie Except [I[**]] were Compelled: affter this his honour and I did agree uppon an Acknowledgement which by my graunt from Mr. Forrett I was to pay yearly to the Lord Sterling, or his Successours a [new] charter and Liberties in it made: grounded upon my first gra[unt and] the resignation of Lord Sterling's heires to his Royall highness etc: thankfully by me accepted there and by all at home

---

*   Richard Nicolls, George Cartwright, Sir Robert Carr and Samuel Maverick (editor's note)
‡   sent
†   decline
+   I meane (?) from
** events

and also at Na[ntuc]kett soe farr as I knew; the generall Court unanimously [passed] Law made a[ccor]ding to Liberties graunted without [
] the next year[e wee w]ent to Nantuckett [with the] * [   ] Us a Book
of w[hich] w[e] had noe Notyce of, or any Instruction [   ] they would
not proceede in the Waye Wee beganne [the great]‡ b[†] after Verry
Much debate Wee Came away resolving speed[ily for to] apply ourselves
to the governor thereabout, but Mathew being up[pon] the way, who was
furnished to pay the Acknowledg[em]ent [the]+ Newes that york was
taken by the dutch; then I hearing Cap[taine] Ny[colls was well,] etc. I
certyfied him at lardg of everything from [which] I [had an An]sewere
to full sattisfaction in every pertyculer: [and lastly by our A]pplycation
to your honour I did and doe still r[est] s[atisfied theri]n to the full it
being absolutely Just in my [Judgment,]** [and such a]s have seene it
that are Verry Juditious: But those of N[antuckett, it] is said they say
noe man had right to a foot of Land before [the Date of the last] Charter
and acte accordingly notwithstanding all the foresaid [and they by the
B]ook Indeavour to overthrow our Liberties; [announcing my Right]‡‡
obtayned from the Earle of Sterling Nothing: also the indian right
[nothing,] my quiett [Occupasion]†† [there of] 29 Yeares Nothing, the
grounding the [ten Partners]++ upon my [first graunt nothi]ng: all other
Transactions — for 29 yeares Nothing the Lawes [now] * [made nothin]g,
which your honour and Counsell saw Reason to put in force; all which
is [most absu]rd Unreasoneable, and most Unwise that which they for
some by end [indeavour to in]terprett away and make voyd, is that which
by generall Nycolls [was judged Good, which] his honour Collonell
Lovelace Confirmed without the least [Scrutiny,]‡ [and Counsel,] that
which Captain Nycolls by his Letter Really approves and tha[t which
your Honour and] Counsell hath determined: I hope your honour will
take some spee[dy Course to] force into practyce what you have

* where
‡ the year
† Howell is guessing "before."
+ with
** unders[tanding]
‡‡ grounding also all
†† possession
++new charter
* we
‡ scruple

established: this is verry cer[taine, that t]heire now Condemned ap-
prehensions and Interpretations and ac[tings in s]ome Degree acordingly
was the first roote of contentions abou[t] [Right]* [t]o Land at Nantuckett and Revoltings from Government here and [crying]‡ [down] power:
And theire Comming hither now and [   ]uring without our doeing
more in punishing ringleaders for crying downe power of government
with theire Comerse with some of them And allso Captaine gardners
sayeing to the Cheiffest of them at his house; that yf he had noe More to
answer for then they had at york he should [sitt]† but little by it but he
had Much more and I say this hath allso turned to our prejudice I have
[one]+ Oath of what Capt: gardner spake as above; And last I saye I have
[doune my] best in settling these Iles; have passed through Many
[difficulties and daungers in i]t, beene at verry Much Coste toucheing
English and Indians which I [shall] [have]** for present to mention;
much desireing yf god please to re[   ] sellf: I beseeche your
honour to [take] [our good Understanding]‡‡ to [   ] [I] wish all
happines to attend your honour and all as I commend your honour and
[yours to] the Lords Direction and protection and rest.

> your honours Most affectionate
> and most humble Servant.

> Thomas Mayhew

The [12 Aprill] I say farther, that Capt: Gardner who seemed to [make]††
[little of the Faults] of the ringleaders: I beseech your honour to
Consider his unfitt[nes to medle with it. Cer]tainely they have need of
al [with all] that were resolved [to owne] noe power of his Royall
Highnes here, and onely one of the six is [come,] who wee have accepted
and remitted his fine to 1 d the other I see noe [readyness] to Render any
Sattisfaction my sonne Saxson is now to sett uppon it I hope our
Ack[nowledgment will] [ ] [taken] speedyly and fined it true that the
[   ] the Uncertainty of interest in Lands at Nantukkett

---

* rights
‡ laying
† sett
+ on
** leave
‡‡ in good my adventurous
†† mind

[   ]
Servant

Tho: Mayhew

May it please your honour to [image]* what I have on these Ilands.

Graundsonnes,	15
My sonnes sonnes sonnes	3
daughters	3
grand daughters	11
	32

I prayse god two of my grand sons doe preach to English and Indians Mathew sometymes John the youngest Weekely.

[ADDRESSED:]   For his Honor Maijor Edmond Andros [the] governour generall for his Royall highn[ess] James Duke
of yorke and Albany over all his Territtories in
America, these Presents At Fort James in New York

[24:93]

[PETITION BY THE TOWN OF SHERBURN ON NANTUCKET ISLAND
FOR PRIVILEGES]

[   ]he right Honorable Edmund Androsse Esquire Governor Gen.
under his Royall Highnesse James Duke of Yorke and Albany of his
Teritories in America.

The Petition and Adresse of the town of Sherbourne upon the Ile of
Nantukkett.

Right Honorable we entreat your favourable acceptance of our real and
heartie Welcome as our Governor which is to us the riseing sunne afer a
darke and stormy night, together with our humble thankfullnesse for your
Honors care of us, as appeares by the renewed Commission and direction
sent our Magistrates which we hope have bin and will be readily
followed: Thus your Honors manifested favour together with our owne
necessity, gives us encouragement Humbly to Petition

---

* injoy

[   ][*] That our real Loyalty to our Gratious Soveraigne our true [   ]sty obedience to his Royall Highnesse, [   ] by our obedience to his Royal Highnesse Laws, and that we may not be excluded the Go. [   ] and use of them by any meanes.

[   ]n: may reteine the Absolute government [   ] and that we may be subordenate to no person [   ] your Hon: onely so long as God and his Royal [.   ]e please, which we hope will be dureing your life [   ]ch we pray God to continue.

[   ] That the liberties and rights graunted us in our Charter by the Honorable Col: Lovelace by Commission from his Royal Highnesse may not be impared or deminished by any pretence of our aversaries whatsoever.

[   ]ly that your Honor would be pleased to graunt us some favour in the manner of our paying our acknowledgment if possible And [   ] graunt us such farther instructions as shall be proposed by our friends, as your Hon: find to be m[   ]derate and rationall.

[   ]ly Your Honors favourable audience and candid heareing of our Friends whom we have soe that end to give your Hon: a full and true accompt of all matters here with us, [   ]use [ ]o believe hath not bin yet donne by those [   ]come and not bin sent There being many [   ]t of Consequence which by writeing we cannot so well do which we have comm[   ] friends, to attend your Honors direction in.

And now right Honorable we beg your pardon for our wea[ ]nesse or impertinencies in this our petitioning protesting it is not out of the least jealosie of your Honors goodnesse to us, or wisdome in ordereing all things so as shall be legal and rigt, but are hereunto mooved perceiving the endeavours of some to bereave us of [   ] all, as Loyalty, Obedience, Laws, Libertyes, all whic[ ] are pretious to us: The father makeing out of thes[ ] particulars: and what else may concerne us we leave our Friends whom we doubt not but will give your Hon[   ] full satisfaction, and information in whose mo[ ] we are Confident will not be found a fals[ ]

---

* It appears that the paragraphs were originally numbered "1st" through "5thly."

g[   ] thus with our prayers etc. we take leave, and [   ] entreat we
may subscribe our selves your [   ] and real servants.

Sherborn the 12 of   Ju[   ]*
Aparell 1675   Edward S[   ]
                            Tho: Macy
                            William Wort[ ]
                            William Bunker
                            Thomas Colma[ ]

[24:94]

[PETITION OF SAMUEL DAYTON AND JOHN LAUGHTON FOR
PERMISSION TO PURCHASE LAND FROM THE INDIANS]

To the Right Honorable Colonell Andrews Governor Generall under his
Royall Highnes James Duke of York and Albina of all his territoys in
America etc.

The humble Petition of Samuell Dayton of Setalcott and John Laughton
of Southampton M[   ]mbly Sheweth and Desireth

That whereas theire is a Certaine Track of Land yet unpurchased of the
Natives Sittuate in A Tray Anglue‡ forme betweene the bounds of
Southampton Southhold and Setalcott: Lying on the South Side of Long
Island and your humble Petitioners Conceiveing it may bee very Convenient both for Whalling and Small fishing and your Petticioners
haveing had some of the first Exp[ ]ience in the Said Desighne and being
Men that want: Land to improve and this being noe way Improved by
any of the Said three townes and the Indians the Native propriators of
the Land haveing Often proffered the Salle of the same unto us Most
humbly beseech: your Honnor would bee pleased to grant A Lysence to
us: and our Coepartners for the Legall Purchasing of the Same of the
Indians that Soe wee might then: take out A Pattnet for the same and for
your Honors helth and Happines Wee Shall Ever as wee in Duty are
bound most humbly Pray.

---

* F. B. Hough states that there were two illegible names above this one. There is certainly
enough room in the original for two more signatures, but they are completely gone, rather
than just illegible. The last three incomplete names are Starbuck, Worth, and Colman;
Alexander Starbuck in *The History of Nantucket* (Rutland, VT, 1969) lists the last name as
Gardner, which is incorrect.
‡ triangle

[ENDORSED:]   The Peticion of Sam: Dayton and
Wm Laughton about some Land at the South.
Apr. 15. 1675.

[24:95]

[LETTER FROM SECRETARY NICOLLS TO RICHARD WOODHULL
ABOUT THE PRECEDING PETITION]

New Yorke Aprill 16th 1675.

Sir:

The enclosed is a Coppie of a Peticion presented Yesterday to the
Governour by our Neighbour Mr. Samuell Dayton, and Mr. John
Laughton of Southton, on the behalfe of themselves and some As-
sociates.

The Governour in answer was pleased to order that it bee recommended
to you to make Enquiry of the Scittuation of the Land mencioned in the
Peticion, whether as yet within no Pattent, and may be granted without
prejudice to any Towneshipp, how the Indians may bee treated with about
it, and you are desired to returne an Account thereof, with the first
Convenience, together with your Judgment of the Quantity and Quality
of the Land; whereupon his honor will give such Graunt and Confirmation, as shall be thought Convenient, the purchase being With leave first
made of the Indian Proprietors in the name of his Royall Highnesse:

I am
Sir
Your humble servant
M.N.

A Copie of my L[   ]
to Mr. Woodhull writt
by the Go: order.

About some land peticioned for by Mr. Dayton
and Mr. Laughton.

[24:96]

Apr. 20. 1675.

This day three of the Indyan Sachems, being invited by th[   ]
Go. Carterett [ ]d came to the Fa[   ] Towne [   ]last night.

Their names[   ]nemas

Porapp[ ] of[   ]

Taptawap[   ]

Porpuppa [   ] the Governor, and
[   ] of the rest for having bee[   ]well[   ]
ready, and bids the [   ] a good morne

The Gov. returnes then thankes for comei[   ] so freindly being
deseired, and that both [   ] and Go. Carteret are willing to continue
friendship with them but the occasion in part for the sending for them
hath beene some Rumors of disturbances amongst their Neighbors but
thinke they have no hand in it, and hope will not.

Mr. Edsall and Thom[ ] Laurence the baker who were sent for them, are
Interpreters. Sam Edsall discour[   ]t large with th[   ] the Governor
on this subje[ ] writing in [   ] bought from N. Je[   ]
[   ]

The Go. tells th[   ] friendship
[   ] that are
ag[   ] not joyne
[   ] the other
[   ] The Go.
[   ]hath
beene pro[   ] by those
sev[   ] He
promises them [   ]ship and Protec[   ] long as they shall
continue.

Mataupis Another Sachem comes and thanks the Go. as the former and
bids him good morne to pre[*blank*] The Governor with 2 large bands of
sewant Saying they come with a good heart from himselfe and his people.

Then h[   ]esents a 3d band in the behalfe of h[   ]lsive than
his againe.

[   ]nswer hee doubts not of there [   ]es
of the Continuance thereof, [   ]pon him.

[   ] Interpreters tell them, that [   ]
with all the Indyans about, [   ] are under his protection.

[   ]arly the Maques have lately desired [   ] and direction
from the Go: and that upon that Consideracion, have preserved 17
Minquas Indyans alive, who they are ready to deliver, that the same
friendship and protection there is for the other Indyans to the North, and
those of Esopus.

Mr. Edsall hath the Maques proposalls and Commissioners of Alb.
answer to relate to them.

The Go: bids them whatsoever agreements of friendship were made by
his predecessors with any of the Indyans, hee will make them good.

After the proposalls were interpreted to them, the [ ] declares his intent
to protect and defend [   ] under his Protection.

[   ] satisfyed with their friendship, and [   ]
engage them in warre with their [   ]xpect they will
not harbor, or de[   ]mies.

[   ] Laur: to tell if any one of
[   ] here, they shall have
[   ] were shall have the like from
[   ]

The [   ]p 2 of the bands and Go: Car[   ]her 2
and assures them of the acceptance of their friendship. The one of 15
wamp: deep. another of 14 — another of 15 — the 4th of 12.

The Sachems promise not onely friendship but not to harbor the Enemyes
of the Engls: or to have to doe with them.

The Go: and Go: Car[   ]ke to them, and the Go: gives them [   ]
duffells mad[   ] and 3 other, so [   ]ired
in token of [   ]

They retu[ ]ne [   ]thers
speech[   ]

Afterwards t[   ] The
Governors ga[   ]

[ENDORSED:]   Indyans from
                   Nevisans etc. being
                   3 Sachems.
                   Apr. 20. 1675.
                   To record.

[24:97]

[LETTER FROM CAPT. JOHN CARR TO MATTHIAS NICOLLS
CONCERNING ASPERSIONS MADE BY CAPT. JOHN MANNING]

Sir.

Understanding that his Honor the Governor was to come to Delaware I
did suppose you would come with him therefore I made bold to leave
thesse few lines with my wife before my departure for England to deliver
to you, Sir I understand by severall that come from your partes, that Capt.
Manning laid great blame upon me to Cleare himsealf, I doe protest to
Allmighty god that I never acted ore did any thing but what was by his
Comaund, he pretending himsealf deputy Governor, and the last th[ ]
was he Camaunded me to desier the Enimy to sta[   ] long and to stope
them untill the Articles was [   ] drawne, but they was att the turnpike
when I wen[ ] out of the gate, and pressing forward to the gate, I was in
the midle of them, and I thought it my best way to gett from them, then
to enter with them this is the greatest Crime that god and my owne
Conscience knowes I ame guilty of, Sir it is upwards of thirty years since
I bore Armes for his Majesty of bleased memory and Continued in his
present majesties service at home and abroad, in which service I have
spent my blood and my youth and lost my Patrimony, all which I shall
produce good Certificats from persons of quality, Sir I hope his Honor
will Consider thosse things as allsoe my present Condition and my wifes
and five smale Children Sir I must acknowledge the former favoures I
have receaved from your sealf, I doe not doubt but you will Continue the
same, my humble request is that you will be pleased to be assisting to
my wife she Comeing there to looke after our Estate which the Dutch
tooke from us, the which I have Patants for, haveing not else to trouble
you, but wishi[   ] you all happines, and Conclude my sealf Sir

Your
very Faithfull and Humble Servant.

John: Carr

Maryland 20th
Aprill 1675

[ADDRESSED:]   Theese.
For his ever Honored
friend Capt. Mathias
Nicols.

[ENDORSED:]   no. 33
Capt. Carre
Maryland Apr. 20th
1675.
Received May 10th 1675.

[24:98]

[PETITION OF INHABITANTS OF NANTUCKET PROTESTING ACTS OF
THEIR LOCAL GOVERNMENT]*

[   ]mond Andros Esquier go[vernor]
[   ]hynes teretoryes in
America hum[bly]

[*Sheweth*]

[*That*] Whearas [w]ee whose names are under written with soum [other]s
of the first purchasers and propriotores of the Iland of Nantu[   ] which
first Began to settell the Iland with Einglish Inhabbitantes soum of us in
person and others with theare Estates whose names ar with your honor
on Record, By Reson of our Application that wee made unto your honor,
soone after your hapie safe Arivall into this land And your honor with
your honnorabell Counsell weare pleased to An[   ] our proposales with
severall Instructiones directed to the Chefe [   ] of nantucket and his
assistantes, which weare according [   ] But wee see littell that
The have doun or willinge to doe. [   ] to your honnores
Instructions) Although in a petition that the [   ] drawne up: as
the say to present unto your honor in which I[   ] that the have dulye

_____
* Part of the following text comes from *NYSHAR* vol.3.

observed and doun accordinge to your honors P[   ]tiones) or words to
that Efect The peettion was Received att a Tow[ ] meetinge and voted
By the major part To bee sent and prese[*nted*] unto your honnor, But wee
whose names ar under writte[*n*] Could not see [   ]in any reson we could
saflye Joyne wit[*h*] Them in [   ]t with
respect to your h[   ]terted to the
lawes of [   ] Established[   ] Royal hynes But our hum[bell
peti]tion Is that we may allso Injoye the liberties [   ]unto us: In
Respect of Keecpinge of a gennaral Co[ ] Amongst our selves: to witt
the Vinyard peopell and our selves accordinge to o[ ] first Instructiones:
for we dout not But wee shall macke It Appeare that Capt. John Gardner
hath indevored to get a partye to act with him soume of each Iland and
so to macke a devition Amongst the peopell And that under a pretenc[*e*]
of standinge for his hynes the duckes Intrest, which wee desire may B[*e*]
upheld: Under which wee hop to Injoye our Intrest and proprietie, and
priv[ ] granted us in our patten and Charter so not doutinge But that
your honor [ ] your honorabell Counsell will Concider of our present
stat and Condition s[   ] wee may live in peace and qietnes which Is
the desier of your humbell serv[   ] Inhabitinge upon the Ilandes of
Nantucket and Marthas Vinyard.

Nantucket the 20th of Aprill 1675.

I toe Like   Richard   Swaine his marc[k]
this petition
[Tho]mas Mayhew   Tristram Coffy[n]
                         John Swaine
                         Nathaniell [barnar]d
                         Nat[haniel Starbuk]
                         Step[hen Coffyn]
                         John C[offin]

[24:99]

[JUDGMENT IN A SUIT BY EMANUEL MANDEVILL AGAINST JOHN
SHAKERLY, AND ORDER FOR EXECUTION OF THE JUDGMENT]

Att the Mayers Courte held in N: Yorke the
21th of Aprill 1675.

Emanuell Mantevile Plt.
John Shakerly Deft.

The Plt. declared against the deft. that hee detayned A Negro woman of his and Proved her to bee his Negro, The worshippfull Court haveing Heard the wittnesses, Paper Red, and the debates of both Partais, giveing the charge to The Jurey who went outt and Brought In thair Verdict as Followeth — the Jurey finds the Negro Woman by Name Ezabella, to bee unjustly detayned by the defendent, from the Plt. tharefore wee find for the Plt., and that the deft. deliver the said Negro Unto the Plt. according to declarasion with Cost of Suite:

Whareupon the Court Accepted of the Verdict, butt orderd Judgment to bee Suspended Untill further Order.

Copia Vera Per

John Sharpe,
Towne: Clearke.

New Yorke SS

You are hereby required in his Majesties name to put the judgment within mentioned into Execution, by Seizing the said Negro and soe much of the goods chattells or effects as will pay cost with such insidentall Charges as are allowed by the lawes of this Government for your soe doing this shall bee to you a sufficient warrant, Dated in N. Yorke etc.

Copia Vera Per

John Sharpe
Towne Clearke.

[ENDORSED:]   Mayors Court Proceedings
                   Shakerly)
                   Hall   }

                   Past

[24:100]

[PETITION ON BEHALF OF THE ORIGINAL PURCHASERS OF
NANTUCKET SEEKING TO REGAIN CONTROL OF THE TITLE]

The humble petition of Tristram Coffin, and Matthew
Mayhew, in Behalf of the Major part of The first purchasers
freehoulders, upon the Island of Nanuckett.

To Your Honour Humbly Sheweth

That your Honours petitioners, having derived Right and interest, unto
the said Iland of Nantucket, from the Right honourable William, Earle
of Sterling; as also for their more sure injoyment thereof, from Ferdinando Gorges Knight; they Began to settle and inhabit the said Iland in
prosecution wherof, they expended, a Considerable summe besides the
many Dangers, they exposed themselves unto in Respect of the Natives
there inhabiting: and findeing necessitie of Necessarie Sea men, and
Tradesmen, they have Given out of their said purchase, certaine parcells
of landes, with cor[   ] injunctions, necessarie to the well being of the
plantation, as [   ]ne Coppies of their hould may appear; and having
obtained a Confirmation of their said interest, from Collonell, Fraunces
Lovelace, the said purchasers and freehoulders hoping to have held their
said interest and proprietie; By the said Tradesmen and Seamen, with the
assistance of some of the first purchasers, have been Damnified to the
value of some hundred of pounds, Nither are the said purchasers
freehoulders there suffered to act in the disposall of any of their landes,
and interests aforesaid; But their said interest and proprietie is ordered
and disposed of principally by the said Tradesmen and seamen; who with
some of the purchasers Being the Major of the [   ]d Iland in persones
though not propriety; have Elected into authoritie some of themselves,
wherby they have presumed to dispose of our said purchase, deviding it
one among another; Niether can your pe[   ]ioners have there redress; they
affirming that Every card they pl[   ]y is an ace: and Every ace a Trump;
and that the said purchasers could have no remedie in law; affirming that
it was his Highness had taken it, and Given it to them; your petitioners
therefore humbly pray, process, against the said intruders; and that it may
pleas your honour to Assist your honours humble petioners, so, that there
may be some means whereby they may Bring their said cause to triall;
not Doubting to make more Enormious actions appear then in this we
can acquaint your honour with; humbly desiring your honour to pardon,
the prolixitie of these unpolished lines; we cease, and are

Your honours humble Servants and Supliants

Apr. 27, 1675.*   Tristram Coffin
                                   Matt: Mayhew

[ENDORSED:]   A Petition and Proposalls
                     from Mr. Coffin and
                     Mr. M. Mahew in N-T.
                     Apr. 27. 1675.

[24:101]

[PETITION OF WISQUANNOWAS, ALIAS ADAM, OF MARTHA'S
VINEYARD ASKING FOR A GRANT OF LAND]

[   ] you Mr. G[ ]vern[ ]

I have much trouble, because I have [   ] I have reason to
have piece land, because m[   ] father and sachim his father of chapa-
quet[   ] brothers, and now I doe know and I see S[   ]
Their own brothers they have share of [   ] their sons after
them, and now I say whe[   ] have no land aswel as them this
first t[   ] next I sayd I have more trouble abou[   ] field Three
yeares agoe the sachim he did lent[   ] land to dwel uppon, so then I
break up new ground and plant upon it, and after hervest hee tel me you
must not plant no mor[   ]at feild you may make new field another
P[   ] where you wil, Then I did tel him [ ]e no like it as you will, but
I must plant upon again my feild, then I did plant again that next summer
and break up new ground more stil, And that time he did give him one
of his sons my field and that he yong man he tel me must not break up
ground no more this time, then I did pray to him to let me break up more
new ground, then he did willing, so I then break new ground last yeare,
and so after indian hervest he come to me, and he said now I doe minde
to come dwel upon your field, that time I won[   ]t that he will
doe it, because he [   ]land, so I said nothing to him[
]time, I did sow that my field [   ]at some, and some leave
itt for [   ]ne this summer, and now this spring [   ]in
to work upon my [ ]ield, then I goe to him speake to him [
]n stay and leave work, and first ta[   ] about it at meeting by indian
magistrats and Mr. Mayhew, then he said I will let be so, then I did went
to Mr. Mayhew and pray to him to help me and

* The date was added by Matthias Nicolls.

Mr. Mayhew [   ]
and if you wil take [   ] now let [   ]rels if you let him have it this summer
I [   ] it very wel, then after take it, because he have [   ] no where or
field therefore you consider [   ] better to use mercy for this man, then
[   ] man say I wil let him plant upon but [   ]re this summer
and no more: another about [   ]my father share and sachim give to [
]mayhew freely I to know how many yeares [   ] one yard at middle of
the whale, but I doe hear alwayes that share was one fathom and I doe
beeleive it was so because severall [   ]lks say was soe, and I doe minde
to hav[   ]gain that share in my hand so far such place this line, for that
share, and one time I went to Mr. Thomas Mayhew and I tel Mr. Mayhew
that sachim he give you that share that myne, and he did say I know this
sachim he is sachim a long time agoe, and he can doe what he wil, so I
can not say nothing that time, and al is while, and now I do hope for help,
pray you consider this busines

Adam my indian na[   ]

[   ]

[24:102]

[LETTER FROM THE MAGISTRATES OF NANTUCKET WELCOMING
GOVERNOR ANDROS AND AFFIRMING THEIR OBEDIENCE]

To the right Honorable Edmund Andros Esquire Gouvenor Gen. under
his Royal Highnesse James Duke of Yorke and Albany etc. of all his
teritories in America.

Right Honorable let our humble and hearty welcome salute Your Hon:
as our Governor: yea thrice welcome let your Honor be whose first
appearance made our hearts rejoyce, and put new strength into our weake
hands, haveing had hard labour, and great opposition in the trust committed to us, being bereaved as it were of all succour except our Loyalty
to our Royal Soveraigne and obedience unto his Royal Highnesse which
we were resolved to part with our lives rather then to loose but now
question not of protection in what is Legal and just Right Honorable your
renewed Commission and instructions sent by Mr. Coffin we received
14 days after his arivall here being first (as we were informed) canvessed
too and fro by such private and inconsiderate persons as he thought good
the which we readily and thankfully received the rules there in prescribed
we have al along followed formerly and since according to the best of
our understanding, and shall be stil[ ] willing to be guided by your Honors
further directions, and for that end have sent our friend and fellow

labourer under the burthen with us whom we hope will find favor with your Hon: that he may give a full and true accompt of all things with us, which is our humble petition: being fully confident your Hon: being rightly and fully informed will have favourable thoughts of us we presume and certainly beleive that very false things and untrue are suggested to your Honor upon selvish and sinister ends: not doubting but they will find acceptance accordingly.

As to particulars we leave to our friend assureing your Hon: you shall always the trueth appeareing find us Loyal obedient ready to heare and follow instructions thus with our prayers etc. we take leave and rejoyce that we may subscribe our selves

Your Honors humble and real servants

Received Apr. 27th 1675   Richard Cavelaer
by C. John Gardner.*   Edward Starbuck
                                   Tho: Macy

[ADDRESSED:]   For the Right Honorabll
                Edmund Andrews Esq. and Governer
                Generall Under his Royall Highnes James Duck of
                Yourck and Allbany
                of all his Territories in America
                These.

[ENDORSED:]   A Petition from
                Nantucket by Capt.
                John Gardner
                April 28. 1675
                From the Magistrates.

[24:103]

[PETITION OF NICOLAES DE MEYER APPEALING A JUDGMENT OF
THE MAYOR'S COURT]

Emanuell Mandevell   To the Honorable Edmund
Attourney to Major   Andros Esquire S[ ]nior of Sans Marez
Nathaniell Kingsland   Plt. Leiftennant And Gov[ ]rnor Generall
                            of all His Royall Highnesses
Nicolas Demier Deft.   Territories in America etc.

*   Note written by Matthias Nicolls.

The Humble Peticion of the Defendant

Sheweth

That your Peticioner being sued by the Plt. in the Mayors Court of this Citty in an accion of the Case (for recovery of a certaine Negro man now in the Possession of your peticioner which the plt. pretends did belong unto the Estate of the said Major Nath. Kingsland) For want of severall Materiall wittnesses and Papers which your Peticioner could not on the heareing of the Cause there produce, the Plt. on the 20th of Aprill last past obtained a verdict against your Peticioner.

> Your petitioner therefore humbly prayes your Honor that he giving security as the Law in such case requires may have the Liberty of an Appeale and that his cause may be heard before your Honor and Councell att the next Generall Court of Assizes.

And your Peticioner shall pray etc.

[ENDORSED:]   28th Aprill 75
Granted as per Petition.

Emanuell Mandevil Plt.
Nichs. de Meyer Deft.
About a Negroe.

[24:104]

[PETITION OF SIMON ATHEARN OF MARTHA'S VINEYARD FOR A CONFIRMATION OF HIS GRANT OF LAND IN EDGARTOWN]*

[   ] most humble wise

[   ] Simon Athearn an Inhabitant of Tisbury on martins vineyard
[   ] make my most humble petition unto the Right honnorable
[Gove]rnor over all his Royall highnesses Territories in america.
[Ri]ght honnorable.

[In] asmuch as I am an inhabitant as abovesaid: and whereas I have [bou]ght sum revertion of Lands as may appeare by deeds I humbly conce[ive it] is my aboundant duty for the good of my posterity: and espetially [conside]ring the perril of these times: to petition unto your

---

* Part of the following text comes from *NYSHAR*.

honnor for [ ] [*Entra*]nce of my deeds in this ofic of records at newyorke and [*that your*] honnor would be pleased to graunt me a Confirmation of [*the Landes*] I have bought and paid for, it being only for my [*n*]esessity (and not superflous,) the Land most of it, but barrin and [*pr*]ofitable* for nothing: and if it do or may appeare, that I have [*not*] veryly bought and paid for the said Land as my deeds expresseth [*I am*] willing your Confermation of it to me shall be voyd and [*of n*]one Efect; or that if it do or may appeare that any person [*or*] persons English or Indians have bought any part or parcell [*co*]ntained in the [*d*]eed: but my selfe only; I am willing your graunt to me shall be voyd and of none efect: or that If it do or may appear I have not bought it the said Lands of the Indians the right owners and paid for it, I am willing your honors confermation of it to me [*shall be o*]f non Efect: or that If it do or may appear [*that I hav*]e related any thing to your honnor which is not tr[u] to my be[*st understanding, I am wil*]]ling your graunt into me shall be of none efect: [*wherefore, I*]] besech youe be not out of charrity with me.

The deeds I [*desi*]er [*to b*]e recorded and graunted are these folloing.

bought of [*france*]s Us[*elt*]on and Lying in the town on martins vineyard now Called Edge[*rtow*]n b[*arin*]g date november the 30: 1667 and a tru coppy out of the toun record[*s*] by phillip watson Clark September 20: 1675.

[bou]ght of william pebo[*di*]e of duxbury who was the man that purchesed [*Tis*]bury of which I ha[*d*] a former graunt and I tooke posesion and [   ]lt and dwelt theron [*th*]ree years before he gave me this dede
[   ]te november 20th 1673

[   ] Jude the s[*o*]nne of Moses (the premises) the deede [   ]
[   ]the thirtie day of August 1674: and acknowledged [   ]
[*a magistra*]t or Asistant August 10: 1675.

[*bought of*] Josias the Indian sachem of tabymmy the deede bareing [*date*] november 10:1674.

[ ] I besech your honnor to pardon me and grant me a remitance [   ]e fine layd on me by the authority at martins vineyard for sum [   ]est in the tim of the duch: for which I besech your honnor Let your [*pard*]oning

---

* *NYSHAR* has "unprofitable," which seems unlikely from the context, as well as being too long to fit in the gap.

marcy bow my heart in all prayer for the Long and [*hap*]py Life of your
honnor heere and Life everlasting Amen.

[   ] [1]675   from your honnors
                                                most obeadiant sarvant

                                                Simon Athearn

[ENDORSED:]   [   ]
                     of Mar[   ]
                     Petition.

[24:105]

[DRAFT OF A LETTER FROM GOVERNOR ANDROS AT DELAWARE,
APOLOGIZING FOR NOT VISITING LORD BALTIMORE]

Right Honorable.

I have received sometime before my comming from New Yorke, your
very obliging Letter, for the which I should have sooner returned you (as
I now doe) my acknowledgment and thankes, but that it mentioned your
Intent of suddenly departing for Engl.;* I should thinke myselfe Very
happy of the honor you intim[ ] of seeing you at N.Y. and am sorry my
extraordinary occasions of going to the severall parts of the Government
will not admit my now waiting on you at St. Maryes, to assure you
myselfe of the sense I have of your Civilitye and my Inclinacion to serve
you.‡ I have beene the more hastned to this place, by the neighbouring
Indyans rudenesse with the Christians of whom they killed 2 in the dutch
time and since some Cattle in a more publick manner then ordinary and
gave great Apprehension of greater disorders, if not open warre. All
which I hope is now remedied; I have setled all publick Concernes here
and give in Particular orders to the Magistrates and officers of this River
and Bay, that they bee very carefull, that they and all others in their
severall precincts comport themselves and keepe that due and friendly
correspondence as they ought with their Neighbors in your province, Not
doubting (which I pray that you'l give like fitting Orders to those of yours
who border upon his R. Hs. Government: I am now hastening away for

* The following was canceled: "which resolution I heare by Mr. Ward you have alter'd; I
should bee glad if my occasions would admit of my Jo . . ."
‡ The following was canceled: "but the late changes of Government in these parts obliges
me to goe to the severall parts of the Government for the resetlement of affayres, which I
have now done for this river and Bay."

N.Y. in order to my goeing up to Alb:, But where ever I am, shall be ready to receive your Commands, Remaining

Right Honorable

For his Excellence Charles Calvert
Esqr. Go. and C. Generall of
Maryland at St. Maryes.
May 15. 1675.

[ENDORSED:]   no. 34
                Copy of a Lettre to my Lord
                Baltimore.
                May 15. 1675.

[24:106]

[PETITION OF GEORGE MORE TO ADMINISTER THE ESTATE OF THOMAS LANE]

To the Right Ho[   ]ajo[   ]ond Andros capt. Generall of all his Royall Highness his territories in America and governor of new Yorke.

The petition of George More

Humble sheweth

That whereas your petitioner was by verball will made heire of som small estate of Mr. Tho Lane deceased as by wittness can be made appeare, upon whose account and in Concideration thereoff Your petitioner hath all reddy paid severall debts of the Decesed, and requesting of the Justices of newcastle priveledge of administring on his estate here in this River was denyed insomuch that your petitioner is Destitute of regaining his Disburstments, Your petitioner humble Craves of your Honor and this Honorable Court to grant him a letter of adminisstration that so he may take posession of whatt is freely given to him

And your petitioner shall for your
Honor Ever pray as in Duty bound.

[ENDORSED:]   George Moores
                Petition about Mr.
                Lanes Estate.
                For Administracion.

Graunted.
May 1675.

[24:107]

[DEED FROM THE MAGISTRATES AT ALBANY TO ADRIAEN GERRITSZ
FOR A LOT IN THE CITY. TRANSLATION]

Copy.

The lords commissioners of Albany, Colony of Renselaers Wyck and
Schanhechtade hereby declare to cede, transport, and convey in rightful,
true, and free ownership to and for the behoof of Mr. Adriaen Gerritsen
a certain lot located and situated in Albany near the plain within the city's
stockade between the lots of Messrs. Slichtenhorst and Rut Aertsen on
the east side of the street, and on the west side facing the street it is three
rods and nine feet wide, on the north by Rut Aertsen it is nine rods and
one foot long, in the back against the other street on the east it is thirty-
six feet wide, on the south side it runs from the front street to the back
street; and that free and unencumbered without they, the grantors, having
the least claim thereon any longer, and acknowledging that they have
been fully paid and satisfied for it, giving full authority for it to the
aforesaid Adriaen Gerritsen, his heirs and offspring, or those who afterwards may receive his right and title, to do and dispose of the aforesaid
lot as he might do with his other patrimonial goods and effects, hereby
granting him permission to petition the right honorable lord governor
general for a patent. Thus done by the honorable magistrates in Albany
on this 27th of May 1675.

Was signed:

Jacob Schermerhoorn
A. Teller

Agrees with the original in the
protocol.

Acknowledged by me
Johannes Provoost, Secretary.

[ENDORSED:]*   Right Honorable. Wt. your Leave
                     These are to Certify that I was
                     Present when Adrian Gerritse
                     bought the Erff‡ from the
                     Commissaries mentiond
                     one the other side, as wittness
                     my hand in Alb.
                     this 17th August 1676

                                          Silvr: Salisbury

                     A Transport to Adrian Gerritse.
                     and Certificate from Capt. Salisbury.

                         Aug. 17. 1677.

                     A Patent for Mr. Peter Jacobs.

[ENDORSED:]†   Transport from
                     Adriaen Gerritsen

[24:108]

[PROCEEDINGS IN THE SUIT OF JOSEPH TOWNSEND AGAINST
JOHN FOXHALL]

At an Especiall Court held on Thursday 27o May, in the 27o yeare of his
Majesties Reigne 1675.

John Rider and)   Attorneys for Joseph Townsend of
John Robinson)   Boston Plt.

John Foxhall Deft.

They produce a lettre of Att: empowering of them and put in a declaracion
in 337 £ 4 sh 5 d.

They proceed to prove their declaracion by an account sworne to before
Go: Leveret. Mr. Cooke Att.

---

*   Endorsed in English.
‡   Dutch for "premises" or "building lot."
†   Endorsed in Dutch.

The deft. by Mr. Leet produces the Judgment of a Court in Virginia against the plt. for 28000 wt. Tobacco and 3000 some hundred wt. of sugar etc.

After Long debate it was referred to a Jury, who brought in their Verdict for the plt., etc.

The Court gave Judgment accordingly.

[ENDORSED:]   At a speciall Court of
                Mayor and Aldermen.
                May 27. 1675.
                John Townsend ⎞
                per Mr. Rider etc. ⎠   plt.

                John Foxhall deft.

[24:109]

[LETTER TO GOVERNOR LEVERETT CONCERNING A DESERTER]

New Yorck the 2d of June 1675

Sir

Where I left all very well setled At my returne from Delawarr I have receav'd yours of the 21th aprill and thanck you for your obligin favor in securing upon so great a suspition john Dobree a soldier of this Garrison, whou thou nott otherwayes guilty did runn away which if sufer'd in them, or others, would very much incourage, all idle and loose poeple, to the prejudice of all colonys, I therefore pray he be sent back I shal be ready Always to make you a sutable returne and further to serve you in whatt else may be in my power I am

                        Sir

                                Your most humble servant.

To Go. Leveret*

---

* The closing and address were added by Secretary Nicolls. The rest of the letter appears to have been written by Governor Andros.

[ENDORSED:]   Copie of a Letter
                     from the Go: to
                     Go: Leverett.

                     June 2. 1675.

[24:110]

[JUDGMENT AND BILL OF COSTS IN THE SUIT OF MICHAL SPICER,
          WIDOW, AGAINST ROBERT COE]

                              Att a Court of sessions Held att Jam[   ]
                              For the north Rydeing of Yorks[   ]
                              on Long Island by his Majesties Au[   ]
                              rity begining on Tuesday the 8th d[   ]
                              of June in the 27th yeare of his
                              Majesties Reigne Annoque Domini
                              1675.

Michall Spicer widd. Plt.
Mr. Robt. Coe. Defendt.

The Plt. Demands Payment of three Bills under the hand of the Deft.
produced in Court, amounting to the sume of 5£ 1 sh 0 d the which were
allowed of by the said Deft. as Sherriffe, for publique Expences att the
Courts of Sessions for the West Rideing att Gravesend the same being
fully debated in Court and reffered to a Jury they Braught in their verdict
for the plt. The Court Agree with the verdict of the Jury and give
Judgment accordingly. Only That the Plt. Discount for what she hath
received, The Deft. to pay Costs of Suite.

                              By Order of the Court etc.

                              John West Cl. sess:

Ent. Accion and sum	00: 05: 00
fil.. declaracion	00: 01: 00
Coppy	00: 01: 00
Sherriffes fees	00: 06: 00
Cryer and Marshall	00: 01: 10
Enter Judgment	00: 03: 00
Coppy to the plt.	00: 01: 06
to the Deft.	00: 01: 06
Jury	01: 04: 06
Publique charge	00: 10: 00
	02: 15: 04

[ENDORSED:]   Coppy Judgment
Spycer ads. Coe
Sessions. Jamaica.
June 1675.

Judgment
Spicer)   Jamaica
vs.   }   Sessions
Coe.)

[24:111]

[MINUTES OF THE COURT OF SESSIONS AT JAMAICA]

Tuesday

At a court of Ses[sions] [   ] Jamaica
beginning June 8th 1675.

Present
Secr . Nicolls
C. Brockles
C. Salisbury high sheriffe
Mr. R. Coe
Mr. R. Cornell.
Mr. John Pell — ab:

The Court called over.

The Causes also called over, but [   ]
pretence of mistake of the day [   ]
till to morrow morning 7 a [   ]

The Constable being called few [   ]
and few of the plts. or defts.

Wednesday.

Wed. June 9. 1675.

[   ] appeared.

The New Constable called upon to bee sworne.

Mr. Cornell excepts against Simon Seryon chosen for Hempsteed, for abusive Language given him for sending his warrant for horses for C. Barton and C. Brockles etc.

Mr. Jackson the old Constable declares upon Oath very ill Language against the Justice.

Its look't upon to bee cause of Exception, and hee is ordered to bee presented for it.

A warrant to bee sent for James Pine, John Williams and Richd Gildersleives wife, to bee here with Sim. Seryon tomorrow morning.

Joseph Thurston complaynes against Humphrey Underhill striking him etc.
ordered to bee brought by the Constable before the Go.

New Constable for Jamaica Sam. Smith, Joseph Thorne for Oysterbay. Nath. Cole.
They are sworne.

A proclamacion and [   ] Councell read.

ordered to bee sett up.

John Sharpe Plt.
Robert Coe Deft.

The plt. putts in a declarac[   ] upon a bill of 18£ and an acc[   ] of 11£

The Deft. makes answer by [   ] of mouth.
The bill of 18£ was fo[   ] boy hee tooke out of prison.
Hee saith hee paid a Cow at 4£ 1[   ] Oxe at 8£ beefe at 4£ a ho[ ] at 3£ 5sh. 0 d.

The plt. alleadges what hee received was for Countrey Rate Exp. at the Assizes etc.

The account read etc.

[   ]ed that the Plt. mend his [   ]count and give it the Deft. for per[   ]all till tomorrow morne.

Micah Spicer Plt.
Mr. Robert Coe Deft.

The pltf. by Mr. Sharpe her Att. for moneys upon bills for sessions Charges.

The bills produced. 51£ 1 sh. 0 d.

The deft. alleadges that part is paid, hee deferrs to Mr. Smiths booke, That he paid Mr. Wells debt in his Sheriffalty, and expected C. Manning should doe the like.

To bee referred to a Jury.

Wm. Hallett plt.
Joseph Thorne deft.

Mr. Leet desires it may bee put off till afternoone.

Tho. Hunt jun[   ]
John Nappier[   ]

The plt. putts in his de[   ] by Mr. Leet, for Trespasse etc.

Wittnesses sworne.

Tho Wandall.
John Jefford
Peter Upton

Its about firing the Woo[   ]ing the plts. fence by which mea[   ]
Corne was spoyled.

The deft. by Mr. Cooke is w[   ] pay for the fence, but no da[   ]

Mr. Tho: Laurence senior declar [   ] have view'd the Ground where
th[   ] was and saith it is much damifyed.
Hee and John Forgeson sworne.
John Forgeson and John Jeffor[ ] say 26 Rod of Fence was burn[   ] as
to the damage they cannot judge.

Peter Tysen saith The Hoggs came in after the fence was made up, but
they gott not in at the New fence, That it was [   ] 16 May when the
Hoggs [   ] when hee was with Mr. Leet [   ]ford.

John Meeker sworne for the deft. saith The fence was up before the Indy:
Corne was planted.
That Tho: Hunt told him upon his asking why leet let the Hoggs bee in
his Corne, hee said hee left them there to eate up the weeds out of the
Corne.

The Plt. saith hee said Now they have eate up the Corne, they may eat
up the weeds.

Mr. Rich: Corn[   ]
Mr. Wm. Laurance [   ]

Mr. Richard Osburne [   ]

The buisnesse to bee hea[   ] the afternoone.

Tho: Crump Plt.
Wm. Foster Deft.

The plt. by Mr. Cooke putts in an [   ] Declaracion To the w[   ]
Leet demurrs.

The plt. is ordered to mend [   ] declaracion and to bee heard in the afternoone.

John Coomes Plt.
Dr. Taylour Deft.

Declares upon a Judgment of the last Court.
To bee heard in the afternoone when. Dr. Taylour is desired to appeare.

The Court adjourne.

Afternoone.

A Peticion of acknowledgment from Simon Seryon.

It's admitted.

Hee is sworne Const.

C. Ponton of W. chester excepted against as Const. last yeare.

A New Election ordered for W: chester and the like for Eastchester.

The wid: of Edw. Farington—Dorothy—enters into a Recognizance of 100£ to performe the will of her husband whereof shee is Executrix.

The Will brought in to day.

To bee proved to morrow, *viva voce.*

The Jury bring in their Verdict,
In the Case of

Micah Spicer Plt.
Mr. Robert Coe Deft.

They bring in for the plt. ordered to be recorded.

In the case of

Tho Hunt, junior [   ]
John Nappier Deft.

They find for the plt. vizt. 30£ damages—and Costs.

Ordered to be recorded.

Tho. Hunt Junior plt.
John Richardsen Deft.

The plt. by Mr. Leet pu[   ] declaracion for Trespasse [   ] wayes
over his Land.

The deft. by Mr. Cooke pleads [   ] Guilty.
The plts. proceed to prove th[   ]claracion.

C. Tho: Laurance
Tho: Hunt Senior
John Forgeson   sworne
Peter Tysen

Tho: Laurence saith hee was an Arbitrator to end the difference about a
highway 6 yeares agoe [   ]t was not attended, This the [   ]ly now is
over the plts. Meado[ ]

Tho: Hunt sends to the last and then the defts. cattle have beene seen By
him upon the plts. land.

John Forgeson speaketh to another high way said to bee appointed, but
not attended that hee hath seene the defts. Oxen and Cattle upon the plts.
land—Meadow, and Upland.

Peter Tysen, That the highway is through The Defts. land and that the
highway appointed by the 4 men is not attended.

That hee hath seene the defts. working Cattle upon the plts. land, and
supposes were turned in there being barres.

Mr. Cooke Att. for the deft.

The deft. pleads.
The Arbitracion to bee Stood to under penalty of 30£.

Referred to a Jury.

Thomas Crum[   ]
Wm. Foster[   ]

The Plt. putts in a declaracion by Mr. Cooke Att. Its about a servant.

An idle suite. Plt. to pay Costs.

William Hallet Plt.
Joseph Thorne Deft.

The Plt. Complaines against the De[   ] for detaininge his wife etc.

Not admitted by reason of the orders etc. past.

Mr. Leete moves for Appeale.

Ordered to be entred and the Go. to bee moved therein.

Susannah Hallet moved to have execution etc.

To bee considered.

A Peticion from John Archer about two cowes taken away by C. Coe, for which hee had Judgment and Execucion. Ordered In regard [   ] Coe lives in another Rid[   ] that it bee referr'd hither.

Wm. Creeds Peticion as Att. to P: Smith for a debt cast in Court in the time of the Dutch. The debt agreed upon. The Charges to bee considered.

John Coomes
Dr. Taylour

Execucion granted to be leveyed if any of N. Davis can bee found to make it good.

In the Case betweene
Tho: Hunt Plt.
John Richardson Deft.

The Jury find for the plt. with 1 sh damage and Costs of suite.

The Court adjourne till tomorrow 8 a Clock.

June 10

The Will of [   ] proved by Joh[   ]

Dorothy the wid: entr[   ]nizance of 100£ to performe t[   ]

To bee recommended to the Go. fo[   ] of Amd:

The Case of
John Sharpe Plt.
Robt. Coe Deft.

Taken ag[   ]ine into Consideracion as ordered yesterday and recommended to the Jury.

Richard Smith Pltf.
Jeremiah Wood Deft.

No declaracion in, so not according to Rules of Court. Mr. leete and Mr. Cooke Att. per Plt.
Mr. Sharpe Per Deft.
The Case already decided in the Dutch Government, so being under the notion of the Go. Pro. for legall Judiciall Proceedings not fitt for the Court to take Cognizance of.

June 10. 1675.

The Oysterbay buisnesse of Rich. Crab and his wife, and their son Gideon, Left to this Sessions.
The Security given for division of the Estate according to Law. Time to bee given for the Debts to be made appeare, which ought to bee authentickely proved.
Alice Crab to have her owne Goods, and Gideon no more then can bee proved to bee Hanahs.

The Commissions to bee delivered: and somewhat said to C. Ponton and those of Westchester.

To speake about the Proclamacion for the Fast, and other Orders of Councell, with some Order of Court about Church and Church affaires.

Mrs. Waters buisnesse.
The Judgment of Court to bee read off; The Trainings to bee publisht.

Joseph Thurstans C[   ] Humphry Und[   ] to be called upon.

Fr. Bloodgood   )
Meyndert Coert   } bound over

Dr. Taylours Complaint against Meynder[ ]

The Westchester mens Custome of [   ]tion

Richard Osburne
Mr. Richard Cornell)
C. Wm Laurence   }

About Roger Townesends Will etc. ordered by the Go. to bee adjudged.

Mr. Leet Att. for R. Osburne produ[   ] a deed made betweene Roger
Townes[ ] deceased and his wife, wherein hee engaged himselfe not to
dispose of any of the Estate from his wife etc. at his decease.

Mr. R. Cornell and Mr. W: La[ ]ren[   ] produce the will, wherein hee
m[   ] them Overseers and disposes to the [   ] Patent land etc. upon
Consider[   ] 60£ to her 3 sons.

To bee considered of by t[   ] the validity of Agreement and Will.

The Peticion of Wright and Townesend Etc.
To bee considered of by the bench for an agreement.

William Foster, and the 2 oth[   ]seers, Mr. Doughty and Mr.Wolls[ ]
Th[ ]mas Fosters Will, for the use of the Children. Recommended by
the Go: to this Court.
The Overseers desire an Account may b[ ] given to the Court of the
former Trust of the Will:

John Sharp Plt.
Mr. R. Coe Deft.

The Jury bring in their Verdict for the Plt. and that the deft. shall pay
what is due and shall appeare to bee due by bill and upon ballance of
acc[   ] and Cost of suite.

A Complaint brought in by Mr. Doughty and [   ] Waters against Mr. Coe
about a bill of 8£ 4 sh. 0 d. per the which hee had Mr. Delavalls bill of

Credit for Mr. Waters [   ] part of 9£ due from Mr. Ely: Doughty to Mr. Coe, for which hee had Mr. Doughtyes note for 9£ and another of double with Mr. Waters.

Its ordered that Anthony Waters wife have Credit for the 8£ 4 sh. 0 d. and Mr. Doughty to pay Mr. Coe the other 16£ so to have up his two bills.

The Trustees of the [ ]hildren [   ] Forster bring in their account ac[   ]ding to the Go: order by Wm. Foster etc.

Joseph Thurston produces Lettres of Administracion for himselfe and wife who is the Mother. Hee owes for the lettre of Adm.

The Court adjourne till 2 a Clock.

Afternoone.

June 10. 1675.

Francis Bloodgood
Meyndert [   ]dert
No Complaint [ ]ppearing since against them they [   ] dismist, and to have their bonds [   ]d.

The order of Court about a new Election of Const. at W: Chester and a Dep: a[ ] Eastchester.

I ratled [   ]ntors before the Court for their abuse [   ] Election.
Mr. Pells pr[ ]sentment of E. chester about fences. [   ] Persons to view and order the best way of [   ]curing both sides.

The orders and Judgment of Court read.

Our opinion upon the Case of Richard Osburne and Mr. Cornell and C: W: Laurence to acquaint the Go. with it.

Gideon Wright his bro: sister and Mothers matter about the Administracion etc. taken into consideracion.[*]

---

[*] Apparently a final page has been lost. There should be a resolution to this case, and the court dissolved.

[ENDORSED:]   Jamaica Sessions
June 8, 1675

[24:112]

[PROCEEDINGS IN THE SUIT OF JOHN SHARPE AGAINST
NATHANIEL BRITTAINE]

At a court of Sessions held att Gravesend for the West
Rydeing of Yorkeshire on Long Island by his Majesties
Authority on Tuesday the 15 day of June in the 27 yeare of
his Majesties Reigne Annoque Domini 1675.

Between John Sharpe   Plt.
Nathaniel Brittaine Deft.

The matter recommended to this Court by his Honor the Governor to be
heard in Equity, between John Sharpe formerly Plt. in this Court and
Nathaniel Brittaine Deft. where the Deft. was then Cast. The Court
haveing heard the same fully debated on both Parts togather with all the
new proofes or Allegacions of the Deft. they Cannot find but the Bargaine
and Agreement betwee[   ] Deft. for the servant in quecion
was a Re[   ] Bargaine and agreement neither doth it appeare that the
Deft. hath Lost the said Servant, any wayes Through the Defect Neglect
or other meanes of the Plts. They doe therefore Order and Decree for the
plt. but in regard of the reall Losse the Deft. hath susteyned by the running
away of the said Servant and his detention by other Persons which
Probably occasioned the same They doe Decree that time be given for
payment of the sume Contracted for and Charges the one Moyety or halfe
to be payed att the next killing time, and the other Moyety in the month
of March next ensueing.

By Order of the Court etc.
John West Cl. sess:

Sharpe   ⎞   Decres all
Brittaine ⎠   Order

Gravesend 1675
Kings County*

---

* Added after the counties were formed in 1683.

[24:113]

[CALENDAR OF THE COURT OF SESSIONS AT GRAVESEND]

June 1675   Att a Court of Sessions held att Gravesend beginning on Tuesday the 15 of the said Month.

Justices Present   Mr. Rich Betts one of his Majesties Justices etc.

present—   Mr. James Hubbard one of his Majesties Justices etc.
Capt. Elbert Elbertson one of his Majesties etc.
Capt. Jaques Cotilliou one of his Majesties Justices etc.

[ ]staffe*
none
the Conste-
able of

{ N. Towne
   Boswyck
   Breucklyn
   Flatbush   noe staffe
   Flat Lands
x Gravesend
   New Utrecht   noe staffe
   Stat. Island

The names of the Jurors [ ] the said sessions
Richard Stillwell
Thomas Wandall
Sam: Holmes
Peter Simpson
Wm Cumphen
Ralph Hunt
Rich: Doddyman
Ralph Wardner
Nath: Whittman
Tho. Stevens

---

* Each constable was expected to present his staff of office upon arrival at court and could be fined for forgetting it.

Accions to be tryed att the said Court as followes,

Agreed	1	Robt. Hollis	Plt.
		Lambert Durlan Jansen	Deft
	2.x	Tunis Dircksen	Plt.
		Annica De Bruis	Deft.
	3.x	Albert Cornelissen	Plt.
		Tys Barents van Lerdan	Deft.
	4 x	Patrick Dowdall	Plt.
		John Boys	Deft.
	5.	John Sharpe	Plt.
		Capt. Jno Manning	Deft.
	6.x	George Wood	Plt.
		Richard Fidoo	Deft.
	x	John Ryder	Plt.
		Garrett Stophelson	Deft.
	7.x	Capt. Tho: Laurence	Plt.
		Cornelis Mattys	Deft.
Agreed	8.	John Robinson	Plt.
		Andries Jurianson	Deft.
	9.x	John Kingdome	Plt.
		Peter Belleiu	Deft.
	10.x	Jacobus Deharte	Plt.
		Minnie Johnson	Deft.
Agreed	11.	The same	Plt.
		Dirck Storme	Deft.
	12.	Laurence Peterson	Plt.
		Hanse Christoffleson	Deft.
agreed	13.	The same	Plt.
		Minnie Johnson	Deft.

14.x	Matthias Deharte	Plt.
	Titus Syrux	Deft.
15.x	The same	Plt.
	John Rowleffson }	Defts.
	Minne Johnson }	
16.x	Nath: Whitman	Plt.
	Jacob de yonge	Deft.
17.x	Ralph Cardiff	Plt.
	Wm Janson van Berkloo	Deft.
18.x	Richard Feyday	Plt.
	George Wood	Deft.
19.x	Engleca Burgers wid	Plt.
	Katherine Hegamen wid	Deft.
20.x	Mr. Justice Betts in the behalfe of the Inhabitants of Mackbeth Kills }	Plt.
	The Towne of Flatbush	Defts.
21.x	Dirck Jansen	Plt.
	Cryne Jansen	Deft.

Complaints {

	Thomas Loulis	Plt.
	Thomas Walto	Deft.
x	John Archer Contra. Capt. Jo. Coe.	
Agreed x	Nath. Britton	Plt.
	Thomas Walton	Deft.
	George Wood	Plt.
Agreed	Josias Ferman	Deft.
Agreed	Ralph Doxey	Plt.
	Jonathan Shrickland	Deft.

x Presentment	Cornelis Coursen	Plt.
	Adam Brower	Deft.

x Complaint	Elias Doughty	Plt.
	Geo: Wood	Deft.
Complaint	Arson Con. Wardner	

| x | Fardinando Van Sickland for a Lycence | |

Pettcon Askew Con. Scott

| Complaint | Stevens con. Inhabitants N. towne | |

| Peticion | Thomas Stevens | |

| Complaint | The towne of Gravesend | Plts. |
| | John Spanieson | Deft. |

| Complaint | Constable and Overseers Gravesend | Plts. |
| | John Griggs | Deft. |

| Complaint | Bardus Juresson P[ ] | |
| | Peter Simpson   Deft. | |

| Complaint | Constable and Overseers Gravesend | Plts. |
| | Peter Simpson Deft. | |

[ENDORSED:]   Dockett for
Gravesend.
1675

[24:114]

At a Court of Sessions held at Gravesend, begun the 15th day of June 1675.

The bench called.
The Const. called. 4 with staves. 4 without—Newtowne neglected, Flattbush, N. Utrecht burn't, Boswyck had none.

New Const. called.
No returne from Newtowne, the same being chosen, and had not notice of a new Election.

The Overseers of the severall Townes sworne, two onely wanting one of Breucklyn—t'other in the place of Auke Jansen.

A Jury sworne for all the Causes.

The Proclamacion and orders of Councell read.

The Causes called over.

John Sharpe
Nath. Brittaine.

The plt. moves by Mr. Leet for Judgment as of last Court; the deft. neglecting to attend the order of Councell to bee heard in Equity, Mr. Cooke his Att. suggests this Court not capable of hearing in Equity. That being over = ruled it is order'd to bee heard in Equity after the first Jury cause to bee gone out upon.

Mattys D'Haart Plt.
Titus Serix Deft.

Judgment by Consent onely with Cost.

agreed

Teunis Dircks Plt.
Annica de Bruyn Deft.

Ralph Cardall Plt.
Wm Jansen Van Berkleu Deft.

The Plt. hath a bill of his hand for 491 G.
Judgment of Court already for it.
June 21. 1671.

Execution graunted upon the former Judgment; with deduction for what is paid.

Inter. since that Judgment to bee considered of.

The Court adjourned till tomorrow. 7 a Clock in the morning.

Unruly horses complained of at New Utrecht etc. proposed that all horses out of the rates to bee confiscated by C. Betts.

To bee considered of.

June 16th 1675.

George Wood Plt.
Richard Fido Deft.

The Declaracion of the plt. put in. It was of Trespasse, but no summe whereupon Mr. Rider Att. for the Deft. moved for a Non=Suite.

Richard Fido Plt.
George Wood Deft.

The declaracion of the plt. upon Trespasse on the Case, and assault—so desires Costs and that the deft. may bee bound to the peace.

Both declaracions agreed to bee mended so to joyne issue.

The first Cause first to bee tryde.

Abrah : Frost ⎫
Tho: Sherman ⎬ sworne

The first to an Agreement about a fence, the other to the Defts. forewarning the plts. setting up the fence according to the Agreement.

John Firman ⎫
Tho: Petit ⎬ sworne

They declare to an Agreement which was drawne up in writing, but refused afterward by Geo: Wood.

Mr. El: Doughty ⎫
Mt. Gershom Moore ⎬ declare
Mr. Robert Field ⎭
to the Agreement.

The 2d Cause about the Assault, The Deft. pleads not Guilty.
Esther Gleene ⎫ sworne before
Hanah Petit ⎬ Justice Betts

Declare in Court their sight of The Assault.

Both referr'd to a Jury.

A Presentment brought in to the Court of reviling words against mee[*] and Mr. Betts.

The first some yeares agoe, so past by.
The latter about belyeing Justice Betts about a Riplevin.

Hee is likewise called in Question by presentment, about selling an Oxe that was none of his owne.

Its very suspicious.
To bee consider'd of by the Court.

A complaint against Tho: Sherman.
An order upon it.

agreed	Laurence Peterson Plt. Hans Christoflesen deft.
agreed	The same plt. Minne Johannes deft.
Non=suited	Jacobus D'Haart plt. Minne Johannes deft.

The Jury find for the Deft. the last Agreement to stand good.

In the next Cause of Assault, They find for the plt.

The Verdicts ordered to bee entred.

Capt. Tho. Laurence Plt.
Niels Mattys Deft.

The Plt. putts in a Declaracion by Mr. Leete and Mr. Cooke his Att. which they proceede to prove;
Tho: Etherington sworne saith that being desirous to goe over to Harlem, from the defts. plantacion, Hee told him, now C. Tho: Laurence must sett people over for hee had sold his land, with divers other Circumstances.

A deposicion of Joris Janse about the sale.

---

* Presumably Matthias Nicolls, since the document is in his hand.

A deposicion of Jan Forgeson to the same purpose.

Another deposicion from Henry Brookes sworne at New London.

The deft. bought other Land of Tho: Lewis, before hee sold this.

The deposicions are most of what was declared out of the Defts. mouth.

The Deft. by Mr. Allard Anthony putts in an Answer, and some Attestacions.

Referred to a Jury.

Alb: Cornelissen
Tys Barents Van Leerdan.

The Plt. declares upon a bill of 202 G.
It being an old Case, wherein John Kingdome, and Sim: Jans. Rom: are concern'd, the former having Judgment and latter found Tar[ ], about Counterfeiting a Release of Younker Voschs.
This to have Judgment against the deft. and John Kingdome to bee paid by Sim: Jans. This the Courts Judgment.

To adjourne till 2 a Clock afternoone.

Afternoone.

C. Tho: Laurence Plt.
Niels Mattys Deft.

The Jury bring in their Verdict for the Plt., Vizt that it was a Bargaine.

Ordered to bee entred.

Mr. Justice Betts etc. on behalfe }
of the Inhabitants of Mashp: Kills. }   Plts.
The Inhabitants of Flattbush   Defts.

The Plts. by Mr. Leet and Mr. Sharpe Att. put in their declaracions.

The Defts. pretend not to have the Decl. time enough, the Clarke being absent when they came for it.

Tho : Petit
Rich Fido
Tho: Wandall   } sworne
Henry Johnson
Gersham Moore

Mr. Wandall saith That about 14 yeares agoe, the Plts. hired and bought of the Indyans the Land in question and enjoyed it quietly severall yeares and never heard to the contrary till of late.

Richard Fido was about 14 yeares agoe at the laying it out and declare as before.

Tho: Petitt, to the same, and that hee mowed there for Mr. Betts.

Mr. Ger: Moore, not at the laying the land out being then very young but that they have possest it quietly 12 or 14 yeares.

Henry Johnson, was there when hee lived with C. Betts about 14 yeares agoe, as his Master bought the land in question of the Indyans and payd for it.

the Indyan deeds read. Recorded in 1664 2 bills of sale.

Go: Stuyvesants Patent.

some of the Plts. have had Patents under Go: Nicolls, as Anth: Gleene etc.

A Patent engrossed to bee signed by Go: Lovelace a litle before the aleracion of Go: Certified by mee.[*]

John Hansen sworne as to the bounds. That hee was there about 4 yeares agoe, when the Indyans were shewing the land they had sold to Flattbush; but it was by accident.

The Defts. plead their purchase and Grant from Go: Lovelace An: 1670.

---

* Here it is more certainly Matthias Nicolls, who was secretary under Lovelace and could certify the authenticity of the document.

Jonathan Hazard ⎫
Sam: Ruscoe   ⎬   sworne
Dan. Whitehead ⎭

Jon: Hazard saith That when the Go: went last to Delaware, hee went to the south to the Indyans, where hee saw them cutt out the Flattbush marke of 0: saying Flattbush had nothing to doe there, and that it was the land within C. Betts bounds. Which hee claymes.

Sam: Ruscoe. one sent by the Town of Jamaica, to view and perambulate their bounds, there was there, C. Betts, and the Indyans, and some of Flattbush, who the Indyans said they had sold nothing to, and finding their 0: upon a Tree, which they cutt out.

Dan. Whitehead—at the same time there from Jamaica, when the Indyans said the land did neither belong to Flattbush nor Capt. Betts.

The tresspasse was forewarning C. Betts and the rest from making use of this Ground; firing the Meadowes and burning their stacks of Hay: severall times. Once in January fired, scorched their cattle and spoyl'd them.

Committed to a Jury after Collection and recitall of the passages.

Matthias de Haart Plt.
John Roeloffsen ⎫
Minne Johannes ⎬   defts.

Judgment against both.

Angleke Burgers pltf.
Catharina Heggeman deft.

Its about a Vendue, John Parsell alias Butcher bought, hath paid 3200– G 900—or thereabout behind.

Angleke Burgers Judgment against Cath: Heggeman, and Cath: Heggeman against Butcher: The last in fault to pay the Charge

Upon payment a good title to bee made for all the Bowery.

Complaint   Patrick Dowdall plt.
                             Jan Buys deft.

About 2 Cowes and a young Calfe

To bee delivered back and 50 s hyre.

A Presentment

The Constable of Breucklyn.
Adam Brower

To bee considered of.

A Complaint.
John Archer ⎫
John Coe   ⎬   About a pair of Oxen
pretended to bee delivered to Dennis Holdren, and Dennis Holdren saith
hee delivered them back to John Archer by whose order hee received
them.
John Coe pleads hee disobey'd no order of Court or Go.

Ordered John Coe to give bond of 40£ to answer it or make it appeare at
the Assizes.

Dennis Holdren in 20£ he made it good.

C. Betts etc. Plt.
Flattbush   Defts.

The Jury find for the Plts.

John Kingdome Pltf.
Peter Billieu Deft.

About 2 Cowes and a Steere taken of the plt., by the deft.

The deft. saith hee did it by Authority.

Dan: Stillwell sworne saith that hee was by John Kingdoms yard, and
saw the deft., goe in and drive out the 2 Cowes and steere or yeareling.

That hee knew them to belong to the plt. for about 2 yeares.

Obediah Holmes sworne saith his knowledge, and relates the whole story.

Mr. Ogden principally concern'd desires by Fr: Barber, the cause bee remitted till next Court. The which was allowed.

Nathan Whittman Plt.
Jaques Guyon Deft.

An Action of Trespasse.

Geo: Cummins
John Kingdome } sworne.
Louis Lackman.

Geo: Cummins saith that hee saw the Deft. take downe the barre of his yard and let in his milch Cowes into the Meadowes or point from whence they might goe to the Hay, In meane time his other Cattle bleateing at the Towne fence the which they forced downe.

John Kingdome saith hee hath seene the defts. Cattle there and hath help't drive them out, at which the deft. only laught.

Louis Lackman saith, That an order being made that what Cattle should bee taken in the Meadowes, should bee put in the pound whereupon Regrenier said, if any carryed his Cattle to the Pound, hee would fetch them back with his Gun.

There was afterwards order of 20 G to bee levyed as a fine for every default.

The Deft. pleads, hee never put in his Cattle, without a woman or someone to looke after them.

That the towne fence is defective.

Its alleadged none trespasse but the Defts. Cattle.

Its referred to a Jury 3 Jury men being alter'd.

The Court adjourned till tomorrow morning.

Thursday morne.
June 17. 1675.

To call upon the Jury for their Verdict.

Nathan Whitman Plt.
Jaques Guyon Deft.

They bring in their Verdict for the plt. 8£ damage and Costs of suite, breach of Town Orders left to the Court.

The verdict to bee entred.

No damage proved.

4£ allowed and 10 sh breach of Towne orders. The publick fence to bee view'd by new Const. and Overseers where defective to bee made good.

The matter of the Cause in difference betweene
John Sharpe Pltf.
Nathaniell Brittaine Deft.

formerly heard in Court here, and now ordered by the Go: to bee heard in Equity.

The Deft. by Mr. Cooke his Att. putts in a Peticion instead of a Bill, with Interrogatories desired upon Oath from the pltf.

It being not the practise of the Government to oblige any to sweare against himselfe, It was over=ruled: but they admitted to bring what new proofes they could.

They proceed to plead—Mr. Leet Att. for Mr. Sharpe.

After pleading on both partes, The bench have ordered to consider and give their Judgment.

Mr. John Sharpe plt.
Capt. John Manning Deft.

The Deft. writte in Excuse, thinking the Isl. not to belong to New Towne. The Go: adjudged it to belong to Newtowne, and gave mee order to grant a summons to this sessions. Mr. Tho: Wandall declares that when Simones the Carrman lived upon the Isl. hee paid Rates to Newtowne, and hee being an Overseer the Corne was brought to his house, which was his part of the Rate. The Court proceede to heare the Cause.

A declaracion put in.
A bill under the plts. hand for 2576 G. 7 st for the publick.

Booke debt. 511 G 19 st.

The pltf. acknowledges to have received a bill of Credit from Go: Lovelace upon the Excise for 1400 G which is to be deducted from the 1st summe.

The bill and booke debt are allowed by the Court, nothing appearing against it, Judgment is desired. To bee taken into Consideracion.

Agreed   Dirck Jansen Plt
                         Rein Jansen Deft.

Mr. Elyas Doughty Pltf.
George Wood Deft.

About a debt under 5£ of John Holden, in his booke. To bee recommended to the Towne Court of N. Towne, to heare and determine If the deft. can prove to have paid any part to bee allowed, and the accounts in the booke to bee allowed, if no just Exceptions against it.

Tho : Case   }
Sam: Scudder }   both to bee bound
to the good behavior in a bond of 40£ a piece, and to appeare at the generall Court of Assizes, to answer to what shall then bee objected against them there.

Two Deposicions sent by Justice Coe from Jamaica about Tho: Case, and Sam: Ruscoes declaracion about hearing the rodes etc. It was in May last about the time of their meeting at Oysterbay. Mr. Tho. Wandall about a scandalous paper directed to Mr. Leveridge signed Sam Scudder.

Sam: Firman bound to the Assizes also in 20£

The Orders and Judgments of Court read And the Court adjourned till afternoone.

Afternoone.

Complaints brought in by the old Const. and Overseers of Gravesend.

Const. and Overseers against Peter Simpson

About Neglect of upholding the Towne Common Fence.

Barent Jurisse Complaynes also against Peter Simpson.

Both ordered to bee view'd and repayred, by the Const. and Overseers and Viewer of the Fences, with the first convenience; and the defaults made good, and fences repaired according to Law, under the same penally.

The towne of Gravesend Complaine against John Hancen about his pulling downe the common fence betweene the Townes, and worrying some Hoggs of the Townes with Dogges upon their owne Ground.
The Agreement between the Towne of Gravesend and De Bruyne to bee observed for the time to come, and the damages to bee enquired after and adjudged by C. Hubbard and C. Jaques as also the damage done to the swine.

Const. and Overseers of Gravesend against John Griggs.
About neglect of Fences and abuse of Const. and Overseers.

The Deft. to pay a fine of five pounds but to bee mitigated to the one halfe, if hee bee submissive, and so adjudged by C. Hubberd, C. Elbert, and C. Jaques, if refractory to bee bound over to the Assizes.

Complaint of John Aertsz against Ralph Warner about the horse that C. Hubbard had. Referr'd to bee examined into and determined by C. Betts, and C. Jaques in 2 months time.

Peticion Askew and Scott about ditching upon Staten Isl.

Ordered to bee paid according to agreement in one Month or Execucion to issue forth against those in default.

Jurors names
Richard Stillwell
Sam: Holmes
Nathan Whitman
Richard Doddyman
Peter Simpson
Wm. Compton
Ralph Hunt.

In the Staten Isl. action changed

Rich. Stillwell
Nath Whitman
Dick Doddyman

For

Thomas Wandall
Thomas Stevens
Ralph Warner.

[ENDORSED:]   Gravesend Sessions
                     June 15–16–
                     1675.

[24:115]

[PROCEEDINGS OF THE MAYOR'S COURT AT NEW YORK]

June 22. 1675

At a Mayors Court.

The Jury sworne.

Mr. Alex. Bryan by C. Nath: Davenport Plt.
Mrs. Eliz: Bedloe   Deft.

The Plt. declares upon an Attachment.

The Deft. demurre that the declaracion is not sufficient, shee being not
named either Executrix, Administratrix etc.

Its the opinion of the Court that shee having acted both in the dutch and
Engl. time as administratrix and disposed of part of her husbands Estate
to pay his debts, shee shall bee look't upon as administratrix, so the
declaracion order'd to bee mended by consent of the Defts. attor. Mr.
Leet and Mr. Cooke.

The plt. put in the account betwixt plt. and deft.

P.D. la Noy sworne—acknowledges the account, but saith Mr. Bedloe
acted for the Go:

The deft. produces Coll: Lovelaces lettre of Att. to act for him etc.

Mr. Elyas Doughty Plt.
Mrs. Eliz: Bedloe   Deft.

The Plt. puts in his declaracion as before the declaracion ordered to bee mended administratrix.

The Deft. puts in her answer and plea by Mr. Cooke and Mr. Leete.

They put the plt. to prove the delivery of the Oxen:

The plt. goes to get proofe.

Mr. Osburne in part about the bargaine.

Mr. Laurens V.D. Spiegle Plt.
Mrs. Eli Bedloo   Deft.

The Plt. puts in his decl. by Mr. West his Att. The account read.

The bookes of Mr. Bedloe to bee viewed.

The Court adjourned till 2 a clock afternoone.

Afternoone the bookes being brought into Court The 3 causes were referr'd to the Jury.

Upon the returne of the Jury

In the Case
Alex: Bryan Plt.
Eliz. Bedloe Deft.

The Jury find per the plt. 129£ 9 sh 6 d. according to the decl. and Attachment.

Elyas Doughty Pltf.
Eliz: Bedloo   Deft.

The Jury find for the deft.
The Court unsatisfyed desire the Jury to goe out againe.

Mr. Laurens V.D. Spiegle Plt.
Eliz: Bedloo   Deft.

The Jury find for the pltf.

[ENDORSED:]   [   ] Mayors Court
                     June 22. 1675.

[24:116]

> At a Court of Mayor and Aldermen etc.
> adjourned to this 24th June 1675.

C. Wm. Dyre on behalfe of his R. Hs. Plt.
Egidius Luyck Deft.

The Plt. by Mr. Leet putts in a declaracion upon 2 bonds, the Copyes attested by mee.

Many accounts produced by the deft. Amongst the rest hee urged the decision of it before in the Dutch Government, confirmed by Go: Colve.

Urges the Go: Proclamacion of legall Judiciall proceedings.

Its Over=ruled—so committed to a Jury.

They brought in their Verdict for the Plt. That the deft. pay 8541 G sewant or value.

The Court adjourned till afternoone.

                     Afternoone.

Judgment Entred in the Jury Actions past.

Mr. Leete on the behalfe of the wid: Bedloe, moves for an Appeale to bee heard in Equity at the Assizes for the 1st 3 accions.

Granted as the law directs.

Nicholas Bayard Plt.
John Rider Deft.

About Dr. Jacob Vervanghers house in the Stone Streete, that was Mary Paulets sold at a Vendu due to Mr. Delavall for Mr. J. Rider. Mr. Delavall gave 5010 G. sewant. Mr. Bayard 4775 G. sewant.

Mr. Rider Credit   5010 G.
for the house.   3407
              due   2613
                          5010

Hughe Barentsz Plt.
Dan: De Haart Deft.

The Jury find for the deft.

[ENDORSED:]   At a Mayors Court
                 June 24. 1675.

[24:117]

[MINUTES OF A VISIT TO THE GOVERNOR OF A PARTY OF
WAPPINGER INDIANS ON AN EMBASSY TO THE
SUSQUEHANNA NATION]

June 28: 1675.

Mawhoscan Sa[ ]h[ ]m of the Wapping Indyans with [   ]f his people
came to give [   ]he [ ]vernor and presenting [   ]
Sewant, by one of his M[   ]h hee is glad to see him,
[   ]s his being Governor Then presen[   ]
Band, declares their Intent t[   ]nor [ ]ke a Peace
between[   ]quehannas Indyans [   ]
Warres his 16 yeares.

Then shewed 24 bands and a round circle of sewant, which they carry
with them as a present.

[   ]ke[   ] of the wapping Indyans being [ ]avest[   ]he
Susquehannas is to have a Passe, and all persons are desired to bee helpe
full to him in putting him over the Rivers, or letting him quarter in their
houses as hee passes along.

Hee is employed [   ]king the P[ ]ce.
This same d[   ]kpoushe the Masapeag [   ] Capt.
Rammurack and d[ ]ds [   ], upon the old Complaint against
[   ] about their lands, that th[   ]heir lands.

The Go: will S[   ] with Hempsteed men about it, and give
[   ] answer in a month or thereabout.

[ENDORSED:]   June 28. 1675.
Indyan Appear[   ]
and visitt.

To be recorded.

Wapping.

[24:118]

[PETITION OF MICHEL HAINELLE TO BE APPOINTED REGISTER OF
HORSES TRANSPORTED FROM LONG ISLAND. TRANSLATION]*

To the High and Powerful Lord, Monseigneur the Governor General in
the name of His Royal Highness James duke of York and Albany and in
all his territories in America—

It is very humbly represented by Michel Hainelle, inhabitant of the town
of Brooklyn, that heretofore, during the time of Governor Lovelace, to
avoid the troubles that sometimes arose in transporting horses out of the
countryside, he had ordered a certain Raeff Waernaer to register the
brand, the notice, the number of horses, and the names of those who
transported or directed the transport of any horses off Long Island, so
that if it should happen that he should lose some horses or that someone
should order to be transported or transport those belonging to another,
one could undertake a search, which the superintendent hopes that
Monseigneur would think a very useful thing to do for the public welfare
and, given the aforementioned Raff Waernaer had no fixed residence or
domicile and as it is an employment that could not be more appropriate
than to a person who lives near the ferry and to him whom Monseigneur
has had the grace to give the appointment of clerk of the Flemish villages
of Long Island—

The superintendent requests Monseigneur most warmly, should it please
him to put a prudent order into the said transport of horses, to be so good
as to accord him the employment of keeping account of the brands and
notices, ordering the owners of the said horses to pay him the regular
wages, and in promising to acquit himself faithfully, he would do what
a good and loyal subject is obliged to do for his lord and in doing this he
will have a new reason to pray to the Almighty for the health and
prosperity of Monseigneur and to be forever

* Translated from the French by Linda J. Pike.

Brooklyn 28 June   His most obedient and faithful
1675 Old Style   servant and subject,
                                 Michel Hainelle

[24:119a]

[LETTER FROM NEW LONDON ANNOUNCING ATTACKS BY
KING PHILIP]

Newlondon June 29: 1675

Yesterday Left:[*] Avery myself and some others went up to Uncas to
understand iff possible we Could, how we stood affected to Phillips
designe he informed us that he heard of much damage done by Phillip,
by killing many English, and burning theire houses But would not be
known that he held any Correspondence with him, but upon Carefull
vew, we have Reason to beleive that most of his men are gone that wa[
] hath very few men att ho[   ] three gunns A mo[
] [   ] hath had great [   ] and many
presen[   ] (that effectuall Cour[   ] parts
into a posture [   ] It is Reported that [   ] [
] Expects farther [   ]

Copye as Subscribed by [   ]an[   ]threll

[ENDORSED:]   Copie of a Lettre from
                   New London about the
                   Indyan Newes
                   June 29. 1675.

[24:119b]

[LETTER FROM JOHN WINTHROP ABOUT THE ATTACKS]

Newlondon June 29 1675.

Sir.

[   ] att Mr. Richards Sm[   ]lett I mett Capt.
Hut[   ]n Boston with [   ]rnor
and Council [   ]enne Craft, and [   ]a,
the Contents [   ]e more particularly [   ]
[   ]ms, which being brought to [   ]ning with the

* lieutenant

said Report of the farther Confirmation of the murthers Committed upon severall English by Phillip; there is preparation for Convayance to your selfe and being something ill myselfe since my Returne, have desired Mr. Witherly what intelligence is passing, to Convay itt:

A coppy as subscribed per J Winthrop

[ENDORSED:]   [   ]py of another
                Letter from New
                [   ]ondon about the In[   ]yans
                Jun. 29 1675

[24:120]

At a speciall Court of Mayor and Aldermen.
June 30th 1675.

Wm. Foresight Plt.
Richd. Hall Deft. upon a Review.

Thomas Johnson
Wm. Disteler   sworne

declare that the Master Conde and Mr. Hall the Masters first and Merchant after, came aboard the ship and calling the Men together told them that those that had in Mind to bee discharged should have their wages.

Edward Williams sworne for the Deft. saith hee heard Mr. Conde say to Mr. Foresight that if hee owed him anything hee might sue him.

Referred to the Jury.

They bring their Verdict for the Plt.
T[   ]rt give Judgment accordingly for the [   ].

[ENDORSED:]   Mayors Court.
                June 30. 1675.

[24:121]

[LETTERS OF THE GOVERNOR TO VARIOUS OTHER GOVERNORS]*

. . . dutyes to bee answered at his or their perills.

You may as you have oppertunityes, (particularly to the Magistrates,) assure all of my acting fairely and candidly as authorized, and of my Inclinations to contribute to my power for their good and of all equall favor in this Government and may hint to them their danger in persisting to act, or countenence others in hi[s] R. Hs territories, without if not contrary to Authority.

You are in your going, stay or returne from thence, to bee very carefull To comport yourselves as you ought, and to give no just Cause of Offence.

You are also to deliver my Letters to Governor Winthrop and Major Winthrop his son (if there) with my service, but in Case Governor Winthrop should bee gone to Boston or elsewhere out of the Colony, you are then to bring back my said Letter, but may send Major Winthrops to New London; I wish you a good Journey and remaine

Yours

E: Andros.

C . Salisburyes
Instructions to bee entred here:
July 2d—the date—

> The Letter from the Go: to the Go: or Dep: Go: and Assistants etc. of Conecticutt and another to Go: Winthrop: the Gov: hath and also the 3d Letter sent by C. Collyer to Go: Dep: Go. etc.

> A Letter from the Go: to Go: Winthrop upon the Indyan Newes.

July 4th 1675.

---

* This duplicates a document in *BGE* 1674–88, pp. 54–58, which has been used to fill gaps. The beginning is a list of instructions to Capt. John Collyer, which appears in the *BGE* copy. The version appearing here consists of pages 5–8 of Matthias Nicolls's copy.

Sir.

This morning about 3 a Clock I received yours of the 1st instant, together with severall Copies of Letters, of the Indyans being in Armes in Plym. Colony, and their having destroyed severall Christians Plans[*] to the Eastward of you as neare as Narrogansett, and apprehension of their tending further to you wards I am very much troubled at the Christians misfortunes and hard disasters in those parts being so over powered by such heathen.

Hereupon I have hastned my comming to your parts and added a force to bee ready to take such Resolucions as may bee fitt for mee upon this extraordinary occasion, with which I intend (God willing) to sett out this Evening, and to make the best of my way to Conecticutt river, his R. Hs bounds there, where at my arrivall you shall heare further from

This was sent in   Sir
post haste from Const.   Your most humble servant
to Const. [‡]   E: Andros

                              A letter to Go: Carteret upon the Indyan
                              Newes: sent July 4. 1675.

Honored Sir:

The severall enclosed Copies came to my hands at 3 a Clock this morning which I thought fitt, as soone as I could to dispatch to you, that you may see the power of, and outrages committed by the Indyans in Plimouth Colony, and as farre as Narrogansett on the Christians, and apprehension of their further proceedings, upon which I have quickened my Voyage that way, and resolve to take a force with me, which I intend (God willing) to embarke this night for Conecticutt River, I am in haste

                              Sir
                              Your humble servant
                              E: A:

---

* Probably an abbreviation for "plantations."
‡ Passed along from one town's constable to another.

A Letter at Saybrooke from the Go: to the Go: or Dep: Go: and Assistants or cheife Magistrates of the Colony of Conecticutt to bee delivered to the cheife of them at Hartford.

July 8, 1675.

Honorable Gent.

I writte to y[ou] at [lar]ge the 28th past by Mr. John Collyer, and a[lso] by another the 4th instant in the morning, by returne of your Express[e] upon your notice of the Indyans Rebellion, and barbarisme, did give you account of my Intent this way and to this place, where I am now arrived, but finding no occasion here upon the Indyan account, I am sending a small vessell further eastward for Intelligence, and do send this by Expresse to you in his Majesties and R. Hs behalfe, to desire your direct and effectuall Answer to my foresaid Lettre which here attend, on discharge of my duty accordingly; In the meane time remaine

Honorable Gent.

Your affectionate friend
and humble servant

E: Andros.

A Letter of the same date at Saybrooke from the Go: to the Go: of Boston.

Honorable Sir.

I cannot omitt this oppertunity by Mr. Andr. Belcher, with my respects to give you an account of my arrivall to this place, being intended to these ports, upon account of the limitts expressed in his Majesties Lettres patents betweene his R. Hs and Conecticutt, but suddenly hasten'd by the Newes from Go: Winthrop by Expresse, of the Indyans Irruption and barbarousnesse of which proceedings hearing no furth[er] I hope there already is or will bee speedily a good Event; And as to the limitts, having proceeded in the fairest manner, according to his Majesties pleasure and Commands I will not doubt a suiteable Issue therein accordingly, for which and the Indyan Concernes, I doe attend here, where I shall bee glad, or at my returne of any oppertuni[ ] to [ser]ve [you.] Remaining

Honored Sir
Your very humble servant
E: Andros.

A Lettre from the Go: to the Go: of Boston
June 2d about a souldyer.

Sir.

At my returne from Delaware, where I left all very well settled, I received
yours of [the] 21th Aprill, and thank you for your obliging favour in
securing upon so great a suspicion John Dobree a soyldyer of this
Garrison, who though not otherwayes Guilty, did run away, which if
suffred in them or others, would very much encourage all idle and loose
people to the prejudice of all Colonyes; I therefore pray hee may bee sent
back, and I shall bee ready allwayes to make you a suiteable Returne,
and further to serve you in what else may bee in my power, I am

Sir.
Your most humble servant.
E: Andros.

[24:122]

[AFFIDAVIT OF ANDREW BALL CONCERNING A MUTINY]

The Examinacion of Andrew Ball Master
of the Ketch Susannah of Jamaica, taken
upon Oath, July the 2d 1675.

The Master being askt, to whom the Ketch doth belong.

Hee saith that Mr. Philip Dickerey of Jamaica, who keepes a house of
Entertainment at the Point there, hath three parts of the said Ketch, and
the other 4th part belongs to the Mate, Peter Gerritz.

That from Jamaica the said Ketch was bound to the Canaryes for wine,
but being not able to ply up to Windward, put into Virginia, and so here
to this Port.

That hee the said Master being trusted with the Cargo, to dispose of for
the best advantage, the which having done, and loaden her with Pipestaves, and cleared at the Custome house, Hee sayled from before this

place June the 22th in order to his Voyage to Fyall,[*] and prosecuted it so farre as New Utrecht, where they came to an Ancher, expecting Wind and Tyde to goe out to sea, and lay there till the 26th, when the Mate mutinyed, and quarelling with the Master, drew his knife upon him, and forced him to deliver up his Lett passe from Jamaica, and his clearing at the Custome house here, with all other papers that hee had Whereupon being affrighted, hee mad[ ] a shift to get ashoare, in a small Ca[ ] belonging to a Sloope thereby, app[ ]hending hee was in danger of his Life by the Steerman or Mate and [ ] other Seamen.

The said Master doth not know that [ ] said Mate, had any Order or authority to medle with the said Ketch or Concernes, And therefore lookes upon this Action to bee no other then a Mutiny, and the Mate and his Complices to bee Robbers and Sea Rovers, and that they will dispose of the said Ketch and Goods accordingly.

Sworne before the Governor
at the Custome house.

[ENDORSED:][‡]   Andrew Ball P[ ]=
                       tended Master of the Ketch
                       Susannah which was condemned.
                       July 2d. 1675

[24:123]

            [THIS IS THE DRAFT COPY OF 24:122]

[SIGNED:]   Andrew Ball

[NOTES:][†]   The Ketch had belonging to her 7 men
                   and a boy—almost all Dutch.

                   Present Mr. Laurence
                   C. Brockles, etc.

---

* Faial, in the Azores.
‡ The endorsement was made on a separate paper.
† The notes appear at the end of the draft copy.

[24:124 (1)]

[INSTRUCTIONS AND ORDERS CONCERNING THE REORGANIZATION
OF COURTS IN THE ESOPUS]*

Magistrates for Esopus.

C. Tho: Del: Justice of the peace for Kingston, Hurley Marbleton and
the new Paltz and precincts.

                                    Edward Wh[   ]

Jan Joosten

Louis du Bois

John
Tho: } Garton

Kingston to have 4   C. Tho: De[   ]
buersiers who with a   Jan Joosten
Justice to keepe a Towne   Edward Whittack[ ]r
Court for small matter not   [*blank*] Garton
exceeding 5£   Louis du Bois

Hurly and Marbleton 4 more—with a J[   ]

A Towne Court at the palts
To try all Causes not above 5£ according to Law.

By the Go.

These are to authorize the J.T.P. to administer the usuall Oathes of
Justices acc[   ] To Law to [the New Justices of Kingston, Hurley
Marbleton] Jan Joosten, Edw. Whitt[ ]ker [*blank*] Garton and Louis du
Bois.
These are to authorize you to administer the usuall Oathes of Justices of
the peace according to Law, for Esopus and precincts to the unde[ ]named
p[   ] there unto [   ].

---

* This is a rough draft by Secretary Nicolls. The abbreviated names include Thomas
Delavall, Stephen van Cortlandt, and Edward Whittacker. J.T.P. is justice of the peace.
Material crossed out in the document is included here in brackets.

J.T.P. John Joosten
C. Louis du Bois; and   Giv etc.*

To C. St. Cortl.
one of the Councell.

[Where in there have beene no later Returnes of officers for the Tr.]

[24:124 (2)]

[A LIST OF APPOINTMENTS]‡

for Kingstowne   for Mombackus
John Cottine   Now Rochister
Geriet van vliet   John Vanete
Tunis Peare   Syman Westphale

for Hurly   for the N. Palse
Matis Blanshan   Abraham Duboys
Houybert Souyland   Luis Bevie

for Marbletowne
Will Notingham
Tho: Hall

[24:125]

[EXAMINATIONS OF ANDREW BALL AND PETER GERRITSZ
CONCERNING THE MUTINY]

[Ju]ly 4, 1675
At a Councell

Present

The Go:
The Mayor
Mr . Laurence
C. Brockles.
C. Dyre.
Andrew Ball Master or pretended to be[   ] of the Ketch Susannah
brought back by [   ]ciall warrant, denyeth the first part of his [   ]

* This is badly scrawled.
‡ Possibly persons appointed as magistrates at the Esopus.

that Phil. Dickerey of Jamaica was 3 part Owner.

Hee denyeth the next part, that they came [   ] from Jamaica, but came from Curacoa, and we[ ] designed for the Canaryes but could not beat up—so went to Jamaica, where they obtayned their Passeport—was there 5 weekes T[   ] of his Oath also false on[ ]y that they came to Virginia and so here and the drawing of the Knife.

That the Ketch doth belong Only to Curac[   ] the Owners being John Hollyford of Curacoa the Mates and 2 others of Holland one of the [   ] named C[   ].* Their loading was salt [   ] 14 Negroes, of which 3 dyed, 2 sold for [   ] at the Hencias‡ and 9 hee brought hith[   ] with the suger.

Peter Gerritz being examined denyes that hee [   ] the Master Andrew Ball of the Ketch or that hee was Master but that hee himselfe is [   ]ster and owner of the Ketch, and that Andrew Ball [   ] [   ] Curacao [. . . one line missing . . .] of Freezland [. . . one line missing . . .] Hollyford.

That from Curacoa they next designed for the Canaryes, but by foule weather could not reach it so came to Jamaica, where they gott their lett Passe, so came to Virginia, and to here.

That hee himselfe was borne at Utrecht in Holland, and is an Inhabitant of Curacoa.

[ENDORSED:]   The 2d Examinacion
                 of Andr. Ball at the
                 Fort before the Councell.
                 July 4. 1675.

[24:126]

[EXAMINATION OF PIETER GERRITSZ]†

[The Examination] of Peter Gerritz brought back by the Governors speciall warrant with the Ketch Susann[ah] from Sandy Point. July 4th 1675.

The Examinant denyes that hee turned out of the Ketch the Master

---

* Reading uncertain: possibly "Coning."
‡ The reading here is uncertain.
† The following text comes in part from NYSHAR.

Andrew Ball, or that hee is Master being onely Cook to the Vessall, But saith that he[e] himselfe is Master and Owner of the said Ketch the which hee bought with his owne money.

Hee farther saith that hee bought the said Ketch at Curacoa, and that his brother in Law, Luycas Volckerts of Freezland, living now at Curacoa hath one Quarter part, and Jan Hollyford another, the other halfe is his.

That from Curacoa they were designed for the Canaryes, but meeting with foule weather could not reach it, so went to Jamaica, where they obtayned their Lett Passe, from thence came to Verginia, and so hither.

That hee himselfe is an Inhabitant of Curacoa, where hee hath a Plant[ation] and servants.

Pieter Gerritz Stofflesz

[ENDORSED:]   The examinacion of
Pieter Gerritsz Stoffle
about the Ketch Susannah of
which hee an Owner.

July 4th 1675.

[24:127a]

[PETITION OF ELISABETH BEDLOO APPEALING A COURT DECISION
WITH UNRELATED NOTES ABOUT PASSPORTS
AND A MARRIAGE LICENSE]

To the Right Honorable Major Edmund Andros Governor
Generall of all his Royall Highnes his Territories in America
etc.

The humble peticion of Elizabeth Bedlowe widowe late the Relict of Isaack Bedlowe deceased sheweth unto your Honor that whereas Alexander Bryan hath layed an Attachment upon A house of your petitioners late husband for 12 G 7s And hath Received Judgment for the same in the Worshipfull the Maiors Court of this Citty and one Elias Doughty att the same Court comensed his accion against your peticioner for 27 G as administratrix to Her [   ] husband per reccorded Judgment thereupon for And one 4[   ] 13 pence att the same Court comenced his accion against your petitioner as beinge administratrix to her late husband, And received Judgment there upon for

Therefore your petitioner humbly prayes your Honor to graunt unto your petitioner her severall appeales in the severall accions att the next severall Assizes she beinge ready and willinge to performe all such things as the Law requires in such cases. And your peticioner as in duty bound shall ever pray etc.

[ENDORSED:]   Mrs . Bedloes
                  Peticion of Appeale
                  July 5. 1675.

                  Request of Letters of
                  Administration.
                  All.
                  Graunted July 26–1675.

                  Elizabeth Bedloe.
                  By the Go:

                  Isack Bedloe
                  Mr . Bryan.
                  Mr. Doughty.
                  Mr. Laur. Vander Spiegle

A Passe for Katherin[ ] Jonassen, and Alice Jonassen to goe in the good Hope,

Geo. Heathcott Master.

Woodgate, Master of the Margarett.

Mr. Thomas Carre.

Jan Hendrickse van Baal, a Passe for himselfe, wife and 5 children and a maid.

Lycence for Marriage between Mr. Fr. Rombouts of this City Merchant and Mrs. Anna Eliz. Wessells of the same place Widdow. 6th August 1675.

[24:127b]

Account of charges for Mrs. Elizabeth de Potter widowe of
Mr. Isacq bedlo—

To Mr. Leete Clearke	£1:02:
To Henry neuton	11:00:
To Peter Shaefbanck	08:00:
To Mr. Sherif	04:00:
To Mr Loues for translating of three dep[ ]sitions	07:06:
To Mary Jo[ ]n for severall days to Come from here plantation to attend the Court of Mayor and Aldermen, as also the High Court of Assizes	07:06:
For charges to the enterring of the negro woman by order of our [ ]our Lovelace	18:09:
To Mr. West attorney fees before Mayor and aldermen, as also before High Court of Assizes	01:10:
To Capt. Nicols as appeare by his account 9.6.7	4:05:04
	£9:14:01

The agreement for the Negro woman whas made for foureteene Hundred
gilders and one ancre special wine word more as one Hundred gilders so
that is together five teene Hundred gilders.

[24:127c]

[MARRIAGE LICENSE: FRANCIS ROMBOUDTS AND ANN ELISABETH,
WIDOW OF WARNER WESSELLS, OF NEW YORK, AUGUST 6, 1675
(LISTED IN CALENDAR, BUT NOT PRESENT)]

[24:128]

[ABSTRACT OF A LETTER FROM GOVERNOR CODDINGTON OF
RHODE ISLAND CONCERNING THE INDIAN WAR]

An abstract of another Letter from the Governor of Roade
Island, dated the 21th of July 1675.

A greate part is Relacion of severall passages of the warre betweene
Plym. Colony and the Indyans, and their owne being in a warlike posture
of Defence;

Then relates the comming of an Army from Boston and Conecticutt
Colonyes into their Colony (without informing them thereof) to bring
the Indyans there, to their owne termes, and to call that part of Roade Isl.
Colony theirs, (vist. Kingstowne in the Narrogansett Countrey) and
having made terms with the Indyans, tooke prisoner one Tho: Gould
appointed a Conservater of the peace in Kingstowne for questioning
whether they should not (rightly) have informed Them of their comming
with an army within their province and pinioned and guarded him, and
the next morne sentenc't him to bee sent from Constable to Constable to
Conecticutt prisone with 8 horsemen, at his owne Charge, but afterwards
tooke bayle, for him. The person so apprehended was a Conservator of
the Peace in the aforesaid Kingstowne, his name Thomas Gould.

And further Those of Conecticutt have also formerly threatned by force
that wee should not use the Kings authority there, and not to maintaine
it for the Kings Province as confirmed to us, It intimates their force was
as much therefore as their pretence against our Indyans, and wee doubt
not but we could have prevailed to have brought our Indyans to greater
conformity than they have done by their Armes and so with Relacion of
some skirmoshe with the Indyans takes leave

signed—W. Coddington

[ENDORSED:]   An abstract of Letters
from the Go: of Roade Isl.
to our Governor.
1674.

[24:129]

[PETITION OF JOHN AND SUSANNAH SCUDAMORE CONCERNING
THE KILLING OF THOMAS BARKER BY THEIR SON]

To the right honourable Edmund Andros Esquire Governor Generall
under his Royall Highnes James Duke of Yorke and Albany etc. of all
his Territoris in America.

Righte honourable the humble request of your poare aflicted petiti[   ]
whose names are here underwritten sheweth that whereas there was such
a sad acsedens fel out at my house your petitioners being both from home
not knoweing any thing of Thomas Barker which is now deade being
there neither did wee knowe of any deferens in the least measure that
was betwene our son and the party deseased therefore had noe grounds
to susspect any hurt being done at that time but to our gret grefe and
truble it fell out soe that my son takeing up a gun, which stoode in the
howse not knoweing it was charged as wee have very good grownds to
beleve for wee can prove that it was charged when the boy was abroade
in the feeld[   ]net presumeing to cok the gun without exsame [   ]hether
it [   ] charged or not it did that mischeevous akt[   ] killing [   ] boy
which hath bene soe gret a greefe to your petitioner [   ] soe much that
wee knowe not well howe to bear our afliction [ ]nd in dede seeing some
of our neighbours manege soe much malis against us and our childe ads
much to our greefe: yet notwithstanding wee hope though there hath bene
meanse used for to make the act as odeous to your honour as may bee
that your honor will be pleased to use the best meanes you can that the
case may be hearde by such persons as are noe wayes prejudissed to us
or our child and allsoe men of understanding for though our childe is
deare to us yet wee are soe far from justef[ ]ing our childe in any evel
act that we shall not in the least measure goe aboute to make the case
better or worse then it is not douteing but if honest understanding men
have the hea[   ] of the thing it will not apeare soe bad as wee suppose
you a[   ] informed it is: and in granting this our petition wee whoe are
your most humble servants and petitioners shall for [   ] honour ever
pray

Jemaicae this 22th of Juely   John Skidmore
Anno Domini 1675

                                                  Her mark

                                 Susanah   S   Skidmor[   ]

[ENDORSED:]   The Peticion of
                John Scudamore and
                Susannah his wife
                about their sons killing
                the young lad etc.
                July 22. 1675

[24:130]

[MINUTES OF A MEETING WITH SOME HACKINSACK INDIANS
DURING A TRIP BY THE GOVERNOR]

A[   ]July 23th 1675.

There was [   ] of Indyans before the Governo[   ]ing to
Hackingsacke etc. on the West side of Hudsons River.

One of them makes a speech to the Go: declaring their comming to give
the Go: a Visitt, and that their hearts are good, and give a present of some
Deere skins.

The Go: thankes them and tells them hee sha[   ] his predesessors bee
glad to live in good frie[ ]ship with them.

They expresse their desire of it, and give another present of Deere
s[   ]firmacion.

The Go: tells [   ] Very well.

Thereupon th[   ] spoke for the rest, with[   ] expressions
of kindnesse gives the Go: a ba[   ] as a token of their hearty
fri[   ]

The chiefe [   ] M[ ]ndawasse and Hoynayhaha[   ]ssaekes
and of Tapp[ ] Ashawocan, o[   ]halfe of their Nations.

This being all they have to say, the Go: acqua[   ] them of his intent of
friendship to all the Indya[ ] and [   ]ints them what hee hath done
in [   ] Young upon Long Isl[   ] and hath for the present taken
away their a[   ] because they paid tribute to the Indyans, but will protect
them against those they paid Tribute to, or any other,

That the Go: doth [   ]tend to doe so by them, but exp[   ]her
their continance in friendship, [   ] late of Long Is[   ] shall
pay any [   ] to the Indyans to the Eastward [   ]

them of his Ennemy. They s[   ] at giving Hostages Its to
[   ]ee for a time onely, and that they shall [   ]ed.
Thereupon [   ]onsent to leave two of their young men for
Hostages, and are very well satisfy'de:

The Go: presents the 3 Sachems each with a Coate of Duffells and gives
them each a dram:
Their Compa: was about 50.

Sam : Edsall
Thom: Laurence the baker   Interpreters

They desire time to speake together at home and will bring[   ]
hostages.

The Go: [   ] from their promise, and gives [   ]
5 dayes time. to pres[   ] or 4 bottles of liquor and
dismisse[   ]

[ENDORSED:]   July 23. 1675
                   Hackingsacke and Tappan
                   Indyans Visitt.

[24:131]

[BILL OF ANNA ELISABETH, WIDOW OF WARNAR WESSELS, AGAINST
FORMER GOVERNOR LOVELACE. TRANSLATION]

The Honorable Lord Francois Lovelace
Governor General

Debit   Credit

1672
November

Accepted by his honor   For the three years'
for the soldiers ac-   lease of the tappers'
cording to the list   excise from 1669 to
shown his honor...ƒ2970:3   May 1672 ...... ƒ30160

Expended afterwards
by the officers and
soldiers according

to the accompanying
list............................ 1327:1

December

Delivered to the
court of assizes 48:16

To the commissary
of the fort 125:15

To the voyage to
the Delaware 127:10

To Mr. *Thomas
Lovelace 152:6

<u>1673</u>

19 July To 4 1/2 barrels of flour,
1066 lbs. net at 36 per
cento; with the barrels,
amounts to 406:15

To the account of Mr.‡
Cornelis van Ruyven,
collector, for the
amount paid to him for
the tappers' excise
from May 1669 to 30
July 1673................ 23695:9

to the account of
Isaacq Bedloo's governor's
account .... <u>2340:8</u>
             Total   31194:3

For the closing
balance   <u>1034:3</u>
        Total   ƒ31194:3
I owe on the lease in
partnership with Pr.
Nys ƒ2091:7
My half amounts
to.   ƒ1045:13:8

---

* The abbreviation "Mr." appears in the original, but it represents the English "mister"
rather than the Dutch *"meester"*; neither of these men is a *heelmeester* (barber-surgeon).
‡ See previous note.

[ENDORSED:]*   Wid: Wessels
                      bill and Account

[NOTATION:]   Some persons to
                      bee appointed to
                      examine and make
                      report of the
                      Accounts
                      July 26, 1675

[24:132]

[PETITION BY CUSTOMS COLLECTOR WILLIAM DYRE FOR, AND
APPOINTMENT OF, APPRAISERS FOR THE SHIP *SUSANNAH*]

> To the worshipfull the Mayor and Aldermen of the citty of
> N. Yorke

> Wm Dyre Gent. Collector of his Majesties Customes in this
> his Royall Highness province.

Sheweth that wheras Mr. Wm. Roadney and Mr. Jos: Lee per their
Atturney as well Et: have sued to Judgment the Ketch susannah now in
this road seazed per speciall warrant from his honor the Governor with
her loading of goods as well Imported as Exported: Therefore in due
process for the leagall Condemnation of which said vessell and goodes
I humbly Crave your Worships writt of Apprisment etc.

> At a Mayors Court held at New Yorke one the thirty first
> day of July 1675.

Upon the above written motion of Capt. Wm Dyre for a writt of
Apraisement etc. as is therein mentioned: the worshipfull Court have
granted it accordingly and doe desire and appoynt Capt. Natt: Davenport
Capt. Tho: Smith Mr. Fran: Smith Mr. Tho: Lewis and Mr. Wm.
Woodgate to be the A[ ]praisers of the said Ketch Susanna: her sailes
Ancker Cables Rigging Vittualls with her goods and mercha[ ]izes
Imported and Exported.

---

* The endorsement and the notation are in English.

[ENDORSED:]   At a Mayors Court
June 27. 1675.
About the Ketch.

15	2.13.4
7	
10/5	8-0-
5.5	1.6.8
1.10	9.6.8
	5.0.0
	4.6.8

[24:133]

[APPOINTMENT OF AUDITORS AND ACCEPTANCE OF THE ACCOUNTS
OF THE EXCISE COLLECTORS]

By the Governor

Whereas Anna Elizabeth the widdow and Relict of Warner Wessells
deceased hath made Application unto mee, desireing that some person
may be appointed to view and examine into the Accounts of her deceased
husband, and her own, touching their farming the great Excise in the time
of the late Governor Col: Lovelace that as farre as they shall be found
balanc't, shee may have a Lawfull discharge for the same, these are to
appoint the present Mayor, and Deputy Mayor, with Mr. William Darvall
one of the Aldermen to view and Examine into the said Accounts, and
to make report unto mee, how they doe find the same, that such order
may be taken therein as shall bee most proper for the Petitioners
discharge in that matter: Given under my hand in New Yorke this 31th
day of July 1675.

The same persons are Likewise to
view and examine the Accounts of
Peter Nys and make report there of.

By the Governor.

Upon the Report of Mr. Matthias Nicolls Mayor, Mr. John Laurance
Deputy Mayor and Mr. William Darvall one of the Aldermen, That the
widdow Wessells and Peter Nys, late Farmers of the great Excise, in Coll.
Lovelaces time, had fully paid or accounted for the said Excise or Packt
with Coll. Lovelace or his Officers, to the time they had it; I doe hereby

signify my allowance therof accordingly. Given under my hand in New
Yorke the 10th day of August 1675.

signed E. Andros.

[ENDORSED:]   The Governors Order
to Mr. Nicolls Mr. Laurence
and Mr. Darvall; to view
and examine the widdow
Wessells and Peter
Nys his Accounts.
July 31. 1675.

[24:134]

[CERTIFICATION OF THE EXCISE ACCOUNTS]

May it please your Honor.

Wee have according to your Honors Ord[ ] viewed and examined into
the Accounts of th[ ] widdow Wessells, relating both to her hus[   ] and
herselfe, as they were successively F[   ] of the great Packt or Excise;
And as w[   ] by what wee have seene and some of us d[   ] very well
know, as by Information from others, who have declared the same unto
[ ] Wee doe find that the severall summes in th[ ] Account produced
unto us, taken out of her bookes by William Bogardus the publicke
Notary, were for the greatest part payments made by her husband and
selfe, to those entruste[ ] by the late Governor Collonell Lovelace, for
the which the Receits have beene produced, and the rest were Summes
promised to bee allowed of by the said Governor, The which together,
doe within a very small That is to say with the summe of 11G 10st sewant
balan[   ] the Accounts due for their farming of the sa[   ] Excise: Wee
doe therefore recommend the sa[   ] to your honor, for your favourable
Allowance, be[   ] fully persuaded of the reality and Truth the[ ]of:

As to the Account of Peter Nys, who was for some time also one of the
Farmers of the said Excise, the same being likewise by your Ho[   ]
referred unto us, Wee have view'd and examined them, and doe find that
the souldyers debts to him in the lyst produced unto us, being allowed,

as wee are credibly informed hee was also promised by Mr. Bedloo and
the Governor himselfe then his account will bee ballanc't:*

This wee also humbly represent unto yo[   ] honors and subscribe
ourselves.
                    Your honors most humble ser[   ]
[   ]ust 4th   Matthias: Nicolls.
1675.   John Lawrence
                                                 Wm: Darvall.

[ENDORSED:]   The Report of Mr. Nicolls,
                Mr. Laurence,
                and Mr. Darvall
                about the wid: Wessells,
                and Peter Nys his Accounts.
                Aug. 4th 1675

                                         Michel Heinelle
                                         clerk

[24:135]
[NO ENTRY IN THE CALENDAR FOR THIS NUMBER]‡

[24:136a]
[INVENTORY OF BOOKS AND PAPERS BELONGING TO ELIZABETH
BEDLOW, ADMINISTRATRIX OF THE LATE ISAAC BEDLOW, TAKEN BY
PETER DE LA NOY, ETC.; AUGUST 12, 1675]†

[24:136b]
[ASSESSMENT ROLLS FOR THE FIVE DUTCH TOWNS
ON LONG ISLAND IN 1675. TRANSLATION]+

* The last five words of this sentence replace the following, which is crossed out: "there
will bee due to him upon that Account 1054 Guilders wamp. for which hee may have his
remedy at Law."
‡ Two business accounts of John Shakerly, which now appear at this number, will be
published with Shakerly's other accounts collected in 1679.
† The document is missing.
+ See appendix for these assessment rolls.

[24:137]

[LETTER OF JOSEPH BAYLY, WARNING OFFICIALS OF OYSTER BAY
TO BE ON GUARD AGAINST THE INDIANS (TWO COPIES)]

September 10 75 to Ca Townsend

or to the constable and oversears and inhabitantes of osterbay gentlemen
and naibours I being at the south and our naibours being inf[   ] an
indian that the indians wo[   ]d bee spedily in action soe that it is my
advice to put your selves in the best posters of defence you can wich is
the advice of your friend

Joseph bayly

Septem 10:75

To the Constable and overseers and inhab[   ]ants oster bay Gentlemen
and Naightbours I being at the south and one of oure Naightbours beeing
informed by an Indian that the Indians would speedily bee in ackcion
soe that it is my advise to put youre selves in the best posture of defense
y[ ]u cane which is the advise of youre loving frend Joseph Baly

This is a true coppie per mee

Abraham Frost

[24:138]

[MINUTES OF MEETINGS WITH SACHEMS FROM ROCKAWAY,
HACKINSACK, AND TAPPAN]

Sept. 18th 1675.

This morning there came to the Governor in the Fort one of [   ] Long
Isl. Sache[ ] that mis't yes[ ]rday[   ]ith Eyes, hee is of Rockway or
t[   ]

The other [   ]rday upon the newes of [   ]
[   ]esse.

Here was at[   ] with
Tom t[   ] and others, and were very well [   ]
[   ]hat was done yesterday by[   ] the
behalfe of the rest.

Here were also two Sachems from the other side one from Hackingsack, the other from Tapan, who hearing of the Go: returne from Alb: came to bid him welcom[ ] h[ ]me and promise all friendship.

[ENDORSED:]   Sept. 18. 1675.
A Meeting of Indyans
before the Go:

Rockway etc.

[24:139]

[MINUTES OF A MEETING WITH INDIANS FROM DELAWARE]

Sept. 22th 1675.

There appeared some of the Indyans toward Delaware before the Governor this morne vizt Mamora[   ] by Millstone river and Auri[ ]Falls. Mr. Edsall and [   ] Baker Interpreters.

[   ] Go: tells the [   ]lcome [   ]
Mamorakickan s[   ]conding a[ ] his
promise, Th[   ]arts of the Engl. good to
[   ]art is good and offers it to
th[   ]res with his people to liv[ ]
quiet, and [   ]ent and eate and drinke and bee qu[   ]e.

The Go: saith againe they are welcome, and tells them that since hee was at Delaware there hath hapned warrs to the Eastward, but that hee hath beene all about the Go: to keepe matters well and quiet and they are so, and that hee is in a Condicion to keepe them so.

The Go: saith as wee punish any that are bad amongst us, so must they doe with theirs, and then the rest will be well.

Hee saith That the next [   ] hee goes to Delaware hee'l come [   ] see [   ] Hee tells them hee hath beene [   ] Indyans, and lay at their Co[   ]

They speake of [   ]cay up the Raritans River [   ]r doe any harme; The G[   ]ll they may g[ ] when they ple[   ] friends.

[ENDORSED:]   Sept 22th 1675.

                   Appearance of Indyans
                   toward Delaware.

[24:140]

[INTERROGATION OF GRIETIE RYCKMANS BY THE COURT
AT ALBANY. TRANSLATION]

Copy—

Interrogatory conducted before the honorable court of Albany, etc., present: Adrian Gerritse and Mr. Pritty, magistrates, and Mr. Siston, sheriff of the aforesaid court, at the request of Jan Gerritse van Marcken, former schout of Schaenhechtady, to examine Grietie Ryckmans,[*] the wife of Jaques Cornelisen.

1. Whether on the 21st of September last she did not hear Marritie Mynderts, when she passed out of her door, say to Jan Gerritsen van Marcken: "You scoundrel, you said that I stole a raccoon coat."

Answer: "No."

2. And whether he did not answer: "No, Marritie, I am not talking about a raccoon coat; certainly not, I am not talking about it."

Answer: "I heard them talk but did not understand what they said. I heard Jan Gerritse say: 'I am not talking about the raccoon coat.'"

3. And whether he did not come into the house then and say: "That is bad of Marritie. She runs to Myndert's house, saying: 'That scoundrel, that thief says that I stole a

---

* In the will of Jacques Cornelissen van Slyck, dated May 18, 1690 (*Early Records of Albany*, 4:119–21), she is called Gerritje Ryckman. She was a daughter of Harmen Jansen Ryckman.

THE ANDROS PAPERS   205

raccoon coat.' God knows that I did not say that."

4. Whether Myndert thereupon did not come into the house with evil intent, saying: "What did you say? That my mother is a thief?"

5. And whether he did not answer: "Why, no, Myndert, I did not say that. Your mother does wrong in saying that."

6. And whether his mother Marritie did not say then: "Now look at the dog; he says that he did not say it."

7. Whether her husband, Sweer Tuenisse, did not say thereupon: "You little scoundrel, you little thief, you slander this woman. You said that she lusted after horses. That has cost her ten nights' sleep."

8. Whether her son Myndert thereupon did not say: "Strike the dog, or I shall strike him. Is he to say that my mother is a thief? It is not true."

9. Whether I, Jan Gerritsen, did not answer: "Myndert, I am not saying that your mother is a thief."

10. And whether Myndert did not grab him by the head and drag him by the hair over the floor and beat him?

Answer: "Yes," she heard Jan Gerritse say so.

Answer: "Yes."

Answer: "Yes."

Answer: "Yes."

Answer: "Yes."

Answer: "Yes."

Answer: "Yes."

Answer: "I saw that Myndert dragged him over the floor but did not see who started it."

11. Whether Myndert, when he let him go and ran out of the door, asking for his hat, did not say: "Why didn't you let me alone? I would have thrown him into the cellar and broken his neck."

Answer: "Yes, but I do not know exactly whether he said broken or wrung his neck but heard one or the other."

12. Whether, further, she did not hear Sweer say: "The court record is so scandalous that we are ashamed when we open it. Yes, so scandalous is it and such [awful] things are written in it."

Answer: "Yes, but I did not hear him say: 'Such [awful] things are written in it.'"

On the 15th of September, or thereabouts, the aforesaid Grietie Harmensen heard Sweer Teunisse in the presence of the whole court say to Jan Gerritse van Marken: "You are a scoundrel and a thief and I shall prove it. We have your signature and it is down here."

Grietie Harmense, aforesaid, also says in the presence of the above mentioned magistrates that when she was at Schaenhechtade to submit to the interrogatory under oath, in the matter of the aforesaid Jan Gerritsen van Marken, the honorable magistrates of Schaenechtade said to her: "You need give no further testimony, nor give him any affidavit of it. It is sufficient for you to have sworn to this interrogatory." All of which Grietie Harmense has confirmed by solemn oath before the aforesaid magistrates, in Albany, on the 29th of September 1675.

Jannetie Schermerhooren, at the request of the said Jan Gerritse and before the aforesaid magistrates, also declares that she heard Jan Gerritse van Marken say to Maritie Mynders, the wife of Sweer Teunise: "I am not saying that the raccoon coat was stolen, nor that the five beavers were stolen; nor do I say that the money of the poor is stolen." She also understood the said Jan Gerritse to say (so she thinks): "I am not saying that the letters were concealed." And he also said to her: "Is that the reward for the favors done by me? I was present when powder and lead were sold here." The deponent knows nothing further of the matter and is ready, in case of need, to confirm what is hereinbefore written by solemn oath. *Actum* in Albany, *dato ut supra.*

After comparison

I find that it agrees with the original minutes.	Acknowledged by me, Ro: Livingston, sec.

Quod attestor
Ro: Living: sec.

Collated by me
Ro: Livingston, sec.

[ENDORSED:]   Copy of an interrogatory
at the request of J: Ger: van marke

[24:141]

[MINUTES OF A MEETING WITH TACKPOUSHE
AND OTHER SACHEMS]

Sept. 30th 1675.

Tackpoushe the Marsapeag Sachem with some other Sachems and severall of their Indyans app[   ]e before the Go: at the Fort.

The occasion of [   ]ng is to make their demands of [   ]d
of theirs [   ]

[24:142]

[COMPLAINT OF GABRIEL MINVIELLE AS ATTORNEY FOR LOUIS DU
BOIS AGAINST LEWIS MORRIS FOR DETAINING TWO NEGROES]

Cytie of New Yorke

Gabriell Minveile of this citty Merchant Atturney of Lewis Debois of Esopus Complaines of Coll. Lewis Morris of a plea that without Delay he Render unto him a Certaine Negroe man Called Anthoney and a Negro Woman Named Susannah which he unjustley deteynes from him and pledges etc. where upon the said Gabrill saith and Declareth that the said Negro Man Called Anthoney and Negro Woman named Susannah were both of them Lawfully bought by the Plt. Lewis Diebois at a Publique out Cry or vendue held in Esopus in the yeare 1673 or 1674 in the time of the Late Dutch Government and paid for according to the Condicions of Sale and the said Negroes were by vertue of said Sale and Purchase quietly Enjoyed and possest by the Plt. untill the Last Spring when upon what Ocasion he knowes not) they absente[ ] themselves and Runn away from the said Masters service and stragling in the woods and after Crosing the River whereby some Indians Dirccted to Coll. Morris their Quandam Masters plantacione where its Supposed they yet still Remaine and though the Plt. by Gabrill Munveale his Atturney hath Often Demanded Restitucion of the said Negroes yet the said Coll. Morris the Deft. hath and still doth Refuse to doe Claiming Right and Interest in them whereby the said Plt. hath lost the Benefitt of the Laboure the Last harvest as well as before and since to his Detriment and Damag[ ] the Sume of Thirty Pounds whereupon desiring sattisfaccon of said Damage and Restitucio[ ] of said Negros and purchased by him he brings his Suite to this worshipfull Court.

> A True Coppy of the Tryiall
> Exam per Abr: Corbett Cler.

[ENDORSED:]   Minvielle do. Clarratie

[24:143]

> The Answer of Gabriell Minvielle Attorney to Lewis du Boise Defendant to the Bill of Compaint of Coll. Lewis Morrice Complainant.

The said Defendant saith that hee beleeves it to be true, as the Complaint alleadges, That the two Negroes now in dispute, were part of the Estate of the Complainant, being a Negro man named Anthony, and a Negro Woman named Susanna, and that they might be taken from the said Complainant in the time of the late dutch warre, but the said Negroes, were justly and Honestly Bought by the Defendant Lewis de Boise at the Sopez, not Clendestinely But In Open Vendue by the Authorized Vendue master there, to whom hee made payment to them According to Condition, they being sent to him as hee is informed, by the then Governor Anthony Colve, or Secretary Nicolas Bayard, the legality of whose Seizure or adjudication of any part of the Complainants Estate is not for the defendant to judge, But he humbly conceives the detaining of the said Negroes, by the Complainant, is contrary to Law, they being run away from their Masters Service, who so Legaly had bought them According to Vendue custome of the Country, and had the Defendant beene so well advised as to prosecute them by Hue and Cry, hee Supposes they might have been sent back to him as his proper estate, wheras now they have been detained for the Space of 13 Months, during which time the Defendant hath not onely lost their Service, in the very Harvest time, but hath been much Damnified and disappointed, there being none at that extraordinary season to bee hired for Money; The Defendant on the behalfe of his principall therfor prays that Your Honour and this honourable Court, will take the Same into Your Serious Consideration, and order that the Judgment past against the Complainants in the Majors Court may be confirmed and the Negroes bee delivered back to their Master, and such damage bee allowed as may bee thought Reasonable for their so long Detainer, and the case Determined by this honorable Court with costs etc.

[ENDORSED:]   The answer of
Gabriell Minvielle Att.
to Lewis de Bois Deft.
To the bill of Complaint
of Coll. Lewis Morris

[24:144]

[RETURN BY THE TOWN CLERK OF THE HEMPSTEAD
PROPERTY VALUATION]

The totall sume of our townes Esteats doth Amount to: 11532–19–4 this yere deated at Hempsted
this 28 day of Agust
in the yere of our Lord 1675

Nathaniell Persall Clar

[ADDRESSED:]   To be delivered into
the offis an
New Yourck

[24:145]

[COVERING LETTER FROM SIMON SEARING FOR THE ABOVE]

Respected Sir

according to your order i have herein sent you the valuation of our townes estate, in the paper inclosed, so with my service to you I rest yours to comand

Hempsted Sept: 7th: 1675.

Simon Saring

[ADDRESSED:]   To Mr Math[   ]
                at New Yor[   ]
                Is[   ]

[24:146]

[LETTER FROM NATHANIEL COLES REPORTING THE OYSTER BAY
PROPERTY VALUATION]

Oyster Bay the 21th August 1675.

Sir.

Your warrant wee have received, dated the 7th Aug[   ]; for the sending,
into your Office, the sum of our Townes Estate, the which wee have dun,
and the Estate of our Towne is 4900£ now sent by this bearrer Mr.
Shakerly not Else to acquaint your Worship with but desiering your
welfare, I rest yours to Comand.

Nathaniell Coles

4900   40 9
12222
  11
        20–8–4

[ADDRESSED:]   To the Worshipfull Matthias
                Nicols, Mayor these
                Presents.
                In New Yorke.

[ENDORSED:]   the Returne from Oyster Bay brought in
                [   ] Aug. 24. 1675

                Valuacions.
                [   ]ast Oct. 25
                [   ]900
                20£.8.4

[24:147]

[LETTER FROM BENJAMIN COE REPORTING THE JAMAICA
PROPERTY VALUATION]

Honored Sir

We have presented to your vew the hole estate of our towne as it is given
in to us the valewation where of doe amount to 5700£ the troopers with
their horsis being includid which deduct if you please

Jemaica Sept. th 8 1675.

By order of the Constable and Overseers

Beniemin Coe

21
196
5700   14/5
1222   23–15
11

[ADDRESSED:]   To the honored Capt. Nicoles
                    at New York

[ENDORSED:]   Jamaica Valuacions
                    Brought in Sept.11th 1675.
                    past Oct. 25
                    5700
                    23. 15. 0

[24:148]

[ASSESSMENT ROLLS OF WESTCHESTER AND EASTCHESTER IN 1675]*

[24:149]

[RETURN OF THE VALUATION OF PROPERTY IN GRAVESEND]‡

[24:150]

[RETURN OF THE VALUATION OF PROPERTY IN EASTHAMPTON]†

---

* See appendix for this assessment roll.
‡ See appendix for this return.
† See appendix for this return.

[24:151]

[LETTER FROM SOUTHAMPTON OFFICIALS RELATING TO THE
VALUATION OF PROPERTY]

Southampton Sept: 28: 1675

Worthy sir.

Wee the subscribed present our best respects to you hopeing of and much
Desireing your good health etc: Wee received your Order or warrant for
the makeing up and sending to you the Estimate or valuation of our
Towne And at length with care and trouble wee have effected it: And it
exactly amounts to twelve thousand five hundred and fourty one poundes
xxi s–viii d: Wee have dilligently accompted every mans estate up, and
that is the just totall according to our best inspection: Wee herein send
up not the particulers, for wee conceive that would bee but lost labour to
us, and noe advantage, Nor more satisfaction, but rather a Cumber to
you: And therefore according to our former maner to the High Shereive
wee send you the summe in gross, which wee hope will bee sufficient
and fully answer your expectation: Wee crave favour and pardon that
wee could not procure it sooner into your hand; But hope it will come
soe seasonably, that wee haveing your Order by the bearer our loveing
friend and much respected Justice Topping at his returne, May make
payment in the most suitable maner wee can to the Cuntries occasions;
But corne is but scarce with most of the Inhabitants, and wee Desire that
specie may not bee enjoyned in your warrant.

Sir wee have presumed to write to the Governor respecting our estimate,
and therein what wee have sett the horse=kinde* at, and have made
request to him touching that subject, If his honor bee not well=pleased,
wee desire your worshipp to bee Instrumentall as you can to excuse our
goeing beside that old law or order (which wee cannot but thinke now
to follow is excessive hard and oppressive) that rates horses and mares
one with another at 12 £ a peece. Sir: there are soe many people every
where, besides ours, Doe soe Exceedingly complaine that mares should
bee rated at 12 £ peece, when hardly the best will give 4 £ and many of
them not 40 s a peece, Emboldened us now to accompt them at 4 £ a
peece one with another which is more then anyone will give. Yet least it
should fall out (contrary to our expectation and beleif) that his honor the
Governoar should bee Dissatisfyed, and that wee may Deale uprightly,
Disscharge our Consience for the Towne and Duty towards the Cuntry
wee have as afforsaid sum'd up the horses and Mares at 4 £ 3 year olds
at 3 £ two year's: at 40 s and yearl: at 20 s peece: And withall wee have

* horses, donkeys, etc.

collected out of all the bills men particulerly brought in, the Just Numbers of horses and mares 3 year olds 2 year olds and yearlings: That for if notwithstanding our honorable Governor shall see cause, and it bee his plea[   ] to continue them still at the old rate of 12 £ a peece etc. wee cra[   ] favour to veiw the inclosed account and ad the Difference, [   ] which remaines (according to the said account) unto our valuatio[ ] And then the Estimate will bee compleated: Sir It is Desir[   ] at the Court you will promove the alteration of valuation[ ] horse kinde: Sir: Wee are yours to Command to our power [   ].

Wee are greived to heare of the
 loss of English blood by the
creull damned Pagans and very
many are Sorry the Indians here
have theire guns returned to them.

Thomas Topping
Henry Peirson
Thomas Cooper
Francis Sayer
John Jaggar

[24:152]
[RETURN OF THE VALUATION OF PROPERTY IN SOUTHOLD]*

[24:153a & b]
[COVERING LETTER AND RETURN OF THE VALUATION OF PROPERTY IN HUNTINGTON]‡

[24:154]
[RETURN OF THE VALUATION OF PROPERTY AT BROOKHAVEN]†

[24:155]
[RETURN OF THE VALUATION OF PROPERTY AT NEWTOWN]+

[24:156]
[RETURN OF THE VALUATIONS OF PROPERTY AT FLUSHING]**

* See appendix for this return.
‡ See appendix for this letter and this return.
† See appendix for this return.
+ See appendix for this return.
** See appendix for this return.

[24:157a]

[LETTER FROM MOSUP, SACHEM AT MONTAUK, ASKING FOR THE
RETURN OF HIS PEOPLE'S GUNS]*

Right Honorable

I and my men understanding that your Honnor was pleased to graunt
Liberty to the other Indians to have their Guns restored to them, but a
restraint was imposed upon us the Montaukut Indians, by reason of some
Complyance we have had with Nenecraft the Muhiggen Sachem, have
sent this our messenger with these few lines to Intreate your Honors
favour towards your poor Supplicants, your Honor may understand my
father and grandfather, have stood [ ]lways loyall to the English in the
Pequot warrs now towards 40 years since [ ] forefather was a great help
to the English, haveing then this whole Island att his Commaund, and
since then upon all occasions manifested his faithfulnes[ ] to the English,
and if any plots were att any tyme against them tymely discovered them
and this is known to many of the English yet alive: and concerning this
plot now on foot against the English, and your honor may be assured (for
we speak it before God the knower of all hearts) that had we been in the
least acquainted with any such matter we should have discovered the
same and though of late years we have had some Correspondency with
Ninecraft, your honor may be assured it was onely with respect to our
own security we being very weak, and few in number, and he being great
and having had wilfull experience of the great disolation he made
amongst us while we stood in termes of hostility against him, but this we
understanding is offensive to your Honor, we shall forbear for the future,
onely Intreate your honor to take some speedy course for our security,
that we may not be molested by the Marhigansits, for our dependence is
wholy upon your honor for protection, as we hope your Honor shall find
us ever loyall subjects to the King and duke of yorke and to your Honor,
and to all authority under you. your Honor may be pleased to take notice
that 4 of our stoutest men have been this tyme of warre with the English
Captaines, and fought under them and helped to doe some execution
upon their enemies, and had their free liberty to returne home being
dismissed upon their desire to retu[ ] to their friends and relations by the
Governor att Boston. we leave our selves with your Honor hopeing your
honors favourable acceptation of us, now is the usuall tyme of our
hunting, and to gett a litle provision, and some skins for Cloathing, and

* The letter is in the handwriting of the Rev. Thomas James and was written on the back
of his letter to the governor (24:157b).

if our humble request herein, may find a gracious answer, we shall take it as a further engagement to your honor.

and shall rest your honors humble servan[ ]

Easthampton Octob: 5th 1675.

Charls   Sachem Mosup Sachem ⟨mark⟩ marke

Jeckonna Couns[ ]   Will⟨X⟩alias
his marke ⟨mark⟩   Wuttauntaquim his mark

Monugabongun ⟨mark⟩
alias Gentleman his mark
Counsellor

In the Name and with the consent of the reste of the Indians att Montaukut.

[ ]de the
other side)

[24:157b]

[LETTER FROM THE REV. THOMAS JAMES SUPPORTING
THE PRECEDING REQUEST]*

Right Honor:

the lines upon the other side I wrote upon the desire of the Sachem and his men, they were their owne words, and the substance thereof they also had expressed before Mr. Backer but since my writeing of them which was alm[ost a] weak since, I perceive that delivering up [   ] armes to the Indians doth not relish well w[   ] the English, especialy since of late we h[   ] of the great slaughter, they have made up[   ] English in other parts of the Country; I perceive [   ] Southampton the English are much troubled the Indians have their armes, and I thinke it doth much disturbe the spirits of those have them not, as for these Indians for my owne part I doe thinke they are as Cordiall friends to the English as any in the Country, and what is written by you is known to many to be the truth though God knows their hearts as their Counseller said: your honors Predecessor wrote severall letters to me to stirre me up about Instructing

* Part of the following text is taken from *NYSHAR*.

the Indians in the knowledge of God and true Religion and that he would
further and encourage the buisnes so farr as lay in his power, I doe thinke
if your Honor be pleased to set in att this tyme it may be a good promotion
of that work which may Conduce to the enlargment of Christs kingdome,
and that which I have seen in severall writeings of his most excellent
majesty the king his pious desires expressed for the putting forward that
worke, but sir I cease further to trouble your Honor att present and for
what the Indians have written I leave to your Hon[ors] prudence to act
for the best, and rest with my humble service to your Honor and honored
Counsell.

Easthampton   Your Honors humble supplicant
Oct. 5th 1675   at the Throne of grace

                                                        Tho: James

[24:158]

[PETITION OF NICOLAES VAN RENSSELAER TO BE APPOINTED
DIRECTOR OF RENSSELAERSWYCK]

To the right honourable
Major Edmond Andros Esqr:
Governour of all his royall highnesse
Territories in America

The Humble Petition of Nicolaus van
Rensselaer Minister of N: Albany etc.

Sheweth

W[   ]s by the death of my brother Jeremias van[   ]aer the
direction of the Colony Rensselaerswyck was vac[ ]nt, and that there is
nobody in these Parts of the family and sonnes of my deceased Father
Kiliaen Van Rensselaer (in his Lifetime Lord Patron of the said Colony)
but myselfe, your Petitioner turns himself to your Honor Most Humbly
craving that the said direction Provisionally may be granted unto your
petitioner, till nearer order and Confirmation of his royall Highnesse in
tha[ ] behalfe, and that your Petitioner may execute the same Priveledges
and Authority in the abovementioned Colony as my deceased brother
Jeremy hath injoyed under the governments of Colonel Nicolls, and
Colonel Lovelace, By severall warrants of his Royall Highness granted
unto us assuring your honor that your Petitioner shall do nothing but what

obedience, equity, and justice shall allowe and that by your honors order
your Petitioner may have a free use of the bookes and Papers of the
Colony and that he may have a Due account of the revenues and accounts
of the Colony, and that your Petitioner may have for the use of his own
family one of the best farmes of the Colony; as three of my brothers have
hadd: of which two of them sold Theirs and my brothers widdowe doth
injoy herrs where she Lives at Present not doubting but your Honor shall
do your Petitioner all right justice and equity

And your Petitioner shall
alwayes be obliged

To
Pray

[ENDORSED:]   [   ] of October [   ]
                 [   ]enseleaers
                 [   ]tition Conserning
                 the Colonye.

[24:159]

[PETITION FROM SIMON ATHEARN CONCERNING HIS LAND TITLE
AND THE NEED FOR REGULATING OF AFFAIRS AT MARTHA'S
VINEYARD][*]

October 8th 1675:

In most humble wise

I Simon Athearn an Inhabitant of Tisbury on Martins Vineyard: do make
my most humble petition under the most Excellent and Right honnorable
Governor over all his Ryel hinesse his Territories in america;   Right
honnorable; I humbly Conceve I am in my way to record the title of my
Land in this ofic of records Considering our neglect; and also the perrills
of these times, if it please your honnor the Case is this: Mr. Mayhew
brought us Charturs from General Lovelesse the which I have paid my
part for, and am a man Concarned therein as my deeds will testifie if you
please to peruse them: and that Land I have bought I humbly Conceve
the Charter for Tisbury doth give me liburty to buy and much more: but
I have not bought any more then mearly for my nessessitie, neither do I
desier to ingrosse more land then I can make use of, for I rather desier

---

*   Material in brackets is taken from *NYSHAR*.

the Iland to be inhabited: now we ware to pay an anuell acknowledgment which hath beene neglected: and what the End may be I know not I onc delivered Six Shilling in mony to Mathew Mayhew for my part of the acknowledgment but It hath not been used with others to buy fish: others had their mony restored to them again: but I had never mine to this day: and now if I must be wise for myselfe, what Can I doe but petition unto youre honnor for a Confermation of my title buy an Entranc in this ofic of Records; or sum other way; whereby my title may be confermed: both that I have bought from the Indians, and of the English: so shall I bee redy to pay my acknowledgment now, and from time to time for the futer if the Lord will: I verily beleeve did your honnor know the broken Confusednesse of the records on martins vineyard your honnor would see it nessessery for all to take a better title;

If it please your honnor I humbly Concive I have recived rong in the lose of my sevant, if not to teadious its thuse; I Took a naked Indian boy to be my apprentic fower years the which term he was to serve me my heirs or assignes; and I my heirs or assigns to provid him sofitiant food and rayment during his servic, and at the end of his servic to give him sofitient duble apparrell and one good young Cowe for his servic, but after about a yeare there Came an Indian of the b[   ]s bindred and utered violant words to the great afrightning of my wife, and Caryed away my boy, but sum days after the Indians brought him againe so about a weeke after I had ocation to goo from whom* and left my boy to doe as I had apoynted him but the same day I went from the Iland the boy run away also but soone after the Indians brought him again; then the boy would have agreed with my wife, that If shee would lett him goe every Satterday and Com on munday then he would tary till I com whom: but my wife said no you shall not go to stink of your Compeny but you shall go to meeting with me and do as your master hath apoynted you, but quickly after my boy runn away: so after the end of three weeks or near a month I Came whom; my boy was then at whom the Indians having brought him two days before: and my wife telling me of his doing I gave the boy two boxes on the Eare with my fist, so sum dayes after the boy run a way again: [then] I complaind to mr. Mayhew our governor and the Justic I had; the boy [wa]s to return to me but I not to requier any thing for lose of time (because I strook him twic) and If I strook him soe again he should be free.) but no punnishment to boy nor Indian soe I never strook the boy before nor since, but when greene Indian Corn was eatable my boy run away again and hath beene gon ever senc, so he hath abscented my servic about fowr month unto my great disopoytment and Lose I would have

---

* Intended for "home."

shewed your honnor a Coppy of the Indenture but James Allin an
assistant the man that hath it in keeping would not let me have a coppy
of it at a tim I said if my boy would not serve me, I would sell him: into
which richard sarson an assistant answared my Indentur was unlawfull
because he was bound to serve me my heirs or assignes: why said I if
not so who shall pay him his ward if I die: then said richard sarson it
should have beene mentioned within this government, and its a known
thing it hath beene Mr. Mayhews Judgment that no master should strick
his servant and that if the servant is not willing to abid the master should
let him goe, I shall not mention the many greeviences which are many
But this I know that if things be not mended, diverc of the inhabitents
will remove their dwelling to goe whare they Can: wherefor I besech
your honnor to graunt us your Law to be our rule and Square to walke
by that we may be delivered from all rible rable* and notions of men
doutlesse if things ware better I should give you a better Carrictor also I
besech your honnor to Consider us your sarvants in our low estat wee
being but about 38 English men on the Iland able to bare arms: and the
Indians a multitud Mr. Mayhews tennants I hope your honnor will in
goodnesse and marcy to us Give order, that all English Lands be
inhabited with a Competant number of English inhabitants: and that no
person or persons be suffered to lett any indian or indians have any
pouder in these perilous times: all I besech your honnor to give order that
each town build [ ]em a meeting house and Call them and maintain them
a minister able [ ]o devid the word of god aright that we may be kept
from profainnesse herosse‡ and vic and a scoolmaster to teach our
children: so both us and our Children shall have your honor in renoun
forever.

if it please your honnor our Condition is such the authority took sum
laws out of boston and plimmouth Law books to be our law, and made
a law that if any Case com to tryell which this law doth not reach it should
be tryed by the law of boston or the law of England: the law of England
non of us know, the law of boston hath been rejected as not the Dukes
Law, and Law confermed above five pounds: Mr. Gardner have the
Dukes Law to Judg by but Mr. Mayhew and Richard Sarson did reject
to keep Court by it at nan tucket, so the Generall Court seaces: yet Mr.
Mayhew gives out warrants and swares Juryes sum times to goe according to Contiance and sumtimes according to Law, and hath not signed
vardicts: I veryly beleve had Gennerall Lovelesse Given and Confined
Mr. Mayhew and us unto the Laws of this Provinc it had prevented all

* Idle and low talk (*The Century Dictionary*, 1890–91).

‡ heresy

disorder which hath fallen out senc. But when good government faills the bauty and honnor of a stat faills: for such and many other Causes as are well known we are keept very few in number and pore in estats and Left to a great annomossitie of spirit which must needs be the cancomatants of such Erreguler proseed[   ]s: But how wonderfull is this citty bautified by your honnors sharpnesse of wisdum and great dilligenc in Executing Justic and Judgment which gives me great hope that your honnor will voutsaf to take dew Care for a better settleing of a pore and a disordry people. I beeing very much desiered by one Jacob Perkins of hoomes hall to relate his Late greevenc before your honnor and that your honnor might know both the Cause and reason if it please your honnor thuse There was a man and Thomas Dogget fell to deferenc in somuch that the man called Tho: Dogget Lyer knave and Theefe so Tho: dogget sewed the man and the man brought Testimony that Tho: dogget had taken goats and sheep that was non of his: so the Case was Like to go hard with Tho: doggett by the Jury; this Jacob parkins being of the Jury: and no favorer of thomas doggets Case Jacob perkins Coming not long after to Thomas doggets house presently tho: Doggets wife Mr. Mayhews daughter, (which woman) the peopl of martins vineyard very Generaly call the Deputy Governor, she being displeased with perkins said if it had not been for hamton men her husband had had the Case to which perkins answered; if an indiferant parson and not a relation had writt the tesstimony or that if Skiffe* had swept all his testimony away; and pleaded to your husbands own confess[   ]n skiffe had prooved his charg: so tha[   ]rted in displeasur: quickly after Mr. Mayhew gave an Indyan a warrant [ ]hich took uppe[   ]ns[   ] them: so after sum weeks perkins Coming where the Indian with others was so he asked the Indian whether it was he that took away his hogs, the indian said no twas mr. mayhew, perkins said twas he so thay tell to; you lye, and lying roag: Then quickly the Indian run on the said perkins and Laid hould with his hands on perkins his heair and plocked him down and swore he would kill him and Called to his fellows for a knife to kill him, so perkins went and Complained to Mr. Mayhew, and mr. mayhew and Tho: Dogget much threatened him that he should answar for it and would have find perkins five pounds for Calling the Indian Lyeing Roag: but thay very mildly tould the Indian that if he Carryed any stick or knife or weapon in his hand for such a tim; he should pay five pounds, so the Indian went away Lauthing: perkins being then much trobled for the unjust taking away of his hogs and meeting with so could releefe from so great an evill he utered words of discontent, to which Mr. Mayhew said if you do not

* James Skiff

like what I doe, you may go to yoark but the man being pore and can not wright did desier mee to shew your honnor the Case as I have dun.

[ENDORSED:]   Martins Vineyard.
              Simon Athearns Peticion.
              Oct. 8. 1675.

[24:160]

[PETITION FROM SECRETARY NICOLLS FOR REDRESS OF LIBEL COMMITTED BY INHABITANTS OF HUNTINGTON]

To the right Honorable Governor and the Honorable Bench Assembled att this Generall Court of Assizes.

The humble Peticion of Mathias Nicolls
Secretary to his Honor the Governor etc.

Sheweth

That whereas the inhabitants of Huntington and Especially Jonas Wood Isaack Platt Tho: Skidamore and Tho: Powell with severall false scandelous and Malicious reports to Detract and take away the good name and reputacion of your Peticioner in the month of Aprill 1674 and Diverse times before and since not only in words but in writting have Charged your Peticioner of falseyfieing the Records of this Colony and foysting in An Order of Assizes Int. Smith and the Inhabitants of Huntington etc.

Therefore Humbly Prayes that the said Wood and his Confederates may prove their Accusacion against your Peticioner or else that they may be bound to their good behaviour and to stand to the Judgment of this honorable Court etc.

And hee etc.

[ENDORSED:]   Capt. Nicolls Peticion

12th of Oct. 1675 granted an order by the Court after reading a Certain letter of the towne dated 20/10 of agust 74 Mr. Nicolls oblig'd to prosecute.

[24:161]

[BOND OF WILLIAM BOWDITCH AND THOMAS DELAVALL TO PAY
SALVAGE ON TWO BOATS AT PEMAQUID]

The Condicion of this Obligacion is such That where=as the above
bounden William Bowditch hath purchased the right and Interest in two
Ketches lyeing at Pemaquid, which were brought in there by the Indyans
upon the Agreement of Peace with them the one named the Willing Mind
of Salem, whose Owner was John Turner, the other The Bette of
Marblehead, formerly belonging to Ambrose Gale, and upon the Applicacion of the said Willm. Bowditch, there being an Order of Councell
for their delivery unto him or his Order Now if the said Willm. Bowditch
and Thomas Delavall their Executors, Administrators or assignes shall
well and truely pay and make good what Salvage or other Charges the
said two Ketches shall bee lyable to and adjudged to pay, by the Governor
of these his R. Hs Territories, upon demand, at his Returne, that then this
present Obligacion shall bee voyde and of none Effect, otherwise to
remaine and bee in full force, power and vertue.

Sealed and delivered in
the presence of
[*blank*]

[ORDER TO SETAUKET TO CLEAR AWAY BRUSH NEAR THE FORT]*

By the Governor

Whereas I am informed that neare the Fort newly built at Seatalcott, there
is a parcell of Brush wood, both in the common and the Lotts of private
persons, which upon occasion may prove very inconvenient These are
in his Majesties name strictly to enjoyne and require the Inhabitants of
said Towne that forthwith they all joyne in cutting down and bringing
the brush in the Commons within 80–perches‡ of the said Fort, and that
the persons who have particular Lotts doe the like in their said Lotts to
that distance, and for soe doeing this shall bee their warrant, Given under
my hand in N.Y. this 22th day of Oct. 1675.

To the Justice of Peace
Const. and Overseers of
Sealalcott.

---

* This document , which appears on the back of the preceding document, has been crossed
out.
‡ E. B. O'Callaghan read this scrawled word as "poles," which is not impossible. Both
words refer to a unit of 16^1/$_2$ feet, so the meaning is not an issue.

[24:162]

October 10th 1675.

This day came before mee John Ambrose Mate of the ship the *Good Hope* lately come from Barbados, and Walter Feverell Boateswaine of the said ship, and doe on the behalfe of themselves and the rest of the shipps Company make their Protest against the Sea.[*]

About 2
a clock in the
afternoone

[ENDORSED:]   Entry of Protest
               by the Mate and
               Boateswaine of the
               Ship the Good Hope
               Oct. 10. 1675.

[24:163]

To the Right Honnorable the
Governor and the Honorable Court of
Assizes.

The petitione of Johannes verveile

In all humble maner

Sheweth: That your honors petitioner brought his accion against John Archer for his nonperformance of a Certaine Contract made with your petitioner wherein the Worshipfull the Mayors Court found for your petitioner but the said Archer has nott yeelded obedience thereunto: but one the Contrary hath Carried away aboute 4 load of hay to the greate Impoverishment of your honors petitioner

Therefore humbly prays that your honor will be pleased to

---

[*] Obviously Secretary Nicolls meant to write something other than "sea"; perhaps, "seaworthiness." The *Good Hope* was condemned by the court of Admiralty a few days after this protest and sold to pay the crew's wages (see *BGE* 2: 91, 157–58).

releife him herein according to Equity = and he as In Duty
bound

Shall Ever pray
for your honors prosperity

[ENDORSED:]   Johannes Verveile
his petitione.
Past 1675.

[24:164]

[PETITION FROM THE COOPERS OF SOUTHAMPTON AND
EASTHAMPTON TO KEEP OUT COMPETITORS]*

To the Right Honorable Coll: Andreas Governor Ge[n.]
of all his Royall Highnes Territtori[es]
in America:

The Humble Petition and Addresse of the Coopers of South:
and Easthampton.

Most humbly Sheweth.

That theire is A Company of Coopers yearely Come in the Winter season
from Boston to worke heere: that neither pay to: Towne nor Country any
Rates and teach young men: theire Trade for: A winter worke or some
small tym[e] more: whereby theire bee many bad workmen in the townes
which is greatly to the Damage both of Townes and Merchants And if
any of our Coopers in the Summer Tyme when w[ee] have noe Employment att whome goe out to B[oston to work if th]ey work under one of
those Coopers h[ere Cannot] bee perm[itte]d to worke because hee
Served not hi[s tyme there] whereby it appeares that they have a Law:
that no[ne but] Such as have served theire tymes in that Jurisdiction bee
permitted to sett up theire.

Wherefore wee most humbly besceech your Honor wo[uld be] gratiously
pleased to Cause an Order to bee made fo[r the] prohibition of any such
that shall Come heere to Set [up that] have into this government: Either
Served theire tym[e or] are inhabitants thereof As also that none might
[bee] permitted to worke for themselves but under some other men that
have not served att least five yeares: And that theire may bee A sworne

___
* The following text comes in part from *CD* 14.

searcher and G[ager] that noe unmarchantable Barrells may bee putt up[on] Merchants as frequently they are: whereby the merchant is f[orced]: by reason of his Dammage with his Casque to sett h[igher] prices of his goods soe that both Plantor and [Merchants are] hereby wronged: which makes us your Honors most h[umble] Pettitioners humbly seeke Releife of your Honor [and we] shall as wee are Ever bound most humbly pray

William Jeane   Char Shawe
                             Phillip Leek
                             Ebenezer [Leeks]

the mark of ⟨Ꝺ⟩   Christopher Lymon

[ENDORSED:]*   A Petition from
                    the Coopers of
                    Easthampton and
                    Southton.
                    1675.

                    Past.
                    Assizes.

[24:165]

[PETITION FROM FARMERS ON RICHARD SMITH'S LAND FOR EQUITY]

To the Right Honorable Edmond Andross. Esquire Governor Generall under his Royall Highnesse James Duke of Yorke and Albany of all his R. Hs. territoryes in America and this honorable Bench.

The humble Peticion of the Poore farmers whoe are Seated on the land latly in Controversy Betweene Richard Smith, and the inhabitants of Huntington.

In all humillity sheweth.

That your honnors poore Peticioners have by virtue of an order of an honorable Court of Assizes held in New yorke in the moneth of October Anno 1670, Satt downe, built upon, Cleared, fenced, Planted, Plowed, and soed upon the Land on the West syde of Nessequauke River, and Cutt and provided Hay for their Cattells Provizion this winter. and your

---

* The endorsement is on a separate paper.

honnor and this honorable Bench, having found the aforementioned Land, etc. doth belong to said Richard Smith and passed a decree accordingly. Not Explaining therein, your honnors intention, how your poore Peticioners Shall regulate themselves, as to the Posessing, renting or purchasing the said Land, which is by them soe seated, cleared, cultivated, and built on. Being by Experience assured, that if Your honnor take not some course, and make some firme order for their releife, in and about the renting or Purchaseing the said Land, Your poore Peticioners, their wives and Children, must of necessity, Inevitably and Irepayreable-ly bee ruined and ondone, it now appeareing the said Smith, hath noe more, than what Huntington Long since tenderd for Peace and Quietness sake to the said Smith, as they are able imediatly and ready to prove and make appeare, which the said Smith refused to accept of, or Embrace, which refusall, hath occasioned all this trouble and charge to the poore towne of Huntington, etc. Now if your poore Petitioners must bee constreyned, to lye at said Smiths mercy imediatly to bee turned off, or in the renting or Purchaseing the said Land, they can promise nothing to themselves but unreasonableness and Cruelty which constreynes them to address themselves to your honnor for releife in the premisses humbly begging and beseeching your honnor seriously to Consider this their said and deplorable Condition, in ordering somthing for their releife, as shall best suite with your honnors Gravity wisdom and Prudence, which will oblidge them and theirs Ever to pray for your honnors Long life and Prosperity etc.

Thomas Skidmor
for the farmers

[ENDORSED:]   Peticion of the farmers Newly
settled, on the Land lately in
Controversy Betweene Richd.
Smith and Huntington.
Past 1675

[24:166]

[PETITION OF GERRIT HENDRICKSZ AT HALF MOON, APPEALING
A JUDGMENT THAT HE PAY COURT COSTS]

To the right Honorable the Governor and
Honorable Bench assembled att this
Generall Court of Assizes.

This humble peticion of Garritt Hendrix

Sheweth

That your Peticioner haveing made good his Title to 16 Morgan of Land in the halfe moone the which one Goosen Garrittsen kept from him and for which he hath now obteyned the Judgment of this Honorable Court humbly conceives under favour of this Honorable Court he had Just cause of accion the said Goosen Garrittsen alwayes refuseing to Lett your Peticioner have any land on the half moone but your Peticioner is informed This honorable Court hath adjudged your Peticioner to pay the Costs which if soe your Peticioner wil be greatly Dampnified he being very poore and feareing the Costs will be more worth then the Land.

Therefore your Peticioner humbly prayes this Honorable Court to Consider the premisses and to Order the Delinquent or party Cast to pay the Costs according to Law and the practice of this Government.

And your Peticioner shall pray etc.

[ENDORSED:]   Gerrit Hendricks peticion.
About the Costs of Court
betweene him
and Goosen Gerritse.
past 1675

[24:167]

[PETITION OF NICHOLAS BLAKE, APPEALING A JUDGMENT]

To the Right Honorable Ma[   ]ond Andros Governor Under his Royall Highness James Duke of Yorke of all his territories in America, or in his absence to his D[   ]tie

The humble Peticion of Nicholas Blake merchant

Sheweth,

That one francis Richardson late master of the wrackt flyboate called the good Hope, coming from the Barbados with pretended power to call your peticioner to an accompt for his acting in order to the fixxing off the goods that came in said shipp, called a spetiall Court, where hee could show no sufficient power for it, but to the Contrary your Peticioner could (and still can) prove the power to be suffitient by which hee loaded the said goods, had the matter gon on to bee cleered out; But being that your Peticioner offered freely to secure (by his owne bond) the said Master from all demages that may accrue unto him or the owners of the Intressed by reason of any act of his in shipping the said goods; The Court thought fitt to heare no farther in the Matter and concluded all with an order that your Peticioner should give the said Francis Richard[   ] security to indemnifie him as above; and now your Peticioner is summoned to performe the same or else to be under Execution; wheras your Peticioner humbl[ ] declareth that hee is not bound to fullfill the order being hee in court protested at the making that order, that other security then his owne hee could not (being a stranger) give, so there was no consent on your Peticioners side, which hee can Amply prove.

Also the said francis Richardson by a Motion of his own procured this last order on Tuesday last, your Peticioner knowing nothing at all of it, nor was sent for by the Court to heare what hee had to say for himselfe.

Wherfore your Peticioner prayes, that seing none ought to bee condemned withour hearing, or surprised without notice in any Legall way, that your Honor would give order for the suspention of said Order for the present, or that hee take What I profered in Court, my single bond, or else that it may come to a faire Tryall the Verry next Court;

And your Peticioner shall pray etc.

The reasons why [N] B. doth not
comply with the Courts order.[*]

1. Whereas tis said the order was [   ]de by Consent of both parties, tis a mistake for N. B. never consented (to the last) to give other then his owne personall security (of which hee can give good proofe) so this not being by Consent, N. B. holds not himselfe bound to give other security Then his owne bond, which hee is still ready to doe, then it may bee demanded why N. B. did nott appeale, to this I answere that hee intended so to doe, but the Governor would first know of Mr. Mayor what had passed, who (by mistake) said that what was sett downe in the order was by Consent, which caused that the Governor (at that time) would conclude upon nothing of an appeale, it being (as hee was Informed) a Mutuall agree-

---

* Appears on a separate page from the petition; however they could have been attached originally.

ment, but I Informed the Governor of the error Mr. Mayor was in (as really he was in) so the thing lay till now, that francis Richardson hath Cautelously[*] and surreptitiously gotten an order to putt in other security with my selfe.

2.This last order was procured and gotten out without the least notice given to N. B. that hee might bee there (by sommons) to speake for himselfe, in case hee had anything to alleage, and tis a Rule in all Courts of Justice, that the defendant should bee heard before hee bee condemned through the meere suggestions of a playntiff;

3. If N. B. should performe this order (which was not by consent as alleag[ ]d) he cutts himselfe off from ever having a full hearing of the case which he desires there may bee, being that hee doubts not of making it out how hee had suffitient order to act as hee did.

[ENDORSED:]   Mr. Blakes reasons
                     of his peticion.

[24:168]

[PETITION OF SAMUEL BARKER TO BE INDEMNIFIED FOR THE LOSS
OF HIS SON]

To the Right Honorable Major Edmond Andross Governor Generall and the rest of the Honorable Court of assizes.

                The Humble peticion of
                Samuel Barker

Shewing Unto your honor, and this honorable bench that since by sadd fate, hee is unhappily deprived of his sonne who was the staffe of his age and onely Comfort, for maintenance hee haveing no other dependance then, but now Since the law is sattisfied, uppon the offender

Your poore peticioner humbly offers to your mercifull Consideracion the poverty of your peticioner and the abillity of the offenders parents, whether or no according to the (Law of God) some restitution ought not to bee made for your peticioners future Releife, according as by your honors Judgment shall bee thought fitt, to the end that his Gray haires, may not altogether goe with sorrow to the Grave

* An obsolete or archaic word meaning "deceitfully" (*Oxford English Dictionary*).

Your honors poore peticioner shall pray etc.

[ENDORSED:]   The humble peticion of
                Samuell Barker.

                Samuell [   ]
                petition.
                Not gr[   ]ed.
                1675.

[24:169]

[PETITION OF ALLARD ANTHONY FOR AN
APPEAL IN EQUITY]

To the Right Honorable Major Edmund
Andros Esq. Sen. of Sans Maritz Leif-
tenant Governor Generall of all his Royall
Highnesses Territoryes in America etc.

The humble Peticion of
Allard Anthony.

Sheweth.

That your Peticioner the Last Mayors Court sued Elizabeth Bedloe
Adm[inistratrix] of Isaack Bedloe Deceased for a Negroe Servant sold
by your Peticioner unto the said Isaack Bedloe for 35£ Sterl. and an
Anchor of wine worth ƒ100, for which your Peticioner never received
one Farthing in Satisfacion where (your Peticioners wittnesses who
could prove the Sale and Delivery of the said Neger being either dead or
Departed this Government) your Peticioner not being able to make Such
Sufficient Proofe as the Strict rules of the Common Law in such Case
requires was Cast.

Your peticioner therefore Humbly Prayes
your Honor to Grant him an Appeale that
his Case may be heard before your Honor
att the next Generall Court of Assizes in
Equity he Performing what the Law in
Such Case requires.

And your Peticioner shall pray etc.

[ENDORSED:]   Mr. A[   ]rd Anthony.
An appeale granted about the
Negroe etc. sold to Mr. Bedloe.
Nov. 25th 1675.

[24:170]

[PETITION OF JACOB MELYN, APPEALING A JUDGMENT]

To the Right Honorable the Governor etc.

Humbly Complaineing sheweth unto your Honor your Orator Jacob
Molyne etc. That your Orator was sued att the Mayors Court of this Citt.
by one Robt. Leprerie where Judgment past against your Orator who
being not willing to abide thereby Is forced to Appeale to your Honor
Desireing your honors releife etc.

[ENDORSED:]   Jacob [   ]
peticion of [   ]
graunted [   ]
16[   ]

[24:171–84]

[RECORDS OF THE COURT OF ASSIZES FOR THE COLONY
OF NEW YORK FOR 1675]*

[24:185]

[PETITION OF JOHN MANNING TO BRING SUIT AGAINST MARTEN
HOFFMAN]

To the Right Honnorable the
Governor and the Honnorable Bench
Assembled at this Court of Assizes.

In all humble maner Complaining Sheweth unto your Honor that your
daily Orator John Manning Late of this City Gent. was seized in fee or
otherwise of a certaine Messuage of tennement with a lott of ground
lyeing and beinge In the High street of this Citty which said House etc.
your Orator did purchase of one Martine Huffeman Late of this Citty

* These documents are published in *CA*, pp. 141–88.

who Conveied the premisses unto your Orator by a firme deed with a Warrantie which beareth date the 21st of November 1668 Now soe it is may it please your Honor that the said Huffeman one purpose to defraude your Orator did Morgage the premisses before Conveiance as aforesaid for the summ of [*blank*] besides intrest and Cost of suite in the Mayors Court thereby occationed Therefore pray that the said Huffeman forthwith may by your Honnor and Honorable Court be Compelled to disingage the said Morgage and that he may pay all intrest and Charges happned theirupon and your Honors Orator as in all Duty bound shall Ever Pray etc.

Generall Courte and part

[ENDORSED:]   Capt. John Manning
                  against
                  Martine Huffeman

                  Not allowed, The
                  Deft being not summoned
                  Past. 1675.

                  1675.
                  John Manning.

[24:186–88]

[RECORDS OF THE COURT OF ASSIZES]*

[24:189]

Due for the last yeares Rate

	£	s	d
Flattbush	13	04	4 3/4
Boswyck	3	00	10 1/2
Newtowne	28	03	3 1/2
Jamaica	23	06	8
	67	15	2 3/4

---

* See previous note.

[24:190]

[LETTER TO THE CONSTABLES CONCERNING THE ABOVE
TOWN TAX RATES]

Gentlemen

By the Governors Order I am to give you notice by this Expresse that his
honor expects you to make Payment forthwith, for the summes due from
your Townes for the last yeares Rate, (the particulars where of you have
here enclosed) and that in Corne, The Governor having Present occasion
for the Garrison, and you shall receive discharges [*one line missing*]-
faction of the sheriffe. I am

Your loving friend
Matthias Nicolls.

New Yorke.
October 20th 1675.

[ADDRESSED:]   To the Constables
of Flattbush Jamaica
Newtowne and Boswyck.
Upon Long Island.

[24:191][*]

[TABLE OF SHERIFF'S FEES AT THE COURT OF ASSIZES]

Sheriffs fees Stated by the Corte	sh d	sh d
For serving A warrant	1.8	
For taking Securyty	2.6	5.0 of Arest or
For returning the warrant	0.10	Atatchment
For Impanilling A Jury	2.6	
For Every Vardicte of the Jury or Corts Judgment	1.0	
For Every Excycution	5.0	
For Every pertickuler Summans of Complaint by order from A magistrate	2.6	

* The original number of the document that is now called 24:192.

	sh.d.	
For Imprisonment of Aney person to the Sheriffe	10.0	
To Mr. Hen. Newton	03.0	16.0
To Sherbanke	03.0	

[24:192]*

[TABLE OF SHERIFF'S FEES GIVEN IN AND COMPARED WITH THOSE FORMERLY ALLOWED]

Sheriffs fees given in by
Mr Aldran Cony‡

	£ s d	
For serving A warrant	0.01.8	of arrest or attachments
For tacking securyty	0.02.6	allowed
For Every Vardicte of the Jury or Corts Judgment	0.01.0	allowed
For Every Exeycutian	0.05.0	allowed
For Every partickler sumance of Cumplaint	0.02.6	allowed

by order from a Magistrate†

Formar Customes of fees	gild stirs	
~~For An Areste~~+	07:10X	
~~For security of the same~~	02:00X	
~~For Atatchment~~	06:00X	
XFor returning the warrant	02:00—	10d allowed
For Impan. A Jury	05:00*	
For Every Vardict of the Jury or Corts ordar	02:00	
For Every partickler sumance of Cumplainte	05:00	
For Imprisonment of Aney person (to the Sheriff)	20:00	allowed 12 sh.

* The original number of the document that is now called 24:191.

‡ This person could not be identified. Perhaps Adriaen Cornelissz, who served on the city court during the Colve administration, is intended.

† This line, the last three lines before the endorsements, and all material to the right of the numbers was added by Secretary Nicolls.

+ The cancelations in this document were made by Mr. Nicolls.

* A "3" is written above the "05" by Mr. Nicolls.

To Hen Newton	06.00	allowed 6 sh
To Sherbanke	06:00	

For warrants of Seartch
[   ] left by your Worships

	sh d	
serving warrant	1 – 8	sh.
security	2 – 8	8. – 0
Returnes	<u> –10</u>	
	5: 0	

[ENDORSED:]   Sheriffes Fees etc
                 allowed   N.Y.

[24:193–94]

[MINUTES OF A MEETING EXAMINING INDIAN CLAIMS TO LAND
ADJOINING HEMPSTEAD]*

At a meeting of Indyans. Oct 21

[ ]tephanus   A Note of land under Hemsted Claimed by
V: Cortland   the Indians as not Paid for.
[ ]riffe

                     A necke kalled Matinnekonck on the sound
                     at the Eastward of Muchitoe Coove.

                     A Small island Called Hoggs island at
                     the Sou[th side] of Long Island.

Merricocke the ind[ian] [   ] [Pl]anting land volontarily left
[   ] Massepeake on [   ] [Tackop]awis and his
Indians did for[merly] Plant, but about three or fo[u]re Year ago were
turned of by one Cheepy who Claimed the said land to bee his as
informed by Indians

Whereupon Tackepawis off Marcepeake [and] [   ]nimham of
Mericocke did remaine [   ] [and] plant upon rockeway where [   ]
have Planted Ever Since.

Decla[ration] by Geo [Hewlett.]
That Cowe Necke has bin fenced in and injoyed by those of Hemsted,

* The following text comes in part from *CD* 13.

this 25 Yeares and doe not knowe, the same to be Claimed, by the Indians Ever sins

That Great Mad Nans [Neck ha]s been Setled about Eight [years agoby the] English with many fo[   ] Setled 30 Yeares ago [by John] Richardson and do not know [that it has] been Claimed by the indians Sin[ce.]

Little Mad Nans Necke Setled by Severall familys about 8 yeares, and neere 20 Yeares reputed to be Purchased under [Hempstee]d [and] is now under flisschingen

all these severall trackes were [spoken] off in Gouvernor Nicolles time after Gouvernor Lovelaces aryval and particulars dicoursed afore them att Mr. Hixes the Indian[s] being sent for, and present, but nothi[ng] fully Concluded onely advised [that if they persi]sted should give to the Indians [a present] to satisfy them.

M[emorandum] The Indians do ouwne they [had] sold the land at the Soudward but not Nortward.

At a Councell—Oct. 21. 1675.

Before noone

Present
The Gov.
The Secr.   C. Dyre
Mr. Philips

Mayor and Ald[   ]

The Indians to follow [the d]irections of the Assizes to remove from Mr. Pells.

No powder nor lead to be sold in this town to the [Indians.]

Afternoon[ ]   [   ] meeting etc.

Present the Go:

The Secr. Mr. Philips.

Mr. Cor[nell] Wm Laurence from Flush[ing] Mr. Gildersleeve and Mr. Geo Hewlett from Hempsteed they came according to order th[is] day from the two Townes.

Tackpousha and the rest came not till [this] Evening; and brought som[e pr]ete[nding] to L[and] with them the persons appeared just agoeing returned with them [. . . *one line lost* . . .]

Mr. Edsall Interpreter.

The Indyans renewed their prete[nces] to the land on the North of Hempsteed [   ] etc.—particularly Cow Neck, Litle Madnans Neck, great [Madnans] Neck the Go: makes offers and [   ] but they not willing to consen[t] [   ] with Cow Neck, so to remain[ ] as it is, but neither Christian nor Indyan to bee permitted to settle there at present.

Tackpousha brought some other p[reten]ders of being Owners etc. to some of the land at the North.

[   ] to consider of it till to morro[ ]

[ENDORSED:]   At a Councell
               Oct 21th 167[ ]
               and Indyan Meeting
               Tackpousha etc.

Oct. 22. 1675

At a meeting of Indyans before the Go: at the Fort

Tackpoushe, his son and some others.
Its about an Agreement for the Lands on th[   ] Hempsteed limitts The [   ]r Gildersleeve [   ]eorge M[   ] and Lt. Tho: Wil[ ]t for Flat[   ].

Mr. [   ] and myselfe.

One of the Indyans claymes 3 Necks to belong to him and an old Squaw. They aske 120 £ againe as before, for the 3 Necks, and to keepe Cow Neck themselves.

All that have pretences must come [   ]gether some other time; and the Go[   ]gree with them.

[ENDORSED:]   At a Meeting of
                   Indyans at the Fort.
                   Oct. 22. 1675.

[24:195]

[MINUTES OF A MEETING AT WHICH INDIANS WERE ORDERED
TO SURRENDER THEIR GUNS]

Oct. 23. 1675.

At a meeting of Indyans in the Fort

Tackpoushe and his son, with Rockways Sachem and 2 or 3 more.

They say they'l come againe [ ]ith the rest con[ ]erned about prete[   ]
land and in ten[   ]

[   ]arges th[   ] their holding In[ ]lligence with the
In[   ] the Maine etc.

They are told that upon their good Comport as was thought they had their
Guns given them, but now upon this they are to bee taken away againe;
but some shall bee lent to the good Indyans.

They deny to have had any Correspondence as is [   ] to their Charge.

They are ordred to bring in [   ]n Tuesday next beetimes to the
Officers at Hempsteed.

[ENDORSED:]   Oct: 28. 1675
                   At a Meeting in the [   ]
                   The Indyan Ch. [   ]kpousha.

[24:196]

[MINUTES OF A MEETING DEALING WITH NICOLAES BAYARD'S
REFUSAL TO SWEAR ALLEGIANCE]

At a Councell etc. Oct. 29. 1675.

Present
The Governor
The Secr.   C. Dyre
Mr. Philips.

The matter under Consideracion is the matter of Mr. Cornelys Steenwyck etc. and their late behavior etc.

Upon Consideracion of the late ill Comport of Mr. N. Bayard etc. since the Judgment of the Court of Assizes.

It is the opinion of the Councell that for securing his Majesties peace the said N. Bayard bee forthwith apprehended, and brought to the Fort, there to bee kept a Prisoner in Order to further Proceedings against him, and the Judgment of the Court of Assizes to bee fully put in Execucion against his Estate.

[ENDORSED:]   At a Councell etc.
Oct . 29. ⎞
Nov. 1st ⎠ 1675.
Mr. Steenwyck etc.

The Andros Papers

1675–1676

The New York Historical Manuscripts Series
Volume XXV

[25:1–2]

Nobr. 1. 1675   At a Councell etc.
                               Present:

The Governor
The Secr.   C. Dyre
Mr. Phillips.

Mr. Nicholas Bayard being a prisoner in the Hole in the Fort, his matter is taken into Consideracion.

Gab : Minvielle.
Gerrit Van Tright.
Cornelys V: Borsum   offred for Security, if
Jacob Teunis Kay.   hee may have his liberty
Rayneer Williams.   etc.
Peter Bayard.

Accepted of for the good Behavior also, but waved by him.

That for this night Mr. Bayard bee releast out of prison in the Fort, and left to Mr. Minvielle to goe to his house, who is to bee responsible for him, and his good behavior.

Ordered that Mr. Steenwyck and all the rest bee sent for tomorrow morne to the Fort, and told, That whereas the Governor is informed that they are dis=satisfyed with the late proceedings against them at the Court of Assizes where they had no Jury it being not then desired, by them: Therefore up[ ] their giving in security of good behavior etc., there shall forthwith bee [ ] speciall Court of Assizes called in whic[ ] the proceedings against them as Delinquents shall bee by a jury etc. But in Case the sai[ ] persons doe desire to abide by their for[   ] sentence and doe comply therewith a[ ] the law doth require (provided it[ ] within three days), they s[   ] bee admitted thereunto.

The Court of Mayor and Aldermen to bee [   ] to, that they bee here likewise, 9 a clock in the morning.

Mary—The wife of Thomas Case is brought by the Sheriffe bef[ ] the Go: and Councell, upon the request[ ] 3 of her daughters and husbands that l[ ] at Aftercull,[*] that shee may have her liberty: Upon her promise of not goei[ ] abroade to unlawfull Meetings,. nor su[ ]ing any at home, shee is ordered to b[ ] releas't; The fine to bee levyed upo[ ] her husbands Estate—Its 5 £—and t[ ] bee of the good behavior.

[25:3]

[NO DOCUMENT ON THIS PAGE AND NO ENTRY IN THE CALENDAR.]

[25:4]

[AGREEMENT FOR SALE OF LAND AT CLAVERACK BY JAN HENDRICKSZ VAN SALSBERGEN TO GERRIT VAN SLICHTENHORST. TRANSLATION]

True copy

Today, this first of November 1675, appeared before me, Adriaen van Ilpendam, notary public, (residing in New Albany) Jan Heyndricsz van Solsberghen, on the one side, and Mr. Gerrit van Slichtenhorst, on the other side, who have come to an accord and agreement in friendship and with affection in the manner as follows: Namely, Jan Heyndricsz acknowledges to have sold and Mr. Gerrit van Slichtenhorst to have bought (about two years ago) a certain piece of woodland, previously owned by the aforesaid seller, lying in Claverrack; to wit, the equal half of all the land which the aforesaid seller has there in Claverrack, beginning from the northerly end of the second *Claveren*,[‡] running eastward to the *Groote Kil*[†] and northerly to Mayoor Abraham Staas' Kil, southerly to the land of Gerrit Visbeeck, including the stream as far as the land reaches; which aforesaid half of this aforementioned land and stream the seller now presently transfers to the aforesaid buyer free and unincumbered (except for the Lord's right); for which aforesaid half of the aforesaid land and stream the aforesaid seller hereby acknowledges to be paid and satisfied in full to his contentment.

Hereunder the aforesaid contracting parties pledge their respective persons and goods, nothing excepted, subject to all lords, courts, judges, and magistrates. In witness whereof they have, together with Barent Meyndersz and Johannes de Wandelaer as witnesses, signed this document with their own hands in the presence of me, notary, in Albany. Dated as above.

---

* Originally *Achter Col*, near the present Elizabeth, New Jersey.
‡ fields or meadows
† Great Stream

After comparison with the original (resting with me, notary) this was found to agree. In Albany the first of November 1675.

Quod attestor
Adriaen van Ilpendam, notary public.

[25:5–7]

[COUNCIL MINUTES CONCERNING THE ACCUSED DUTCH LEADERS]

At a Councell etc. Nobr. 2d. 1675.

[ ] against	Present.
[ ]lle	The Governor
[ ] Cortlandt	The Secr.—C. Dyre
	Mr. Philips.

Mr. Steenwyck etc. having notice to bee here this morning—appeared all but Mr. Bayard and Antonio de Mill, both being ill.

The Go: related to them the former part of the order last night, but they being refractory or foolish had no more said to them after a long discourse, and they insisting on an Appeale from the sentence of the last Court, but could not endure to heare to bee tryde by another Court and a Jury, then that they should give in their Answer what they would stand to by 4 a Clock in the afternoone.

I gave out 2 orders of the Court, one to them present, t'other to Mr. Minvielle for Mr. Bayard.

[ENDORSED:]   At a Councell
Nobr. 2d., 1675.
Before noone.

At A Councell etc.
No: 2d 1675—Afternoone

Mr. N. De Meyer	The Governor
D. Mayor*	The Secr.—C. Dyre
Mr. Minvielle	Fr: Philips
Mr. Gibbs	
Mr. Steph: V: Cortlandt	
Aldermen.	

* deputy mayor

The persons before the Go: and Councell in the morning, appeare againe—and deliver in a joint Answer under their hands in Dutch. Mr. Luyck talkes of an Appeale still. etc.

They desireing time till tomorrow, to make a more direct Answer, have it graunted upon giving security of the good behaviour, to appeare tomorrow morning by 10 a Clocke to give a more direct answer each apart and in English.

The sheriffe to take it without writing or summe mencioned so they bee good men.

[ENDORSED:]   At a Councell
Nobr. 2d. 1675.
Mr. Steenwyck etc.
Afternoone.

At A Councell

No. 2d. 1675.

Mr. Cor: Steenwick, Mr. Johannes V. Brugh Mr. Egid: Luyck, Mr. Wm. Beeckman and Mr. Jacob Kip being by order before the Go: and Councell It is ordered That if the said persons bee

If not satisfyed with the former Judgment

A Rehearing and Review shall bee granted them, for which a speciall Court of Assizes to bee called where both the matter of their Estates and the other Causes of their Commitment to bee tryed by a Jury, etc. Their Answer to bee given in by 4 a Clocke afternoone.

By order etc.

[ENDORSED:]   Nobr. 2d 1675.

No. 1st 1675
At a Councell

Ordered that Mr. Cornelys Steenwyck etc. bee sent for to come to the Fort tomorrow morning by 9 a Clocke, and then told, That whereas the Governor is informed that they are dis=satisfyed with the late proceeding against them at the Court of Assizes, where they had no Jury, It being not then desired by them, Therefore upon their giving in security for the good behavior etc. there shall forthwith bee a speciall Court of Assizes called, in which they shall be proceeded against as Delinquents, the which to bee by a Jury.

But in case the said persons doe desire to abide by their former sentence, and doe comply therewith as the Law doth require, they shall bee admitted thereunto, Provided it bee done within three dayes after this Notice given them.

[ENDORSED:]   No. 1st 1675. At a Councell
                   Mr. Steenwyck etc.

[25:8]

[PETITION BY CORNELIS STEENWYCK, JOHANNES VAN BRUGH, AEGIDIUS LUYCK, WILLEM BEECKMAN, AND JACOB KIP. TRANSLATION]

Noble, highly Esteemed, Wise Lord, the Noble Lord Major Edmund Andros, Noble Governor General of all His Royal Highness's territories in America, and His Noble highly Esteemed Lords Councillors.

Highly Esteemed Lords,

Pursuant to your honors' highly esteemed order placed today in our hands, we, your honors' undersigned subjects, show that our intention and desire has never been to petition your honors for a rehearing or review before another court of assizes, because it is well known that the power and authority of this court of assizes is equal to the former court; therefore, we petition again, as we have humbly done by previous petitions, that your honors mercifully pardon us from the previous severe sentence. Awaiting hereon your honors' favorable disposition, we remain

1675 the 2nd of November,   Your highly Esteemed Lords'
New York.   faithful subjects,
                            Corn. Steenwyck
                            Johannes van Brugh
                            Agidius Luyk
                            Will. Beeckman
                            Jacob Kip

[25:9–13]

[25:9]

> To the Right Honnorable Edmund Andro[ ] Esquire Gouvernor General of all his Roya[ ] Highnesses Territoris In America and his Honnorable Councill.

Right Honnorable Sirs:

Uppon the orders of Your General Court yesterday Rece[ ] to answer:
—I doe Submit m[ ] selffe wholy to Jour Honnor and the court off assizes Judgment, given aganst mee, at the said court of assizes held at Niew Jorke in october 1675: Prayingh jour honnors wil bee please favorabley to moderate te said Judgement and to admitte him to take te oath of fidellity and hee Schall pray: and Remayne

1675: 3 Nov.	Jour Honnors Most humble subjeckt
Niw Jorke	and Servant
	Jacob Kip

[ENDORSED:]   Mr. Jacob Kipps
Answer and submission
Nobr. 3d 1675.

[25:10]

> To the Right honorable mayor Andros Esquier Gouverneur of al his Royal Heignes territorie In America and Councel

the peticion Of Corn. Steenwyck

Humble Sheweth

That In Answer upon your honnours Ordre Of the 2: instant Y do wholy submit to the Judgement given against mee by the grand Court of assises held at nie yorke from the 6: to the 13 of October laest and do humbly desier that your honnour pleas to leth him take the oath as other Subjects have done and hi shal pray

November 3: 1675

Your fuitful servant
Corn. Steenwyck

Mr. Cornelius Steenwycks
Answer and submission.
Nobr. 3d 1675
The Answer of Mr. Steenwyck etc.
Nobr. 2d. 1675.*

[25:11]

To the Right Honorable Edmund Andros Gouv. off all his
Royall Highnes Territories in America and his honorable
Councel

Right honorble Sir:
In all due submission to jour Honnors order off the second off this instand
moneth the underwritt suppliant answeeres that jour suppliant wholy
submitt to the Judgement off the former Court off Azzizes and in all
Humblenes Craves that no further proceedings may bee made against
him and that jour honnour favourabl please to admitte your Suppliant to
take the oath off fidellity as the Rest off the Inhabitants have done.

Nieuw Jorcke 1675   And your petitioner
de 3 novemb.   Johannes van brugh
                           shall pray

[ENDORSED:]   Mr. Johannes van Brughs
Answer and submission.
No. 3d 1675.

[25:12]

To the Right Honorable Mayor Andros Esqu. Gover. In al
His Royal Hignis Territoris In America and his Honnob.
Counsel.

Honnorabel Sirs.
Upon the Ordre I Receved yisterday the Answer I declar and submit to
his Honnor and the Honnorab. Court off Assizes Jugement met at the

* These last two lines are from a separate wrapper.

layt Court off Assizes and Humble prayes that no further proceding may
bee against my and admitt to take the oath of fidelite

[   ]w Jorck this 3 day Nov.   I remaine your Honn[   ]
1675.   Most Humble Servant
                                   Will Beeckman

[ENDORSED:]   William Beeckmans
                    Answer and submission.
                    Nov. 3 1675.

                    Papers relating to Mr. Steenwick

[25:13]

            To the Right Honnorable Mayor Edmund Andros Esqr: and
            Governor Gennerall of all his Royall Highnesses Territories
            in America; and his Honnorable Councill

Right honnorable Sir.

In all due obedience to Your Honnors order of the 2d of this instant
month, the under written Suppliant gives for answer to Your Honnor that
Your Suppliant wholy submits himselfe to the judgement of the last Court
of Assizes, an in all humbly manner supplicates that no further proceed-
inges may bee made against him, and admitted to take the oath of
fidellity.

                    And Your Petitioner
                    Agidius Luyk shall pray

New Yorke the 3d
of Novemb: 1675.

[ENDORSED:]   Mr. Egidius Luycks
                    Answer and submission.
                    No: 3—1675.

[25:14–15]

[COUNCIL MINUTES AND ORDER CONCERNING THE PROPERTY
            OF THE ABOVE PERSONS]

            At a Councell etc. Nov. 3d 1675.

The Governor
The Secr.   C. Dyre
Mr. Philips.

Mr. D. Meyer D. Mayor[*]
Mr. Minvelle
Mr. Gibbs   Aldermen
Mr. Cortlandt

The 5 persons that were ordered yesterday to appeare, come and bring in their severall answers apart.

They all submitt to the former Judgment etc. without appeale for Engl., or desire of a New Tryall here.

Whereupon its ordered That they have 3 dayes time to make their Composicions with Mr. Leete, according to the former order of the 1st inst., in which if not then done to have Execucion against their Estates.

Nov. 3. 1675.
At a Councell
Mr. Steenwick etc.

At a Councell held in New Yorke Nov. 3d 1675

Upon the answer and submission of Mr. Cornelys Steenwyck Mr. Johannes Van Brugh etc. to abide by the Judgment of the late Court of Assizes, without Appeale for Engl. or desire of a New Tryall here: It is ordered that the said persons have three dayes time to make their Composicion with Mr. Leete for the one third of their Estates according to former Order of the first instant which if not then done Execucion is to issue forth against them for the whole.

By order of the Gov. and
Councell.

No. 3. 1675.
Order of Councell about
Mr. Steenwyck etc.

* Nicolaes de Meyer, the deputy mayor.

[25:16]

[ORDER FOR THE ARREST OF SARAH MINTALL* IN A SUIT AGAINST
THOMAS HATFIELD]

To the Constable of Mamaronock

Whereas Sarah Mintah late the servant of Thomas Hatfeild hath this daye
brought before me the person of Thomas Hatfeild her said Master whom
she doth afirme att severall times to have had Carnall knowledge of her
bodye and doth suspect her selfe by the said Thomas Hatfeild to be with
Childe and she the said Sarah Mintah Nott finding secarity according to
law for the prosecuting of the said Thomas Hatfeild accordingly Att the
next Court of sessions to be held att Jaimaica on the second Wednesday
in December next these are therefore in his Majesties name to require
you to deliver the person of the said Sarah Mintah into the Custody of
the sheriffe of the Citty of New Yorke for her personall appearance att
the Court sessions att Jaimaica to prosecute the said Thomas Hatfeild
according to Law hereof faile nott dated att Anhookes Neck this 3d of
Novemb. 1675.

John Pell

[ENDORSED:]   A Mittimus
for Sarah Mintah

To the Constable
of Momoronock

[25:17]

[MEETING WITH LONG ISLAND INDIANS CONCERNING THEIR TERMS
FOR VACATING VARIOUS LAND TITLES]

Nobr. 5th 1675.

At an appe[   ]ance
of Indyans.

Present

The Governor

* This name is variously spelled here and in document 21. It does not appear in the Jamaica
town records, but the Hempstead records mention persons named Minthorne.

The Secr.
Mr. Philips

Tackpousha [   ] Indyans [   ] the land [   ]d they [   ]t payd
for a [   ]psteed. They say they ar[   ] Owners of three Necks of land
and aske 120 £. Nanashewe is one of them, and claymes the great Neck.

Chaperacke—another, great Mad Nans Neck

Nannawatuck the 3d l[   ] MadNans Neck.

Cow Neck is said to belong to Tackpousha, the which they will not sell.
Hempsteed hath beene long in possession. their patent from Go: Kieft is
about 30 yeares agoe rather more.

One of them sayes they aske this [   ] onely for the [   ] not for the
[   ] within. [   ] having never [   ]posed before is thought
u[   ]able, And would create new disputes, if the one part should
bee bought and not the other.

Their demand for all is

05 Ten long Guns
 5 Ten pistolls
 8 Twenty Kittles, ten great, ten small
 6 Twenty blancketts
12 Th[   ] Duffell Coates
 6 [   ] Coates of D[   ]ns
10 [   ] shirts
12 Twen[ ]y pairs of stocking[ ]
20 Sixty Hooes.
20 Sixty Axes.
40 Sixty knives.
30 Sixty staves of lead
40 Sixty pound of pouder.
[ ] Hundred and twenty fathom of wam[   ]

That in the Margent offered

They will consider of it.

20	beaver	10	beaver
8		4	
20		[ ]6	
40		2	
34		2	
30		[ ]	
10		5	
6		4	
20		8	
20		8	
2		2	
5		3	
7		5	
20		7	
242		99	

[ENDORSED:]   Att a C[   ]
etc.
Novemb. 5. 1675.
About the Indyans
[   ]mand for the
[   ]nds about Hempsteed.

[25:18]

[NARRATIVE OF BENONI STEBBINS'S CAPTIVITY AMONG AND
ESCAPE FROM INDIANS]

Benonie Stebbins which was taken Captive by the Indians at dearfield
12 miles from hatfield retorned to hadlie the fifth of occtober Instant

related as followeth

That the Indians that tooke him weare al Norwootuck Indians save only
one which was a naraganset they were 26 in al 18 of them fighting men
the rest 2 squas old men and boys. they told him that they had lived at
the french and intended to retorn there Again to sel the Captives to them
which had Incouradged them that they should have eight pound per peece
for them And the french Indians did Intend to come with them The next
time either in the spring or in winter if they had sucses this time   The
manner of his Escape was thus when they came 2 days Journey above
Squakheag they sent part of their compeny to wotchuset kills to fetch
away a smal compeny of Indians that had lived theire al this war time

with whome they sent this captive and he being sent with 2 squas and a mare to fetch some hucleburies a litle way from the compeny then he got upon the mare and rid away til he tired the mare and then run on foot and so escaped to hadly being 2 days and 1/2 without victuals

This relation was taken from his mouth at Northampton 6th Instant

per me Samll. Eells

[ENDORSED:]   [   ]
                     The honnor gov.

[25:19]

[PETITION OF JOHN HEADY FOR INHABITANTS OF YONKERS TO
REMAIN AT HOME TO RESIST THE INDIANS]

To the Right honorable Edmond Andros Esquire Governor Generall under his Royall Highnesse of all his Territoryes in America.

The humb. peticion of John Heady Inhabitant of the place called Younkers land, on the behalfe of him and his neighbours consisting in 4 familyes.

Sheweth with all submissions your honors Peticioner living at a distance of a lone mile from the towne Fordham as that being comanded by Mr. John Archer proprietor of the said Towne Fordam to come hee and his neighbours into his Towne and there to make such fortificacions as hee shall order.

But your honors Peticioner and his neighbours being removed from the said Mr. Archer his Towne above a mile, and wee being strong enugh (or though so) to resist this heathenish warr, having a good and strong blockhouse: And To remove and retire their selfes to Fordham should bee but an occasion of pry* to the Heathens.

Therefore it's your Honors Peticioners Request that hee and his Neighbours may not bee bound to leave their houses, and goods and to please the humour of the said Mr. Archer and thereby perhaps to loose all what they have: But that your honor bee pleased to graunt to your honors

* prey (?)

Peticioner and to his neighbours to Joyne togather and to make such defences as (with the helpe of God) to secure them selfes.

Your honors Peticioner and neighbours being at all tyme ready to bee helpfull to their neighbours in a Christian way, shall expect from your honor an order which shall be observed from

Nobr. 8. 1675.   Your honors humb. Peticioner
which shall ever pray

[MARGINAL   [ ] men
NOTE:]*   2 boyes
Arm'd

[ENDORSED:]   The humb. Peticion
of John Heady, and
Neighbours.
ordere d etc.
Nov. 8. 1675.

[25:20]

[RESPONSE TO THE PRECEDING PETITION]

Whereas a peticion hath beene presented unto the Governor by John Heddy on the behalfe of himselfe and the other Inhabitants upon the plantation at the Younckers Land, That in regard of their Distance from the Village of Fordham, and their having for the defence of their wives and Children already [ ]ade a Block house at their owne plantacion and also given assistance to their Neighbours at Fordham they may bee excused from further trouble about their Fortificacions, These are to certify that the said Inhabitants upon the Younckers land are by the Go: order excused from any further worke at Fordham, they being Vigilant at their owne place and keeping watch upon all occasions. Dated in N.Y. this 8: Day of Nov. 1675.

[ENDORSED:]   Copie of Certificate given by mee‡
to John Heddy by the Go: order
to excuse them from working at
John Archers Fortificacion.

* Written in pencil in the governor's hand.
‡ Matthias Nicolls

[25:21]

[BOND OF SARAH MINTALL TO PROSECUTE THOMAS HATFIELD]

N. Yorke ss

Know all men by these Presents that I Sarah Mintall, doe stand firmly bound unto our Soveraigne Lord the king in the full and Just summe of Twenty Pound sterling payable on demand, to which payment well and truly to mee made I binde mee my heyres and Executors firmly by these Presents, in Wittness whereof I have hereto sett my hand and Seale in New Yorke this Eighth day of November in the 27th yeare of his Majesties reigne. Annoque Domini 1675.

The condition of this obligacion is such that whearas the abovesaid Sarah Mintall hath complained that one Thomas Hatfeild her late master, hath gotten her with Childe, and denyeth the same, and Mr. Justice Pell having sent her to bee secured in the Goale of this Citty untill shee finde suretyes to prosecute the said complaint against the said Thomas Hatfeild, Now if the said Sarah Minter shall personally appeare at the next Court of Sessions to bee held in Jamaicoe on long Island, for the North Rideing of Yorkesheire and there prosecute the said Thomas Hatfeild for his misdemeanor aforesaid, then this present obligacion is to bee Voyd and of none effect, otherwise to bee of full Force and Virtue

Signed sealed and Delivered   Sa[   ] Mintarh   [*seal*]
In Presentia,
Henry Newton

John Sharpe
Sherriff

[ENDORSED:]   Tho: Hatfeilds case
                    about his servant with Childe.
                    Recognizance.
                    Nov: 1675 for
                    Jamaica Sessions

[25:22–23]

[RECEIPTS FOR GOODS FROM RICHARD BRYAN ON BEHALF OF ALEXANDER BRYAN TO GABRIEL MINVIELLE AND MATTHIAS NICOLLS]

Bee it knowne unto all Men by these presents that I Richard Bryan of Milford in the Colony of Conecticutt Merchant have received of Gabriel

Minvielle of New Yorke Merchant upon the Account of Matthias Nicolls Secr. to the Colony of New Yorke, and for the use of Mr. Alexander Bryan senior of Milford aforesaid in severall sorts of Merchandize to the value of two thousand Guilders sewant which at forty Guilders to the pound, amounts to the summe of fifty pounds, for which said summe I doe promise to procure an Acquittance or discharge from the said Mr. Alex: Bryan to the said Matthias Nicolls for so much of the debt due from him unto the said Mr. Bryan by obligacion: In witnesse whereof I have hereunto sett my hand and seale in N.Y. this 22th day of Novemb. 1675.

Sealed and delivered in
presence of [*blank*]

Be it knowne unto all men by these presents that I Richard Bryan of Milford in the Collonye of Conetecutt Marchant have received of Gabriell Manveale of New yorke marchant for the Account of Mr. Alexander Bryan senior of Millford In severall sorts of marchandize: to the valewe of five thousand sixe hundred eightye seaven guilderes three stivers which at fortye guilders to the pounds amounts to the sume of one hundred fortye two pounds thrcc shillings and sixe pence: For and In Consideration of the said sume I doe promis and Ingadge that the afforesaid Mr. Alex: Bryan shall send a Letter of attorney: to Receive of Mrs. Elizabeth Bedlowe of this City the sume of one hundred twenty nine pounds nine shillings and sixe pence: as appeares by the Judgement of the Courts of Mayor and Aldermen and Assizes and For the remaine of the abovesaid sume: I doe promis to pay unto the said Gabriell: Manveale or his order good marchantable porke at three pounds per Barrell or soape at twelve shillings per Ferkin to bee delivered free of all Charges at the bridge in this City. In wittness whereof I have hereunto set my hand and seale in new yorke this 19th day of November 1675.

Sealed and delivered
in presence of: [*blank*]

[ENDORSED:]   Mr. Bryans Receits to Monsr.
Minvielle and mee.
Sale draughts.
Milford.

[25:24]

[BOND OF SAMUEL SCUDDER FOR GOOD BEHAVIOR]

Know all Men by these presents, that I Samuell Scudder of Mashpeth Kills upon Long Island, Husbandman, am holden and firmely bound, unto our Soveraigne Lord the King, in the summe of Twenty-pounds of good and Lawfull money of England, or the value; to the which payment well and truely to bee made, I doe hereby bind mee my Heyres, Executors and Administrators firmely by these presents, Sealed with my seale Dated the 10th day of November, in the 27th yeare of his Majesties Raigne Annoque Domini 1675.

The Condicion of this Obligacion is, that the abovebounden Samuell Scudder, bee of the Good Behavior, which if hee the said Scudder doth truly observe, and not act contrary thereunto, for the space of one yeare and a day, Then this Bond to bee void, and of none Effect, otherwise to stand and bee in full force.

Sealed and delivered   Samuell Scudder
in the presence of   Seal*
Henry Newton.

John: Sharpe.

[ENDORSED:]   Samuell Scudders
bond of 20£ to bee
of good Behavior.
Nob. 10th 1675.
To pay for the taking up
his bond.

* This document is cut so that a flap is folded over the seal to which it adheres. The reason is unknown.

[25:25]

[BILL OF LADING TO LEWIS MORRIS BY CAPTAIN FRANCIS
RICHARDSON]*

Shipped in good order, and well conditioned by Coll.
Lewis Morris *in and upon the Ship called the* good
Hope *whereof is Master for the present Voyage* Francis Richardson *and now riding at Anchor in the* Bay
of Carlisle *and bound for* London *to say* Twenty
M x 1 to   hogsheads of Clayd Sugar for the proper Account
20   and Advent of the Said Coll. Lewis Morris *being*
marked and numbered as in the Margent, *and are to*
be delivered in the like good order, and well condi-
tioned, at the Port of London (*the danger of the Seas*
only excepted) unto Cap. John Bradenham *or to* his
Assigns, he or they paying Freight for the said Goods
after the sale of Six pounds Sterl. per tunn Caske *with*
Primage and Average accustomed. In witness
whereof, the Master or Purser of the said Ship hath
affirmed to three Bills of Lading, all of this tenor and
date; the one of which three Bills being ac-
complished, the other two to stand void.

Dated in Barbados July the 28th 1675.

Parsells reseved Insids and Contents not knowne
to

Francis Richardson.‡

[ENDORSED:]   Coll. Lewis Morris
his bill of Loading.

---

* The document is partially printed. The printed portions are here italicized as in the
original.
‡ The signature and the preceding line are in a different hand from the rest of the document.

[25:26]

[REPORT OF CARPENTERS ON THE CONDITION OF THE SHIP
GOOD HOPE]

New York this 10th of November 1675.

These may sartifie whome itt may conserne thatt wee whose names are heere under written according to the governors order have bene one borde the shipp hope and have veiwed and survaied the said ship and have found the principall of her upor work alltogather unsofitiant for the seas and ase wee Judge will not be repaireed sofitiantly under the vallu of six hundred pounds sterling as to the defects wee have seen besids whatt defects may bee that wee could not see may amount to a very great charge of mony.

The truth of the Contents in this paper written, is by the persons who have hereunto signed, sworne to, according to the best of their knowledge, this 11th day of Nov. 1675. Before mee	the marke **W** of william Jinens Elias Pudington John Comte Abram mo Roger Pooly Abraham Robines

Matthias Nicolls. Secr.

[ENDORSED:]   The Report of the
Carpenters about
the Ship Good Hope.
Nobr. 11th 1675.

[25:27]

[PETITION BY OFFICERS AND CREW OF THE *GOOD HOPE*
FOR THEIR WAGES]

To the Right Honorable Major Edmond Andross Governor Generall of all his Royall Highness his Territoryes in America etc.

The humble petition of John Ambrose Stephen Mextead Mates of the Ship Called the Good hope Walter Feverall Boatsman William Jennings Carpenter and the rest of the said ships Company.

In humble manner sheweth That since it was Your Honors pleasure to graunt Your Petitioners A Warrant for Surveying of the Ship Good=Hope in order to the payment of your petitioners wages etc. And the Surveyors haveing made Report thereof unto your Honor

Therefore humbly pray That out of a Deepe
sence of your petitioners sufferings will be
pleased to order and Direct a way for their
speedy payment as your Honor in your
Grave Judgment seemeth most meete

And your petitioners
shall Ever pray etc.

[ENDORSED:] A Petition of the
Mates, and other
Officers and Marriners of
the shipp Good Hope.
No: 12. 1675.

[25:28]

[COMMISSION OF A COURT OF ADMIRALTY TO ADJUDICATE THE
SUIT CONCERNING THE *GOOD HOPE*]

Edmund Andros Esquire, Seigneur of Sausmarez
Lieutenant and Governor Generall under his Royall High-
nese James Duke of Yorke and Albany etc. of all his
Territoryes in America.

Whereas the shipp the Good Hope of London came into this Port in
distresse, and at the Request of Francis Richardson the Master, some
Masters of shipps and Vessells here, were appointed to view the stowage
of the said Shipp, as to the Goods and Merchandize, then on board her,
since the which (upon the Peticion of the mates and other Officers and
Marriners belonging to her) severall Carpenters have been also ordered
to View and make a Survey of said shipp; The reports whereof have been
returned unto mee; And Application being now made by the Officers and
seamen, that they may have their wages paid them, the shipp being found
insufficient, and their Voyage disappointed, The Master also refusing to
make them satisfaction, unlesse Constreyned or Ordered thereunto by
the Law; These are in his Majesties name to constitute, authorize, and
appoint you Mr. Matthias Nicolls, Capt. William Dyre, Mr. Fredrick
Philips, Mr. Gabriel Minvielle, Mr. Thomas Gibbs, Mr. Thomas Lewis,
Mr. Stephanus van Cortlandt, Mr. Johannes De Peyster, Capt. Nicholas
Blake, and Mr. Samuell Leete, or any five of you, to bee a Court of
Admiralty to meet together to=morrow, being the 13th instant, and at any
other Convenient time or times during the space of six days from the

Date hereof at the City Hall, to heare and examine into the matter in question between the Master and the shipps Company, and what other Matters shall relate unto the said Shipp; In order to which you Mr. Matthias Nicolls being sworne before mee, are hereby empowered to take the Oath of the rest in Commission. And you the said Commissioners as above are authorized to call before you, and examine any Person or Persons upon Oath, and to heare and adjudge, and give your Determinacion therein according to the Lawes and Customes of the Sea in such Cases provided: For the doing whereof this shall be your sufficient Warrant. Given under my hand and sealed with the Seale of the Province in New Yorke the 12th day of November in the 27th yeare of his Majesties Reigne Annoque Domini 1675.

This is a true Copie   E. Andros. s.
Matthias Nicolls Secr.

[ENDORSED:]   A Copie signed of the Go: Comission
                   for a Court of Admiralty.
                   No: 12th 1675.
                   About the shipp the Good hope.

[25:29]

[PROCEEDINGS OF THE ADMIRALTY COURT IN THE ABOVE SUIT]

Saturday   At a Court of Admiralty
Afternoone   etc.   No: 13th 1675.

The Commission read—all present.

The peticion from the mates, seamen etc. read.

The Masters peticion to the Governor.

The Master desires a Copie of the Mates etc. peticion—which was ordered, the directions being mended, It wanting the direction to the Court of Admiralty.

They put in also the demands for their wages, A copie whereof was also to bee given to the Master.

The Master desired subpoenas for the freighters here, which was granted.

The Court adjourned until Tuesday morning—8, or 9 a Clock.

Nov. 15. A Subpoena was given forth to the Marshall to summon—Coll. Lewis Morris, Abraham Whirly and Wm. Wayte.

Before noone   Tuesday Nov. 16th 1675.

I[*] was this morning sworne before the Governor as to the court of Admiralty.

At a Speciall Court of Admiralty then held about the ship the Good Hope, and the Master and Mariners.

The bench sworne.

The Mates etc. put in their peticion or declaracion, with a demand of their wages in a bill annext.

The Master makes objection against James Parkers wages—for neglect of duty here.

An Agreement under the Masters hand with two of the seamen to advance their wages.

Severall of the others clayme the like advance. But in that and the rest Both Master and Seamen referre themselves to the Court.

The Master and seamen relate the Condicion of the shipp, and their distresse at sea. The mast broake atop while they were cutting the Mast by the board a quarter through.

The master referrs the Consideraction of the freight when hee will answer the matter of wages.

Coll. Morris being subpoenaed appeared in Court, and Abraham Whirly. Hee putts in severall objections of which hee had the heads[‡] in writing. Denyes paying any freight here, produces his bill of Loading.

Abraham Whirly the like refusing to pay fraight here.

---

* Matthias Nicolls.
‡ The chief points to be raised.

They produce their Protest made before John Sharpe, by master Mates etc.

After all persons had declared to the Court what they had to say, All were ordered to withdraw out the court.

Its agreed that the seamen are to have their wages, for the payment whereof the ship is lyable, or what freight shall become due.

Proposed whether the Mast being begun to bee cutt by the Master, and afterward carryed overboard, The Merchant is lyable to pay only part of the damage.

Its agreed That beginning to cutt the Mast by the Master with the mutual Consent of the ships Company is as much as if really cutt down, and the Cutting of the weather shrouds was the occasion of the breaking of the Mast aloft and carrying it overboard, and that the Merchant is lyable to beare part as in all Cases of that Nature.

Proposed whether Goods put on board a ship for one Port and by misfortine is driven into another, Fraight is to bee paid or what.

The Court adjourned till 4, or 5 afternoone.

Afternoone.

All appeared but Mr. Leete.
The Question put to the Vote.

1 Mr. Lewis—If Average no Freight.
1 Mr. Gibbs—No freight.
1 Mr. De Peyster No freight.
0 Capt. Blake. Freight proporcionably as they have gone.
0 Mr. Cortlandt. Freight some part.
1 Monsr. Minvielle—No freight.
0 Mr. Philips—some part of Freight.
0 C. Dyre—Freight proporcionably to time and distance etc.
1 M. N. Average—No freight.
0 Mr. Leet—freight proporcionably etc.

To bee considered the Equality of Votes.

The prices desired to bee sett upon Cotten Sugar etc. not thought practicable and not in our Commission.

The Court adjourne till Thursday 9 in the morning.

> At the special Court of Admiralty
> etc. Tuesday before noone.
> Nov. 16–1675.

Upon the Proposall whether the Master and seamen belonging to the ship Good Hope etc. are to have their wages and how to bee paid. Its agreed by all, That they deserve their wages, and that the ship, as farre as shee will goe to make satisfaction is lyable, In default whereof the freight or other Concernes of the Owners is to make it up.

About the Question of Average, when lyable to bee paid.

| Not lyes before us | The direction in *Lex Mercatoria*,[*] about cutting of a Mast, is judged to bee practicable, the like of a Cable etc. |
| Not be-fore us | To the 3d thing Proposed, Whether Goods put on board a shipp etc: with bills of lading for one Port, and by misfortune driven into another, the Fraight is to be paid, or what. |

The Court adjourned till afternoone.

The Question then not being agreed upon was put to the Vote, as followes.

Mr. Lewis—No Freight if Average.

Mr. Gibbs—No Freight unlesse brought to the Port.

Mr. De Peyster the like.

Capt. Blake Freight proporcionably

Mr. Cortlandt—some part.

Monsr. Minvielle—No Freight as before

Mr. Philips some part
C. Dyre—Freight to bee paid proporcionably to the time and distance

---

[*] commercial law

sayl'd before the storme fell upon them.

Mr. Nicolls. No freight without being the Goods to the Port mencioned in bill of loading.

Mr.Leete, (who came in after all had given their Votes)—freight proporcionably.

The Votes being found to bee equall as to Numb. of the Commissioners—The Court adjourned untill Thursday the last day of the Commission.

The prices desired in the masters peticion to bee sett upon Cotten, Sugar etc. being not directed in the Commission nor adjudged practicable, layd aside.

Thursday   At a Court of Admiralty by speciall Commission
                  from the Governor

                  Afternoone Nobr. 18th 1675.

The master putts in his Account of wages.

And an account of things lost from on board in this harbor out of the Cabbin.

The 8 persons that were upon the watch, or undertook it, of which 2, that sayl'd were on shoare, shall have so much of their wages stop't in the Masters hands or the Value of the goods doth amount unto. The master to proove the losse of the Goods.

The Master desired the Protest might bee read, hee thinking there may bee some ommission therein.

In the first part hee takes notice of the shipps Compa. being omitted, with the Master and Officers.

In another part omitted 4 foot water in the Hold as Master and Mates averre.

Mr. Sharpe referrs himselfe to his Notes and is advised to mend it.

The Court proceeded to give Judgment, the which they desired Mr.

Nicolls to draw up, and to meete at 2 a Clock at Mr. Dyres. The time limited in the Commission being expired after this day.

The Court is dissolved.

[ENDORSED:]   Proceedings at the
Court of Admiralty.

[NOTE:]*   Freight to be paid proportionable to the time,
and Distance saild before the storm Fell upon them.

[25:30–31]

[LETTER OF CONSTABLE THOMAS TOPPING TO SECRETARY NICOLLS
CONCERNING TAXES AND AN ACCOUNT]

Southampton November the 15: 1675.

Worthy Sir.

My service presented etc. I with the Overseers of this Towne received your warrant for this yeares Cuntry rate of 56£ 18s: 11d 3/4 as alsoe your Manifestation of the Governors pleasure to accept our proportion in fatt cattle, Accordingly wee have put forth utmost endeavours to procure the best wee could for that use and have sent them to you by the hands of our Neighbors Joseph Rainer and Charles Sturmy; That is to say Soe much as to make up the value of the rate, with the payments Due here, unto particuler persons on the Cuntries account with which Dues, the bearer hereof Joseph Rainer will fully acquaint you: But Sir: in that accompt of the Cuntries Debts, I must crave your pardon In that I have presumed to adventure to sett the summe of small particulers my self, as that particuler of sending two men in the night season Post to Seatauk with a letter from Mr. Barker to the Governor etc. The true reason whereof is because I endeavour to make up a Just account to you, and I cannot come at the men to know what they Demand Nor at your self to know your allowance; Soe, I have done therein according to my best Judgment and am in hope of your approbation yet leave it to your Worships Correction if need require, And if you please to accept my said accompt of the Cuntry Debts here, and send mee a discharge of the rate, (and your owne 40 s which is alsoe now sent in the cattle) I shall Dilligently take spetiall care to take in the shereifs bills, and cleere accompts with the particuler persons specifyed with those bills till they

* The note is on a separate paper.

have theire pay. By which meanes, with your favour the Cuntry may have good cause to satisfaction, and particuler persons [   ] Soe hopeing you will accept my true intent and endeavours in the premises with my Constant prayers to the Almighty for the Cuntries peace and your happines I take my leave at present and Ever Rest   Sir

Your Servant to Comand

Thomas Topping

Mr. Wells agreement
9 head of Cattle
50£ 12s 6d.

Charges of comming up with the Cattle[*]

[ADDRESSED:]   To the Worshipful his
                 good Friend Capt.
                 Matthias Nicolls Secretary
                 At New Yorke
                 theise Present

[ENDORSED:]   Mr. Tho. Topping Constable
                 of Southton
                 With the bill of
                 Charges for the
                 sheriffe.
                 No: 15. 1675.

Out of which is to bee paid here as followeth

	£	s	d
To Joseph Fordham for expence at the Sessions in March 74/5	14	00	00
To Leiftenant Phillips due before the Dutch came	04	07	00
To Tho: Mapes for his service on the Jury at March Court 72: assigned to Henry Peirson	00	07	00
To Tho: Shaw and his boat attending the Court	00	06	08
to 3 Jurymen from Southton at June Court 75 4 Dayes from home at 3 s etc.	01	16	00
4 other Jurymen 1 Day assigned to Mr. Jennings	00	12	00
John Jessup Juriman March Court 72	00	03	00

* The preceding four lines of notes were added by Matthias Nicolls.

To James Herrick per Capt. Salisburyes order March the 6th 1674	00	14	08
more per Capt. Manings Order	00	10	00
more for his sonnes attendance of Justice Topping to the Court of Assizes 15 Dayes out, 40 s horse meat 5 s is	02	05	00
per Order of Mr. Barker 2 men prest to goe Post to Seatauk with a letter for the Governor from Mr. Barker they went in the night season	01	10	00
for Collecting the Cuntry rate	02	17	00
	29	08	04

Your friend Thomas Topping

[25:32]

[SUBPOENA OF MERCHANTS WITH FREIGHT ABOARD
THE *GOOD HOPE*]

These are in his Majesties name to require you to Summons Coll. Lewis Morris, Abraham Whirly, and William Wayte, to appeare before the Court of Admiralty, to bee held tomorrow morning, being Tuesday the 16th instant, at the City Hall to Answer to the Complaint of Francis Richardson, Master of the Shipp the Good Hope, now in this Harbor, concerning the Freight of some Goods putt on Board the said shipp, by the said Persons, or their Agents in the Barbados; Hereof they are not to faile, as they will Answer the contrary at their utmost Perills: Given under my hand in New Yorke, this 15th day of November, 1675.

Matthias: Nicolls. Secr.

To Henry Newton,
  Marshall.

[ENDORSED:]   Subpoena returned.
                   Nov. 16th 1675.

[25:33]

[AN ACCOUNT OF WAGES DUE THE COMPANY OF THE *GOOD HOPE*]

An Account of men Shipt on board the Ship Good hope of London Francis Richardson Comander etc.

Jno Ambrose cheifmate from the 25th June to the 5th
  November being 4 mos. 11 dayes att 3£ 5s per mo.   £14:03:10
Stephen Mextead Second Mate from the 1st June to the
  5th November being 5 mos. 5 dayes att 55s per mo.   £14:04:00
Walter Feverell boatswaine from the 26th June to the
  5th November 4 mos. 9 dayes at 50s per mo.   £10:13:00
Wm. Jennings Carpenter from the 1st July to the 27th
  October 3 mos. 27 dayes at 3£ 5s per mo   £12:13:06
Wm. Bastard purser from the 29th June to the
  13th November 4 mos. 14 dayes at 40s per mo.   £08:18:08
George Hayes Boatswaines Mate from the 24th June to
  the 5th November 4 mos. 11 dayes at 45s per mo.   £09:16:06
Thomas Smith from the 18th June to the 5th November
  being 4 mos. 17 dayes att 36s per mo.   £08:04:06
Francis Jones from the 24th June to the 5th November
  being 4 mos. 11 dayes at 36s per mo.   £07:17:00
Robert Wilson from the 14th Aprill to the 5th
  November being 6 mos. 21 dayes at 30 s per mo.   £10:01:00
Hugh Williams from the 28th June to the 5th November
  being 4 mos. 7 dayes att 30s per mo.   £08:01:00
Robert Narron from the 28th June to the 5th November
  being 4 mos. 7 dayes att 40s per mo.   £08:09:04
Zachariah Mitchell from the 28th June to the 9th
  October being 3 mos. 11 dyes at 38s per mo.   £06:07:00
Wm Glasse from the 29th June to the 5th November
  being 4 mos. 7 dayes at 30s per mo.   £06:07:00
Thomas Mansfeild from the 2d July to the 24th October
  being 3 mos. 22 dayes att 37s per mo.   £06:18:00
Rowland Christian from the 6th July to the 5th
  November being 4 mos. at 30s per mo.   £07:04:00
John White from the 6th July to the 5th November
  4 mos. at 24s per mo.   £04:16:00
Timothy Higgings from the 9th July to the 5th
  November being 3 mos. 27 dayes at 32s per mo.   £06:04:00
Harmon Swan from the 8th July to the 5th November
  3 mos. 28 days at 34s per mo.   £06:13:06

Wm. Bryar from the 19th July to the 5th November
   3 mos. 17 dayes at 38s per mo.   £06:15:06
Thomas Pilgrim from the 14th July to the 5th
   November being 3 mos. 21 dayes at 27s per mo.   £04:19:06

John Hall from the 2d August to the 5th November
   3 mos. 3 dayes at 26s per mo.   £04:00:06
James Parker from the 13th July to the 9th October
   2 mos. 27 dayes at 27s per mo.   £03:19:00
Wm. Cooke from the 5th July to the 5th November
   4 mos. 1 day at 30s per mo.   £06:01:00

                                   176:17:8:[*]

[ENDORSED:]   The bill or Request
                 of the Mates etc
                 with their demand
                 of wages.
                 delivered in Court.
                 Nobr. 16th. 1675.

[25:34]

[DEPOSITION OF COMMISSIONERS HAVING INSPECTED THE
GOOD HOPE]

These May Certifie Whome itt may Concerne that wee whoes names are
hereunto subscribed have by order of his honnor the Governer (of this
Place) been on board the shipp Good Hope of London which is lately
Putt into This port in distresse, wherof Francis Richarson is Comander
and have viewed her hould, both att the feirst opening The Hatchis, and
allso att the breakeing of the ground teer.[‡] And find the hatchis wear well
fast and Thite, The goods that lay in The Hatch way, we found to be in
good order and well Condicioned. And we whoes names are hereunto
subscribed do farther testefie, that upon View we found The ground teer
to be allsoe well stowed, and sufficiently Dennaged[†] Butt Never The
lesse found There was much Damage sustained in the ground teer given
under our hands in New york

---

* These figures appear at the bottom of the page and may have no connection with the list
of wages, which totals £183:7:4.
‡ Ground tier: the lowest tier of articles stowed in a ship's hold (*Webster's Third New
International Dictionary*).
† Dunnage: wedge or chock, as cargo (*The Century Dictionary*).

October the 23th 1675.   Rob. Jones

                                          Benjam Blagge
                                          1675

                                          Francis Smith

Mr. Robert Jones and Mr. Francis Smith
sworne to the truth hereof, this 25th
day of October 1675.
                    Matthias Nicolls.
                    Secr.

Mr. Benjamin Blagge sworne to the truth
hereof this 28th day of Oct. 1675.
                    Matthias Nicolls Secr.

Entred in the Office of Records in New Yorke
the 29th October1675.

                                   Matthias Nicolls Secr.

[ENDORSED:]   Certificate for
                    the ship the
                   Good Hope
                   about her Stowage.
                   Oct. 23. 1675.
                   Ent.

[25:35, 36]

[NO DOCUMENTS ON THESE PAGES AND NO ENTRIES
IN THE CALENDAR]

[25:37]

To the Honorable Major
Edmond Andros Governor of New York etc:

The humble peticion of francis Richardson, Commander of the ship
Good hope of London

Sheweth

That your peticioner being bound from the Iland of the Barbados to
London, in the said ship Good hope, did there take in his ships lading of
sugar and other Commodities, from severall merchants and factors
resident in the Barbados, to bee delivered (the danger of the seas
excepted) at the said port of London; But it hath pleased God to send
such tempestuous and stormy weather about the degrees of 37 and 38
that your peticioner could not possibly proceed on the Intended Voyage,
his Mayne mast being broken, and his ship so extreamly bruised, that for
savegard of the mens lives and goods, your peticioner was fayne to come
unto this port of New yorke, and to unlade the said ship; which since
upon search is found to bee unable and Unfitt to proceed on her intended
Voyage: And wheras some part of the said goods laden in the said ship
belongeth to some passengers, who are now heere and have their goods
on shore in their custodies, the said passengers refuse to pay your
peticioner freight for the said goods according to bill of lading (which
hee humbly conceaveth to bee his due) or any thing at all but what shal
bee ordred by Authority; Although your Peticioner hath done to the
Utmost of his power, even to the spoyling of his ship to attayne his port.

Your Petitioner wherfore humbly prayes, that as your honour, is heere
Vice Admerall, and cheife in this high Court of Admiralty, You would
Issue out a Commission to some knowing and able men in marchant and
maritim affaires, such as your Honor shall think most fitt, to waygh and
concider your peticioners case and sad Condiction, and to allott him such
freights (after they shall have heard all parties) as in their prudence and
conscience shall seeme fitt and Just: And your Peticioner is the more
earnest in supplicating to have it speedily ordred, because his seamen
Importune him for their Wadges, which your peticioner shall not bee in
any capassity to pay them, Unlesse hee have freight paid him heere, by
those who have their goods already in their possession; which otherwise
may prove to the Utter Undoing of your peticioner.

And your peticioner shall ever pray etc:

The parties that have had their goods on shore, are
Coll. Lewis Morris, Abram Whirley, and Wm. Wayte.

[ENDORSED:]   The Peticion of Francis Richardson
Master of the ship Good Hope.
No: 12–75.

[25:38–39]

[ANOTHER PETITION OF FRANCIS RICHARDSON, CONCERNING THE
WAGES OF THE SHIP'S COMPANY, WITH AN ACCOUNT]*

New Yorke.   To the court of Admiralty sitting at the
Towne Hall In this City of New Yorke
November the 16th 1675.

The humble Peticion of Francis Richardson Master of the
ship Good Hope of London.

Sheweth

That in Answer to a Complaint putt into this Court against your Peticioner
by John Ambrose, and Stephen Mextead, Walter Feverall, and the rest
of the said Ships Company for Non-payment of their Wages, your
Peticioner humbly conceives That Marriners Wages are due to bee paid
where Freight is paid, and not otherwise. And whereas your Peticioner
by his Petition to the Governour (being Vice Admirall, and Cheife in this
Court of Admiralty) did desire to have Commissioners Nominated who
might call all Partyes Concerned to shew Cause why they refused to pay
Fraight for their Goods which they have received in to their Power and
Custody, which Petition it pleas'd the Governour to referr unto you to
consider and conclude on what shall bee most suitable to bee done in this
Case, both in reason and Conscience, and according to the Merchant and
Maritine lawes. Your Petitioner therefore saith, that hee humbly conceives, Hee can noe way declare what Wages hee oweth untill hee know
what this Court will conclude in poynt of Fraight to bee paid him; which
when tis concluded on, then your Peticioner will humbly submitt himselfe to pay the said Marriners Wages in that proportion you shall
Ordaine: And to make all things plaine, your Peticioner doth herewith
present a Paper annexed of the full Wages which would have been due

* See appendix for debit-credit account associated with this document.

to each particular Man of the Ships Compa. to this day, in case this Disaster had not befallen.

And whereas, when this Court shall have settled what Fraight is to bee paid, and what Wages also, it may soe happen that Money cannot bee procured in this place to pay that and other Vast incident Charges your Peticioner hath and shall bee at, nor any other Commodity save Muscado. Sugar and Cotton Wooll, on which to value themselves;

Your Peticioner therefore further desires, That the Court may please to settle such a fitt price on Sugar and Cotton, wherewith to make payments of (as shall bee Ordered) as to your Judgments shall seem equitable and just for all Partyes.

And your Peticioner shall pray etc.

[ENDORSED:]   The Peticion of Francis Richardson Master of the shipp the Good Hope to the Court of Admiralty.

[25:40]

[JUDGMENT IN THE CASE OF THE *GOOD HOPE*]

At a Court of Admiralty held in New Yorke, by speciall Commission from his Honor Edmond Andros Esquire Lieutenant and Go: Generall under his R. Highness James D. of Yorke and Alb: etc. of all his Territoryes in America the 13th 16th and 18th dayes of November in the 27th yeare of his Majesties Reigne Anno Domini 1675.

The Commissioners Present
vizt.

Mr. Matthias Nicolls, C: Wm. Dyre Mr. Fredrick Philips, Mr. Gabr: Minvielle Mr. Thomas Gibbs. Mr. Thomas Lewis—Mr. Stephanus Van Cortland— Mr. Johannes De Peyster Mr. Nicho. Blake, and Mr. Sam: Leete.

The matter under Consideracion, recommended by the Governors Commission to this Court, being the wages of the Officers and Marriners belonging to the shipp the Good Hope of London which came into this Port in distresse, and hath here beene adjudged insufficient, with other matters relating to the said Shipp.

The Court having heard what could bee said and alleadged, as well on the part of Francis Richardson the Master, and the other Officers on the behalfe of themselves and the shipps Company, and likewise Viewed the papers or writings relating thereunto, Having with mature deliberacion considered of the same; They doe adjudge That the Master with the other officers and Marriners belonging to the said shipp the Good Hope, ought to have their full wages paid them, It appearing not to the Court, that they have fayled in their dutyes. And that the said shipp the Good Hope with her Tackle, Furniture and Apparell together with her Cables, Anchors and appurtenances are lyable, to make satisfaction to the said Master etc. and shipps Company for their wages, In default whereof, (if they shall not bee found sufficient for the same,) any other Concernes of the Owners in the Masters hands, are to make it good.

As to the Masters Proposall, That the Goods on Board should bee brought into an Average for the Damage the shipp and Cargoe may have susteyned by the distresse of weather at Sea, and cutting their Mast etc.

As also for the payment of freight in this Port, the shipp being designed for another Port.

The Court having taken due Consideracion thereof, Doe give their Judgment that those matters, doe not properly lye before them, but leave them to a determinacion therein at Common Law if not otherwise agreed either where the persons most concerned doe reside, or otherwise as they shall thinke good.

Concerning a parcell of Goods taken away or stolne from on Board in the night out of the Masters Cabbin, since the shipp came into this Harbour, there being then a watch appointed, and the Master desireing releife therein.

The Court doth thinke it reasonable, that the persons who were, or ought to have beene upon the Watch that Night or time that the said Goods were lost, should make satisfaction for the value, and that the Master may stop so much of their pay in his hands as it will amount unto; In the which if they shall thinke themselves aggrieved, they may have their Recourse at Law for Remedy.

And for the Case of James Parker the Marriner complayned of by the

Master to have fayled of his duty, since the ship came into this Port, and therefore objected against payment of his wages, Hee is lyable to the usuall Customes and practice of the Seas for saylers in such Cases provided.

[ENDORSED:]   Judgment of the
                   Court of Admiralty.
                   Nov. 18–75.

                   M.
                   N.*

[25:41a]

[OATH ADMINISTERED TO THE ADMIRALTY COURT]

You do sweare by the everliving God, that according to the best of your understanding, you will well Examine and give true Judgment in the case now depending before you concerning the Shipp the Good Hope etc. whereunto you are Authorized by this Commission, So help you God.

[ENDORSED:]   The Oath of the
                   Court of Admiralty.

[25:41b]

[AN ENGROSSED COPY MADE FROM 25:40, LACKING THE
LIST OF COMMISSIONERS]

[25:41c]

[PETITION OF EASTHAMPTON WHALERS FOR PERMISSION
TO EMPLOY INDIANS]

To the Honorable Edmond Andross Esquire Generall of all his Royall Highnes his Teritories in America: And Governor at New Yorke:

The Humble Peticion of Jacob Schallenger, Stephen Hand, and James Soper, and others adjoyned with them in the whale Designe at Easthampton.

---

*   Matthias Nicolls. The document is in his handwriting.

Humbly Shewing to your honor that the last Spring your Peticioners appoynted or agreed to Joyne together in one entire Company for whaleing: For the carrying on of which theire Designe they agreed together to Indent with 12 Indians to man=forth Your Peticioners two boats they prepared with all suitable Craft thereunto: According whereunto, your Peticioners seeing the Indians Yearely imployed by other men both of theire owne Towne, Southampton and elcewhere: And knowing Nothing but that they might assume like liberty, and doe therein as themselves and others used to doe in former yeares, They hired, and Covenenated with 12 Indians, about June last, to goe to Sea in theire said boats with Craft this whale season soe Nigh at hand, upon terms which your Peticioners and the said Indians agreed on: But it fell out soe that fowre of the said Indians (competent and experienced men) belonged to Shelter Island, whoe with the rest received of your Peticioners in part of theire hire or wages 25s a peece in hand at the time of the contract, as the Indians Custome is, and without which they would not engage themselves to goe to sea as aforesaid for your Peticioners: After all which premises had passed your honors Order come downe to Easthampton (as they say) requireing all Indians to keep at theire owne usuall quarters for winter though your peticioners understand it relates onely to the Indians at Mr. Pells Plantation: And some of the Towne of Easthampton wanting Indians to make up theire Crue for whaleing they take advantage of your honors said Order thereby to hinder your Peticioners of the said fower Shelter Island Indians, One of the Overseers being of the Company that would Soe hinder your Peticioners: And Mr. Barker warned your Peticioners Not to entertaine the said fowre Indians without licence from your honor: And although some of your Peticioners opposites in this matter of great weight to them seek to prevent your Peticioners from haveing those said fowre Indians under pretence of zeale in fullfilling your honors order, yet it is more then apparent that they endeavour to break your Peticioners Company in that maner that soe they themselves may have opertunity out of the other eight Easthampton Indians to supply theire owne wants.

The premises Considered, And for that your supplicants designe is utterly broke for this whale season if they cannot enjoy the help of the said fowre Indians, which will bee to theire great loss and disappoyntment: Alsoe for that there is now noe hope of supply by home Indians, because all capable are by others already hired: Alsoe It is hopefull in reason, that fowre poore knowne Indians belonging to a place soe neere adjacent will not, nor can they doe much harme to the Towne if reall trouble should come, which is hopefull may not come, however not this winter season: And alsoe for that your Supplicants are like to bee deprived of the pay before mentioned which they were necessarily exposed to imparte to the said Indians upon Indentment with them.

Your Supplicants most humbly and Earnestly beseech your honor to take this theire address and weighty concerne into your Serious Consideration, And of your goodnes grant liberty unto your Supplicants of the help of the said fowre Indians this Imediate ensueing whale=Season according to theire honest contract with them, And alsoe bee pleased to voutsafe your Supplicants an Order from you to that effect: And your Most humbly devoted Supplicants as Duty bindes them shall ever pray for your honors happines etc.

[ENDORSED:]   1676
                 A peticon
                 From Easthampton.

[IN PENCIL:]   Granted 18 Nov. 1675[*]

[NOTE:]   Granted
                 EAS[‡]

[25:42a]

An account of Goods lost from on Board the Goodhope, (Francis Richardson Master) Notwithstanding that wee had a Watch upon the Deck, of foure men all the Night.

	£ s d
One Beaver Hatt, worth	02:15:00
One Caster Hatt	00:15:00
One broad Cloath Coate lined with silke	02:05:00
One paire of Breeches	00:16:00
Two Stuffe Coates, One New, the other not	03:00:00
One Box that was Stolen, and afterwards recover'd	00:10:00
againe, the Charge	10:01:10

---

[*] It is not known when this note was added.
[‡] Note and initials are in the governor's hand.

One Bundle, the which I was told was
Linnen, that I gave a Receipt for to
deliver it in England, that I know not
the valve of, which I desire that
Sufficient value, may bee left in my
Wm. Cooke, sworne   hand, in Case they bring it not to
the 23d November   light, it was About a Foot, every way
1675.

Francis Richardson

[ENDORSED:]   The Goods lost from
                on board the ship the
                Good Hope.

[25:42b]

Wm Cooke sworne the
23d November 1675 to each
particular:
M:N: Secr.

[25:43]

[LETTER FROM SECRETARY NICOLLS TO RICHARD SMITH,
EXPRESSING THE GOVERNOR'S VIEWS ABOUT SOME DISPUTED HAY]

Mr. Richard Smith.

Your Neighbours Thomas S[c]udder John Golding Benjam[ ] Jones and
William B[rot]hert[on] [   ] their Applic[   ] unto the
Go[   ] they may have the hay they have mowed, The which
was stop't by Attachment from C. Brockholes it being in a manner their
whole provision of fodder for their Cattle this winter they being willing
to make any reasonable satisfaction for the same to bee adjudged by
indifferent m[ ] I am ordered to write to you about it that Upo[ ] their
so equitable proposall you will doe [   ] to suffer them to have that
parcell of [   ] the Condicions aforemencioned, th[ ] their
Cattle may not perish and they bee altogether disappointed of their labor,
The Go: being likewise informed that you are otherwise someh[ ]
provided per your owne stock that you have no absolute Necessity
thereof: The Go: would have spoken with you about it but you were gone
before hee was acquai[ ]ted with the matter; your Moderacion [   ]ein

[   ] your other [   ]nes wi[   ] not
one [   ] commendable but redound to your ow[   ] quiet and satisfaction, which I doe earnestly rec[   ]mend to you being

Your Loving friend
M N

No. 13. 1675
I writt also to Mr. Woodhull
who was to see my letter to Mr. Smith
to favour them about the Hay

[ENDORSED:]   A lettre by the Go:
order to Mr. R. Smith
and another to Mr.
Woodhull about the
men at the Farme

[25:44a]

[DECLARATION BY LUDOVICUS COBES CONCERNING THE LAND PATENT AND MURDER OF JAN REYERSZ. TRANSLATION]

Whereas one is obligated to attest to the truth, especially when summoned thereto; therefore, I, the undersigned, upon the request of Mr.
Gerrart van Slichtenhorst and Jan Hendricxs van Solsbergen declare how
it was that some years ago Jan Reyers, deceased, asked me to accompany
him on a trip to Claverrack late in the autumn and to record the sale of
land, which he bought from the Indians, named Preeuwen Hoeck, from
about the Claver until the kil of Mr. Abraham Staes and extending in
breadth until the kil on the east side. However, when we reached
Claverrack by boat that same night, the river froze and we were unable
to cross the kil. Therefore fruitlessly we had to return overland to Albany.
In addition to this I know of the confirmation of the aforesaid sale, in
that I myself submitted it to the Lord Stuyvesant, former general, who
replied that he approved of the sale; however, the aforesaid Jan Reyers
was to live there with at least five to six families, as some had already
done, and he was to pay the Indians in full for the aforesaid land. Indeed,
I also know that at the same place the aforesaid Jan Reyersz with his wife
and another man with wife and children were murdered by two Onon-
daga Indian murderers at the time of the Mahican and Mohawk war. I
am prepared to confirm this, my deposition, by solemn oath (if required).

Done at Schaenhechtede   Ludovicus Cobes, secretary
the 22nd of November 1675.

[25:44b]

[DECLARATION BY JAN TYMENSZ VALENTYN TO THE SAME AS
ABOVE. TRANSLATION]

True copy

Jan Thymensz, inhabitant of Schaenhechtede, attests and declares, upon
request as above, that he knows that Jan Reyersz, deceased, bought the
aforesaid land from the Indians and that he personally lived on a piece
of it with his family, which Jan Reyersz had granted and sold to him and
had already paid on it two and a half beavers in goods; also that a certain
Adriaen de Vries and Ryck Riddersz had settled there on the aforesaid
land with their families. In concluding his deposition he is prepared to
confirm the same by solemn oath (if required). Done at Schaenhectede,
dated as above.

Was signed:
Jan Tymenssen Valentyn

the mark ∌ made
by Benamin Robberts summoned
hereto as witness.

After comparison this was found to agree
with the original.

Quod attestor
Ludovicus Cobes, secretary.

[ENDORSED:]   For Mr. Slichtenhorst

[25:45]

[PETITION OF DANIEL DE HAART, APPEALING A DECISION
OF THE MAYOR'S COURT]

To the Right Honorable Major Edmund Andross Esquire
Governor Gennerall of all his Royall Highnes his Territories
in America.

The humble petione of Daniell De Heart Administrator unto
Balthazer De Hearte Deceased.

Sheweth
That your peticioner was sued at the Mayors Court of this Citty by John
Hendrik van Bommell Jacob Tunison Kay and Jaques Cousseau trustees
to the Esteate of Balthazer De Heart aforesaid for the summe of 5000
gilders they pretending soe much due for their Comission and Exteror-
dinary Expences in selling and disposeing of the testators Esteat[ ]
Contrary to will; att which Judgment passed against your petitioner for
the summ of 3656 gilders they haveing besides that discounted from your
petioner out of the said testators Estate above 16000 gilders upon that
account.

Therefoere humbly prayes that your Honor will be pleased
to grant him an Appeale And that his case may be heard
before your Honor att the next Gennerall Court of Assizes
and that in the meane tyme all further proceedings on the
said Judgment in the Mayors Court may be stayed he
performing as the Law in such cases required.

And your peticioner as in Duty bound
Shall pray etc.

[25:46]
[PETITION OF FORMER SHERIFF (ROBERT COE?) TO CAUSE THE
SETTLEMENT OF HIS OFFICIAL ACCOUNTS][*]

To the right Honorable [   ]
Governor Generall of [   ]
Territories In A[   ]
The petitione of [   ]

In all humble manner

Sheweth that your petitioner was sued Gra[   ] the widow Spicer
for Considerable sumes for [   ] petition was high sherffe such
etc. May it please [   ] Jon. Ryder of this Citty was Clarke of the
[   ] petition and sherffe: and doth des[   ] fees

_____

* The Calendar dates this document as Nov. 23, 1675. A penciled note of that date also
appears on the document, but when the document itself was written is unknown.

and publique Charg: The s[   ] pay your petitioner
his just right [   ]

Therefore most[   ] be pleased to grant
an[   ]ed [   ] Ryder May appeare before your Honor to [   ] Clause why he hath not
paid and satisf[   ] petition and that upon his [ ]efusall
soe to doe Your honnor will be pleased to grant tym[   ] to
your petitioner for payment of said [   ]and
[   ] be forced therunto

and your [   ]
as I shall duly [   ]
shall [   ]

[25:47]

[MINUTES OF A MEETING WITH THE INDIANS CONCERNING
LAND AT HEMPSTEAD]

Nov. 25: 1675.

Tackpousha and severall other Indyans appeared before the
governor.
It was about the land claymed by them which Hempsteed men have so
long enjoyed, for the wh[   ] have made their demand [   ]nor
his proposall.
They say that the [   ]e spoken with those concerned, but have not their
answer.
The governor tells them, That they must have patience, untill they shall
make it, when a conclusion may be resolved on.

[ENDORSED:]   Tackpousha [   ]
                [   ]her Indyans

[25:48]

[NO DOCUMENT IS LISTED FOR THIS NUMBER IN THE CALENDAR.
TWO ITEMS NOW FILED HERE BELONG WITH JOHN SHAKERLY'S
ACCOUNTS IN VOLUME 29]*

* See appendix to the final volume of *The Andros Papers.*

[25:49]

Condicions of the Weighhouse Ordered by the Governor to be lett to Farme in the Publicke and usuall manner this 25th day of November 1675 and to be entred upon the Next day being the 26th.*

The former Regulacion and payments (a Copie whereof is hereunto annext) shall be punctually observed, and to that end it shall be sett up in the Weigh house for everybodyes View.

The highest bidder for the same, to be preferred, giving sufficient security to make good the payment.

The Rent to be paid quarterly, and in Case of Failing fifteene dayes after each quarter, the sheriffe shall have power to distreyne for the same.

The weigh=House is this day taken by Mr. John Sharpe at six thousand two hundred Guilders sewant or value, to bee paid according to the Condicions, In testimony whereof hee hath hereunto sett his hand, the day and yeare above written.‡

wittnesse   John Sharpe.

Matthias Nicolls.
fredryck flypsen
Giulain Verplanck

[ENDORSED:]   The Farme Lett
                     of the weigh house
                     Mr. Sharpe f:6200
                     No: 25. 1675.
                     155£.

---

* This was crossed out on a later occasion. The dates were changed to read: "10th day of December 1680 . . . Next day being the 11th." Apparently the office was put up for bid again.
‡ The last paragraph was added by Matthias Nicolls. It is not certain whether "the date above written" refers to 1675 or to 1680, although the earlier date is suggested by the quality of Nicolls's handwriting and by Sharpe's having dropped out of sight politically by 1679.

[25:50]

Orders to bee observed for payment of the Weigh money.

All Goods and Merchandize which are subject to be weighed shall nott bee imported within this City, neither exported out of the same Except they be weighed by the Sworne Weigh Master, and the charges of the Weighing shall bee satisfyed; and all Goods and Merchandize are to pay for the Weighing in Wampom or beaver, or otherwise to the Wheigh Masters Satisfaction, before the Carrying away of the Goods.

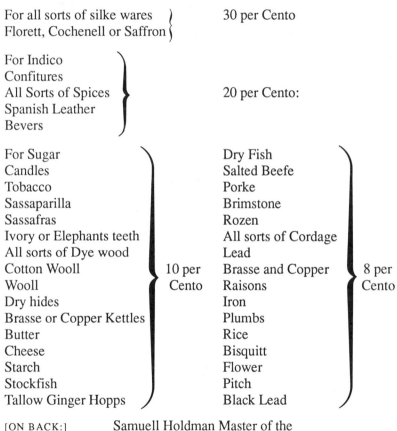

For all sorts of silke wares ⎫
Florett, Cochenell or Saffron ⎬   30 per Cento

For Indico ⎫
Confitures │
All Sorts of Spices ⎬   20 per Cento:
Spanish Leather │
Bevers ⎭

For Sugar		Dry Fish	
Candles		Salted Beefe	
Tobacco		Porke	
Sassaparilla		Brimstone	
Sassafras		Rozen	
Ivory or Elephants teeth		All sorts of Cordage	
All sorts of Dye wood		Lead	
Cotton Wooll	10 per	Brasse and Copper	8 per
Wooll	Cento	Raisons	Cento
Dry hides		Iron	
Brasse or Copper Kettles		Plumbs	
Butter		Rice	
Cheese		Bisquitt	
Starch		Flower	
Stockfish		Pitch	
Tallow Ginger Hopps		Black Lead	

[ON BACK:]   Samuell Holdman Master of the
Recovery for Jamaica

[ENDORSED:]   Condicions for the
Weigh=house.

[25:51]

[CONDITIONS RELATING TO THE AUCTION OF THE POSITION OF
COLLECTOR OF THE ALCOHOL EXCISE]

Condicions of the great Pact or Tappers Excise, by the
Governor to bee lett to Farme in the publicke and usuall
manner this 4th day of December and to bee entred upon at
the Expiracion of the former, being the 8th day of January
next. Anno 1675/6.

The former Regulacion and payments (a Copie whereof is hereunto
annext) shall bee punctually observed, and to that End it shall bee sett
up at the Farmers Office, expressing the time of its being, Upon Mornings
and Afternoones.

The highest bidder for the same, to bee preferred giving sufficient
security to make good the payments.

The Rent to bee paid Quarterly and in Case of failing fifteene dayes after
each Quarter, the Sheriffe shall have power to distreyne for the same.

The great Packt is this day taken by Otto Gerrittsen at ten
thousand three hundred Gilders sewant or Value, to be paid
according to the Condicions, In Testimony whereof he hath
hereunto sett his hand this 4th day of december Annoque
domini 1675.

Wittnesse   Otto Gerrittsen

Matthias Nicolls

Wm Dyre   fredryck flypsen
                                 G: Minvielle

[ENDORSED:]   Condicions of the
                   Great Packt
                   let out.
                   Dec. 4. 1675.

[25:52]

[AN ENGROSSED PARTIAL COPY OF 25:51, THE ENDORSEMENT
OF WHICH IS DATED JAN. 8, 1675/6]

[25:53]

[BIDDERS ON THE PRECEDING]

The Great Packt farmed the 4th of December 1675.

ƒ10	Paulus Turk 4000. 9000.
	Tho: Carr 5000.
	Mr. Sidenham 5200.
ƒ5.ƒ5.	Otto Gerrittsz 6000. 7500. 8500. 10000 a beaver.
	Mr. Humphrey Davenport 6500.
	Mr. Roadsby 7000.
ƒ5.	Mr. Sharpe 8000.
ƒ10.	Capt. Dyre 9500.
3 beavers	Otto Gerrittsen 10300.

2000 Gld. Advance

t'was lett att 10300 Guilders.

Expence 4 beavers.
35 Guilders sewant.

18 Cans of sack and some burn't wine.

The small Excise lett before, for 6000 G.,
These Expence [*illegible*]* 16 Cans. besides burn't wine.

[ENDORSED:]   Bidders at the
letting of the
pacht,
Dec. 4 1675.

* This scrawl may say "were neere," or "which were." Secretary Nicolls wrote this entry
and the previous three lines.

[25:54a]

[NOTES (COUNCIL MINUTES?) ABOUT TIMBER TO BE LOADED ON
THE SHIPS OF CAPTAINS GRIFFITH AND BURTON AND ABOUT THE
BOUNDARY BETWEEN CONNECTICUT AND NEW YORK]

Dec. 7th 1675.

It was R[   ] That in regard no present Fre[ ]ht [   ]d either
in this Port, or the [   ] for to lode the Castle
[   ] most advantageous loading [   ]
timber for knees, * Standards, etc. to be had [   ]
there was store in

[   ]enters and Masters Advice [   ]
Castle Frigotts, and approbacion of the [   ] ships [   ]
Griffith and Capt. Burton with The Gove[   ] his Councell.

In the month of November 1664 Governor Winthrop, with severall
Commissioners from the Generall Court of Hartford in the Colony of
Conecticott came [   ] New Yorke, to congratulate the Arrivall [   ]r
Nicolls and the rest of the [   ] for the affayres of New
England [   ] for the reducement of the [
]ence, and withall to agree [   ] [   ]ts
of the two Colonyes: [   ] the one upon the other [
]t was Verbally agreed on [   ]   [   ] limitts
of the Dukes Government [   ] [   ]Westerne of
Conecticutt Colony shoale bee [   ] to the Eastward of Hudsons
River and [   ]nhatans Island, but to make the said limitts more
certaine It was afterward concluded that a small Creeke at a place called
by the Indyan name of Momoronock bet- weene 18 and 20 miles off the
River should bee the bounds, betweene the Governments the which was
set [   ] downe in writing and given into charge [   ] and it being sug[
]sted that Hudsons River did goe up North [   ] likewise
mentioned that th[   ]ld goe up so too, either No[
] it was found and it [   ]p North and Easterly, wit[
] [   ]y must cutt neare the Esopus not halfe way up to Alb:
The same being Contrary to all the discourse about the said Agreement,
It being urged and at length [   ] the limitts of Conecticutt
[   ] 120 mile of the River, or at least not neare[ ]the the
mouth of Momaronock Creeke, however omitted in 2d writing.

---

*   A piece of naturally bent timber used in supporting structures coming together at an angle
(adapted from *Webster's Third New International Dictionary*).

[ON THE BACK:]

[MINUTES OF A MEETING OF GOVERNORS ANDROS AND CARTERET
WITH SOME NEW JERSEY INDIANS]

New Yorke—Apr. 20th 1675.

This day three Indyan Sachems belonging t[ ] the Province of New Jersey
t[   ]rds Delaware being se[   ] into the Fort to the [   ] and
making [   ]t of 4 bands of sewant [   ] in
friendship, the [   ] Upon the Governor[   ]
[   ]urning them above d[   ]ent,
they promised [   ] with the Govern[   ]
[   ]not take part with [   ]nemies.

Capt. Philip Carteret
Go: of New Jersey was
present with the Go:

T[   ] were
M[   ]—sachems of Toponemus.
Poruppa sachem of Nevesans.
Taptawapamum sachem of Kackowackin.

[ENDORSED:]   The Appearance of 3
                   Indyan sachems of and to
                   the south of the Nevisan[ ]
                   to conclude and confirme
                   a peace.
                   Apr. 20, 1675.

[25:55]

[PROCEEDINGS OF THE COURT OF SESSIONS AT JAMAICA]

                        At a Court of Sessions held at Jamaica for
                        the North Riding etc. Dec. 8th 1675.

The bench called over
Mr. R. Cornell
Mr. J: Pell.
Mr. W: Laurence
Mr. T. Hicks.

The Constable of the Townes all appeare.

A Jury returned and sworne.

The Causes called over.

Nath: Spratt   plt
Mich: Clarke   deft. } agreed

Asser Levy   plt.   } Judgment by
Elyas Doughty deft. } Consent.

Richa. Smith   plt.
Geo: Codner   deft.
Mr. Leete for the   plt.
Mr. G: Cooke for the deft.

put to a Jury upon the defts pleading to a certaine bill of 12£
Non est factum

Mr. Leet takes oath that the deft. confest his bill to him at Oysterbay.

Asser Levy   plt.)
Peter Jansen deft. } agreed

Richa Smith   plt) no
Jeremiah Wood deft } warrant

An Execucion upon some smiths Tooles in the hands of Anthony wright of Oysterbay at the suite of John Coomes against Nichs. Davis, the summe 9£ 15s 0d. the Tooles apprized at 15£—Anth: Wright 1/3.

Jacob Leysler   plt.)
Anth: Wright   deft. } No Goods
left there.
The Constable of Oysterbay saith hee can find other Effects there. Ordered to bring a new declaracion.

Mr. John Pell   plt.)
Tho: Squire   deft.} An attachment

The Const. of Westchester to make his returne tomorrow morne.

The Court dismist till tomorrow morning—7 a

---

* The plea of the general issue in an action of debt on bond or other specialty and on any written instrument in some states (*Webster's Third New International Dictionary*).

Dec. 9th.

Richa Smith plt.
Geo: Codner deft.

The returne of the Jury they find for the plt for the bill, what is paid to bee discounted.

A Review proposed
Security demanded
Referred to the latter End of the Court whether a Review or no.

John Robinson and ⎫
Wm. Sidenham Att. ⎬ plt.
unto Jos: Knott   ⎭

Tho: Davis   deft.

The Declaracion upon a bill of the defts hand for 12£ in the specie therein mencioned.

Jos: Knotts letter of Att. to John Robinson—Robinsons to Sidenham.

Mr. Cooke Att. for the plt.
Mr. Leete Att for the deft.

The wittnesses not present. Mr. Leet moves for a Non=suite.

The deft. pleads the Goods taken were in trust.

Tho: Hunt sworne declares the Goods were stolne.

Elyas Doughty sworne—declares the like and that hee made an Agreement with Mr. Holden for 7£.

The court order a Non-suite (upon want of proofe)

Allan Anthony plt.
Francis Doughty deft.

Tho: Davis answers upon an Attachment having had his Oath, to have some goods of the defts, but inconsiderable, that hee hath them still, hee is ordred to produce the Invoyce.

Wm. Osburne sworne saith That hee was shewne by Tho: Davis an Account of Goods in His hands from Mr. Doughty which hee thought would buy 12 Mares besides his Commission. That hee had seene the Invoyce of the Goods which was in Tobacco as hee thinkes to the Value of betweene 30 and 40£.

A letter from Mr. Fr: Doughtye to Mr. Sharp acknowledging the debt, and promise of satisfaction.

The warrant of arrest in N.J.

Proceedings in Court there etc.

The originall debt was to Nath: Brittaine for 1900 wt. of Tobacco.

Referr'd to the Jury. Mr. Elyas Doughty being of the Jury is excused in his bro: Cases, and Gideon Wright sworne in his place.

John Coe and ⎞
Ben: Coe   ⎠   plts

Richa Crabb   deft.

The declaracion of the plt for 2 Mares or Equivalent.

The summons call'd for to the Const. of Oysterbay—signed by Mr. Robt. Coe.

The bill from the deft, signed anno. 1661.

The summons put to the Vote whether good or no. Over=ruled to bee good.

The bill urged to bee prooved.

A Non-suite.

Ariaen Van Laer   plt.
Peter Jansz Schol   deft

Judgment by default. the debt. confess't.

C. Anth: Brockhurst plt.
Sam: Ruscoe   deft.

Judgment acknowledged and ordred to bee entred.

Mr. John Pell plt.
Richa Ponton deft.

A declaracion upon account for 10£ Due upon his Uncles bookes.

Judgment for what shall appeare to bee due upon the booke.

Ephraim Hermans   plt.
Westchester   deft.
Upon a bill of Court Charges from the Assizes etc.
Judgment for what shall bee adjudged by Mr. John Pell and C. Wm.
Laurence.

Mr. John Pell plt.
Tho: Squire   deft.
Upon attachment by the Cour: of Westchester neglected (as alleadged)
by the Const., who returnes hee found no Effects.

The Action 10£.
Judgment given for so much as shall appeare to bee of the summe in the
hands of Sam: and John Palmer To bee adjudged by any two Justices of
the Ridinge, The Const. of Westchester for his default lyable to make
good the damage if Effects embezled.

Geo: Mills   Complt.
Humphry Underhill)
Abell Gale   } defts.

Assault upon the highway.

to bee considered of by the bench.

John Caster plt.
Tho: Hunt   deft.
The plt not appearing—A Non=suite.

The Court dismist till afternoone.

Afternoone

Allard Anthony   plt.
Francis Doughty   deft.

The Jury find for the plt. that the Goods attach't bee lyable to make satisfaction to their value.
That the Goods and Invoyce bee delivered up by Tho: Davis into the hands of the next Justice of Peace and ordered to bee sworne value by two apprizers apprized by the Court.

Thomas Hunt   Plt.*
John Richardson Deft.
George Cooke for the Plantiff.
Mr. Leett for Deft.
Mr. Leet pleads against new Evidence upon a review. Mr. Cooke pleades thatt matteriall evidence is wanting by executing of the Governeurs speciall order.

The bench taking the case in Consideracion the plantiff wanting materiall evidence the case referd Till tomorrow morning.

Mr. William Osborn Plantiff
Ebenezer Jones Deft.
Mr. Osborne for himselfe.
Mr. Cooke for the Deft.
Mr. Cooke pleades thatt the Declaration is nott aggreable with the Warrant.

Mr. Leett in the behalfe of the Plantiff requires non suite upon Consideration that the warrant and declaration did nott aggree the Court did grant a non suitt the Warrant being for Debt. the Declaration for an action upon the case for tresspasse.

Ebinezer Jones Plantiff
Richard Osborne Deffendant

Mr. Cooke for the plantiff
Mr. Leett for the Deffendant.
Mr. Leett prayes a non=suitt for thatt the plantiff declaration is nott according to the Warrant.

*   From here to the end this document is in a different hand from that of the first part, which was written by Secretary Nicolls.

Samuel Riscoe   plt.
Mr. Robert Coe   Deft.
Mr. Leett for the plantiff.
Mr. Leette delivers in Court Samuel Riscoes Account for 21£ 19s 09 signed Robert Coe.
The Account shewen Mr. Robert Coe he Can nott owne the hand.
Samuel Riscoe Declares for 124 £
Delivers his Account in Court
Mr. Leett declares the ballance desire is 24£
The Plantiff delivers in an order of Mr. Coes signed and owned in Court Directed to Mr. Anthony Watters to pay Samuel Riscoe fifteen poundes 12 sl for severall s due in the former sherriffes time.
Mr. Coes Attorneye desires Samuel Riscoe to sweare to his account
Samuel Riscoe sweares to his account and saith that upon ballance there is due to him 23£
The Jurye are to give in there report tomorrow morning.

For Misdemeanor.
Humphrey Undrill and Abell Gale called; refferred till tomorrow Morning.
Mrs. Waters Petition taken into Consideration.
The Court doth order to be Consider of in private.
Mr. Coes complaint against Edward Watters of Westchester
Mr. Coe desires an account of two yeares rates from the Constable of Westchester to the value of 50£
The Court takes the bussinesse into consideration till tomorrow.
In the Action between Samuel Riscoe Plantiff Mr. Robert Coe Deffendant the Jury finde for plantiff.

Thomas Hunt Plantiff
John Richardson Deft.
Mr. Leet Att. for the Plantiff
Mr. Cooke Att. for the Deft.
An Speciall Order from the Governour to have a reveiw.

the first declaration read over.

the former judgment read over.

Samiel Drake
William Heydon   Wittnesses for John Richardson
Richard Ponton
Edward Watters

Articles produced and read over concerining a Division of the land they
live upon signed by Thomas Laurence Samuel Drake William Heydon
Jonathan Hazard

John Richardson pleades that this way is upon the land exepted in the
Articles of agreement agreed upon by the foure men.

Mr. Thomas Laurence declares upon his oath thatt the foure arbitrators
did appoint a highway and did appoint Thomas Hunt to make* severall
trees and itt was don before the signing of theire arbitration.

The case is left to the Jury to bring theire verdict.

The jury finds for the Deffendant.

Mr. Leett moves for an appeale in the behalfe of the Plantiffe.

Jacob Leisler Plantiff
The estate of Nicollas Davis Deft
Mr. Cooke Attor. for the Plantiff
Mr. Leett for the Deffandants
Mr. Leette moves for cost of suitt
Mr. Cooke desire continuance of the Attachmentt

The Court saw cause to continue the Attachment and the plantiff to pay
costs.

Thomas Daniel ⎱ both prosecuted by the Constable
Cornelis Mott ⎰ of Hempstead for stealing a hogg

They plead nott guilty and putt themselves upon God and the Country.
Cornelis Mott saies that Thomas Daniel had kild a swine and itt lay in
the Woodes reddy dressed the haire was of and he help Daniel To bring
halfe of the Hogg home and Daniel the other halve.

Thomas Daniel saith that Cornelis Mott told him he had kild a racoone
and itt lay in the woodes and desired him to help him home with itt and
when he came to the place itt was a dead hogg.

The Jurye find the prisoners both Guilty.

[ENDORSED:]   Jamaica Sessions
                Dec. 8th 1675.

                1675 Queens County‡

---

* He probably intended "mark."
‡ Added after the counties were formed in 1683.

[25:56]

Accions to bee tryed att Jameca December 1675.

x 1   John Robinson and Wm. Sidnam
          Attorneys unto Joseph Knott   against Tho: Davis   2

   2 x Thomas Hunt against John Richardson   5
   3 x Wm. Osborne against Ebinezer Jones   0
   4 x Ebinezer Jones against Richard Osbourne   0
x 5   George Mills against Humph. Underhill
x 6   Nath: Spratt against Michael Clarke
x 7   Samuel Rescoe against Robt. Coe.
x 8   Richard Smith against Geo Codner
x 9   Asser Levy against Elias Doughty
x 10 The same against Peter Janse schol
x 11 Richard Smith against Jer Wood
x 12 Arian Van Laer against Peter Janse Schol   5
x 13 Mr. Jno Pell against Rich: Panton1
x 14 Capt. Antho: Brockhurst against Sam Rescoe
x 15 John Carter against Tho: Hunt
x 16 Jacob Leisler against Anth: Write
x 17 Allard Anthony against Fran Doughty   3
x 18 Jno Coe and
          Benjamine Coe   against Richa. Crabb   4
x 19 Ephram Harman against the towne of Westchester
x   Thomas Hatfield
x   Cornelis Mott Presented Tho Davis
x 20 Jno Pell against Tho: Squire Attach.
x   Coe against Waters Complaint.
      Rachel Waters wid. Peticion.

[ENDORSED:]   Dockett Jameca
           December 1675.

[25:57][*]

[PROCEEDINGS OF THE COURT OF SESSIONS AT GRAVESEND]

Wed: At a Court of Sessions held at
                        Gravesend Dec. 15th 1675.

The Court of Justice, for the West-Riding—called over—all 4 Present.

The Const. the like, appear'd with their staves all etc.

A Jury empanell'd and sworne.

The Cause call'd over.

Elyas Doughty   Plt.

Tho: Janse Van Dyke ⎞
Hendr. Mattysen etc. ⎭   Defts

A declaracion against the defts of N. Utrecht—about stopping some horses of Mr. Fr: Doughtyes.

They gave an obligacion for 1600£

Damage is pleaded.

Mr. Leete—Att. for the plt.

Mr. Cooke for the Deft.—to bring his plea in writing.

Putt off till tomorrow morne—the first Cause.

The Court dismis't till tomorrow morning 8 a Clocke.

                    Thursday Dec. 16–1675.

The Jury called over.

The Constables also.

The Orders of the Last Court of Assizes read.

---

* This document and 25:133 are presently reversed. We have restored them to their correct order.

Elyas Doughty   plt.
Tho: Jansen van Dyke etc. defts.

Hendryck Mattysen Smacks all Pix-start.[*]

To bee referr'd to the Jury.

Mr. Tho: Wandall
C. Richa. Stillwell.
Sam: Holmen
Jon: Hazard   } Jurors
Wm. Compton
Roloffe Marte
Sim: Jansen

Dan: de Haart   plt.
Derrick Jansz Hooglands deft.

A declaracion putt in by Mr. Leete his Att. upon a sale and Morgage.

	The morgage read.
4200	The debt 4200 G. upon the house.
641–17	641£ 17st.—by bills.
4841:17	

Jan Van Kirke sworne—saith hee paid 2 Oxen at 5500 G—the booke but 500 G.

Referr'd to a Jury—both Causes.

Derrick Jansz Hooghland   plt.
Reyn Jansen   deft.

1481 G by agreement.

Confes't—Judgment issued.

Tho: Morgan etc. plt.
Ralph Cardall   deft.

---

* The word "all" may be an abbreviation, perhaps for "alias." However, we have not found the term "pix-start" used elsewhere in connection with Hendrick Mattysz Smock, and the meaning of the term is uncertain. Charles Gehring suggests that it may represent "pig's start"; *start* in Middle English and Dutch meaning "tail." In the late seventeenth century "pigtail" referred to a twist of tobacco, not to a hairstyle.

A declaracion by Mr. Cooke.Their fathers will read. Its about 4 Oxen. The deft. ordered to putt his answer in writing.

Nich: De Myer plt.
Claus Clausen Ils (?) Defts.

798£ tobacco in Caske.306£–4 s wampum and a Cow.

Hee is removed to Stat: Isl.

An Attachment granted upon Effects in the hands of the Vendue Master.

Agreed	Asser Levy plt.	Min: Joannes—Deft.
	Do. plt.	Jan Barents—deft.
	Do. plt.	Barent Egbertsz deft.

Agreed   Cor: Coertsen—plt. Ad: Brower—deft.

Const. of Newtowne—Sam: Moore
Geo: Wood—upon Execucion.

The Apprizers to take their Oathes if required and the others not satisfyde. Review to bee considered of.

Mr. N. De Meyer craves Execucion against Aukes Jansen upon a Judgment the last Court for 1300 G 7 st. Granted.

Mr. N. De Meyer, craves Execucion against Laurs Jansz upon a Judgment 238 G bound in wheat, 1694 G in wheat. Execucion already granted.

Sam: Leet—an Endictment against Flattlands, about the high way being block't up. To bee considered of.

Mr. Heynells buisnesse of his having a salary; to bee consider'd of.

Angeltye—Jan's complaynes against Butcher—that hee doth not performe his collaterall agreement—after Judgment and Execucion.

Referred to the later End of Feb: the last payment—if not then Execucion, as before—Mr. Betts and another Justice to bee acquainted with it.

John Kingdome moves a determinacion of a former order, about wintering a Cow etc. The title to bee made appeare by order of the last Court.

To bee consider'd of.

Tho: Morgan etc.   plt.
Ralph Cardall etc. deft.

The deft. brings in an Answer in writing.

Its an old buisnesse, The former order to bee observed.

The Jury bring in their Verdict in the Case of

Elyas Doughty   plt.
Tho: Jansen etc. deft.

They find for the plt. with costs of suite.

Dan: de Haart   plt.
Dirck Jansz Hoogeland deft.

They find for the plt. what can bee proved to bee paid by the End of Feb. to bee discounted.

The Jury dismist.

Mr. Cooke moves for an Appeale in the former Cause.

Granted as the Law directs.

Dismis't till afternoone.

Afternoone.

The peticion of Geo: Wood taken into Consideracion: To have a Review as the Law directs.

Mr. Doughtys buisnesse with New Utrecht, proposed to conclude it for 1000 G—if immediately agreed to.

Respited for halfe an houre.

John Kingdome to have Judgment against Bilieu, none appearing to answer at this Court.

Mr. Heynelles Commission considered of, for a setled salary: An order upon it, that the Towne doe pay for publick or private buisnesse.

Ralph Cardall   plt.
Richard Harvey deft.

It was about Harvey's comming into his house and taking away the Keys of his doores which were found about him.

It was examined in private and composed the deft. being in drinke and begging pardon for what hee did comitte but protests not to know how hee came by the Keys and was sorry promising to comport himselfe better hereafter. The Court chid him and Cardalls wife and advised them to give no occasion of future scandalle so were dismis't. Harvey to beare the Charge.

Severall other small [   ]

So the Court dismis't and dissolved in the Evening.

[ENDORSED:]   Graves End Sessions.
               Dec. 15. 1675.

[25:58]

[DOCKET OF THE COURT AT GRAVESEND]

Accons to be tryed att Gravesend the 15th December 1675.

Jury   x Dan: de hart Administrator unto Balthazer Dehart
               against Derick Jansen Hougland.
         x Asser Levy against Minne Johannes
         x The same against Jan Barentsen
         x The same against Baren Engbert
        —Ralph: Cardall against Rich: Harvey
         x Nicho: Demeyer against Clausse Clausen etc.
to mor. x Tho: Morgan Jno Morgan and Daniel Morgan Orphans
               against Ralph Cardall
         x Cornelis Coursen against Adrien Brewer
to mor. x Elias Doughty against Tho: Jansen Van dyke Hendricke
Jury   Mattysen Smack and Jan van Deventer.
         x Derick Jansen Houghland against Ryere Jansen.

[ENDORSED:]   Accions
               Dec. 15–75
               Gravesend Court.

[25:59a]

[INVENTORY OF THE ESTATE OF THOMAS SEABROOKE]

Thomas Seabruck dyed at westchester the 17th desembar 1675 an inventory of the estate of the desesed.

1 houce and homelot
9 akers land in the feeld
2 akers medow
2 mares 2 colts to yeer old
2 yong colts
5 Cous 2 three yeer olds
2 steers to yeer old
3 yeerlings 5 Calves
3 swine
1 feather bead
5 blankets
2 sheetes
1 Iron pot
3 guns

this inventory taken the 18 as above by the Constable and to of the ovarseers witness our hands

Edward Waters
Tho Molleenex
Nicoles bally

at the desire of the widow this estate prised by the Constable and to ovarseers

	£	s	d
the whole acomadations prised at	90	0	0
to mares and 2 to year old colts	9	0	0
to young colts	1	10	0
5 cous 2 three yeer olds	26	0	0
2 steers to yeer-olds	5	0	0
3 yearling 5 calves	7	0	0
3 swine	3	0	0
the feather none of thomas sea brucks nor to blankets			
3 blankets	1	4	0
1 sheet	0	12	0
1 Iron pott	0	10	0
3 guns	2	10	0

this estate prised as above
witness our hands
Edward Watars

Tho Mollennex
Nicolles balle

[ENDORSED:]   Letters of Administration
hereupon.
Inventory of Tho:
Seabrookes   graunted
Estate
Entred
Dec. 17. 1675

[IN PENCIL:]   Mary the wife of
Tho: Seabrooke lettres
of Administracion to mem.

[25:59b]

[RECEIPT FROM THE CONSTABLE OF EASTHAMPTON TO JOHN
COMBS]

Easthampton, December the 17th 1675.

Received of John Combs of Brookehaven (alias) Seatalcott, the full and
just summe of five pounds, being in full of all Fines and Court Charges
whatsoever, either layd on him the said John Combs, or caused by him,
by entring any Action or Actions, Complaint or Complaints in any of this
Towne Courts, all the time of my Constableship, I say received the
abovesaid summe of five pounds.

William Perkins *q per mee Thomas Dyment
Robert $R.D.$ Dayton

A true Copie taken by mee Febr. 21th 1678.

M. Nicolls.

[ENDORSED:]   [   ]charge from the Const.
of Easthampton to Jo:
Combs for 5£ Court charges there.

* The marks are copies made by Secretary Nicolls.

[25:60][*]

Albany, the 18th of December 1675

Worthy friend Captain Nicolls,

I deeply desire that your honor will do as much as is possible for the village of Schaenhechtede, and concerning my other friends at New York, which is only to please tell Maritie Jacobsz, on behalf of Geertruyt Jeronimus, that she has already offered silver and gold as security and mortgage for her legal debt, and that she will not pay the difference in question, except upon investigation by honest men such as Hendrick de Backer etc. I can do no more on my part, and if *Juffr*. Maria Jacobsz wants to have me do something, I expect a special power of attorney not only for this but also for other matters which she may be pleased to propose. In closing I commend your honor and his family to the merciful protection of God Almighty.

Your honor's humble and
obedient friend,

Ludovicus Cobes, schout

[ADDRESSED:]   Mons. Capt. Nicolls
Secretary of
New York

[25:61]

Albany, 18 December 1675

Cordial friend and lord, Captain Nicolls.

These few lines concern a certain Jan Thomasz, present magistrate of the colony Rensselaers[wyck], truly a very good friend, who bought a certain farm from Mr. Jan Baptist van Rensselaer some years ago for no small quantity of beavers, and who afterwards also bought from the native

---

* This is the calendar number. The document is now numbered 25:60(1).

Indians an island nearby which he turned into productive farm land with great effort. This aforesaid purchase is evident by the attached papers, and is apparent and known to the whole world.

It is now the case that the aforesaid Jan Thomasz, residing in the jurisdiction of the Colony, finds himself thereby aggrieved that in this matter, especially the island, measuring twenty-seven morgens and 315 rods for which he paid the native owners out of his own pocket, he is being taxed for tenths as one does for leased land. Therefore, he claims that he cannot be constrained to pay anymore in this same matter than as a recognition to his royal highness the duke of Yorck, together with all granted, sold and possessed lands, plots, lots, and farms which are not taxed higher annually than twenty morgens at four bushels of wheat. This right he also requests most earnestly.

On the other hand, the aforesaid Thomasz does not desire any more such prerogatives and privileges than his neighbors have; and at the same time may it be taken into consideration that he not be required to tithe or tenth the other land situated on the farm or properties but pay the recognition to the same degree as stated above.

Therefore the aforesaid Jan Thomasz can presently find no better means or expedient than to refer the matter for your honor's recommendation so that these matters may be considered at one time or another; and he promises to compensate your honor honestly for all labor, work, and efforts. Herewith awaiting a favorable reply, I remain in the meantime

Your honor's loyal friend

John Thomasz

My lord and friend, please do your best in this [matter], for which there shall be no lack of compensation. Without a doubt you shall advise the honorable lord general of everything. Relying thereon I commend your honor to the merciful protection of God Almighty.

Your honor's humble
servant,

Ludovicus Cobes, schout

[ADDRESSED:]   To the honorable Lord
Capt. Matthias Nicolls

Secretary of
N. Yorke

[ENDORSED:]   Mr. Lodovicus
Cobez
Alb. Dec. 18–75

[25:62]*

[INDIAN DEEDS TO VOLCKERT JANSZ AND JAN THOMASSZ FOR
ISLANDS IN THE HUDSON RIVER. TRANSLATION]

Copy

Have come to an accord and agreement, as they do accord and agree
hereby Syme, Calcoen, so named by the Dutch, the second and the third,
Capachick, and the fourth, Nachonan, as sellers on the one side, and
Volckert Jans and Jan Thomasse as buyers on the other side, over the sale
and purchase of a piece of the island situated to the east of the Binnen
Kil in front of the aforesaid buyers farm, beginning in the north along
the aforesaid Binnen Kil by a thick old ironwood tree proceeding directly
south to an ash tree standing about in the middle of the island, going from
there to the post placed directly opposite the aforesaid ash tree, going
again as before to the Kil to an elm and a water beech tree; where the
sellers are completely satisfied and promise the buyers to keep the same
place ever free and without any claim either from them or their heirs.
Thus done without fraud and in acknowledgment thereof the parties have
signed this before me, secretary, which I confirm with my own hand, this
27th of December 1658 in R:Wyck.

Was signed:‡ The Mark of ⎛⌐ Syme done
with his own hand.

The Mark of ✕ Calcoen done
with his own hand.

The mark of Capachick ⟍⟍
done with his own hand.

---

* Calendar number of the document now numbered 25:60(2).
‡ The marks and signatures are copies made by Secretary Cobes.

This is ✝ marked by
Calcoen for Nachonan.

Volckert Jansz
Jan Thomasse
Jeramieas van Renselaer
Abram Staets, as witnesses

Done before me D. V. Hamel, secretary.

Agrees with the original, *quod attestor*

Ludovicus Cobes, secretary.

Today, the 25th of January 1661, Folkert Jans and Jan Thomasse acknowledge and declare to be in accord and agreement with the Indians named Syme, Capachick, and Nachonan, so for themselves as for their blood relatives and co-owners, over the sale of the half of the island, or the rights that they still have thereto, situated east of the Binnen Kil in front of the farm of the aforesaid Folckert Janse and Jan Thomasse; in addition to a small island close by, called in Indian Nanosech, otherwise in Dutch *het cleyne cuypers eylantie,*[*] and that in this manner the aforesaid Folckert Jans and Jan Thomasse shall from now on possess and make use of the entire aforesaid island with the aforesaid little island in free ownership, without them, the Indians, having any further claim whatsoever in the world on it, in any manner, as they, the Indians, acknowledge to be completely satisfied and paid for it, with the promise never to do anything contrary to this nor have anything done nor allow anyone to do anything contrary. As token of the truth these contents have been translated clearly for the aforesaid Indians by Mr. Abram Staets and Sr. Ruth Jacobse, and affixed with their signatures together with those of the buyers in the colony of Renselaerswyck, dated as above. Was signed:

Folckert Jans
Jan Thomasse

 the mark made by the
Indian Syme, aforesaid.

 the mark made by the Indian
Capachick, aforesaid.

* Little Cooper's Island

The mark ―┼― made by the
Indian Nachonan, aforesaid.

In addition to Abram Staets,
Rutgers Jacobs, and in my
presence D. V. Schelluyne, secretary.

Below was written:
Agrees with the original kept by me,
which was signed as an attestation:
                    D. V. Hamel, secretary

Agrees with the true copy. *Quod attestor*,
                    Ludovicus Cobes, secretary.

[25:63]

[LETTER FROM JOHN BARNES, JR., TO JOHN SHAKERLY
CONCERNING A CONSIGNMENT]

Mr. John Shakerley.   Barbados December 22th. 1675.

Sir. in the moneth of July 1674 did Consigne to Mr. Roger Rugg a parcell
of Rumme amounteing with the Charges to Five thousand nine hundred
and Six pounds of moscovadoe Sugar as appeares by the Inclosed
Invoyces, I have allsoe Inclosed his letters the First gives mee an account
of his Safe arrivall and that hee had Received the Contents of my Bill of
loadeing and paide the maister his Fraight, the Second that hee had Solde
all my Rumme for 3s 6d per gallo., now by your Fathers Ketch I did
Receive a parcell of goods amounteing to (by his Invoyce) 22£ 05s 01d
and that hee woulde indeavour to Send mee the Rest, Seince this hee
deceases and am highley incoureaged by my Friend Mr. Charles Pope to
give you the trouble of this inconsiderable Conceerne the which (Sir) if
you please to take itt upon you Shall thanckfulley owne itt as a greate
Favour and assure your Selfe if I cann Serve you or any of your Friends
I will punctualley performe itt and pray in the leaste measure Scruple
nott to Impose your Commandes, I have Sent the third bill of loadeing
and a Coppey of my orders which I gave with him and the attor-
ney=shipp, all which I hope will be authinteiek to Recoover by, Pray
Mrs. Shakerley bee mindefull of this my affaire and Send mee the
proceeds accordeing to the Coppie of my orders to Mr. Rugg and you
will highley obleige,

Your Readey Fr. and humble Servantt

The letter off attorney ⎫   John Barnes
I have gott the merchant ⎬   1675 Junior.
and the maister to Wittness. ⎭

[25:64a]

[STATEMENT OF AN ACCOUNT OF JOHN SHAKERLY AND MR. LEE]

1675 Mr. Shakly and Mr. Lee deptors
October 20 To Mr. Shackly 125 Sticks
              of wood at 7s per 100   00–08–09
No: 2   To mending of your Sales   00–10–00
  30   To 900 Stickes of wood at 7s   03–03–00
Dece: 10 To Mr. Lee 1100 Stickes
              of wood   03–17–00
    29   To Will: Holmes by order of
              Mr. Shackly   01–05–00

Contra Credar.

July 9: by one Voyag ⎫
made in the Scow   ⎬   02–10–00
to muskete Cove   ⎭

No: 2 by the hire of   ⎫
the scow from   ⎪
the 2 of november to the ⎬   09–07–06
20 of december   ⎪
5 weekes 2 dayes   ⎪
at 35 s per week   ⎭

[25:64b, c, d, e]

[NO DOCUMENTS ARE LISTED FOR THESE NUMBERS IN THE
CALENDAR. FOUR ITEMS THAT NOW FILE HERE BELONG WITH
JOHN SHAKERLY'S ACCOUNTS IN VOLUME 29][*]

* See appendix to the final volume of *The Andros Papers*.

[25:65]

[MINUTES OF A MEETING WITH WESTCHESTER INDIANS]

At the Fort.   Jan. 7. 1675.

Severall Indyans from Wickers creeke with Claes the Indyan, came with a present of Deere skins and Deere to the Governor.

The skins be[   ] three parcells [. . . *one line lost* . . .] and give one P[   ]

Then another [   ]ven—declaring and desiring to continue in friendship.

Then the 3d was given.

A sachem of Wisckers creeke was pres[   ] and another of Kictohan with 16 or 17 in Company besides Claes.

T[   ]ha[ ]ke them, and willing to [   ]f[   ]ndship, and would protect t[ ]m, but now they are gone out of his reach to mind them as before, but hee would willingly see them sometimes.

The Go: in returne would give them Coates but they desired drinke- which is order[   ] for them.

[ENDORSED:]   Wicke[ ]s [   ]
Indyans.
Jan. 7. 1675.

[25:66]

[MINUTES OF THE MAYOR'S COURT CONCERNING A SUIT BY JOHN TUDER AGAINST JOSIAS HELMAN AND WIFE HANNAH]

Jo: Tuder   SS. Att a Mayors Court held the
against   xi[th] January 1675 etc.
Jos: Helman etc.

Jury finde for the plt damages [   ] fourty pounds. Court agree with Juryes verdict and give Judgment accordingly.

Deft. moves for an Appeale to the Court of Assizes which the Court graunts.

Plt. moves that the deft. give in security which the Court order and accordingly Mr. Isaacke Melyne became baile etc.

Examined per me Sam: Leete Cler.

[25:67]

[LETTER OF REPROACH FROM THE GOVERNOR OF RHODE ISLAND TO OFFICIALS OF MASSACHUSETTS AND THE UNITED COLONIES]

The Governor and Councell of the Mathacusetts and Commissioners of the United Collonies writing to us to give us thanks for transporting their souldiers and provision and that our sloops transported their wounded and desired us to sett out 100 or 200 souldiers answering them denying so to doe and gave them grounds, This was our postscript.

Friends

Since our writing the abovesaid to you is Come to our hands, certaine printed lawes or orders of yours of the 3th November 1675 set forth by the authority of your generall assembly of the Masaashusetts your secretaries hand being to them wherein you say you have apostated from the Lord with a great backsliding. To which I doe consent so great hardly to be parallel'd all things considered, we were a people professing the feare of the Lord in England against Bishops and ceremonies in tender love to all that professed godliness and soe departed from the land of our nativity declaring the ground of our removall into New England Vizt: to seeke out a place for our brethren where we might enjoy the liberty of our consciences that the sons of wickedness might vex us noe more as was then publikely preached and declared.

2dly—For the propagating of the gospell converting the Indians etc.

3dly—That we might enjoy such as preached the gospell (the power of God to salvation) for the Bishops did then silence our best ministers these and others in 1630 was printed and dispersed both in England and Holland which I have by me in print the Governor and Deputy Governor and assistants hands being to it, my selfe and Simon Broadstreet being two of the then assistants our hands is to it I have them at large in print to be seene.

How well this hath bin performed by you let your print lawes declare, and this amongst the rest our houses are now open to receive your wounded and all in distress we have prepared an hospitall for yours, but you a house of correction for all that repaire to our meetings, is this to doe as you would be done by. your Ministers with us have not bin molested, ours with you have bin persecuted, is this a time for you to Establish iniquity by a law, will not the Lord be avenged on such a motion as this that set up ministers that are not so made ministers by the power of an endless life, but of the letter that kills, but not the Spirit that gives life and a worship that is not in spirit and truth, set by Christ above 1600 yeres agoe; we cannot come to you, but depart from the Lord as you have done, Therefore desiring your returne to the power that made you the true light that is in you.

This is written to you by one who above 45 yeares Past was one of you and now is one that desires your true good both aeternall and Temporall as I did when I was with you and am

yours in True Love

Rhoad Island January   William Coddington Governor
the 9th, 1675/6.
              Vera Copia:

[ENDORSED:]*   The Go: of Rhode Isl. to the Go:
                   and Councell of Boston
                   Jan. 9. 1675/6.

                   A Copy of a letter sent by the
                   Governor of Kings Province
                   being then Wm. Coddington Esq.
                   to the Commissioners of the
                   United Collonies at Boston

These

[25:68]

[LICENSE TO THOMAS SMITH TO TEACH THE USE OF ARMS]‡

By the Governor

[Wher]eas [Applicacion hath been made unto] mee, I doe consent [and

---

* The first endorsement is by Secretary Nicolls, the second by the copyist.
‡ Partly from *BGE* 2.

allow] Capt. Thomas Smith to admitt and teach any Gentlemen or other Free Men the use or Exercize of Armes, for which to meet at any fitt times and Places within this City, without any Lett or Molestation: Comporting themselves as they ought. Given und[er] my Hand in New Yorke this 18th day [of Decem:] 1675.

[to] all Magistrates,
Officers or others whom
[it] may Concerne.

[ON THE BACK:]
    [MINUTES OF A MEETING WITH LONG ISLAND INDIANS]

January the 12th. 1675.

Memo

60 G wamp.	That the Indyans that came now to the Governor with a Present (the Chiefe of whom is Tackpuch) doe engage a Friendshipp for themselves, and also for all the Indyans soe farr as beyound Seatalcott etc. and desire onely t[ ] live quietly to eate and drinke and enj[ ]es and childr[ ]

[ENDORSED:]   [   ]
                  Indyans [   ]
                  Governor

[25:69]
    [PETITION OF JOSIAS HELMAN APPEALING A JUDGMENT]

To the right Honorable Major Edmond Andross, Governor Generall of all his Royall Highnes terretoryes In America etc.

                  The humble peticion of Josias Helman

In all humility sheweth unto your honor,
                  That upon some words betwixt Your peticioners wife and John Tudor, your peticioner hath bene arrested, sued and Condemned, by the Common law, forty pounds dammages with Costs, upon which, your peticioner finding himselfe agreived, well Knowing the said Tudors Reputation, your peticioner moved the majors

Court,[*] for his appeale att the next assizes, To which your peticioner humbly prayes your honors assent your peticioner being ready to putt in such security for the prosecution thereof, as the law doth direct, also your humble supplicant doth pray that the said Tudor, may putt in security to answer such costs and dammages, as may happen, hee being not a free Burgar of this Citty, The which your peticioner is,

>   And your peticioner as in Duty bound
>   Will Ever pray etc.

>   Jos. Hillman

[ENDORSED:]   The humble petition of Josias Hillman.
                     The order of Court to bee produced.
                     Appeale granted,
                     Jan: 24. 1675.
                     Helman and Teudor.

[25:70a]

[WARRANT TO THE CONSTABLE OF STATEN ISLAND TO SEIZE
PROPERTY OF NATHANIEL BRITTAINE]

These are in his Majesties name to require you to put in Execution the order and judgment of the last Court of Assizes by levying upon the Estate Goods and Chattells of Nathaniel Brittaine of Staten Island the summe adjudged him to pay unto John Sharpe of this City, being the one halfe of the debt demanded together with the one halfe of the Charge of that Court, As al[ ] the Incidentall Charge of the Execucion and that you make returne of the due service and levy hereof at the secr. Office in the Fort within the space of one moneth after this date, Of which you are not to fayle. Dated in N.Y. the 26th day of January 1675.

To the Const. of   By order of the Go: and
Staten Island or   Generall Court of Assizes
his Deputy.

[ENDORSED:]   Execucion against
                     Nath: Brittaine
                     Jan. 26. 1675.

---

* court of mayor and aldermen at New York

[25:70b]

[PROCEEDINGS BEFORE THE COUNCIL CONCERNING WILLIAM
PINHORNE, BOOKKEEPER FOR JOHN WINDER]

New Yorke   Febr. 6th. 1675.

Mr. John Palmer appearing before the Governor in Councell, with the
bookes kept by Mr. Wm. Pinhorne for Mr. John Winder deceased and
Compa., Mr. Pinhorne likewise present, according to an order of Councell, Mr. Palmer upon his producing the bookes alleadges formerly to
have offerr'd the said bookes to Mr. Pinhorne to make up particular
persons accounts, but hee refused the same, the which is now owned by
Mr. Pinhorne, Hee being now ask't, what hee had to say.

Answers That hee is not nor will bee concerned therein, and that no such
thing or any account Thereof can bee made out of the said bookes. Nor
will medle or have to doe with them. Hee also recedes from and denyes
what hee formerly attested of wrong or injury done, particularly in
Councell the last Councell day whereupon ordered That

Mr. Palmer dismis't from any further attendance in this matter and Mr.
Pinhorne to pay all the Charges the said Palmer hath beene at in his
attendance on the Councell on this account and likewise that hee pay a
fine of five pound to pious or Charitable uses.

Hee justifyes himselfe upon the reading of the sentence, not to have said
those words the last Councell.

Hee was by the Go: advertized that being of the good behavior hee had
herein broken his bond, and had Caution for the future to take Care
thereof.

Hereupon hee submitted and desired that no ill Construction might bee
putt upon his words.

[ENDORSED:]   Palmer and Pinhorne.
                Feb. 6. 1675.

[25:71]

[PETITION OF SEVERAL MERCHANTS FOR HELP IN RECOVERING
GOODS SEIZED AS PRIZE OF WAR AT BOSTON]

To the Right honorable Edmond Andros Esquire Lieftenant and Governor Generall under his Royall Highness of all his territories in America.

The humble Peticion of Christopher Hoghland, Francis Rumbout, and Gelyne verplanck, of this Citty, Merchants

Sheweth,

Unto your honnor with all humillity that in the moneth of June, 1673, one Mr. William Greenow, Master of the shipp the blessing shipt on board the said shipp in the Port of London a Certaine parcell of Merchantdize for th[ ] Propp[   ] account of your honors peticioners, the which hee [   ] there from Mr. Christopher Dynout, of London Merchant, with order (as per bills of Lading may appeare) to deliver the same to the peticioners in this place.

But may it Please your honnor soe it is, that as the said Greenow was on the way bound to sea, hee had notice that this Citty of New Yorke was taken by the Duch, upon which hee altered his Voyadge and went to Boston: where being arived the Government there Ceized upon your honnors Peticioners goods as belonging to their Enemies, and soe deteyned, and still doe deteyne, Notwithstanding that the Peticioners made instant solicitacion for theire restoring, And that the goods and Merchantdizes belonging to Severall of the Inhabitants of Boston in this place under Arrest by the Duch Government were releast upon the account, that the Peticioners [   ] there [   ] freed.

> Your honnors Peticioners doe therefore most humbly pray the Premisses being [ ]pen into your serious and Prudent Consideracion, that your honnor will bee pleased favourably to write in your Peticioners behalfe to the Governor and Magistrates of Boston, that the Peticioners goods or produce of them may bee restored unto them, together with Consideracion of dammage and interest.

> Your humble Peticioners presenting to your honnor that the Peticioners were the subjects of his Majestie when their goods were shipt on board from his Majesties Port of London, and that then this Place was likewise his Majesties is by Gods providence it is now become soe Againe, Your honors favourable Appostell hereupon is most h[   ]bly de[   ]d, whereby the Peticioners most humbe[   ] to regulate themselves in this affayre,

> And Your honnors Peticioners as in duty bound shall ever Pray etc.

Christo: Hoogland
Francis Rombouts
Guilain Verplanck

[ENDORSED:]* Petition of Christor. Hoghland,
Francs. Rumbouts
and Gellyne Verplanck.

[25:72]

[NO DOCUMENT IS LISTED FOR THIS NUMBER IN THE CALENDAR.
ONE ITEM NOW FILED HERE BELONGS WITH JOHN SHAKERLY'S
ACCOUNTS IN VOLUME 29][‡]

[25:73]

[RECEIPTED STATEMENT OF SAMUEL ANDREWS'S ACCOUNT]

```
8- 5–6
    3–6
    2–6
    3–9
    1–6
    6–0
    2–6
9- 5–3
    2–6
9- 7–9
7–17–6
£1–10–3
```

Samuell Adres is Dr.
To the Ballance of the ould
accompt   £1.10.3
To 25½ yds of Carsey
    at 7 s per yd   £8.18.6
To soe much Paid Robert Story   £5.0. 3.6
                                                      £15.12–3
To 19 Paid Wm. Asten   £00.19.0
                                                       16.11.3

---

* The endorsement is on a separate paper.
‡ See appendix to the final volume of *The Andros Papers*.

Received this 24th of Febr. 1675 From John Shakerly the Juste Sume of
Sixteen Pounds Eleven Shillings
I say Received

                    Per mee
                    Sam: Andrews

[ON BACK:]   25½
               7
              175
               3
              178

[25:74]

[BILL OF SALE FOR A SLOOP FROM SAMUEL ANDREWS TO JOHN
SHAKERLY AND REYNIER WILLIAMS]

This day being the 24th of Febr. Anoque Domini 1675/6 Its agreed and
Concluded upon by and betwenn Samll. Andrewes of Long Island on the
on part and Reineer Williams and John Shackerly both of the Citty of
New Yorke on the other part:

1o —The said Samll. Andrewes for and in consideracion of thirty pounds
in hand paid before the ensealing and delivery hereof unto him by the
said Reineer Williams and John Shackerly the receipt thereof he doth
hereby acknowledg = and for and in consideracion of thirty pounds 10s
more to be paid in Manner and forme followeing = he the aforesaid
Samll. have bargained sould and Made over unto the said Reineer
Williams and John Shackerly a sloope or vessell being Now opon* the
stockes In oyster bay aforesaid Conteyning thirty on‡ foote by the Keele
= and twelfe foote fouer inches by the bame sixe foote and on† inch deep
in the hould = the bulke head to be built two foote English Meeasure
higher then the Maine deck And the sterne to be made sutable Togeather
with sufficient Coakeing+ prehing = wha[ ]fitting Maste = and the same
to besett: with boom bowsprite winles and all other Meterialls belonging
unto Carpenters worke to Compleate and finish the said vessell fitt for
the sea to be done by the said Samll. Andrews = and that he the said
Samll. Andrews is to Lanch the said vessell att or before the first day of

* upon
‡ one
† one
+ "Calking"; the next two words are indecipherable.

May next ensueing date hereof = the said vessell to remaine and Continue the said Samuells untill she is fully Compleated and Lanched as aforesaid.

The said vessell being Compleated and finisht as aforesaid = and Lanched as aforesaid they the said Reineer Williams and John Shackerly doth Covenant and mise:* and agree and engage joyntly and severally to pay or cause to be paid unto said Samll. Andrews or his order the summ of thirty pounds and tenn shillings seaven pounds thereof to be paid in bread and flower answerable to Boston Mony = the last payment being twenty three pound = to Compleate the aforesaid summ of sixty pounds and ten shillings to be paid att Lanching of the said vessell as aforesaid to be paid in good Marchantable goods as he the said Samll. can buie for pork and beefe or any Marchants inhabittance and burger of the said Citty or upon difference That then the said Samll. shall have his said 23 £ 10s in Marchantable Goods at the price that two men shall sett: = persons indifferently Chosen by the said John Shackerly = and said Samll. Andrews In Wittnes whereof the parties to these presence have sett their hand Enterchangably and afixed their freely the day and yeare first above wryten.

signed seald and delivered in   Samll Andrews—O
presenc of   Jon. Shackerly—O
Danll. de heart   Reineer Williams—O
Tho: Lovell
                                 verte‡

Memorand. the words = be done enterlyned in the 22 Lyne in said Samlls. Covenant and the words = aforesaid in the 10 Lyne of Mr. Reineers and Jon. Shackerlys Covenant and the word: enterchangably was enterlyned in the orriginall before the ensealing and delivery thereof.

> This is a true Coppie
> of the orriginall
> taken by mee G. Cooke
> True copy.

---

* "Mise," as a noun synonymous with "agreement" is listed in several dictionaries, but nowhere do we find it as a verb.

‡ True copy. The "O" after each signature probably represents the place of the seal in the original.

[25:75]

To the Right Honorable Edm. Andros Governor of all his Royall Highness Territoris in America.

The Petition of the Constable and Overseers of the towne of Huntington humbly

Sheweth

That Whereas wee received your Honors Letter wherin your Honor was pleased to recomend to your Consideration the Case of those farmers now dispossesed of their farmes, and That [   ] should Supply them with suitable Lands to what [   ] have now lost according to the Judgment of the last Court [   ] Assizes. Though wee acknowledge ourselves both [ ]ivilly and morally obliged to yeild ready obedience to all your Honors Commands Yet that your Honor may bee more fully informed in this matter wee humbly beseech your Honor to take Cognisance of these following Considerations

Imprimis The towne was not the first Cause of the farmes setting forth neither did wee willingly Consent to it but the Consideratio[ ] of the after inconvenience that would therby happen to the town made us very averse to it and if the Courts decree Concerning it Could have been answered by any summ of money that we were Capable of paying we would rather have done it then to have set out any one farme but the Courts decree was absolute and the verdict and Judgment.

2d. Neither did the Towne enforce any man to take up those farms but they went out voluntary for their own (excepted) advantage.

3d Neither did the greatest part of the Towne (proprietors in those then Common lands upon which the farms are built) sell the Land to them farmers at any other price then that the whole ten farmes Should pay to the proprietors only what Charges they had expended at Law in defence of their title to their Land; which was an incon[ ]siderable Summ for so much Land, and some of those four farmers [ ]ver payed any thing, and those that did pay have now demanded [   ] some have received what they before payed, so that wee humbly [   ]hat the Loss of that Land now falls upon the first suposed owners [   ] on the farmers: and one of those farmers hath a house and [   ] in the Towne and all other accomadations eaquall with our [ ]elves but went out to take up a farm there for his greater Enlargement, but wee humbly Conceive that the greatest Dammage that those farmers Sutaine is in the Loss of so much Labour and Charge that they have been at in building, fenceing, Clearing, and manuring of Land which is indeed very great: And Mr. Smith only doth reap the benifitt of that Labour and Charge. And some of them had made some Considerable beginings before that order of Court Desember 6th 1672. Wee also humbly beceech your Honor to Consider the ground of that order or means by which it was procured which was as wee Conceive a falce information of Mr. Smiths by which wee Conceive the Court was misled. And that his information was untrue which doubt not [ ]ut wee are able to prove to your Honors Satisfaction.

Yet the Court Judiciously ordered that a fuller understanding of the perticularities of it Should be indeavour'd for in the Spring following, and that a Respit Should be made for the present till the Spring and we humbly Conceive that the intent of it was not to put a stop to the Farmers proceedings (For the seting [   ])farmes was Absolutely Commanded by the former Courts that [   ]that wee should not press to hard for our Charges wh[   ] werein persuance of and that Mr. Smith might Cea[   ] the Governorand Councell with his dayly pititions, som[   ] haveing before that order, according to former orders [   ]siderable beginings upon their farmes.

Now our humble Petition to your Honor is that your Hono[   ] not inforce us to give out any more farmes to these men or any other for wee are very sensible of the intollerable prejudice the town sustaines by them wee have been forced to set out allredy and adding more would be a great addition to our present burthen. We have already tendred to those of them that have not already in the towne Eaquall with ourselves, that wee will give them in the towne, Land Eaquall with ourselves so far as wee are Capable. Wee hope your Honor will Conceive our Innders(?) to bee rationall and not inforce our towne to setle any more farm[   ] abroad which doth and will prove very destructive to the well bei[ ]g of the town.

Thus prostrating ourselves at your Honors feet for your favorable acceptance of these our requests as in Duty bound wee shall ever Pray etc.

[SIGNED:]*   Epent[   ]
              tom [   ]
              [   ]
              Sam[   ]

---

* The signatures seem to be those of Epenetus Platt, Thomas Powell, Samuel Titus, and at least one other person. The published Huntington Town Records do not indicate who served as constable and overseers, April 1675–March 1676.

[ENDORSED:]   1st of Feb.[   ]
                 from Hunt[   ]
                 factions.
                 sent for the wit[   ]
                 the 17th feb. 1675.
                 [   ]Isl. to[   ]
                 To begin—Tuesday
                 come fortnight.
                 A Petition [   ]
                 the Const.
                 and Overse[   ]
                 Huntington ref[   ]
                 upon the Court of [   ]
                 Anno 167[ ].
                 they are bound over
                 to the next Assizes.
                 Feb. 27th 1675.

[ADDRESSED:]   To the right Honor[   ]
                 Edm. A[   ]s Governor
                 of all his Royall Highnes
                 Teritories in America
                 these.
                 At James-fort
                 New Yorke.

[25:76]

[PETITION OF DANIEL DE HAART RELATIVE TO A DEBT OWED TO
HIS BROTHER'S ESTATE BY HUGH BARENTSZ DE KLYN]

To the Right Honorable Mayor Edmund Andross Esquire
Senior of Sause Marees Leftenand Governor Generall of all
his Royall Heyghness his Territories in America.

The Petition of Daniel De Haert

Humble Manner

Sheweth that Huygh Barentson De Klyn stands Justly indebted unto your
petitioner as administrator unto his Brother Balthasr. De Heart Deceased
in the Summe of 2771 guilders in Wampum as per Morgage bearing date
the 6 [ ]f Aprill 1667 appearred now So it is may it please [ ]ur Honnor

that the said barentson obtained an Order [   ] this Heigh Court of assises
for the summa of 1357 gl. [   ]or [   ]ueenst your petitioner, as hee
whas agcnt of his [   ] Brothcr Balthasr. and that all future trouble [
]ease.

> There for your Petitioner humbly prays that your Honnor
> will bee pleased to take the premisses into your Grave
> Consideration and that upon your petitioner making the
> Said debt appear and he allowing unto the said Barentsen
> what he has paid thereupon, humbly prays that your Honnor
> will order therein for a discount or other wayes as your
> Honnor Semeth meet and your petitioner Shall
> ever Pray: etc.

[25:77]

[CERTIFICATE OF JOHN STANTON TO THE SERVICES OF THE PEQUOT
INDIANS DURING THE WAR]

These may Certifie all whome it may Conserne that the pecoietes
Indianes have bene out with the Endelesh armye against the neragansits
and have aproved themselves very faithfull to our english intrest the
Enemey fled before the army and in the persute those pequets indienes
did very good serves: we slew in all neere about fower score persons and
followed them neare about thre score and ten mille the enemies having
noties* of our armyes aproching the sachems fleed and their wimen and
Chilldren and lefte sixtye pe Kom tonk indians and three hundred fitteing
men to waylay the army by the amboscadoes but weare by the providence
of god timly discovered by our endyins they wounded five endglish men
in the reare of the army after they weare beaten in the fronte by our
Endelish and our endyians we slew at that time five of the uplanders and
kiled on‡ of there Chefe Captaines and the same day tooke the towne
and badyed† there all night the next day burned the towne and then
morchet to the metropolitente glace+ and found it deserted soe fiered**

---

* notice
‡ one
† bided
+ Perhaps he means "glacis." F. B. Hough read this as "place," which makes sense, but the
first letter is almost certainly not *p*.
** fired

nere five hundred widgwames this scalpe cared by the beorer was a endyion of greate accounte and was taken by with 25 persanes more by the pecaits indjans upon there retirneing home after they ported with the Endglish [   ]* and his men killed two men nere noradg‡ and took away a boy alive this 6 feberry this is short but cannot in lorge febery 9 = 1675.

your loving frind
John Stanton

[ENDORSED:]   Mr. S[ ]anto[ ]
                  feb 9 1675.
                  About Indyan Newes.

[25:78]

[BOND OF SIMON BARENTSZ TO APPEAR AT THE ASSIZES]

Know all men by these Presents that I Symon Barnson of New Yorke Marriner, doe Stand firmly bound unto the Mayor of the Citty of New Yorke his heyres and Successors in the full and just summe of Fifty Pounds Boston silver Payable on demand, to which payment well and truly to bee made, I bind mee my heyres Executors and Administrators firmly by these Presents In wittness whereof I have hereunto sett my hand and seale in New Yorke this 9th day of February in the 27o yeare of his Majesties reigne Annoque Domini 1675/6.

The condition of this Obligation or Recognizance is such that if the above bounden Symon Barnson shall personally appeare at the next Generall Court of assizes to bee holden in this Citty of New Yorke to answer to such matters as shall bee objected against him by Jan Scholtir to doe and receive that which by the Court shall bee then and there enjoyned him and that hee in the meane tyme doe keepe the peace of Our Soveraigne Lord the King towards the Kings Majestie and all his leidge people, and especially towards the said Jan Scholter and all his, that then this present obligacion is to bee voyde and of none effect, otherwise to stand in full force and virtue.

Signed sealed and Delivered   Symon barentsz

---

* Captain Stanton was having problems with his pen when he wrote this name; it appears to be "Scne" or "Srne." It is possible that he was trying to write "Sam." "Sagamore Sam" was the name by which the English referred to Usatuhgun, sachem of the Nashaway.
‡ Norwich

In presentia
Henry Newton
John Sharpe Sherriff.

[ENDORSED:]　Symon Barnsons Recognizance for the Peece and
good behaviour. £50. 00. 00.

Feb. 9. 1675.
From the Mayors Court To appeare
at the Court of Assizes
and answer to Jan Scholter etc.

To the Mayors Court again. 1676.

[25:79]

[MEMORANDA CONCERNING AN APPEAL BY JOHANNES VERVELEN]

on a petition of vevaele[*]

The petitioner having given suficient security to abide the determination
Mr. Jo: Rider is hiereby requiered without delay, to give me an Answer
to the above petition.

N.Y.
12th February. 1675/6.

EAS.[‡]

Aldolfe Peeterson become security for the above.

[ENDORSED:]　To speake to Mr. Rider about this
buisnesse Concerning Vervelen.
Its the Go: answer to his peticion,
and his security, Adolph Peters.

Johannes Vervelen appealing from the Mannor Court of Fordham to the
Court of Assizes, hee having in that Court beene fined 20£, and other
matters complayned of in his peticion, his Appeale was allowed of by
the Governor, hee having given security to prosecute.

Feb: [blank]—1675　　　　　　　　　　Mr. Adoph Peters
The day before the Go. went for Alb:　　Security

* Johannes Vervelen
‡ This document appears to be in the governor's hand.

[ENDORSED:]   Mr. Johannes Vervelens
Appeale allowed of Feb. 1675.

[25:80]

[AN ACCOUNT OF ISAAC MELYN AND A NOTE
ABOUT PASSPORTS]

Mr. Isaack Melyne is Dr.			
To Severalls bought	£	s	d
in Vendue	17"06"00		
	16"17"00		
Due to Ball:	00"09"00		

Per contra is	Cr.	£	s	d
By 4 hogsheads of Tobacco				
per Capt. Andrew Bowne		£	s	d
qt 1500 lb. gr Neate 1257 lb.		10"09"06		
at 2 d per pound is				
By Ditto Received in Ditto		£02"17"04		
By paid Mr. Corbett		£01"10"02		
		£10"17"00		

[ENDORSED:]   Mr. Isaack Melynes Account.

[MEMORANDUM   John Helmes.
ON BACK:]*   John Hill.
Their names to be sett up,
to goe in the ship
the [blank] of [blank]
for Barbadoes
C. [blank] Moore
Commander

___

* Obviously this note has nothing to do with the rest of the document. *BGE* shows that a
pass was issued for John Hill and various family members on July 27, 1676, but none appears
for John Helmes or Captain Moore.

[25:81]

[STATEMENT OF THOMAS WARNER CONCERNING
HIS CAPTIVITY WITH THE INDIANS]

Feb. 25: 1675.

born in
Barbadoes.
Young man

Thomas Warner one of the two that came downe
from Albany and had beene prisoners with the Indyans who arrived here this morne, being Examined;
saith, That hee was one of 9 persons that being sent
out from Hatfield where the English Army lay to
discover the Ennemy, but a party of Indyans way
layed them, and shott downe 5 of their Company, and
tooke 3 of which hee and his Camerade are two, the
3d they put to death, the 9th was an Indyan that came
with them, and escap't away:

That the Indyans lay still two dayes after they were
taken, and then a party of about 30 with whom hee
was march't to a River North East from thence about
80 miles called Ousuck, where about a fortnight after
the rest of the Army came to them, having in the
meane time burn't two Townes; they kill'd one of the
prisoners presently after they had taken him, cutting
a hole below his breast out of which they pull'd his
Gutts, and then cutt off his head.

That they put him so to death in the presence of him
and his Camerade, and threatned them also with the
like.

That they burn't his Nayles, and put his feet to scal'd
them against the fire and drove a stake through one
of his feet, to pin him to the Ground, The stake about
the bignesse of his finger, this was about 2 dayes after
hee was taken.

[   ]
f[ ]hting

That about 5 weekes agoe they continued at Ousuck
sending out partyes severall ways and that at one
oftheir meetings [hee held?]* 2100 Indyans, of which
5, or 600 french Indyans, with strawes in their Noses.

---

* The corners of the paper are damaged, affecting the text, and the correct order is uncertain
for material written between the lines in the first part of this sentence.

When hee was taken the party were abo[   ] 600
Indyans.

That the River Indyans received those Indyans kind-
ly, furnish't them with provision, and som[ ] of those
Indyans were with them that h[   ] him.

That there were 5 or 600 of the Indyan[ ] with strawes
in their noses, which they call'd the french Indyans.

That hee was made to tell the number by the Indyans
themselves, which hee did 3 times over.

That there were about 300 horse of them

That they were most young men—the oldest not 40
yeares old.

That they were supplyed with pouder from the french
Indyans.

That they said their designe was with the spring to
goe to Hadly, Hatfield etc. and Conecticut Col., and
having destroyed them to goe to Ber[(?)] * in the
Hem[(?)]‡ and then after this they [will?] destroy the
[Indyans?] etc. but the french I [   ] they allso were
Indyans etc. they supplying the[ ] with pouder(?) and
what they n[eeded?]

[ENDORSED:]   The Examinacion of Tho: Warner
that had beene a prisoner with
the Indyans. Feb. 25. 1675.

Mr. Jacob Walker livingh att the Maine, wrote the letter for them att their
Desire.

[ON BACK:]†   James fortt
1675. 22 feb.
first they

---

* Many words in this paragraph are uncertain, with letters half formed or omitted,
suggesting that the scribe (Secretary Nicolls) had writer's cramp. F. B. Hough reads this as
"Boston" which is in the wrong direction to be an immediate objective.
‡ Hough has "dutch," which is a possible but most unlikely reading because an attack on
Albany would almost certainly have brought the Mohawk into the war on the English side.
† The note is written in a Dutch hand.

acknoledge to
be their ouwne
[   ] Fry
had Put unther
the letter.

[25:82]

[MINUTES OF A MEETING WITH TWO RAHWAY INDIANS]

Tuesday. Feb: 29. 1675.

[ ]his day two Indyans came to the Fort from Rahway, and brought with
them an Indyan scalp with the hayre on, to [ ]resent to the Go: Their
names—War[   ] [   ] Cattcus, T[   ] head was [   ]
Pequid [   ] to them [   ]
hand [   ] in the [   ] Indyans.

[   ]t thought fitt to take notice of it, wee [   ]ng at peace with all
the Indyans, but [   ]ll acquaint the Go: with it at his re[   ]e.

Present.

[   ] Carteret
[   ] Billop.
and 3 of the councell.

They say their sachem Tackpousha bad them bring it to the Go: if hee
did not accept of it, th[ ]y [   ] though it a [   ] what they [   ]
[   ] so they have [   ] [
]back with th[ ]

[25:83]

[PETITION OF MATTHEW HILLER FOR ESTABLISHING A SCHOOL]

To the Right Honourable Major Edmund Andross Governour Generall of all His Royall Highnesses Territories in
America: And this Honourable Court of Assizes:

The Humble Petition
of Matthew: Hiller:

Humbly Sheweth:

That whereas your humble petitioner haveing been, and still is desirous to serve your Honour, and this Worthy City in what he may or can, the petitioner haveing already with humble Submission, endeavoured to Inform your Honour and The Worshippfull the Mayor and Aldermen, of the great want of a convenient Settlement for a Schoole, and the great inconveniences and neglects that have arose thereby, Upon which an Order for the same was made, but as yet noe Care taken for it,

Your humble petitioner beggs your Honour would be pleased to take it into consideration, Humbly supposeing your Honour is acquainted with the expedition it requires,

> And Your Petitioner Shall Pray as in Duty bound etc.

[ENDORSED:]*   The Humble Petition
of Matthew: Hiller:
1676.

For the Court of Mayor
and Aldermen.

[25:84–85]

[PETITIONS OF RICHARD WOOD FOR A DIVORCE]

To the Right Honourable Mayor Edmond Andross: Governor Generall of all his Highness Territories in America:

The Humble Petition of: Richerd: Wood:

Humbly Sheweth:

That whereas your Honours Petitioner haveing lived under his Highness Jurisdiction in Westchester about fifteen years, dureing which time your petitioner hath endeavoured to demeane himselfe as a true and loyall subject, and serviceable in his generation to the best of his power, but Through the inchastity and disloyalty of the petitioners wife, by name Mary Wood, sustained great detriment and endured a very troublesome

---

* The first endorsement is written in the same hand as the text; the second is by Matthias Nicolls.

and vexatious Liveing, to the Dishonour of God, and repugnant to the holy bond of wedlock, she haveing as much as in her lay endeavoured the totall ruine and destruction of your petitioner, by her most abominable words and actions, haveing openly confessed she hath defiled her marriage bedd, and that purposely to breed difference between your petitioner and her selfe, notwithstanding your petitioner endeavored to reclaime her, by all means lawfull, who yet continues the same and rather worse, and now purposely absented her selfe by reason she knows her selfe guilty and to prevent that shame and punishment due to her base and wicked actions.

Your Petitioner humbly beggs your Honour would bee pleased to take your petitioners sad Case into Consideration, and if it shall seem good in your Honours sight a seperation may bee made, otherwise noe otherwise can bee expected but a sad event of such deplorable doings

> And your Petitioner shall for
> Ever Pray as in duty bound

[ENDORSED:]*   1676.
The Humble Petition
of Richerd: Wood
A Presentment
New Towne.

> [   ] Right honorable Edmund
> Andrews Esquire Governor
> of New Yorke etc:

The humble Petition of Richard Wood alias Consider

Most humbly Sheweth

That your Petitioner haveing presented one other Petition to your Honor incerting a difference betwixt your Peticioner and his Wife, for the which your Peticioner humbly desired a hearing in Court in Reference to a Bill of Divorsment.

> These therefore are most humbly to beseech your Honor
> that your Peticioner maye have a Speedy heareing; by
> Reason of the great Charge your Peticioner is at here and

---

* The first endorsement is by the writer of the text, the second by Matthias Nicolls.

the dammage hee is like to Sustaine at home in his Absence and your Peticioner shall

Ever pray etc.

Rich: Wood
                       Peticion.

[25:86]

[PETITION BY JOHN TUCKER TO BE COMPENSATED FOR
HAVING BEEN WOUNDED]

To the Right Honorable Major Edmond Andross Leiftenantt and Governer Generall of all his Royall Highness his Territories In America and to the Honearable Bench assembled att this Court of Assize etc.

The Humble Petition of John Tucker Junior of Seatalcoott Alius Brookehaven upon Long Island: Sheweth unto Your honor and his Honorable Courte that whereas aboute the firste of november 1675 One Samull: Seyward of the same with a Gunn (Vizt) a fowling Peice att the day and place afforesaide being then Charged Loden and Prymed did fire in and upon your Peticioner and with the same did suite him through the Right thygh with three Bulletts by which his life was not onely in greate danger but alsoe Cost your Petitioner for the Chirurgeons Charges and feese thirty three Poundes besides the Charges of your Peticioner lying from the time afforesaid till March following (all which was Occationed by the neglect of one Thomas Basely deceased who Carelessly left the said gunn Loaden)

Therefore humbly prayes your honor and this honorable Courte that the said Samuell Seyward or Thomas Baseley may by the order of this honorable Courte not Onely pay unto your Peticioner his Costes and Charges afforesaid butt alsoe allow him the Dammage hee sustayned by Reason of the said wounding and loss of time thereby and hee as in Duty bound Shall Ever Pray.

[ENDORSED:]   Jon. Tucker Junior
               Peticion.
               1676.

[25:87]

[PETITION OF JOHN HART FOR A SHARE OF HIS FATHER'S ESTATE]

> To the Right Honorable Edmund Andros Esquire Governor
> of all his Royall Highness Territoryes in America, and to
> the Honorable Court of Assizes.

> The humble Peticion of John Hart.

In all humility sheweth.

That your Peticioners Father (John Hart) was formerly an Inhabitant and freeholder, in Mashpeth Kills, within the precincts of New Towne.

That in the yeare 1671 your Peticioners Father deceased, without making any formal Will in Writing, onely Verball, before some certaine witnesses of the Neighbourhood (who are now in being) Your Peticioner being the Eldest Son, was then in Maryland, and in the time of his absence, the matter hath been so carryed, That your Peticioner (being the principall Heir of the Inheritance) is shutt out, and totally dispossest, of his part, or porcion, therof, and the same sold unto Thomas Case, by Samll. Hart your Peticioners younger Brother, by what Right, or Authority, your Peticioner knowes not, but since the said illegall Sale, your Peticioners Brother hath transported himselfe to England, and the said Thom: Case continues in the possession of the said Estate, to the great prejudice and endamagement of the Peticioner.

Hee therefore humbly Prayes your Honor and this Honorable Bench, to cause the said Thomas Case to appeare before you, to Answer the Complaint of your Peticioner, and to graunt him such reliefe in Equity, as your Honor shall thinke meet.

> And hee shall ever Pray etc.

[ENDORSED:]   John Harts Peticion.
              For the Sessions.
              1676.

[25:88]

[ORDERS TO LT. GERRIT TEUNISSZ CONCERNING THE INDIANS]

Copia

By the Governour

You are hereby authorised, and required with the Indian guide orderd with you, forthwith to goe eastward, to the furthest pairt of the Government, or as farr as Coneticut river, to finde out Phillip or other north Indians, lately within this Government, and lett him or other Sachems or Commanders in Chief know that haveing heard of there being in Warr-li[ ] Posture, intruded, and brought some Christian Prisoners in our Pairts, I have therfore sent you, to demand the said Christian Prisoners, brought by them into this Government, and to Command and forewarne them, from, or returning unto any Pairt, of the government, or Confines.

If they should be divided, into severall partyes or Parts You are then as you see cause, and have opportunity, to goe to each, but to make no longer stay, in any, then to deliver your messadge, and receive such Prisoners as they shall deliver, and refresh and rest your self, and without delay to return and make the best of your way to me, given under my hand and seall in albany the 4th march 1675/6.

Was signed E Andross.

Aggrees with the Principall
Quod attestor R Livingston

[IN MARGIN:]   To Gerrit Teunise
Left. to Capt. Volkert

[ENDORSED:]   A copie of the Go: ord.
from Alb.
to command the
North Indyans
to bee gone
etc. by Lt. Gerrit Teunis.

[25:89]

[AN ACCOUNT OF THE INDIAN WAR, BY LT. GOV. JOHN EASTON
OF RHODE ISLAND]*

a true relation of what I kno and of reports, and m[y Understanding] conserning the begining and progress of the war now betwen the Engl: and the indians.

in the Winter in the year 1674 an indian was found dead, and by a Coreners Inquest of Plimoth Coleny judged murdered he was found dead in a hole thro ies‡ broken in a pond with his gun and some foulle by him, sum English supose him throne in sum indians that I judge intelegabell and impartiall in t' Case did think he fell in and was so drouned and that the ies did hurt his throat as the English said it was Cut, but acnoledged that sumtimes natv† indians wold kill others but not as ever thay herd to obscuer as if the dead indian was not murdered, the dead indian was Caled Sausimun and a Christian that could read and write, report was he was a bad man that king Philip got him to write his will and he made the writing for a gret part of the land to be his but red as if it had bin as Philip wold, but it Came to be knone and then he run away from him, now one indian informed that 3 indians had murdered him, and shewed a Coat that he said thay gave him to Conseall them, the indians report that the Informer had played away his Coate, and these men sent him that Coate, and after demanded pay and he not to pay so acused them, and knowing it wold pleas the English so to think him a beter Christian, and the reporte Came, that the 3 indians had confesed and acused Philip so to imploy them, and that the English wold hang Philip so the indians wear afraid, and reported that the English had flatred them (or by threts) to bely Philip that thay might kill him to have his land, and that if Philop had dun it, it was ther law so to execute home ther kings judged deserved it that he had no Case to hide it.

So Philip kept his men in arems, Plimoth Governer, required him to disband his men, and informed him his Jealosy was falce Philip ansered he wold do no harm, and thanked the Governor for his information The 3 indians wer hanged to the last denied the fact, but one broke the halter as it is reported, then desiered to be saved, and so was a litell while then confesed thay 3 had dun the fact and then he was hanged and it was reported Sausimun before his death had informed of the indian plot, and that if the indians knew it thay wold kill him, and that the hethen might

---

* Material in brackets in the text is from the published text edited by F. B. Hough (1858).
‡ through ice
† Perhaps intended for "native."

destroy the English for their Wickednes as god had permited the heathen
to destroy the iserallits of olde, so the English wear afraid and Philip was
afraid and both incresed in arems but for 4 years time reports and jelosys
of war had bine veri frequent that we did not think that now a war was
breking forth, but about a weeke before it did we had Case to think it
wold, then to indever to prevent it, we sent a man to Philip, that if he
wold cum to the fery we wold Cum over to speke with him about four
Miles he had to Cum thether our messenger Come to them, thay not awar
of it behaved themselefs as furious but sudingly apeased when thay
under[stood who he] was and what he [came] for, he Called his
Co[unse]ll and agred to Cum to us Came himself unarmed and about 40
of his men armed then 5 of us went over 3 wear magestrats we sate very
frindly together we told him our bisnes was to indever that thay might
not reseve or do rong thay said that was well thay had dun no rong, the
English ronged them we said we knew the English said the indians
ronged them and the indians said the English ronged them but our desier
was the quarell might rightly be desided in the best way, and not as dogs
desided ther quarells, the indians owned that fighting was the worst way
then thay propounded how right might take plase we said, by arbit[ratio]n
thay said all English agred against them, and so by arbitration thay had
had much rong mani miles square of land so taken from them soe English
wold have English Arbetrators, and once thay wer perswaided to give in
ther arems, that therby Jelosy might be removed and the English having
ther armes wold not deliver them as thay had promised, untill thay
Consented to pay a 100 po., and now thay had not so much land or muny,
that thay wear as good be kiled as leave all ther Livellyhode, We saied
thay might Chuse a indian king, and the English might Chuse the
Governer of new yorke that nether hat Case to say ether wear parties in
the Diferans thay saied thay had not herd of that way and said we onestly
spoke so we wear perswaided if that way had bine tendered thay wold
have acsepted we did endever not to here ther Cumplaints saied it was
not convenient for us now to consider of, but to indever to prevent War
said to them when in war against English Blud was spilt that ingaged all
Englishmen for we wear to be all under one King, we knew what their
Cumplaints wold be, and in our Coleny had removed sume of them in
sending for indian rulers in what the Crime Conserned indians lives
which thay veri lovingly acsepted and agreed with us to ther execution
and saied so thay wear abell to satesfie their subjects when thay knew
an Indian sufered duly, but said in what was only betwen ther indians
and not towneshipes that we had purchased, thay wold not have us
prosecute and that thay had a great Fear to have ani of ther indians should
be Caled or forsed to be Christian Indians, thay said that such wer everi

thing more mischivous, only disemblers, and then the English made them
not subjects to ther kings, and by ther lying to rong ther Kings we knew
it to true, and we promising them that however in goverment to indians
all should be alicke and that we knew it was our King's will it should be
so that alltho we wear wecker then other Colenies, thay having submited
to our king to protect them others dared not otherwise to molest them so
thay expresed thay tooke that to be well, that we had litell Case to doute
but that to us under the King thay wold have yelded to our Determena-
tions in what ani should have Cumplained to us against them,

but Philip Charged it to be disonesty in us to put of the hering the [just
C]umplaints, therf[ore] we Consented to he[ar them] thay said they had
bine the first in doing good to the English, and the English the first in
doing rong saied when the English first Came, their kings father was as
a great man and the English as a litell child he Constrained other indians
from ronging the English and gave them Corne and shewed them how
to plant and was free to do them ani good and had let them have 100
times more land, than now the king had for his own peopell, but ther
kings brother when he was king came miserabely to dy by being forsed
to Court, as thay judge poysoned, and another greavanc was if 20 of there
onest Indians, testified that a Englishman had dun them rong, it was as
nothing, and if but one of ther worst indians testified against any indian
or ther king when it plesed the English it was sufitiant, another Grivanc
was when ther kings sold land the English wold say it was more then
thay agreed to and a writing must be prove against all them, and sum of
ther kings had dun rong to sell so much he left his peopell none and sum
being given to drunknes the English made them drunk and then Cheted
them in bargens, but now ther kings wear forewarned not for to part with
land for nothing in Cumpareson to the valew therof, now home the
English had owned for king or queen thay wold disinheret, and make
another king that wold give or seall them there land, that now thay had
no hopes left to kepe ani land another Grivanc the English Catell and
horses still incresed that when thay removed 30 mill from wher English
has anithing to do, thay Could not kepe ther Coren from being spoyled,
thay never being iused to fence and thott when the English bott land of
them thay wold have kept their Catell upone ther owne land, another
grevanc the English wear so eger to sell the indians lickers that most of
the indians spent all in drunknes and then ravened upon the sober indians
and thay did belive often did hurt the English Catell, and ther kings Could
not prevent it we knew before these were ther grand Cumplaints, but then
we only indevered to perswaid that all Cumplaints might be righted
without war, but Could have no other answer but that thay had not herd

of thet way for the Governer of yorke and a indian king to have the hering
of it, we had Case to thinke in that had bine tendred it wold have bine
acsepted we indevered that however thay should lay doune ther arems
for the English wear to strong for them, thay saied then the English
should do to them as thay did when thay wear to strong for the English
so we departed without ani discurtiousnes, and sudingly had leter from
Plimoth governer thay intended in arems to Conforem Philip, but no
information what that was thay required or what termes he refused to
have their quarell desided, and in a weckes [t]ime after we had bine with
the indians the war thus begun plimoth soldiers [w]er Cum to have ther
head quarters within 10 miles of Philop then most of the English
therabout left ther houses and we had leter from Plimuth governer to
desier our [h]elp with sum boats if thay had such ocation and for us to
looke to our selfe[s and from] the genarell at the [quarter]s we had leter
[of the] day thay intended to Cum upon the indians and desier for sum
of our boats to attend, so we tooke it to be of nesesity for our Ieslanders
one halef one day and night to atend and the other halef the next so by
turens for our owne safty in this time sum indians fell a pilfering sum
houses that the English had left, and a old man and a lad going to one of
those houses did see three indians run out thereof, the old man bid the
young man shoote so he did, and a indian fell doune but got away againe
it is reported that then sum indians Came to the gareson asked why thay
shot the indian they asked whether he was dead the indians saied yea a
English lad saied it was no mater, the men indevered to inforem them it
was but an idell lads words but the indians in hast went away and did not
harken to them, the next day the lad that shot the indian and his father,
and fief English more wear killed so the war begun with Philop but ther
was a queen that I knew was not a party with Philop and Plimoth governer
recumended her that if she wold Cum to our Iesland it wold by well and
shee desiered shee might if it wear but with but six of her men—I Can
sufitiantly prove, but it is to large here to relate that shee had practised
much the quarell might be desided without war, but sum of our English
allso, in Fury against all indians, wold not Consent shee should be
reseved to our Iesland alltho I profered to be at all the Charg to secuer
her and those shee desiered to Cum with her, so at length prevailed we
might send for her, but one day acsedentaly we wear prevented, and then
our men had seased sum Canneos on her side suposing thay wear
Philopes, and the next day a English house was there burned and mischif
of ether side indevered to the other and much dun hir houses burned so
we wear prevented of ani menes to atain hir the English army Cam not
doune as informed thay wold so Philop got over and they Could not find
him, 3 days after thay Came doune had a veri stormy night, that in the

morning the foote wear disabled to returen before they had refreshment, thay wear free to acsept as we wear willing to relive them, but bonten[*] trupers sayed of ther Captaine they despiscd it and left the foote after the foote had refreshed themselefs thay allso returned to their head quarters and after hunt[ing] Philop from all sea shoers that thay Could not tell what was becum of him, the naroganset kings informed us that the queen aforesaid must be in a thicket a starving or conformed to Philop, but thay knew shee wold be glad to be from them so from us had Incuregment to get hir and as mani as they Could from Philop. After the English army, without our Consent or informing us Came into our Coleny, brott the narogenset indians to artickels of agreement to them Philop being flead about a 150 indians Came in to a Plimoth garreson volentarely. Plimoth authority sould all for slafes (but about six of them) to be Caried out of the Cuntry,

It is true the indians genaraly ar a very barbarus peopell but in this war I have not herd of ther tormenting ani but that the English Army Cote an old indian and tormented him he was well knone to have bine a long time a very decreped and harmles indian of the Queens as Philop flead the foresaid queen got to the narogansets and as many of hir men as shee Could get, but one part of the narogansets Agreeme[nt t]o boston was to [kill or deli]ver as many a[s the]y Could of Philops peopell, therefore boston men demanded the fore said queene and others that thay had so reseved for which the indians wear unfree and made mani excuses as that the queen was none of them and sum others wear but Sudieners with Philop becase removed by the English having got ther land, and wear of their kindred which we kno is true not but we think thay did shelter mani thay should not, and that thay did know sum of ther men did asist Philop but acording to ther barbarus ruells thay acounted so was no rong or thay Could not help it, but sum enemis heds thay did send in and told us thay wear informed that however when winter Came thay might be suer the English wold be their enemies, And so thay stood doutful for about 5 months the English were jelous that ther was a genarall plot of all indians against English and the indians wear in like maner jelose of the English I think it was genarall that thay wear unwilling to be ronged and that the indians did judg the English partiall against them and among all a philthy Crue that did desier and indever for war and those of ani Solidety wear against it and indevered to prevent the war, for Conserning Philop we have good intelegenc that he advised sum English to be gon from ther out Plases wher thay lived or thay wear in Danger to be killed but whether it wear to prevent a war, or by their Prests informed if thay begun thay

* band

should be beaten and otherwise not so we have good intelegenc for I do think most of them had a desier the English wold begin, and if the English be not Carefull to manefest the Indians mai expect equity from them, thay mai have more enemies than thay wold, and more Case of Jelosy, the report is that to the estward the war thus began by supposing that sum of those indians wear at a fight in these parts and that thear they sa a man wonded so authority sent sum forth to discufer having before disarmed those indians and Confined them to a place which the indians wear not ofended at, but those men Cuming upon them in a warlike postuer thay fled that the men Cote but 3 of them, those in authority sent out againe to excuse themselefs but thay Could only Cum to the Spech with one man as he kept out of ther rech thay excused themselefs and said his father was not hurt one of them thay had taken he said he Could not belive them for if it was so thay wold have brott him thay had bin desaitfull to disarem them and so wold have killed them all and so he run away, and then English wear killed, and the report is that up in the Cuntri here away thay had demanded the indians Arems and went againe to parell with them and the indians by ambushcado tretcherously killed, 8 that wear going to treat with them.

When winter was Cum we had leter from boston of the iunited Comitioners that thay wear resolved to reduse the narogansets to Conformity not to be trubled with them ani more and desiered sum Help of Botes and otherwise if we saw Case and that we should kepe secret Conserning it our governer sent them word we wear satesfied Narogansets wear tretcherous, and had ayded Philop and as we had asisted to relive ther army before so we should be redy to asist them still, and advised that terems might be tendered that such might expect Compation that wold acsept not to ingag in war and that ther might be a seperation betwene the gilty and the inosent which in war Could not be expected we not in the lest expecting thay wold have begun the War and not before proclaime it, or not give them Defianc, I having often informed the indians that English men wold not begin a war otherwise it was brutish so to do I am sory so t[he ind]ians have Case [to think me] desaitfull for the [En]glish thus began the war with the narogansets we having sent ofe our Iesland mani indians and informed them if thay kept by the water sides and did not medell that however the English wold do them no harem alltho it was not save for us to let them live here, the army first take all those prisoners then fell upone indian houses, burned them and killed sum men, the war without proclemation and sum of our peopell did not kno the English had begun mischif to indians and being Confedent and had Case therfore, that the indians wold not hurt them before the English begun, so did not kepe ther gareson exactly, but the indians having reseved that mischif Came unexpected upone them destroyed 145 of them beside other gret lose but the English army say thay suposcd Conetecut forses had bine there, thay solde the indians that thay had taken as afoersaied, for slafes, but one old Man that was Caried of our Iesland upone his suns back he was so decriped Could not go and when the army tooke them upon his back Caried him to the garison, sum wold have had him devouered by doges but the tendernes of sum of them prevailed to Cut ofe his head, and after came sudingly upone the Indians whear the indians had prepared to defend themselefs and so reseved and did much Mischif and for aboute six wecks sinc hath bine spent as for both parties to recruet, and now the English army is out to seecke after the indians but it is most lickly that such most abell to do mischif will escape and women and Children and impotent mai be destroyed, and so the most abell will have the les incumbranc to do mischif.

But I am Confident it wold be best for English and indians that a peas wear made upone onest terems, for each to have a dew propriety and to injoy it without opretion or iusurpation by one to the other but the English dear not trust the indians promises nether the indians to the Englishes promises and each have gret Case therfor, I see no way lickly but if a Sesation from arems might be procured untill it might be knone what terems king Charles wold propound, for we have gret Case to think the naroganset kings wold trust our king and that thay wold have acsepted him to be umpier if it had bine tendered about ani Diferanc for we do kno the English have had much Contention against those Indians to invaled the kings Determenation for naroganset to be in our Colony, and we have Case to think it was the gretest Case of the war against them, I see no menes likely to procuer a sesation from arems exept the Governer of new York Can find a way so to intersete and so it will be lickly a pease mai be made without so trubling our king not but it allwais hath bine a prinsipell in our Coleny that ther should be but one supreme to English men and in our natief Cuntry wher ever English have jurisdiction and so we know no English should begin a war and not first tender for the king to be umpier, and not persecute such that Cannot Conforem to ther worship, and ther worship be [w]hat is not owned by th[e k]ing the king not to mind to have such things redresed, sum mai take it that he hath not pouer, and that ther mai be a wai for them to take pouer in oposition to him I am so perswaided, of new England prists—thay are so blinded by the Spiret of persecution, and to maintaine to have hyer, and to have name to be more hyerlings that thay have bine the Case that the law of nations and the law of arems have bine violated in this war, and that the war had not bine if ther had not bine a hyerling that for his maneging what he Caleth the gospell, by voiolenc to have it Chargabell for his gaine from his quarter and if any in magestrasy be not so as ther pack horses thay will be trumpating for inovation or war.

John Easton

5th: 12m: 1675. Rhoadiesland.

[ENDORSED:]   A Relacion of the Indyan Warre,
                By Mr. Easton of Rhoade Isl.
                1675.

[25:90]

[ORDER FOR THE HOLDING OF WILLIAM LOVERIDGE UNTIL HE
     PROVES CHARGES AGAINST ALBANY]

Copia Vera

By the Governour

Whereas Mr. Wm. Loveridge did 2d Instant, afore me magistrates and cheef officers of these pairts, alleadge and Confidently affirm that the north Indians have been lately here this last winter, supplyed by the (Dutch as he termed them) Inhabitants of this Place, with ammunition, notwithstanding the Law and strict Prohibicon; but could not make it appear, by any evidence, or Circumstance, or named any Persone, whatever, he could Suspect, and therefore was Committed, and not haveing yett, and it being a Generall Imputation and reflexion, You are in his Majesties name, further orderd, stell to keep the said Wm. Loveridege, untill he give sufficient Security, at the Secretary or Clerks office, to answere the Same, at the next generall Court off Assisses, and to be in the mean time of the good behavior, for which this shall be your Sufficient warrant; Given under my hand in albany this 11th day of March, 1675/6.

To Mr. Michel Siston Sherriffe   was Signed
or Schout in albany   E Andross

This is a true Coppy examined
By me
Ro. Livingston Secr.

[25:91a]

[LETTER FROM SIMON SARING CONCERNING
THE CAPTURE OF A FUGITIVE]

Capten Nicoulls

sur thes are to give youer whorshipe A Counte That In order to the Huencrye that I have Reseved from youer whorshipe I have aprehended this parsonne sent doune to yorcke upon good grounds his agge and statuer and Huire all agree with the huencrye and upon Exsamashoun is found to bee in manye lyes and denyes that He Came from dillwer by water which did apeer to bee fouly for one In ouer towene sa this mane at yorke when he Came ashour or soune after and the master of the sloupe and this mane did booth declaire that he Came from dillwer which mackse me greetlye mistroust that hee is gilltye of the Crime that hee is Charged with hee was apprehended at ouer towen but had bine at osterbay and Heerd of the Huencriye and was Reetourninge backe I thoughte good to leet youer worshipe understand the Cause and grounds for what I have dune and when his name was asked Hee sayed his name was Roburt Williams and soune after was asked againe and sayd his name was Thomas Williames and In sevrall outher things was found to Contriydike himsellfe so havinge nothing moor to trobell youer worshipe with at this tim Reest youer lovinge frind and sarvant to Command

Hempstid march the 14 1675/6   Simon Saring

[ADDRESSED:]   These for Chapten Mathias Niccouls Esquire
                  In Neuyorke

[ENDORSED:]   Simon Seryon.
                  Hempsteed.
                  Mar. 14–75.
                  about the Murderer

[25:91b]

[MINUTES OF THE EXAMINATION OF THE ABOVE PRISONER]

[   ]house.
[   ]675
[   ]ouncell in the
[   ]since
[   ]Alderman Lewis
[   ]ris and severall others

The meeting was upon oc[ ]asion of a person be[   ] apprehended by vertue of a Hue and Cry at Hempsteed and sent downe hither.

Being asked his name	Hee saith it is Richard Honch but upon Long Isl. hee said It was Robt. Williams and Th[ ] Williams some other times.
Hee was pursued by the name of Richa. Perrot	Hee acknowledges to bee a servant to one Geo. Freshwater of Maggotes bay in Accomack River in Virginia, and that hee is run away from his Master. Denyes the knowledge of the persons murder, Hee says hee hath beene out of Engl. 3 years, but hee told Mr. Edsell hee had beene 7 years out.

Hee confesses that hee came from the Whorekill in Dirck Francens Sloope, who was present to justify it; and could not deny his leaving a horse and sadle for his Passeport.

According to the discription hee is lookt upon and is very much saspected to bee the person accused.

Whereupon hee is Ordred to bee committed a close prisoner in Irons in to the Dungeon.

And this notice bee given of his app[ ]hensi[ ] to C. Cantwell by a Massage giving the[ ] this order may bee further taken about hi[ ] Transportation where the fact was committed.

[ENDORSED:]   The Examinacion
of the person accused
for Murder at Maryland.

[25:92]

[MINUTES OF A MEETING WITH TWO WICKERS CREEK INDIANS
ABOUT TO JOIN THE NORTH INDIANS]

Present   Mar: 29: 1676.
C. Brockholes
Mr. Mayor
Mr. Philips.
The Secr.

The Indyans of Wickerscreeke having beene sent to the 27th Inst. came
now this day here. Their names are Wissakano and Ammone the 2
Sachems sent for to come. The occasion of their sending for was Upon
a Letter from the Go: intimating a mistrust of them by reports above.

Mr. Sam: Edsall Interpreter.

The matter being told them by the Interpreter They deny to have had any
thoughts of joyning or treating with North Indyans or others not friends
to this Government, under whose protection they desire to live, according
to their Engagements to the Go.

The sachems had each of them a Counsellor with them, without whom
they were not willing to speake.

They declare rather to suffer either by Christian or Indyan, before they
strive then to offer any harme to any they desiring to live quietly.

They promise when they certainely know of any disturbance or like to
bee, they will give notice to the Go: and they hope to have notice from
here of any hurt intended against them, but they promise to bee true to
their Engagement to the Go.

They desire as before from Mr. Philips, to have leave to come upon this
Island and hereabout oystering.

They are promist to have a Note to certify that they have liberty behaving
themselves as they ought.

They desire liberty to send some young men with Canooes to Mr. Pells
for the Remainder of their Corne, (having had but one half from thence
already) and to fetch about halfe a dozen old men, women, and boyes,
from Greenwich that they left behind there.

They are told, wee shall speake to the Governor about it, but referre it to the Go, who was daily expect.

They say they shall stay till then, when they will come againe.

Upon their friendly Comport and for that they came so willingly being sent for, they are presented with 2 Coats for the 2 sachems.

They pretend not to expect or deserve them, their hearts being good without them, but they being desired to accept of them for that reason, receive them.

They are appointed to goe to Thomas Laurens the baker in Pearle streete to stay all night.

[ENDORSED:]   Wickerscreeke Indyans at Mr. Philips
Mar. 29. 1676.

[25:93]

[NO DOCUMENT IS LISTED FOR THIS NUMBER IN THE CALENDAR. ONE ITEM NOW FILED HERE BELONGS WITH JOHN SHAKERLY'S ACCOUNTS IN VOLUME 29][*]

[25:94]

[LIST OF APPLICANTS FOR LAND]

The names of the persons For Land upon Manhatens Island.

Imprimis.

Wolferd Webber Constable }
Jno. Peterson: wheelemaker }   2
Arien Cornelius Son
Tunis Edisse
Bastian Elson
Henry Corneliusson
Spunge Yonson
Claus Manuell a Negro
Jon: DeFreeze Molatt [‡]
William Antonis Molatt

---

* See appendix to the final volume of *The Andros Papers*.
‡ Mulatto

David Defore and his son Jon: Defore 2
Garrat Cozensee
Solomon Peterse
Andrews Vriance
Old Mingoe:
Severeene Laurenson
Ebbert Foctuse
Arnold Webber
Assent Negroe
Michaell Negroe
Old Franciscoe Negroe
Lewis Smith Negroe
Jon. Bennue
Daniell Clarke
Theophilus Elsworth
Clement Elsworth
Marcke de Susswaie Senior
Marcke De Susswaie Junior
Marten Hardwen

[ENDORSED:]   Persons for land upon
Manhatans Isl.
1676.

[25:95]

[BOND OF SEVERAL PERSONS TO APPEAR IN COURT AT JAMAICA]

Know all men by these presen[ ] that wee Samuell Rusco of Jemaica and William Creed Abell Gaile and Humphrey Underhill all of Jemaica aforesaid Doe bind ourselves in the full and Just Som of an hundred pownds starlling money of England: unto our soveraigne lord the King.

The Condition of this obligation is such that if the above bounded Samuell Rusco William Creed Abell Gaile Humphrey Underhill; if they shall make theire personall appearence at the next court of Sessions held at Jemaica, then and there to anser the suite of Roulfe Johnson in an acction of Case:

That then this presents shalbe of none Effect, otherwise to stand in full power fource and vertue as wittness our hands this 11th of Apriell, Annoq: Domine 1676.

Signed in the
presents of us:
Thomas Hickes
A Gleane:[*]

Samuell Ruscoe
Humphrey Underhill

William ⚔ Creed
   his marke
Abelle ⋔ Gaile
   his Marke.

[ENDORSED:] The Obligacion of the
persons of Jamaica
bound over to answer
at the Court about
a steere being kill'd
claymed by Roeloff
the Butcher.
May [*blank*] 1676

[25:96]

[RECEIPT OF THOMAS WILLIAMS TO LAURENCE VAN DER SPIEGLE
FOR MONEY DUE THE ESTATE OF JOHN COOKE]

Whereas Capt. Thomas Williams, heretofore of New Haven, now of
Flushing on Long Island, was proved and allowed of By Coll. Francis
Lovelace, then Governor here, to bee Lawfull Attorney of Nathaniel
Clare, of the Island Barbados, Executor of the last will and Testament of
John Cooke, of the same Island Merchant; By vertue whereof, hee had
Power to receive the Goods or Effects belonging to the said John Cooke
or Nathaniel Clare, in the hands of Mr. Laurence Vander Spiegle of this
City, who by the said Governors Order, bearing date July the 5th 1671
was to bee acquitted from whatsoever hee should Pay unto the said
Thomas Williams upon the Account; Now these presents witnesse and
Declare, That the said Thomas Williams hath received full Satisfaccion
from the said Laurence Vander Spiegle, of what Debts, dues or Accounts
there were left by the afore named John Cooke or Nathaniel Clare, in the
hands of the said Laurence Vander Spiegle, of the which hee doth hereby
exonerate Acquitt and discharge the said Laurence Vander Speigle, his
Heires, Executores and Administrators for ever. In testimony whereof,
hee hath hereunto sett his hand and Seale in New Yorke, this 12th day of
Aprill, 1676.

* The intial is lost in its own flourishes; we presume it is *A* for Anthony Gleane.

Sealed and delivered in presence of
    M. Nicolls.

[ENDORSED:]   C: Tho: Williams
                     Acquittance to Mr. Laurence Vander Spiegle,

                     for what received of Mr. Cookes Estate of
                     Barbados etc.
                     Apr. 12. 1676.

[25:97]

[MINUTES OF A MEETING WITH WICKERS CREEK SACHEMS]

Apr. 14. 1676

There appeared the two Sachems of the Wickerscreeke Indyans that were
here last in the Go: absence.

They desire to know of the Go: how matters above at Alb: are with the
Indyans, for that they have had no Newes of it.

The Go: tells them that when hee came up hee found the Maques returned
from following the North Indyans, that the Mahicanders were fled, but
hee sent to them to come backe, and that one of the Mahicanders
prisoners being taken by the Maques hee demanded him and being
delivered sett him free, that some of them were come backe upon the Go:
promising the protection if they should come, and if any of them wanted
land that hee would supply them.

That hee left all well there.

That the Go: comming at the Sopez, the Sachemacks were with him and
all things were well there also. And that some of them desiring land by
the Redout Creek, the Go: consented to it.

They pretend they would come upon this Island or any where neare, but
being neare the Christian plantacions their Cattle and horses would
allwayes bee trespassing upon them.

Its answered if they receive Injury they may complaine and then bee
relieved. They are offered to find out some Necke easy to serve either
upon this or Long Island.

They pause upon it; After desire to joyne with the Stamford Indyans and to plant upon a Neck at Wickerscreeke together, and that they may have liberty to fetch some Corne from Stamford that they left.

Its a fallacy, and no way belongs to them. They are offred all freedome of fishing or Oystering any where here about.

Their Corne at Stamford is offer'd to be bought. They will come againe 12 dayes hence.

[ENDORSED:]   April 14. 1676.
                       Some Wickerscreeke Indyans
                       appear before the Go:

[25:98(1)]
[MINUTES OF A MEETING WITH THE CARPENTERS FOR THEIR RECOMMENDATIONS FOR BUILDING THE GREAT DOCK]

Aprill 15. 1676.

At a meeting at Peter Nys house, of the Governor with the Carpenters etc. about the agreement for their worke concerning the frame of Timber for the harbor, for the which Notice hath beene given this particular time.

Present.

> The Governor
> Capt. Brockholes—C. Dyre
> Mr. Phillips—The Secr.

Aldermen
> Mr. G: Minvielle
> Mr. N. De Meyer
> Mr. Steph: V: Cortlandt

Adolph the Carpenter and a great many of them being present etc.

All the Carpenters being present afterwards doe unanimously agree and give their opinion as followes—That Groundcills beneath and plats above.

That at each end of a Groundsill one beam to come athwart.

That for every ten foot—a Stud—and a beame over it will be necessary.

The upper beames to bee layd at high water marke; and every other beame to bee under braced.

[ENDORSED:]   1676.

[25:98(2)]

[ADDITIONAL NOTES ON THE ABOVE MEETING]*

To make the forme of the prop[   ] wharfe the carpenters opinion to be substentiall.

Groundsels and planes att the End of Each Groundsell a beame a thwart and Every ten foot a Stud, and a beam over itt.

The uper beames to be placed att ordinary hye water marck and Every other beam Braced downward.

To be fill'd with wood [   ] stone, the wood all undermost and the stone togeather upermost.

[ENDORSED:]   The Go: with the Carpenters at Peter Nys.
                  Apr. 15.–76.
                  About the Harbor

                  28 Cans of wine

                  Wee met there by
                  the Go: order once before
                  Expences then.

[25:99]

[MINUTES OF A MEETING WITH SACHEMS FROM THE WEST
END OF LONG ISLAND]

Apr. 17. 1676.

There was an Appearance of some of the Sachems of the west End of Long Isl. before the Go:—Tachpousha etc. They appeare for Rockway, Mashpeage, Mericock, Unchachauge and Sequetauke.

The Go: tells them, hee was above when they were here last, but had

* The document appears to be in the governor's handwriting.

heard of their being here and offering to come to live in the Towns and for protection. That they shall bee welcome, and order shall bee taken for their Armes, that their hearts being found to bee well, they shall chuse what place they will to come to, or to make a Fort for themselves.

Tackpousha first presents a string of white wampum, in token of friendship, and after on behalfe of himselfe and all the rest, gives a large band most of black wampum 18 deepe and about a yard and 1/2 long as a token of their fidelity.

The Go: promises them land where they shall come, if not already planted by others, and for their owne land they shall keepe it still also.

That the Go: left the Indyans all well above, and stopt the Maques from coming upon the Mahicanders and others, and sent for the Mahicanders to come back to their lands.

They desire time to answer till morrow morne which is given them.

Apr. 18. 1676

Tackpousha and the other Indyans came againe to the Governor this morning, to whom the Go: presented 5 Coates of Duffells, with some Tobacco and pipes.

They pretend not to expect any thing, but in friendship accept of what was given.

The Go: will send for all their Guns, and they shall in a litle time have them all againe.

They say their feare being over they have no cause to remove now, but if there shall bee occasion they will come and desire to remove.

[ENDORSED:]   Apr. 17. 18–76.
                Tackpousha and
                other Indyans.

[25:100]

[PETITION OF DANIEL DE HAART, APPEALING A JUDGMENT]

To the right Honnourabell Mayor Edmund Andross Esquire Governour Generall of all his Royall Heighness Territories in America.

Humbly Shewes unto your Honnour that your petitioner in the Worshipfull the Mayors Court was Cast, at the Suite, of Huygh Barentsen, in the Summe, of therteene houndred fifthy seaven guilders sixtenne stuyvers, therefor your petitioner humbly prays your Honnour to be pleased to graunt your petitioner his Appeall, to the next Generall Court of assises he beinge ready to performe what the law doth direct in suche Cases

And your Petitioner Shall Ever Pray etc.

Daniell De Haert

[ENDORSED:]   An appeale allowed for Mr. Daniel De Haart against Hugh Barnesen.
Apr. 26. 1676.

[25:101]

[LETTER FROM JACOB THEYSEN VAN DER HEYDEN, SEEKING A LAND PATENT]

Albany the 23 April 1676

Honored Sir

These are to begg your assistance in the Procureing of a Patent or ground brief for the lott of Land In closed, and have sent hereby a bever for your fees, I haveing sold said Platt of ground and with out the Ground brief cannot attain to my Pay, Pray good sirr send me the Patent up by the verry first and you will Infinitly oblidge

Sir
Your humble servant   [*seal*]

Jacob Theysen vander heyden

[ADDRESSED:]   For Capt. Mat: Niccolls Secr.

at N. York.
With a Bever.

[ENDORSED:]   A letter from Alb: for a patent.
Apr. 23. 1676.
Received May 29. 1676.

[25:102]

[AGREEMENT BETWEEN ELISABETH BEDLOO AND CAPTAIN JAMES
CARTERETT FOR THE SALE OF LOVE ISLAND]

We underwritten Captain James Carterett and Elizabeth bedloo, doe
acknowledge, to have been agreet in a bargine about an Island Called
Love Island, in Condition and manner as followeth, Vizt.—

Captain James Carterett doth acknowledge to have bought from
Elizabeth bedloo the said Island Called Love Island with all the depen-
dances belonging thereunto for the sume of eighty and one Pound Boston
money; to bee paid at Boston in the month of September next ensuing to
Richard Middlecoete merchant at Boston, or his order.

Elizabeth Bedloo relict and administr. of Isaak bedloo doth acknowledge
to have sold the said Island, upon Condicion as is Expressed in the
Premisses, unto the said Captain Carterett, and to make to him or his
order a Just and a true title to the said Island, and to give possesion of
the same on demand,

Done without fraud, and to the Confirmation of the Premisses, both
Partyes have to these Present sett theire hands and fixed theire Seales.

In N: Yorke the 20th Aprill 1676.
Sealed and Delivered   John Carterett   [seal]
in the presence of
                              Elizabeth bedloo   [seal]
Daniell De Haert
Dederich Gysbers

[ENDORSED:]   The Agreement betweene Capt. James Carteret
and Mrs. Eliz: Bedloo for Love Island
20; of Aprill, 1676.

[25:103]

[MINUTES OF A MEETING WITH CONNECTICUT AND
LONG ISLAND INDIANS]

Apr. 27. 1676.

Present.

All of the Councell.
The Mayor and some of the Aldermen
and others of which 2 Justices.

About 50)   Severall Indyans appeared before the Governor in
the Fort;

They say they belong to a place called Wayattano, at
the head of Stratford River, with them were some of
Wickerscreeke and some Stamford Indyans. The
sagamore of Wickerscreeke (Wessecanoe) came
with them.

They declare themselves to bee good friends and
desire to continue so and make a present of about ten
deerskins, a beareskin and 4 small beavers, given at
three times repeating their desire of friendship;

The Governor accepts of it, and promises protection
to them within this Government but will not undertake anything without;

That hee had heard from the wickerscreeke Indyans
that they are good Indyans, and now findes them so,
and they may have all friendship and freedome here,
so long as they behave themselves well.

The Governor presents them with three Duffells
Coates. one to the Wickerscreek sachem, the other
two, to the two cheife from Stratford river.

[ENDORSED:]   Apr. 27. 1676.
At a Meeting of Indyans in the Fort.
Stratford River and Wickerscreeke.

[25:104]

[LETTER FROM WILLIAM NOTTINGHAM TO SECRETARY NICOLLS
REQUESTING A WRIT OF APPEAL]

Honored Sir after my sarves[*] with my wifes presented to you and your
good Ladey these Few Lines ar to in treat you to Do me the faver as to
get me a pertision wret and would Desire you to Delever it to his honer
the govener that I may have a hering of my sut at the sises and I shall
mack you satesfaction and think my self, your Ever ableaged sarvant,
For my wife hath ben grosley abused in so much that I Fear that it may
Cost her Life and our good Cort is plesed to give my wife ten sk of wheat
but I hope shee may get ten Lashes or mor or else here will be no Leving
here for sevel pepel For my wife was speeking in the Corthowse and her
hosband told my wife if shee held not her tongue that shee should have
more oppon her Face and my wife mad her Complant to the Cort but hee
had no check for it sir Mr. hall will give you an acount of it to the foll.
not else at

present but rest your homble sarvant

William Nottingham

1676.
Aperel 29:
Esopes

[ADDRESSED:]   Thes For Cap Nicols
in New Yorck
delivered.

[ENDORSED:]   Mr. Nottingham.
Kingston in Esopus.
Apr. 29–1676.
To speake to the Go:
about an appeale.

Granted
E A S.[‡]

* service
‡ This last portion of the endorsement is in the governor's hand.

[25:105]

To the Right Honnorable Major Edmond Andros Governor
Generall under his Royall Highnesse James Duke of Yorke
etc: of all his Territories in America;   And to this honnorable Court of assizes now sitting—

The Humble Petition of Margareta
Stuyvest. in the submittest Manner praying
that your honnor Graciously will be
pleased to graunt a favorable hearing unto
your present petitioner=

Humbly shewing, that Your Petitioner in all obedience doth submit unto
your honnors decree and Jugement pronounced against hur on yesterday
at the suit or appeale of Daniel De Haert administrator to the Estate of
his deceased brother Balthazr. de Haert; But soo it is that of the full rigour
of the said Jugement (as it was understood by your Petitioner) must stand
in force, it will unavoidebly tend to the utter ruine of Your Petitioner and
family; shee being thereby deprived not only of some part of her account,
but alsoo of the whole debt due unto hur from the said d'Haert; Now
Whereas Your Honnors said Jugement (as Your Petitioner in all humility
Conceives) was Cheifely grounded because the Balthazr. d'Haert by his
last Will did acquit Your Petitioner from the debt she might be Charged
or Indebted in his bookes; Which said acquiettance Your Petitioner
hoopes and in all submission prayes that it may not be an argument that
muste force hur to do the like, or to loose what he was indebted unto hur
being of a verry more Conciderable vallue, as Your Petitioner sufficiently
hath proeved to the full satisfaction of Arbitrators, the Jury and Court of
Mayor and aldermen, and still is able to proeve shall be pleased to Graunt
Your Petitioner the favour of a hearing and examitation of the particulers
of the said account,   And as Concerning what the said d'Haert may
alleadge that it is not probable that his Deceased Brother who was
possessed of a large Estate would live uppon the suett* and meane portion
of Your Petitioner, In answer to Which Your petitioner shall only say,
that shee being with the said d'Haert uppon agreement of Marriage, it is
Evident and knowne that the said Balthaz' d: Haert in his life time made
use of the Estate belonging to this petitioner, as his owne particuler, And

* sweat?

his sudden deceaze preventing the accompleshing of the said Marriage Your Petitioner was thereby forced to draw to hur selfe the rest of hur said Estate, the greatest part of which was before his decease Converted to his owne use and by him melted and mint in his owne Estate, Whereuppon Your Petitioner for the recovery of some part was forced to Commence hur suite at Common Law, and uppon due proofe, obtained soo ample an Award, Verdict and Jugement in hur behalfe as is manifested unto your honnor, Which said Verdict and jugement of the mayors Court as for the Generall part thereof being now repealed by your honnors said Jugement—

It is the most humble Petition Prayer and Supplication of your Petitioner that your honnor (In Compassion and Comiseration to the Petitioner and families total ruyne) Will be pleased soo farre to review the said matter by takeing an Inspect and examination of the particulers of Your Petitioners account with the said De Haert, and to allow Your distressed Petitioner such small reliefe therein as your honnor in Justice and Equity shall judge meete.

And Your Distressed Petitioner shall ever pray.

[ENDORSED:]   Mrs. Backers peticion[*]
1676. not granted.

[25:106]

[PETITION FROM DANIEL DE HAART SEEKING A POSTPONEMENT OF THE SETTLING OF HIS BROTHER'S ESTATE]

To the Right honorable Major Edmund Andros Esquire senieur of Sauce Marees Leuetenant Governor Generall of all his Royall Highnes his Teritories in America etc.

The petition of daniell dehart Administrator of Balthezar dehart deceased etc.

Humbly sheweth
That whereas your honors peticioners wittnesses to prove a legal demand made in the behalfe of your peticioner; Mathias and

* Margaret Stuyvesant was the half sister of the former Dutch governor and the wife of Jacob Backer, according to E. B. O'Callaghan, cited in the *Records of New Amsterdam* (6:255–56).

Jacobus his two bretheren cannot be here presently produced untill
the widd: and Relict of the said Mathias shall come here to give
notice who they are that can testifie the same since the Testators
Estate Lyes bleeding and all concerned therein must inevitably be
ruind if not by your honor releeived—

In tender Consideracion whereof your peticioner humbly prayes that
your honor would please to give a longer day for producing such
Wittnesses as may without all doubt be found to give their Evidence in
the case before such persons as your honors grave wisedome shall
nominate and appoint which will encause your peticioner and all con-
cernd in the Testators estate To pray for your honors happines in this life
and eternall happines hereafter.

[ENDORSED:]   The peticion of daniell dehaert for and
                in behalfe of himselfe and others etc.
                1676.

[25:107]

[PETITION OF JOHN MANNING FOR AN AUDIT OF HIS ACCOUNTS AS
HIGH SHERIFF OF YORKSHIRE]

To the Right Honorable Major Edmund Andross Esquire Senieur
of Sans Mareze Governor and Lt. Generall of all his Royall
Highness Teritoryes in America and the Rest of his Majesties
Justices of the peace now Assembled in Court.

The Petition of John Manning

In all Humble Manner

Sheweth, Whereas your Petitioner was in the yeare 1671 and 1672
high Sherrife for Yorkesheir upon Long Island, And hath since he
came last into the Country beene sued for publick debts, and
Judgement is graunted Against him for the same:

Your Petitioner therefore humbly prayes your Honors to
take his Case into serious Consideration, and to Appoint
such persons as your honors shall thinke meet to Auditt your
petitioners Accompts whereby he may be the better Enabled
to pay his publique debts by receaveing what is Justly due
from the publicke to your petitioner And your petitioner as

in Duty bound,

Shall ever pray etc.

The humble Petition of John Manning
to the Governor and Court of Sessions.
1676.

[25:108a]

[PETITION OF THE CHILDREN OF CORNELIS MELYN TO BE INVESTED
OF THEIR INTEREST IN STATEN ISLAND]

To the right honorable Major Edmund Andros Esquire,
Seigneur de Saus=Marez, Governor and Liftenant Generall
of his R: Highnesse the Duke of Yorke, of all his Territoryes
in America together with the honorable Councell and Worshippfull Justices of Peace, the Generall Assembly now
conveined as a Generall Court of Equity in the Citty of New
Yorke.

The humble adresse of Jacob and Isaac Melyn in the behalfe of
them selves and sisters, all the children and issue of Cornelius
Melyn the Equitable proprietor of Staten Island late deceased.

Humbly present to this honorable Assembly their oppressed State, that
by reason of warr, and revolution of Government in this Colony, that
before your Suppliants could according to law bee invested in their
interest on Staten Island, by the authority then being; were necessitated
to Suspend their proceedings: The Change of Government hasting
thereon; By reason of which, your Suppliants as poore Orphans were
Left deprived of their just and equitable interest in the Said Island; where
their Father was at the Charge and Expences of many thousand pounds
in the first settling therof.

Therefore your Suppliants, not being versed in Law with the
perticular wayes to proceed in it; being Confident of the kindnesse
of this honorable Assembly, to show how ready they are to relieve
the fatherless, and widowes, and pleade the Cause of the Orphans;
And therein bee in all Equitable account and matter of Justice, as
Nursing Father to them; and accordingly as matters of Justice
appeares before your honors to give releive; This honorable
Assembly being the onely authority before whome this Case is
Cognizable, Therefore are bound with submission and Leave to
present their greevances to your honors by way of Remonstrance

hereunto anexed, it containing the truth and merit of their present Case; And accordingly hope for a favorable construction therein. And your honors graunting your Suppliants Releife: And that wisdome may bee your honors directory in all matters of Justice in the premises;

And your honors Suppliants shall ever pray

Jacob Melyen
Isaack Melyen

[ENDORSED:]   Melynes Peticion.

[25:108b]

[REMONSTRANCE AND GRIEVANCE OF THE HEIRS IN THE ABOVE MATTER]

The Remonstrance of the present Case and Greevance of Jacob and Isaac Melyn in behalfe of themselves and sisters, the Equitable proprietors of Staten Island in brief sett forth.

With Leave and Submissions.

First, That your Suppliants are apt and not without ground to persuade themselves that the most, or all the ancient Inhabitants of this honorable Assembly, cannot but bee both Sensible and well Satisfyed, that your Orators Father was for many yeares possessed of Staten Island; and was at great Expences upon the Same for many yeares, it being his owne propriety: And therefore not trouble this honorable Assembly with needles writtings to cleare up that, wherein is no reason to suspect, doubt, or question of the ancient propriety our said Father had in the Land, it being So well knowne to all Ancient Inhabitants, and doubtless to a great part of this honorable Assembly.

2ly But, that which your Suppliants are desirous to make your honors Sensible off, is, that the said propriety of the said Land, was neither by our late Father, or any derived from him allienated; And therefore your Suppliants humbly conceives, that the right in the Land of the said Island, that did formerly belong to your Orators Father, doth now in Equity belong to your honors poore Suppliants, his Children; And therefore doe move this honorably Assembly for reliefe in the premises.

3ly   And iff it should bee alledged that the propriety was sold by our said Father to the West India Compa. For reply your Orator sayes not so; for our said Father sold only the Jurisdiction and prerogatives and priviledges thereof and not the soyle of the Land or Plantacions improvement; but on the contrary in the very writting of Convenyance and Contracts with the Compa. in Holland, is a binding Article for your Suppliants late Father his Sons and Daughters to continue, possess, and enjoy, not only what they were then possessed off, and manured, without any taxe; but alsoe for soe much as their father may bee able to improve in the like kind alsoe, Which evidently cleare up, that the Interest of the Land of that Island, was never allienated; But only it hath beene your Suppliants misfortune, together with the many revolucions of time, that hath prevented and suspended our duty to renew the said Interest for the future good of our Family's. However, as the way to excuse a fault, is not longer to continue in it, Therefore your suppliants are willing to improve the present oppertunity of this Generall Assembly, to consider of the Equity of our Case, and the greatnesse of our Sufferings; and accordingly to Lett your Suppliants to bee Shareing in your grace and favour, in vouchsafeing us a grant at Least of some Considerable lotts in the said Island according to the number of our Familyes. And when your honors have heard your Orators, not only their verball pleadings and allegacions, but your honors haveing had alsoe a sight of these Credencialls upon Record, that in Conclusion, your poore Suppliants cannot but to have good ground to hope your honors will so farr consider the promises in good Justice as they may have allwayes Cause to bless God for your honors wisdome herein.

Whilst in the Interim Subscribe

Jacob Melyen
Isaack Melyen

[25:109]

[LETTER FROM THOMAS MACY RELATIVE TO THE CONDITION AND THE TREATMENT OF THE INDIANS AT NANTUCKET]

Nantukket May:9:1676

May it please your Honor where your goodnesse have bin such as to send so aften to us to knowe how lie with us in these troublsome and dangerous times wherein our neighbours have so greatly sufferred and we as yet through the goodnesse of God are free: these are to returne thanks the same of your vigilances we doubt not hath conduced to our peace: These rude lines are to give your Honor an accompt how things are and have bin with us: a consederable company of our Indians have formerly ownd themselves Philips men, but since the warrs began theis have seemingly (at least) declard themselves against him: we have carried ourselves to ward them manifesting no [ ]rust and things have bin ordearly carried among them: onely we have heard now and then a word from single persons the which we have not liked but have overlooked the same. And I doubt not but we may enjoy peace (if our sins hinder not) so long as we can keepe strong liquor from them: your Honor may understand that some that dwell elsewhere have some yeeres past sent goods to trade with the Indians: upon the accompt of fishing and otherwise and great quantities of strong liquor have bin sent and notwithstanding all orders and care about it to prohibit, it hath bin one way or other disposed to the Indians which hath ocasioned great abuse and disorder but since the warrs began they have not had much; the last fall the Court tooke into their possession all on the Iland and disposed of it by small [ ]antities, as the owners and the English neighbours had need, and because of the late scarcity little hath lately Come: the Agent here that carries on the trade for the Gentlmen hath barganed with the Indians to give each man a dram before they go out to fishing in the morning: but under that pretence much abuse hath bin, and respecting the present voyage a small quantity came, about 16 gallons which was carried to the Indians, It so came to passe that a sloope came to my Honored Cousin Mr. Mayhew from the Honorable Councell and Mr. Mayhew sent to me the order that prohibitted strong drinke being carried to any Indian plantation, which order came to my hand and I presently went to the house of him that had carried the liquor aforementioned to the Indians: and carryed the order with me but finding him not at home left a warrant at his house requireing him on his Majesties name to fetch away the liquor carried to the Indians: but slited and not at all obeyed but the liquor spent there as understand the monday following I caused the order to be read in the town meeting which some greatly disliked: as I understood: my humble request is a word or to from your Honor about it. Sir concerning the peace we hithertoo enjoy I cannot immagine it could have bin if strong liquor had bin among the Indians as formerly: for my owne part I have bin to the utmost an apposer of this trade these 38 yeares, and I verily believe (respecting the Indians) tis the only ground of the miserable present ruine to both nations: soe that hath kept them from Civility, thes have bin by this drinkin trade kept all this while like wild Beares and woolves in the wildernesse: Concerning my understanding in this matter I have now sent to Governor Leverett that which I hope may come to publike view etc. But respecting the present times and state of things I humbly entreat if in your wisedome you shall see meet to make a strict Law or order respecting our Iland to prohibit any vessel whatsoever that shall come into the harbour to sell or give any strong drinke more or lesse to any Indian under a penalty and to Command or order the Goverment here to search all vessels for strong drinke and either to Cause the master or merchant to carry away or take into Custody so much as they judge may be needfull for the moderate use of the English here or for Indians in case of sicknesse etc. and according to the discression of the court to put it i[ ] t[   ] hands of some man or men that may be judged faithfull by [   ]all quantities dispose as lie needed for tho the traders it may be do not dispose of much to the Indians yet many of the Inhabitants do frequently purchase it pretending for their owne use and sel it to the Indians: an order from your Honor will be of greater force then any we can make tho lest to a liberty herein: and whereas in your letter to Mr. Mayhew you give liberty to dispose of powder to trusty Indians for their necessary use, we judge it were better soe as wholely to prohibit for tho some here we apprehend may be confided in yet so to distinguish will give great offence: yet by private instructions your Honor may referre something to the discression of this Government respecting Contigent accidents in refferrence to [   ] and peace, not farther trouble at present I Commend you [   ]esly the weighty affaires Committed to your mannagement to the [   ]easeing of the onely wise God and remaine

Your Servant at
Commaund
Tho: Macy

[ADDRESSED:]   To the [   ]rable
Edm[   ]
Go[   ]rnor at the Citty
of New yorke
these.

[ENDORSED:]   Nantukett 9th May 76
from Mr. Macy.

Mr. Macy to the
Go: Nantucket
May 9 [seal] 1676.

[25:110]

[MINUTES OF A MEETING WITH SACHEMS FROM HACKINSACK
AND TAPPAN]

May: 13th. 1676.

There appeared before the Governor in the Fort, The sachem of Hack-ingsack and another of Tapan, with long Claes the Indyan and others.

Mr. Sam: Edsall Interpreter.

They desire to continue good friends and to live in peace, and promise to doe their Endeavors to bring some of the other Neighbor Indyans hither.

[ENDORSED:]   May 13. 1676.
                 At a meeting of some Indyans befor the Go:
                 Hackingsack
                 Tappan

[25:111]

[DEPOSITION OF JOHN CLARKE AND PENELOPE COOKE CONCERNING
THE ORAL WILL OF THOMAS SEABROOKE]

The Testimony of John Clarke of Westchester aged about 29 years.

This Deponent saith that when there was an alarme of Indians being att Castell Hill loaden with aminition last summer this Deponent was then a sojurner in the House of Thomas seabrooke and itt being in the night; the said Thomas seabrooke was Commanded among others to goe to Capt. Osbornes House. And att his going away he the said Thomas Seabrooke tooke his Wife (the now present Widdow Seabrooke) by the hand in the doore as he was agoing out and said Wife I am agoing out I know not butt I may be knott o' the head; if I never come again I give all that I have to thee, Meaning his Wife and further said to this Deponent pray take notice; what I say And further saith nott. Sworne before me

John Pell

May 15th 1676

The Testimony of Penelope Cooke aged about 50 yeares.

This Deponent saith that Thomas Seabrooke of Westchester the late

Husband of the Widdow Seabrooke being some time last Winter att Consider Woodes he did declare that he was going over to Long Island And then att the same time did say that when soever he did die he would make his Wife full and whole Executor And give all to her; his Wife And no body else should have nothing to doe with any thing he had but his Wife and further saith nott.

sworne before me John Pell

Westchester 1676
May 15th

[ENDORSED:] Deposicions of Tho: Seabrooke, leaving his Estate to his wife, May1–5–1676.

[25:112]

[SALE OF A LOT IN ALBANY FROM THE MAGISTRATES TO JACOB TYSSZ VAN DER HEYDEN. TRANSLATION]

Copy*

The honorable magistrates of Albanie, the colony of Renselaerswyck and Schaenhechtady hereby declare, in rightful, true and free ownership, to cede, transport, and convey to and on behalf of Jacob Tyse van der Heyden a certain lot located and situated in Albany near the plain within the city's enclosure at the corner of the plain street; twenty-seven feet in width at the road, and eleven feet at the road in the back by the new churchyard; three rods in length on the south [side] at the city's enclosure, and three rods on the north [side] at the churchyard; and [declare] that it is free and unencumbered, without them, the grantors, making any further claims on it (being granted to him in recompense or compensation for his lot and house which he had outside the city's gate near Rooseboom's); giving as a result *plaenum actionem celsam* and complete power to the aforesaid Jacob Tyse van der Heyden, his heirs and descendants, or those who afterward might inherit his right and title, in order to do and dispose of the aforesaid lot as he would do with his other patrimonial goods and effects; granting hereby permission to request a patent‡ from the right honorable lord governor general. Thus done by

---

* The original, a translation of which appears in *ERA* 1:125–26, has a few details not included in this copy. Van der Heyden sold the property on the same day to William Loveridge (*ERA* 1:126).

‡ groundbrief

the honorable court in Albany on this 20 May 1676. Was signed: Adriaen
Gerritse

Richard Prittie   Agrees with the original in the protocol
                   quod attestor, Ro. Livingston, secr.

[25:113]

[PETITION OF REBECCA SADLER FOR POSSESSION OF LAND OF HER
    HUSBAND ON STATEN ISLAND HELD BY JONAS HALSTED]

To the Honorable E[   ] of his Royall Highnes Collony
[   ]rica.

The Humble petition of Rebecca Sadl[   ]iveinge in the Towne
of Portsmouth on Rhode: Island in his Majesties Collony of Rhode
Island and providence plantations in New England

Most Humbly Sheweth

That whereas your poore petioner the wife of Thomas Sadler (whoe
formerly lived upon Staton Island) haveinge been for severall Yeares in
a widow-like Condition left by her said husband with three small
Children to Maintaine, with only the labour of her owne hands, not
haveinge any Releife from her husband thereto, and alsoe your poore
petioner for this four yeares past, not heareinge nor haveinge any
information whether her said husband be liveinge or Dead:

And beinge certainely informed that her husband when he went away
from Staton Island (as she is informed intending for Merriland) he left
some small Estate on the said Island in the custody of one Joanas Holsted,
whoe though he can lay noe just claime to it in any respect yet the said
Joanas doth keep and with-hold the same from your poor petioner, whoe
with her children are in great wants for their lively-hood:

And your petioner not only liveinge remote, and of soe poore a Condition
not able to prossicute in the law whereby she is dissabled to follow the
said Joanas Halsted in a course of law for Recovery of her just Right.

Therefore your poore and distressed petion[ ]r most Humbly prays your
Honor that you will cast an eye of tender pitty upon your petioner and
her poore childrens deploreable Condition, and in your clemency grant
the favour to your Supplicant that the said Joanas Halsted may be

constrained by your Honors Order to surrender up and deliver what is in his custody left by your petioners husband that it may be Restored to your poore supplient, which will be a great Comfort to her and her Children whoe are also her said husbands Children, And your petioner shall still pray for your Honors happines and prosperity etc.
portsmouth the 22th of May 1676.

[25:114–15]

[NO DOCUMENTS ARE LISTED FOR THESE NUMBERS IN THE CALENDAR. TWO ITEMS NOW FILED HERE BELONG WITH JOHN SHAKERLY'S ACCOUNTS IN VOLUME 29]*

[25:116]

[LETTER FROM GOVERNOR ANDROS TO THE GOVERNOR AND COUNCIL OF MASSACHUSETTS RELATING TO THE INDIAN WAR]

Gentlemen

Having unask't, acted beyond Expectacion, in your Indyan Warre, though all friendly proffers slighted by nearest Neighbors, However out of Commiseration, and upon Account of your Letter of the 5th past, I shall not bee wanting in any thing fitt for mee; according to, and with due Regard to your said Letter, and particularly am ready (if you resolve and desire it) to endeavour to procure you, an honourable and safe Peace, with said Indyans; As to the powder, I have well examined, and cannot find the least Cause: This is by Mr. William Darvall, Mayor of this City, who will informe you, of the state of things here; so thanking you for your above Neighbourly Letter, I remaine

Gentlemen

New Yorke   Your affectionate Neighbour
May 22th 1676.   and friend

[ADDRESSED:]   For the Honorable the Governor
                and Councell of the Colony
                of Massachusetts—
                These.
                At Boston.

[ENDORSED:]   Copie of the Go:

* See appendix to the final volume of *The Andros Papers.*

Lettre to Boston.
May–22–1676.
By Mr. Mayor.[*]

[25:116a]

[NO DOCUMENT IS LISTED FOR THIS NUMBER IN THE CALENDAR.
ONE ITEM NOW FILED HERE BELONGS WITH JOHN SHAKERLY'S
ACCOUNTS IN VOLUME 29][‡]

[25:117]

[LETTER FROM SECRETARY NICOLLS TO EDWARD RAWSON,
SECRETARY OF MASSACHUSETTS, CONCERNING
MERCHANTS' GOODS SEIZED AT BOSTON]

Worthy Sir.

Being very much importuned by Mr. Christopher Hoogland, Mr. Francis
Rombout and Mr. Guylaine Verplanck, (his Majesties subjects and
Inhabitants of this place) who with some others had Goods seized on in
Boston in the beginning of the Dutch Warre, which were shipt on board
Mr. Greene's Ship in London for this Port, before knowledge of the said
Warre, concerning the which Applicacion hath been made to your
Government for redresse, and withall was recommended in Mr. Leets
and my Instructions when there to speake to your Governor about, from
whom though we received but little Incouragement, Yet had no positive
Denyall; the same being referred for determinacion to the Generall
Court, or Court of Assistants, (if I am not mistaken,) of whose result, or
whether any notice was then taken of it or no, wee are hitherto ignorant;
Upon the request of the said persons, I desire You'l doe them and me the
favour to let me know in a line or two what was don therein at the Court,
and if Nothing, that you will procure an answer in writing under the
Governors hand or yours by his and the Councells or Courts Order, what
they must trust to, whether to have any restitucion or satisfaction made
for their said Goods or not, that having no further expectacion from your
parts, they may bee at liberty to endeavour the recovery of the same
otherwise as they shall see cause or be advised by their friends; I hope
my request is so reasonable that you will please to comply with mee
herein, and upon all occasions I shall endeavour to approve my selfe.
Worthy Sir

---

* William Darvall
‡ See appendix to the final volume of *The Andros Papers*.

New York
May [*blank*] 1676.
By Mr. Mayor.*
I pray give my best respects
to your honorable Governor.

Your very affectionate
humble servant.
M.N.

[ENDORSED:]   Copie of a Letter to Mr. Rawson Secr. at Boston.
By Mr. Mayor May 1676.

[25:118]

[MINUTES OF A MEETING WITH UNCHECHAUG INDIANS
CONCERNING FISHING RIGHTS]

May 23. 1676.

At a meeting of the Unchechaug Indyans of Long Island—before the Go:
at the Fort.

They give thankes for their peace, and that they may live, eate and sleepe
quiet, without feare on the Island, They give some white strung seawant.

They desire they being free borne on the said Island, that they may have
leave to have a whale boate with all other materiells to fish and dispose
of what they shall take, as and to whom they like best.

They complaine that fish being driven upon their beach etc. the English
have come and taken them away from them per force.

The Go: Demands if they made complainte of it to the Magistrates in the
Townes, who are appointed to redresse any Injuryes.

They say no, but another time will doe it.

The Go: will consider of it and give them Answer tomorrow.

May 24. 1676.

The Indyans come againe to the Governor in presence of The Councell.

What they desire is granted them as to their free liberty of fishing, if they

* William Darvall

bee not engaged to others; They say they are not engaged.
They are to have an Order to shew for their priviledge.

[ENDORSED:]   May 23.24 1676.
                   Unchechaug Indyans.

[25:119a]

[ORDER GRANTING THE ABOVE FISHING RIGHTS]

At a Councell held in N.Y. the 24th day off May 1676.

Upon the request of the Ind[   ]s of Unchechauge upon Long Island

Resolved and ordered that they are at liberty and may freely whale or
fish for or with Christians or by themselves and dispose of their effects
as they thinke good according to law and Custome of the Government
of which all Magistrates officers or others whom these may concerne are
to take notice and suffer the said Indyans so to doe without any manner
of lett hindrance or molestacion they comporting themselves civilly and
as they ought.

                             By Order of the Go: in Councell

[ENDORSED:]   Order of Councell may 24. 1676.
                   Unchechaug Indians.

[25:119b]

[LIST OF OWNERS OF VACANT LOTS IN NEW YORK]

Mr. Steenwyck   The vacant Ground etc.
Mr. V: Brugge   Mr. Allard Anthony
Mr. de Peyster   X Mr. Sam: Edsall
Mr. Hoogland   Mr. Guylayne Verplanck
Mr. Ebbing   X Adolph Peterse.
Mr. Rombout   X Seuart Olferts.
Mr. Ver Plancke   X Mr. Thomas Lewis
Mr. Gerrit V: Tright   X Peter Stoutenberg
Mr. Winder etc.   Jan Vigné
                                 Mr. Ebbing
                                 Mr. Rombout
                                 Cor: V: Borsum
                                 Mr. Hoogelandt
                                 6 or 7

[NOTE ON BACK:]   Lot and his wife in John Watkins house.

[25:120]

[ORDER ABOUT VACATED LOTS]

At a Councell held in New Yorke
this 26th day of May, 1676.

Upon Consideracion of the returne of the valu[ ]cions of the vacant Land about this City, brought in by the Apprizers.

Resolved, that all vacant Land without Fence, not Improved as directed by the Law, shall bee deemed Vacant, and disposed of according to Law.

That all decayed Houses, or lotts of Land to the Streetes, convenient for Building, shall be ascertain'd to any, that will bee willing to Pay the Purchase to the right Owners, according to the Apprizement, unlesse the owners will build themselves; Which Building so to bee made by the right Owners or Purchasers, are to bee Sufficient dwelling Houses, and to bee built within one yeare after the Publicacion hereof, or otherwise to bee rendred uncapable of Building upon the said Land hereafter; And the Land to bee look't upon, as other vacant Land, and Valued accordingly, and disposed of by the Government for the Publicke good.

By Order of the Governor in Councill

To the Mayor, or Deputy Mayor and Aldermen
of the City of New Yorke, to Publish this Order.

[ENDORSED:]   Order of the Councell about Vacant
Land in this City. 1676

[25:121]

[INSTRUCTIONS TO THOMAS DELAVALL TO ARRANGE FOR INDIANS
TO MEET WITH THE GOVERNOR AT ALBANY]

No. 10.   C. Delavalls Instructions

You are hereby authorised and desired att your arivall att Albany having aquainted Capt. Sharp principal Commander there and togeather with

him by arnold the interpreter* to send by a good maquase notice to the
maquase and sineques that I am designed next weeke for Albany, and
desire and order somme of them to meet me there as soon as Convenient-
ly they cann, perticularly Caraconty.

If no good maquase be found that will undertake the whole journey for
which must be well rewarded, then to Consult your best mean's of
sending said mesage forward from Castle to Castle, and that they returne
Answer the same way.

Also to send some good mahicander Eastward to let the indians that live
that way know that all of them that will Come in to live under this
Goverment shalbe admited under the protection thereof and that I intend
being att Albany as above next week where they may then freely comme
and speake with me and returne if they will without any Restraint or
harme from the Goverment.

To Capt. Tho: Delavall May 30. 1676.

[ENDORSED:]   C. Delavalls Instructions
                   for Albany May. 30. 1676.

[25:122]

[PETITION OF DANIEL DE HAART APPEALING A JUDGMENT]

> To the Right Honorable Major Edmund
> Andros Esquire Senieur of Saus Marez
> Leiftenant and Governor Generall of all his
> Royall Highnesses Territoryes in America
> etc.

The humble Peticion of Daniel Dehart etc.

Sheweth

That your Peticioner was Sued at a Mayors Court holden in this Citty the
9th day of May 1676 by Margarett Bakers of this Citty widdow for the
Summe of 12849 gilders 10 stivers pretended to be due from your
Peticioners late Brother Balthazer Dehart Deceased where Judgment

---

* Arnout Viele

passed against your Peticioner for the said Summe your Peticioner not being willing to acquiesse with the said Judgment.

Graunted
E Andros S*

Humbly prayes your honor to grant him an appeale that his Cause may be hear'd before your Honor att the next Court of Assizes he performing what the Law in such Case Directs etc.

And your Peticioner shall
ever Pray etc.

[ENDORSED:]   Mr. Deharts Peticion for appeale against Uffroe‡ Bakers.
Granted June 1676.

[25:123]
[DOCUMENT HAS BEEN MISSING SINCE BEFORE 1866]

[25:124]
[MINUTES OF A MEETING WITH SUSQUEHANNA SACHEMS]

June 2d
1676

At a Meeting in the Fort of some Susquehanna Indyans from Delaware and the head of the bay and those parts, having beene sent for by the Go:

Conachoweedo.
Sneedo.
} 2 Sachems

Jacob
Loockerman
Interpreter
}

The Go. tells them they are welcome and hee is glad they are come hither to see him, and saith that if hee can doe them or any of their Nation Courtesy hee will doe it.

Mr. Edsall also present but understands them not well, nor Mr. Steph: V: Cortland.
}

They are told that if they will come and live any where within the Government the Go: will protect them, but cannot undertake at great distance.

*   Penciled note written by Gov. Andros.
‡   *Juffrouw*, Dutch term of respect, meaning "Lady" or "Madam."

They speake)
Maques.   )

The Governor saith hee hath spoken to the Maques already about them, and they told him these were their brothers and children.

The Governor bids them to thinke what hee can doe for them with the Maques now at his goeing up (which will bee in five dayes).

That having heard a good Report of them hee is sorry from his heart at their Troubles, and would willingly help them out.

They are wish't to goe eate and drinke and thinke upon what they have to say, and come againe tomorrow.

They are told further that if they are afraid and not well where they are, if they will come into this government, they shall bee welcome and protected from their Ennemys.

That the Go: will take Care the Maques and Sinneke shall bee at peace with them, and will also make peace for them with Virginia and Maryland.

The Go: gave the 2 sachems 2 Coates and to eate and drinke.

June 3d 1676.

The same Indyans appeare againe.

They being demanded what they have now to say, They answer that they have no mind to goe up to Alb: but to returne to the South River, to their folkes.

The Go: saith t'is well and further—tells them that the Maques shall doe them no hurt, for hee hath spoken with the Maques about them already, and they have promis'd it, calling them brothers and Children and if they will they may goe and live with them.

The Go: asks them if they will goe and speake with their owne Nation about it, and returne an Answer.

They say they are but two so can give no other answer then that they will goe to the rest of their people and tell them what the Go: saith, and will returne with an answer.

The 2 sachems will returne themselves.

They say they will when they come againe bring some present with them to appeare like themselves.

The Go: tells them Its no matter, Hee hath heard a good Report of them, and they shall bee welcome whither they bring any thing or not.

The Go: saith further that they should say whether they will come into the Government or no, if they will not t'is well, if they will hee will make provision for them, and they shall bee protected and welcome: so that when they returne—They should make answer whether they will come or no in briefe.

They had given them to eate and drinke, so they departed well satisfyed.

[ENDORSED:]   At a Councell or Meeting with the
                Indyans of the Suskehanno's
                June 2d and 3d.
                Cunachoweedoe.

[25:125]

[PASS TO EMMEN, A WICKERS CREEK SACHEM]

These are to certify That the Go: hath given leave to Emmen—one of the Wickerscreeke sachems who hath lived quietly and well within this Government, to passe with some of his Indyans in two Canooes through the Sound to Stamford to fetch his Corne, or about other his lawfull occasions, and to returne againe without any manner of Lett or Molestacion: Dated in N.Y. this 6th day of June 1676.

To all whom this
may concerne.

[ENDORSED:]   A Certificate and passe for
                a Wickerscreeke sachem.
                Jun: 6. 1676

[25:126a]

[NO DOCUMENT IS LISTED FOR THIS NUMBER IN THE CALENDAR. ONE ITEM NOW FILED HERE BELONGS WITH JOHN SHAKERLY'S ACCOUNTS IN VOLUME 29][*]

[25:126b]

[ACCOUNT OF MATTHIAS NICOLLS WITH JOHANNES NEVIUS. TRANSLATION]

In Book No. A

Anno 1670	Capt. Nicolls, debit to the late Johannes Neevius, ferryman	
28 May	For ferry fee of a hogshead of tobacco belonging to Jaques Coreljouw	ƒ1.10
20 June	For a *pintie* brandy by written order and two *pintie* beer	ƒ4.08
4 July	For taking over the horse and ferry fee of Tho. John	ƒ2.08
26 do.	For four *mut.*[‡] brandy by written order	ƒ4.
25 October	For ferry fee of 2 horses and a *pintie* beer	ƒ4.04
31 do.	For ferry fee of 12 persons and for what he agreed to pay on his account	ƒ2.08
	For nine *mut.* brandy	ƒ8.02
6 November	For ferry fee of an animal[†] belonging to Richard Smidt	ƒ2.
11 do	For ferry fee of an animal[+] belonging to Will Wilkens	ƒ2.

---

* See appendix to the final volume of *The Andros Papers*.
‡ *mutjes*
† Dutch *beest*, literally a beast, usually a cow.
+ ibid.

	For a cow belonging to Mr. Coo .... ƒ2.
18 do.	For ferry fee of a hog belonging to Mr. Coo ƒ–.06
22 do.	For taking over his horse, over and back
	with which an Englishman was to travel to
	Dillever bay and agreed to
	pay on his account.. ƒ4.
20 december	For ferry fee of his horse..................................... ƒ2.
24 do.	For ferry fee of two sheep.................................... ƒ–.12
	Carried over to folio 70....................................... ƒ39.18

continued

Anno 1671

15 January	For taking over his horse..................................... ƒ2.
	For six *mut.* rum.. ƒ4.
	For ferry fee of Thom. John................................ ƒ–.08
16 February	For ferry fee of his servant Roeloff..................... ƒ–.08

	Tho. Teller and Pieter Smidt
	drank three *kanne* beer with the
	aforesaid Roeloff.. ƒ1.04

	For ferry fee of his horse..................................... ƒ2.–
First March	For ferry fee of his servant Roeloff..................... ƒ–.08
8 do.	For ferry fee of his brother................................. ƒ–.08
9 do.	For ferry fee of his horse..................................... ƒ2.
20 do.	For ferry fee of Tho. John and a
	paertie beer ƒ–.16
25 do.	For ferry fee of a horse....................................... ƒ2.
	For ferry fee of his brother................................. ƒ–.08
	For ferry fee of Roeloff...................................... ƒ–.08
7 April	For ferry fee of two horses and a *paertie*
	beer and three *mut.* rum.................................... ƒ6.14
8 do.	For ferry fee of 2 horses..................................... ƒ4.
	For 1 1/2 *mut.* rum ƒ1.01
11 do.	For ferry fee of 7 skipples grain belonging to
	Bartlet Claesse.. ƒ1.07
	Carried over to folio 129 .... ƒ69.12

15 do.	For ferry fee of his brother and Negro ƒ–.16
18 do.	For ferry fee of Tho. John when he drew
	hay and one half *mut.* rum and beer

	with Roelandt *f*–.08
5 May	For ferry fee of his servant Roeloff *f*1.10
8 do.	For ferry fee of his brother, Capt. Car
	Jan Lauwer, his servant Roeloff
	and Negro boy, each 4 st .... *f*1.
	For Mr. Dairl and John Geerlen, over
	and back *f*–.16
	For three and one half *mut.* rum *f*2.09
	For his horse.. *f*2.
11 do.	For ferry fee of his brother and Capt.
	Car Jan Laurens and his daughter, the
	widow of doctor Tieleman; Mr. Dairl, John
	Greerlen; his servant Roeloff and Negro boy,
	Pieter Smidt.. *f*2.08
	for his horse.. *f*2.
12 do	for ferry fee of the Negro boy *f*–.08
15 do.	For ferry fee of a cow and for Wel
	Brunckely and 1/2 rum drunk by him................... *f*2.15
17 do.	For ferry fee of a horse and for Thom. Jans
	and 1/2 *mut.* drunk by him................................. *f*2.15

These above mentioned charges came to *f*89.05

Carried over to the other side.

	The amount on the other side is *f*89.05
19 do.	For ferry fee of Mr. Scharp and his horse,
	over and back, come to *f*4.08
25 do	for ferry fee of 2 servants and 3 children. *f*1.04
	Carried over to folio 134.................................. *f*94.17

5 June	For ferry fee of the horse and Thoms Johns......... *f*2.8
	For 3 *Kanne* beer... *f*1.4
10 do.	For ferry fee of Tho. Johns and a *Kan* beer *f*–.16
	Carried over to folio 1 in book B. *f*99.05

17 do.	For one *mut.* rum to Will Brinckely *f*–.16
6 July	For ferry fee of a *vaatie* butter *f*–.06
17 August	For ferry fee of Jonathan Stuckely...................... *f*–.08
18 do.	For ferry fee of two horses................................. *f*4.£
19 do.	For ferry fee and for five *mut.* rum
	and three *Kanne* beer.. *f*5.
26 do.	For ferry fee of said brother and Negro .... *f*–.1[ ]

	For five *mut.* rum .... *f*4.	
29 do.	For one *pintie* rum to Raelf Warnar *f*3.04	
3 September	For ferry fee of said brother and Geerlen and six *mut.* rum presented to the sailors of the ship *De Gratie* *f*5.04	
22 do.	For ferry fee of Tho. Johns and 1/2 *mut.* rum... *f*–.[ ]	
25 do.	For ferry fee of a horse.................................... *f*2.	
28 do.	For ferry fee of two horses and on the 29th for 3 horses.. *f*20.	
3 October	For ferry fee of a horse... *f*2.	
31 do.	For ferry fee of 2 horses...................................... *f*4.	
First November	For five *kanne* beer for him and 4 *pintiens* to the sailors of N. Verbraack's ship *f*2.16	
	Carried over to book C, folio 6. .... *f*154.15	
3 November	For ferry fee of an ox belonging to Mr. Coo .... *f*2.	
14 do.	For ferry fee of 9 sheep belonging to Adriaen Heegem[an].. *f*–.09	
	For ferry fee of his brother and boy *f*–.16	
15 do.	For ferry fee of an animal .... *f*2.	
16 do.	For ferry fee of an animal .... *f*2.	
18 do.	For ferry fee of said brother and boy, and for the same a horse and a cow *f*4.16	
14 December	For ferry fee of 2 hogs... *f*1.04	
20 do.	For ferry fee of a horse... *f*2.	
29 do.	For ferry fee of Tho. Johns and his horse............. *f*2.04	
30 do.	For ferry fee of an animal .... *f* 2 .	
Anno 1671/2	continued	
9 February	For ferry fee of a cow................................. *f*2. [ ]	
	Carried over to folio 48................................. *f*176.[ ]	
15 do.	For ferry fee of Tho. Johns................................. *f*–.[ ]	
	For one Evaen beer drunk by him................... *f*–.[ ]	
	For ferry fee of two horses................................. *f*8.	
4 March	For one *mut.* rum and one *kan* beer..................... *f*1.04	
	For ferry fee of Tho. Johns................................. *f*–.04	
	Account cleared hereof *f*186.16	

Anno 1672

First of May	For ferry fee of a horse	f2.
7 do.	For three *paertie* beer for the sailors of the ship and one parthye for him	f2.
18 do.	for ferry fee of Waitil	f–.08
22 do.	For ferry fee of 2 cows	f4.
25 do.	For ferry fee of a horse	f2.
26 do.	For ferry of a horse	f2.
21 June	For Capt. Mathias Nicolls's honorable wife and maid, fee for	f–.16
do.	For ferry fee of Capt. Nicolls and Tho. Johns	f–.08
	Carried over to the other side	f200.08

The amount on the other side comes to f200,8

24 June	For ferry fee of a cow	f2.
26 do.	For ferry fee of a horse belonging to Nathanael Denthen	f2.
5 July	For ferry fee of the aforesaid's son and Tho. Johns	f–.16
15 do.	For ferry fee of Thom. Johns	f–.08
	The amounts total up to	f205.12

By order of your honor's subject
Jan Aertsen, husband and guardian
of the widow of the deceased Joh. Neevius,
Ferryman.

At the ferry,
the 12th of June 1676.

[ENDORSED:]*   Mr. Nevius his bill
brought by his wid:
June 12, 1676.

Mr. Nevius bill
at the ferry.

---

* The endorsement is written in English.

[25:127]

Citty of   )   SS The Court of Record of the Citty aforesaid holden
New Yorke)   at the Citty hall within the said Citty the 13th day of
                June 1676 Before Nicho. Demyer deputy Mayor etc.

Ezekiell Fogg)   SS decl. Letter of Attourney bond all Read the deft.
  against   ownes his hand and seale to the same.
John Ryder   )

Plea Read that he never entred into any such Condition as in the
decl. mencioned Court give Liberty to the plt. to mend his decl.
and give the plt. Judgment for 62£ and interest since itt was due
by the Condicion of the said bond.

The deft. moved for an appeale to the generall Court of Assizes
Court grants the same performinge such things the Law Requires.

Compared per me

S. Leete cler.

[ENDORSED:]   Att a Court
              the 13th of June
              1676.
              Ezekiell Fogg
                against
              John Ryder.

              Allowed by
              the Go:
              July. 25th. 1676.

              Mr. Humphrey Davenport
              security.

[25:128–29]

[DOCKET FOR THE COURT OF SESSIONS AT JAMAICA]

Jameca sessions June 1676.

agreed	1	Joseph Smith	Plt.
X		Tho: Davies	Deft.
Jury	2	Jno. Burch	Plt.
X		Nico: Wright	Deft.
X	3	The Same	Plt.
Jury		Rich: Crabb	Deft.
X	4	Sam: Shrimpton	Plt.
		Trustees of Nico: Davies	Deft.
agreed	5	Wm. Sydenham	Plt.
X		Tho: Davies	Deft.
agreed	6	David Whitehead	Plt.
X		Humphry Underhill	Deft.
X	7	Thymothy Gabry	Plt.
by the Court		Wm. Sympson	Deft.
X	8	Tho: Wandall	Plt.
		Richard Harcatt	Deft.
X	9	Capt. Nico: Demyer	Plt.
by the Court		Wm. Smith	Deft.
X	10	Bezaleel Osborne	Plt.
		Jno. Ashman	Deft.
X		Capt. N. Demyer	Plt.
		Peter Jansen Schol	Deft.

[ENDORSED:]   The Docket.

June 1676.

Complaints Peticions etc. this sessions.

X Humphry Underhill to answer for a Colt by Order of the last
   Sessions.

X Augustine Herman. report to be made to court.

X Geo: Codners Businesse.

X Constable and Overseers of Westchests Complaint against
   Tho: Hunt senior.

X Sam: Andrues request.

X Wm. Heidens Presentment.

X Wm. Smiths Peticion.

— Mr. Robt. Coe in Edward Waters report.

X Humphry Underhill and Abell Gale fin'd 50s each last
   Sessions.

X The Omission for Stocks

X Md. to make Order about Overseers of Flushing

X Constables Jameca: presentments

X Cons. Flushing @ Wm. Pidgeon

X Rich: Smiths Peticion

Cast out X Laurens Mott for Execucion

X Mrs. Waters Peticion.

[25:130]

[PROCEEDINGS OF THE COURT OF SESSIONS AT JAMAICA]

Afternoone.

At a Court of Sessions held at Jamaica for the
North Riding—June 14. 1676.

The bench called over, who all appeared.

The Constables called over, who appeare, but some without staves[*] who
are reproved, and threatned to bee fined.

The Jury returned.

Elyas Doughty   Foreman.
John Symons
George Hewlett
Nicholas Passell
John Foster
John Man
John Baily

They are sworne.

Joseph Smith   Plt.
Tho: Davis   Deft

The first Cause, tomorrow morning, by 7 a Clock.

Tuesday Morning
June 15th 1676.

The Constables Election irregular, therefore ordered to have a new
Election both of Constables and Overseers according to Law.

Joseph Smith   Plt.
Tho: Davis   deft.

The plaintiffe sues upn a bill of 9£.

The deft confesses Judgment which is ordered to bee enter'd.

---

[*]   symbols of office

Wm. Sydenham   Plt.
Tho: Davis   Deft.

The pltf. sues upon a bill of 12£ to Mr. Knot whose Att. hee is.
The Deft. confesses Judgment, which is ordered to bee enter'd.

John Burd   Plt.
Nicholas Wright   deft.

Mr. Leete   The Plt. declares that Anthony Wright did let a shop
Att.   and smiths Tooles to him, and that the deft. came and
    by violence tooke away the bellowes and tooles out
    of his shop.

The deft. Pleads hee acted by vertue of his being eldest Overseer, the
Constable out of the way, and by order of Anthony Wright, and that the
tooles were not let to him.

By the deposicion of Gideon and Caleb Wright, the tooles were let to the
plt.

Referr'd to the Jury, how legally the Plt. was possest of the Tooles and
how legally they were taken away.

John Burd.   plt.
Richard Crab   deft.

The plt. declares upon an accion of Defamacion, That the deft. should
say the plt. had stoln his Gun.

Two wittnesses sworne to that Purpose.

The deft. by Mr. Cooke answers and denyes the words.

Referr'd to a Jury.

Agreed   David Whitehead—plt.
    Humphrey Underhill deft.

Tho: Wandall   plt.
Richard Harcker   deft.

The Plt. by Mr. Leete putts in a declaracion about an old Debt referr'd
to arbitrators who burn't the bill. It was assigned to Tho: Wandall.

The Award signed by John Underhill, and Richard Harcker, written by C. Underhill. Strange reasons for its burning, but one that it was not a true bill, Jonas Halsteeds hand being not rightly spell'd.

Jonas Halsteed sent for.

Richa. Harcker declares That upon Jonas Halsteeds denying the bill to bee his hand, they ordered it to bee burn't.

Jonas Halsteed denyes that ever hee gave his hand to any such bill, or to that bill which t'was then produced, but confesses to have had dealings with [blank] Felthouse to whome the Originall bill was made. And they had a bargaine about a Cow and Calfe but not as alleadged.

Referr'd to the Jury.

Timothy Gabry   Plt.
Wm. Simpson   deft.

The plt. puts in a declaracion by Mr. Cooke, for Goods bought in Vendue to the value of 204 G. 9 st. which delayd sueing for by reason of his poverty.

Order'd That The deft. do make payment of the debt by the 1st of Dec. next.

Nicha. De Meyer   plt.
Wm. Smith   deft.

Mr. Cooke puts in a declaracion—clayming 900 G upon a Morgage of his house and Mill at Flushing.

The Morgage produced and read dated Aug. 30th 1671.

Another bill of 360 G. for Int. and otherwise, 3 Dec. 1674.

The deft. answers by a peticion for time to come and make up his accounts.

The Plt. to have Judgment but what shall appeare to bee payd to bee deducted: The Deft. to have 3 mo. time to make it appeare before any 2 Justices of the Riding.

Sam. Shrimpton by Mr. Leysler   plt.
The Trustees of Nich: Davis etc.   deft.

The Plt. by Mr. Cooke his Att. putts in a declaracion upon an Attachment of a small piece of land upon Hogg Neck at Oysterbay valued at about 10£.

The plt. hath his account produced proved and certifyed under the seale of Boston.

His letter of Att.
The assignment to Nich: Davis.

None appeare to defend, However the Court give Judgment for the plt. upon the attachment, the value thereof not amounting to above one third of the debt claymed by the Plt.

The Report brought into Court by Mr. Justice Pell and Mr. Justice Laurence, concerning a matter referr'd to them about Court Charges be-tweene Westchester and Aug: Hermans—Its allowed by the Court and Judgment graunted Mr. Hermans.

The court dismist till 2 a Clock afternoone.

Afternoone.

An order of the last Court of Sessions for C. Newton against Cornelius Barnsen, with Execucion if the condicions not performed.

Execucion to bee issued forth, if Cornelius doe not forthwith shew cause to the contrary.

John Burd   Plt.
Nicholas Wright   deft.

The Jury find for the plt,. unlesse the deft, can make it appeare that the tooles and bellowes were taken away after the time of the 6 mo. hyre were expired, Otherwise for the Deft. For the damage its referr'd to the bench, as well as the time to bee made appeare.

John Burd   plt.
Richa. Crabb   Deft.

The Jury find for the Deft.

Mr. Leete moves for an Appeale. To bee consider'd of.

Bezaliel Osburne   plt.
John Ashman   deft.

Mr. Leete for B. Osburne plt. declares upon attachment of Cattle and Goods, in the hands of Robert Ashman for the summe of 35£.

Severall Assignments of bills neare the summe produced with Divers Certificates relating to the same.

The summes come to 32£ 10s. 0d.

Robt. Ashman Puts in a peticion to desire time for his sons comming or sending to him; and besides claymes an Interest in the Goods for debt and for his sons childs dyet.

The attachment call'd for—which brought in and the particulars attach't.

Referr'd to the Jury.

C. N. De Meyer   plt.
Peter Jansz Schol deft.

Mr. Cooke putts in a declaracion for 1315 G 10 st. in beaver and 321 G 6 st. wamp: as per sentence.

Hee confesses judgment for the whole, Recommended for the plt. to give time.

A Complaint of the Const. and Overseers of Westchester against Tho: Hunt senior.

Upon breach of Covenent, about maintaining a fence and ditch. Tho: Hunt denyes the Covenant: Referr'd to Mr. Pell, Mr. Will: Laurence and Mr. Cornell or any two of them to view and determine within 15 dayes.

Geo: Codners Case referr'd by the last Court for farther Evidence His peticion with a Reference from the Go: read.

Upon proposall of the Att. Mr. Leete and Mr. Cooke, They come to collaterall Agreement. Mr. Coole engaging that Codner shall in 6 weekes time give security to pay the Judgment being 12£ or prosecute his bill in Equity by the returne of Mr. Richa. Smith from Engla., In meanetime to Pay all past Costs.

Wm. Heydens of Eastchester a Presentment against Moses Hoyte, John Jackson, Richa. Hedley Richa. Shute: suspended (for want of timely notice) till next Sessions.

Sam: Andrews—a Peticion to bee excused being Const. as chosen, for that hee will not take an Oath; Its of no force, the Election being voyde.

John Ockeson of Mad Nans neck presented by the Const. of Hempsteed for killing Hoggs in the Woods etc. There appearing no intent of fraude, hee is dismis't.

Will Pidgeon, is presented by the Const. of Flushing upon the Compaint of Dan: Patrick, about killing of Hoggs none of his owne. Hee saith that hee came to Pidgeons while hee was killing of hoggs, and saw one newly killed that had not his marke, about which hee had discourse with him. Hee saith hee saw another in his keeping the yeare before, that had not his marke, which caused him to suspect him.

Will Pidgeon saith hee had kept this hogge 2 yeares.

It appeares not that it was his Hogge.

To bee condider'd of, whether the hogge shall bee for his use or the Countryes.

Ordred That hee returne the value of the hogge to the Const. of the Towne for the publicke use and to bee fined 20s.

John Lumme's peticion against Mr. Coe for 6£ 10s 0d. about C. Seamans wherein he was cast.

The Execucion was served upon his Cattle and delivered into Mr. Coes Custody as sheriffe: Hee is ordered to pay the debt.

Thomas Wandall plt.
Richard Harcutt deft.

The Jury find for the plt. That the defts burning the bill was the occasion
of the plts. losse of his debt, so hee to make it good and pay Costs.

Mr. Cooke moves for a Review.

Osburne   plt.
Ashman   deft.

The Jury find for the Plt [   ] 32£ 10s proved in Court with [   ] but in
regard of the Attachme[   ] upon his Goods, and the hopes [   ] the defts.
being here in sho[   ] time, payment to bee deferr'd till Michaelmas day,
and if security bee given, by Robt. Ashman, the Goods to continue with
him till then.

A presentment brought by the Constable and Overseers against D:
Denton about taking up a Letter that wa[   ] sending to Boston for a
Minister.

Against John Scudamore for ill language upon the same Account.

To bee considered of tomorow m[   ] and the Presentment against
Abigail Darling.

The Court dismis't till tomorrow mo[   ] 7 a Clock.*

[ENDORSED:]   Jamaica Sessions
                   June 14th 1676.

                   Mr. Jackson upon his desire,
                   hadtime to bringe in
                   the returne about
                   their lands till Monday
                   come sennight.‡

---

* There is no record here of the last day of the session.
‡ Seven night: one week.

[25:131]

[COURT MINUTES OF A SUIT BY NICOLAES DE MEYER
AGAINST WILLIAM SMITH]

Att a Court of Sessions held att Jameca in the North Rydeing
of Yorkshire on Long Island the 14th day of June by his
Majesties Authority in the 28th yeare of his Majesties
Reigne Annoque Domini 1676.

Nicolas Demyer   Plt.
Wm. Smith   Defendant

The Plt. Declared for the summe of 900 guilders due by Mortgage dat
30th Augyst 1671: and likewise for 360 gilders by bill Dat: 3d December
1674 the Deft. Nott appeareing in Court but sending a Peticion thereby
desireing time to make up accounts with the Plt. The Court gives
Judgment for the Plt. but what the Deft. Cann make appeare to be Paid
within three Months before any 2 Justices of the Peace to be Deducted
the Deft. to Pay Costs.

By Order of Court etc.
John West Cl. Sess.

[ENDORSED:]   Judgment of Court
                     Demyer
                       vs.
                     Smith
                     June 1676 Jamaica Sessions.

[25:132]

[COURT MINUTES OF A SUIT BY JOHN ROBINSON AGAINST
THOMAS DAVIES]

Att A Court of Sessions held att Jameca in
the North Rydeing of Yorkshire on Long
Island the 14th day of June by his Majesties
Authority in the 28th yeare of his Majesties
Reigne Anno Domini 1676.

Wm Sydenham Attourney }
unto John Robinson   } Plt.

Tho Davies   Deft.

The Plt. declared against the Deft. in an accion upon the Case for the Summe of £12 payable in good wheat neat Tobacco or Porke att Price Currcnt due to him from the Deft. by Bill under his hand for the which the Deft. confessed Judgment and the Court Ordered the same to be Entered accordingly with Costs.

Execucion Past August 2d 1676.
Ex. Per
John West Cl. Sess.

[ENDORSED:]   Flushinge.
Constable hath Received the Debts but
taken horses upon accompt which are
not worth soe much.

Pray that they may take them upon their
apprehend: debts and costs.

[25:133]

[PROCEEDINGS OF THE COURT OF SESSIONS AT GRAVESEND]*

At a Court of Sessions held at Gravesend the
Before noone.   21th June 1676.

The bench called over and Constables who all appeared with their staves.

The Jurors returned. A Jury empannell'd and sworn.

The names of the new Constables returned.

The Actions called over, and the Court dismis't till 3 a Clock afternoone.

Afternoone.

The New Constables sworne without Exception, but with Charge to observe the Law for the future punctually in their Election.

The Overseers returned and sworne onely the 2 Overseers of Gravesend and 1 of Newtowne who as Quakers refused the Oath but are admitted upon offering to take an Engagement as the Law directs.

---

* This document and 25:57 are presently reversed. We have restored them to their correct order.

Cornelys Coertsen   plt.
Adam Brower   deft.

The plt putts in a declaracion by Mr. Cooke his Att.

for an Oxe of 250£ value delivered in 1673.

Andries Juriaensen, John Pieterse Macklick, and Hendrick Mattys
sworne as wittnesses, to prove the declaracion.

Andries declares it fully.

Jan Pieters by hearesay.

Hendrick Mattys, about an agreement, and some Circumstances.

Mr. Anthony	The Deft. acknowledges the debt, but saith hee hath
the defts. Att.	paid the greatest part, and particularly that hee paid
retained in Court.	125 G. to the plt. and the rest hee owes yet to Andries
	the payment already made was in wheate and Rye.

but nothing proved.
Referr'd to the Jury.

John Roeloffsen   plt.
Adam Brower   deft.

The declaracion for 400 G damage about a servant, to bee Prentice for 3
yeares, of which hee served neare halfe the time.
The Indenture produced, and owned; to bee brought up a Shoemaker.

The deft by Mr. Anthony his Att. putts in an answer. That hee was
employed in Country worke. The father kept him, without complayning
to any Magistrate.
Refferr'd to the Jury.

Ralph Cardall   plt.
Caarsten Jansen   deft.

Mr. Cooke Att. for the deft pleads the declaracion not put in till this
morne.
The plt. Nonsuited.

Angeltye Borgers brought in a Complaint against John Butcher alias Passall that having Judgment of the Court for the summe of 900 G or thereabout the last June sessions, shee did at the instance of some friends, come to a New agreement of which no part being performed, shee desires new Judgment with Interest Costs and damages, The which was allowed of.

The damage to bee considered of by the Court.

Mr. Wandall and James Way complaine against Tho: Sherman,— Ordered to bring it in writing, tomorrow.

In the Case betweene—Cor: Coertsz plt. and Adam Brower deft.

The Jury find for the plt. with Costs.

In the Case betweene John Roeloffsen and Adam Brower.—

The Jury find for the plt. with Costs of Court.

The Court desires them to consider of the damage.

And adjourne till tomorrow morning 7 a clock.

In the   Thursday. June 22th 1676.
morne.

The will of Margaret Toe offred to bee proved.

Jacob Reader admitted Administrator.

The Jury being desired to give their opinion touching the damage, which was referr'd to them last night, bring in 200 G damage, instead of 400 G. demanded.

Geo: Wood   plt.
Richa. Fido: deft.

The plt by Mr. Leet and Mr. Cooke his Att putt in a new declaracion, and the old one read. This being review. Its for a piece of meadow of 1/2 an ancker.
C. Tho: Laurence, John Smith, Abram Frost, and John Ethrington sworne.

C. Laurence, declares that Geo: Wood desired him since the last Tryall to goe with him to see a piece of fence, upon the land which formerly was his, and that hee very well knowes it was upon Geo. Woods land.

John Smith declares that hee made the ditch that passed the plts. and defts. land, which this (being about 7 yeares agoe) was one Richard Smiths, and they were then both agreed about it.

Abram Frost sworne saith that hee being one of 6, or 7, that had Interest in a piece of boggy meadow there for its Improvement they agreed to put it to the Towne Surveyors to lay out everyones proporcion and to ditch it in, which was by some of them accordingly done.

Tho: Ethrington saith That before the agreement spoken of, hee saw the plt. and Richard Smith the defts. predecessor mowe the swarth together.

A former judgment of Court read.

A draught shewne.

The plt. claymes to have his Lott to run from the front to the Creeke as the Neighbours doe, It was double 10 acres Lott sold by Mr. Laurence to the plt. The defts. is a greater Lott as Mr. Betts relates.

The deft being disappointed by Mr. Rider his Att. pleads himselfe, to a Collaterall Agreement.

Tho: Petitt) produced as wittnesses, to the Agreement, which was
John Firman } onely Verball.Mr. Elyas Doughty a wittnesse.

Reffer'd to a Jury.

John Kingdome plt.
Peter Bilieu deft.

A Review by the Go: order.

The old declaracion read.
A bill of sale from John Wootton and Ned Shackleton signed by one. Its about a heyfer kept by the plt 3 yeare, and the Encrease.

Nicolas De Meyer   plt.
Claes Claesen.   deft.

The plt putts in a declaracion upon a Morgauge account booke debt, and Cow.
The Deft not appearing, though notice given him, Judgment to passe for what is unsatisfyed, for the which hee hath 2 mo. time. the Cow to bee adjudged by indifferent men.

Nicha. de Meyer   plt.
Peter Simpson   deft.

Upon a bill for 225 G.
C. Cortelyau demands preference for 150 G. vendue money which is granted, hee making his debt appeare by his booke.
Judgment for the plt.
Another for Cow the deft sold to Lambert Doorlars.
The Court adjourned till afternoon 3 a Clock.

Afternoone.   July 22th 1676.

George Wood—A Complt. against Jonathan Hazard of Newtowne. Upon account of taking away a Cow and some Corne without warrant or apprizement.

John Ketcham   )
                         } sworne
Thomas Doxey)

Ketcham complaines against Hazard for 160 acres of common land layd out to him which is against damage to each particular Inhabitant.

The deft. saith hee makes use of none but his owne Land, and it was due to his father 24 yeares agoe.
That hee hath not given leave to any to barke Trees upon the Common but upon his owne land.

Tho: Doxey saith thee was at Geo: Woods when Jon: Hazard came to take the Cow, and refused to shew by what authority he did it: It was for Charges at the Towne Court, but hapned to bee after the expiracion of his time.

The distraint for the wheate was for the Rates.

To bee consider'd of by the Court.

Geo: Wood—Complains against John Borroughs.
For taking away a Cow, 2 Calves 3 sheepe the one a lambe.

Burroughs Const. then and produces severall orders of Court for what hee did.

The Const. of Newtowne presents a lame single woman for being with Child of her owne Confession etc. and that John Lorrison gott it, who is gone to Southton out of the Riding, shee is look't upon as no Inhabitant of New Towne, but of Huntington. Ordered to bee sent to Huntington, and recommended by the Court to bee bound over to the sessions by the Const. and Overseers of that place.

The Complt. about the horse that John Aartsen, Mr. Hubbard and Dirck had.

Ordered That Dennis Holdren who tooke away the horse in the Dutch time, without order doe returne the horse or Value to John Aartsen the last possessor, and to have liberty to try his title at the next Court.

George Wood   plt.
Richard Fido   deft.

The Jury find for the plt. with Costs.

John Kingdome   plt.
Peter Bilieu   deft.

The Jury find for the Deft. that what hee acted was by order so justifyable.

The buisness of Mr. De Meyers Cow, valued at 109 G.

Allowed of, or 1/2 if the Cow miscarryed.

The Court dissolved after divers Complaints and Peticioners answer'd.

Mr. West the present Clarke hath order to draw up the orders and Judgments of Court at large.

[ENDORSED:]   At a Court of Sessions held at
                   Gravesend June 21th and 22th
                   1676.

[25:134]

[STATEMENT OF THOMAS DELAVALL'S ACCOUNT]*

1669.   Captain Thomas De Lavall

               Debet‡   tob.   Zeewant Bevers

Octob.18   To Sundry goods in tob. 5741£

November 3   To 32 Blanketts at f40   ƒ1280:—
1670 June 13   To 1 ditto   40:
               To 184 1/2 ell duffles at ⎞
               13 1/2£ tob. per ell   ⎬ 2490 3/4
                                         ⎠

1671
June 13   To 302 deall boards   ⎞
               at 35 pieces wampum   ⎰   528:10
               do.To divers goods as duffles ⎞
               and blanketts as per account ⎬   4451:
               delivered in bevers   ⎠
23 November   To 215 blanketts and 7 pieces ⎞   2844:
               duffles in bevers   ⎠   _____
                                         8231 3/4lb ƒ1848:10 ƒ7295
               signed   tobacco zeewant bevers

                        Errors Excepted

                        Tho: De Lavall

---

* Compare his account with Daniel de Hondecoutre at 25:154.
‡ The sums represent payment in tobacco, seawant (wampum), and beaver skins. Deal
boards are pine planks; duffel is blanket cloth much used in the Indian trade.

[ON THE BACK:]*

[ ]as De Lavall Credit		bev[ ]
1674 14 June	by 50 bevers and 11 Lapps from	
	Joris	ƒ424
	By 7 Elke Skinns	28
	By 5 Otters	30
25 ditto	By 25 ell Carsay‡	
	3 Coates	
	1 house	
26 do.	By Joris Davids 12½ ell duffles	49
29 do.	By advis that the bill of Exchang	
	is pind	1866

[   ] hath drawne a bill of Exchange
[   ] hollands as by the bills of Exchanges
[   ] notice, that the same is paid, then
[   ] for the Sume of f 1866:13 bevers, which
[   ] with the ship the James, wherefore I have
[   ] for the said sum

[. . . ending lost . . .]

[25:135]

[AFFIDAVIT OF JANNETIE CORNELIS VAN VOORHOUT CONCERNING
A SUIT BETWEEN SWEER TEUNISSZ VAN VELSEN AND JAN GERRITSZ
VAN MARKEN. TRANSLATION]

Today, this 23rd of June 1676, appeared before me, Adriaen van Ilpendam, notary public, residing in N. Albany, Jannetie Cornelis, wife of
Jacob Schermerhoorn, about 45 years old, who acknowledges to have
testified, as she hereby does, upon the petition of Grietie Rijckmans, wife
of Jacques Cornelisz, without guile or deceit by anyone, but for the
promotion of justice, that it is true and certain that she was in Schanechtade at the house of Jacques Cornelisz during the dispute between Jan
Gerritsz van Marcken and Sweer Teunisz and heard and saw that Sweer
Teunisz and Jan Gerritsz fought with one another and that one lay atop
the other; and to the best of her knowledge could neither see nor notice
anything else except that they were both drunk and that she heard Jan
Gerritsz say, "I am not saying that Harman Vedder was given a phony

---

* The left margin has been trimmed by about one inch, the bottom of the page by an
unknown amount.
‡ kersey: a type of cloth.

conveyance and sent to a village where there were no houses; also, I am not saying that the money for the poor was stolen." Whereupon Sweer Teunisz replied, "Listen to what the scoundrel is saying." Thereupon Douwe Auckes replied, "Whose money is it?" To which the aforesaid Sweer replied, "Mohammed's* money."

In closing this her deposition she is ready (if so requested) to affirm the aforesaid further, and in my presence has signed the original of this with her own hand in Albany on the above date.

After collation this was found to agree with the original (kept by me) in Albany the 23rd of June 1676.
    Which I witness,

Adrian van Ilpendam, notary public.

[ENDORSED:]   Deposition of Jannetie Cornelis
upon the petition of Grietie Rijckman.

[25:136]
[ACCOUNT OF PROVISIONS SUPPLIED THE INDIANS AT ALBANY.
TRANSLATION]‡

6 ditto   To the River Indians who were taken prisoner when Juryen was killed and who escaped from the enemy, 2 3/4 ells of duffels, 1 shirt, 1 pair of stockings; the duffels was mine; by order of Col. Schuilaer. two pounds of gunpowder, two staves of lead.

ditto   To Awans a piece of duffels for his claim that he had

* Spelled *mochomus* in the original.
‡ This document is out of place and is probably from 1696 or 1697. The reference to the Oneida points to a time not long after the burning of their castle by Count de Frontenac in August 1696 at the conclusion of his campaign against the Iroquois Confederacy in King William's War. Peter Schuyler was promoted to colonel between August 1696 and December 1697. The only Mr. Bancker in Albany at that time was Evert who could have ordered the dispensing of supplies during his term as mayor, October 1695–September 1696 (or in some later position of trust). Peter Schuyler contracted in September 1696 to supply the regular soldiers and in October 1698 was called the commissary for the fort: since he was also a senior militia officer he had more than enough authority to dispense supplies to the Indians. The writer of this document was not a native speaker of Dutch and was perhaps French; his spelling renders some words unrecognizable.

on the French woman and her child that she had two yards of my duffels; by order of Col. Schuilaer.

ditto	To Wallansachkes one shirt, one pair of stockings; by order of Col. Schulaer.
6 ditto	To Quaquendaron's son one kettle, one pair of stockings, one knife, two staves of lead; by order of Col. Schuilaer. It was for his father sending him from the Suskihannes[*] River to hear about the situation at our place.
ditto	To Quaquendaron's son upon his departure to the country[‡]; and he also took along two pounds of gunpowder for his father, ditto three staves of lead.
ditto	One pair of stockings.
27 November	Col Schuilaer had two staves of lead drawn from the store nortselwylt,[†] six pounds of gunpowder.
3 ditto	Given to Kanadagereax, Onnederse[+] sachem, for his assistance in urging the Oneida to occupy their castle again in the spring, one quarter pound of paint, one shirt, one hat, one pair of stockings, twelve staves of lead, six pounds of gunpowder from the store, one hatchet
18 ditto	To Towenjouwe and Hendrick who went with the French women to Kanyda, each a shirt, each a hat and kettle from the store by [order of] Mr. Bancker; for three pounds of gunpowder for the expedition to Kanyda; three staves of lead to ditto
18 ditto	To the Indian who was also on firewatch, one knife; To ditto another who was on ditto firewatch, one knife.

[*]   Susquehanna
[‡]   home to his homeland
[†]   Probably an attempt at Dutch *noortsewilt* (i.e., "for the northern Indians").
[+]   Oneida

[25:137]

[POINTS OF LAW SUBMITTED BY COLONEL LEWIS MORRIS]

to the Juris Decktion of the Cort.
to plead in bar to the acktion
to dennie to ought thats Contrary to Laue

Imprimas Query if Cast hear whether an apeall For England be not good.

Iff this be a Cort of Coman ples then we ought to have a Declaration of what we ar somand heare and sued For.

If a Cort of Chansery then a bill of Complaint.
If Cort of admarallity then we should have a Liebill Declarying ouar transgretion.

If any part of the Frait be Due tis all Due.

If thay be a Cort of Chansery thay may Metigat if not then all or Noen is Due.

I had not Lawffull warning as per the Corts of Admarallity. They ar not adbytratars indeffarently Chossen so not bound to stand to thair award

A man connot be Constrained to pay ought to any man but what he is obliged to by promis by word or obligation or som ovart ackt obliging herunto: and in all Caisses ther ought to be quid pro Coe: but in this Nosoch thing.

The Covinants Not per Hermen the consedaration not Due.[*]

[ENDORSED:]   Coll: Morris—
              his paper.

* Perhaps this concerns Harmen Vedder; see 25:153.

[25:138]

[PETITION OF MARTIN GERRITSZ VAN BERGEN FOR A LAND PATENT
AT ALBANY. TRANSLATION][*]

Memorandum for his honor the highly esteemed lord governor general
of Nieuw Jorck for awarding a patent of a parcel of pastureland granted
to me; to wit, beginning from the fort's pasture westward up the hill,
south of the Bever's Kill, along the fence of Cornelis Segersz, northward
above the fall; to wit, into the woods and from the fall north of the Bever's
Kill, eastward to the pasture of Rinselaer.

Albany, the 28th of June
1676.

Marten Gertsen

800—yards long[‡]
500 yards broad

recalled

[ENDORSED:]   A patent past.
Smithfield or
Smithstowne
to bee distinguish't.[†]

[25:139]

[NO DOCUMENT IS LISTED FOR THIS NUMBER IN THE CALENDAR.
ONE ITEM NOW FILED HERE BELONGS WITH JOHN SHAKERLY'S
ACCOUNTS IN VOLUME 29][+]

* A patent was granted November 12, 1677 for 12 morgens and 3 rods of pastureland; see
Patents 4:2:62 in the New York State Archives.
‡ Beginning with this line, the remainder of the document is written in English, in part by
Governor Andros.
† This note by Matthias Nicolls has no bearing on the present document. It may refer to
the Smithtown Patent issued March 25, 1677; see Patents 4:1:128, *loc. cit.*
+ See appendix to the final volume of *The Andros Papers*.

[25:140]

[LETTER FROM HENRY EASTON AT BARBADOS TO JANE RIDER
ABOUT BUSINESS MATTERS AND ABOUT CHARGES AGAINST
JOHN TUDOR]

July 5. 1676.

Deere Maddam beeing now by the providence of god safly arived in
Barbadoes I am now with my faithfull friend Coll. Bate, with whome I
shall continue untill you will bee pleased to make returne to mee of that
which is yet remaining in youre handes: I hope Mr. West and Mr. Sturt
have paide you that eleven shillings and six pence which they promised
to pay when I came awaie in all I conceive it amountes to foure poundes
seventeene shillings and six pence, which I would intreate you to make
returne theere of unto Coll. William Bate at the Bridge toune whoo will
give order to recevit to my use. I suppose the Collonell will wright to my
cosen Leete which makes mee forbare to trouble him at this time bee
pleased to present my sirvis to him and tel him all his freinds heere are
in good health. I pray send no beefe but porke, or flower will doe
resonable well. I am desireed to intreate you to send a rundlot* of
cranburies which will bee received welcume heere.

I pray present my humble sirvis to Mr. Winder with thanke's for his greate
kindnes to mee, remember my love to youre husband and to Mr. Helman:
and tel him that upon inquirie I finde Mr. Tudor had counterfeted the
governors hand, and if I can learne anithing more you shall bee sure to
have an accoumpt of it by the first opportunitie.

I shall not trouble you anie further but expect youre returne by the first
opportunitie, with my prayers to god for youre prosperity espetially in
the thinges that leade to a better life. I rest

from Polly Bates   Your faithfull freind to sirve
at the bridge toune   you
toune   Henry Eston

it is reported heere that Mr. Tuder whoo once lived heere hath plade the
knave with divers people.

if you can procure anie garden seedes as cabbige, lettis, readish: or anie
other: and put them to my accoumpt they will bee verie acceptable heere
for my wantes such thinges.

* rundlet: a keg

[ENDORSED:]   Mr. Eastons Letter.

453
 96
549

[25:141]

[MINUTES OF A MEETING WITH WICKERS CREEK INDIANS WHO
SEEK PAYMENT FOR THE YONKERS PATENT LAND]

July. 25th 1676.

There appeared Claes the [   ]dyan with others before the [   ]ckers-
creeke Indyans etc.) [   ]etend not to bee paid for the Youncke[   ] land.

Mr. Delavall [   ]duces the patent to H. Oneale—and deed from Ely:
Doughty, The Record viewed of th[ ] Indyans acknowledgment to have
r[   ]ed satisfaction, Claes was then on[   ].

The Go: will speake with Mr. D[ ]ughty about it, in a few dayes, when
hee will answer them further.

[ENDORSED:]   Wickerscreeke Indyan
                   appearance.
                   25 July 1676.

[25:142]

[LETTER FROM HENRY EASTON TO JANE RIDER ABOUT JOHN TUDOR]

Deere and loveing cosen, youres of the thirtith of may I have received
and was much rejoysed thereat. Now whereas you desire to heere from
mee by the first opportunitie, I have theerein answered youre expectation; for I have wrighten one letter and sent it by Mr. Knot, wherein I
gave you to under stande that upon inquirie I was informed that John
Tuddor had not only counterfeted the governors hand, but hath allso
cheated divers persons which will more at large appeare when you
speake with Mr. Bisshop, with whome I have had sum discorse: and hee
saide hee had spoken with his master, whoo had promised him to give
him a testimoniall under his owne hand: and the assertion of severall
others whoo will avoach the same which my former letter did informe
you. I pray therefore present my sirvis to Mr. Hellman and let him know
the substance heereof, and that for your sake I will bee readdie to sirve

him, or anie freinde of youres that so I may approove myselfe youre faithfull kinsman.

As to my owne busines I refer you to my former letter only let mee acquaint you that I am with such a freinde whoo is to mee all one as a father, with whome I intende to spende moste of my time untill you make returne to mee of that which remaines in youre handes, and upon recept theere=of I intende to goe for england, wherefor let mee intreate you to bee minde-full of mee. No more at present but my tru love to youre husban, and youre selfe with my daily prayers for youre prosperitie heere, and eternall happines heere after: which is, and ever shall bee the prayer of him whoo is

Barbadoes   youre assured loveing
July 26. 1676.   Kinsman

                                                         Henry Eston

[ADDRESSED:]   HELPD.*
                        to Mrs. Jane Rider
                        liveing in the Stone
                        Streete neere the fort
                        in new Yorke
                        give This.
                        from Barbadoes.

[ENDORSED:]   Mrs. Rider from Mr. Easton
                        about Tuder, from the Barbados.
                        July 5 and 26 1676
                        A tryall with Mr. Helmont

[25:143]

[PASS TO SOME INDIANS FOR LONG ISLAND]

Wickapeag and Wattoweetto and some other Indyans with them to goe to the south of Long Isl. by Gr[ ]send and as farre as the bay to take of th[ ]hells called Clipcunts and to pas and repasse freely comporting themselves as they ought.

                        dated July: 28. 1676.

---

* The reading is very uncertain. It may be HE 4S 2D, which would mean that Henry Easton (HE) paid four shillings two pence (to send the letter?).

signed by the Go:
and deliv[ ]d.

A Passeport to [   ]
                   Indyans
                   July 28. 1676.

[25:144]

[LETTER FROM THE MAGISTRATES OF ALBANY NOMINATING
NEW MAGISTRATES]

                                   Nieu Albany the 21 July 1676

Right Honorable Sir

According to your honors order we have sent doun the names of four
men Whom we Conceive are fitt to be Magistrates, and desires your
honor to Nominate and choyce some or all of them as your honor shall
think Convenient. There names are as follows

          Andries Teller
          Dirk Wessells
          Cornelis Van Dyck
          Marte Crigyer

This is all at Present wishing your honor all helth and happiness, doe
Remain

                         Your humble Servants
as for the Commissaries   The Commissaries off albany
of the Colony Renselaers-
wyck dom. Renselaer,   Adriaen Gerretsen
doth send there names
doun to your honor herein
Inclosed.

[ADDRESSED:]   To The Right Honorable Major
                   Edmund Andross Esqr. Governor
                   Generall off all his Royall
                   highness Territories in America
                   at Fort James—

[ENDORSED:]   Albany.
                     July 21th 1676.
                     Commissaryes nominated.

[25:145]
     [LETTER FROM NICOLAES VAN RENSSELAER NOMINATING
                     MAGISTRATES]

                                        N Albany 22 July 1676

Much Honoured Sir

Whereas the Commissaries, upon tuesday Last made a nomination of
new Persons to be magistrates in Lieu of those that shall go off, i have
Chosen Teunis Spitsenbergh and juriaen Theunissen, for to bee, Com-
messaries for the ensuing year, humbly desiring your Honours
approbation, to the end, that the aforesaid Persons, in its time may take
place in the bench jan Thomassen, is to remaine, but i should think it
fitter, and more serviceable, that either marten Gerritsen, or Pieter winne
schould remaine, being Jan Thomas is an ancient man i have several
times spoken of it but they complaine, and protest very much against a
Longer Continuation, and told me it would be their ruine and they would
rather Leave their farmes, but i shall exspect your honours, wise advise
about it all things are here in Peace, the boores* are very bussie, in
gathering in their Corn, and i hope it will proove a good harvest, if the
Lord Please to blesse us with the Continuance of peace and quietnesse i
shall take Care for your Honours wheat, and if here is anything further
of your Honours service pray Sir Command but and as much as Layes
in my hand, shall be contributed thereunto, i shall add no more for this
present but that i remaine as i am

Sir Pray remember my   Sir
respect to my Lady the   Your Honours Dutyfull
governesse, and Mrs. Francis   and Humble Servant

                                   Nicolaus van Rensselaer

[ADDRESSED:]   For the Right Honoura[   ]
                     Edmond Andros Esquire Governour
                     generall of N yorck and albany
                     At Fort James.

* Dutch *boeren*, "farmers."

[ENDORSED:]   Do. Renslaer
Alb: July 22.1676.

[25:146–48]

[NO DOCUMENTS ARE LISTED FOR THESE NUMBERS IN THE
CALENDAR. THREE ITEMS NOW FILED HERE BELONG WITH
JOHN SHAKERLY'S ACCOUNTS IN VOLUME 29]*

[25:149]

[PETITION OF SCHENECTADY MAGISTRATE SWEER TEUNISSEN
APPEALING REMOVAL FROM OFFICE]

To the Right Honorable Major Edmund Andross Esquire Governor
Generall of all his Royall Hignes his Territories in America

The humble peticion of Sweer Thuneson

Sheweth

That your Honors peticioner Commenced his suite against John Garrett-
son=for reparatione of his good Name etc. at a Court held at Albaney on
the sixth of May last Where the Jury found=(That your peticioner had
taken noe good Oath) The Court approved the oppinione of the Jury; and
concluded he had taken a false Oath. And declared him uncapable, of
discharging the office of a Commessary from which hard Sentence your
honors peticioner Appealed to New Yorke.

Therefore most humbly prays=that your Honor will bee
pleased to grant his Appeale; And a hearing of the whole
matter before your Honor and Honorable Councell=Or att
the next Gennerall Assizes as your honor seemeth meet and
that an order may Issue forth for the appearance of the said
John: Garrettson to answere your petioner etc. he performing as the Law in such Cases require: And he shall

pray etc.

Sweer theonussen

* See appendix to the final volume of *The Andros Papers*.

The peticioner hath entred unto a Recognizance of fifty pounds to appeare and make good his allegacions against John Gerritson, before the Governor and Councell on Thursday next the 27th Inst. in the forenoone: Dated the 24th July 1676.

Matthias Nicolls.[*]

[ENDORSED:]   The peticion of Sweer Teunissen
for an Appeale.

An Order to bee heard by the Go:
July. 27. 1676.

Remitted to Aug: 4th.

The deft. to have Copyes
They were given.

[25:150]

[SUMMONS FOR JAN GERRITSZ VAN MARCKEN AT FLATBUSH TO
ANSWER THE COMPLAINT OF SWEER TEUNISSEN]

These are in his Majesties name to require you John Garretson van Marcken to make your personall appearance before the Governor and his Councell on Thursday next before Noone being the 27th instant, to make answer to what shall then and there bee alleadged against you by Sweer Teunissen of Schanechtade, upon account of some difference heretofore tryed betweene you at a Court at Albany from the which hee hath appealed: Hereof you are not to fayle at your perill, Dated in N.Y. this 24th day of July 1676.

To the Constable of Flattbush who
is to cause this warrant to bee
serv'd etc. Returne thereof made
at the time prefix't.

[ENDORSED:]   Copie of warrant sent to
John Garretsen Van Marcken.

---

* The preceding note is in Nicolls's handwriting.

[25:151]

[ORDER TO TRANSMIT THE PAPERS RELATING TO THE ABOVE SUIT]

To a Generall Court: houlden by his Majesties authority upon the 20th of June, at albany: in the 27 jare of aer Sover-aing Lord: Charles the Second King of Great Brittaine france and Yerland, Defender of the faith Annoque Dom: 1676.

Sweer Teunissen Plaint:
        Contra
Jan Gerritsen van Marken Defnd:

it is ordred that all the papers of Sweer Teunisen and Jan Gerrisen Van Marken in Cause of appeall of Injurie shall be send downe to New Yorke, within the time of 14 Dayes shall then be Examined: with the parties and that for reasons that the Defendant is absent

Agreed with the Origenell
in wittnesse of me

Ro: Levingston Secret.

[ENDORSED:]   sentense of the 20 of June 1676
                out of the register of Albany.

                Order of Court att Albany
                to be heard att Yorke.

[25:152]

[DECLARATION OF JAN GERRITSZ VAN MARCKEN IN
THE ABOVE SUIT]

Extract.

Translated out of   Out off the Records off
the dutch Originall   Albany the 2d may 1676.

Jan Gerritse doth declare before the Bench that Sweer Theunise now for the Present Commissary off Shinnechtady, hath sworne a false oath, which shall appear upon the Records off Skinechtady, namely thus, that the foresaid Sweer hath sworn that Van Marken should have said, that harme Vedder hath given forth a false Oath; and desired that this might be Recorded

By order off the Court

Ro: Livingston
Secr.

[ENDORSED:]   Judgement
of the Court
2d May 1676
N.A.*
N. 4

[25:153]

[COURT MINUTES OF THE ABOVE SUIT]‡

Att Ane Court hold in Albany the 6th May 1676.

Sweer Tunesen Commissary of Skhenechtady
against
John Garetsen van Marken deffendant

The Plentiff demands of the deffendant reparation of Honor, or good name, by resone that hee did slander him before the Court, m[   ]lling him a perjured persone as is extent upon the Records and sheweth the Interogoter Wherupon he as deffender relayeth Extant out of the records of Skhenechtady the 27th of September 1675.

Ro: Livingston Secr.

Interagatory for to demand rightlie or justly Sueer Tunesen Commissary, Douwe Aukes, and Geritie Harmans, that wchich they did hear at the house of Jacqwes Corneleisen, upon tuesday, being the 21th of September, and to give thar oathes of the varectie of the same.

---

* New Albany
‡ Another translation of the original prepared by A. J. F. Van Laer can be found in the *Minutes of the Court of Albany, Rensselaerswyck and Schenectady*, 2:99–105.

Sueer Tunesen Answered not to have hard the same. Douwe Aukes to have hard the same and that Markin did most Vilanouslie break foorth, with words, and that amongest the rest said I will say what I know, and not Know.

Gritie Harmans Ansuers, not to have hard the same.

Sweer Tuesen van Velsin ansuereth that he did, hear of fyve beawer which John Garetsen was speaking off bot nothing of the person.

Douwe Aukess anssuereth to have hard van Merkin speak of beawers bot not Knowing whom he named only that he said, I will not say thet the beawers are changed.

Gretie Harmans Ansuereth that van Marken did say that the Fyve beawers are stolen.

Sueer Tunesen Ansuers that he hard the same bot not knowing whither he meaned Sanders Landertse or his wyff.

Douwe Aukes Ansuers that van Marken said, I doe not say that the poore money is stollen.

First whether yea Sueer Tunesen was not present on the day afore-said at the house of Jaqwes Van Cornelisen, wher John Garete van marken was who brust out, vorie vilanouslie, with all passionat expressiones saying, I will say what I think and not think.

Secondlie whether yea did not hear that van merken said, I will not say that Sanders or his wyff hath stollen the fyve Beawer.

Thridlie whither yea did not hear van Mirken say, that Sanders Lendertse haith stollen the poore money.

Geertie Harmans Ansuereth that van marken said I doe not say that the poore money is stolen, wherwpon Douwe Aukes asketh whom doeth that concern, sueer Tunesen Ansuereth, tharwpon, that it Concernes Machoumus, and I will tell him, Douwe beare Witnese.

Sueer Tunesen ansuereth yes Douwe Aukes ansuers that he did hear somthing spoke of ane false obligacion, or leter, and that van Marken spoke lykwayes, of Harme Vedder.

Greitie Harmon Ansuers that van Marken said, I will not say that thar is ane false transport, given to Harme Vedder, showen upon a dorp or village, wher thar is no houses.

Sweer Tunesen Ansuers that he said therewpon, how that rogue who did sitt president at that tym, and therewpon req- wyred to witnese, Douwe Aukes and Janakye Shermer- horn sitting nixit him.

Douwe Aukes anssuereth that he did not hear of the false sentance; bot that Sueer Tunesen said unto him, hew what that Rogue sayeth beare witnese of it Greitie Harmone Ansuereth, that she did not hear the same.

Sueer Tunisen Ansuereth that he did heare the same bot others can give you better tes- timonie seeing that it is his wyff.

Fourthly whether yea did not heare van Marken say I will not say that Herme Vedder haith recawed ane false obligation, or morgage from Sanders Leen- derts.

Fyftly Whither yea did not hear that van Marken said I will not say that Herme Vedder haith given foorth ane false sentance.

Sixthly whether you did not heare van Marken say to your wyff she being in the yeard and he befor Jacqwes Cornelisens door these words, I say nothing of the Racoan Coat.

The Interagotoryes the deponents have declaryed Wpon oth

Aggreith with the Records by me
sec subscribitur*

Ludivicus Cobes Sectry.

The Plentiff desyreth that Adrian Appell may bring foorth the aggreiment which was depositat in his hands, togedder, with Peiter Masson, of the deat the 7 September 1675 which containeth as folloueth, that the Deffendant did confesse from his heart, to have wronged the Commissaryes of Shennechtady in some Caises giving by these a declaration wnder his hand befor witnesis that they are all honest peopell in Generall and in particular.

Therefore the plantiff concludes that the deffendant is a rogue, by resone of the Injurys done to ther Court, For which they compleand to the Leat‡ Commander Brokholes. And therefter he put of his Visorn, and sent good Men, unto them as is mentioned herebefor, Never the lesse the Plentiff desyrethe to be purged; and refereth himself to the abowewritten Interragotorys, and that the Deffendant may be punished lyk ane rogue and Infamous person to be ane example wnto all others. Cum expenssis

The deffendant desyreth, that Greitie Harma[   ] may heir the Interragotorys read, wchich was granted, bot shee knew nothing else bot what she Ansuered to the abow written, Inte[   ]gatorys, only that they wer drunck and qwarel[   ]

The deffendant bringeth in two Attestationes, who declareth that at Sturum Vanderzee house, he did slander the Plantiff by Calling him severall tymes ane perjured persone and said he wold make it good, and reqwyre[ ] the Plantiff to tak witness tharwpon, which he did not doe bot was silent.

The abowwritten Process is refered to a jurie of tuelve Men, who haith taken thar othes to give their true Verdict therewpon viz:

Gerrit Swart	Jan Blyker	Ary van Ilpendam
Marten Crigeir	Jacob Shermerhoorn	Jan Hend: Bruyer
Dirick Weeselsen	Willem Tiller	Johannes Provoost
Cornelius van Dyck	Jan Verbeck	Hendric Cuyler

*   A misspelling for Latin *sic subscribitur*: thus it was signed.
‡   lieutenant

The Jurie Men having pondered and seriously considdered the Cause, doe give in ther Verdict, that no, Man can be Interogat in his oun Cause, much lese to sueer, and as to the aggreiment which the Plantiff doeth ground himself wpon can not serve in this Cause.

Seeing that they doe find that the Interragatory doeth stryve against itself, and plaine evidences of a fault, A Civill Moderation may be brock the More becaus the deffendant declareth that he did not know off that othe; In the thrid Article of the forsaid Interragotorye wher he sayeth to have heard the same bot not knowing whither he meanet Sanders Glen, or his wyff; and Efterwards by the declaration of Greitie Harmans Wherupon Douwe Aukes Ansuered how doe yea mean by that, Sueer Tunesen ansuered that he meaneth Machomus, and that he did mean it, he can not Swear that he heard it, and per contrary if he heath hard it, he can not suear that he meanet it. Ergo false, what concerneth the 5th Article wherin is demanded of van Marken whither he did not say that Herme Vadder did give foorth ane false sentance, whereupon Sueer Tunesen said, hear that rogue, and requyred Douwe Aukesse and Janetky Shermerhoorn to be wittnes, who declareth, that they did not hear of the land; that van Merken haith said off the false sentance, bot that Sueer Tunesen said wnto him hear what that rogue sayeth, Concluding therfor, that A partie can not be taken for a wittnese, much lesse in the Matter of slander, being in such a Maner against his partie bot contrarie the other Attestators Douwe Aukese and Janakie Shermerhoorn most be beliveid; soo it is that the Jurye out of the third and fift Article of the Interagatory Togidder with the Laufull attestion of Janaky Shermerhoorn, and the declarationes of Douwe Aukess and Greitie Ryckmans.

Wee Conclude that the plantiff Sueer Tunesen haveing suorn the forsaid Interagatory haith taken no good othe.

The Court having heard both partys and taken the Cause into serious deliberation, doe Approve in all Respects the oppinion of the Jurye, Men, Therfor doe conclude that the Plentiff Sueer Tunessen hath taken ane false oath and doe declare him Incapabille and Unable to discharge the place of bein a Commissary at Schennechtady which he hath bein heither, and Condemes him in all the charges of this process.

Aggreith with the Records

In Knouledge of me.

Sic Subscribitur
Rob: Livingston Secr.

Translated per me
Ro: Livingston
Secr.

[ENDORSED:]   Judgement
of the Court
6 Mey 1676
N: D.
No: 2

[25:154]

[THOMAS DELAVALL'S ACCOUNT WITH DANIEL DE HONDECOUTRE.
TRANSLATION]

<u>1670</u>   *Credit*

                                        Tobacco Seawant Beavers

		Tobacco	Seawant	Beavers
18 January	By Isaacq Bedtloo		1280	
8 March	By tobacco	1072		
11 do.	By tobacco	410		
21 May	By tobacco	318		
26 do.	By tobacco	531		
1 June	By tobacco	1826		
3 do.	By tobacco	277		

<u>1671</u>

10 April	By Tobacco	1202		
23 November	By beavers received through Van Cliff as well as by a promissary note			2526:17

	Tobacco	Seawant	Beavers
lb.	5636	ƒ1280	ƒ2526:17
Receivable to close this	2595 3/4	568:10	4768: 3
lb.	8231 3/4	1848:10	7295:

Done in Albany, 10 Aug. 1673.

Your humble servant, Daniel de Hondecoutre.

Debit   Capt. Thomas DeLavall

                                Tobacco   Seawant Beavers
To balance of account from other side

                                2595³/4 568:10   4768:3

1674
22 May, to Joris Davitsz for freight
        earned by your honor's order . . .   144—
                                                                4912:3

Credit   Tobacco Seawant Beavers

1674
14 June   by [*illegible*] 50 beavers   424
               by 7 elk skins   78¹/2
               by 5 otters   30
25 th   by 25 ells kersey
                  3 coats
               by one house
26th   by Joris Davits for 12 ¹/2 ells duffels   41
29 June 1679   received information that the bill of
                  exchange has been paid   1866:13

Note: 23 Nov. 1671, Capt. DeLavall executed a bill of exchange for the
sum of 1866:13 in beavers or 1400 *Hollants* as appear by the bills of
exchange and when word is received that it has been paid, then Capt.
DeLavall must be credited for the aforesaid sum of f1866:13 in beavers,
which we have now received on the 29th of June 1674 with the ship *St.
James* and therefore credit him accordingly above this.

[NOTE:]*   In Albany 16 June 1676, Capt. DeLavall submitted
                  the same account; a copy thereof.

1669   Mr. Thomas DeLavall   Debit

                                    tobacco seawant beavers

18 October   To diverse goods in tobacco 5741 lb.
9 November   To 32 blankets at 40 guilders
                  sewant each   1280

* This note directly follows the preceding note.

1670

13 June	To one blanket	40
do.	To 184$^1/_2$ els duffel	
	13$^1/_2$ lb. tobacco, totals	2490 $^3/_4$

1671

13 June	To 302 planks 35 stivers		
	seawant each	528:10	
do.	To diverse goods, duffels		
	as well as blankets, according		
	to submitted account in beavers	ƒ4451	
23 November	To 215 blankets and 7 lengths of		
	duffel, altogether in beavers	2844	
	lb. 8231 $^3/_4$ ƒ1848:10 ƒ7295		

errors excepted Tho. DeLavall

[25:155a]

[TRIAL BY A SPECIAL COURT OF ALBERT HENDRICKS FOR
LIBELING THE KING]

At a Meeting in the State house,
July. 29. 1676. by order of the Go.

Present

Brockholes ⎫		Mr. De Meyer Dep. M.
Dyre ⎬ of the Councell		Mr. Minvielle
Nicolls ⎭		Mr. V: Cortlandt
		Alder[ ]

Dr. Hartman Wessells, being examined saith, that hee heard Albert
Hendricksz (who came here with Mr. Peter Bayard, about the midle of
June) say, tha[ ] there would come ships here in short time from Holl: to
take this place, this hee heard him say at severall times both drunke and
sober; whereupon the said Hartman advised not to talke afte[ ] that
manner, yet the other persisted th[   ]in; Hee said moreover (being sober)
that the King was dead, and that ther[ ] had beene Roguery done, either
by the K: or to that purpose.

Part of this was spoken at Andries Rees where hee lodges. The like at
[   ] Mathews; and at Long Isl:[*] That at Andries Rees was in
his p[   ] who declares this.

Other Testimonies there are.

Albert Hendricksen being brought out of the prison, pretends Ignorance,
and that hee was drunke, but was sorry if hee spake any such things and
other foolish Excuses.

It is the unanimous opinion of all, That the said Albert is guilty of what
is layd to his Charge, and do condemne him to pay th[ ] summe of five
pounds and charges or 200G of[‡] Imprisonment or receiv[ ] 39 stripes.

[ENDORSED:]   At a Meeting [   ]
                   the State House.
                   July. 29th 1676.

                   About Albert Hendricksz
                   that reported severall idle
                   storyes etc.

                   By order of the Governor.

[25:155b]

[MEMORANDUM BY MATTHIAS NICOLLS OF ITEMS TO BE DISCUSSED
    BY COUNCIL MEMBERS AND MAGISTRATES]

              X   To call Albert the prisoner and dispa[   ]

Time   X   About Shooemakers and Tanners.

              X   About butchers slaughter[ ]buth to b[   ] of Towne.

C. Delavall   To thinke of some fitt persons to ag[   ]
Mr. John Laur: with workemen and to supervize the making
Mr. Ol: Stevens   of the Mole for the Harbor
Mr. Fredr. Phil.
Mr. V: Brugh.   The Officers of Militia to take turnes.
Mr. Steenwyck

---

* This is probably the island in the Hudson near Albany.
‡ Probably "or" was intended.

P. Stouten= X The Magistrates to appoint a Towne Treasurer.
berg.

> Referr'd by the Governor for C. Dyre, C. Brockholes and
> myselfe to meete the Magistrates of the Towne about the
> above matters.

[25:156a]

[PROCLAMATION AFFIRMING THE ACQUITTAL OF SAMUEL
GAINPAINE]

> At a Court of Assizes held in the City of N.Y. beginning on
> Wednesday the 6th day of Oct. 1675 and ending [*blank*].

Samuell Gainpaine, having beene formerly acquitted by a Coroners Jury
of Enquest for the casuall death of Laurence Robinson, was upon the last
day of the Court of Assizes cleared by Proclamacion.

> By order of the Generall
> Court of Assizes.

July 29. 1676—   sent the Law booke that came from Boston of Mr.
Wharton, to Michael Siston.

[26:156b]

[NOMINATION OF MAGISTRATES FOR SCHENECTADY. TRANSLATION]

> Schaenhechtede, the 31st of July 1676

Right Honorable Lord General

Pursuant to your honor's order and customary practice we have made
nominations and cannot find more than six suitable persons for the
administration of the magistrates' office. We hope that this will not
displease your honor and that he will be pleased to effect election from
them. The persons are:

X Theunis Cornelissen Swart
X Daniel Janssen
   Claes van Petten
   Pieter Jacobssen Borsboom

Adam Vromans
Johannes Pootman

Those who are leaving:

    Alexander Glen
X Sweer Theunissen
X Herman Vedder
    Jan van Eps

In closing we commend your honor to the merciful protection of Almighty God, and we remain,

> Your honor's
> devoted and humble
> friends and servants,
> the magistrates of Schanecht.
> Jan van Eps
>
> By order of the same,
> Ludovicus Cobes, secretary.

[ADDRESSED:]   To the Right Honorable
Lord, My Lord Major
Etmont Andross governor
general of N. Jorcke,
on behalf of His Royal Highness,
James, over all his territories
in America. Fort James,
N. Yorck.

[ENDORSED:]   Schanechtada
July 31, 1676.

[25:157]

[NO CALENDAR ENTRY OR DOCUMENT APPEARS FOR 25:157]

[25:158]

[TERMS FOR A SALE AT AUCTION BY GERRIT VAN SLICHTENHORST TO HENDRICK KOSTER VAN AECKEN OF PROPERTY AT ALBANY. TRANSLATION]

Conditions and stipulations by which Mr. Gerrit van Slichtenhorst intends to sell at public auction to the highest bidder both his houses and his lots located in Albany; to wit: the house in which he is living and the one situated near the gate by the plain. Each shall be auctioned off and sold separately.

The buyer or buyers, whether they be one or two, shall be consigned the aforesaid houses and lots, unrestricted free and unencumbered, on the first of May 1677, except for the Lord's right; and that it is in length and width as follows: The large house and kitchen or the place where he presently resides is in length on the north seven rods, on the south at the street also seven rods; in width, on the east two rods and four feet, on the west two rods and five feet. The house near the gate by the plain, including the ground upon which the house stands: the lot is in length on the south nine rods and eight feet, on the north along Adriaen Gerritsz's lot ten rods; in width on the east [   ]* feet, on the west as wide as the house, with an alley on the south side of the house of two and a half feet Rhineland measure.

Payment shall be made, for the one as for the other, in equal installments in good, whole, merchantable beaver skins at ƒ8 a piece; to wit: the first on the first of June 1677—the true half of the promised sale price—and the second payment being the other half on the first of June 1678, punctually and without any delay.

The buyers shall furnish for the sale price two suitable sureties, jointly and severally as principals, to the satisfaction of the auction master.

If the buyers or buyer cannot furnish the aforesaid sureties within the appointed time, then the house and lot which has been purchased shall be auctioned and sold again at his charge and expense; whatever less it brings he shall be obligated to compensate for, whatever more he shall not realize as a profit.

The fees are to be charged to the buyer in payments as aforesaid. The last of August 1676 in Albany.

Hendrick Koster remained the buyer of the house near the gate by the plain for the sum of six hundred guilders, and Gerrit Goossens and Sijbrant Goossens van Schaick presented themselves as sureties and principals according to the aforesaid conditions. Done in Albany the last

---

* The document is damaged at this point. The deed to Slichtenhorst from the city magistrates, dated May 27, 1675, gives the width on the east as six feet (*ERA* 1:116–17).

of August 1676. Was signed: Hendrick Koster, Gerrit Van Schayck, Sijbrant Goossens van Schaick.

Agrees with the auction book,
to which I attest,

Johannes Provoost, auction master

[25:159]

[WARRANT FOR THE SEIZURE OF PROPERTY AND ARREST OF
THOMAS DAVIES AT FLUSHING]

Jameca Sessions

Whereas att a Courte of Sesions held att Jameca in the North rideing of yorkeshere on Long Iland the 19th day of June last past Wm. Sydenham Attorney unto John Robinson obtained a Judgement against Thomas Davies of Flushing on the said Island for the sume of twelve pounds payabell in good wheate nett Tabacco or Porke at price Currant with Costs of sute as by the records of the said Courte appeareth these are tharefor in his Majesties name to Charge and Command you That you seize levey and Distrayne soe Much of the Goods and Chattells of the said Thomas Davies as will amount to and sattisfy the said sume of twelve pounds in Manner aforsaid and two pounds tenn shillings Costs of sute together with the Incedentall Charges allowed of by the law of this Goverment occasoned by the service of this Excecution And for want thereof to take the bodey of hime the said Thomas Davies and Commit hime to the Custodey of the shreefe and Make retorne to the secr. Office of the due Excecucion heareof within fifteene days after the date heareof faile not att youre Perell Given under my hand this 3d day of Augut 1676 Anno Reg: Cs.* Carl. 2d xxviijo.

Matthias Nicolls

To the Constable of Flushing.

[ENDORSED:]   Execucion ag. Thomas Davis
of Flushing.
1676.

---

* This is an error by the clerk; "Rs." (regis) was intended. The entire phrase means "In the 28th year of the reign of King Charles."

[25:160]
[LIST OF DOCUMENTS IN THE SUIT BETWEEN SWEER TEUNISSEN
AND JAN GERRITSZ VAN MARKEN]

The Judgment of Court and Proceeding in Dutch.

An extract out of the Prothocall in dutch wherein Jan Gerritze declares
that Sweer Teunissen hath taken a false oath.

An agreement of the matter in English.

An attestation of 2 Persons in Engl. Isack de Truce and Jan
Pietersz Meable.

Another Attestacion in Engl. for 3 persons vizt. Joris Aertsz, Elyas
Gyseling and Gysbert Gerritsz.

Sweer Teunissen desires liberty to sell some small matters of merchandize at Schanechtade to the Christians, and not to the Indyans.
Not Granted.

[ENDORSED:]   Papers d. Sweer
               Teunissen.
               Aug. 19. 1676.

[25:161a]

[NOTE ABOUT A CASE ON APPEAL FROM THE WHOREKILL]

Aug. 10. 1676

The Go: granted, that onely the plt. Henry Smith, John Avery the
President and Foreman of the Jury to appeare at the Assizes.

[25:161b]

[PETITION OF PETER GROENENDYCK, APPEALING A JUDGMENT
AT THE WHOREKILL]

To the Rigt Honorable mayor Edmund Andros Governor Generall
of all his Royall highnis terrytoris In amereca.

the humbl. Petition of Peter Groendyk

In all humbl. maners

Sheweth that your Petitioner was sued at a Court held at the Whorkill the 14th of march anno 1675/6 for 3540 £ of tob. at the suitel of henry Smith but so it is that the Just debt due to the said Smith your Petitioner had Paid unto Jhon Storey his Attorny Whoe Was then President of the said Court: lang before the said Smith Was Commenced: for Which your Petitioner hath his discharges in full may Please your honor the Jury and President upon forther Consideration hath owned their procedingh therupon Erronious all Which your Petitioner can Proeve.

Therfor humbl. Prease your honor to grant your Petitioner a Review of the said action at the Whorkill at the second Court ther to dellawer bay as your honor seemeth meet.

And he as in duty bound shall Pray

Pieter Groenendyck

[ENDORSED:]   Peter Groenendykes request.

The persons are to appeare
at the Assizes. Aug 10. 1676.

[25:162a]

[SUMMONS TO (ENGELTIE PIETERS?) AND WILLIAM FISHER OF
ESOPUS TO APPEAR AT THE ASSIZES]*

These are in his Majesties name to require [*blank*] and William Fisher, of Esopus, that they make their appearance at the next Generall Court of Assizes to bee held in this City to make answer to the Complaint of Anne the wife of William Nottingham of the same place upon account of Battery and slander, of the which they are not to fayle at their perills Dated in N.Y. this 18th day of Aug 1676

By order of the Gov.

M. N. Sec.

---

* At a court of sessions held at Kingston April 26, 1676, Engeltie Pieters was convicted of having threatened and beaten Anna Nottingham and was ordered to pay the plaintiff ƒ60. On the same date in a separate case Mrs. Nottingham sued William Fisher for calling her a cheat; after hearing various claims and counterclaims the court granted the plaintiff a stay. The suit is mentioned neither at the next sessions, nor at the assizes.

To Mr. Geo: Hall Sheriffe
at Esopus, who is to make service and returne hereof

[ENDORSED:]　　　A warrant of sundry to the Esopus.
　　　　　　　　To the Assizes October 3d. 1676.
　　　　　　　　Aug 18. 1676.

[25:162b]

[MINUTES OF A MEETING WITH SEVERAL MOHAWK REPORTING ON
A CONVERSATION WITH THE GOVERNOR OF CANADA]

At a meeting in the Fort before the Governor and Councell of some
Maqu[　　　　　] sachems vizt Coniaco and deha[　] of [　　　　]
[　　　] Cast[　　　] Aug [　　]76.

Cornelys Arnout
Interpreter.

Coniaco sa[　　　]hat he[　　　]me downe to the Go: [　] having
[　]ard st[　　]lle 10x* above.

The Inter-　　That an Indyan now present by name Tayandorab
preters name　hath beene at Canada, where the Go: there told him
was Oqueeto　 by his Interpreter that the Gov: of N.Y. was not right
in french,　　and then when hee had writte to him a letter when
major Le Mon. the warr was done with the North Indyans hee[　　]
　　　　　　[　　]the Maques and deft not‡ the[　　　　　]

That the [　　　] unusuall presents given them was
[　　] blind them.

That if s[　　　　] 12 of [　]s the name with the
North Indyans [　　　　　　]future upon them
beefore now.

That they shall have anoth[　] great present given
them yet before they bee destroyed.

That the Go: of Canada gave Cananondage son of the said Castle a[　]
packet of lettres which hee was to deliver with his but knowes not [　]

* This may not be an "X" at all. Matthias Nicolls's rough notes are barely decipherable
when the text is complete, but in this document rodents have made the task insuperable.
‡ destrot? defttnet?

him they were whether for the [   ] or Jes[   ] or who else—the
[   ] Indy[   ] gone with a party of 20 more to the [   ]ard to
fight, and is not come home.

[   ] thi[   ] left them some dayes [   ] have [   ] part of the
way with [   ] and ha[   ] some letters from Jesu[   ] Canada, to the
Jesuite abov[   ]

That the Go: of Canada was to coming with 1000 men to Cataraguy and
had 3 Indyans with them, which hee intends to send out one of the
Maques, another of the Onondagues, another of the Huwerons which hee
intended to send to the [   ] Nations to come to him, other[   ] that
[   ] will fall upon them[   ]had th[   ]ein to give memory to
the Ma[   ]hat they should not refuse or d[   ]heir comming when
he shoul[   ]d It.

T[ ]e furt[   ]le him, that the [   ]ekes had so misbehaved the en[   ]
to the Jesuites, of which hee had two letters from them and doubted it
yet a lie so was now resolved to goe and destroy them said Sinnekes and
Cayukes.

That the Sinnekes were upon the way to Alb: where heering the Rumours
and newes returned back, [   ]d to the Onondagues
and Hu[   ] presents of [   ]hat they [   ]
the[   ] Cause, therefore w[   ]end themselves as well
as they [   ] and they might doe as they please.

That heering th[ ] wens[   ] Maques land the Go: did very mu[   ]
[   ] them that Curler should prove so to [   ] who they tooke to
bee all one there heart and that Conaico said he could not believe it, but
would come and see, which they approved of whereupon hee is now
come in the beheste of all the 4 Castles, and therefore desires to know if
there bee any the[ ] of sep[ ]icion which for h[   ]
net Credit.

That Hee do [   ] the [   ]ll, that the Go: is Curler
was who never did [   ]ve them. Conaico saith [   ] no b[ ] was
so concerned to [   ] those rep[ ]ts as hee was. and therefore under
to[   ] voyage to know the truth of it. [   ] ashamed to
thinke of such reports and thinke the Go: to bee to se[   ] and gives
a band of sewant on behalfe of the Maques.

The Go: tells them, It is a wonder the Go: of Canada should talke of

things of so great Import to a private Indyan, [   ] sachem, and the
more it being [   ]

[   ] Go: int[   ]end up Answer[   ] writing [   ]
shew that his heart is good, and is [   ] read to them here first.

The marke of
Tayandoras

In acknowledgment of the
Truth of what hee hath related.

Canjegkoo hath a blancket given him, and the other sachem, and other
two Indyans, which were all that were Present each, a Case of Duffells.

[ENDORSED:]   At a Councell
                   etc. Aug. 10. 1676.
                   the Maques
                   Sachem etc.

[25:163]

[PETITION OF ABRAHAM CORBETT FOR A DISTILLERY LICENSE]

To the right honorable the Governor of New Yorke and other his
Royall Highnes the duke of Yorke his Teritories in America etc.

The peticion of Abraham Corbett late of Shipscott and now
resident in New Yorke aforesaid.

Humbly sheweth that whereas your peticioner lately lyeing to the
Eastward parte of New England; about seaven Weekes since; he and all
other his neighbours were enforced by the Barbarous and cruell Heathen
to Fly for their lives and to leave a[ ] their habitations and Estates, both
Reall and Personall to the burning and spoyle of the furious Enemy;
insomuch tha now your peticioner is destitue of all meanes to releive
himselfe, wife and Fowre children; and haveing sinc[ ] that unhappy
stroake, had a great desire to come to this place; to live under your honors
proteccion; and where the Rubricke of the Church of England is soe
settled and Established; under which hee was brought Upp; and being
very unwilling to presse or intrude upon your honors Clemency and
goodnesse for releeife:

Humbly desires and intreates; that your honor be pleased to consider his sad Condicion: and to give him a licence to distill strong Liquors; unto which trade and profession he served to obtaine, not doubting; but that by your honors gratious favor towards him, in granting this his request: in some few yeares, hee may by Gods blessing upon his endeavor, be raised to live comfortably, and Credibly, amongst thes people, as formerly hee hath done elsewhere; and upon grant of your honors licence as aforesaid; shall and will bind and oblige himselfe in any summe your honor please to impose upon him, that he shall not, nor will not; work distill nor Convert, any Corne or Grayne whatsoever into Spiritts; but upon the first Conviccion, shall willingly undergoe; any fine or punishment, as your honor shall inflict upon him; the granting of this his request, will more deepely Engage him to pray, for your honors hapines in this life, and eternall happines in the life to come

Abra: Corbett

[ENDORSED:]   3 September 1676.
Mr. Abraham Corbets
petition of shipscots
river Eastward.
Graunted.

Abr: Corbetts
peticion
Sept: 3d: 1676.

[25:164]

Persons for land in harlem bonds given in by the Constable and overseers as free persons the 4th of September 1676.

Conrad Hendrickson
Jean Hendricksen
Jean Naegell
Arent Harmensen
Jean lameter
Lourence Jeanson
X Cornelis Jansen
Niclas de vou
David de mares
Samuell de mares

Adolf mayer
frederick devou
barne Waldron
Jean Dickman Constable
Resolve Waldron
Jose van Oblines
Jeon Loe
Peeter oblines
John bignoux
Daniell Clarck

[ENDORSED:]   Persons for land in Harlem bounds by the Go: order
Sept. 1676.

[25:165]

At a Meeting of the Southton Indyan sachems.
Sept. 15th 1676.

The Go: gave the two sachems each a Coate, and thankt them for their Visitt, recommending a good Correspondence between them and the Constable etc.

The Go: hath promis't to write that they shall have their Armes delivered.

Tackpousha and other Indyans with them.

[ENDORSED:]   At a meeting of Southton
Indyans etc. Sept. 15. 1676.
Easthampton Indyans came
here Sept. 19th 1676.

[25:166]

[LETTER FROM THE GOVERNOR TO OFFICIALS AT ALBANY CONCERNING CHARGES BROUGHT BY JACOB LEISLER AND JACOB MILBOURN AGAINST DOMINE NICHOLAES VAN RENSSELAER][*]

Gentlemen

I have receav'd aplicacion, and seen the order of the Court in a diference

* Van Rensselaer was accused of heterodox theology. The present rough draft is in Gov. Andros's handwriting.

betweene Mr. Jacob Leisler and Jacob Milborn whou accuse D. Reinslaer
for words in a sermon preached by him the 13th past and the said D:
demanding reparation on them for the same and have also by letters and
aplication from both partys heard much of said mater, by which the great
distraction itt hath acasioned in your parts, which I think you might in a
great measure if not whole have remedied and brought it to a fitting isue
on the place or Colmely sent itt hiere, I Canott tell you howe sensible
and troubled I am att itt, have and shall by the best advice indeavor to
take a fitting and doe Course in't and doe desire and require you that youl
as Christian magistrates use your utmost indeavour to asuage [and
prevent all animosity whatever and to that End stop all disputes arrtes*
or argueing in the said mater]‡ and [   ]† of [(?)   ] to doe ther[ ]
duty and use their utmost [ ]vors therein and punish any [   ]ell or violent
[   ] and desire the min[   ], I have herd and order'd Mr.
Leisler to give suficient security hiere and Mr. Milburn with you as per
order which you are to see presently observed and doubt nott a good isue
from then will [   ] their admenitions acordingly

Your afectionate friend

To the Comander and
Magistrats att albany
N.Y. Sept. 1676.

[ENDORSED:]   the Commander and Magistrates
                   of Albany by C. Delavell.
                   Sept. 16. 1676.

[25:167]

[PETITION BY JOHN PARSELL, APPEALING A VERDICT]

To the Right Honorable Major Edmund
Andros Esquire Senieur of Saus Marez
Leiftenant and Governor Generall of all his
Royall Territoryes in America etc.

The humble Peticion of Jno. Passall alias Butcher.

---

* Arret: court decision.
‡ The material in brackets was written in the margin to be inserted in the text. The exact
place or places, the correct order of phrases, and the amount of text lost in three places where
the paper is torn away, are all uncertain.
† Andros's scrawl at this point is entirely unreadable.

Sheweth.

That your Peticioner att a Court of Sessions holden att Gravesend the 15th day of June 1675 was sued by Angletie Burgers for the Arrearage of the Purchase mony due for a Plantacion bought by your Peticioner of the said Burgers late husband, where Judgment passed against your Peticioner and Execucion Issued out thereon, but before it was served your Peticioner and the said Burger came to an Agree for the payment of £900 att such time and in such species as therein is Expressed the which Agreement your Peticioner not being able to Comply with all the said Burgers Adressed herselfe to the next December Court where your Peticioner was Ordered to performe the Agreement else the Execucion to be served, your Peticioner then Could not performe the same, nor was the said Execucion served, But att the next June sessions the said Burgers Peticioned to have a new Execucion on the former Judgment etc. upon which the Court Considering your peticioners neglect in not performing the Agreement Ordered the former Judgment to stand good and Execucion to issue thereon for the debt Interest Cost and 100 gilders Damage for the which persuant to the said Order your Peticioner hath severall times tendered payment but she hath absolutely refused Declareing she will be satisfied with nothing but her land againe and although your peticioner hath already paid above ƒ3000 she refuseth to make him any title.

> Your Peticioner therefore humbly prayes your honor to grant him an Appeale to the next Court of Assizes that his Cause may be Examined before your Honor he performing as the law in such Case Directs and your Peticioner shall pray etc.

[ENDORSED:]   Peticion of Appeale
John Parsell alias Butcher
against Angletie Burgers.

Graunted upon security.
Sept. 16. 1676.

John Wolstoncroft and hee saith Tho:
Wandall security upon an Appeale made by him.

from the Judgment of the last Court of
Sessions held at Gravesend for a
certaine difference betwixt them

touching the payment for a certaine
parcell of land at Mashpeth Kills.
Hereof etc.

[25:168a]

[OBLIGATION OF NICOLAES BAYARD TO PAY JOHN SHAKERLY]

I do hereby bond and oblidge myselfe unto Mr. Jno. Shackerly, that if
the said Mr. Shackerly within the space of four Months after this date
can make appeare that the Custome for which his account by Governor
Colve was Charged the 31th day of May 1674 to the summe of sixty
gilders, by him the said Shackerly was then paid in specie, That I:
underwritten will repay the said summe of sixty gilders uppon demand;
In Wittnesse Whereof I have hereunto set my hand In New Yorck 16th
of September 1676.

N. Bayard.

[25:168b–169]

[NO DOCUMENTS ARE LISTED FOR THESE NUMBERS IN THE
CALENDAR. TWO ITEMS NOW FILED HERE BELONG WITH
JOHN SHAKERLY'S ACCOUNTS IN VOLUME 29][*]

[25:170]

[INVOICE OF GOODS]

Invoice of good Loden one Borde the Sloope Edmond of Niueyorke
(Petter Lorance Master for Delaway) Being for the Proper Accompt and
Risque of John Shakerly and Renar Willson In Comp. September the
23th 1676.

To Sundyr Accompt For Marchandizes Bought of Mr. Edward Grifing	£72"05"6
To 92 gall. of wine att 3s per gall	£13"16"0
To one Peece of Carsey at	£ 4"10"0
To one Peece of whit singell thicks } qt. 38 yds at 3s per yd }	£ 5"14"0
To one Peece of Sarge att	£ 3"10"0

* See appendix to the final volume of *The Andros Papers*.

To one Peece of Carsey at	£ 3"10"0
To 192 Gallons of Rume att 4s per g	£38"08"0
To 3 Tearses* of Mallasses att	£ 9"00"0
To 50 Scifell‡ of salte att	£ 5"00"0
To 10 Barrells att	£ 1"10"0
To 3 grose of Cotte Buttons att	£ 0"18"0
To 4 ditto of Brest ditto att	£ 0"15"0
To silke 1/4 s att	£ 0"10"0
To silver Cupp att	£ 1"10"0
To A sarge Cootte att	£ 1"00"0
To one Blankett att	£ 0"10"0
	£162"16"6

[25:171]

[LETTER FROM GOVERNOR ANDROS TO COMMANDER JACOB
BENCKES OF THE DUTCH FLEET. TRANSLATION]†

at York, this 25th Sept. 1676

Sir,

I received yours of the 24th of August by Commander Rutger Righwin, who had, without delay, every freedom to take provisions and, I believe, left satisfied but took so little that it merited in no way your recognition or to be mentioned to my lord His Highness and prince of Orange, whom I shall always be ready to serve as I must in all occasions in my power. As I understood your dispatch from Europe, I had not in the least doubted the continuation of your good fortune, and you may imagine that I am quite pleased at present to hear the effects of it and thank you for your obliging letter, which will always oblige me at every opportunity in which I can prove how much I am,

Sir,
Your very humble and very obedient servant,
E. A.

Captain Righwin will tell you about the departure in Holland of Domine Larik, who should have had (like all others) every liberty to go to see you.

---

* Tierce: a cask holding a third of a pipe.
‡ Skipple (Dutch *schepel*): 1.29 bushels of salt.
† Translated from the French by Linda J. Pike.

[25:172]

[LIST OF DEBTORS TO THE ESTATE OF COL. FRANCIS LOVELACE, IN JAMAICA, LONG ISLAND, WITH WARRANT TO THE CONSTABLE AND OVERSEER OF THAT TOWN TO NOTIFY THE PARTIES TO PAY THE SAME; SEPT. 25, 1676 (*MISSING*)]

[25:173]

[COVERING LETTER FROM SOUTHAMPTON ENCLOSING THE DOCUMENT FOLLOWING]

Southampton Sept: 28o: 1676.

Honorable Sir.

Wee the subscribed, the present Constable and Overseers of this Towne, hereby present to you our humble service etc. wee have had some Intelligence by Mr. Justice Arnold, very lately, That it is your honors Pleasure, our Towne and Southhold should send up against the Next Court of Assizes, the reasons why wee take not out a Pattent for our lands as some other Plantations in this Jurisdiction have done: Sir wee alwayes are, and shall bee most cheerefully willing and ready to render you duty, and the best satisfaction whereof wee are capable, But in reference to the premised occation being streightned by time wee are bold to present you (here inclosed) a Just coppy of our reasons, which sometime upon like Injunction Our Towne and the Towne of Southhold sent to Colonell Francis Lovelace Esquire, then Governor whoe (for ought wee know) accepted them; as wee hope your honor will; Soe humbly Craveing your pardon, with our constant and sinceere diseires of your happines wee rest

Sir   your Servants

Joseph Hayner
Edward Howell
John Jagger
Francis Sayer
John Foster

[ADDRESSED:]   To the Honorable Edmond Andross Esquire
Generall of all his Royall Highnes his
Teritories in America, and Governor at
New York: theise
Present.

[25:174]

It hath pleased your honor to require of us the Inhabitants of Southampton to receive a Pattent from you for our lands which wee have long possessed, and alsoe to Demand of us the reasons of our delay: Our reasons, some of them, are these:

1—Because wee apprehend that wee have a Just and lawfull right and title to our lands already, without such a Pattent For at our owne cost and charge (and not at any others) wee transported our selves into these forraine parts, and here purchased our lands wee now possess of the Natives, the then proper owners of them, and that by the approbation of the Lord Sterlings Agent: And alsoe have with long and hard labour subdued parte of these lands with the perill of our lives, espetially in those times when wee were few in Number, but the heathen numerous:

2—Wee have Possessed our lands (some of us) about the space of 30 yeares without any mans laying claime to them, which is Esteemed a matter of some weight in law.*

3— Because it seemeth a New and strange thing to us that each Plantation on this Island should bee enjoyned to take a Pattent for theire lands: Wee never heard of any such practice in England, or in any of his Majesties Dominions, that every Towne or Parish is enjoyned a Pattent: although the Englis[ ] under the Dutch Government have had theire land breifs.

4— We apprehend that where Pattents are made use of, the Termes and Conditions are Expressed betweene him whoe grants, and them to whome the grant is made, But it doth not seeme to us, to bee soe in the Pattents here imposed But Persons are upon uncertaineties, and at the will of theire Lord, to make such acknowledgments and payments from time to time as seemeth good to him to appoynt soe that men know not what to looke for, or to trust unto.

5— Lastly, wee conceive that the proclamation made by his Majesties Commissioners here in the yeare 64 assure us of as much, if not more then this Pattent will Doe: the substance of which Proclamation was this, That the People here should enjoy whatsoever Gods blessing and theire owne honnest labours had furnished them with. And after this Governor

* Written in the left margin next to this paragraph in the same hand is "1670."

Nicolls gave another his hand that wee should have equall priviledges freedome and Immunities (if not greater) as any of his Majesties Collonies in New England: the truth is (to speak plainely) wee cannot bee free to pass over our owne proper rights to our lands into other mens hands, and put ourselves and successours into a state of servitude, which, if soe, whoe will pitty or help us: But that wee may not bee further troublesome to your honor at this time, wee humbly take our leve of you, and rest ready to our abillities to render all such dues and duties as either the law of God or Nature binde us to.

[ENDORSED:]   Southton and Southold Papers.
1676. Assizes.

[25:175]

[REASONS WHY SOUTHOLD RESIDENTS DID NOT TAKE
OUT A LAND PATENT]*

Lastly we conceive that the proclamation made by his Majesties Commissioners here in the yeare 64 assurs us of as much, if not more then this patent will doe. Our conclusion, is, that if we could be firmly assured, upon sufficient grounds, that the takeing of a patent will doe us good, and no hurt be an advantage to us, and ours and no disvantage, then we would not be long without one: but if by takeing of a patent we should bring ourselves, and Successors into a state of servitude, then who shall pitty, or help us, but that we may not be further troublesome to your honour at this time, we here humbly take leave of you, and rest ready to our abillities, to render all such just dues and duties, as eyther the law of God, or nature bind us.

[ENDORSED:]   Sept. 28. 1756 [sic]
the People of
Southamptons
Reasons against
taking out a Patent.

* This document, a petition from the inhabitants of Southold, reads almost word for word the same as 24:174 (the petition from the inhabitants of Southampton) through the first four petitions. Only the fifth petition is given here.

[25:176]

[25:177]

Bookes taken out of the great Chest at Mrs.
Bedloo's Sept. 30th. 1676.

A. Great Leidger. 1. Journall: 1. Wastebooke

B. Great Leidger. 3. Journalls. 1. wastebooke

C. Great Leidger. 2. Journalls. 1. Wastebooke

D. Great Leidger 1. Journall. 2. wastebookes

E. Great Leidger. 1. Journall. 2. wastebookes

A copy booke of Accounts drawne out beginning 1mo. December 1672.

A file of bills and Accounts delivered in the Dutch time.

Sept. 30th 1676.   Lest of Mr. Bedloo's bookes
                    with Mr. Steph: V: Cortlandt.

A Leidger. Litt F.

The Journall. L: F:

The Waste booke. F and Alphabets.

Another wastebooke out of the Chest.

A leidger and Journall in short with the Alph. in Go: Colves time.

A short Abstract made by P:D:L. Noy when Mrs. Bedloe
administred.

* Published in *Records of the Court of Assizes*.

A list of Debts abstracted by P.D.L. Noy.

These sent for by the Go: from the Fort.

[ENDORSED:]   Papers and bookes delivered to Mr. Stephanus
Van Cortlandt and Mr. Guylaine Ver Planke.
Sept. 30th 1676.
I* gave the key to the Go:

[25:178]

[LOST PRIOR TO 1866, SINCE THERE IS NO ENTRY IN
E. B. O'CALLAGHAN'S CALENDAR]

[25:179]

[SUBPOENA FOR WITNESSES IN THE SUIT BETWEEN ALLARD
ANTHONY AND ELIZABETH BEDLOO]

These are in his Majesties name to require you to make your personall
Appearance at the Generall Court of Assizes to be held in this City,
begining on Wednesday the 4th day of this instant Month, then and there
to testify the truth of your knowledge in a matter or cause in question
between Allard Anthony Plt, and Elizabeth Bedloo Deft, Hereof you are
not to fayle at your utmost perills. Dated in New Yorke this 2d day of
October 1676.

To/ Marritje Jans
X / Jacob Cornelisen Stille
X / Anthony Anthony Cornet
/ Pieter de la Noye

Matthias: Nicolls Secr.

[ENDORSED:]   Subpoena for 4 persons.
1676
Anthony
against
Bedloo.

*   Matthias Nicolls

[25:180]

[RECEIPT FROM STEPHANUS VAN CORTLANDT TO SECRETARY
NICOLLS FOR CERTAIN BOOKS BELONGING TO THE ESTATE OF
FRANCIS LOVELACE, OCT. 2, 1676 (MISSING)]

[25:181]

[COURT PROCEEDINGS]*

[25:182]

[PETITION BY FOUR RESIDENTS OF HUNTINGTON FOR EQUITY IN
FEES ASSESSED BY RICHARD SMITH]

To the Right Honourable Major Edmond Andross Governor of all
his Highnes the Duke of Yorke his Territorys in America and the
Rest of the Honourable Court of Assizes now Assembled humbly
showeth

That wee Your poor Peticioners Thomas Scudder William Brothertone,
Benjamine Jones, and John Gowlding being seated upon a tract of land
which is now fallen to Mr. Smith of Neassequage to your humble
Peticioners great damage, haveing Expended A great deale of charge and
Labour, which wee are like to lose, if Your Honour and the Rest of the
Honourable Court grant us not some releife. And further wee humbly
desire that it may be taken notice of that we in setling intended not the
least dissobedience to the power that was then here established; but
severall of us sold ourselves out elsewhere and tooke possession severall
months of the lands we have lost before the last order dated in December
1672 came forth, for we had provided meat for our Cattle, built shelltars
for our winter quarters, and provideing for A Crope the next summer so
that we were at that pass that we knew not how to stop as that order
required which was two yeares full after that Judgement past for Hun-
tingtowne for that order comeing forth in winter as may appeare by the
Records that to come off the land some of us haveing sold our Selves out
of our former livings wee knew not where to goe, and for our Cattell we
knew not what to doe with them, haveing there provided for them, and
at as great a Loss we were what would become of our families if wee
provided not bread for them being in the wilderness which we humbly
beseech your Honour and the Rest of the Honourable Court to Consider
our Condition and grant us releife for bound we were to the Towne to
Settle in the time the high Court of Asizes perfixed Also we humbly

* Published in *Records of the Court of Assizes.*

Conceive that Mr. Smith doth deal Verry hardly with us Concerning the hay we gott last there makeing us pay eight shillings a load for Grass when we were at charge of mowing and makeing and stacking besides other charge he demands above the hay; it is true he did Atach the grass belonging to three of the aforesaid farmers but for your humble peticioner John Gowldings part Mr. Smith did not stack his; yet he demands twelve shillings a Load for the grass, and it being Valued at three load he demands thirty six shillings and eight shillings for two mens comeing to Aprise it the which forty foure shillings for three load of grass he stops money due to my father in law for payment, your humble peticioner being at all charge in mowing and makeing stacking and fencing etc. Soe humbly leaveing our Selves and Conditions to your Honour and the Rest of the Honourable Court in hopes to find releife and we shall ever pray

Thomas Scudder
William Brotherton
John Gollgurd
Beniamin Joness

[ENDORSED:]   A Peticion from Thomas Scudder
[*blank*] Brotherton etc. Huntington 1676.

[25:183]

[PETITION OF JOHN ROBINSON TO CAUSE THOMAS DAVIS TO ABIDE
BY THE TERMS OF A JUDGMENT]

To the Right Honorable Major Edmund Andross Governor of iiis Royall Highnesses Teritorys In America and to the Honorable Bench of Assizes etc.

The humble Peticion of John Robinson of the Citty of New Yorke Merchant humbly shewes unto your Honors that the 14th of June 1676 att a Sessions held att Jameca: hee by his attorny William Sydenham sued Thomas Davis for twelve pounds payable in good Wheate neate tobacco or Porke att Price Currant due to him and Recovered Judgment and Execution for the same directed to the Counstable of flushing to Execute the same: Who hath levyed the debt and Costes in horses: hee giveing Men there Oathes to apprize the same who hath Valued the horses att such a high rate that thereby your Peticioner will have little or nothing for his Debt and should your Peticioner Accept the horses att the apprizers Value and Render an accompt thereof to his Corispondance in Barbados it wold not Onely bee a Ruine to his future Employ but in your

Peticioners weake Judgment devert those Merchants and Others from Employing there Estates in the trade of this Collony.

Therefore humbly Prayes that the said Davis may pay your Petioner according to his note under his hand or Else that the appraizers may bee forced to take the said horses as they have valued them and pay your Petioner acording to his Contract: and your Petioner as in duty bound

Shall Pray etc.

[25:184]

[JUDGMENT AGAINST WILLIAM LOVERIDGE FOR MAKING
UNSUBSTANTIATED CHARGES AGAINST DUTCH
INHABITANTS OF ALBANY]*

[25:185]

[COURT COSTS FOR WILLIAM LOVERIDGE; VARIANT COPIES]

A bill of Court Charges for William Loveredge
At the Generall Court of Assizes held in Oct. 4th etc. 1676.

	s d
The Returne from Alb: of his being bound over to this Court with the Cause	6. 8
Entry in the docket for a hearing	5.—
The deposicions and testimonies of 5 persons against him to prove what hee was charged with	10.—
The sheriffes Fees	12.—
The Cryer and Marshall	3. 8
Toward publicke Charge	10.—
The one and Judgment of the Court	10.—
The Copie	2. 6
	2–19.10

* Published in *Records of the Court of Assizes.*

[ENDORSED:]   Mr. Loveredges bill.
              Assize Charges 1676.

          A bill of Court Charges for William Loveredge at the
          Generall Court of Assizes held in Oct. 1675.

William Loveredge.   s. d.

The Returne from Albany of the Cause of his being
bound over to this Court   6. 8

Entry in the Docket for a hearing and Tryall   5. 0

The deposicions and Testimonies of five persons,
taken in Court to prove what was alleadged   10. 0

X The Sheriffes Fees   12. 0

X The Cryer and Marshall   3. 8

X Towards the publike charge   10. 0

The Judgment of Court and Order   10. 0

The Copie   2. 6

X Withdrawing the bond of Appearance   5. 0
    12.–   Matthias: Nicolls.   2 19.10
    3.8   Secr.   5.
    10.–   2 14.10
    5.0
1.10–8

          I desire a bill of him but for 1£ 13s 0d.

          Received for his passe 10s and 2s over
          which makes the abatement

[ENDORSED:]   A bill of Court Charges
              at the Assizes 1676
              Mr. Loveredge.

[25:186]

[REQUEST BY DANIEL DE HAART THAT A SUBPOENA BE ISSUED TO
WILLIAM BOGARDUS]

Sir.

I intreat the favour that a supenee may be made for William Bogardus
his Appearance att next Court of Assizes then to give his Evidence in a
Matter depending Betwen Danll De Heart administrator unto Balthazar
D: Heart deceased and Margarett Stephenson,* alias Bakers=and allsoe
att said Court that he shall produce the orrignall will of said Balthazar
D: Heart. Togeather with the bill of Seale of the Howse Lyeing neer the
Heer Graft in this Citty which he sould unto the said Margarett Bakers
=and the same shee sould unto the said Balthazar D Heart and allsoe the
bill of seale of the Negro Woman Sarah from the said Magerett Stephenson unto the said Balthazar De Heart: which will oblige

Oct. 2d 1676   Your Humble Servant
                                        to Comand

                                     Daniell De Haert

[ENDORSED:]   Mr. D: De Haarts direction for a
                   Subpoena for Wm. Bogardus.
                   Oct. 2d in the accion of
                   Mrs. Marg: Stuyvesant.

[25:187–90]

[SUBPOENAS ISSUED IN THE SUIT OF DANIEL DE HAERT AGAINST
MARGARET (STUYVESANT) BACKER]

These are in his Majesties name to require you Willm. Bogardus, to make
your personall Appearance at the Generall Court of Assizes to bee held
in this City, beginning on Wednesday the 4th day of this inst. month, then
and there to testify the truth of your knowledge in a matter or cause in
question betweene Daniel de Haart Administrator of the Estate of Balthazar de Haart deceased, and Marguerite Stuyvesant alias Backer, and
particularly that you produce the Originall Will of the said Balthazar de
Haart at the said Court, Together with the bill of sale of the house lyeing
neer the Heer Graft in this City, which he sold unto the said Margaret
Backer, and the same she sold unto the said Balthazr. de Haart, and also

* An error, or at least an English attempt at the name "Stuyvesant."

the bill of sale of the Negro woman Sarah, from the said Margaret unto the said Balthazr. if in your Custody: Hereof you are not to fayle at your utmost perill: Dated in N.Y. this 2d day of Oct. 1676.

To William Bogardus.

[ENDORSED:]   Copies of Subpoena for Wm. Bogardus.
                   D: de Haart Plt.
                   M. Stuyvesant Deft.
                   Assizes—1676.

                   Sept. 25 1676.

Nicolas Bayard
Jaques Cousseau.
Jacob Teunissen Kaey.
Caarsten Liersen.
Jan Hendricks Van Bommel.
William Bogardus.
Boel Roeloffsz.
Jacob Lunen.
Mr. Evert Pieters.
Jochem Beeckman
Nicolas Anthony.

These are in his Majesties name to require you to make your personall Appearance at the Generall Court of Assizes to bee held in this City, beginning on Wednesday the 4th day of this instant month then and there to testify the truth of your knowledge in a matter or cause in question betweene Daniel de Haart Plt. and Marguerite Stuyvesant alias Backer Deft., Hereof you are not to fayle at your utmost perills: Dated in N.Y. this 2d day of Oct.1676.

                   To Nicolas Bayard etc.

Elias provoost
grietien leune
Mr. John Laurence
Mr. Johannes van brugge
Mr. Nicklas bayard

Abraham lussena
anna roemers interlake boss*

[ENDORSED:]   Mr. D. de Haarts
                     direction of subpoe[   ]
                     for the within writt[   ]
                     in the action against t[   ]
                     Trustees.

These are in his Majesties name to require you [Anna Roemers] to make
your personall appearance at the Generall Court of Assizes to bee held
in this City, beginning on Wed: the 4th day of this inst. month, then and
there to testify the truth of your knowledge in a matter or cause in
question betweene Daniel de Haart Administrator of the Estate of Balthazr. de Haart deceased, and Jacob Teunis Kay, Jan Hendrick Van
Bommell and Jaques Cousseau, Executors in Trust to the Will of the said
Balthazr. de Haart, Hereof you are not to fayle, at your utmost perills.
Dated in N.Y. this 2d day of Oct. 1676.

to Mr. John Laurance
   Mr. Johannes Van Brugh
   Mr. Nicholas Bayard
   Elyas Provost   } of this City
   Abraham Lucena
   Gretien Leunen

Another of the same Forme for Anna Roemers—which the Constable of
Flattbush is to serve, and returne.
her name to be mencioned at first, after require you.

[ENDORSED:]   Copie of Subpoenas
                     D: de Haart plt.
                     The Executors defts.
                     1676.

Marritje jans
Jacob Cornelys Stille
antony antony Cornet
pieter de la noye
In the Case betweene Allard Anthony and Eliz: Bedloo.

---

* *Interlake boss* appears to be Dutch but its meaning here is obscure; perhaps the writer
wished to indicate that she lives in the woods between the lakes.

Suppoenes desired in the Case betwixt Mrs. Baker and Mr. Daniel
d' haert—

Carsten Luersen
Jacob teunissen Kaey
Nicolaes Bayard
William Bogardus
Boele Roelofs
Nicolaes Antony
Jacob Leunen
Jochum beekman
Mr. evert pieters
jacques Cousseau
jan Henddricksz van bommel

subpoenas.

[ENDORSED:]   Mrs. Backers
                     note For
                     subpoenas

[25:191–97]

[COURT PROCEEDINGS]*

[25:198a]

[PERMIT TO THE SHIP *MARGARETT* OF NEW YORK, GILBERT PACK
COMMANDER, TO SAIL FOR ENGLAND,
OCT. 27, 1676 (*MISSING*)]‡

---

* Published in *Records of the Court of Assizes*.
‡ A damaged copy is published in our *Books of General Entries of the Colony of New York,
1674–1688*, 136–37. For a related document see 25:214(1).

[25:198b]

A bill of Court Charges
at the Generall Court of Assizes
1676.

Wm. Roadesby Complainant
Capt. Wm. Dyre deft.

		s	d
	The peticion to bee heard in Equity	10.	0
	The Entry in the Docket.	5.	0
	Filing the Declaracion.	2.	6
	A Copie.	3.	4
	Filing the Answer.	2.	6
	A Copie.	3.	4
abated	High Sheriffes Fees	12.	0
	Cryer and Marshalls Fees	3.	8
abated	Charge of the Action	10.	
	Order and Judgment of Court	10.	0
	Copie	2.	6
		3 4.10	

[ENDORSED:]   Mr. Roadesbyes bill
Court of Assizes Charges
1676.

[25:199]

A Bill of Court Charges at the
Assizes. 1676.

Capt. Silvester Salisbury Plt.
John Sharpe   Deft.

	£ s d
The speciall warrant of summons	00:10:00
The Entry of the Action for tryall	00:05:00
Coppy of Declaracion	00:03:04
Fileing	00:02:06
Coppy of answer	00:03:04
Fileing	00:02:06
High Sherriffes Fees	00:12:00
Cryer and Marshall	00:03:08
The two Agreements produced and given in Evidence	00:04:00
Charge of Action according to law	01:15:00
Orders and Judgement of Court	00:10:00
Coppie	00:02:06
	04:13:10

Matthias: Nicolls. Secr.

[ENDORSED:]   Bill of Court Charges at the
               Assizes Anno 1676.
               For Mr. Sharpe.

[25:200]

[PETITION OF DAVID DES MAREST APPEALING A JUDGMENT]

To the right Honorable Major Edmund Andross Esq. Governor
Generall of all his Royall Highnes his Territories in America.

The humble petitione of Davis Des Marees

In all humble manner

Sheweth

That your peticioner was sued by John Archer: att the last Court
of Assizes held in this Citty; att Common Law=for a Lott of

Meadow ground at or neare Fordam by spiting Devill, where your peticioner was cast.

Granted for
giving suficient
security
E Andros S[*]

Therefore humbly prays that your Honor will be pleased to grant him An appeal att this Next Court of Assizes=hee performing all things the Law in such Cases requires.

And your Honors peticioner
shall Ever pray etc.

[ENDORSED:]   David Des Mares petitione for an appeale.
Sept. 18 1676.
Granted.
Paulus Richards
    security.

[25:201–3(1)]

[JUDGMENTS AND COURT PROCEEDINGS][‡]

[25:203(2)]

[JURYMEN AT A SPECIAL COURT OF ASSIZES, OCT. 25, 1676]

Mr. Elias Doughty
Henry Taylor
Wm. Laurence Junr.
Edward Griffeth
Joseph Smith
Thomas Smith
Thomas Ogly   Jury men
Daniell Whitehead
Jonathan Hazard
Gershom Moore
Thomas Stevens
Thomas Barker

[ENDORSED:]   The Jurimens
names.
Returne of Jury.

---

* The grant and signature are in the governor's hand.
‡ Published in the *Records of the Court of Assizes.*

[25:204]

[ORDER FOR THE SURVEYING OF LAND, WHICH WILL BE GRANTED
TO JOHN CORNELL]

By the Governor

Upon the Peticion and Request of John Cornell, that being driven by the
Indyans from his habitacion to the Eastward and desireous to live under
his Royall Highnesse's Government if he may have a Competent peice
of land assigned him to improve for his subsistance with his Wife and
five Children, I have Given and graunted unto the said Jno. Cornell the
quantity of one hundred acres of improveable land, not already taken up
and improved, with Meadow proporcionable if there bee so much
adjoyning, on the west side of Cow Neck, the which the Surveyor is
hereby required to survey and lay out in Order to a farther Confirmacion
according to law: Given under my hand in New Yorke, this 3d day of
October 1676.

[ENDORSED:]   Copie of Order for Mr. John Cornells
settlement at Cow Neck .
Oct. 3d 1676.

[25:205(1–5, 7)]

[JUDGMENTS]*

[25:205(6)]

[SUBPOENAS TO JOHN ARCHER AND HENRY LUDLAM
AND A WARRANT OF IMPRESSMENT]

By the Governor

These are in his Majesties name to will and require you Mr. John Archer
to appeare at the next Generall Court of Assizes to bee held in this City,
beginning on the first Wednesday in October being the 4th day of the
said month, then and there to make answer to the Complaint of Mr.
Johannes Vervelen upon an Appeale brought by him the said Vervelen
from the mannor Court of Fordham where hee was fined the summe of
20£ for Non=appearance, Hereof you are not to fayle at your perill: Given
under my hand and seale in New Yorke this 23d day of Sept. 1676.

* Published in the *Records of the Court of Assizes.*

To Mr. John Archer
at Fordham.

[ENDORSED:]   A speciall warrant for
              Mr. John Archer
              to appeare at the suite of John
              Vervelen at the Assizes.
              Sept. 23. 1676.

Hennery Ludlam the sun of Will. Lud. of Southampton at the suite of R.
Smith of Nesaq: Sept. 24 a warrant from the Go:
A warrant to presse horse and men from mee by the Governor by Mr.
Cooke.
     *

[25:206]

[COURT FEES OF JOHN GREENE]

A Bill of Charges for John Greene at the Assizes 1676
about killing Isaak Scudder.

	£ s d
Entry in the Dockett	00:05:00
The Indictment	00:10:00
The Sherriffes Fees	00:12:00
Cryer and Marshall	00:03:08
The Jury	02:02:00
The Judgement of Court	00:10:00
Coppy	00:02:06
	£04:05:02

[   ] Greene is poore and desireth   Matthias: Nicolls
[   ]the till next Cropp.   Secr.

[ENDORSED:]   A bill of [   ]
              the Assizes 1676 for
              John greene.

---

* These notes are on the back of the document and in a different hand from the rest, which
had been written by Matthias Nicolls.

[25:207]

[DECLARATION OF WILLIAM AND ANNA NOTTINGHAM OF KINGSTON
AGAINST WILLIAM FISHER FOR SLANDER]

Citty of
New Yorke.

William Nottingham and Anne his Wife Complaine of Wm. Fisher of a
Plea of Trespas on the Case and Pledge that and Whereupon the said
Wm. and Ann by Jno. West their Attourney Say That whereas the said
Wm. and Ann are true honest and faithfull Subjects unto his Majestie of
Great Brittaine and of good name fame and Creditt and Reputacion and
soe have been accounted and Reputed as well amongst their Neighours
as other good and honest People and from the time of their Birth heither
to have Justly and honestly behaved and Demeaned themselfes without
the Least Suspicion Stane or Blott of any Felony Robbery Larceny
Deceite Cusening* or Cheateing or any other meanes and endeavours to
gett a Livelyhood for themselves and family by buying and selling by
true and Just weights and Measures the which Occupacion is wholy
managed by the said Ann the said Wm. being a very weake and sickly
man not able to performe or looke after the Same, Notwithstanding the
said Wm.‡ not Ignorant of the Premisses but falsely and malitiosly
without Cause to vex and Molest the said Wm. and Ann And them not
only to wound in their good name fame Creditt and Reputacion, but also
to disenable them to Mentaine themselves and family, on Easter Munday
last past att Esopus within the Jurisdiccion of this Court Certaine false
scandalous and Injurious words of the said Ann did Publiquely report
reharse and Declare as followeth (vizt.) That she (meaning said Ann) was
a Cheat, and that he the said Wm. would prove her (meaning the said
Ann) to be a Cheater both in weights and Measures, by Reason of the
said Wm. Publishing Reporting and Declareing the said Words the said
Wm. and Ann are not only absolutely Blasted in their Creditt and
Reputacion but alsoe Deprived and frustrated of their future Livelyhood
and Maintainance and its true might have brought them under the Lash
and punishment of the Law the which they lay to their Damage 100£
Whereupon they bring their Suite and pray Judgment with Costs and
Damages.

John West Clerke

[ENDORSED:]   Declar.

* Cozening: fraud.
‡ Fisher. In the course of this document both men are referred to as "the said Wm.," but in
each case the context indicates who is meant.

Nottingham
vs
Fisher.
Ended and withdrawne.
1676.

[25:208]

[DOCUMENT MISSING; NOT LISTED IN E. B. O'CALLAGHAN'S
CALENDAR IN 1866]

[25:209]

[COURT ORDERS]*

[25:210]

[COURT FEES OF WILLIAM GRAVES]

A bill of Court Charges at the Assizes

| The Const. of Newtowne | plt. |
| Wm. Graves | deft. |

Entring the presentment	5–0
The Enditement	10–0
The sheriffes fees	12–0
The Cryer and Marshalls fees	3–8
Three wittnesses sworne and their deposicions taken	6–0
To the Cryer for giving the Oath ‡	3–2–0
The Charge of the Jury	2–2–0
The Judgment of Court 10–0	
The Copie	2–6
	4–13–2

Quere of young Scudamore.

[ENDORSED:]   Assizes bill.
Wm Graves.
4.13.2.

---

* Published in the *Records of the Court of Assizes*.
‡ This is undoubtedly a mistake in copying. Since this amount throws the total off by exactly
£3, the cryer must have been paid 2 shillings—a more reasonable fee for this position.

[25:211]

The Order of Assizes concerning Hempstead men to be read in court and they told that whosoever acts by the Combinacion, run themselves into a new premunire, they to pay Charges of the Court of Sessions.

To tell Mr. Cornell, Doughty etc. that if they will not immediately settle on L. Island, there are them that will.

[ENDORSED:]   Memo.

[25:212a]

A bill of Court Charges at the Assizes—1676.

Josiah Helmont plt.
John Teudor   deft.

	s.d.
The peticion of Appeale	10.0
Entry of Action	5.0
Returne of proceedings from the Mayors Court	6.8
Copie of Declaracion	3.4
Filing it.	2.6
Copies of Answer	3.4
Filing it	2.6
The high sheriffs Fees	12.0
The Cryer and Marshall	3.8
Three deposicions and 2 papers given in Evidence	0.0
The Charge of the Action to the publick	10.0
The Judgment of the Court	10.0
The Copie	2.6
	4–1.6

[ENDORSED:]   Accounts about the Ketch Susannah.[*]

A bill of Court Charges
Helmont and Tudor.
1676.

* This endorsement does not relate to this document, but to 24:122–23, 125.

[25:212b–213]

[COURT ORDERS]*

[25:214(1)]

[COURT FEES OF JOHN ARCHER]

A bill of Court Charges at the Assizes 1676.

Johannes Vervelen plt.
John Archer   deft.

	s d
	s d
The peticion of Appeale	10.[0]
Entry of Action	5.[0]
Returne of Proceedings from the Mannor Court of Fordham	6.8
Copie of bill in Equity	3.4
Filing	2.6
Copie of Answer	3.4
Filing	2.6
The high sherrifes Fees	12.0
The Cryer and Marshall	3.8
Severall deeds and papers produced in Evidence	8.0
The Charge of the Action	10.0
The Judgment of Court	10.0
The Copie	2.6
	3.19.6

[ENDORSED:]   Bills of Court Charges.
Vervelen against Archer.
Des Maretz against Archer.
1676.

[25:214(1)]

[PASS FOR THE SHIP *MARGARETT*, GILBERT PACK COMMANDER]‡

Edmund Andros Esquire Seigneur of Sauz-
marez Lieutenant and Governor Generall
under his Royall Highnesse James Duke of

* Published in the *Records of the Court of Assizes.*
‡ This document was canceled and the preceding draft written on the back. Another copy
(damaged) is in *BGE* 2:136.

Yorke and Albany and of all his Teritories in America.

Permit and suffer the ship Margarett, of New Yorke whereof Mr. Gilber[t] Pack, is Commander, bound for England, freely and quietly to passe out of this Port with her Goods, Merchandizes, Pa[ssengers] and Loading, And to proceed on her intended Voyage without any manner of Lett, Hinderance or Molestacion whatsoever, She haveing Cleared and given Security according to Law, Given under my hand and Seale in New Yorke this 27th day of October 1676.

Past the Office

To all His Majesties Officers
or others whom this may Concerne.

[25:214(2)]

[COURT FEES OF HENRY SMITH]

A bill of Costs at the Court of Assizes 1676.

Peter Groenendyke—plt.
John Avery etc.
and Henry Smith—defts.

	s.d.
The order of Councell to bee heard this Assizes	10.0
The Entry in the Dockett.	5.0
Returne of proceedings at the Whorekill.	6.8
Filing the bill or declaracion	2.6
A Copie	3.9
Filing the Answer of John Avery etc.	2.6
A Copie	3.9
The sheriffes Fees	12.0
The Cryer and Marshalls fees	3.8
Severall deposicions and papers giving Evidence	10.0
Charge of the Action to the publick	10.0
Order and Judgment of Court to bee put off to the next Assizes	10.0
Copie	2.6
Credit at Fredr: Gysberts for 3£.10s.0d	3.9

Oct. 23. 1677   Rec'd $\dfrac{4\text{--}1.6}{1\text{--}0.0}$ *

$3\text{--}1.6$

Order this Court $\dfrac{10.0}{3\text{--}11.6}$

[ENDORSED:]   Order of Court of Assizes
about Simon Gibson. Delaware‡

[25:215]

[COURT ORDER]†

[25:216]

[PETITION OF JOHN ROBSON FOR CLEMENCY]

To the Right honorable Major Edmund Andros Esquire Senior of Sauce Mares Leftenant and Governor Generall of all his Royall highnes his Teritories in America etc.

The humble peticion of John Robson now in Custody etc.

In all submissive manner sheweth

That your honors peticioner is deservedly cummitted and upon the bended knees of his hart beggs your honors pardon for his Unbridled and presumpteous sayings which proceeded from Unruly Youth But as to anything forethought or premeditated sedition hopes your honor conceives him not Guilty of such a deepe Dyed Crime but hath noe plea but inocency, or to be purged by his oath May it please your honor suer it is that your peticioner relyes wholy upon your gentle Clemency and goodnes in that his Creditt for the present for the future support his Confinement it being now in the heights of his busines ruine must be his porcion if not prevented by your honors favor.

Humbly prayes that your honor out of the bowells of Compassion wilbe pleased to admitt your peticioner unto your personne and that the whole matter may be fully and wholy Determined before

---

* This should be 4:6:1, which changes the final to 3:16:1.

‡ This endorsement concerns a case heard in 1677 (26:97), not this document.

† Published in the *Records of the Court of Assizes.*

your honor to the which he humbly and gladly submitts himselfe
and for your honors prosperity shall ever pray etc.

John Robson

[25:217]

[PETITION OF ELLEN WALL FOR HELP IN COLLECTING DEBTS]

To the Honorable Sir Edmund Andros; Seigneur of Sauze
Mares Governor Generall under his Royall Highnesse of all
his Territoryes in America.

The humble Peticion of Ellen Wall.

With all Submissions

Humbly Sheweth your humble Peticioner, an Inhabitant of the Towne of
Flushing about 24 yeares, That 3 yeares agoe by an unexpected mis-
chance her house was burnt; whereby became needy, and destitute of
what shee formerly enjoyed; and was forced in her old age (allmost
against nature) to beginn the world againe; And whereas at the said
Towne of Flushing and thereabouts, severall small debts are due to your
Peticioner, which (If received) could confort her, But to the contrary;
although all sorts of good meanes used, cannot attaine to, notwithstanding haveing beg'd right and justice of the Magistrates there; they still
delay and neglect the same.

Therefore your Peticioner humbly prayes your honor be pleased
to take the Estate of your Peticioner into consideracion in graunting few lines for the said Magistrates, ordring them to dispatch
your Peticioners small buissnesses; that thereby shee may recover
her debts; and to enjoy in her old age, what shall hereafter doe her
noe good.

And your honors Peticioner shall ever pray.

[ENDORSED:]   The humble Peticion of Ellen Wall.
               1676.

[25:218]

[INDEMNITY BOND OF TIMOTHY GABRY. TRANSLATION]

Appeared before me, Willem Bogardus, notary public residing in N. Yorke, appointed by the right honorable lord Edmund Andros, governor general of New Yorke etc., and before the witnesses named below, Mr. Timotheus Gabry who declares that according to the judgment received in the last court of assizes, held in this city the 5th, 6th, and 7th of this month of October, on the charge of Jan Jansz Veryne for the sum of seven thousand seven hundred guilders in seawant, he has been ordered to post security for the sum of seven thousand guilders, Holland's value, before he shall be allowed and able to receive the aforesaid sum. For which he then requested Messrs. Gabriel Minvielle and Nicolaes Bayard, who also appeared and committed themselves thereto and promised to let themselves be so recorded by the secretary, Matthias Nicolls. They then came to an agreement thereon in the form and manner as follows: First, the aforesaid Thimotheus Gabry, does promise and bind himself, his heirs, and progeny at all times to the aforementioned Messrs. Gabriel Minvielle and Nicolaes Bayard for the indemnification and compensation of their pledged surety, and for their maximum security he transports and conveys to the aforementioned Messrs. Minvielle and Bayard out of the initial sum of money of the aforesaid judgment to the amount of six thousand guilders, seawant's value, to be received and held by them until the time that the aforementioned Gabry completely and absolutely releases them by further order of the same court of assizes or by sufficient counter security of their aforesaid pledged security. When this is done, then the aforementioned Messrs. Minvielle and Bayard are obligated and beholden to the aforesaid Mr. Gabry or his order and to those who should inherit his obligations, to return here and restore all the money received by them, namely, the aforesaid six thousand guilders, seawant's value. Mr. Gabry is also obligated to deliver into the hands of the aforementioned gentlemen all papers and documents, none excepted, concerning the proceedings between him and Jan Janse Veryn, aforementioned, which shall also be returned to him when the aforementioned gentlemen are released and discharged from their security in the aforesaid manner. For execution thereof the respective parties further pledge their persons and goods, none excepted, submitting the same to the constraints of all magistrates and courts. Signed in the protocol as testimony of the truth of these minutes by the parties involved, Mr. Balthasar Bayard and Pieter Symkam as witnesses and me as notary in N. Yorcke the 11th of October 1676.

Agrees with the minutes,

to which I attest,

W. Bogardus, not. pub.

[25:219]

[NOMINATION BY THE MAYOR, ALDERMEN, ETC., OF NEW YORK OF
TWO SETS OF CANDIDATES, OUT OF WHICH THE GOVERNOR IS TO
SELECT THEIR SUCCESSORS FOR THE ENSUING YEAR;
OCTOBER 14, 1676 (*MISSING*)]

[25:220a]

[AFFIDAVIT OF HENRY CLARKE CONCERNING A LIBELOUS PAPER]

Oct. 16. 1676.

Mr. Henry Clarke being this day sworne to declare the truth of his
knowledge concerning a certaine Pamphlet or libell, saith That at his
coming home Thursday night last about nine a Clock having open'd the
katch to come in, and shutting of it againe, hee trod on a paper which
hee tooke up, and the moone shining very bright hee went out againe to
read it, where at first hee tooke it to bee Dutch, but finding some English
words in it of which hee could then make nothing, hee came in againe
and layd it upon a Chest of Drawers in his Chamb. and went to bed
presently. Next morning hee with much adoe (being an ill hand) read it,
and not apprehending on whom it reflected, or Consequence of it, Hee
unadvisedly show'd it to severall, but being told it was not well done,
hee gave it the governor without delay, having refused to give any Copie:
Further that hee doth not know directly or indirectly the Author or
Contriver of the said Paper, nor how it came into his house, a place where
hee found it:

Sworne before mee the day and
yeare above written.

Matthias: Nicolls Secr.

[ENDORSED:]   Mr. Henry Clarkes Oath about
the libell hee found.
Oct. 16. 1676.

[25:220b]

[PETITION OF WILLIAM LOVERIDGE FOR REMISSION OF A FINE]

To the Right honorable Edmund Andros Esquire, Governor Generall of all his Royall Highnesse Territoryes in America.

The humble Peticion of Wm. Leveredge.

Sheweth

In all submission and humility; that your Peticioner is much troubled and very sensible of his haveing incurred your honors displeasure against him, for uttering that indiscreet report to your honor at Albany concerning the North=Indyans being supplyed with amunicions from the Inhabitants there; For speaking the which, hee humbly acknowledges his great fault; That your Peticioner doth humbly submitt to the Justice and censure of the Court, in imposing the fine on him: which they were pleased to order, in regard of the ill consequence of his Report; However, since what was said by your Peticioner not proceeding from a malicious heart; but out of a plaine and honest meaning; declaring only his thoughts, being ask't, and not his knowledge of the thing; and your Peticioner being a poore Man, having the Charge of a Family; iff the said Fine of twenty bevers, should bee levyed upon him, itt would bee very hard with him.

In tender consideracion of the premises, your Peticioner doth humbly implore, that your honor would bee pleased to accept of his acknowledgment of his fault to your Honor, as hee hath allready done in Court; praying that his Fine may bee remitted; And alsoe bee excused of his Bond of Good Behaviour; Promising for the future to live quietly and peaceably, without giveing offence to any Man.

And your Peticioner shall
(as in duty bound) ever pray etc.

[ENDORSED:]   16 Oct. 1676.
Mr. Loveridges Petition

the humble Peticion of Wm. Leveredge.

[25:221]

[SUBPOENA OF SEVERAL PERSONS TO TESTIFY IN A SUIT OF
SHERIFF THOMAS ASHTON AGAINST GEORGE HEATHCOTT]

[   ]y of
[   ] Yorke

By Vertue of an act of Parliament made in the 5th yeare of our most gratious soveraigne lady queene Elizabeth these are therefore in his majestyes name to Charge and Comand you Fredrick Phillips Capt. Thomas Delavall Wm. Darvall Wm. Roadsby John Robinson John Robson Richard Travis Peter Jacobs and Claas Bording that you and every of you be and Personally appeare before the Mayor or deputy Mayor and aldermans of this Citty att the Citty hall on tuesday the 24th day of this Instant octob. by nine of the Clock in the morning of the same day then and there to testifye the truth of your severall knowledges in a matter of Variance depending betweene Tho: Asheton Cheriff Plt. and George heathcott deft. one the behalfe of the deft. and hereof faile not att your Perrills Given under my hand this 19th of octob. 1676.

C[   ]pia   upon the Penalty of one hundred pound sterling
                per Cor[   ]

                                                    N d: meyer Mayor

[ENDORSED:]   Copie of Supoena of severall persons
                  by George Heathcott. Oct. 19.–76.

[25:222]

[LETTER FROM SOUTHAMPTON OFFICIALS WILLING TO TAKE OUT
A LAND PATENT]

Whereas the honorable Court of Assizes held in New York the 4.5 etc. Dayes of this Instant October, Adjudged our Towne of Southhampton to send up by the 23 Instant theire resolves to fullfill the law for takeing out Patent or Confirmation of our properties Interests and liberties Wee the subscribers the Constable and Overseers of the said Towne of Southampton, In Obedience unto our honorable and Esteemed Governor and the said Act of the Court of Assizes, doe in behalf of our said Towne hereby Depute our friends Mr. Justice Topping and Capt: John Howell with all possible convenient speed make address to his honor Our Governor for such said Pattent or Confirmacions. Alsoe to present the Townes service to his honor and to crave his pardon wherein soever the Town or ourselves have any way accidentally though not Intentionally made Default. And since by devine providence his honor is now in singular capacity to contribute to our Townes wellfare in respect of concernes both Civill Eclesiasticall, To beseech his honor that in both respects hee would please to bee propitious unto us in this soe weighty concerne, since God onely knowes whoe may hereafter succeed him to Governe us or ours. Soe shall wee and ours have cause to bee ever most thankfull unto him, and to God for Him, and to our said Deputies for theire paines:

> Joseph Hayner
> Edward Howell
> Francis Sayer
> John Foster
> John Faggar

[ENDORSED:]   23th October 1676.
from Southampton for a patent.

[25:223]

[RATES AND CREDITS OF SEVERAL TOWNS ON LONG ISLAND]

[ ]sthamton rats	Credite	Fieskeep[	] threue Credit
18–18– 2 1/2	33–13–6	14–17–3 1/2	
	44–18–0		

Southampton Rates	Credet		
61–00–00	71–18–2		
02–08–00	84–07–2		
23–08–00	156– 5–2	32–17–[ ]	
Soughould Rate	Crediete		
39–11–0	42–01–00		
38–17–5	41–13– 7		
78–8–05	83–14–07	05–06–02	
Setaket Rate			
12–18–08	20–16–06		
14–10–00	16–12–00		
27–08–08	37– 8–06	09–19–10	
Huntinton Rate	Credit		
20–00–00	21–14–00		
16–15– 6 1/2	18–08–04		
36–15– 6 1/2	40–02–04	0[ ]–06–[ ]	
		51–10	
		15–[ ]	
		36 0[ ]	

[ENDORSED:]   [   ] of Long Island Eas[ ]hampton Matthias: Nicolls.
                    Report from the Justices about Mannings Accion
                    By order of the Court of Assizes. Oct. 1676.

[25:224]

[NOTES FROM THOMAS BACKER AND RICHARD WOODHULL,
AUDITORS OF THE ACCOUNTS OF SHERIFF JOHN MANNING]*

Captain Nickales Secetery.

Whereas we were Agreed the Honered Corte to Audete the Hight Shreffe
Captaines Manings account: we have balanced: and if anythinge Conserning wontes‡ or hew and cries or else that the law or Amendments
given (?) noteries Allowe not we cannot allowe oto[   ] by us.

New Yorke   Tho Backere
9 October 1676   Richard Wodhull

Sir ther was a proclammation made that all that lane was indepted to
shrife maning in ther acount but Mr. Peeter Smith william foster Mr.
Jacson and Dork Smith requier 12 pounds which I know to be ther due
was omitted they not hering of the proclammation it being charges about
his imprisonment which I hope may be alowed them.

October the 9–1676.   Richard Wodhull

[25:225]

[ORDER OF HEMPSTEAD TOWN OFFICIALS FOR JEREMY WOOD AND
ABRAHAM SMITH TO WARN AWAY SETTLERS AT COW NECK]

Hempsted September the 29: 1676

We the Inhabitants of Hempsted due Imply Jeremy Wood and Abraham
Smith to Go and forwarn any Parson or Parsons that doth offor to make
any bilding or Preperration thereunto or fenceing or any way Go about
to take Poseshon of any land within theire towne bounds and in Perticulor
upon cow neck or any Part thereof We huse Neames eare under written
in the behalf of the toune

Nathaniell Pearsall Clarck   simon Sareing
                                        Richard Gildersleve.

___

* The document is poorly written and in places is very faint.
‡ warrants?

[ENDORSED:]   Hempsteads Order to Jeremy Wood etc.
to warn Mr. J: Cornwall.

[25:226–42]

[PUBLISHED IN THE *RECORDS OF THE COURT OF ASSIZES*.]

[25:243]

[ORDER TO THE CONSTABLE OF NEWTOWN TO SEIZE GOODS OF
RICHARD FIDOE]

Gravesend Sessions ss

Whereas att A Court of Sessions held att Gravesend in the West Rydeing
of Yorkeshire on Long Iland the 24th day of June last Past, one George
Wood obtained a Judgment against Richard Fidoe for a Certaine Parcell
of Meadow then in Difference between them togather with Costs of Suite
as by the records of the said Court may appeare, These are therefore In
his Majesties Name to Charge and Command you That you Seize Levy
and Distreyne soe much of the Goods Chattles or Estate of the said Rich:
Fidoe as will amount to and Satisfie the Sume of twelve pounds seven
shills. and six pence being the Costs of Suit, Together with the Incidentall
Charges allowed of by the Lawes of this Government occasioned by the
Service of this Execucion and that you make returne of the Due Execucion hereof att the next Sessions whereof you are not to faile att your
Perill Given under my hand this 27th day of October 1676 Anno Reg.
Rs. Car. 2di. xxvijo.[*]

To the Constable of New Towne.   Matthias: Nicolls.

[ENDORSED:]   Execucion
Wood
v.
Fidoe
Oct. 27. 1676.
Kings County. [‡]

---

[*] The twenty-seventh year of the reign of King Charles II.
[‡] Added after the formation of the county in 1683.

[25:244]

[ASSESSMENT ROLLS]*

[25:245]

[BIDS AND CONDITIONS AT THE AUCTIONING
OF THE POST OF WEIGHMASTER]

N: Yorke Dec. 2d. at farming the
Weigh house 1676.

1 beaver	Mr. Sidenham	ƒ2000.	5000.
	Judge Leet.	3000.	
	Mr. Tho: Sharpe	3500.	
1 beaver	Mr. Tho: Clarke	4000.	
1 beaver	Mr. Darvall.	4500.	

ƒ3000 advanc't. fell to Mr. Sidenhams at
ƒ5000.
Time given to get Security till Munday Morning.

Condicions Whereupon the Weighouse is to be Lett to
Farme this 3d day of Decem. 1677 and to be Entr'd upon
to Morrow by the Person that shall take the same to Farme.‡

Mr. John Robinson first security, upon his goeing for Engl.
Mr. Stephanus Cortlandt but the bonds taken up hee having
paid.†

[ENDORSED:]   Bidders at farming
the Weigh house

Nov. 2d. 1676.
Mr. Sydenham 5000—
or 125.+

---

* See appendix for these assessment rolls.
‡ The paragraph is in a second hand; probably that of the clerk Ephraim Hermans.
† The paragraph was written by Secretary Nicolls.
+ According to *Money and Exchange in Europe and America, 1660–1775*, by John J.
McCusker (Chapel Hill, 1978), the exchange rate in 1676 at Amsterdam for ƒ36.19 (average)
was £1 sterling. If ƒ5000 equaled £125 at New York, the rate there was ƒ40 for £1.

[25:246a]

These are in his Majesties name to require you to levy upon the Goods
and Chattells of Mrs. Elizabeth Bedloo the summe in the which shee was
cast at the Mayors Court of this City at the suite of Capt. Nath: Daven-p[
]e Attorneys of Mr. Alexander Bryan; [   ] in the Colony of
Conecticutt who appealing from the said Court to the Generall Court of
Assizes: Anno 1675, had likewise the Judgment within written given
against her there by the said Court in Confirmacion of the former, as also
all the Charges of suite and service of this Execucion according to Law,
the same to bee payd to the Atturneys or Assignee of the said Mr. Alex:
Bryan and for soe doeing this shall bee your warrant: Dated in New York
the 22th day of Nov. 1676.

[   ]ffe of the
City of New yorke or his
Deputy.

[ENDORSED:]   Copie of Execucon
against
Mrs. Eliz: Bedloo

Mr. Bryan:
No: 22. 1676

[25:246b&c]
[PUBLISHED WITH THE *RECORDS OF THE COURT OF ASSIZES*]

[25:247]
[REASONS PRESENTED BY JOHN LAURENCE FOR REJECTING
CHRISTINA VEENVOS'S PETITION FOR HIS PROPERTY]*

Resons wherefore Cristina Venvos shuld not have hir petition in all respects granted are as followeth

* This undated document seems to belong to a later period. There was no Christina Veenvos
and no Queen Street in 1676. Daniel Veenvos married Christina van der Grist, widow of
Cornelis Jacobsz, on April 24, 1681 (New York Reformed Church Records). Queen Street
(now Pearl Street) was named on October 13, 1694 (*Minutes of the Common Council of New
York, 1675-1776* (1905), 1:370.

Imprimis   because she Covets and desires as Ahab did A Con-
                           siderable part of my Inheritance as Appears by
                           sundry deeds which I have heare to demonstrate

2ly   because I have had an uninterupted possesion of what
                           is my proper and personall Right this thirty eight
                           years

3ly   because I have been at great trouble and Charge to
                           preserve from the violence of Stormes by sea and
                           flouds by land this thirty years and more to A Con-
                           siderable Expence neare one hundred pounds

lastly   Dout not from my observations of that Justices which
                           are the Inherent princeaple of your Excelency and by
                           your Assistance to Keep it still from this Averitious
                           and Coveteous woman and hir Abettors from all
                           there violent and tumulteous practices god Almighty
                           direct your Excelency in wisdome and Justice in this
                           and all other Cases to doe that which is Right without
                           partially is the prayer of sir your humble

                                            Servant

                                            John Lawrence.

[ON THE BACK:]   For Miles Foster had noe land to Queans Streat to
                           se[ ] that which he bought of the City was vacent
                           land to [ ] mark and not Apropriated pattened and
                           possesed 38 years as [ ] upon the whole of what she
                           Desires in hir petition I hun[ ] she ought not to have
                           a Confermation for Directly Des[   ] and intrench
                           upon Anothers Lawfull Rights as mine is which [ ]
                           and has used all Unlawfull wayes and means to
                           Effect by [ ] violence severall Kinds of wayes by
                           hir Agents and Abetors C[   ] prompted there unto
                           to get possession but prevented as I hop[ ] Still be
                           [. . . *unfinished* . . .]

[25:248]

[LETTER TO MATTHIAS NICOLLS FROM PETER SMITH WITH A
COMMISSION]

Jamaica No: 11th 1676.

Sir.

I have enclosed sent you a Copy of my Commission*according to your
Desire: I hope you will please to speake to the Governor about it by the
first convenient opportunity, and Let mee know how hee resents‡ it: I
hope you got well and safe home the last night. I shall not forget what
you spoke to me about; but shall be ready (not only now) but upon all
occasions to expresse myselfe Sir.

> Your most faithfull friend, [   ]
> humble servant.
>> Peter Smith.

[ADDRESSED:]   For Capta. Matthias Nicolls Secretary at
New Yorke with Care.

[25:248]

[MEMORANDUM OF THE SEVERAL TOWNS TO WHICH COURT ORDERS
WERE SENT AND BY WHOM]†

Orders of Assizes. 1676

Easthampton ⎫
Southton   ⎬   in a packet to Seatalcot
Southold   ⎭
Seatalcott   ⎫
Huntington   ⎪
Oysterbay   ⎪   All sent by Nath: Coles—Constable of
Hempsteed   ⎬   Oysterbay Novemb. 17th. 1676
Flushing   ⎪
Jamaica   ⎭

---

* Not present. He was commissioned clerk of the court of sessions at Gravesend on
November 28, 1674, and collector and surveyor of the rates and duties sometime prior to
June 26, 1675. At the assizes on October 9, 1675, he is called the deputy of Sheriff Robert
Coe.

‡ To be sensible of; to take something well or ill (obsolete) (adapted from *Webster's Third
International Dictionary*, 1964).

† Written by Secretary Nicolls on the letter preceding.

X Newtowne
X Gravesend
X Westchester ⎞
X Eastchester ⎰
X Breucklyn
X Flattbush
X New Utrecht
X Boswyck
X Flattlands

These all but Westchester and Eastchester sent to Mr. Heynelle Nov. 20: 1675.

[ENDORSED:]   Orders of Assizes 1676
                   sent and by whom.

                   Westchester by my son[*]
                   Eastchester Mrs. Hunt

[25:249]

[LETTER FROM JOSEPH KNOTT IN PRISON, ALLEGING HIS INNOCENCE
OF SHIPPING UNCULLED STAVES]

May it please your Honor

I am not only like Moses of an unredey tongue but at present a prisner
which to resons, Constraine mee to borrow the Assistance of Aron and
make my penn my orrator Sir I sometimes sence bought a parcell of pipe
staves at New Jersey which staves I tooke farre what lay in mee should
bee good to which end I sent mony by Mr. Fogge to Governer Cartwights
Culler to have them Culd which was accordingly donn and a receaipt
sent mee by that Culler that those staves were Culd and lay redey by the
watters side to be shipt when ever I should send for them, Next I made
a Contrackt with Capt. Clarke to take those staves on borde and Carry
them to Barbados the first bote Came upp brought 15. cwt. staves nether
I nor the Master at that time Knowing of this Order heare In dispute
nether did I Know it tell the second bote Came upp then the Culler heare
told mee those staves might be Culd heare, to home I said thy ware Culd
allredey, and I Knew no reson why I should bee at a dobell Charge to no
purpose, ware on I whent to Mr. Maior that now is and desierd hime that

* Referring to Matthias Nicolls's son William.

I maight put them on borde hee told mee I maight not, wareopon I landed
those staves of the second bote and what Came afterwards ware Culd
over againe beefor they whent on borde; by the Cullers heare, Now Sir
the Cullers heare haveing Made Complaint to the Maior, I ware sent for
by the Maior to his house ware I ware accusd that I had shipt staves
Contrary to order to the dishonner of this Collony; when I call God to
record with mee that I tooke all the Carre lay in mee to reserve the
Collonys Repute and my owne Intrest the order saith all staves shipt or
Transeported from this Collony shall bee Culd by Cullers deputed by the
Cunstabells of the towne from whence those staves should bee shipt, on
forfiture of the staves; or the vallew (why then a fine) Except all such
staves as shall bee shipt for Dry Caske, which Gives mee to Understand
that this order strickes only att such staves as shall bee shipt for the Ilands
ware none but tite Caske are usd and not to Barbados ware more dry
Caske are usd then tite as your honor well knows, the order further saith
that if any master of a vesell shall presume to lode any staves befor thy
are Culd as aforsaid shall pay five pounds for every thousand soe taken
on borde, by this Order I may shippe Nine hundred Ninety Nine without
breach of the order, its not said they shall pay proportionabell for the
quantity more or less; then pray Sir why seven pounds tenn shilling for
15 cwt. staves; Lastly all staves by this order shall bee Culd, yet by this
order all staves are allowed to bee shipt, May it plese your honner soe it
is, then pray Sir what dishonner hath the Master or I donn the Collony
or warein have ether of us Injured any Man all Cann bee said is the
deputed Collers, of this Citty want Imployment, and ould willingly have
had three shillings for on owers Imploy, when those staves ware never
landed within the Jurisdiction, which had I Knowen I should never have
made a dispute of as suffishently appeares by my ordering the staves to
bee Culd heare that whent on borde after I ware acquainted of this Order
to my unnecesary and dobell cost, Sir I have acted no otherwaise now
then I have donn for six yeares past unquestiond, I never see this order
tell now Mr. Maior shewed it mee nor Could I well when scarse five of
the bookes are to bee found within the Collony, Why than should bee a
differance Made beetweene the faith of the Culler of New Jersey and the
faith of the Culler of this place both beeing subjects to on King and
profesing Christians is past my Understanding, Sir for this Crime If it
bee a Crime I Am Committed to prison to pay seven pounds tenn shillings
and cost befor I have had any legall summonds to any Courte or am
Condemned by A Jury of My peares of a breach of this order and Contrary
to the order the Courte red to mee in Courte last Courte themselves which
was to loose the staves or vallew, which vallew is but thirteene yeardes
of Doffells no More did those staves Cost mee I cann now by duffells

for fower shillings the yeard, Sir I aver that it is Contrary to Law to prosecute the rigor of the law on any man that hath performd the Intention of the law of this I thought good to acquaint your honor beefor I paid this fine, haveing this laid my Cause befor your honor I leve the hole to your Christian Considderation Not douteing but that your Honor is a parson that soe farr Minds Honor and Justice as that you will not see the Master or mee suffer in soe greate A Mesure, On a Quibell, in a Matter of soe small a Concerne, Sir In My weake Judgement I may without pregadis to my Contience use the words of St. Paull in another Case, Nether against the laws of my Nation nor against Ceaser have I offended to what your honors orders I shall submitt I am

From prison 15th November   Your Honors humbell sarvant
1676.
                                 Joseph Knott 1676.

[ADDRESSED:]   To the Right Honorable Edmond
                Andross Governor Genarall under
                his Royall highnes of all his
                Territoreys In Amerrica.

[ENDORSED:]   Mr. Joseph Knotts Letter
                to the Go: Novemb. 15th 1676.

[25:250]

[MINUTES OF JOSEPH KNOTT'S APPEARANCE BEFORE THE COUNCIL]

15 November 76

Mr. Joseph Knotts leter Receav'd att noon Complaining of the Court of major and Aldermen for a fine for non Culling pipe staves the very reflecting sent for my* counsell To meet att 5 a clock and heard and Examined said knott on Every perticulor of said letter which he no wayes Excuses but still pleads wrong Contrary to Lawe the all proceedings vieued saith that if he would have given the Culler 3s he needed nott have had this trouble Scarce 5 lawe books in the Colony fined without a legall sumons or tryall Contrary [   ] lawe

Resolved so much of import as fitt for a more publick hiering and that itt should be putt of till next day or longer if he desired itt and then heard att the toune holl

* The document appears to have been written by Governor Andros.

Mr. Knott being called in doth desire no longer time then tomorrow morning and that itt may then be heard without any further delay

Tomorrow Thursday the 16th att 10 a Clock apointed for hiering the same att the toune hall.

16 November 1676

Mr. Knott Called att the toune hall afore me and Counsell remaines obstinate as afore, that he was wronged the[ ] speakes of a jury

[ENDORSED:]   Part of the papers relating
to Mr. Knotts being examined before
the Councell in the Fort, and at
the City hall. No: 15 and 16. 1677.[*]

The rest amongst the Councell Orders.

[25:251]

[JUDGMENT OF GOVERNOR AND COUNCIL IN THE ABOVE CASE]

At a meeting of the Governor and Councell
at the Citty hall the 16th day of November:
1676.

Upon Application of Mr. Jos: Knott Concerning A Judgement of the Court of Mayor and Aldermen for Pipe staves unduly shipt by him; All proceedings being produced and himselfe and Attorney fully heard.

It is Ordered that the Judgement of the Mayors Court as to the fine of seven pounds ten Shillings do Stand good.

And further that the said Joseph Knott shall according to Law forfiett the said staves so illegally Shipt to be delivered one Shoar here or Ship being loaden to pay the Vallue as Valued by himselfe at two pounds twelve Shillings, but if the said Staves bee not delivered here, besides paying the said Value, that hee give Sufficient Security of [   ]at the said Staves shall nott bee sold, or Exposed to sale but as Rough unculled Staves, of the which to make a due Returne from the Secretaryes Office or Governor of Barbadoes, that they were so disposed of, which

* Secretary Nicolls's error for 1676. It would appear from the council minutes that the records were organized in June 1677.

Returne to bee made within the space of one whole yeare or the Recognizance to bee Forfeited.

That the said Joseph Knott doe likewise Stand upon the Stepp before the Whipping post this afternoone by three a Clocke, for the Space of one hour with a paper on his breast with this Inscription.

For Falsely and Notoriously reflecting on the Magistracy and Law.

And that hee the said Joseph Knott doe remaine in Custody of the Sherriffe untill he hath given Sufficient Security or Comply'd with the Order as before the Court of Mayor and Aldermen and Sheriffe to see the ord[ ] put in Execucion.

To the Sherriffe of the   By order of the Gov[   ]
Citty of New Yorke.   in Councell.

This is a true Copie[*]
Matthias Nicolls. Secr.

[25:252]

[PETITION OF JOSEPH KNOTT FOR REMISSION OF
A PORTION OF HIS SENTENCE]

To the Right Honorable Major Edm: Andros Esquire Senieur of Saus Marez Leiftenant and Governor Generall of all his Royall Highnesses Territoryes in America etc.

The humble Peticion of Joseph Knott

Sheweth

That your Peticoner in all humblenesse Submitts to your Honors Judgment past against him, And is hartily Sorry that he gave any occasion for

---

* The document is a fair copy upon which a number of changes have been made, not by Secretary Nicolls. As it is unclear whether Nicolls is certifying the first or the second version, the original text is here noted. In the first paragraph: "Mr. Joseph Knotts Letter to the Governor and whole Case Concerning A Judgement of the Court of Mayor and Aldermen about Pipe staves; being examined and himselfe and Attorney fully heard"; in the third prior to the phrase "the Vallue as Valued by himselfe" appeared: "And further that the said Joseph Knott shall forfeit the Fifteen hundred Pretended Pipe staves Shipt by him to be delivered one Shoar here or . . ."; in the last "and sheriffe" was added after "Aldermen."

Justice soe to Proceed by his Undiscreetly and unhandsomly writeing to your honor or by any other way or thing that might Deserve the same for the which he humbly beggs your honors Mercy and Pardon.

> Therefore humbly Prayes your Honor That he may be Excused from that Parte of the Sentence which will bring him to open and Indigne though Deserved Punishment the same maying Prove his Future Ruine, etc., and for the time to Come he will take Care not to Offend Your Honor in the Like Nature.

> But will Ever Pray for your Honors Prosperity etc.

[ENDORSED:]   Mr. Joseph Knotts
peticion after Sentence.

[25:253]

[STATEMENT OF CAPTAIN JOHN COSTER'S ACCOUNT]

1676	Capt. Joh Coster is Debtor	Per Contra is Creditor
Oct: 9th	To the Fraight of 3 Packs of Ingen Cootes* at	ƒ36
	To one Large Chiste of goods	24
	To ditto for 3 Ankers of Rume	12
	To ditto for 4 Chares att	16
	To youer Pasaige att	40
	To a Caske of Pouder att	06
	To John Homes Pasaige	30
November	To 2 Pare of woolen Stokings	14
the 4th	To 3 Tearses of Mast pcas‡ att	440
ditto 18	To 49 [(?)]† of Sugar att	49
	To 2 Ankers and 3 gll:+ of Rume att 120 gild. per Anker	276

---

* Indian coats

‡ tiers of mast pieces

† Unreadable, but intended for pounds, since the price given in other documents is ƒ1 per pound.

+ Apparently gallons. A Dutch anker was 10.128 English gallons. If rounded off to 10 gallons per anker, then 2.3 ankers would indeed be ƒ276.

[25:254]

[PETITION OF WILLIAM PINHORNE, AS ATTORNEY FOR JOHN
JACKSON OF LONDON, APPEALING A JUDGMENT]

To the Right Honorable Major Edmund Andros Esquire Senieur
of Saus Marez Leiftenant and Governor Generall of all his Royall
Highnesses Territoryes in America etc.

The Humble Peticon of Wm. Pinhorne Attourney unto Jno. Jackson of London Merchant Sayler

Sheweth

That one Samuel Wilson of this Citty Merchant being truly Indebted unto
the said Jno. Jackson by two severall bonds, The one 124£: 11s sterl. and
the other 106£: 3s ster. your Peticoner by vertue of a Lettre of Attourney
etc. att a Mayors Court holden in this Citty the 7th Instant sued the said
Wilson where the Jury found the said bonds, Notwithstanding the which
the Court thaught not fitt to give their Judgment for the Defendant your
Peticoner not haveing the Originall bonds.

Your Peticoner Therefore humbly prayes your honor to grant him
an Appeale to the next Generall Court of Assizes. That his Cause
may be fully heard and Examined before your honor and that he
may have such releife therein as to your honor shall seeme meet
(he performeing what the Law in such Case Directs)

And your Peticoner shall pray etc.

[ENDORSED:]   Mr. Pinhornes peticion
                    for an Appeale.
                    Graunted. Dec. 1st 1676.

[25:255a]

[AUCTION OF THE ESTATE OF EDWARD RAWLING]

Att a Vendue held in New Yorke of Severall Goods belonging to Mr. Edward Rawlins deceased, December, the 2d and
4th 1676

Payment to bee made in four monthes in wheate, Floure, pease, or porke
(nott above halfe in one Specie except by allowance of Vendue Master)
at price Current when payable.

	£	s	d
To John Cavileer			
A Stuffe Coate and two pair of breeches	02	03	00
To Mr. Tho: Clarke			
A Stuffe Coate and pair of Breeches	01	13	06
a pair of Slippers	00	04	00
Two Whisks	00	07	00
To Mr. Tho: Delavall			
A Cloath Coate and pair of Breeches			
thirty one pieces of Fancy Ribbon	02	12	00
	06	17	06

[25:255b]

[A DOCUMENT OF MARCH 10, 1678/9, WHICH WILL BE
PUBLISHED IN VOLUME 28]

[25:256]

[JUDGMENT OF THE COURT AT ALBANY IN THE SUIT OF GERRIT
VAN SLICHTENHORST VS. ANTONIA VAN CURLER. TRANSLATION][*]

Extract from the register of court proceedings held in Albany on the 5th
of December 1676

Sr. Gerrit van Slichtenhorst, plaintiff
against
Juffrou Curler, defendant

The plaintiff persists with his previous request.

The notary public Ludovicus Cobes appearing at the session shows
power of attorney and petitions that the matter not be deliberated on
before and until she has received proof from those who shall help support
her in her justifications and until the time that God may restore her to
health; also, that the plaintiff has given her no credit for all the documents; and in addition that he has a diamond ring as security which he
refuses to accept for such value as the defendent places on it.

* Another translation by A. J. F. Van Laer can be found in the published *Minutes of the
Court of Albany, Rensselaerswyck and Schenectady* (Albany, 1928), 2:180.

The plaintiff responding insists upon preference and requests a final judgment because he has been without his money so long.

Their honors of the court, having heard the parties, condemn the defendant to pay the plaintiff the aforesaid promissary notes, which she has outstanding; the one amounting to the sum of twelve hundred thirty- nine guilders three stivers, the other on behalf of Gerrit Rees amounting to twenty-six beavers and thirty skipples of wheat for Mees Hoogeboom, discounting what she has honestly paid thereon; and that as a consequence of the nature and content of the same, also a sum of seventy-one guilders in beavers and eight guilders sixteen stivers seawant, private debt, discounting three beavers earned by her Negress, and for the expense of these proceedings.

> Agrees with the original minutes,
> as attested by me
>
> Robert Livingston, secretary.

[ENDORSED:]   Gerrit Slichtenhorst plt.
Jeuffrow Curler deft.
Albany

[25:257]

[PROCEEDINGS OF THE SESSIONS IN THE NORTH RIDING]

At a Court of Sessions held at
Afternoone.   Jamaica the 13th day of Decemb. 1676.

The Generall Commission of the Justices read, and the bench calld
over
The Const. calld over, most absent though in Towne, appeare
afterwards.
The Jury call'd over and sworne.
The Causes call'd over.
Hempsteed mens buisnesse to bee heard first.

Tho: Wandall plt.
Richa. Harker deft.
A Review. next.

The Court dismist till tomorrow morning, 8 a Clock.

Morning.   Dec. 14th 1676.

All the Go: paps. to the Constables about horses etc. delivered
for the 2 Ridings North and West.

A warrant for Richa. Ponton sent by the Const. Mulliner.

The Hempsteed men call'd, most doe appeare.
They declare to have had no ill Intent, but legally to beare
equall Charges, and are dismist paying Court Charges.

The proclamacion about Staten Isl. settlement read.

Tho: Wandall plt.
Richa. Harker deft.
A Review.

The proceedings of last Court read.
Mr. Leet for the plt.
Mr. Cooke for Deft. and pleads the Statute of limitacion as long
since pretended to bee due, and not demanded.

To bee considered by the Court whether to bee allowed.

C. Delavall plt.
Joseph Ludlam deft.

The Deft. pleads that hee is not prepared for want of timely
Service—it being but on Saturday last that the Const. summoned him.
put off till next Court.

Adam Mott jun. plt
John Ashman deft.
An attachment for Tobacco.
putt off till afternoone.

Abr: Frost plt.
Laurence Mott deft.
Agreed.

John Skidmore plt.
John Lynus deft.
Nonsuited.

John Emmery plt.
Nath: Selleck deft.
A declaracion upon attachment.
Judgment.

Robt. Williams plt.
John Buro deft.
Non est inventus[*] returned

Tho: Hunt jun. plt.
Edwa. Waters deft.

The defendant ordered, to pay the plaintiffs Charges before notice that the action was withdrawne.
The deft. bound over by Mr. Pell to prosecute the plt. for felony.
To have time till the Court bee dismis't to make good his Charge.
The Court adjourned till afternoone.

Afternoone.

Richa. Smith plt.
Jeremiah Wood deft.

About some suite tryde in the Dutch time for 200 G. etc. fine.

Mr. Leete and Mr. Corbet Att. for the Deft.

The plt. mistakes in his declaracion pretending debt, etc. but appeared not.

The Court to consider.

Adam Mott jun. plt. }
John Ashman deft. } Attachment.
The last Court order'd Mr. Ashman to have next preference of attachment after Bezaliel Osburne.

* "He has not been found." The return of a sheriff on a writ when the defendant or person to be served or arrested is not found in his jurisdiction (*Webster's Third New International Dictionary*, 1964).

By Mr. Leet Robt. Ashman putts in a declaracion demanding 60£ for his sons dyet 8 years and 1/2 and 30£ for 2 horses and 4 mares.

Edwa. Titus a Quaker saith hee kept the Child a yeare and a half and had 10£ a yeare as hee remembers and then the Child went to his grandfather.

The Court order both actions to bee referr'd to the Jury.

Mr. Wm. Osburne sworne saith hee beleives the bill was signed by John Ashman, and that Ralph Hutchinson was employed to demand it, but hee told him hee could not procure it That John Ashman confes't the debt to him.
Mr. Mott declares to have received 1500 wt. of Tobacco, and 350 lb. wt. for a horse.

Referr'd to the Jury.

Mr. Ponton sent for by order of Court for abusing Mr. Justice Cornell and the Justices saying there was no law to bee had against them, as Mr. Pell likewise declared, and that Mr. Cornell owed him 40s which hee could not get, though hee had summoned him to the Towne Court at Flushing, but hee would not appeare.

To bee consider'd by the Court.

Abigail Darling and Zachariah Mills bound over by the last Court for having a bastard.
To appeare againe tomorrow morne.

The Court dismis't till tomorrow morning.

Fryday Decemb. 15th. 1676.

Tho: Wandall and Harker.
The statute of limitacion and award consider'd of.
Adjudg't for the deft.
An Appeale to the Assizes if the Go: allowes of it, being under the value.

The Jury about Mott and Ashman, and Ashman and Ashman.
The Jury find for Robt. Ashman to have the preference, but allow

Motts bill.

Richa. Ponton—fined 3£ and is to make an acknowledged[*] at a Towne Court.

A fine of 5£ a piece on Abigail Darling and Zach: Mills, or 10 stripes a piece and hee to maintaine the Child and give security.

Richa. Smith plt.
Jeremiah Wood deft.
The plt. nonsuited, as not proving his declaracion.

Mr. Cooke moves for a Review.
Graunted.

Edwa Waters ⎱
Thomas Hunt ⎰   Accusacion of
Theft pretended to bee done 4, or 5, yeares agoe.
Its thought to bee vexatious.
Waters ownes hee hath done him wrong in that particular.
To bee cleared by proclamacion.

Severall other papers and peticions read and answered.
Mr. Delavalls Judgment never entred, and defective, so refused to bee entred.

The Court dissolved.

[ENDORSED:]   Sessions papers at Jamaica.
Dec. 13th 14th 15th 1676.

Queens County[‡]

[25:258(1)]

[NOTICE THAT ANDREW GIBB OF OYSTER BAY HAS GIVEN SECURITY
FOR A COURT APPEARANCE]

These are to certify all whom it may concerne that whereas warrants of Arrest and Attachment have beene given out against the persons, Goods

---

* A mental lapse by Secretary Nicolls, who obviously intended to write "acknow-ledgement."
‡ Added after the counties were formed in 1683.

and Chattells of Samuell Edsall and Andrew Gibb of the City of New Yorke, in the North and East Ridings of Yorkeshire upon Long Island, the which hath beene served upon the person of Andrew Gibb at Oysterbay, and Upon the Goods and Chattells of both the said Samuell Edsall and Andrew Gibb in the said two Ridings, Security hath this day beene given here to answer the suite of Samuell Blagge of this City in either of the said Ridings at their next Court of Sessions for the sume of 1521£ sterling, for which said summe the warrant of Arrest and Attachment were granted, so that the person of the said Andrew Gibb is to bee releast, and the Attachment in either of the Ridings to bee taken off, and a stop to all pretences, there on this Account untill a determinacion bee had upon the same according to Law, Dated at N.Y. this 30th day of Dec. 1676.

To any of the Justices of the
peace, Constables and Overseers
upon Long Isl. or where else this
may Concerne.

[25:258(2)]
[THE CONDITIONS OF THE ABOVE SECURITY]

1000£ besides about 1500 bushells of salt 8£ to bee shipt 1800—overcharged the most of the Goods 50 per Cent. by S: Blaggs Confession and to bee prooved etc.
Paid back to S. Blagge in specie and Returnes 1300 lb. or thereabout.

For the remainder Effects are or will be ready this season by the Spring.

William Osburne, Jonathan Smith, and Jeremiah Smith of Hempsteed, Stephen Jarvis, and John Finch jun. of Huntington, and William White of New Yorke.

The Condicion etc. that if Sam: Edsall and Andrew Gibb of the City of N.Y. shall appeare and abide by the determinacion of the Court of sessions to bee held at Southton for the East Riding of Yorkeshire upon Long Isl. in the month of March next, or at the Court of Sessions to bee held for the North Riding in the mo. of June following at Jamaica, in answer to an Arrest layd upon the person of Andrew Gibb at Oysterbay and an attachment layd or to bee layd on the Goods and Chattells belonging to the said Sam: Edsall and Andrew Gibb both in the East and

North Ridings aforesaid upon pretence of a debt due from both or one
of the said persons for the summe of fifteene hundred twenty one pounds
sterl. and bee answerable for the value of such Goods as upon this
security are Replevinde, if adjudged thereunto by the Court, that then
this Obligacion bee voyd and of none effect otherwise etc.

Wittnesses
Tho. Gibbs
Walter Webley.
W: Nicolls.

[ENDORSED:]   Copyes of papers given out about
                   Mr. Sam: Blagge and Mr. Sam: Edsall etc.

                   Dec. 30th 1676.

[25:259]

[DOCKET OF THE SESSIONS FOR THE NORTH RIDING]

                   Accons to be tryed at jameca Sessions
                   the 13th December 1676.

X 1   Tho. Wandall   Plt.
        Richard Harcutt   Deft.

X 2   Rich: Smith   Plt.
        Jeremiah Wood   Deft.

X 3   Capt. Tho: Delavall   Plt.
        Joseph Ludloe   Deft.

X 4   Adam Mott Junior   Plt.
        Jno. Ashman   Deft.

X 5   Abram. Frost   Plt.
        Lorus Mott   Deft.

X 6   Jno. Skidmore   Plt.
        Jno Linas   Deft.

X 7   Jno. Emery   Plt.
        Nath Selleck   Deft.

X 8   Robt. Williams   Plt.
        Jno. Burd.   Deft.

Complaints

X   Tho: Hunt Junior v. Edw: Walters

Peticons

X   Nico: Bayard v. Dr. Henry Tayler
X   Jno Watkins v. Sam: Riscoe

X   The men of Hampsted bound over by Order of assizes.
X   Abigall Darling bound over by Sessi[   ]
X   Zachery Mills bound over ditto

X   accion Robt. Ashman v. Jno. Ashman

Appendix

[24:136b]

[ASSESSMENT ROLLS FOR THE FIVE DUTCH TOWNS ON
LONG ISLAND IN 1675. TRANSLATION]

Assessment roll of the land and property in Boswyck taken on the
19th of August 1675

Pieter Parmentir:
3 heads,* 2 horses, 3 oxen, 6 cows, 2 ditto of 3 yrs.,
3 ditto of 2 yrs. 2 ditto of 1 year, 4 hogs £148.10
32 morgens of land and meadow . . . . <u>64.00</u>   212.10

Jan Cornelise Dame:
1 head, 4 horses, 6 cows, 1 ditto of 3 years, 2 ditto
of 2 yrs. 3 ditto of 1 yr., 16 sheep, 8 hogs £124.00
28 morgens of land and meadow . . . . <u>56.00</u>   180.00

Joost Koeckwytt:
1 head, 2 horses, 8 cows, 2 ditto of 3 yrs., 1 ditto
of 2 yrs., 2 ditto of 1 yr., 6 sheep, 1 hog £99.00
15 morgens of land and meadow . . . . <u>300.00</u>   129.00

Pieter Janse Witt:
3 heads, 3 horses, 1 do. of 3 yrs, 7 cows, 3 do.
of 3 yrs., 4 ditto of 2 yrs., 8 ditto of 1 yr., 3 hogs,
13 sheep £175.10
50 morgens of land and meadow . . . . <u>100.00</u>   275.10

Woutter Gisberse:
1 head, 3 horses, 4 cows, 3 ditto, 3 yrs. 2 ditto of
2 yrs., 3 ditto of 1 yr., 2 sheep £96.00
18 morgens of land and meadow . . . . <u>36.00</u>   132.00

* The number of people in the household

Jan Paris:
1 head, 2 horses, 6 cows, 3 ditto of 2 yrs.,
15 sheep £86.00
23 morgens of land and meadow . . . . <u>46.00</u>   132.00

Charles Fonttein:
1 head, 1 horse of 3 yrs., 2 oxen, 10 cows, 4 ditto of
3 yrs., 6 ditto of 2 yrs. 2 ditto of 1 yr., 4 hogs . . . £122.00
40 morgens of land and meadow . . . . <u>80.00</u>   202.00

Evert Hedeman:
1 head, 1 horse, 2 oxen, 2 cows, 1 hog £53.00
13 1/2 morgens of land and meadow . . . . <u>27.00</u>   80.00

Jaques Cossartt:
1 head, 2 cows, 1 hog, 5 sheep £31.00
5 morgens of land . . . . <u>10.00</u>   41.00

Pieter Schamp:
1 head, 2 cows, 1 sheep, 3 morgens of land 34.10

Adriaen de La Forge:
1 head, 1 cow, 1 ditto of 2 yrs. 25.10

Gisbertt Theunisse:
2 heads, 3 horses, 2 ditto of 2 yrs., 2 ditto of 1
yr., 4 cows, 2 ditto of 3 yrs., 2 ditto of 2 yrs., 2
ditto of 1 yr., 1 hog, 10 sheep £129.00
22 morgens of land and meadow . . . . <u>44.00</u>   173.00

Charles Housman:
1 head, 1 horse, 3 cows £45.00
11 morgens of land and meadow . . . . <u>22.00</u>   67.00

Stas de Groott:
1 head, 1 horse, 1 cow 3.00

Cornelis Jansen:
1 head, 1 horse of 3 yrs., 1 cow, 1 ditto of 3 yrs.,
1 ditto of 2 yrs. £37.10
[*blank*] morgens of land and meadow . . . . <u>8.00</u>   45.10

Jan Cornelise Zeuw:
1 head, 2 horses, 2 cows, 5 sheep £54.00
17 morgens of land and meadow .... <u>34.00</u>   88.00

Caspeert Jansen:
2 heads, 2 horses, 1 ditto of 1 yr., 1 cow £73.00
3 morgens of land .... <u>6.00</u>   79.00

Pieter Jansen Zeuw:
1 head, 1 horse, 1 ditto of 2 yrs., 1 cow 40.00

Onfre Kley:
2 heads, 2 horses, 3 ditto of 3 yrs., 6 cows,
3 ditto of 2 yrs., 3 ditto of 1 yr. £126.00
12 morgens of land and meadow .... <u>24.00</u>   150.00

Jan Jansen:
2 heads, 1 cow of 2 yrs., 1 hog 39.10

Jan Joorese:
1 head, 2 horses, 5 cows, 3 sheep, 1 hog £80.10
5 morgens of land .... <u>10.00</u>   90.10

Alexander Coquevertt:
1 head, 1 horse, 2 sheep, 1 hog £32.00
2 morgens of land .... <u>4.00</u>   36.00

Volckert Dierckse:
2 heads, 3 horses, 1 ditto of 3 yrs., 1 ditto of 1
yr., 5 cows, 4 ditto of 3 yrs., 3 ditto of 1 yr.,
6 sheep, 2 hogs £129.00
25 morgens of and meadow .... <u>50.00</u>   179.00

Jan Areiaensen:
1 head, 3 cows, 1 ditto of 3 yrs., 2 ditto of
1 yr., 3 hogs, 2 sheep £44.00
3 morgens of land .... <u>6.00</u>   50.00

Arie Cornelise Vogel:
2 heads, 3 sheep 37.10

Amador Foupier:
1 head, 2 horses, 1 ditto of 2 yrs. £47.00
21 morgens of land and meadow .... <u>44.00</u>   91.00

Seimen Haeckx:
1 head 18.00

Jabecq Jansen:
1 head 18.00

Nelttie Jans:
2 cows, 3 sheep 11.00

Jan Jansen Kuiper:
1 head 18.00

Dierck Volckerse:
1 head, 3 horses, 1 of 2 yrs., 2 of 1 yr., 3 cows,
1 of 3 yrs., 1 of 1 yr., 6 sheep £88.00
36 morgens of land . . . . <u>72.00</u>   160.00

Jabecq Dierckse:
1 head, 1 horse, 1 ditto of 3 yrs., 1 sheep £43.10
5 morgens of land . . . . <u>10.00</u>   53.10

Hendrick Barense Smit:
1 head, 4 horses, 2 ditto of 3 yrs., 2 ditto of
2 yrs., 6 cows, 4 ditto of 3 yrs., 2 ditto of 2
yrs., 5 ditto of 1 yr., 3 hogs, 3 sheep £154.00
20 morgens of land and meadow . . . . <u>40.00</u>   194.00

Joseph Hael:
1 head, 1 cow 23.00

Willem Jacobse:
1 head 18.00

Theunes Gisberse Bogaertt:
8 morgens of meadow . . . .   <u>16.00</u>

The assessment of the property in Boswyck amounts to   <u>£3174.10</u>

Assessment of the land and property of the inhabitants of
Bruecklen taken on the 20th of August 1675

Theunes Jansen:
3 heads, 4 horses, 1 ditto of 1 yr., 2 oxen, 4
cows, 4 ditto of 3 yrs., 2 ditto of 2 yrs., 4 ditto
of 1 yr., 5 hogs £169.00
23 morgens of land and meadow 46.00   215.00

Claes Aerense:
3 heads, 1 horse, 4 cows, 1 ditto of 3 yrs.,
1 ditto of 2 yrs., 1 ditto of 1 yr. £94.00
14 morgens of land and meadow 28.00   122.00

Mattheis Brouwer:
1 head, 2 cows 28.00
1$\frac{1}{2}$ morgen meadow 3.00   31.00

Paulus vander Beeck:
2 heads, 2 horses, 4 cows, 3 ditto of 3 yrs.,
1 ditto of 1 yr. £93.10
20 morgens of land and meadow 40.00   133.10

Jan Pietterse the Elder:
1 head, 4 oxen, 6 cows, 3 ditto of 2 yrs.,
4 ditto of 1 year. £85.10
16 morgens of land and meadow 32.00   117.10

Jan Cornelise Buis:
1 head, 2 horses, 2 cows. 1 ditto of 2 yr.,
1 ditto of 1 yr., 12 sheep 59.00

Dierck Stoorm:
1 head, 2 cows, 1 ditto of 3 yrs., 1 hog 33.00

Nicklaes Backer:
1 head, 1 horse, 3 cows, 3 ditto of 2 yrs.,
2 ditto of yr., 6 hogs. £61.10
18 morgens of land and meadow 36.00   97.10

Joostt Fransen:
1 head, 2 horses, 4 cows, 1 ditto of 3 yrs.,
3 ditto of 2 yr., 2 ditto of 1 year £76.10
10$\frac{1}{2}$ morgens land and meadow 21.00   97.10

Cornelis Corse Vroom:
1 head, 2 horses, 1 ditto of 1 year, 3 cows,
2 ditto of 2 ycars, 1 ditto of 1 ycar,
4 sheep, 2 hogs £70.00
22 morgens of land and meadow 44.00 114.00

Jan Pietterse Mackelyck:
1 head, 4 oxen, 4 cows, 1 ditto of 1 yr., 2 hogs. ..£65.10
12 morgens land and meadow 24.00 89.10

Dierck Cornelise Hooglantt:
3 heads, 2 horses, 6 cows, 2 ditto of 2 yrs.,
3 ditto of 1 yr., 2 hogs £119.10
8 morgens of land and meadow 16.00 135.10

Paulus Mickielse Vander Voortt:
1 head, 1 horse of 3 yrs., 2 oxen, 3 cows,
1 ditto of 3 yrs., 1 ditto of 1 yr. £58.10
10 morgens of land and meadow 20.00 78.10

Willem Willemse:
1 head, 2 horses, 2 oxen, 6 cows, 2 ditto of 2 yrs.,
4 ditto of 1 yr., 1 hog £96.00
13 1/2 morgens of land and meadow 27.00 123.00

Dierck Hattum:
1 head, 2 oxen, 1 cow, ditto of 2 yrs. 37.10
1 1/2 morgen of land 3.00 40.10

Rhem Jansen:
3 heads, 5 horses, 8 cows, 4 ditto of 3 yrs.,
4 ditto of 2 yrs., 4 ditto of 1 year, 2 hogs £188.00
19 morgens of land and meadow 38.00 266.00

Frederick Lubberse:
1 head, 6 cows, 1 ditto of 2 yrs.,
2 ditto of 1 yr., 7 sheep.....................£56.10
15 morgens of land and meadow 39.00 86.10

Pietter van Neestt:
1 head, 5 cows, 2 hogs £45.00
5 1/2 morgens land and meadow 11.00 56.00

Pietter Jansen:
1 head, 2 horses, 5 cows, 3 ditto of 2 yrs.,
4 ditto of 1 yr. £80.10
8 morgens of land 16.00   96.10

Groott Jan:
2 heads, 2 oxen, 2 cows, 1 ditto of 2 yrs.,
1 ditto of 1 yr. £44.00
2 morgens of meadow 4.00   48.00

Johannes Christeffel:
1 head, 2 oxen, 2 cows £40.00
6 morgens of land and meadow 12.00   52.00

Thomes Jansen:
1 head, 2 horses, 2 cows 52.00

Conradus vander Beeck:
1 head, 2 oxen, 3 cows £45.00
14 morgens of land and meadow 28.00   73.00

Ackeys Jansen:
1 head, 1 cow 23.00

Paulus Dierckse:
2 heads, 2 horses, 2 oxen, 7 cows,
2 ditto of 2 yrs., 5 ditto of 1 yr., 3 hogs £122.10
12 morgens of land and meadow 24.00   146.10

Dierck Pauluse:
1 head, 1 horse of 3 yr. 3 cows, 4 ditto of 2 yrs.,
3 ditto of 1 yr., 1 hog £56.10
12 morgens of land and meadow 24.00   80.10

Weynantt Pietterse:
1 head, 2 horses, 3 cows, 1 ditto of 2 yr.,
2 ditto of 1 yr. £62.10
5 morgen of land 10.00   72.10

* "big" or "large" in Dutch

Adam Brouwer:
2 heads, 2 cows, 3 ditto of 3 yrs., 3 sheep, 1 hog . . £60.00
1 1/2 morgen of meadows 3.00   63.00

Johannes Marcuse:
1 head 18.00

Evertt Hendrickse:
1 head 18.00

Gerritt Croessen:
1 head, 2 oxen, 4 cows, 2 ditto of 3 yrs.,
3 ditto of 2 yrs., 2 ditto of 1 yr., 3 hogs £71.10
14 morgens land and meadow 28.00   99.10

Egbertt Stevense:
1 head 18.00

Seimen Aersen:
1 head, 2 oxen, 3 cows, 2 ditto of 1 yr., 3 hogs . . . £51.00
10 morgens of land and meadow 20.00   71.00

Pietter Pietterse:
1 head, 1 horse 30.00

Lambert Jansen Dortlantt:
1 head, 4 cows £38.00
8 morgens of land and meadow 16.00   54.00

Jerom de Rapallie:
3 heads, 3 cows, 1 ditto of 1 yr., 1 horse £82.10
8 morgens of land and meadow 16.00   98.00

Daniel de Rapallie:
1 head, 1 horse, 1 cow 35.00

Seimen Claessen:
1 head, 1 horse, 1 cow, 1 ditto of 3 yrs., 2 hogs. .   £41.00
6 morgens of land 12.00   53.00

Theunes Gisbertse Bogaertt:
3 heads, 4 horses, 1 ditto of 1 yr., 2 oxen,
14 cows, 6 ditto of 3 yrs., 6 ditto of 2 yrs.,
10 ditto of 1 yr., 6 hogs £247.00
40 morgens of land and meadow .... <u>80.00</u>   327.00

Susanne Dubbels:
2 oxen, 5 cows, 3 ditto of 2 yrs., 3 ditto of 1 yr. ...£49.00
8 morgens of land and meadow .... <u>16.00</u>   65.00

Pietter Corse:
1 head 18.00

Hendrick Corse:
2 heads, 2 horses, 2 sheep £61.00
10 morgens of land and meadow .... <u>20.00</u>   81.00

Hendrick Theymese:
1 head, 1 horse, 3 cows £45.00
3 morgens of land .... <u>6.00</u>   51.00

Thomas Lamberse:
2 heads, 3 horses, 1 ditto of 1 year, 6 cows,
2 ditto of 3 year, 4 ditto of 2 yrs., 2 ditto of
1 yr., 6 sheep, 1 hog £129.10
23 morgens of land and meadow .... <u>46.00</u>   175.10

Jan Gerritse:
1 head, 2 horses, 1 ditto of 2 yrs., 3 cows,
1 ditto of 2 yrs., 3 ditto of 1 yr., 2 sheep, 1 hog. . £71.00
11 1/2 morgens of land and meadow .... <u>23.00</u>   94.00

Jean Aersen:
1 head, 4 horses, 3 cows, 1 ditto of 2 yrs.,
2 ditto of 1 year, 1 hog 87.10

Juff.* Potters:
1 horse, 1 ditto of 2 yrs., 4 cows, 1 ditto of
2 yrs., 2 ditto of 1 yr., 2 hogs £44.10
18 morgens of land and meadow .... <u>36.00</u>   80.10

---

*   Abbreviation of Dutch *Juffrouw*: madam or lady.

Dierck Janse Voertman:
1 head, 2 horses, 3 cows £57.00
9 morgens of land and meadow .... <u>18.00</u>   75.00

Maerten Ryerse:
1 head, 4 horses, 1 ditto of 3 years, 6 cows,
1 ditto of 3 years, 2 ditto of 2 yrs.,
1 ditto of 1 yr., 1 hog £155.10
31 1/2 morgens of land and meadow. .... <u>63.00</u>   178.10

Catharine Jeronimus:
1 ox, 1 cow 11.00

Jabeck Gisberttse:
1 head, 2 horses, 3 cows, 1 ditto of 3 yrs.,
3 ditto of 2 yrs., 1 ditto of 1 yr., 2 hogs £67.00
8 morgens of land and meadow .... <u>16.00</u>   83.00

Jan Fredrickse:
1 head, 2 cows, 1 morgen of meadow 30.00

Baerentt Hegberttse:
1 head, 1 cow, 3 ditto of 3 yrs., 1 ditto
of 2 yrs., 2 ditto of 1 yr. £40.10
4 morgens of land and meadow .... <u>8.00</u>   48.10

Jan Hansen:
1 head, 2 horses, 4 cows, 2 ditto of 3 yrs.,
2 ditto of 2 yrs., 1 ditto of 1 yr., 4 hogs £80.10
10 morgens of land and meadow .... <u>20.00</u>   100.10

Pietter Jansen:
1 head, 1 horse, 3 cows £45.00
8 morgens of land and meadow .... <u>16.00</u>   61.00

Michil Hansen:
1 head, 2 horses, 4 cows, 2 ditto of 3 yrs.,
2 ditto of 2 yrs. £75.00
20 morgens of land and meadow .... <u>40.00</u>   115.00

Wouter Geisse:
1 head 18.00

Andries Jurianse:
2 heads, 4 horses, 6 cows, 3 ditto of 2 yrs.,
1 ditto of 1 yr., 4 sheep £124.10
28 morgens of land and meadow 56.00   180.10

Jan Gillese:
1 head, 1 hog 19.00

Joores Jacobse:
3 heads, 5 horses, 1 ditto of 1 yr., 5 cows,
3 ditto of 3 yrs., 2 ditto of 2 yrs.,
4 ditto of 1 yr., 2 hogs £167.00
40 morgens of land and meadow 80.00   247.00

Total amount of valuation of
the jurisdiction of Breuckelen £5,204.00

Assessment roll of the land and property of the inhabitants
of Middelwout taken on the 22nd of August, anno. 1675

Tittus Sirix:
3 heads, 3 horses, 3 ditto of 1 yr., 7 cows,
6 ditto of 3 yrs., 4 ditto of 1 yr., 9 hogs £173.00
25 morgens land and meadow 50.00   223.00

Dierck Jansen vander Vliett:
2 head, 3 horses, 4 cows, 2 ditto of 2 yrs.,
1 ditto of 1 yr. £98.10
16 morgens of land and meadow 32.00   130.10

Stoffel Probasky:
1 head 1 horse, 1 ditto of 3 yrs., 3 cows,
1 ditto of 3 yrs., 2 ditto of 1 yr., 1 hog £61.00
16 morgens of land and meadow 32.00   93.00

Gerritt Luberse:
1 head, 3 horses, 6 cows, 5 hogs £89.00
20 morgens of land and meadow 40.00   129.00

Seimen Hansen:
1 head, 3 horses, 3 cows, 2 ditto of 3 yrs.,
2 ditto of 2 yrs., 1 ditto of 1 yr., 1 hog £84.10
13 morgens of land and meadow 26.00   110.10

Aucke Janse:
1 head, 2 oxen, 4 cows, 5 sheep £52.00
20 morgens of land and meadow 40.00   92.00

Reyn Jansen:
2 heads, 3 horses, 3 cows, 2 ditto of 1 yr., 2 hogs . £92.00
13 morgens of land and meadow 26.00   118.00

Dierck Jansen Hoglant:
1 head, 2 horses, 4 cows, 1 ditto of 2 years,
1 ditto of 1 yr., 1 hog £67.00
20 morgens of land and meadow 40.00   107.00

Arie Reyerse:
1 head, 4 horses, 1 ditto of 3 yrs., 5 cows,
1 ditto of 3 yrs., a ditto of 2 years,
1 ditto of 1 yr., 2 hogs £109.00
20 morgens of land and meadow 40.00   149.00

Dierck Jansen:
1 head 18.00

Claes Willekes:
1 head 18.00

Jan Harmense:
1 head 18.00

Aers Jansen:
1 head, 3 horses, 3 cows, 2 ditto of 3 yrs.,
2 ditto of 1 yr., 2 hogs £83.10
20 morgens of land and meadow 40.00   123.10

Jan Barense:
1 head, 1 horse, 3 cows 45.00

Hans Christoffel:
1 head, 2 horses, 3 cows, 1 hog 58.00

Hendrick Willemse:
1 head, 2 horses, 3 cows, 2 hogs £59.00
15 morgens of land and meadow 30.00   89.00

Joores Willemse:
1 head, 2 horses, 2 cows, 2 ditto of 3 yrs.,
2 hogs £62.00
15 morgens of land and meadow 30.00   92.00

Barteltt Claesse:
1 head, 2 horses, 1 ditto of 2 yrs., 2 cows,
4 ditto of 3 yrs., 2 ditto of 1 yr., 1 hog £77.00
12 morgens of land and meadow 24.00   101.00

Jabecq Hendrickse:
1 head, 4 horses, 3 cows, 3 ditto of 2 yrs.,
1 ditto of 1 year £90.00
16 morgens of land and meadow 32.00   122.00

Eldertt Luberttse:
1 head, 3 horses, 4 cows, 2 hogs £76.00
16 morgens of land and meadow 32.00   108.00

Louis Jansen:
1 head 18.00

Jockem Woutters:
1 head, 1 horse, 6 cows, 1 ditto of 2 yrs., 1 hog . . . £63.10
17 morgens of land and meadow 34.00   97.10

Minnie Johannes:
3 heads, 1 horse, 1 cow 71.00

Reyn Aersen:
1 head, 2 horses, 4 cows, 2 ditto of 3 yrs.,
1 ditto of 1 yr., 1 hog 73.10

Jan Jansen:
1 head, 2 horses 1 ditto of 3 yrs., 2 oxen, 5 cows,
5 ditto of 3 yrs., 2 ditto of 1 yr., 3 hogs £113.00
17 morgens of land and meadow 34.00   147.00

Arie Lambertse:
1 head, 3 horses, 4 cows, 1 ditto of 3 yrs.,
2 ditto of 2 yrs., 1 ditto of 1 yr., 4 hogs £88.10
24 morgens of land and meadow 48.00   136.10

Annetie de Bruin:
2 horses, 2 cows £34.00
7 morgens of land . . . . <u>14.00</u>   48.00

Pietter Loott:
1 head, 2 horses, 6 cows, 4 ditto of 3 yrs.,
2 ditto of 2 yrs., 1 ditto of 1 yr., 2 hogs £96.10
16 morgens of land and meadow . . . . <u>32.00</u>   128.10

Leffertt Pietterse:
1 head, 2 horses, 2 cows, 1 ditto of 3 yrs.,
1 ditto of 1 yr. £57.10
17 morgens of land and meadow . . . . <u>34.00</u>   91.10

Jan Jansen Feyn:
1 head, 2 oxen, 2 cows, 3 ditto of 2 yrs. 47.10

Willem Jacobse:
2 heads, 2 horses, 1 ditto of 3 yrs.,
1 ditto of 1 yr., 2 oxen, 7 cows, 2 ditto of 2 yrs.,
1 ditto of 1 yr. £124.10
24 morgens of land and meadow . . . . <u>48.00</u>   172.10

Jan Auckes:
1 head, 1 horse, 1 cow 35.00

Pietter Guilliamse:
1 head, 6 oxen, 5 cows, 2 ditto of 2 yrs., 3 hogs. . . £87.00
19 morgens of land and meadow . . . . <u>36.00</u>   123.00

Willem Guilliamse:
1 head, 2 horses, 3 oxen, 7 cows, 2 ditto
of 2 yrs., 3 ditto of 1 yr. £104.10
16 morgens of land and meadow . . . . <u>32.00</u>   136.10

Lambertt Jansen:
1 head 18.00

Jan Streicker:
3 heads, 3 horses, 1 ditto of 1 yr., 12 cows,
2 ditto of 3 yrs., 3 ditto of 2 yrs., 5 ditto
of 1 yr., 2 hogs £178.00
30 morgens of land and meadow . . . . <u>60.00</u>   283.00

Hendrick Streicker:
1 head, 2 horses £42.00
12 morgens of land 24.00   66.00

Barent Barense:
1 head 18.00

Arie Hendrickse:
1 head, 2 horses of 1 yr., 1 cow, 1 ditto
of 2 yrs., 1 ditto of 1 yr., 1 hog 34.00

Arie Andriese:
1 head, 1 horse, 1 cow 35.00

Gerritt Snedeger:
1 head, 4 horses, 1 ox, 6 cows, 3 ditto of 2 yrs.,
2 ditto of 1 yr., 5 hogs £117.10
20 morgens of land and meadow 40.00   157.10

Cornelis Janse Zeuw:
1 head, 3 horses, 5 cows £79.00
30 morgens of land and meadow 60.00   139.00

Caterine Hegemans:
3 heads, 5 horses, 4 oxen, 10 cows, 6 ditto of 3
years, 4 ditto of 2 yrs., 2 ditto of 1 yr., 4 hogs . . £229.00
36 morgens of land and meadow 72.00   301.00

Hendrick Joorese:
1 head, 3 horses, 11 cows, 3 ditto of 2 yrs.,
5 ditto of 1 yr. £124.00
17 morgens of land and meadow 34.00   158.00

Gisbertt Jansen:
1 head 18.00

Cornelis Berry:
1 head, 4 horses, 1 ditto of 1 yr., 7 cows,
2 ditto of 1 yr., 3 sheep £108.00
23 morgens of land and meadow 46.00   154.00

Cornelis Jacobse:
1 head 18.00

Hendrick Cornelise Slechtt:
1 head, 2 cows, 1 ditto of 3 yrs., 1 ditto of
1 yr., 4 hogs £37.10
3 morgens of land 6.00   43.10

Jacob Jansen:
1 head 18.00

Cornelis Barense:
1 head, 3 horses, 1 ditto of 1 yr., 5 cows, 3 ditto
of 3yrs., 2 ditto of 2 yrs., 3 ditto of 1 yr., 1 hog . £104.10
15 morgens of land and meadow 36.00   140.10

Jan Sebringh:
2 heads, 4 horses, 1 ox, 6 cows, 2 ditto of 2 yrs.,
2 ditto of 1 yr., 4 hogs £132.00
19 morgens of land and meadow 38.00   170.00

Balttes Barense:
1 head, 2 cows 28.00

Claes Barense:
1 head, 1 horse of 3 yrs., 1 cow of 2 years 28.10

Stoffell jansen:
1 head, 1 horse of 3 yrs. 26.00

Total amount of the valuation of the property
of Middelwout £5079.10

Assessment roll of the land and property of the inhabitants of
Amsfort taken on the 24th of August 1675.

Gerritt Remmers:
2 heads, 4 horses, 7 cows, 2 ditto of 2 yrs.,
1 ditto of 1 yr. £125.10
23 morgens of land and meadow 46.00   171.10

Harmen Hendrickse:
1 head, 3 horses, 5 cows, 1 ditto of 3 yrs.,
1 ditto of 2 yrs., 1 hog £86.10
25 morgens of land and meadow 50.00   136.10

Albert Alberttse:
2 heads, 3 horses, 2 ditto of 3 yrs., 6 cows,
3 ditto of 2 yrs. £125.10
29 morgens of land and meadow 58.00   183.10

Steven Coertten:
2 heads, 4 horses, 1 ox, 8 cows,
6 ditto of 2 yrs., 2 hogs £147.00
30 morgens of land and meadow . . . . 60 .00   207.00

Hans Jansen:
1 head, 2 oxen, 4 cows, 1 ditto of 1 yr. £51.10
17 morgens of land and meadow 34.00   85.10

Pietter Hendrickse:
1 head, 1 horse 30.00

Swaen Jansen:
1 head, 2 horses, 2 cows £52.00
5 morgens of land 10.00   62.00

Dierck Jansen:
1 head, 2 horses, 3 cows £57.00
7 morgens of land 14.00   71.00

Abraham Joorese:
1 head, 2 horses, 1 ditto of 1 yr., 2 oxen,
14 cows, 3 ditto of 3 yrs., 2 ditto of 2 yrs.,
5 ditto of 1 yr. £151.10
35 morgens of land and meadow 70.00   221.10

Willem Jansen van Berckelo:
1 head, 1 horse, 1 ditto of 2 yrs., 2 cows 45.00

Hendrick Pietterse:
1 head, 3 horses, 4 cows, 3 ditto of 3 yrs.,
2 ditto of 2 yrs., 1 hog. £92.00
19 morgens of land and meadow 38.00   130.00

Seimen Jansen:
2 heads, 4 horses, 1 ox, 8 cows, 3 ditto of
3 yrs., 3 ditto of 2 yrs., 3 ditto of 1 yr.,
6 sheep, 2 hogs £158.10
32 morgens of land and meadow 64.00   222.10

Coertt Stevense:
1 head, 4 horses, 3 oxen, 6 cows, 2 ditto of
3 yrs., 3 ditto of 2 yrs., 3 ditto of 1 yr. £134.00
44 morgens of land and meadow . . . . <u>88.00</u>   222.00

Pietter Monfortt:
1 head 18.00

Jan Kiersen:
2 heads, 2 horses, 2 ditto of 2 yrs., 4 cows,
4 ditto of 3 yrs., 1 ditto of 1 yr., 4 sheep £105.00
31 morgens of land and meadow . . . . <u>62.00</u>   167.00

Willem Gerrittse:
2 heads, 3 horses, 2 ditto of 3 yrs., 1 ditto of
2 yr., 6 cows, 2 ditto of 4 yrs., 3 ditto of 3 yrs.,
3 ditto of 2 yrs., 2 ditto of 1 yr., 2 hogs £157.10
28 morgens of land and meadow . . . . <u>56.00</u>   213.10

Dierckie Roeleffse:
1 horse, 2 cows, 1 ditto of 2 yrs., 1 hog £25.10
4 morgens of land . . . . <u>8.00</u>   33.10

Willem Davittse:
1 head, 2 horses, 1 ditto of 1 yr., 4 cows,
2 ditto of 1 yr. £68.00
12 morgens of land and meadow . . . . <u>24.00</u>   92.00

Jan Roeleffse:
2 heads, 4 horses, 1 ox, 10 cows, 1 ditto of
3 yrs., 2 ditto of 2 yrs., 2 ditto of 1 yr.,
6 sheep, 2 hogs £156.10
52 morgens of land and meadow . . . . <u>104.00</u>   260.10

Albert Alberttse the Young:
1 head, 1 horse, 3 cows, 1 ditto of 2 yrs. 47.10

Jacob and Gerritt Streycker:
3 heads, 3 horses, 5 cows, 2 ditto of 3 yrs.,
6 hogs, and 1 1/2 morgens of land 132.00

Pietter Cornelise:
2 heads, 4 horses, 1 ditto of 1 yr., 6 cows,
2 ditto of 3 yrs., 4 ditto of 2 yrs., 3 ditto of
1 yr., 2 hogs £141.10
24 morgens of land and meadow .... <u>48.00</u>   189.10

Jan Theunisse:
1 head, 1 horse 30.00

Hendrick Assuerus:
1 head 18.00

Adam Michilse:
1 head 18.00

Fernandes van Cickel:
1 head, 2 horses, 3 cows 57.00

Luyckes Stevense:
1 head, 3 horses, 4 cows, 1 ditto of 1 yr. £75.10
20 morgens of land and meadow .... <u>40.00</u>   115.10

Jan Poppen:
1 head, 2 horses, 1 cow 47.00

Jan Maerttense:
1 head, 2 horses, 3 cows, 1 ditto of 2 yrs.,
2 ditto of 1 yr.............................£62.10
10 morgens of land and meadow .... <u>20.00</u>   82.10

Claes Pietterse:
2 horses, 1 ox, 4 cows, 1 ditto of 3 yrs., 1 hog £55.00
7 morgens of land.........................<u>14.00</u>   69.00

Willem Willemse:
1 head, 4 horses, 4 cows £86.00
11 morgens of land and meadow .... <u>22.00</u>   108.00

Willem Huycken:
1 head, 3 cows 33.00

Jan Brouwer:
1 head, 1 horse, 1 cow, 1 ditto of 1 yr. 36.10

Pietter Claessen:
2 heads, 4 horses, 1 ditto of 2 yr., 10 cows,
2 ditto of 3 yrs., 3 ditto of 2 yrs., 4 sheep, 2 hogs £158.00
59 morgens of land and meadow 118.00   276.00

Gilles Jansen:
2 heads, 2 horses, 2 oxen, 3 cows,
1 ditto of 1 year £88.10
10 morgens of land and meadow 20.00   108.10

Ariaen Pietterse:
1 head, 2 horses, 2 cows £52.00
8 morgens of land and meadow 16.00   68.00

Total amount of the whole property of Amsfort £4008.10

Assessment roll of the land and property of the inhabitants of New
Uytrecht taken the 24th of August 1765

Jan Hansen:
1 head, 3 horses, 4 cows, 2 ditto of 2 yrs.,
1 ditto of 1 yr. £80.10
40 morgens of land and meadow 80.00   160.10

Barent Joosten:
1 head, 3 horses, 1 ditto of 2 yrs., 7 cows,
4 ditto of 2 yrs., 5 ditto of 1 yr., 3 hogs 114.10

Anthony Theunisse:
1 head, 1 horse 30.00

Theunes Jansen van Peltt:
2 heads, 4 horses, 4 cows £104.00
32 morgens of land and meadow 64.00   168.00

Jacob Bastiense:
1 head 18.00

Crein Jansen:
1 head, 2 horses, 1 ditto of 1 yr. £45.00
12 morgens of land 24.00   69.00

Jan Gisberttse:
1 head 18.00

Jean Van Cleff:
1 head, 1 horse, 4 cows, 2 ditto of 1 yr. £55.00
40 morgens of land and meadow 80.00   135.00

Jan Jansen van Dyck:
1 head, 2 horses, 2 cows, 1 ditto of 1 yr. £53.10
16 morgens of land 23.00   85.10

Gisbert Theyse:
1 head, 2 horses, 2 cows, 1 ditto of 3 yrs.,
2 ditto of 2 yrs. £61.00
18 morgens of land and meadow 36.00   97.00

Hendrick Mattheise:
1 head, 4 horses, 3 cows, 3 ditto of 2 yrs.,
3 ditto of 1 yr. £93.00
20 morgens of land and meadow 40.00   133.00

Carel Jansen van Dyck:
2 heads, 2 horses 3 cows, 3 ditto of 2 yrs.,
1 ditto of 1 yr. £84.00
24 morgens of land and meadow 48.00   32.00

Huibertt Jansen Stock:
1 head 18.00

Jan Jansen van Rheyn:
2 heads, 1 horse of 2 yrs., 5 cows,
2 ditto of 1 yr. £69.00
20 morgens of land 40.00   109.00

Pietter Jacobse:
1 head, 2 cows 28.00

Theys Jansen:
1 head, 2 oxen, 2 cows, 1 ditto of 3 yrs.,
1 ditto of 1 yr., 1 hog £46.10
12 morgens of land 24.00   70.10

Jan Clement:
1 horse, 2 cows, 1 ditto of 1 yr. 41.10

Jan Musserol:
1 head, 2 oxen, 2 cows £40.00
12 morgens of land 24.00   64.00

Anthony van der Eycke:
1 head, 2 horses, 2 cows, 2 ditto of 3 yrs. 1 hog .. £61.00
12 morgens of land 24.00   85.00

Jan van Deventer:
2 heads, 2 horses, 1 ditto of 3 yrs., 3 cows,
1 ditto of 1 yr. 2 hogs 86.10

Luyckes Mayerse:
1 head, 2 horses, 1 cow, 4 ditto of 3 yrs.,
2 ditto of 2 yrs., 3 hogs £67.00
20 morgens of land 40.00   107.00

Jan Verckerck:
3 heads, 5 horses, 2 ditto of 1 yr., 4 cows,
10 sheep £144.00
72 morgens of land and meadow 144.00   288.00

Rutger Joostten:
1 head, 5 horses, 4 cows, 8 ditto of 3 yrs., 2 ditto
of 2 yrs., 2 ditto of 1 yr., 13 sheep, 1 hog £144.10
72 morgens of land and meadow 144.00   288.10

Jan Gerrittse:
24 morgens of land 48.00

Jacob Gerrittse:
24 morgens of land 48.00

Ackeys Jansen:
12 morgens of land 24.00

Laurens Jansen:
1 head, 2 horses, 2 cows £52.00
24 morgens of land 48.00   100.00

Hans Harmense:
1 head, 3 horses, 5 cows, 3 ditto of 2 yrs.,
3 ditto of 1 yr., 5 sheep, 1 hog £94.00
24 morgens of land 48.00   142.00

Arie Willemse:
1 head, 4 horses, 6 cows £96.00
24 morgens of land and meadow 48.00   144.00

Total amount of the entire property of New Utrecht ..   £2,852.10

Assessments of the five Dutch villages in August 1675

Pounds sh.		Guild st.	Pound Shielling Pence		
3,174.10.0,	assessment of Boswyck,				
	at 1 stiver in the pound 158.14.8	£13.	4.	6	
5,204.	assessment of Breuckel .... 260. 4.	21.	13.	8	
5,079.10.0,	assessment of Middelwout 253.19.8	21.	3.	4	
4,008.10.0	assessment of Amsfortt 200. 8.8	16.	14.		
2,852.10.0,	assessment of New Uytrecht... 142.12.8	11.	17.	8	
Total:					
20,319.	assessment of the 5 villages 1 stiver per pound 1015.19	£84.13.2			

The assessment of all the five Dutch villages amounts, as you see above, to 2031 pounds sterling reckoning the county rates at 1 penny in the pound, they amount to 84 pounds 13 shillings and 2 pence sterling, or in current pay to 1,015 guilders 13 shillings; property being rated as follows:

Each man @ .... £18.	Each cow @ .... £5.
Each horse @ .... 12.	Each 3 year old @ .... 4.
Each 3 year old .... 8.	Each 2 year old @ 2.10
Each 2 year old @ ... 5.	Each yearling @ 1.10
Each yearling @ ...... 3.	Each hog @ .... 1.
Each ox @ .... 6.	Each sheep @ 8, 6

Each morgen of land @ 2 pounds Sterling.

The whole account, errors excepted
    most carefully examined by

Your affectionate servant.
Michel Heinelle
clerk

[ENDORSED:]*   Returne of the 5 Dutch
                    Townes by Mr. Heynelle
                    Aug. 29th 1675.

* Endorsed in English.

[24:148]

[ASSESSMENT ROLLS OF WESTCHESTER AND EASTCHESTER IN 1675]*

Parsons	horses	Oxen	Cows	3 yeer olds	2 yeer	1 yeer	Swine	land	Medow	Sheep
Henry Gardenar	1	0	3	0	3	1	2	4	8	0
Isack Dicarman	0	0	3	0	3	1	2	4	12	0
Willm Shippard	—	—	—	—	—	—	—	—	—	—
Joseph Tailar	1	0	3	1	0	2	1	5	6	0
John Wintar	—	—	—	—	—	—	—	—	—	—
John Qinby	4	4	6	3	3	3	3	20	23	4
Joseph Palmar	1	2	3	4	2	3	4	6	24	6
Samuell Palmar	0	2	2	2	0	0	3	14	13	0
Richard Ozbun	1	2	3	2	2	4	1	8	12	0
Widow Plat	0	0	4	0	0	0	2	9	0	0
Thomas Mulenex	2	8	8	6	3	6	4	14	22	10
Edward Hubard	1	2	2	2	0	1	2	15	13	2
John Turnar	1	0	2	0	0	3	0	5	6	0
Nicles Bayly	0	4	6	1	3	2	10	8	15	0
Robart Huestus	1	0	2	0	2	2	0	19	17	0
John Wilye	0	0	4	2	0	1	2	3	6	0
Thom Seabruck	2	0	6	3	0	3	2	5	12	0

* Some of the numbers are difficult to read and should be verified against town records. We have followed E. B. O'Callaghan's reading in *CD* 13, except where he is clearly wrong. Illegible numbers have been recovered from O'Callaghan and indicated in boldface type.

Parsons	horses	Oxen	Cows	3 yeer olds	2 yeer	1 yeer	Swine	land	Medow	Sheep
John Firis	2 1/2	4	6	1	1	6	5	2	50	10
Timothi Wintar	0	0	3	0	1	1	1	2	9	0
Nathan Bayly	1	0	1	0	1	2	0	2	3	0
James Ryly	—	—	—	—	—	—	—	—	—	—
John Hitchcock	1	2	1	0	1	1	3	0	6	—
Richard Pontun	1	4	5	2	0	1	3	5	18	0
Wilm Colard	3	0	2	0	0	0	1	1	1	0
Thoms Faringtun	0	2	4	0	0	2	0	2	6	[ ]
Thomas Vaill	1	2	3	2	2	0	0	6	8	0
Edward Watars	0	4	4	2	3	1	3	20	20	6
Miles Okely	0	0	2	2	0	1	0	4	4	8
Ditrick Garetson	1	0	1	1	0	1	0	3	6	5
Joseph Hunt	2	2	5	0	2	2	2	7	10	0
John Hunt	0	2	4	2	2	2	4	6	6	4
Francis Peak	1	0	1	3	1	1	1	5	0	0
Considar Wood	1	0	3	1	4	0	5	3	12	0
Thos. Hunt Senior	3	5	6	4	6	6	6	15	30	5
John Forgasonn	—	—	—	—	—	—	—	—	—	—
Robart Maning	2	2	8	6	7	5	2	6	60	0
Thos Hunt Junior	1	4	4	5	4	1	2	8	20	0

Parsons	horses	Oxen	Cows	3 yeer olds	2 yeer	1 yeer	Swine	land	Medow	Sheep
John Richard	—	—	—	—	—	—	—	—	—	—
Thom Baxtar	0	2	3	0	0	3	0	0	0	0
John Palmar	1	2	3	0	3	0	5	0	12	0
Josia Hunt	2	0	5	1	1	4	0	4	0	0

Westchester September the 12th 1675
by mee Edward Watars

Parsans	horses	oxen	[ ]	3 year	2 year	1 year	swine	land	medow	Sheep
Samuell Drake	—	4	3	3	2	2	3	14	12	—
Samul Drake Jr.	1	0	0	0	0	0	0	0	3	—
John Drake	—	—	—	—	—	—	—	—	—	—
William Hayden	3	2	4	3	4	1	4	12	12	—
Moses Hoyt	2	2	8	6	4	1	6	11	15	—
Nathanl. Tomkins	0	2	3	1	0	0	4	6	6	—
John Hoyt	2	4	7	3	0	2	1	15	15	—
John Jacksonn	2	2	2	2	0	1	7	2	7	—
John Goden	1	0	3	0	2	3	0	2	0	—
Ebenesar Jones	1	0	3	0	2	1	0	5	8	—
Richard Hedly	0	0	2	0	0	0	2	0	0	—
Wilm Sqire	0	2	3	0	2	0	5	0	0	—
Samuell Goden	0	0	1	0	0	0	1	4	5	—
[T]homas Sherwod1	1	1	2	0	0	0	4	4	—	

Parsons	horses	Oxen	Cows	3 yeer olds	2 yeer	1 yeer	Swine	land	Medow	Sheep
John Tomkins	0	2	3	0	0	0	1	8	10	—
Richard Shoot	2	2	4	4	2	2	8	10	15	—
David Ozbun	2	4	5	1	1	4	10	15	15	—
Philip Pinkny	0	2	8	0	3	0	9	14	15	—
John Pinkny	2	0	4	2	2	0	0	5	4	—
John Helyard	0	0	1	0	0	2	0	0	0	—

EstChestar

The List of John Richardson estate foure oxen Eaight couese Six three
year oulds foure too year oulds three yearlings one hors one Mare seven
swine twenty Eakers of meddoe three Eakers of upland.

[ENDORSED:]   Westchester Valuations
                       brought in by
                       Mr. Palmer:
                        Sept. 16 1675
                       Ex rate 22£ 5sh 8d

                       [ ]his to be left
                       in the ofes at
                       new york for the
                       use of the
                       high shreeff

[24:149]

The A[   ] Anno
1675 [   ]
Law, as allso of there Land [   ]pland and[   ]Meadow
Ground, With the Number of their Cattle namely: Oxen, Cows, horses,
Mares and sheepe as followes

Imprimis: of: personns the troopers excepted   30
of: Oxen there is 26
of: Cows there is to the number off 107
of: Cattle of three yeares Ould there is 20
of: Cattle of twoe yeares Ould there is 32
of: Cattle of one yeare Ould there is 55
of: Horses and Mares there is 62
of: Horses of three yeares ould 05
of: Horses of two yeares ould 08
of: Horses of one yeare ould 16
of: Sheepe to the number of 60
of: Acers of upland and Meadow ground 932

By mee Nicholas Stillwell constable and the Overseers
.13£: 14sh: 3d

[ADDRESSED:]   This to secretarie
                     Nicolls att: N: Yorke
                     Lett bee delivered.

[ENDORSED:]   Gravesend Valuacions
                     brought in Sept. 20th 1675
                     Rate 13 £–14sh. 3d.

[24:150]

[RETURN OF THE VALUATION OF PROPERTY IN EASTHAMPTON]*

The List of Easthampton august the 24th: 1675

	£	s	d
Jeremiah Conckling	193	10	0
Stephen H[o]dges	243	10	
Joshua: garlick sen:	104	13	4
Tho: Hand	097	3	4
Wm: Mulford	164	3	4
Tho: Edwards	091	3	4
Mr Tho Chatfeild	238	16	8
Tho: Osborne senr:	166	10	
John Cerle	100	10	
Wm Miller	090	13	4
John Hoping	169	00	
[Ro]bert Daiton	205	00	
[Ph]illip Leekie	043	6	8
[ ]n Hand	[11	0]	
[Joshu]a garlick Ju:	056	0	
[Rich:] Shaw	146	13	4
[Rich:] Brooke	142	6	8
[W]m fithian	180	3	4
[S]amuell Parsons	085	0	
[A]rthur Creasy	048	0	
[T]ho: Osborne Ju:	175	0	
John Parsons	126	0	
Abraham Hauke	033	10	
[Joh]n Miller	103	0	
[James] Bird	028	0	
[John] Tkeller	173	3	4
[Benjamin Os]borne	067		
[ ]er	138	0	
[ ]	233	0	
[ ]	146	6	8
[ ]	318	0	
[John Richeso]n	027	10	
[Capt. Tho Tal]mag	255	10	

* Partly from *CD* 14

[John Stretto]n Sen:	291	06	8
[John Strett]on Jun:	090	00	
Mrs. Codner	025	00	
Reneck garison	042	00	
Nath: Bushup	177	34	
James Hand	058	10	
James Loper	076	00	
Samuel Mulford	083	00	
Joseph Osborne	044	00	
Richard Stretton	264	13	4
Tho diment	225	00	
Ebenezer Leek	034	00	
Natha. Domeny	091	00	
Samuel Brooke	066	68	
Wm Perkins	23	00	
John Miller Junear	03	00	
John: Osborne	196	13	4
Enock fithian	067	00	
Benia: Conckling	103	00	
John feild	040	00	
Joanah Hodges	045	00	
Tho: diment June:	030	00	
Tho: Chatfeild	018	00	
[Edward] [ ]	018	00	
The totall summe	6042	16	8

[   ]mtpon Retur
[   ]heir Valuacion
[   ] Sept. 17. 167[ ]
past. October. 25. 1675.
68421–6–8
2810–2—

[24:152]

[RETURN OF THE VALUATION OF PROPERTY IN SOUTHOLD]*

Southoulds Estimate the 16th September 1675

John Paine

1 heade	18 – –
10 acors land	10 – –
2 oxen	12 – –
5 cows 1: 3 yr. old ...	29 – –
3:2 yr. old	07 10 –
2 yerlings	03 – –
3 horses	36 – –
10 gotes	04 – –
	119.10 –

Wm. Robinson

1 heade 1 horse	30 – –
12 acors land	12 – –
3 oxen	18 – –
3 cows	15 – –
2:3 yr. old	08 – –
3:2 yr. old	05 – –
3:yerlings.	04 10 –
	92 10 –

John Greete

1 heade	18 – –
30 acors land	30 – –
2 oxen	12 – –
6 cows	30 – –
1:3 yr. olde	04 – –
2:2 yr. olds	05 – –
4:yerlings	06 – –
2 horses	12 – –
1 yerling horse	03 – –
4 swine	04 – –
	124 – –

Calib Curtis

1 heade 12 acors of land	30 – –
2:oxen: 5 cows	37 – –
1:3 yr. old: 2:2 yr. olde	09 – –
4 yerl	06 – –
1 horse: 1:3 yr. old	20 – –
4 swine	04 – –
	106 – –

Wallter Jones

1 heade	18 – –
12 acors land	12 – –
1 ox 3 cows	21 – –
½ a horse	06 – –
2:2 yr. olds 4 yerlings	11 – –
	68 – –

Giddion Yongs

1 heade	18 – –
35 acors land	35 – –
2 oxen: 5 cows	37 – –
1:3 yr. 3:2 yr. olds ...	11 10 –
4 yerlings	06 – –
2 horses 1 yerling	27 – –
7 swine	– –
	141 10 –

Abraha. Whithere

1 heade 25 acors land	43 – –
1 ox: 5 cows	31 – –
3:3 yr. old	12 – –
2:2 yr. old 2 yerlings ..	08 – –
4½ horses	54 – –

* Some gaps in the original have been filled in from *CD* 14.

1 yerling horse . . . . . . 03 – –
8 swine . . . . <u>08 – –</u>
                159

Tho: Terry
1 heade . . . . 18 – –
8 acors land . . . . 08 – –
2:oxen 4 cows . . . . . . 32 – –
2:3 yr. olds . . . . 08 – –
3:2 yer old 2 yerlings   10 10 –
3 horses 1:3 yer old . . 44 – –
1:2 yr. yerling horse . 08 – –
1 swine . . . . <u>01 – –</u>
             129 10 –

John Tuthill
2 heades . . . . 36 – –
40 Acors land . . . . 40 – –
2 oxen 7 cows . . . . . . 47 – –
5:3 yr. olde . . . . 20 – –
7:2 yr. olde 2 yerlings   20 10 –
3 horses and 1 yerling   39 – –
9 shepe . . . . 03 – –
1 swine . . . . <u>– –</u>
            206 10 –

Richard Browne
4 heads . . . . 72 – –
50 acors land . . . . 50 – –
8 oxen . . . . 48 – –
10 cows . . . . 50 – –
6:3 yr. old . . . . 24 – –
7 2 yr. old . . . . 17 10 –
5 yerlings . . . . 07 10 –
6 horses . . . . 72 – –
1:3 yr. old 1 yerling . . 11 – –
25 shepe . . . . 08 – –
10 swine . . . . <u>10 – –</u>
            370 – –

Samll King
1 heade . . . . 18 – –
40 acors land . . . . 40 – –
5 oxen . . . . 30 – –
6 cows . . . . 30 – –
2:3 yr. olds . . . . 08 – –
5:2 yr. olds . . . . 12 10 –
4 yerlings . . . . 06 – –
2 horses 1 swine . . . . <u>25 – –</u>
            169 10 –

Joseph Maps
1 heade 1: 2 yr. old . . <u>20 10–</u>

Samll Grover
1 heade . . . . 18 – –
2 acors land . . . . 2 – –
1 horse 1 cow . . . . <u>17 – –</u>
            37 – –

Tho: Moore Junr
1 heade . . . . 18 – –
40 acors land . . . . 40 – –
4 oxen . . . . 24 – –
9 cows . . . . 45 – –
2 yerlings . . . . 03 – –
4 horses . . . . 48 – –
18 shepe . . . . 06 – –
2 swine . . . . <u>02 – –</u>
            186 – –

Jonathan Moore
1 heade . . . . 18 – –
40 acors land . . . . 40 – –
2 oxen 6 cows . . . . . . 42 – –
1:3 yr. old 1:2 yr. old . 06 10 –
4 yerlings . . . . 06 – –
2 horses 1:2 yr. old . . 29 – –
6 swine . . . . <u>06 – –</u>
            147 10 –

Capt John Yongs

3 heads 10 acors land   64 – –
2 oxen 4 cows . . . . . . 32 – –
4:3 yr. 2:2 yr. old . . . . 21 – –
4 yerlings . . . . 06 – –
8 horses . . . . 96 – –
9 shepe 6 swine . . . . . 09 – –
                          228 – –

Mr. John Yongs Jur
1 heade . . . . 18 – –
24 acors land . . . . 24 – –
4 oxen: 7 cows . . . . . 59 – –
6 yrlings . . . . 09 – –
2 horses . . . . 24 – –
2 yrlings . . . . 06 – –
15 shepe . . . . 05 – –
3 swine . . . . 03 – –
                          148 – –

Peter Simons
1 heade . . . . 18 – –

Mr John Conklin
1 head 80 acors land   . 98 – –
8 oxen . . . . 48 – –
9 cows . . . . 45 – –
5:3 yr. olds . . . . 20 – –
9:2 yr. olds . . . . 22 10 –
6 yerlings . . . . 09 – –
5 horses . . . . 60 – –
3:2 yr. olds . . . . 15 – –
21 shepe . . . . 07 – –
20 swine . . . . 20 – –
1:3 yr. old bull . . . . . . 04 – –
348–10£ 358£–10s–358 10

Jacob Conklin
1 heade . . . . 18 – –
40 acors land . . . . 14 – –
2 oxen 4 cows . . . . . . 32 – –
4:3 yr. 5:2 yr.
3 yerling . . . . 33 – –
2 horses . . . . 24 – –
3 shepe 8 swine . . . . . 09 – –
                          130 – –

John Cory
1 heade . . . . 18 – –
1 ox . . . . 06 – –
1 horse 1 3 yr. old . . . . 20 – –
                           44 – –

Thomas Rider
2 heads . . . . 36 – –
30 acors land . . . . 30 – –
4 oxen 8 cows . . . . 64 – –
1:2 yr. old 1:3 yr. old . 06 10 –
4 yerlings . . . . 06 – –
24 shepe 10 swine . . . . 18 – –
                          160 10 –

John Franklin and John Wigins
2 heads 40 acors land . 76 – –
4 oxen: 6 cows . . . . . . 54 – –
1:2 yr. old 5 yerlings . 10 – –
2 horses 1:2 yr. old . . . 29 – –
9 shepe . . . . 03 – –
4 swine . . . . 04 – –
                          176 – –

Jeremy Valle
3 heads . . . . 54 – –
10 acors land 2 oxen . . . 22 – –
6 cows 3:3 yr. olds . . . 42 – –
1:2 yr. old 3 yrlings . . 07 – –

1 horse 12 shepe .... 16 – –
11 swine .... 11 – –
                     152 –

Edward Petty
2 heads .... 36 – –
10 acors land .... 10 – –
2 oxen 5 cows .... 37 – –
1 horse .... 12 – –
                    95 – –

Simon Grover
2 heads 5 acors land .. 41 – –
2 cows .... 10 – –
1:2 yr., 1 yerling ..... 04 – –
1 horse 3 swine ..... 15 – –
                     70 – –

Nathall. Moore
1 head .... 18 – –
4 acors land 2 cows .. 14 – –
                      32 – –

Mr. Thomas Moore Senr.
1 heade 10 acors land   28 – –
6 oxen 5 cows ...... 61 – –
2:3 yr. 2 yerlings .... 11 – –
2 horses 3 swine .... 27 – –
                      127 – –

Joseph Yongs
1 heade 12 acors land . 30 – –
2 oxen 5 cows .... 37 – –
2:3 yr. old 2 swine ... 11 – –
                       78 – –

Isack Reeves
1 head, 1 horse ..... 30 – –
                      30 – –

Samll Yongs
1 heade 8 acors land . 26 – –
2 cows .... 10 – –
2:3 yr. 2:2 yr. .... 13 – –
1 horse .... 12 – –
1:3 yr. 1 yerling .... 11 – –
                       72 – –

Stephen Bayly
1 heade .... 18 – –
13 acors land .... 13 – –
3 cows 3:3 yr. old ... 22 – –
1 horse 1 yerling .... 15 – –
3 shepe .... 01 – –
                      69 – –

Mr John Yongs mariner
1 heade 2 acors land . 20 – –
4 cows .... 20 – –
1 horse 1 swine ..... 13 – –
                       53 – –

Samll Glover
1 heade 1 ox .... 24 – –
3 cows .... 15 – –
4:3 yr. old 3:2 yr. old . 23 10 –
1 horse 1 swine ..... 13 – –
                       75 10 –

Beniam. Yongs
2 heads .... 36 – –
18 acors land .... 18 – –
6 oxen 3 cows ...... 51 – –
2:3 yr. olds 2:2 yr. olds 13 – –
1 horse: 1 yerling hors 15 – –
21 shepe: 2 swine ..... 09 – –
                        142 – –

Christopr Yongs senr

1 heade 12 acors land .	30	– –
2 oxen 4 cows	32	– –
1:2 yr. old	02	10 –
4 horses	48	– –
12 shepe 1 swine	08	– –
	120	10 –

Richd Clarke

1 heade	18	– –
4 acors land 1 cow	09	– –
3:3 yr. olde 2 yerlings	15	– –
1 horse	12	– –
6 shepe 6 swine	08	– –
	62	– –

John Booth

2 heads	36	– –
17 acors land	17	– –
3 oxen	18	– –
4 cows	20	– –
2:2 yr. olds 2 yerlings .	08	– –
3 horses 1:2 yer old ..	41	– –
3 shepe	01	– –
6 swine	06	– –
	147	– –

John Curwin

2 heads 21 acors land	57	– –
6 oxen 6 cows	66	– –
3:3 yr. old	12	– –
1:2 yr. old	02	10 –
5 horses	60	– –
2:3 yr. olde	16	– –
1:2 yr. old 1 yerling ..	08	– –
5 swine	05	– –
6 shepe	02	– –
	228	10 –

Barnabs. Horton

2 heads	36	– –
37 acors land	37	– –
9 oxen	54	– –
8 cows	40	– –
4:3 yr. old	16	– –
4:2 yr. old	10	– –
4:yerlings	06	– –
69 shepe	23	– –
6 horses	72	– –
1 yerling	03	– –
8 swine	08	– –
	305	– –

Jonathan Horton

1 head	18	– –
36 acors land	36	– –
2 oxen 6 cows	42	– –
3:3 yr. olds	12	– –
5:2 yr. olds	12	10 –
2 yerling	03	– –
3 horses 1 yerling	39	– –
9 shepe 6 swine	09	– –
	171	10–

Richd Benjamin

2 heads	36	– –
39 acors land	39	– –
8 oxen 6 cows	78	– –
2:3 yr. old: 6:2 yr. old	23	– –
4:yerlings	06	– –
4 horses	48	– –
2:2yr.: 1:yerling	13	– –
4 swine	04	– –
	247	– –

Beniam. Moore

1 heade	18	– –
14 acors land	14	– –
4 cows: 2:3 yr. olds ..	28	– –

2:2 yr.: 2 yerlings .... 08 – –
4 horses .... 48 – –
2 swine .... 02 – –
                    118 – –

Mr John Bud not being at home
is lumpt at by the last yeres
accompt at .... £ s d
                    300 – –

Abraham Cory
1 heade 4 acors land .. 22 – –
2 oxen .... 12 – –
2:3 yr. old 1:2 yr. old . 10 10 –
1 horse: 1 yerling .... 15 – –
5 swine .... 05 – –
                    64 10 –

Joshua Horton
1 heade 20 acors land   38
8 oxen 4 cows .... 68 – –
7:3 yr. 3:2 yr.
3 yerlings .... 40 – –
3 horses: 1 2 yr. old .. 41 – –
10 swine .... 10 – –
                    197 – –

Barbabs: Wines
1 heade 15 acors land . 5[3 – –]
2 oxen 9 cows ...... [57 – –]
5:3 yr. olds .... [20 – –]
2:2 yr. 6 yerling ..... 1[4 – –]
6:sheep 6 swine ..... 08 – –
                    15[2– –]

Isack Ouenton
2 heade 24 acors land . 60
5 oxen: 6 cows ...... 6[0   ]
4: 3 yr. olds .... 1[6   ]
8: 2 yr. 6 yerlings .... [29]

4: horses 1 yerling ... 5[1]
20 sheep 9 swine ..... [16   ]
                    23[3–]

Mr Tho Hucisson
1 heade 14 acors land . 32 –
5 oxen 5 cows .... 55 –
4:3 yr. 3:2 yr. 2 yerlings 22 10 –
4 horses 19 swine .... 67 – –
                    176 10 –

Jacob Cory
1 heade 10 acors land . 28 –
4 oxen 2 cows .... 34 –
3:3 yr. 2 yerlings ..... 15 –
1 horse 4 swine ...... 16 – –
                    93 –

[Tho] Reeves
[1 h]eade 23 acors land 41 – –
[4 o]xen 5 cows ...... 49 – –
3 yr. 3:2 yr. 2 yerlings 18 10 –
2 horses 5 swine .... 29 – –
                    137 10 –

John Reeves
1 heade 1 ox .... 24 – –
1:[3yr.] 1 yerling ..... 0510 –
[1 horse]1:3 yr old horse 20 – –
[5 swi]ne .... 05 – –
                    54 10 –

Peeter Paine
[1 head]e 6 acors land . 24 – –
[2 co]ws .... 10 – –
[2:2] yr. old: 2 yerlings 08 – –
[1 hor]se 4 swine ..... 16 – –
                    58 – –

[Dain]ell Terry
[1 hea]de 12 acors land   30 –
[4 oxe]n 5 cows . . . . . . 49 –
[3:3 y]r:3:2 yr. 3 yerlings 24 –
1 horse 1 yerling . . . . 15 –
[8 s]wine . . . . 08 – –
                          126 – –

Peeter Dicisson
[2] heads 20 acors land   56 – –
[8 ox]en . . . . 48 – –
[12 c]lows . . . . 60 – –
[3:3] yr. olds . . . . 12 – –
[6:2] yer olds 3 yerlings 19 10 –
[1 ho]rse . . . . 12 – –
[1:3] yer 1:2 yr. old . . . 13 – –
gotes . . . . 16 – –
swine . . . . 14 – –
                          250 10 –

Richard Cozens
[1] heade 18
[4] acors land 4
                           22 – –

Nathall: Terry
2 heads 20 acors land . 56 – –
7 oxen 8 cows . . . . . . 82 – –
2:3 yr. old . . . . 08 – –
5:2 yr. 5 yerlings . . . . 20 – –
2 horses . . . . 24 – –
1:3 yr. 1 yr.ling . . . . . 11 – –
18 swine . . . . 18 – –
                          219 – –

Samll Wines
1 head 9 acors land . . . 27 – –
2 oxen . . . . 12 – –
4 cows 3 yrlings . . . . . 24 10 –

1 horse 3 swine . . . . . . 14 – –
                           78 10 –

Mrs Mary Welles
26 acors land . . . . 26 – –
4:oxen 6 cows . . . . 54 – –
5:3 yr. old . . . . 20 – –
7:2 yer 2 yrlings . . . . . 20 10 –
27 shepe . . . . 09 – –
5 horses . . . . 60 – –
1:3 yr. 1:2 yr. 1 yerling
horse . . . . 16 – –
12 swine . . . . 12 – –
                          217[10–]

Simieon Beniam.
1 heade 10 acors land . 28 – –
2 oxen 3 cows . . . . 27 – –
4 3 yr. old 1 yerling . . 19 – –
2 horses 1 yr. . . . . 27 – –
3 shepe 4 swine . . . . . . 05 – –
                          106 – –

Wille. Colleman
1 heade 4 acors land . . 22 – –
2 cows . . . . 10 – –
2:2 yr. olds . . . . 05 – –
2 yerlings . . . . 03 – –
1 horse 1:2 yr. old . . . . 17 – –
2 swine . . . . 02 – –
                           59 – –

Calib Horton
1 heade 80 acors land   96 – –
6 oxen . . . . 36 – –
12 cows . . . . 60 – –
5:3 yr. olds . . . . 20 – –
7:2 yr. olds . . . . 17 10 –
7 yerlings . . . . 10 10 –

2 horses 1:3 yr. old
horse .... 32 – –
1:2 yr. old 1 yerling
horse .... 08 – –
2 swine .... <u>02 – –</u>
282 – –

Tho Maps Junr
1 heade 15 acors land . 33 – –
1 ox: 3 cows .... 21 – –
2:3 yr. 4: 2 yr. 2
yerlings .... 21 – –
1 horse 12 swine .... <u>24 – –</u>
99 – –

Thomas Tusteene
1 heade 6 acors land .. 24 – –
2 oxen, 1 cow .... 17 – –
1:3 yr. 2:2 yr. 1 yerling 08 – –
1 hors 3 swine ...... <u>15 – –</u>
64 – –

Thomas Maps Senr
2 heads 24 acors land . 60 – –
6 oxen 8 cows ...... 76 – –
3:3 yr. olds .... 12 – –
3 horses 2 yrlings
horses .... 42 – –
20 swine .... <u>20 – –</u>
227 10 –

Thomas Terrill
1 heade 14 acors land . 32 – –
2 oxen 3 cows .... 27 – –
3:3 yr. olds .... 12 – –
2:2 yr. old 2 yerlings .. 08 – –
2 horses 6 swine ..... <u>30 – –</u>
109 – –

James Reeves
1 heade 24 acors land . 42 – –
10 oxen 7 cows ...... 95 – –
6:3 yr. olds .... 24 – –
5:2 yr. 2 yerlings .... 15[10 –]
3 horses .... 36 – –
1:3 yr. old 1 yerling .. 11 – –
3 shepe 20 swine .... <u>21 – –</u>
24[4 10 –

Will Reeves
1 heade 5 acors land .. 23 – –
3 cows 1:3 yr. old .... 19 – –
2:2 yr. 3 yerlings ..... 09 10 –
1 horse 6 swine ...... <u>18 – –</u>
69 10 –

John Swasie Senr
2 heads .... 36 – –
12 acors land .... 12 – –
6 oxen 6 cows ...... 66 – –
1:3 yr. old bull ...... 04 – –
5:2 yr. old 1 yerling .. 1[4– –]
4 horses .... 48[– –]
20 swine .... <u>20 – –</u>
200[– –]

John Swasie Jun.
1 heade 10 acors land . 28 – –
2 oxen 2 cows .... 22 – –
1:2 yr. old 4 yerlings .. 08 10 –
4 swine .... <u>04 – –</u>
62 10 –

Joseph Swasie
1 heade 8 acors land . . 26 – –
2 oxen 2 cows . . . . . . 22 – –
1:2 yr. 1 yerling . . . . . 04 – –
1 horse . . . . 12 – –
2 swine . . . . 02 – –
66 – –

Will Halloke
3 heads . . . . 54 – –
70 acors land . . . . 70 – –
8 oxen . . . . 48 – –
[14] cows . . . . 70 – –
[4:]3 yr. old . . . . 16 – –
[10:]2 yr. old . . . . 25 – –
[9 y]erlings . . . . 13 10 –
[2 horses] . . . . 24 – –
[4:2 yr. old 1] yrling . . 11 – –
30 swine . . . . 30 – –
361 10 –

John Hallock
[1] heade . . . . 18 – –
4 acors land . . . . 04 – –
2 oxen 2 cows . . . . . . 22 – –
2 yerlings . . . . 03 – –
2 horses 1:2 yr. old . . . 29 – –
[6] swine . . . . 06 – –
82 – –

[Ric]hard Howell
[1 he]ade 6 acors land . 24 – –
[2 o]xen 1 cow . . . . . . 17 – –
[1:3] yr. old . . . . 04 – –
2:2 yr. 2 yerlings . . . . 08 – –
1 horse 1 yerling . . . . . 15 – –
5 gotes 7 swine . . . . . . 09 – –
77 – –

Thoms Osman
[ ] heads 8 acors land . . 44 – –
4 oxen 4 cows . . . . . . 44 – –
5:3 yr. olds . . . . 20 – –
6:2 yr. . . . . 15 – –
6 yerlings . . . . 09 – –
4 horses . . . . 48 – –
1:2 yr. old horse . . . . . 05 – –
9 swine . . . . 09 – –
194 – –

Will Poole
2 heads 7 acors land . . [25 – –]
2 oxen 8 cows . . . . [52 – –]
1:3 yr. old 1:2 yr. old . [06 10–]
7 yerlings . . . . [10 10 –]
1 horse 8 swine . . . . . . [20 – –]
114 – –

Christopher Yongs Junior
1 heade 1 horse . . . . . . 30 – –
2:3 yr. olds 2:2 yr. olds   26 – –
56 – –

John Sallmon
1 heade . . . . 18 – –
1:3 yr. old horse . . . . . 08 – –
[26 – –]

James Lee
1 heade . . . . 18 – –

Benin. Horton
1 heade . . . . [18 – –]
70 acors land . . . . [70 – –]
4 oxen . . . . 24 – –
8 cows . . . . 40 – –
4:3 yr. olds . . . . 16 – –
5:2 yr. old . . . . 12 10 –

4 horses . . . . 48 – –
4 swine . . . . 04 – –
                            232 10 –

Sarah Yongs
8 acors land . . . . 08 – –
2 oxen 4 cows . . . . 32 – –
4:3 yr. old . . . . 16 – –
1:2 yr. old . . . . 02 10 –
1 horse . . . . 12 – –
2 swine . . . . 02 – –
                            72 – –

The totall sume is

£.   s.   d
10935: 10: 00

[ENDORSED:]

Southold Valuacions
past October 25 1675
10935–10– 0
45–11–3 1/2

Southoulds Estimate
the 16th September 1675.

[24:153a & b]

[COVERING LETTER AND RETURN OF THE VALUATION OF
PROPERTY IN HUNTINGTON]

Much Respected Sir I have attended your warant truly and
faithfully to the best of my Understanding: not els but Rest
yours to Comand in what I may

Epenetus Platt

[ADDRESSED:]   For the Right worshipfull
Cappt. Mathias Nickalls
Secretare [   ] at
New Yor[ ]
To be devered to the
Secreteres ofes in New
York delivered with [   ]

[ENDORSED:]   The Returne from
Huntington brought
in Aug. 28. 1675.
Valuacions.
past
Oct. 25
26.10. 9$^1/_2$

A List of the Estate of the Towne of Huntington
for the yeare 1675.

	H	3	2	Y	O	C	3	2	Y	Sh	Sw	V	L*
Capt. Fleet	01	00	00	00	00	01	02	02	02	00	08	40	21
Tho: Fleet Junr	00	00	00	00	00	00	00	00	00	00	00	00	00
Steph Jarvis	00	02	01	00	02	03	03	01	01	00	05	05	16
Robt Cranfeild	01	00	00	01	04	02	02	02	04	00	00	00	18
Tho: Scudder	04	03	01	00	06	04	05	05	05	06	28	00	28

* For lack of space we have abbreviated these column headings as follows: H=Horses, 3=3
yeares, 2=2 yeares, Y=Yea[rlings], O=Oxen, C=Cowes, 3=3 yeares, 2=2 years, Y=Yearr-
ling[s], Sh=Sheepe, Sw=Swine, V=Vessells, L=Land & Meadoe.

	H	3	2	Y	O	C	3	2	Y	Sh	Sw	V	L
Isaak Scudder	00	00	00	00	00	00	00	00	00	00	00	00	00
Jno Scudder	00	00	00	00	00	00	00	00	00	00	00	00	00
Ja: Chichister Sen.	02	00	00	01	06	04	01	02	04	12	03	00	27
Ja: Chichister Junr.	02	01	00	01	00	00	00	00	00	00	00	00	00
Nathll Foster	02	02	00	00	04	02	01	04	02	00	05	00	19
Jno Finch Senr.	03	00	00	01	02	02	02	00	02	00	05	05	26
Jno Finch Junr.	00	00	00	00	00	00	00	00	00	00	00	00	00
Joseph Baily	02	00	02	00	00	04	02	03	02	02	05	00	25
Tho: Whitson	02	00	00	00	00	03	02	02	02	03	01	00	20
Jno Weekes	03	00	00	01	04	05	01	03	00	08	09	00	18
Mr Jonas Wood Senr.	04	00	00	02	06	07	04	04	03	17	10	00	48
Jno Wood	00	00	00	00	00	00	00	00	00	00	00	00	00
Isaak Platt	01	00	00	00	05	06	06	02	04	10	19	00	25
Tho: Powel	02	01	00	00	05	09	04	04	05	06	09	00	30
Caleb Wood	04	00	00	00	05	03	04	01	03	02	00	00	08
Joseph Wood	02	01	00	00	00	01	01	02	00	00	00	00	07
Samll Wood	02	00	00	00	06	05	02	00	02	06	16	00	24
[Jn]o Green	01	00	00	00	00	01	07	00	00	00	01	00	12
Tho Weekes	02	00	00	01	04	04	02	01	01	07	06	00	28
Jno Corye	00	00	00	00	02	03	00	02	01	06	06	00	12
[Epen] Platt	03	00	00	00	02	03	03	04	04	07	20	00	39

	H	3	2	Y	O	C	3	2	Y	Sh	Sw	V	L
[Walter] Nokes	01	00	00	00	00	01	00	00	01	00	12	00	08
Richd Brush	01	00	00	00	02	03	00	00	04	02	05	00	16
Jonas Wood Junr	01	00	00	00	04	05	00	02	02	06	09	00	20
Joseph Whitman	01	00	00	01	04	06	02	01	00	13	16	00	27
[T]homas Brush	03	00	00	01	06	06	01	04	02	22	17	00	36
[J]no Brush	00	00	00	00	00	00	00	00	00	00	00	00	00
Abigail Titus	02	00	00	00	02	04	03	02	03	04	07	00	18
Samll Ketcham	03	00	00	00	04	04	04	04	00	05	15	00	16
Rich: Williams	00	00	00	00	00	06	00	06	01	00	10	00	11
Samll Titus	02	00	00	01	04	05	00	02	02	03	03	00	34
Jothan Scudder	00	00	00	00	00	00	00	00	00	00	00	00	00
David Scudder	00	00	00	00	00	00	00	00	00	00	00	00	00
Moses Scudder	00	00	00	00	00	00	00	00	00	00	00	00	00
John Tedd	01	01	00	01	02	01	02	00	02	00	04	00	16
Timo. Conklyn	03	00	00	00	02	04	03	00	01	06	11	00	18
Saml Messenger	01	00	00	00	02	02	00	02	01	00	00	00	12
Jno Samwayes	02	00	00	00	04	02	04	01	04	07	05	00	18
The Land of Jacob Walker	00	00	00	00	00	00	00	00	00	00	00	00	18
Henyr Sooper	01	00	01	00	02	03	00	02	02	14	00	00	14
Jona: rogers	03	03	00	00	07	04	03	05	02	40	20	00	45
[George B]aldwin	01	00	00	00	00	00	00	00	00	00	01	00	00
Edwd Bunce	01	00	00	00	04	06	02	02	02	00	08	00	18

	H	3	2	Y	O	C	3	2	Y	Sh	Sw	V	L
John Page	00	00	00	00	00	02	00	00	01	00	00	00	09
Tho: Martin	01	00	00	00	00	02	00	00	02	00	02	00	09
Jno Inkerson	02	00	00	00	04	06	00	04	02	00	08	00	16
Adam Whithead	00	00	00	00	00	00	00	00	00	00	00	00	00
Tho: Scidmore Sen	02	00	00	00	04	07	00	00	02	00	02	00	21
Tho: Scidmore Junr	00	00	00	00	00	00	00	00	00	00	00	00	00
[P]hilip Udale	00	00	00	00	00	03	00	00	01	00	01	00	—
[Jno Goulden]	01	00	00	00	00	04	00	00	02	00	02	**00**	**10**
Peeter Floid	01	00	00	00	00	00	00	00	00	00	00	00	00
Wm Brotherton	01	00	00	00	00	03	00	00	00	00	00	00	06
Brenj: Jones	01	00	00	00	00	05	00	00	03	00	00	00	07
Jonath Hernit	02	00	02	00	00	02	00	01	00	00	00	00	11
Jno Everit	00	01	00	00	00	00	00	00	00	00	00	00	00
Roger Quint	00	00	00	00	00	00	00	00	00	00	00	00	00
Richard White	00	00	00	00	00	00	00	00	00	00	00	00	00
Widow Jones	06	00	00	00	04	08	00	04	06	10	14	00	48
Jno Jones	01	00	00	00	00	02	01	00	01	00	00	00	13
Jno Ketcham	02	00	00	00	04	03	01	00	00	06	02	00	09
Johannes Race	01	00	00	00	00	00	00	00	00	00	00	00	00
Mr Bryans Estate	00	00	00	00	04	10	00	00	00	00	00	00	00
Mr Kane	00	01	00	00	00	00	01	00	00	00	00	00	00

Memorandum Mr byran and Mr wake[rs]
parsons are not heir

[24:154]

[RETURN OF THE VALUATION OF PROPERTY AT BROOKHAVEN]

A valuation for the contry parte of brookhaven in the yere of our lord god 1675.

	H	O	C	1	2	3	H	1	2	3	Sw	L	Sh*	
Thomas Ward	1	2	1	2	2	2	1				9	10		0–91–0
John Thomas	1		1								4	4		0–31–0
Nath Norten	1	2	2	2	2	2	2	1			4	11		0–84–6:8
Saml Daiton	2	5	2	3	2						6	11		1–17–0
Andr Miller	1	4	3	3	2	4					6	14		1–17–0
hen Rogers	3	4	5	3		2	1	1	2		8	18		1–55–0
John Roe	1	3	4	4	1	3	2				5	7		1–12–10
Rich Floyd	1	4	4	2	2	2	3				16	28	15	1–63–0
Thomas Thorp	1	4	3	4	1	2	1				3	11		0–99–10
Zak hawkens	1	4	3	1	1	2	1				2	10		0–83–0
Rich Ffarr	1	2					1				2			0–42–0
Willi Satterly	2	3	2	1	1	3	3				6	10		1–24–0
John Tooker	2	6	7	3	1	5	1				18	20	15	1–89–0
Sargent Bigs	1	4	2	2			3				2	12		1–02–0
Robert Akerly	1	2	2									7		0–47–0

* For lack of space we have abbreviated these column headings as follows: H=heads, O=oxen, C=cows, 1=1yere, 2=2yere, 3=3 yere, H=Horses, 1=1 yere 2=2 yere, 3=3 yere, Sw=swine, L=meadow lands, Sh=sheep.

	H	O	C	1	2	3	H	1	2	3	Sw	L	Sh	
Sam Akerly	1	0	3	4								3		0–42–0
Mr longbothem	2	6	7	5	6	3	5				20	15		2–36–10
John Davis	1	1	1									3		0–28–
Widow Smith	1	2	7	4	1	2	2			1	11	16		1–40–10
Robart Smith	1	2	2	2	1						5	4		0–54–10
Will Salyer	1		3			3	1					3		0–60–0
Joseph Daves	1	2	3	1	1		1		2		2	4		0–72–0
Abr Daiton	1	2	2				5				1	3		1–04–0
Obed Seward	1	3	3	2	2			1				5		0–67–10
Thomas Bigs	1	4	3	3	2	5	2				5	5		1–20–10
John Bigs	1				4		1	1						0–39–0
Tho Smith	1	2	3	2			1		2	1	7	6		0–85–0
Rich Waring	1		2	1	2						4	3		0–49–10
John Jeners	3	3	4	1	1	5					5	13		1–70–10
John Tomson	2						2					6		0–66–0

[ENDORSED:]   Seatalcotts Valuacion
of the Estats, brought in
the 22d Day of Sept. 75
Oct 25 past 3065–16–8
  £ s d
12–15–5 3/4

[ADDRESSED:]   [this] to be left at the Secretary
offes in the fortt at new
yourk

[24:155]

A List off the Estate of Newtowne.

	M	L	H	3	2	Y	O	C	3	2	YO	Sh	Sw[*]
Jonathan Hazard	1	16	1	0	0	0	0	6	0	0	0	0	1
John Farman	0	16	0	0	0	1	2	3	0	0	5	2	4
Gershom hazard	1	3	1	0	0	0	2	2	0	0	0	0	0
Samuell Gray	0	12	2	0	0	0	0	2	0	1	2	2	2
Jacob Reder	2	26	2	0	0	1	2	5	2	2	2	2	3
Lambert Woodward	1	8	1	0	0	0	2	3	0	2	2	6	7
Elaser Leaveridg	1	0	0	0	0	0	0	0	0	0	0	9	4
John Burrougs	2	40	1	0	0	0	4	4	0	0	2	24	6
Nath: Pettet	1	08	1	0	0	1	0	1	2	0	0	2	4
James Way	1	20	1	0	0	0	2	4	6	6	3	20	0
Jerimi Burrouges	1	6	2	0	0	0	2	3	0	1	2	00	1
Joseph Reder	1	15	1	0	0	0	2	3	0	1	3	00	2
Calib Leveridg	2	29	1	0	0	0	2	4	0	2	1	14	1
Content titus	1	20	1	0	0	0	2	3	1	2	2	10	1

* For lack of space we have abbreviated these column headings as follows: M=Males, L=Up land & Meadow, H=Horses, 3=3 yer oulds, 2=2 yer oulds, Y=Yerlings, O=Oxen, C=Cowes, 3=3 yer oulds, 2=2 yer oulds, YO=Yer. Oulds, Sh=Shep, Sw=S[wine].

	M	L	H	3	2	Y	O	C	3	2	YO	Sh	Sw
Dannell Blomf	1	30	1	0	0	0	4	4	2	2	1	4	3
[Joseph] Sackett	1	03	1	0	0	0	0	1	2	2	2	**3**	**1**
[I]sack Reeder	1	13	1	0	0	0	2	3	0	2	**4**	**12**	**1**
John Scudder	1	36	1	0	0	0	4	5	4	4	0	**18**	**4**
Robart Colwell	1	03	0	0	0	0	0	1	0	0	0	00	0
Richard Owen	1	14	1	0	0	0	2	5	0	0	0	4	3
[T]homas Robarts	1	09	1	0	0	0	0	3	1	2	1	1	4
[T]ho: Morrell	1	09	0	0	0	0	0	0	2	0	0	0	0
[J]ames Way Junor	1	10	1	0	0	0	4	0	1	0	2	3	1
[Jo]hn Denan	1	12	1	1	1	0	0	1	0	0	0	0	2
[ab]ram Frost	1	07	1	0	0	0	0	2	1	1	0	0	0
[Joh]n alburtis	1	20	0	0	0	1	4	4	4	1	0	12	3
[Jo]thor alburtis	1	8	1	0	0	0	0	1	1	0	0	00	2
[Tho]mas pettit	1	15	1	0	0	0	2	3	2	0	0	5	4
[Joh]n scudder Jur	1	12	1	0	0	1	2	4	4	1	1	5	4
[H]endrick Jonson	1	03	1	0	0	0	0	0	3	1	0	0	1
[Jo]hn Reder	1	16	1	0	0	0	2	3	0	2	2	6	3
Theophi: Philips	1	6	1	0	0	0	2	2	0	0	0	2	6
John Ramsden	2	30	1	0	0	0	4	5	3	4	3	8	3

	M	L	H	3	2	Y	O	C	3	2	YO	Sh	Sw
John Coe	4	22	2	0	1	0	2	4	0	1	0	6	9
Joseph phillips	1	12	1	0	0	0	0	3	1	0	1	2	1
Thom: Wandall	1	93	1	0	0	0	8	5	6	5	5	81	**6**
Georg Steavenson	1	45	2	0	0	1	4	6	4	3	3	10	[ ]
James Lawrason	1	10	1	0	0	0	2	1	2	0	0	11	00
Thomas Etherington	1	04	0	0	0	0	0	1	0	0	0	20	00
Nathan Fish	1	8	0	0	0	0	0	1	0	0	0	0	3
Nath: Baly	1	5	0	0	0	0	0	0	0	0	0	0	[ ]
John pettit	1	8	1	0	0	0	2	2	0	0	0	2	2
Georg Wood	0	20	0	0	0	0	2	2	1	0	2	10	0
Joshua hazard	1	9	1	0	0	0	0	0	0	0	0	0	0
Thomas Larenc	1	40	2	0	0	0	4	8	4	3	5	00	14
John Kitcham	3	45	1	0	0	0	4	5	3	2	3	30	00
William Graves	0	16	1	0	0	1	0	2	2	3	0	10	5
harrik Sibartson	0	30	2	2	0	0	2	4	0	0	0	00	1
Sibart harickson	1	24	1	0	0	0	2	3	0	0	0	00	1
Hendrik Marteaceson	1	16	2	0	0	1	2	2	0	1	0	2	0
Cornelus Mateace	1	10	0	0	0	0	2	4	0	0	2	0	0
John Smith	2	29	1	0	0	0	2	5	4	3	2	15	[ ]

	M	L	H	3	2	Y	O	C	3	2	YO	Sh	Sw
Jeri: Reader	1	14	1	0	0	0	1	1	0	0	1	02	[ ]
Samuell Scudder	1	1	0	0	0	0	0	0	0	0	0	00	0
William Burtis	1	0	0	0	1	0	0	0	0	0	0	00	0
Thom: Case	1	20	1	0	0	0	2	4	0	2	2	20	3
John parsell	2	40	2	0	0	0	2	4	2	4	4	10	4
Johanes Lorus	1	10	0	0	0	0	0	1	1	2	1	0	1
John Woodstoncraft	1	10	1	0	0	0	0	2	4	0	[		]
[ ] Buckhood	1	5	0	0	0	0	0	1	1	1	0	0	[ ]
John Lorus	0	12	0	0	0	0	2	2	0	1	1	0	[ ]
Lores Peterson	1	8	0	0	0	0	2	2	0	1	0	0	0
Gershom More	2	20	1	0	0	1	2	2	2	3	0	30	3
Joseph Reide	1	00	0	0	0	0	2	0	0	0	0	00	0
Edwa: Stevenson	0	30	0	0	0	0	2	4	0	0	1	[	]
William hallit	1	25	4	0	0	3	2	5	2	2	0	14	3
Will: hallet Juner	0	13	1	0	0	1	2	3	2	2	3	3	2
peter Roulson	1	12	1	0	0	0	2	4	0	2	2	0	0
Tho: Riders bore	1	15	2	0	0	0	2	2	0	0	2	0	3
Jona: Strickland	1	15	1	0	0	1	2	4	1	2	2	4	2
John Copstafe	0	00	0	0	0	0	0	0	0	0	0	[0]	[ ]

	M	L	H	3	2	Y	O	C	3	2	YO	Sh	Sw
Josiah Farman	2	15	1	0	0	0	2	4	0	0	2	4	[ ]
Robart Feelde	1	30	1	0	0	0	2	5	3	2	1	20	2
Frances Hendricks	1	10	2	0	0	0	0	3	0	2	2	00	1
Tho: Stevenson	1	34	0	0	0	0	4	7	3	2	1	9	5
peter pangburn	1	00	0	0	0	0	0	0	0	0	0	0	0
Jospeh burrougs	1	00	0	0	0	0	0	1	0	0	0	0	0
John Bull	1	4	0	0	0	0	0	0	1	0	0	0	0
Samuel More	0	14	1	0	0	0	2	3	0	2	1	5	3
John Graves	1	00	0	0	0	0	0	2	3	0	2	6	4
Richard Fidoe	1	18	1	0	0	1	0	3	0	1	1	3	3
Ralph Hunt	2	30	1	1	1	0	4	4	4	3	2	16	2

[Newtowne Valuations brought in Sepr Beginning]
[ex————1675.]
[Rate—26–6–8.]

[24:156]

[RETURN OF THE VALUATIONS OF PROPERTY AT FLUSHING]

	N	L	M	H	3	2	Y	O	C	3	2	Y	Sw	Sh*
Charles bridges	08	50	60	07	00	02	00	12	12	10	04	04	06	00
John Furbosh	03	18	40	04	00	00	00	06	08	03	03	03	00	30
Alias douty	01	12	20	00	00	00	00	00	12	00	13	00	04	40
John Thorn	00	06	10	01	00	00	00	02	08	00	02	02	03	06
william noble	01	05	20	01	00	00	00	02	04	02	01	01	03	12
Daniell patrek	00	04	00	01	00	00	00	00	00	02	02	01	00	00
dorythy farington	00	12	30	03	00	00	00	02	08	03	00	05	16	30
James Clamenes	00	04	00	00	00	00	00	00	03	00	01	01	02	00
anthony fellde	00	07	20	02	00	00	01	02	05	00	01	00	00	00
Thomas stilles	00	12	10	00	00	00	00	02	04	00	02	03	07	00
[ri]chard tew	00	04	00	01	00	00	00	00	01	00	00	00	00	00
william danfard	00	04	05	01	00	00	00	00	02	00	00	00	00	00
John tere	01	04	10	01	00	00	00	00	02	00	00	**00**	**00**	**00**
Richd willde	00	07	05	01	00	00	00	00	03	02	01	**01**	**04**	**08**
adward grifen Jun	00	12	10	01	00	00	00	02	07	04	02	**02**	**00**	10

* For lack of space we have abbreviated these column headings as follows: N=negeres, L=Landes, M=madoes (meadows), H=horses mares, 3=three yer oldes, 2=to yere oldes, Y=yerlinges, O=oxen and boles (bulls), C=Cowes, 3=thre yer oldes, 2=to yere oldes, Y=yerlinges, Sw=swine, Sh=shepe

	N	L	M	H	3	2	Y	O	C	3	2	Y	Sw	Sh
richard Stockton	01	12	00	01	00	00	00	04	04	00	01	04	05	00
Jonethon wright	00	06	00	01	00	00	00	00	04	00	01	04	00	00
dennes Holdren	00	00	00	01	00	00	00	00	04	00	04	00	00	00
derek Areson	00	00	00	00	00	00	00	00	01	02	00	00	00	00
John Adames	00	08	00	01	00	00	00	01	04	00	01	02	01	—
John depre	00	06	00	01	00	00	00	02	03	02	02	01	00	12
moses browne	00	08	00	01	00	00	00	00	02	01	01	01	06	00
william yates	00	02	05	01	00	00	00	02	00	00	02	00	00	00
Thomas Whittecur	00	08	00	02	00	00	00	00	02	00	00	01	03	00
Johne mere	00	04	00	00	00	00	00	02	03	00	00	00	00	00
nickles Parsel	01	14	15	00	00	00	00	02	08	00	05	02	01	25
Thomas Cimse	00	04	00	01	00	00	00	00	02	00	00	00	00	00
Thomas ford	00	01	00	01	00	00	00	00	02	00	00	00	01	00
Erien corneles	00	06	00	02	00	00	00	00	03	00	00	00	00	08
samuell Thorn	00	04	05	01	00	00	00	02	00	03	01	00	04	00
[h]enry teyler	00	20	10	02	00	00	00	00	04	00	00	00	01	20
[John] bowne	00	20	30	04	01	02	02	04	07	07	03	04	10	50
[ ]orrys Smith	00	14	10	02	00	00	00	02	04	04	00	00	08	11
[Joh]n hinchman	01	10	15	02	00	00	00	04	04	04	00	02	04	40

	N	L	M	H	3	2	Y	O	C	3	2	Y	Sw	Sh
[w]illiam haverland	00	15	10	06	00	00	00	04	05	07	00	00	01	00
Thomas lawrance	01	02	30	01	00	00	00	02	04	02	00	00	02	00
Frances bloodgood	00	03	10	01	00	00	00	12	04	00	04	02	05	40
david Row	00	16	06	00	00	00	00	02	06	01	02	01	06	16
william Chdderton	00	04	05	00	00	00	00	00	01	00	02	00	00	00
simon thewall	00	03	00	00	00	00	00	02	03	00	02	00	04	12
John gelime	00	03	00	01	00	00	00	00	02	00	00	00	03	00
nicklas snethen	00	02	10	01	00	00	00	02	03	00	02	02	00	00
John hoper	00	01	00	00	00	00	00	00	02	00	00	00	00	00
minderd Corto	00	00	10	01	00	00	00	00	02	02	01	00	00	00
gerret hendrekes	00	00	00	00	00	00	00	00	03	00	00	00	00	00
Thomas williames	01	00	00	00	00	00	00	00	00	00	00	00	00	00
william begen	00	02	00	00	00	00	00	02	00	02	00	00	00	00
Joseph Thorn	00	03	10	00	00	00	00	00	04	01	02	02	01	14

[ENDORSED:]   Valuacons of Est[ates] at Flushing
brought in Oct. 9. 1675.
Exd   £ s   d
Rate 18.3.10

hed mone for singel men[*]

Elias purrington
John farrington
Edward farrington
Jonethon fillepes
Andres depro
pole denorman
Edward grifen Junyer
richard tendoll
Thomos mam
John tayler
Jospeh heverlend
John fellde

flushing
september 29
1675.

Capt. Thoms hikes hath not yet prought in a list of his estate

* head money for single men

[25:39]

John Ambrose Do.
To money paid him at tymes £01:15:00
    Balla. £12:08:10
      14:08:10

Per Contra Cr.
By 4 mos 11 dayes wages att
 3£ 0s per mo. £14:03:10

Stephen Mextead Do.
To Sundrys payd him £00:13:06
    Balla. £13:10:06
      14:04:00

Per Contra Cr.
By 5 mos 5 dayes Wages at
 55s per mo. £14:04:00

Walter Feverell Do.
To money paid him £01:02:06
   Balla £09:07:06
     10:10:00

Per Contra Cr.
By 4 mos 6 dayes Wages at
 50s per mo. £10:10:00

William Jennings Do.
To Sundrys paid him 01:11:06
    Balla. £11:02:00
      12:13:06

Per Contra Cr.
By 3 mos 27 dayes Wages at
 3£ 5s per mo. £12:13:06

William Bastard Do.
To Money paid him £01:06:10
    Balla. £07:11:10
      8:18:08

Per Contra Cr
By 4 mos 14 dayes Wages at
 40s per mo. £08:18:08

George Hayes Do.
To money pd him and other Comes.
     04:13:00
   Balla £05:03:06
     9:16:06

Per Contra Cr.
By 4 mos 11 dayes Wages att
 45s per mo. £09:16:06

Thomas Smith Do
To sundries pd him and for
him amo. to £05:04:05
    Balla. £03:00:01
     8:04:06

Per Contra Cr.
By 4 mos 17 dayes Wages at
 36s per mo. £08:04:06

Francis Jones Do.   Per Contra Cr.

To Sundrys pd him Cr.	£01:19:06	By 4 mos 11 dayes Wages at
Balla	£05:17:06	35s per mo. £07:17:00
	7:17:00	

Robert Wilson Do.   Per Contra Cr.

To Sundrys pd and to be

allowed of by him	£05:11:11	By 6 mos. 21 dayes Wages at
Balla	£04:10:01	30s per mo. £10:01:00
	10:01:00	

Hugh Williams Do.   Per Contra Cr.

To Sundrys per Cr.	£03:04:00	By 4 mos 7 dayes wages at
Balla.	£04:17:00	38s per mo. £:08:01:00
	8:01:00	

Robert Narron Do.   Per Contra Cr.

To Sundrys per Cr.	£03:04:09	By 4 mos. 7 dayes Wages at
Balla.	£05:04:07	40s per mo. £:08:09:04
	8:09:04	

Zachariah Mitchell Dr.   Per Contra Cr.

To Money paid him	£01:00:00	By 3 mos 11 dayes Wages
Balla.	£05:07:00	38s per mo. £:06:07:00
	6:07:00	

Wm. Glasse Dr.   Per Contra Cr.

To Sundrys delivered him	£00:04:06	By 4 mos 7 dayes Wages at
Balla.	£06:02:06	30s per mo. £: 6:07:00
	6:07:00	

Thomas Manfeild Dr.   Per Contra Cr.

To Soe much discounted

for him	£01:10:00	By 3 mos. 22 dayes Wages at
Balla.	£05:08:00	37s per mo. £:06:18:00
	6:18:00	

Rowland Christian Dr.   Per Contra Cr.

To Sundries paid him Cr.	£01:09:06	By 4 mos wages att
Balla.	£05:14:06	36s per mo. £:07:04:00
	7:04:00	

John White Dr.   Per Contra Cr.
To Sundrys paid him   £00:08:06   By 4 mos Wages at
              Balla.   £04:07:06   24s per mo. £:04:16:00
                          4:16:00

Timothy Higgins Dr.   Per Contra Cr.
To Sundrys paid for him   £00:12:01   By 3 mos 27 days Wages att
              Balla   £05:11:11   32s per mo. £:06:04:00
                         6:04:00

[ENDORSED:]   The Account given in by Francis Richardson
                       of the seamens wages, to the Court of Admiralty.

Harman Swan Dr.   Per Contra Cr.
                                s. d.
To Sundrys paid him Cr.   £01:08:06   By 3 mos 28 dayes Wages at
              Balla.   £05:05:00   34s per mo. £:06:13:06
                          6:13:06

Wm Bryar Dr.   Per Contra Cr.
To money paid him   £01:00:00   By 3 mos 15 dayes Wages at
              Balla.   £05:13:00   38s per mo. £06:13:00
                          6:13:00

Thomas Pilgrim Dr.   Per Contra Cr.
To Sundryes paid him Cr.   £01:10:06   By 3 mos 21 dayes Wages at
              Balla.   £03:09:00   27s per mo. £04:19:06
                          4:19:06

John Hall Dr.   Per Contra Cr.
To Soe much paid him   £00:01:00   By 3 mos 3 dayes Wages at
              Balla.   £03:19:06   26s per mo. £04:00:06
                          4:00:06

Wm. Cooke Dr.   Per Contra Cr.
To sundries delivered him £00:08:06   By 4 mos 1 dayes Wages at
              Balla.   £05:12:06   30s per mo. £06:01:00
                          6:01:00

[ENDORSED:]   The Master of the Good Hope, his
                       Answer, with his Account of wages.
                       Delivered in Court. Nov. 16. 1675.

[25:244]
[ASSESSMENT ROLLS OF THE FIVE DUTCH TOWNS ON LONG ISLAND.
TRANSLATION]*

Assessment Rolls
of the Five Dutch Towns on
Long Island;

primo October, Anno
1676

Assessment [Roll of Middelwout Made up] 20 September 1676

[No.]		£	s	d
[1]	Baerteltt [Claessen]			
	1 poll, 2 horses, 1 ditto of 3 yrs.,			
	2 cows, 1 hog .... £61.			
	1 morgen of marshland .... 2.			
	....	63.		
[2]	Gerritt Snedeger			
	1 poll, 2 horse,s 2 do. of 3 yrs., 6 cows,			
	4 ditto of 2 yrs., 3 do. of 1 yr., 3 hogs £105.10			
	20 morgens of land and marshland .. 40.			
	....	145.	10	
[3]	[Auwke Janse]			
	1 poll, 4 horses, 4 cows, 6 sheep £88.10			
	18 morgens of land .... 36.			
	....	124.	10	
[4]	Gerrit Luberttse			
	1 poll, 4 horses, 5 cows, 3 do. of 1 yr.,			
	1 hog £96.10			
	20 morgens of land and marshland ... 40.			
	....	136.	10	
[5]	Reyn Aersen			
	1 poll, 2 horses, 4 cows, 3 do. of 1 yr. ...	66.	10	
[6]	[Stoffel] Jansen			
	[1 poll 4] horses.	30.		

* Supplied in part from E. B.O'Callaghan's *DHNY*, vol. 2.

[7]   [Cornelis Jansen Zeuw]
       [6 cows 4 do of 1 year] .... £99.
       [   ] marshland .... 60.
       ....   [159.]

[8]   [*ms. destroyed*]

[9]   [Jan Baer]entse
       [1 poll 2] horses, 2 cows [1] ditto of
       1 yr., [1] hog 54. 10

[10]   Jan C[oer]ten
       4 polls, 4 cows, [3 hogs] ....   95.

[11]   Arie Lamberttse
       1 poll, 4 horses, 5 cows, 2 do.
       of 3 yrs., 4 hogs .... £103.
       22 morgens of land and marshland ..   44.
       ....   147.

[12]   Jan Jansen Van Ditmerch
       1 poll, 4 horses, 4 oxen, 8 cows,
       2 do. of 2 yrs., 3 do. of 1 yr. £139.10
       30 morgens of land and marshland ..   60.
       ....   199. 10

[13]   Hans Cristoffel
       1 poll, 2 horses, 5 cows, 2 do. of 1 yr.,
       3 hogs ....   73.

[14]   Arie Reyerse
       1 poll, 2 horses, 3 do. of 1 yr.,
       5 cows [1] do. of 3 yrs. 2 do.
       [of 2 yrs.], 2 do. of 1 yr., [2] hogs .... £90.
       [20] morgens of land .... 40.
       ....   130.

       ....   1454.[*]

       *   subtotal

15   Aert Jan[sen]
       1 poll, 3 [ ] [cows] 2 do. of 3 yrs.,
       3 do. of 2 yrs., [ ] [of 1] yr., 1 hog ... £88.10
       20 morgens of [land] and marshland . 40.
       . . . .   128. 10

16   Jan Jan[sen]
       1 poll, 2 oxen, 3 cows . . . . £45.
       7 morgens of land and marshland . . . . 14.

17   Pieter Loott
       2 polls, 2 horses, 10 cows, 2 do.
       of 2 yrs., 2 do. of 1 yr., 2 hogs . . . . . . £120.
       16 morgans of land and marshland . .   32.
       . . . .   [152.]

18   Jan Streyc[ker]
       3 polls, 4 horses, 2[   ], 2 Horses,
       [   ] cows, 3 do. of 3 yrs., 4 do.
       of 1 yr., 1 hog . . . . £196.
       30 morgens of land and marshland . .   60.
       . . . .   256.

19   Hendrick Streycker
       1 poll, 2 horses, 1 sheep £43.14
       12 morgens of land and marshland . . . 24.
       . . . .   [67. 14]

20   Willem Guilliamsen
       1 poll, 2 horses, 2 oxen, 7 cows, 2 do.
       of 3 yrs., 2 do. of 2 yrs., 2 hogs . . . . . £104.
       19 morgens of land and marshland . .   38.
       . . . .   [142.]

21   Hendrick Corn: Sle[cht]
       1 poll, 2 cows, [1] hog . . . . [*ms. destroyed*]
       3 morgens of land . . . . [   ]

[22]   Harmen [Key]
       [   ] [horses] . . . . [   ]

[23]   Jacob Hendricks
1 poll, 4 horses, 3 cows ......[   ]
2 do. of [1 yr, 1] hog .... [   ]
20 morgens of land and marshland ... [40].

24   Stoffel [Probasky]
1 poll, [2 horses], 1 do. [of 2 yr 5 cows],
1 do. of [2 yr 2] do. of [1 yr.] ....[£78].
12 morgens of [land] and marshland . [24].
....   [102.]

25   Corn: Jansen Berry
1 poll, 4 horses, [1] ditto of 1 yr., 8 cows,
2 do. of 2 yrs., 3 do of 1 yr., 2 sheep . £119.7
23 morgens of land and marshland .. 46.
....   [165. 7]

26   Lambertt Jansen
1 poll ....   [18.]

27   Ruth Albertse
1 poll ....   18.

28   Seymen Hansen
1 poll, 4 horses, 3 cows, 2 do. of 3 yr.,
3 do/ of 2 yrs., 1 do. of 1 yr., 1 hog ... £99.
14 morgens of land and marshland ... 28.
....   [127.]

29   [C]la[es Willems]
1 poll [   ] ....   [18.]

[30   Willem Jacobsen]
[2 polls, 2 horses, 1] do. of 3 yrs.,
1 do of 2 yrs., [2 oxen 7 cows 2 do of]
[ ] do. of [ ] yr., [6] hogs ....£[1]37.
24 morgens of land[   ] .... 48.
....   185.

31   Hendrick [Willemsem]
1 poll, 2 horses, 5 cows .... £67.
20 morgens of land .... 40.
....   107.

32   Jan Harmense
      1 [poll] . . . .   18.

33   Arie Hendrickse
      1 [poll], 1 horse, 2 do. of 3 yr . . . .   43.

34   Gysbert Jansen
      1 poll . . . .   18.

35   Jabecq* Jansen van de Bildtt
      1 poll . . . .   18.

36   Flores Croom
      1 poll, 2 horses, 3 cows, 1 do, of 2 yrs.,
      1 do. of 1 yr., 1 hog . . . . £62.
      16 morgen of land and marshland   . . .   32.
      . . . .   94.

[37] Dierck Jansen Hoglant
      1 poll, 3 horses, 1 do. of 1 yr.,
      6 cows, 1 hog . . . . £89.
      [13 mor]gen of land and marshland   . .   26.
      . . . .   115.

38   [Corns. Seb]ringh
      [1 poll], [ ] horses, [1 do of 4] yrs.,
      3 cows, 3 do. [   ], [2] do. of [1] yr. . [   ]
      [   ] of land and marshland . . . . [   ]
      . . . .   [   ]

39   [   ] [jan]sen
      [1 poll] . . . .   18.

40   Minne Johannes
      3 polls, 1 horse, 1 [cow] . . . . £71.
      16 morgen of land and [marshland] . . .   32.
      . . . .   103.

* Jacob?

41   Caterine Hegeman[s]
        3 polls, 4 horses, 1 do. of 1 yr.,
        4 oxen, 11 cows, 4 do. of 3 yrs.,
        2 do. of 2 yrs., 4 do. of 1 yr., 4 hogs . £215.
        36 morgens of land and marshland ..   72.
        ....   287.

42   Cornelis Baerentse
        1 poll, 4 horses, 1 do. of 2 yrs., 7 cows
        3 do. of 3 yrs., 3 do. of 2 yrs.,
        2 do. of 1 yr., 1 hog £129.10
        18 morgens of land and marshland ..   36.
        ....   165. 10

43   Dierck Jansen Van der Vliett
        1 poll, 3 horses, 5 cows, 3 do. of 2 yrs.,
        2 do. of 1 yr. £89.10
        14 morgens of land and marshland ...   28.
        ....   117. 10

[44]   [E]ld[e]rtt Luykerse
        [1 poll 4 horses 4 cows] [ ] [hog] .... £87.
        [16 morgens of land and marshland]. .   32.
        ....   119.
        ....   4492. 11*

45   Leffertt Pieterse
        1 poll, 2 horses, [cows 1 do of 3 yr]
        [4] do. of 2 yrs., [ ] [do of 1 yr] ..... £70.
        17 morgens of land [and marshland]   .   34.
        ....   [104.]

46   [T]ittus [Str]ix
        [1 poll 1 horse 2 do of 2 yr] 4 cows,
        6 do. of 3 yrs., 3 do. of 2 yrs.,
        5 do. of 1 yr, 4 hogs .... £103.
        25 morgens of land and marshland ..   50.
        ....   153.

*   subtotal

47   Pieter Guilliamsen
        1 poll, 6 oxen, 5 cows, 2 do. of 2 yrs.,
        3 hogs . . . . £87.
        19 morgens of land and marshland   . .   36.
        . . . .   [1.23]

The whole Property of Middelwout amounts to £4872. 11

Taxed @ 1d. in the pound [Sterlg]
should amount to 20 pounds 6 shgs

                                        your obedient Servant
                                        Michil Hainell

[Assessment Roll] of [Breuckelen] Made up [September] 1676.

[1]   Claes Aerense
        3 polls, 1 horse, 5 cows, []2 of
        2 yrs., 2 do of 1 yr. £96.10
        14 morgens of land and marshland . . .   28.
        . . . .   124. 10

[2]   Jan de Swede
        1 poll, 1 horse, 1 do. of 1 yr., 4 cows,
        1 do. of 1 yr., 1 hog £55.10
        2 morgens of land . . . .   4.
        . . . .   59. 10

[3]   Baerent Hegbertse
        1 poll, 2 [horses 1] cow . . . . £62.
        3 morgens of land . . . .   6.
        . . . .   68.

[4]   Joostt Fransen
        1 poll, 2 horses, 1 do. of 1 yr., 5 cows,
        1 do. of 2 yrs., 3 do. of 1 yr., 2 hogs . . £79.
        19 morgens of land and marshland . . .   38.
        . . . .   117.

[5]   [Andries Ju]riaense
        1 poll, [2] horses, 2 do. of 3 yrs.,
        8 cows, 1 do. of 2 yrs., 2 do. of 1 yr. . £103.10
        28 morgens of land and marshland . .   56.
        . . . .   159. 10

[6]   [Lambert Jansen Dor]lant
        [1 poll 3 cows] . . . . £33.
        [8 morgen land and marshland] . . . . . .   16.
        . . . .   49.

[7]   [   ] [Hendrickse]
        1 poll . . . .   18.

[8]   [. . . .   ]

[9]   [Wouter Geisse]
        [1 poll . . . .   18].

[10]   [S]eimen Aertsen
        1 poll, 2 oxen, 4 cows, [1] do. of 2 yrs.,
        1 hog . . . . £56.
        8 morgens of land and marshland . . . .   16.
        . . . .   72.

[11]   Jean Piettersen Mackelyk
        1 poll, 4 cows . . . . £38.
        8 morgens of land . . . .   16.
        . . . .   54.

[12]   Jean Fredrickse
        1 poll, 2 horses, 2 cows . . . . £52.
        7 morgens of land and marshland . . . .   14.
        . . . .   66.

[13]   Johannes Christoffel
        1 poll, 2 oxen, 2 cows, 1 do. of 2 yrs. . £42.10
        7 morgens of land . . . .   14.
        . . . .   56. 10.

[14]   Mr Paulus van der Beeck
        2 polls, 3 horses, 4 cows, 2 do. of 2 yrs.,
        2 do. of 1 yr. . . . . £100.
        2[0 morgen la]nd a[nd marshland] . .   40.
        . . . .   140.

[15]   [Theunes Gisberttse Bogaert]
        3 polls, 4 horses, [1 do of 2 yrs 5 oxen
        Cows], 5 do. of 3 yrs., 10 do. of 2 yrs.,
        8 do. of 1 yr. 9 hogs . . . . £251.
        40 morgens of land and marshland . .   80.
        . . . .   331.

        . . . .   1361.*

16   Seimen Cl[aes]
        1 poll 1 horses [Cows 1] do. of 2 yrs.,
        2 do. of 1 yr., [1 hog] £46.10
        7 morgens of land and marshland . . . .   14.
        . . . .   60. 10

17   Juffrouw Pott[ers]
        1 horse, 1 do. of 3 yrs., 4 cows,
        1 do. of 2 yrs., 3 hogs . . . . 4[5.]

18   Jean Aersen
        1 poll, 3 horses, 2 Cows, 1 do. of 3 yrs.,
        2 do. of 2 yrs., 1 do. of 1 yr. £74.10
        18 morgens of of land and marshland .   36.
        . . . .   11[0. 10]

19   Thomas Jansen Van dyck
        1 poll, 2 horses, 3 cows . . . . £57.
        1 morgen of land . . . .   2.
        . . . .   59.

20   Acheis Jansen van deick
        1 poll, 2 oxen, 1 do. of 1 yr. £41.10
        1 morgen of land . . . .   2.
        . . . .   43.

* subtotal

21   Dierck Hattum
1 poll, 2 oxen, 2 cows, 2 do. of [3 yrs
1] do. of 2 yrs. £50.10
2 morgens of land . . . .   4.
. . . .   [54. 10]

22   Jurian Blancke
2 horses, 1 cow, 2 do. of 1 yr. . . . . . . [£32.]
6 morgens of land . . . .   12.
. . . .   [44.]

23   Daniel de Rappallie
[1] poll, 1 horse, [ ] cow[s] . . . . [   ]

[24   Jerm de Rappallie]
[2 polls 2 horses] [ ] [cows]
3 morgens of land . . . . [   ]

[25]   Pieter Jansen
1 poll, 2 horses, [2] oxen, 6 cows,
[4 of 2 yrs], 3 do. of 1 yr. £98.10
25 morgens of land and marshland . . .   50.
. . . .   [148. 10]

26   Jan Jansen
1 poll, 2 oxen, [Cows] 1 do. of 2 yrs.
3 do. of 1 yr. £45.10
2 morgens of land . . . .   4.
. . . .   [49. 10]

27   Hendrick Corsen
1 poll, 3 horses, 2 cows,
1 do. of 2 yrs. 66.10
12 morgens of land and marshland 24
. . . .   90. 10

28   Pietter Corsen
1 poll . . . .   18.

29   Casper Cornelisse
1 poll . . . .   18.

30   Willem Willemse bennett

1 poll, 2 horses, 2 do. of 1 yr., 2 oxen,
5 cows, 4 do. of 2 yrs., 3 do. of 1 yr. .. £99.10
13 1/2 morgens of land and marshland   27.
....   126.

31   Rhem Jan[sen]
      3 polls, 4 [horses], cows, [5] do. of 3
      yrs., 2 do. of [2 yrs do of 1 yr 2 hogs] [£148.]10
      19 morgens of [land and marshland]
      ....   [222 . 10]

      ....   2573. 10[*]

[32]   Dierck S[t]oo[rm]
       1 poll, 1 horse .... £30.
       morgen land and marshland .... 22.
       ....   52.

[33]   Maerten Ryerse
       1 poll, 4 horses, 8 cows, [ ] of 2 yrs.,
       3 do. of 1 yr., 2 hogs £117.10
       31 1/2 morgens of land and marshland   63.
       ....   180. 10

[34]   Aerent Isaeck
       1 poll ....   18.

[35]   Susanne Dubels
       2 oxen, 6 cows, 3 do. of 2 yrs.,
       3 do. of 1 yr...................... £62.10
       18 morgens of land .... 36.
       ....   98. 10

36   Theu[nis] Jan[sen]
      3 poll, 3 horses, [ ] do. of 2 yr., 2 oxen,
      4 cows, 4 do. of 3 yrs., 4 do. of 1 yr.,
      2 hogs .... £151.
      23 morgens of land and marshland .. 46.
      ....   197.
[37]   Jan Hansen

* subtotal

1 poll, [2] horses, 4 cows, 1 do.
of 3 yrs., 1 do. of 2 yrs., [1 hog] £69.10
18 morgens of [land and marshland] . .   36.
. . . .   105. 10

[38]   Dierck P[auluse]
1 poll, 2 horses, [4] cows, 4 do.
of 2 yrs., [3] do. of [1 yr] £76.10
[12 morgen] land [and] marshland . . .   24.
. . . .   100. 10

39   [Thomas Lam]ber[tse]
[1 poll 2 hor]ses, [1 do] of 3 yrs., 4 oxen,
8 cows, [ ]yr., [2 do. of 1 yr], 4 sheep . 147.4
[23 morgen land and] marshland . . . . .   46.
. . . .   [193. 4]

[40]   [name destroyed]
[1 poll 1 horse of 1 yr] 1 ox, 4 cows
1 do [of 2 yrs sheep] . . . . £51.
[15 morgen land and] marshland . . . . .   30.

41   [Paulus Dierc]kse
[2 polls 2] horses, [2 oxen 5 cows],
2 do. of[3 yrs 5 do] of 2 yrs.,
[3 do. of 1] yr., [5] hog[s] . . . . £127.
2 morgens of land and marshland . . .   24.
. . . .   151.

[42]   Jean [G]errittse
1 poll, 2 horses, 2 cows, 2 do. of
3 yrs., 2 do. of 2 yrs., 2 do. of 1 yr.,
2 sheep, 1 hog . . . . £70.
11 1/2 morgens of land and marshland   23.
. . . .   93.

43   Bourgon Brouchaert
1 poll, 2 cows . . . . £28.
11 1/2 morgens of land and marshland .   23.
. . . .   [51.]

[44]   Adam Brouwer

1 poll, 3 cows, 4 sheep
1 1/2 morgens of marshland 37. 14

[45]   Willem Brouwer
       1 poll . . . .   18.

[46]   Jabecq Brouwer
       1 poll . . . .   18.

47   [C]onradus Vander [Beeck?]
       [1 poll 2 oxen 2] cows, 1 do. of 1 yr.   . £43.
       14 morgens of land and marshland . . .   28.
       . . . .   71.

       . . . .   4039. 12*

48   Capt. Cornelis [ ]
       1 poll, 3 horses, [ ] [cows], 2 do. of
       3 yrs.,1 do. of 2 [yrs], [ ] do. of 1 yr. . . . £84.
       22 morgens of [land and] marshland . .   44.
       . . . .   28.‡

49   Weynand [Pietterse]
       1 poll, 2 horses, 3 cows . . . . £57.
       5 morgens of land . . . .   10.
       . . . .   [67.]

50   Paulus Michilse van der Voort
       1 poll, 2 oxen, 3 cows, 1 do. of 2 yrs.,
       1 do. of 1 yr. £49.
       12 morgens of land and marshland . . .   24.
       . . . .   [73.]

51   Pietter Ven Neeste
       3 polls, 4 cows, 1 do. of [ ] [yr],
       [ ] hogs . . . . £80.
       5 1/2 morgens of land and marshland .   11.
       . . . .   [91.]

*   subtotal
‡   This total should be "128."

52   Michil Hansen
      1 poll, 2 horses, 5 cows, 1 do. of 3 yrs.,
      2 do. of 1 yr. . . . . £74.
      20 morgens of land and marshland . . . 40.
      . . . .   [114.]

53   Hendrick Theunisse
      1 poll, 1 horse, 2 cows, 1 do.
      of 2 yrs. £42.10
      4 morgens of land . . . . 8.
      . . . .   [50. 10]

54   Jores Jacobse
      3 polls, 4 horses, 3 do. of 2 yrs., 2 oxen,
      3 cows, 2 do. of 3 yrs., [4] do. of
      [2 yr], [ ] do. of 1 yr., 2 hogs, 3 sheep . [£6.]
      30 morgens of land[   ] . . . . 60.
      . . . .[   ]

55   Dierck Corneliss[e Buis]
      [1 poll], 2 horses, 3 cows . . . . [   ]
      15 morgens of land . . . . [   ]
      . . . .[   ]

56   Jan Cornelise Buys
      1 poll, 2 horses, 3 cows, [1 do of] [ ]
      2 hogs,12 sheep . . . . [   ]
      8 morgens of lands and marshland
      . . . .[   ]

57   Gerrit Croes
      1 poll, 2 oxen, [ ] cows, 3 do. of 3 yrs.,
      2 do. of 2 yrs., 3 do.1 yr. £76.10
      14 morgens of land and marshland . . . 28.
      . . . .

The whole Property of Brueckelen amounts to . . .   [£5067. 18]

Taxed at 1d in the pound st[erlin]g
should amount to £21.2.4d   Your obedient servant
                                         Michil Hainelle

[Assessment Roll of Boswyck Made Up] 23 September [1676]

[1   G]isbert [Theuni]ss[e]
       [2] polls, 3 horses, [2 do of] [ ] yrs., 5
       cows, [2] do. of 3 yrs., 4 do. of
       [2 yrs do. of 1 yr. 1] hog, 8 sheep .. [£]138.8
       22 morgens of land and marshland .... 44.
       . . . .   182. 8

[2]   Woutter Gisberttse
       1 poll, 3 horses, 8 cows, 2do. of 3 yrs.,
       4 do. of 1 yr., 4 sheep £109.14
       18 morgens of land and marshland .... 36.
       . . . .   145. 14

3   Volkert Dierckse
       2 polls, 3 horses, 1 do. of 2 yrs., 8 cows,
       2 do. of 3 yrs., 3 do. of 2 yrs.,
       4 do. of 1 yr., 8 sheep, [2] h[ogs] £143.8
       25 morgens of land and marshland .... 50.
       . . . .   193.18

[4]   Charles Housman
       1 poll, 2 horses, 6 cows, 2 do. of 1 yr.,
       2 sheep £75.18
       11 morgens of land and marshland .... 22.
       . . . .   97.18

[5]   Cornelis Jansen
       1 poll, 2 cows, 1 do. of 3 yrs.,
       1 sheep £32.8
       4 morgens of land . . . . 8.
       . . . .   40. [8]

[6]   Pietter Jansen
       1 poll, 2 horses, 1 cow . . . .   47.

7   [Claes] Cornelisse
       1 poll, 5 morgens of land . . . .   28.

8   [Adriaen De La Forge]
       [1 poll 1 horse 2 cows] . . . .   40.

9   [*ms. destroyed*]

10   [*name illegible*]
         [1 poll 1 horse], 4 oxen, 11 cows,
         4 do. of 3 yrs., [1 do of] 2 yrs., 3 do.
         of 1 yr., 4 hogs .... £136.
         [40 morgen] land and marshland ...... 80.
         ....   216.

11   [Albert] Hendrickse
         1 poll ....   18.

[12]   Jan Caerlese
         1 poll ....   18.

[13]   Amador Foupier
         1 poll ....   18.

14   Jan Cornelise [Z]eu[w]
         1 poll, 2 horses, 2 cows, 5 sheep 54.2
         17 morgens of land and marshland .... 34.
         ....   88. 2

[15   E]vertt Hedeman
         1 poll, 2 oxen, 2 cows, 7 sheep, 3 hogs 46.
         13 1/2 morgens of land and marshland . 27.
         ....   73.

[16]   Jan Koorm
         1 poll, 2 horses, 1 do. of 1 yr., 3 cows,
         1 do. of 1 yr., 2 hogs, 2 sheep 64.8
         3 morgens of land .... 6.
         ....   70. 8

         ....   1329. 6[*]

17   Alexa[nder Coquer]
         1 poll, [1 hog 2 sheep] £19.18
         2 morg[en land] .... 4.
         ....   [23. 18]

* subtotal

18   Jan [Lesquier]
      2 polls, [2 horses 5] cows, 2 do. of
      3 yrs., 1 do. [of 1 yr 1] sheep . . . . £103.
      28 morgens of land and marshland . . . . 56.
      . . . .   [159].

19   Capt. Pietter Jansen Witt
      3 polls, 4 horses, 2 do. of 2 yrs., 1 do. of
      1 yr., 9 cows, 4 do. of 3 yrs., 2 do. of
      2 yrs., 7 do. of 1 yr., 18 sheep, 7 hogs £206.3
      50 morgens of land and marshland . . . 100.
      . . . .   30. 63

20   Jabeecq Dierckse
      1 poll, 2 horses, 1 do. of 1 yr.,
      2 sheep £45.18
      10 morgens of land . . . . 20.
      . . . .   65. 18

21   Pietter Schamp
      1 poll, 3 cows, 1 do. of 1 yr. £34.10
      9 morgens of land . . . . 18.
      . . . .   5[2. 10]

22   Joost Coec[k]wytt
      1 poll, 2 horses, 7 cows, 2 do. of 2 yrs.,
      3 do. of 1 yr., 7 sheep, 1 hog £90.10
      15 morgens of land and marshland . . . . 30.
      . . . .   [120. 10]

23   Siemen Haeckx
      1 poll . . . .   [18.]

24   Nelttie Janse[n]
      2 cows, 1 ditto of 2 yrs., 3 sheep, [2 hogs] [   ]

25   Jan Jansen
      [2 poll]s, 1 h[orse 2 cows] [   ]   [   ]

26   Hendrick Baerentse
      1 poll, 3 horses, 3 ditto of 3 yrs.,
      5 cows, 2 do. of 3 yrs., 4 do. of 1 yr.,
      5 sheep, 3 hogs . . . . [£141].
      20 morgens of land and marshland . . . . 40.
      . . . .   [181].

27   Jan Corn. D[amen]
      1 poll, 3 horses, [1] do. of 1 yr., 6 cows,
      1 do. of 3 yrs., 3 do. of 2 yrs., 4 do.
      of 1 yr., 16 sheep, 3 hogs £113.3
      28 morgens of land and marshland . . . . 56.
      . . . .   [16. 93]

28   Jan Ariaense
      1 poll, 3 cows, 1 do. of 1 yr., 4 sheep.   £37.4
      3 morgens of land . . . . 6.
      . . . .   43. 4

29   Cornelis Harmense Vogel
      2 polls, 3 sheep 37. 5

30   Pietter Parmentier
      2 polls, 3 horses, 2 oxen, 5 cows,
      2 do. of 3 yrs.,2 do. of 2 yrs.,
      3 do. of 1 yr., 4 hogs £130.10
      20 morgens of land and marshland 40. 10
      . . . .   [170.10]

31   Jacob Laro[ille]
      1 poll, 2 [horses . . . .   [   ]

      . . . .   [   ]*

32   Philip [Berckelo]
      1 poll . . . .   18.

33   Matthei[s] Jansen
      1 poll . . . .   18.

* The subtotal has been destroyed.

34   Theunis Gisberttse Boga[ert]
      8 morgens of marshland . . . .   16.

35   Ofie Cley
      2 polls, 2 horses, 6 cows, 3 ditto
      of 3 yrs., 3 ditto of 1 yr. . . . . £102.
      12 morgens of land and marshland . . . . 24.
      . . . .   <u>126.</u>

The assessment roll of Boswyck amounts to £2960 14
Rated at 1d. in the pound St[erlin]g
should amount to £12.6.9d.

Your ob[edien]t servant
Michil Hainelle.

[Assessment Roll] Of [New] Utrecht Made [Up 29 Septr] 1676.

[1   Hans] harmense
      1 poll, 3 horses, [4 cows of] 3 yrs.,
      4 do. of 2 yrs., 2 do. of 1 yr. £97.2
      24 morgens of land . . . . 48.
      . . . .   145. 2

[2]   Jan van Dev[ent]ere
      2 polls, 1 horse of 2 yrs., [3 cows 1] do.
      of 3 yrs., 1 do. of 2 yrs. £62.10
      12 morgens of land . . . . 24.
      . . . .   86.10

3   Jan Verckercke
      3 polls, 6 horses, 2 do. of 2 yrs.,
      4 cows, 20 sheep £164.10
      96 morgens of land and marshland . . . 192.
      . . . .   356. 10

4   Gisber[t]t Theyse
      1 poll, 2 horses, 1 cow, 1 ditto 2 yrs.,
      1 ditto of 1 yr. . . . . £51.
      18 morgens of land . . . . 36.
      . . . .   87.

5   Hendrick Matheyse
        1 poll, 4 horses, 3 cows, 3 do. of 3 yrs.,
        3 do. of 2 yrs., 3 do. of 1 yr. . . . . £105.
        30 morgens of land . . . . 60.
        . . . .   165.

6   Laurens Jansen
        1 poll, 2 horses, 2 cows . . . . £52.
        12 morgens of land . . . . 24.
        . . . .   76.

7   [   ] Joosten
        [1 poll 3] horses, 6 cows . . . . £84.
        [20 morgen land] . . . . 40.
        . . . .   124.

[8]   [   ]
        [6] cows . . . . £104.
        [20 morgen land] . . . . 40.
        . . . .   [144].

[9]   [   ] [Rhein]
        [1 poll] [ ] [horses 3] do. of 2 yrs.,
        2 do. of 1 yr. . . . . £46.
        [20 morgen land] . . . . 40.
        . . . .   86.

10   [J]an [Jansen Va]n Deyck
        1 poll, 2 horses, 2 cows,
        3 yrs., 1 do. of 2 yrs. . . . . £52.10.
        16 morgens of land . . . . 32.
        . . . .   84. 10

11   Carel jansen van deyck
        1 poll, 2 horses, 3 cows, ... £57.
        24 morgens of land . . . . 48.
        . . . .   105.

12   Rutger Joosten
        2 polls, 4 horses, 6 cows, 2 oxen, 2 ditto
        of 3yrs., 3 do. of 2 yrs., 4 do. of 1 yr.,
        12 sheep £152.12
        100 morgen land . . . . 200.
        . . . .   352. 12

13   Jean Clement
        1 poll, 1 horse, 2 cows, 1 do. of 3 yrs.,
        1 do. of 2 yrs. 46.10

14   Jacob Bastiansen
        1 poll, 1 cow . . . .   23.

[15]   [T]heys Jansen
        [1] poll, 1 horse, 2 oxen, [ ] cows,
        1 ditto of [3] yrs., 1 hog . . . . £80.
        15 morgen land 30
        . . . .   110.
        . . . .   1991. 14 *

16   Theys Lubbert
        1 poll, [2 horses], [ ] [cows of] 2 yrs.   . [£44.10]
        12 morgen land . . . . 24.
        . . . .   [68 .10]

17   Jean van [   ]
        1 poll, 2 h[orses 4 cow]s,
        4 ditto of 2 yrs. . . . . £72.
        40 morgen l[and] . . . . 80.
        [. . . .   152.]

18   Crein Jan[sen]
        2 polls, 2 horses, 1 do. of 2 yrs. . . . . . £65.
        24 morgen land . . . . 48.
        . . . .   113.

* subtotal

19   Arie Willemse
      1 poll, 3 horses, 5 cows, 2 do. of 2 yr.,
      3 do. of 1 yr. £88.10
      24 morgens of land .... 48.
      ....   136 . 10

20   Pietter Jacobse
      1 poll, 2 cows .... 28.

21   Theunis Jansen Van Peltt
      [2 polls 3 horses 5 cows 1 do of 1 year],
      4 Sheep £100.4
      24 morgens of land .... 48.
      ....   148.[4]

22   Huibert Stoock
      1 poll
      ....   [18].

23   Luyckes Mayerse
      1 poll, 3 horses, 5 cows, 1 do.
      of 3 yrs., 2 do. of 1 yr. .... £74.
      20 morgens of land .... 40.
      ....   [114].

[24] Anthony Van der Eycke
      [1] poll, 2 horses, 3 cows ....[   ]
      12 morgens of land ....   [   ]

25   Jores Bourier
      1 poll, 2 cows, 2 oxen .... [   ]
      12 morgens of land ....   [   ]

26   Zegertt Gerrittse
      1 poll ....   18.

27   Hendrick jan[sen] van deyck
      1 poll ....   18.

28   Jean Muserol
        1 poll, 2 oxen, 4 cows . . . . £50.
        12 morgens of land . . . . 24.
        . . . .   [.74]

The Property of N[ew] Utrecht amounts to   £30.[24 18]
Rates @ 1d per pound St[erlin]g
should amount to £12.12.1d.   Your ob[edien]t Servant
                                               Michil Hainelle

[Valuation Of Amsfortt] Made Up September [1676]

[1]   Claes Pietterse
        1 poll, 2 horses, [1 do of [ ] yrs 6]
        cows . . . . £75.
        7 morgens of land . . . . 14.
        . . . .   89.
[2]   Gilles Jansen
        3 polls, 3 horses, 2 oxen, [ ] [cows] . . £105.
        10 morgens of land and marshland . . . . 20.
        . . . .   125.

3   Gerritt Reinerse
        2 polls, 4 horses, 7 cows, 2 ditto
        of 1 yr., 1 hog . . . . £125.
        23 morgens of land and marshland . . . . 46.
        . . . .   171.

4   Willem Van Berckelo
        1 poll, 2 horses, 1 cow . . . . 47.

5   Dierckie Willemse
        1 horse, 2 cows, 1 do. of 2 yrs., 4 morgen land   32. 10

6   Willem Willemse
        1 poll, 2 horses, 4 cows 1 do. of 3 yrs.,
        1 ditto of 1 yr. £67.10
        11 morgens of land and marshland . . . 22.
        . . . .   89. 10

[7]   Hans Jansen
       1 poll, 2 oxen, 5 cows,
       1 ditto of 2 yrs. £57.10
       17 morgens of land and marshland . . . . 34.
       . . . .   91. 10

[8]   Albert Albertse
       2 polls, 4 horses, 1 do. of 1 yr.
       7 cows do. of 2 yr. 2 hogs . . . . £129.
       [29 mor]gens of land and marshland . . . 58.
       . . . .   187.

9   [   ] Stevense
       [1 poll], [ ] [horses, 1] ditto of 2 yrs.,
       4 cows, [ ] ditto of 1 yr. £84.10
       [20 morgen land] and marshland . . . . . . 40.
       . . . .   124. 10

10   [name destroyed]
       [1 poll 1] horse, 1 cow . . . .   47.

[11]   [Albert] Albertse the younger
       1 poll, 1 horse, 3 cows . . . .   45.

12   Dierck Jansen
       1 poll, 1 horse, 3 cows . . . . £57.
       7 morgens of land . . . . £14.
       . . . .   [71.]

13   Pietter Claessen
       2 polls, 5 horses, 13 cows, 3 do.
       of 3 yrs., 2 oxen, 2 sheep £186.5
       59 morgens of land and marshland . . 118.
       . . . .   304 .5

14   Laurens Cornelisse
       1 poll, 1 horse . . . .   30.

15   Fernandes Van Eickel
       1 poll, 2 horses, 2 cows . . . .   52.

16   Jan Brouwer
        1 poll, 2 horses, 4 cows, 3 hogs . . . .   65.

[17]   Abraham Joorese
        1 poll, 2 horses, 1 do. of 2 yrs.,
        14 cows, 2 do. of 3 yrs., 4 do. of
        [2 yrs] 4 do. of 1 yr. . . . . £141.
        35 morgens of land and ma[rshland] . . . 70.
        . . . .   211.

[18]   Roeloff Maertense
        [2] polls, 4 horses, [1 do of] yrs.,
        10 cows, [2] do. of 2 yrs., 4 ditto
        [of 1 yr 3 hogs] £152.14
        [52] morgens of land and marshland   . 104.
        . . . .   256. 14
        . . . .   2038. 19[*]

19   Steven Coe[rtten]
        2 polls, 4 ho[rses], [ ] [cows, 5] ditto
        of [2 yrs] . . . . [£129.]
        55 morgens of land[ ] . . . . 110.
        . . . .   [239.]

20   Jan Kiersen
        2 polls, 2 horses, [ ] cows
        2 do. of 1 yr. £103.
        31 morgens of land and marshland . . . . 62.
        . . . .   [165.]

21   Willem Gerrittse
        1 poll, 4 horses, 2 do. of 1 yr., 1 ox,
        7 cows, 3 do. of 3 yr., 2 do of 2 yr.,
        1 do. of 1 yr. £131.10
        28 morgens of land and marshland . . . . 56.
        . . . .   187. 10

22   Pietter Monfortt
        1 poll, 1 horse, 2 cows . . . .   40.

* subtotal

23   Jan Monfortt
      1 poll ....   18.

24   Ariaen Pietterse
      1 poll, 2 horses, 2 cows .... £52.
      8 morgens of land and marshland ..... 16.
      ....   68.

25   Pietter Hendrickse
      1 poll, 1 horse ....   30.

26   Seiman Jansen
      2 polls, 4 horses, 8 cows, 3 do. of
      3 yrs., 1 do. of 2 yrs., 2 do of 1 yr.,
      4 sheep, 1 hog £144.4
      32 morgens of land and marshland .... 64.
      ....   [208 .4]

27   Pietter Cornelise
      2 polls, 5 horses, 1 do. of 3 yrs., [ ]
      [cows], 2 do. of 3 yrs., 3 do. of [2 yrs],
      [ ] do. of 1 yr., 4 hogs ....[   ]
      [24 morgen land and marshland] ....[   ]
      ....[   ]

28   Swaen Jansen
      1 poll, 2 horses, 1 cow, 2 hogs ....[£49].
      5 morgens of land [and marshland] ....[10].
      ....   [59.]

29   Hendrick Pietterse
      1 poll, 3 horses, [2] oxen, 5 cows,
      1 do. of 1 yr., 1 hog £93.10
      19 morgens of land and marshland .... 38.
      ....   [131. 10]

30   Coertt Stevense
      1 poll, 4 horses, 1 do. of 2 yrs., 2 oxen
      6 cows, 4 do. of 2 yrs., 4 do. of 1 yr. . £127.
      44 morgens of land and marshland .... 88.
      ....   215.

31   Jacob and Gerritt Streycker
        3 polls, 2 horses, 7 cows, 2 hogs .... £115.
        1¹/₂ morgens of land .... 3.
        ....   118.

32   Jan Martense
        1 poll, 3 horses, 1 do. of 2 yrs.,
        2 do. of 1 yr., 3 cows, 2 do. of 1 yr. .... £83.
        10 morgens of land and marshland .... 20.
        ....   103.

33   Willem Hu[lett]
        1 poll 1 h[orse 2 cow]s ....   40.

        .... subtotal   3865. 13

[34]   Willem [ ]ittsen
        1 poll 2 horses 1 do [ ] [yrs] 5 cows
        2 do of 1 yr 2 hogs .... £77.
        12 morgens of land and marshland ...   24.
        ....   101.

The whole valuation of [Amsf]ortt amounts to   £3966. 13

        Property Rate

The property is rated as follows
        Each Poll ....£18.
        Each horse over 4 yrs. old ....12.
        between 3 and 4 yrs. ....8.
        between 2 and 3 yrs ....5.
        between 1 and 2 yrs. ....3.
Each ox above 4 yrs old ....6.
Each cow above 4 yrs old ....5.
        between 3 and 4 yrs. old ....4.
        between 2 and 3 yrs. old 2.10
        between 1 and 2 ....1.10
Each hog above 1 yr. old ....1.
Each sheep above 1 yr. old 8.6
Each morgen of land ....2.

The property above mentioned of 3,966 pounds 13 shillings @ 1d per pound Sterling should amount to 16 pounds 10 shillings 6¹/₂ pence.

Your Obedient Servant
Michil Hainelle

[Rate Bills of the Five Dutch Towns; 1st October 1676.]

£ 4872.11............... Rate Bill of Middelwout................... £20.06.—
    5067.18 .... Rate Bill of Breuckelen...................... 21.02.04
    2960.14 .... Rate Bill of Boswyck. 12.06.09
    3024.18 .... Rate Bill of N[ew] Utrecht 12.12.01
    3966.13 .... Rate Bill of Amsfort.......................... 16.10.06½
£19892.14 assessment of the 5 towns @ 1d per pound ... £82.17.08½

[22:156]

[COPY OF A LETTER FROM KING CHARLES II TO GOVERNOR PHILIP
CARTERET OF NEW JERSEY ENJOINING HIM TO ENFORCE THE LAWS
AND GOVERNMENT ESTABLISHED BY THE PROPRIETOR,
SIR GEORGE CARTERET]*

Charles R.

Trusty and welbeloved, Wee greete you well, Whereas our right Trusty, and well beloved Councellor Sir George Carteret Knight and Baronet, by Grant derived under us, is seized of the Province of New Cesaria or New Jersey in America, and of the Jurisdiction thereof, as Proprietor of the same; In the plantacion of which said Province, The said Sir George Carteret hath beene at great Charge and Expence: And Whereas of late great Troubles and disorders have hapned there by some ill affected persons, Wee being willing and desirous to encourage the inhabiting and planting of the said Province, and to preserve the Peace and welfare of all our Loving Subjects residing there, Wee doe therefore hereby require you in our name to use your utmost Endeavors to prevent all troubles and disorders here for the future, and strictly to charge and command all persons whatsoever, inhabiting within the said Province forthwith to yield obedience to the Lawes, and Government, which are or shall bee there establisht by the said Sir George Carterett, who hath the sole power under us, to settle and dispose of the said Countrey, upon such Termes and Condicions as hee shall thinke fitt; And wee shall expect a ready Complyance with this our Will and pleasure from all persons whatsoever dwelling or remaining within the same, upon paine of incurring our high displeasure, and being proceeded against with due Severity, according to Law, Whereof you are to give publick notice to all persons that are or may bee concerned, And so wee bid you farewell: Given at our Court at Windsor the 13th day of June 1674, In the 26th yeare of our Raigne.

[ENDORSED:]   **By his Majesties Command**
Arlington

---

* This document appears out of chronological order in volume 22 of the "Colonial Manuscripts." It was previously published in the *Administrative Papers of Governors Richard Nicolls and Francis Lovelace, 1664–1673* (Baltimore, 1980), 216-17. Together with a similarly worded letter of December 9, 1672, from the king to Deputy Governor Capt. John Berry of New Jersey [22:144a], this document was undoubtedly exhibited at Carteret's trial in May 1680 before a special court of assizes. He was accused of having "without any Lawfull Right power or Authority . . . Presumed to Exercise Jurisdiccion and Government over his Majesties Subjects" (*Records of the Court of Assizes*, 258–66).

[ADDRESSED:]   Sir George Carteretts Lettre

To our trusty and well beloved Philip
Carteret Esquire Governor of New Jersey
in America, and to the Councell there.

Copia vera compared with the Originall.

James Bollen Secr.

[ENDORSED:]   Copyes of The Kings Lettres
for New Jersey.

Bibliography

Brodhead, John Romeyn. *History of the State of New York*; 2 vols. New York: Harper and Brothers (rev. ed.), 1872.

Christoph, Peter R., ed. *Administrative Papers of Governors Richard Nicolls and Francis Lovelace, 1664–1673*. Baltimore: Genealogical Publishing, 1980.

————, and Florence A. Christoph, eds. *Books of General Entries of the Colony of New York*; 2 vols. (1664–1673, 1674–1688). Baltimore: Genealogical Publishing, 1982.

————, ————. *Records of the Court of Assizes for the Colony of New York, 1665–1682*. Baltimore: Genealogical Publishing, 1983.

Evans, Thomas Grier, ed. *Records of the Reformed Dutch Church in New Amsterdam and New York: Baptisms (1639–1730)*. New York: New York Genealogical and Biographical Society, 1901.

Fernow, Berthold, ed. *Documents Relating to the Colonial History of the State of New York* (vols. XII–XIV). Albany: Argus, 1877–83.

————. *The Records of New Amsterdam from 1653 to 1674 Anno Domini*; 7 vols. New York: Knickerbocker Press "under Authority of the City of New York," 1897 (reprint, Genealogical Publishing, 1976).

Hough, Franklin B., ed. *Papers Relating to the Island of Nantucket, with Documents Relating to the Original Settlement of That Island, Martha's Vineyard, and Other Island Adjacent, Known as Dukes County, While Under the Colony of New York*. Albany: J. Munsell, 1856.

————. *Narrative of the Cases Which Led to Philip's Indian War, of 1675 and 1676*, by John Easton of Rhode Island. With Other Documents Concerning This Event in the Office of the Secretary of State of New York. Albany: J. Munsell, 1858.

McCusker, John J. *Money and Exchange in Europe and America, 1660–1775.* Chapel Hill: University of North Carolina Press for the Institute of Early American History and Culture, 1978.

New York. *Minutes of the Common Council of the City of New York, 1675–1776*; 8 vols. New York: Dodd Mead, "Under Authority of the City of New York," 1905.

New York State Historian. *Third Annual Report*, 1897. Appendix L: New York's Colonial Archives. Transcriptions of the Records Between the Years 1673 and 1675. New York and Albany: Wynkoop Hallenbeck Crowford, 1898.

O'Callaghan, Edmund B., ed. *Calendar of Historical Manuscripts, in the Office of the Secretary of State*, Albany, NY, Part II, English Manuscripts: 1664–1776. Albany: Weed, Parsons, 1866 (reprinted with the title, *Calendar of British Historical Manuscripts in the Office of the secretary of State, Albany, New York 1664–1776*. Ridgewood, NJ: Gregg Press, 1968.

O'Callaghan, Edmund B., ed. *Documentary History of the State of New York*; 4 vols. Albany: Weed, Parsons, 1849–51 (octavo ed.); 1850–51 (quarto).

Pearson, Jonathan, transl. *Early Records of the City and County of Albany, and Colony of Rensselaerswyck*; 4 vols. (vols. 2–4 rev. and ed. by A. J. F. van Laer). Albany: (vol. 1) J. Munsell, 1869; (vols. 2–4) University of the State of New York, 1916–19.

Purple, Samuel S., ed. *Records of the Reformed Dutch Church in New Amsterdam and New York: Marriages.* New York: New York Genealogical and Biographical Society, 1890 (reprint, 1940).

Ritchie, Robert C. *The Duke's Province; a Study of New York Politics and Society, 1664–1691.* Chapel Hill: University of North Carolina Press, 1977.

Starbuck, Alexander. *The History of Nantucket, County, Island and Town Including Genealogies of First Settlers.* Boston: C. E. Goodspeed, 1924 (reprint, Rutland, VT: Charles E. Tuttle, 1969).

van Laer, A. J. F., transl. and ed. *Minutes of the Court of Albany, Rensselaerswyck, and Schenectady, 1675–1680*, vol. II. Albany: University of the State of New York, 1928.

Webb, Stephen Saunders. *1676: The End of American Independence.*
New York: Knopf, 1984.

Index

Aartsen; *see* Aertsz

Abrahams, Jacob, sues Smith 51

Accomack River, Virginia 347

Achter Col; *see* Aftercull

Adam, alias Wisquannowas, seeks land grant 138–39

Adames, John, assessed 545

Addington, Isaiah, clerk at Boston 94, 97, 99, 101; witness 95

admiralty court; *see* New York (Colony) court of admiralty

Adolph, the carpenter 353

Aerense, Claes, assessed 497, 557

Aertsz/Areson, Derek, assessed 545

Aertsz/Aerse/Aertsen, Jan/Jean/John, assessed 501, 559; bill for 119; complaint against Warner 163, 174; horse 401; husband and guardian 384

Aertsz, Joris, deposition 329

Aertsz/Aersen, Reyn, assessed 505, 551

Aertsz/Aertsen, Rut, lot in Albany 145

Aertsz/Aersen/Aertsen, Seimen, assessed 500, 558

Aftercull/Achter Col, New Jersey 244

Akerly, Robert, assessed 537

Akerly, Sam, assessed 538

Albany/New Albany, accused of supplying guns to Indians 345; business accounts 421; collector 59; commissioners 132; court secretary 121; governor at 337; Indians on way to 432; Indians supplied at 404–5; land patent at 356–57, 407; land sold at 145–46; letter to officials from Andros about charges against van Rensselaer 435–36; magistrates nominated 411–12; meeting with Indians arranged at 375–76; property sold 426–28; residents 447; sale of land 369–70; sheriff 345; sol-

diers sent to New York 68; supplies Indians 467; troops at New York from 76, 77; mentioned 8, 58, 59, 216–17, 244, 282, 290, 307–9, 330, 331n, 352, 378, 403–4, 414

Albany, Colony of Rensselaerswyck and Schenectady, court, costs 448; secretary 121; hears suit 204–7, 413–21; judgment 483–84

Albertse, Albert, assessed 509, 574

Albertse, Albert, the younger, assessed 510, 574

Albertse, Ruth, assessed 554

Alburtis, Arthor, assessed 540

Alburtis, John, assessed 540

Allin, James, official 219

Alrichs/Alricks, Peter, sued by estate of Morris 114; suit with Darvall 39

Ambrose, John, chief mate, suit about wages 223, 261–62, 270, 275, 548

Amersfort/Amsfortt, assessment rolls 508–12, 573–77; minister's salary 93

Ammone, Indian, meets with Andros 89, 348–49

ammunition, lead for Indians 253, 404–5, supplied at Albany 345; gunpowder, 253, 371, 481, given to Indians 367, 404, 405

Amsterdam, ship from 9; mentioned 31, 33

Amyes, Christop., property in New York 116

Andrews, Samuel, account 320–21; court case about land 50; excused from being constable 393; sells sloop 321–22; mentioned 387

Andriese, Arie, assessed 507

Andriesz, Lourens, signs Lutheran petition 17

Barense/Barnsen/Barnson, Symon, mariner, sued by Scholtar, to appear at assizes 327–28

Barker, Mr., commissary, orders mail delivery 270; sends letter to Andros 268; to provision fort 68; warns whalers 279

Barker, Samuel, son killed 228–30

Barker, Thomas, killed 194–95

Barker, Thomas, auditor, 470; juror 455

Barnard, Nathaniel, signs petitions 25, 135

Barnard, Robert, rights to Nantucket land 25–30

Barnard, Thomas, original settler of Nantucket 25–30

Barnes, John, Jr., letter to Shakerly about consignment 311–12

Barnsen; see Barense

barrels, see also coopers; pipe staves 186; pipes 355; price of cask 439; regulations on value 476–81

Barton, Capt., horse 150

Basely, Thomas, left gun loaded 335

Bassett, Thomas, soldier, court witness 71

Bastard, William, purser, suit about wages 270, 548

Bastiense, Jacob, assessed 512, 571

Bate, William, col., mentioned 408

Bates, Polly, mentioned 408

Baxtar, Thomas, assessed 518

Bayard, Balthasar, sues Tayler 491; witness 465

Bayard, Nicolaes, accused, ill 245; appeals verdict favoring Lawrence 120; as attorney 33–34, 59–60; bond and bondsman 112; demands of 35; former secretary and receiver general, power of attorney from Colve 31; obligation as customs officer, to pay Shakerly 438; petition against oath of allegiance 107–8; prisoner 110; prisoner in the Fort 243; property in New York 115; as secretary 208; subpoena 450, 451, 452; sued by Laurance 112–13; sues Rider 177; to be arrested, refuses to swear allegiance 238–39; warrant about his

papers 110; mentioned 31–32, 46, 465

Bayard, Peter, bail for N. Bayard 243; mentioned 423

Bayly, Mr., sued by Woodhull 53

Bayly/Baily, John, juror 388; trustee of Lane's estate 51

Bayly/Baily, Joseph, assessed 534; warns officials about Indians 202

Bayly/Baly, Nathan, assessed 517, 541

Bayly/Bally, Nicoles/Nicles, assessed 516; takes inventory 305–6

Bayly, Stephen, assessed 526

Bayly; see Baily

Baynes, Sgt., court witness 64

Beagle, Mathew, sues Thickston 51–53

beavers, bears; see peltry

Beaver's Kill, mentioned 407

Bedloe/Bedloo, Elisabeth (de Potter) widow, administratrix 201, 230–31, sued by Anthony 444, 451, to pay 258; appeals 177; charges for settling estate 192; goods seized by sheriff 473; petition about letters of administration 190–91; sells island 357; sued by Bryan 175 by Doughty 176, by van der Spiegle 176–77; mentioned 443, 473

Bedloe, Isaac, deceased, bill 197, 201; books to be viewed 176; debt 421; estate account 175; estate inventoried 210; lists of account books 443–44; widow settles estate 190–91; mentioned 230–31, 357

Bedloe's Island; see Love Island

Beeckman, Jochem, subpoena 450, 452

Beeckman, William, appears before governor and council 246; petition against oath of allegiance 107–8; prisoner 110; property liable for confiscation 250–51; seeks pardon 247; submission 249–50; mentioned 112

beer; see liquor

Begen, William, assessed 546

Belcher, Andrew, envoy 184

Bellieu; see Bilieu

Benckes, Jacob, commander of Dutch fleet 439

Beniam, Simieon, assessed 529

Benjamin, Richard, assessed 527

de Vou, Frederick, mentioned 435
de Vou, Niclas, land grant 434
de Vries, Adriaen, settler 283
de Vries; *see also* de Freeze
de Wandelaer, Johannes, witness 244
de Yonge, Jacob, sues Whitman 162
Dicarman, Isack, assessed 516
Dicisson, Peeter, assessed 529
Dickerey, Philip, of Jamaica, part owner of ketch 189; tavern keeper, ship owner 185
Dickman, Jean, constable 435
Dierckse, Jabecq, assessed 496, 567
Dierckse, Paulus, assessed 499, 562
Dierckse, Volkert, assessed 495, 565
Diment, Thomas, constable, assessed 522; receives fines 306
Diment, Thomas, Jr., assessed 522
Dirck, property in New York 117
Dirck, horse of 401
Dircks/Dircksen, Tunis, deposition 48; sues de Bruen 161, 164
Disteler, William, court witness 181
divorce, legal separation 54; mentioned 334–35
Dobree, John, runaway soldier 147, 185
doctor, *see also* Henry Taylor; at fort 44; Tieleman, widow of 382; Wessells, court witness 423–44
Doddiman/Doddyman, Richard, elected Staten Island constable 41–42; juror 160, 175
Dogget, Thomas, dispute with Perkins 220
dogs, mentioned 174
Domeny, Natha., assessed 522
domine; *see* ministers
Dorlantt/Durlan, Lambert Jansen, *see also* Jansen, Lambertt; assessed 500, 558; sued by Hollis 161
Doughty, Mr., to settle on Long Island 460
Doughty/Douty, Elias/Alias, coronet, complaint against Coe 157; court witness 165; letter from Manning concerning Dutch invasion 81; ordered to assemble troops 80; reporting military readiness 82; sues Bedloe 176, 190–91,

Wood 163, 173; to defend New Utrecht 72
Doughty, Elias, assessed 544; deed at Yonkers 409; excused from jury 294; foreman of jury 388; juror 455; sued by Levy 292, 299; sues Jansen (Van Dyke) 300–301, 303–4, and Mattysen (Smack) 300–301, 304; sues van Deventer 304; witness 293
Doughty, Francis, horses 300; sued by Anthony 293, 296, 299
Dowdale, Patrick, sgt., court witness 64, 70; sues Boys 161, 170
Doxey, Ralph, court witness 400; sues Shrickland 162
Drake, John, assessed 518
Drake, Samuel, assessed 518; court witness 297
Drake, Samuel, Jr., assessed 518
Drisius, Domine, property in New York 116
Dubbels/Dubels, Susanne, assessed 501, 561
Du Bois/Duboys, Abraham, magistrate 188
Du Bois, Louis/Lewis, justice 187; sues Morris 207–9
Dudley, Capt., meets the king 61
duke of York; see James, duke of York
duke's laws 219
DuSchelluyne; *see* van Schelluyn
Dutch crew, mutinies 186
Dutch fleet commander, Andros's letter to 439
Dutch government of New York, suit at time of 155, 156, 401, 486; mentioned 207, 208
Dutch lords or college of admiralty, mentioned 31, 33
Dutch navy, marines, etc., attack New York 67–84
Dutch residents, oppose oath of allegiance 107–8
Dutch war, mentioned 372
Duxbury, Plymouth Colony, mentioned 142
Dyer; *see also* Dyre
Dyer, Edward, witness 95, 96

Garton, Thomas, justice 187
Geerlen/Greerlen, John, mentioned 382, 383
Geisse, Wouter, assessed 502, 558
Gelime, John, assessed 546
Gentleman Councellor; see Monugabongun
Gerratt, John B., soldier, court witness 70
Gerritsen/Gerritse/Gerritsz, Adriaen, land at Albany 145–46; magistrate 204–7, 369–70, 411–12; mentioned 427
Gerritsen/Garetson, Ditrick, assessed 517
Gerritsen, Goossen; see van Schick, Goossen
Gerritsen, Gysbert, deposition 329
Gerritsen, Jacob, assessed 51
Gerritsen, Jan/Jean, assessed 501, 514, 562
Gerritsen, John; see van Marcken, Jan
Gerritsen/Gerritsen, Marten, land patent 407; nominated as Rensselaerswyck magistrate 412
Gerritsen, Otto, bids for position of tax collector 289; farmer of tappers' excise 288
Gerritsen/Gerritsz, Pieter/Peter, examined about mutiny 188–90; ship's mate 185
Gerritsen/Gerrittse, Willem, assessed 510, 575
Gerritsen/Gerrittse, Zegertt, assessed 572
Gibb, Andrew, sued by Blagge 488–90
Gibbons, Edmund, complaint against de la Noy 85
Gibbs, Thomas, alderman, member of court 245, 251; ambassador to Dutch fleet 73–75; member of admiralty court 262, 265–66, 276; New York sheriff 19, 21–22, 106–7; prisoner 70; witness 20, 65–66, 490
Gibson, Simon, mentioned 463
gifts, coats to Indians 349, 378; deerskins, bearskins, beavers; duffel, duffel coats, wampum 355; bearskins, beavers, deerskins, duffel coats 358

gilders; see guilders
Gildersleeve, Richard, deposition 52; Hempstead official, order 470; his wife court witness 150; represents Hempstead 237; signs petition for minister 36
Gildersleeve, Richard, Jr., signs petition for minister 36
Gillese, Jan, assessed 503
Gisberttse; see Gysberts
Glasse, William, seaman, suit about wages 271, 549
Gleane/Gleene, Anthony, patent from 168; mentioned 350–51
Gleene, Esther, court witness 165
Glen, Alexander/Sander Leendertse, gives mortgage to van de Water 8; retiring magistrate 426; and wife 420; and wife accused of stealing beaver 417–18
Glover, Samuel, assessed 526
Goden, John, assessed 518
Goden, Samuel, assessed 518
gold, mentioned 307
Golding/Goulden/Gowlding/Gollgurd, John, assessed 536; hay and cattle 281; petitions for relief 446
Good, Peter, soldier, court witness 71
Goossens, Gerrit; see van Schaick, Goossen Gerritsz
Gorges, Ferdinando, knight 137; land title in Maine 123, 124
Gospel, converting the Indians 314–15
Gould, Thomas, peace officer, taken prisoner 193
Goverts, Mrs., property in New York 116
Graves, John, assessed 543
Graves, William, assessed 541; sued by Newtown constable, court costs 459
Gravesend, agreement with de Bruyne 174; assessment roll 520; constable 160; constable, agent 47; constable and overseers sue Griggs 163, 174, Hansen 174, Simpson 163, 173, court orders sent to 476; petition for cattle fair 47; Quakers refuse oath 396; sues Spanieson 163; troops to be drawn to 80; mentioned 211

238; take captives 254–55, 337; tenants of Mayhew 219; threaten residents of Yonkers 255–56; to be Christianized 314–15; to be employed as whalers 278–80; to have guns 355; treatment of at Nantucket 356–67; wars 193, 213, 282, 366, account of 338–45; letter from Andros about 371; of Wickers Creek receive pass 379; mentioned 54, 138–39, 195–96

Indians, land dealings, at Catskill 58; of eastern Long Island offer land 129–30; give deeds to Jansz and Thomasz 309–10; give mortgage to Clute 121; grant land to Col. Nicolls 5; land 217–20; land at Martha's Vineyard bought from 218; land claims 235–37; land sold to Southton 441; sell land 168; sell island in Rensselaerswyck 307–8; sell land at Catskill 58, Claverack 282–83, Nantucket 11

Indians, meeting with Andros and council, from Connecticut and Long Island 358; from Delaware 202–3, 207, 377–79; from Hackensack and Tappan 368; about land at Hempstead 238, 285; from Long Island 316; from Rahway 332; sachems 40, 89, 178; sachems from New Jersey 291; of Westchester 313; of Wickers Creek 348–49, 352–53, 409; with Andros and Carteret 131

Inkerson, John, assessed 536

inventory, of books and papers belonging to Bedlow 201; of the estate of Thomas Seabrooke 305–6

iron, weighing fees 287

Isaeck, Aerent, assessed 561

ivory or elephants' teeth, weighing fees 287

Jackson, Mr., constable 150; rates 470; mentioned 393–94

Jackson, John, accused by Heydens 393; assessed 518; merchant sailor 482

Jacobse/Jacobsz, Cornelis, assessed 507; mentioned 473n

Jacobse, Joores/Jores, assessed 503, 564

Jacobse/Jacobsz, Maritie/Maria, *Juf-*

frouw, seeks payment 307

Jacobse/Jacobs, Pietter/Peter, assessed 513, 572; land patent 146; subpoenaed to testify 468

Jacobse, Rutt/Ruth (Rutger), translates 310; witness 311; mentioned 107

Jacobse/Jacobsen, Willem, assessed 496, 506, 554

Jagger, John, Southampton official 213, 440

Jamaica, Long Island, assessments 211; court orders sent to 475; estate at 440; informed of Dutch attack 72; killing at 194–95; land 169; rates 232–33; residents petition for representation 36–38; tavern keeper's bill 55; troops sent to 82; troops to assemble 78; mentioned 118, 169, 173, 223

Jamaica, constable, position established 36; presentments 387; sworn 149

Jamaica, court of sessions for North Riding, bonds to appear before 350–51; costs 55–56, 148–49; docket 299, 386, 490–91; judgment at 428; judgment ignored 446–47; minutes 49–55, 149–59, 252, 257, 291–98, 388–96, 484–88; orders for holding 99–100, 257, 489

Jamaica, West Indies, ketch from 185, 189; ship bound for 190

James, ———, and wife, lodging 87

James, duke of York, duke's laws 219; grant to Barkley and Carteret 4; hears Manning 61–66; land grants at Martha's Vineyard 23; Manning appears before 77

James, Thomas, rev., supports Indians in request for return of guns 215–16; writes letter for Montauk Indians 215

James Fort; *see* Fort James

Jansen, [ ], assessed 555

Jansen/Janse, Abraham, bondsman 112

Jansen, Aert/Aers, assessed 504, 553

Jansen/Jans, Angeltye, sues butcher 302

Jansen/Janse/Jans, Auke/Aucke/Auwke/Aukey/Aukes/Ackeys, assessed 504, 499, 551; Brooklyn overseer 164; Flatbush overseer 41–43; sued by de Meyer 302

Nesaquake River, farmers at 225

Neversink/Nevesan sachems, meet with governor and Carterett 131–33; mentioned 291

Nevius/Neevius/Nefius, Johannes, ferryman, deceased, account with Nicolls 380–84; widow 384

New Albany; see Albany

New Albion, mentioned 4

New Aroyna; see New Orange

Newcastle, mentioned 39, 145

New Cesaria; see New Jersey

New England, refugee from 433; mentioned 290

Newfoundland, mentioned 75

New Haven, mentioned 109, 351

New Jersey, governor 291; laws and government of 579–80; pipestaves at 476; sachems of 291; mentioned 4, 131, 294

New London, Conn., reports of attacks by King Philip 180–81; mentioned 167

New Netherland, see also Colve, Anthony; mentioned 31

New Orange/Aroyna/Orania/Orangien, see also New York City; court at 98–99; weighhouse 100; mentioned 96, 98

New Paltz, court 187; justices 187–88; magistrates 188

Newton, Henry/Herry, capt., complaint against Scudamore 53; court witness 63, 65–66; debt owed to 192; marshall 270; payment 234–35; sues Barnsen 391; witnesses documents 22, 257, 259, 328

Newtown, assessment rolls 539–43; assessments 539–43; court orders sent to 476; cow and corn taken 400; informed of Dutch attack 72; island belongs to 172; jurors 44; meadows in dispute 44; Quakers refuse oath 396; rates 232–33; to send woman away 401; town court 173; troops to assemble 78; mentioned 38, 213, 334, 336

Newtown, constable, presents suit 401; to be elected 164; to seize goods 471; suit against Graves 459; mentioned 160, 163, 302

New Utrecht, assessments 512–15, 569–73; constable 160, 163; court orders sent to 476; horses 164; residents advise Dutch fleet 75–76; ship anchors at 186; suit 303; troops 72, 80, 82; mentioned 300

New York City, attacked by Dutch fleet 67–84; building of great dock 353–54; building sites 115–18; constable 87, to search for stolen goods 19–20; distillery license at 433; Dutch fleet at 439; Dutch property sold 34; Dutch residents petition against oath of allegiance 107–8; examinations about surrender 65–66; fort surrendered 64; governor's stables 116; great dock (mole) 424; house in 177; house sale 7–8; meeting about vacant lots 375; meeting at state house 423; merchant 446–407; militia officers to be appointed 118; minister for Lutherans 17; petition to build 15; plundered 112–13; property attached in 106–7; property disputed 231–32; residents aid enemy 76–77; school 333; seized by Dutch 319; Mr. Sharpe, clerk 86; ship at 274; ship at customs 85; ship examined 272; ship to sail from 461; state house property 115; stock company headquarters 101–2; town hall, 89, 263, 270, 275; treasurer 425; vacant lots to be viewed 88; weigh house 97, 286–87, 472, fees 287; weighmaster, auction for position 286–87, bids for office, 472; mentioned 130, 136, 147, 207, 209, 307, 321, 327, 464–65, 468

New York City, court of mayor and aldermen, called 243; court of record 385; decision 190, 258, 482; hearing about a ship 198; judgment appealed 140–41, 230–32, 283–84, 316–17, 356, 375–76, 385, 478–80; minutes 110, 175–78, 313, 327–28; orders attachment of property 21; payment for attending 192; to publish order 375; writ of apprisement 198; mentioned 39, 106–7, 113–14, 120, 135–36, 146–47, 177–78, 181, 192, 198, 209, 224–25, 333, 360, 460, 468, 473, 493

Perkins, ———, assessed 522; attacked by Indians 220

Perkins, William, witness 306

Perrot, Richard, alias Robert Williams, Thomas Williams, Richard Honch, captured 346; questioned about murder 346–47; servant 347

Perry, [   ], soldier, court witness 71

Persall; see Pearsall

Peters/Peterse, Adolph/Adolf, appraiser 107; owns land in New York 375; security for Vervelen 329–29

Peterson; see also Pieterse

Peterson, John, wheelmaker, applies for land 349

Peterson/Peterse, Solomon, applies for land 350

Peterson, Laurence, sues Storme 162

Peterson, Lores, assessed 542

petitions 6–11, 15–17, 33, 36–39, 58–60, 67, 82, 89–91, 93, 107–8, 120, 127–30, 134–35, 137–39, 140–43, 144–45, 179–80, 190–91, 194, 198, 216–21, 223–32, 247, 255–56, 261–62, 274–76, 278–80, 283–85, 316–17, 318–20, 323–26, 333–37, 356, 360–64, 370–71, 376–77, 413–14, 429–30, 433–34, 436–38, 445–47, 454–55, 463–64, 467, 480–82, 407

Petteschall, Richard, shipmaster 13

Pettit, John, assessed 541

Pettit/Pettet, Nath., assessed 539

Pettit/Petitt, Thomas, assessed 540; court witness 399

Petty, Edward, assessed 526

Philip/Phillip, king, Indian, attacks 180–81; father and brother of 340; his Indians 366; war 338–45; warning to North Indians 337–39

Philips/Phillips, Frederick, account due to 269; alderman, property in New York City 117; Indians ask permission for oystering 348; at meeting 424; member of admiralty court 262, 265–66, 276; member of council 245, 251, 253, 348; subpoenaed to testify 468; mentioned 236, 238, 243, 353

Philips/Phillips, Joseph, assessed 541

Philips, Theophi., assessed 540

Pidgeon, William, accused of killing hogs 393; charged by constable 387

Pieterse; see also Peterson

Pieterse, Ariaen, assessed 512, 576

Pieterse, Claes, assessed 511, 573

Pieterse/Pieters, Engeltie, convicted of having threatened and beaten Anna Nottingham 430n; summoned to appear at assizes 430

Pieterse/Pieters, Evert, subpoena 450, 452

Pieterse, Hendrick, assessed 509, 576

Pieterse/Pietersz, Jan, deposition 429

Pieterse, Jan, the elder, assessed 497

Pieterse, Leffertt, assessed 506, 556

Pieterse, Pietter, assessed 500

Pieterse, Weynantt, assessed 499, 563

Pike, Robert, signs petition 25

Pike, William, original settler of Nantucket 25–30

Pilgrim, Thomas, wages 550; mentioned 272

Pine, James, court witness 150; signs petition for minister 36

Pinhorne, William, attorney 482; bookeeper for Winder, charged with neglect 318

Pinkny, John, assessed 519

Pinkny, Philip, assessed 519

pistols, Indians request 253

Platt, Mr., of Huntington, tavern bill at Jamaica sessions 56

Platt/Plat, Widow, assessed 516

Platt, Epenetus assessed 533, 534

Platt, Isaac, accused of libel 221; assessed 534; mentioned 324n

Plymouth Colony, governor requires Indians to disarm 338–41; Indian killed in 338; Indians at arms there 183; soldiers 341; war with Indians 193; mentioned 219

Polhemus, Johannes Theodorus, domine, petitions for payment of salary 93

Pollexfen, Henry, member of council 6

Ponton, Richard, capt., accused of abusing Cornell 487; assessed 517; commission delivered 156; fined 488; objection

and Ludlow 456; suit with Rider 328–29

Viele, Arnout/Arnold Cornelissen, interpreter 375–76, 431 (name reversed)

Vigne, Jan, brewer, bondsman 112; land in New York 375

Virginia, attacked 76; cost of passage to Boston 86; court 147; fleet bound for 68; fugitive from 347; passage from 87; relations with Susquehannah 378; ship docks in 185; ship to 85; mentioned 190

Visbeeck, Gerrit, land 244

Voertman, Dierck Janse, assessed 502

Vogel, Arie Cornelise, assessed 495

Vogel, Cornelis Harmense, assessed 568

Volckerse, Dierck, assessed 496

Volckerts, Luycas, of Curacao, ship owner 190

Voschs, Younker, release counterfeited 167

Vriance, Andrews, applies for land 350

Vromans, Adam, nominated as magistrate 425

Vroom, Cornelis Corse, assessed 498

Waerner; see Warner

Waitil, his ferry fee 384

Wakers, Mr., mentioned 536

Waldron, Barne, mentioned 435

Waldron, Resolve, mentioned 435

Walker, Jacob, assessed 535; mentioned 331

Wall, Ellen, petition for help in collecting debt 464

Wallansachkes, Indian 405

Wallebockt, land purchase at 92

Wallop, Richard, member of council 6

Walton, Thomas, court witness 42; Staten Island constable 41; sued by Britton 162, by Loulis 162; sues Bilieu about guns 42–44

wampum; see seawant

Wandall, Mr., complaint against Sherman 398

Wandall, Thomas, assessed 541; court witness 152, 168, 172, 173; juror 160, 175, 301; sues Harker 386, 389–90, 484–85, 487, 490; verdict 394

Wantenaar, Albert Cornelissen, see also Cornelssen, Albert; sues Juriansen 47, 57

Wappinger Indians, visit Andros 178

Ward, Thomas, assessed 537

Waring, Richard, assessed 538

Warner/Warnaer/Wardner, Ralph/Raeff, complaint by Aertsz against 163, 174; juror 160, 175; petition about land at Brooklyn 92–93; register of horses 179; mentioned 383

Warner, Thomas, statement concerning captivity with Indians 330–31

warrant, of impressment 457; to attach property of Lovelace 21, and appraise 106–7; to seize goods of Bedloo 473; to seize property and arrest Davis at Flushing 428; to seize property of Brittaine 317

Waters, Mr., declaration 53

Waters, Mrs., court business 156; mentioned 297, 387

Waters/Watters/Walters, Anthony, accused 488; clerk of sessions 100; sued by Hunt 486, 491; sues Coe 157–58; takes inventory 305–6; to pay Riscoe 297

Waters, Arth., attorney 45

Waters, Edward, assessed 517, 518; court witness 297; sued by Coe 297, 299

Waters, Rachel, widow 299

Watkins/Wattkens, John, soldier, court witness 71; land in New York 375; sues Riscoe 491

Watson, Phillip, clerk 142

Wattoweetto, Indian, pass to Long Island 410–11

Way, James, assessed 539; complaint against Sherman 398

Way, James , Jr., assessed 540

Way, Richard, witness 103

Wayattano, Conn., Indians from, meet with Andros 358

Wayte, Richard, marshall at Boston 97

Wayte, William, goods 275; subpoenaed 270; summoned by admiralty court 264

Webber, Arnold, applies for land 350

THE ANDROS PAPERS, 1674–1676

was composed in Times Roman on a Northgate 286/16
by New Netherland Project;
printed by sheet-fed offset on 50-pound, acid-free P&S Smooth Offset
and Smyth-sewn and bound over binder's boards in Holliston Roxite B
by Braun-Brumfield, Inc.;
and published by

SYRACUSE UNIVERSITY PRESS
SYRACUSE, NEW YORK 13244-5160